Robert Lilleaasen & Christof Sauer (eds.)

Religious Persecution

Christians under Pressure:
Studies in Discrimination and Persecution

Volume 3

- Vol. 1 Bernhard Reitsma (Ed.). Fruitful Minorities – The Witness and Service of Christian Communities in Predominantly Islamic Societies
- Vol. 2 Kay Bascom. Overcomers – God's Deliverance through the Ethiopian Revolution as Witnessed Primarily by the Kale Heywet Church Community
- Vol. 3 Robert Lilleaasen & Christof Sauer (eds.). Religious Persecution – Perspectives from Theology and Missiology

Robert Lilleaasen & Christof Sauer (eds.)

Religious Persecution

Perspectives from Theology and Missiology

WIPF & STOCK · Eugene, Oregon

Wipf and Stock Publishers
199 W 8th Ave, Suite 3
Eugene, OR 97401

Religious Persecution
Perspectives from Theology and Missiology
By Lilleaasen, Robert and Sauer, Christof

Softcover ISBN-13: 979-8-3852-6533-6
Hardcover ISBN-13: 979-8-3852-6534-3
Publication date 10/6/2025
Previously published by Verlag für Kultur und Wissenschaft Culture and Science Publ., 2025

This edition is a scanned facsimile of the original edition published in 2025.

Contents – Overview

Contents – in Detail

A. Opening Section

Editorial introduction

Religious persecution – Theological and missiological perspectives

Robert Lilleaasen & Christof Sauer

Religious persecution has been a defining feature of the Christian story from its earliest days to the present. From the martyrdom of early believers to the contemporary suffering of Christians, persecution has shaped the identity, theology, and mission of the Church. Today, religious persecution continues to manifest in various forms, ranging from social exclusion and legal penalties to the destruction of places of worship, imprisonment, and even death. It is a global phenomenon that affects millions and challenges both the Church and society to respond with wisdom, courage, and compassion.

Theologically and missiologically, persecution is not merely a sociopolitical issue but a deeply spiritual and ecclesial one. The experience of suffering for one's faith has shaped Christian theology across centuries, influencing doctrines of discipleship, ecclesiology, and mission. Missiology, too, must grapple with the realities of persecution, as it seeks to understand and support the Church's witness in hostile environments. Theology and mission are not developed in a vacuum – they are forged in the lived experiences of believers, including those who suffer for their faith. Therefore, they must be equipped to address the challenges of persecution, discrimination, and harassment in both historical and contemporary contexts.

In response to the growing need for theological engagement with the topic of religious persecution, Fjellhaug International University College launched the research project *Religious Freedom and Religious Persecution* in 2019. This initiative is designed to foster interdisciplinary and international collaboration, bringing together scholars from theology, missiology, and related fields to explore the respective dimensions of persecution and religious freedom.

The project serves as a platform for researchers to apply their academic expertise in the service of the persecuted Church and those who minister to it. It is also aimed to bridge the gap between theological reflection and practical ministry, encouraging a multi-voiced and collaborative approach. While legal and political scholars have long contributed to the study of religious persecution, this project has opened a door for a broader range of theological voices to enter the conversation.

Three research symposiums – held in 2021, 2023, and 2025 – have been key milestones in the project. These gatherings have not only fostered academic exchange but also built relationships and networks among scholars and practitioners. Many of the contributions in this volume were first presented at these symposiums, reflecting the project's commitment to cultivating new research and dialogue in this vital area.

Religious Persecution: Perspectives from Theology and Missiology is a direct outcome of the Fjellhaug research project. This volume brings together scholars from a range of theological disciplines – including biblical studies, systematic theology, church history, practical theology, and missiology – to offer a rich and multifaceted exploration of religious persecution. With contributors from nine countries, the book reflects a truly international and ecumenical effort to deepen our understanding of this pressing issue.

Organised into thematic sections, the chapters address a wide array of topics, from biblical and historical perspectives to contemporary case studies and theological reflections. The volume includes contributions from both seasoned scholars and emerging voices, offering a balance of depth, innovation, and diversity in approach. The aim is not only to expand academic knowledge but also to provide theological resources for those preparing for or engaged in ministry, especially in contexts where persecution is a lived reality.

This book is written for students, pastors, missionaries, and scholars who seek to understand the theological and missiological dimensions of religious persecution. It is also intended to inspire further research and reflection, thereby contributing to a more robust and compassionate response to the suffering of believers worldwide. In doing so, it seeks to fill a gap in current scholarship by offering a consolidated theological perspective on a topic that is both historically rooted and urgently contemporary.

The structure of this anthology reflects a purposeful progression through theological and missiological perspectives on religious persecution. The volume opens with a foundational section on definitions, establishing conceptual clarity and framing the discourse. The final section presents applied theology, aiming to translate academic reflection into faithful practice.

I Foundations

Christof Sauer, an expert on persecution studies from Germany, and Werner Nel, a legal scholar from South Africa, jointly lay the foundations for this anthology. In a broad survey, they seek to inform Christian theologians and missiologists about definitions, scales and spectrums of persecution available in scholarly and professional discourse. Legal definitions and uses tend to be very narrow and restrictive, but serve best to establish recognised rights and prosecutable crimes. Sociological definitions, in contrast, are broad and cover the full existential dimension of persecution. This is shared by theological definitions, which add metaphysical interpretations beyond secular perceptions. Across disciplines, overarching definitional elements of persecution can be established. Therefore, the authors call for a reflective use of definitions. Based on this foundation, definitions by selected Christian agencies are considered, as well as terminological scales involving persecution employed among NGOs. The latter aims at establishing distinct terminology for different levels of severity. As even these do not sufficiently and comprehensively grasp the diversity of persecution phenomena and aspects, an array of spectral aspects of persecution needs to be simultaneously considered. Sauer and Nel provide the most thorough and comprehensive survey of contemporary definitions, scales and spectrums of persecution currently available, and even suggest a sociological definition of their own on persecution.

2 Biblical studies

Håkon Sunde Pedersen, a Norwegian scholar in the field of Old Testament studies, investigates the troubling intersection of religious zeal and violence in the Hebrew Bible. In his essay, Pedersen focuses on the figures of Phinehas, Elijah, and Jehu, who, in their fervour for YHWH, commit acts of violence against those seen as threats to exclusive worship. While these characters are often either celebrated or condemned in theological discourse, Pedersen argues that the biblical narratives present them in a far more ambiguous light. His analysis suggests that the authors or redactors of these texts may have been more critically attuned to the dangers of zealotry than is often assumed. Through this nuanced reading, Pedersen contributes to the ongoing development of a biblical theology of religious persecution, offering a thoughtful and constructive perspective.

Geert W. Lorein, a Belgian scholar in Old Testament studies, examines the motives of the Maccabees in the second century BC in their conflict with the Hellenistic king Antiochus IV Epiphanes. He inquires about the reasons why Antiochus IV started his repression and the reaction of the Jews: what exactly were the points that could not be accepted, and the motives that prompted action? Reactions varied, and opinions within the group about the use of violence differed. Not only theological convictions, but character traits and practical considerations too, played a role. Although the main motives were broadly the same, varieties in viewpoints and expression existed within the movement. Lorein's contribution may challenge readers to make comparisons between Hellenistic and contemporary times at several points, and to query for transferable lessons.

Daniel Röthlisberger, a German and Swiss New Testament scholar, addresses the ambiguity inherent in the term "persecution of Christians" by seeking a philologically and theologically grounded definition based on New Testament texts. He employs a systematic semantic and lexical analysis of key Greek word pairs διωγμός/διώκω, θλῖψις/θλίβω, and πάθημα/πάσχω. These terms are central to Jesus' teachings and the lived experience of early Christian communities. His research uncovers a broad and nuanced spectrum of meanings and manifestations of persecution within the New Testament. Röthlisberger's findings contribute to a more accurate and contextually sensitive understanding of persecution of Christians, bridging philological, theological, and sociological approaches.

Christoph Stenschke, a German New Testament scholar, examines the Book of Acts, which contains the first systematic account of some strands of the earliest Christian mission. At first sight, the book abounds with conflicts of various kinds and the suffering of Christ-believers that, on occasion, resulted from their missionary efforts. However, taking inspiration from some recent theorising about religious conflict, Stenschke also detects other aspects in these accounts: Amid intensive missionary activities and, at times, serious conflicts, there are not only instances of de-escalation or resolution of conflict but also instances of relatively peaceful coexistence and even co-operation between Jews and Jewish Christ-followers in the Jewish diaspora. Such coexistence created, or at least allowed for, a climate that was conducive to transition and co-operation. Stenschke identifies some of these instances and analyses them to understand what factors enabled these more desirable forms of interactions between representatives of different convictions and practices, and at what points conflict arose and why.

Håkon Leite, a Norwegian scholar specialising in New Testament studies, investigates the theological significance of persecution in the Pastoral Epistles, focusing on Paul's exhortations to Timothy to suffer for the gospel (2 Tim 1:8; 2:3). In his essay, Leite explores how Paul's positive attitude toward persecution aligns with the broader view of Christian existence presented in these letters. He challenges the interpretive framework of "*Christliche Bürgerlichkeit*", which suggests a diminished eschatological urgency and a socially respectable form of Christianity. Instead, Leite argues that persecution should be understood within the eschatological tension between the present age and the age to come, a dynamic that also shapes Paul's understanding of the role of persecution in Christian mission. Through this lens, Leite offers a compelling re-evaluation of suffering as a vital component of faithful witness.

3 Historical studies and systematic theology

Klaus Wetzel, a German church historian specialised on mission history, explores how Christians have dealt with persecution. He uses examples from three periods of church history (antiquity, the Reformation and Pietism) to show the far-reaching consequences for piety, religious practice and theology, and particularly in church historiography. We observe the development of veneration of relics, the esteem in which Tertullian held persecution, the typologisation in Eusebius of Caesarea and the application of the act-and-consequence scheme by Lactantius. As a result of the theology of the Christian empire, the church itself becomes a persecutor, later through the Inquisition and in the face of the Reformation. The Reformation reacted with books of martyrs and a theology of suffering. The Anabaptists are robbed of their missionary impetus by persecution. While separatist Pietism was unable to find a viable response to the situation of persecution, it was precisely the spiritual heritage of a church wiped out by persecution, the Moravian Brethren Unity – conveyed by Comenius – that, in cooperation with mainline Protestant Pietism, brought about a spiritual awakening in the Herrnhut Moravian Church with a significant impact. Wetzel thus demonstrates the great variety in processing persecution and contributes valuable lessons from church history that might otherwise be overlooked.

Finn Aa. Rønne, a Danish scholar in Church History, explores the emergence and evolution of reform movements within the Ethiopian Orthodox Tewahedo Church (EOTC) over the past five decades. As one of the world's oldest Christian institutions, the EOTC has long been a central pillar of Ethiopian identity and a guardian of the nation's cultural and historical legacy. In his essay, Rønne examines how various renewal movements – some expelled, others operating discreetly within the church – have challenged the status quo, often facing suppression from powerful internal factions. These movements not only reflect theological and ecclesiastical tensions but also raise critical questions about religious freedom in contemporary Ethiopia. Rønne situates these developments within the broader context of the EOTC's historical authority and the growing influence of Protestant churches, which have played a significant role in shaping Ethiopia's modern religious and social landscape.

Christof Sauer, as a mission theologian from Germany, revisits the evangelical consensus statement on suffering, persecution and martyrdom emanating from a global expert consultation in Bad Urach, Germany, in 2009. Fifteen years later, he reviews its impact and briefly reminds us of its genesis and architecture. The Bad Urach Statement is generally appreciated by numerous missiologists and has impacted some major Christian statements. It continues to be affirmatively used beyond its signatories, as well as ignored or – more seldom – criticised. More than half of its specific content has been referred to in various works. The essay closes with desiderata and suggestions for a future upgrading of the statement. As the lead drafter, Sauer has reintroduced this benchmark evangelical interpretation framework, which emphasises a mission perspective.

Sara Afshari, a Christian scholar specialised in media studies, exiled from Iran to the UK, develops a theology of persecution through the lens of Holy Saturday, the silent day between crucifixion and resurrection. She argues that the persecuted church dwells not only in Good Friday's suffering or Easter's hope, but in the in-between space of fear, abandonment, and sacred waiting. Grounded in the story of the Episcopal Church in Kerman, Iran, the essay frames persecution through three interwoven narratives: the disciples' fear and disorientation, Christ's descent into abandonment, and the Triune God's shared suffering. Holy Saturday is revealed as a theological space where faith endures in silence, identity is tested, and hope is gestated in obscurity. This descent is not defeat, but sacred solidarity with Christ. The essay invites the global church into deeper empathy – not through triumphalist narratives, but by dwelling with the persecuted in their silence, waiting, and wounds, where the seeds of resurrection are quietly sown. Afshari thus uniquely contributes a theological interpretation shaped by first-hand contextual experiences.

Věra Miláčková and Kamila Veverková, theological scholars from the Czech Republic, explore the theological reasoning behind fleeing from religious persecution. In their essay, they respond to contemporary concerns about the legitimacy and purpose of Christian flight from the Middle East, particularly in contexts such as Iraq and Egypt. By comparing biblical narratives of flight with modern testimonies of persecuted Christians, the authors identify four distinct theological approaches: the *Salvation at Stake* approach, the *Altruistic/Common Sense* approach, the *Hearing God's Voice* approach, and the *Opportunistic* approach. Their aim is to provide both persecuted individuals and those who support them with a nuanced framework for understanding the diverse theological motivations that shape the decision to flee.

4 Practical theology

Henrik Nymann Eriksen, a Danish scholar specialising in Practical theology and Christian leadership, explores the multifaceted pastoral role of Danish ministers who support Christian converts facing persecution upon repatriation to their Muslim-majority countries of origin. Drawing on interviews with pastors and Christian leaders, Eriksen identifies three key dimensions of pastoral identity: pastor, mentor, and prophet. As pastors, ministers offer care through presence, prayer, blessings, biblical teaching, and practical support, extending traditional Lutheran pastoral responsibilities. The mentor role involves guiding converts through discipleship and helping them navigate the challenges of their Muslim backgrounds and the risks associated with persecution. The prophetic role, meanwhile, reflects a form of public theology, as pastors advocate for vulnerable refugees and engage in critical reflection on leadership and authority. Eriksen's study highlights the need for contextual sensitivity and a balanced approach to leadership that is both culturally aware and theologically grounded.

Robert Lilleaasen, a Norwegian scholar in Practical theology, explores the often-overlooked role of followership within Christian congregations facing religious persecution. In his essay, Lilleaasen integrates perspectives from ecclesiology, leadership theory, and persecution studies to examine how persecution reshapes the leader-follower dynamic and the broader leadership process. Drawing on Chaleff's model of courageous followership and theories of crisis and extreme context leadership, he highlights how followers under pressure become increasingly vital, offering both supportive presence and constructive challenge. Lilleaasen argues that persecution intensifies the need for shared leadership and resilient congregational structures, emphasising the importance of theological and cultural preparation. His study contributes to the emerging field at the intersection of followership and religious persecution, calling for deeper theological and empirical engagement with the role of followers in sustaining church identity and mission under duress.

Tonje Belibi, a Norwegian scholar specialising in Practical theology and faith education, examines how persecuted Christians are represented in Norwegian Sunday school curricula for children aged 3-9. In her essay, Belibi analyses three educational programs – *Ordets liturgi for barn* (Catholic), *Sprell Levende* (Evangelical Lutheran), and *Awana* (adapted for the Norwegian Evangelical Lutheran context) – through the lens of theological perspectives on persecution and child development theory, including Fowler's stages of faith. The study reveals that while all three curricula address the topic of persecution, they do so with varying degrees of depth and frequency. *Awana* offers the most vivid and direct portrayals, often linking persecution to themes of mission and discipleship, while *Ordets liturgi for barn* and *Sprell Levende* tend to soften or omit more challenging content, focusing instead on God's love and comfort. Belibi's research underscores the importance of integrating difficult biblical narratives in age-appropriate ways to foster resilient faith and global awareness among young children.

Knut Kåre Kirkholm, a Norwegian scholar in Practical theology, explores how persecution is addressed in the preaching of Norwegian Lutheran Evangelical congregations. His essay analyses twelve sermons delivered between 2019 and 2021, focusing on how theological themes of persecution are represented and how preachers navigate these themes within a context largely free from religious pressure. Kirkholm examines how factors such as lectionary text selection and the preachers' ministerial contexts shape their messages. A notable finding is the connection between persecution and the "inner cross", a concept rooted in Lutheran theological tradition. The study suggests that certain theological aspects of persecution may be difficult to emphasise in a Norwegian setting and critiques the tendency to portray persecution in overly simplistic terms, ranging from mild discrimination at home to violent oppression abroad. Kirkholm calls for further homiletical reflection and research to better equip preachers to engage with the complexities of persecution in a meaningful and theologically grounded way.

5 Missiology and religious studies

Joel Hofer, a German scholar in Missiology and Religious studies, investigates the complex relationship between conversion to Christianity and religious persecution. Both topics have been widely studied independently but not together. Converts often represent the most intensely persecuted group within Christian communities. In his essay, Hofer explores how these two phenomena intersect by analysing the Regnum Edinburgh Centenary Series – one of the most comprehensive missiological collections of the 21st century. Through this analysis, he identifies five thematic patterns: (1) conversion as a trigger for persecution, (2) reciprocal influences between persecution and conversion, (3) anti-conversion motives as drivers of persecution, (4) pro-conversion actors as both victims and advocates, and (5) other groups situated between these dynamics. Hofer's study offers a nuanced and far-reaching perspective on the theological, historical, and sociopolitical dimensions that shape the interplay between Christian conversion and persecution in global contexts.

Meiken Buchholz, a German scholar of missiology specialising on China, examines "sinicisation" in the tension between political and theological interpretation. "Sinicisation of religion" is a widely used term for contextualisation in China. Its basic meaning is "making religious faith Chinese" and, in a broad sense, can apply to any form of contextualised Christian faith in China. At the same time, it is a political term. Since 2015, "sinicisation of religions" is the ruling principle of religious policy in the People's Republic of China and the official umbrella organisation of Protestant churches in China (Three-Self Patriotic Movement). Using Bevans' contextualisation-models as analytical tools, Buchholz discusses red lines beyond which the sinicisation-concept turns from a *theological* blueprint of a contextualised Chinese Christianity to a *political* guideline of religious policy.

Frank Ole Thoresen, a Norwegian scholar of Missiology and Religious studies, examines the intricate landscape of religious diversity and tolerance in post-revolutionary Tunisia, with a particular focus on the experiences of Jewish and Protestant Christian minorities. Despite Tunisia's reputation for relative religious freedom, highlighted by the awarding of the Nobel Peace Prize in 2015, challenges persist. Through combining religious freedom categories with ten anonymised interviews conducted in the Spring of 2023, the essay aims to understand the current perceptions of tolerance and freedom of belief among these groups, shedding light on the broader implications for religious coexistence in Tunisia amidst its shifting political and social landscape. He seeks to answer the research question "How do members of selected religious minority groups experience tolerance for freedom of religion and beliefs in Tunisia at present, and how do these experiences reflect the broader social and political dynamics of post-revolutionary Tunisia?"

James Bultema, an American scholar in Missiology and Religious studies, explores the deeply contested perceptions surrounding the Turkish Protestant movement, which has been gradually emerging since 1961. In his essay, Bultema argues that the movement has often been misconstrued, shaped by polarised narratives about its mission and the persecution it faces. On one side, missionaries view themselves as faithful and vulnerable messengers of the gospel, frequently subjected to governmental and societal hostility. On the other hand, many Muslim citizens of Turkey – both nominal and devout – perceive these missionaries as threatening outsiders, with converts seen as victims of foreign influence. These conflicting perspectives reveal the complex interplay between evangelistic mission and persecution, which resists simplistic interpretation. Drawing on historical and contemporary insights, Bultema introduces the concept of "wild wisdom" – a contextual and adaptive approach aimed at reducing missionary attrition, enhancing fruitfulness, and fostering a more culturally sensitive portrayal of national Christians.

6 Applied theology

Sara Afshari, a scholar in mission studies from Iran, reflects in this short essay on her experience at the Fourth Lausanne Congress in South Korea in 2024, focusing on how the Congress approached the issue of persecution of Christians. As someone who has personally faced persecution as a convert from a Muslim-majority country, she found that the Congress often reduced persecution to emotional appeals for evangelism or support. This approach, she argues, risks turning the suffering of Christians into a tool for marketing and evangelism rather than recognising it as a sacred and shared experience within the Church. She therefore calls for a shift in how we think about and respond to persecution. Instead of viewing it as just a problem to solve or a story to tell, we should see it as a sacred witness, a powerful way the Church bears the cross together. In short, Afshari suggests that we need a more thoughtful and holistic approach that honours the sacred, communal dimensions of suffering.

Duane A. Miller, a scholar of missiology and Anglican priest from the USA, explores the theme of unmerited suffering through a theological and pastoral reading of the book of Job, connecting it to the lived reality of persecuted Christians today. He begins with a biblical-theological reflection on Job, focusing on the heavenly court, the figure of the satan, and Job's anguished protest against divine silence and apparent injustice. He reflects on the difference between law and wisdom, the challenge of redemptive suffering, and Job's unwavering integrity. Drawing on his pastoral experience with persecuted Christians, particularly in Islamic contexts, he argues that Scripture-centred theology can offer true comfort and strength, far more than abstract academic analysis. He then explores how Job's insights resonate with the challenges these believers face today. Miller concludes by affirming that their suffering is seen, remembered, and honoured by God. Job's yearning for a redeemer ultimately finds fulfilment in Christ, and his story offers a pattern of faithful endurance and hope.

– – –

We, the editors, extend our heartfelt gratitude to all the contributors whose scholarly work forms the foundation of this volume. Your research and willingness to collaborate have made this book possible. We are deeply thankful for your insights and the theological and missiological depth you have brought to the subject of religious persecution. We also wish to express our sincere appreciation to the anonymous peer reviewers,[1] whose thorough academic evaluations and constructive feedback have enhanced the quality of this work. Your careful attention and thoughtful suggestions have been invaluable. We would also like to extend our thanks to the publisher and the series editors for the opportunity to bring this anthology to publication and for the professional support provided throughout the process. It has been a privilege to work with each of you, and we are grateful for all that we have learned along the way.

This book was born out of a serious and sobering context: the lived reality of religious persecution. Our motivation has been shaped by the desire to offer theological and missiological perspectives that speak into this reality. Ultimately, this book is written to serve Christians who are under pressure for their faith. We hope it will inspire, encourage, and equip.[2]

July 2025
Robert Lilleaasen and Christof Sauer

---

1 All contributions have undergone double-blind peer review by at least two independent reviewers in addition to the scrutiny of the editors. Anonymity of an author was hard to achieve in the few instances where the author is widely known in a small community of researchers. The peer review of the contributions of an editor was managed by the other editor, thus maintaining the same standards. Peer review was not applied to the one short opinion piece in the section "Applied Theology".

2 Eight contributions of the 2023 Fjellhaug Symposium have been published under the title *Christian mission and FORB*, as a special issue of the *International Journal for Religious Freedom* (18/1), freely available at iirf.global. In some respect these papers are complementary to the present anthology.

1 Religious persecution

Definitions, scales, and spectrums reflected for the context of theology and missiology

Christof Sauer[1] *& Werner Nel*[2]

Abstract

This survey serves to inform Christian theologians and missiologists about definitions, scales and spectrums of persecution available in scholarly and professional discourse. Legal definitions and uses tend to be very narrow and restrictive, but serve best to establish recognised rights and prosecutable crimes. Sociological definitions, in contrast, are broad and cover the full existential dimension of persecution. This is shared by theological definitions, which add metaphysical interpretations beyond secular perceptions. Across disciplines, overarching definitional elements of persecution can be established. A reflected use of definitions is therefore called for. Based on this foundation, definitions by selected Christian agencies are considered, as well as terminological scales involving persecution employed among NGOs. Such scales aim at establishing distinct terminology for different levels of severity. As even these do not sufficiently and comprehensively grasp the diversity of persecution phenomena and aspects, an array of spectral aspects of persecution needs to be simultaneously considered.

Keywords: Religious persecution, persecution of Christians, definitions, scales, spectrums.

---

1 Christof Sauer (*1963) is part time Professor II at Fjellhaug International University College, and Consultant for its Research Project "Religious Freedom and Religious Persecution"; resident in Germany. As a professor of religious studies and missiology, he is particularly interested in the intersection between FORB and mission. He takes particular responsibility for sections 3, 5, 6 and the overall design and drafting of the essay. Email: christofsauer@icloud.com, ORCID iD: 0000-0002-4976-7574.

2 Werner Nel (*1985) is a senior lecturer at the Faculty of Law, University of Johannesburg, South Africa. His primary research focuses on the intersection of religious persecution and religious freedom with international criminal and human rights law. He takes particular responsibility for sections 1.2, 2.3, 4.2, 7. Email: wnnel@uj.ac.za, ORCID iD: 0000-0002-8679-8417.

I Introduction

The study of religious persecution as a topic of theology and missiology happens in the context of diverging definitions among various other academic disciplines and Christian agencies or NGOs. Three different layers of specificity need to be distinguished: persecution in general, religious persecution, and persecution of Christians in particular, in which theologians are most often interested. There are broad and narrow uses of the terms, and these are influenced by different interests, perspectives and contexts, and in part also by misperceptions, distortions or reductionism. There also exist dissatisfaction about the inflationary use of the term persecution and calls for a scaled and differentiated terminology.

Therefore, this essay[3] inquires about the benefits and limitations for the context of theological and missiological study of the various definitions, scales and spectrums of persecution available in scholarly and professional discourse. At the outset, the colloquial use of the term persecution and the ambivalent role of religion in defining religious persecution will be briefly considered.

In a first step, the definitions of persecution in various disciplines outside theology will be examined, briefly passing psychological perspectives, and then proceeding to broad sociological definitions and more specific legal definitions and uses of the term. Thereafter, theological terminology and definitions will be considered, focusing on church historiography and New Testament scholarship. The examination of scholarly definitions concludes with the identification of divergences and commonalities by characterising broad and narrow uses of the term persecution and isolating overarching definitional elements of religious persecution.

Moving to the operational level in a second step, the understanding of the term persecution among selected Christian agencies is critically examined. Thereafter, various "scales of persecution" are introduced and characterised, leading to critical conclusions about their usefulness and limitations. This naturally leads to the final query, whether the complexity rather requires a model describing a scattered spectrum of concurrent persecution phenomena, which is subsequently pursued.

Accordingly, this essay is a scoping review, adopting a critical multidisciplinary survey approach, with its primary value lying in the integration and contextualisation of existing scholarship, adding critical remarks and also several new contributions. It constitutes complementary teamwork,

---

3 For a more extensive version of this essay, see Sauer & Nel (2025), also including a section on language use.

combining the missiological and theological reflections of Christof Sauer (2021: 25-33; 373-380) on definitions of persecution with those of Werner Nel (2020; 2023) on the characteristics of persecution in legal fields, and presents results of their joint engagement with professionals in the field of advocacy for the persecuted.

1.1 Persecution – general meanings and colloquial use

The term *persecution* in general has three meanings, namely, the act of persecuting, the state of being persecuted, and a program or campaign to persecute certain people.[4] The verb *to persecute* (including *persecuted* and *persecuting*) means to pursue with harassing or oppressive treatment, or to annoy or trouble persistently. *Persecution* may refer to unfair or abusive treatment toward a person or group of people because of race, religion, ethnicity, sexual orientation, gender, or social status. Synonyms of persecution in colloquial use are vilification, hustle, (criminal) investigation, pursuit, hunt, and chase. A popular understanding almost always equates *religious persecution* with physical violence, state involvement, and the presence of a religious motive.

A closer examination of more precise definitions below will reveal that the defining characteristic of persecution lies in unjustified differential treatment - particularly when it stems from intolerance toward the victim's beliefs, convictions, or membership in a specific identifiable group.

1.2 Religion – its ambivalent role in a definition of persecution

"Religion is a powerful motivator for both positive social change and mass violence" (Guiora 2009: 9). Therefore, it is no surprise that communities across all religious and belief traditions have, in varying historical and geopolitical contexts, both suffered discrimination, intolerance, violence, and persecution *by reason of their beliefs*, and, at times, perpetrated similar atrocities *in the name of their belief.*

From a phenomenological perspective, it is important to recognise both the distinctions and the overlaps between these two paradoxical effects of religion, particularly in relation to religious persecution (Nel 2023).[5]

---

4 Dictionary.com

5 This distinction is of utmost importance in the context of the criminalisation and prosecution of systematic attacks on fundamental human rights, particularly in relation to persecution as a crime against humanity under international law.

Crucially, words and concepts are not universally understood in the same way; rather, their meanings are often shaped by distinct sociocultural and geopolitical contexts. This divergence in interpretation can exacerbate the conceptual gap between *persecuting in the name of religion* – a perpetrator-driven perspective, and *being persecuted by reason of religion* – a victim-focused perspective. Theologically, this implies that religion or belief, like other ideological systems, may be implicated in persecution in two distinct, yet often intersecting, ways.

First, for religious fundamentalists, their "[r]eligion has priority over all other considerations" (Guiora 2009: 12), and may therefore act as the subjective motive, catalyst, or justification for persecuting others. In instances where persecution is committed *in the name of religion* – that is, religiously motivated persecution – the persecutor's religious ideology plays a central role in shaping victim selection. Frequently, such persecution manifests as intolerance toward dissenting religious ideologies and results in the discriminatory targeting of individuals based on their religious affiliation or lack thereof. However, the persecutor's religious ideology may also drive victim selection along other, often intersecting, grounds of victim identity. Depending on the underlying ideological "truth" asserted by the persecutor, religiously motivated persecution is not automatically or exclusively limited to targeting victims of other religious identities.

Second, persecution may be "directed at" (Tieszen 2008a: 41) individuals or groups on the grounds of, or by reason of, their religious identity or behaviour (Petri 2021: 19.37). In such cases, religion does not serve as the motivating catalyst for persecution but rather as the identifying basis for the selection of victims. In other words, the particular victim or victim group is targeted primarily on account of their actual or perceived religious identity or behaviour – or absence thereof. Here, religion functions as an identifying element, regardless of the persecutor's own religious beliefs or motives. The religious affiliation or behaviour of the victim may become the basis for persecution for a variety of reasons unique to the persecutor.[6] Importantly, the motive of the persecutor is not determinative for establishing religion as the ground or mode of persecution. Furthermore, religious intolerance or motive is not a required element to constitute religious persecution. For ex-

---

[6] To make matters even more complex, for control-obsessed governments issues of faith and identity are much less threatening than questions of political loyalty and communitarian autonomy. Thus, being a Christian and churches operating openly might not be a problem for the government, as long as these groups can be controlled and do not insist on independence by refusing registration or going underground to resist government instrumentalisation and infiltration (Email by Heiner Bielefeldt to C. Sauer, 2 April 2019).

ample, in parts of Latin America such as Colombia, criminal syndicates involved in drug and human trafficking have used targeted violence to silence and intimidate religious communities that oppose, report, or expose their criminal activities (ODI/WWR 2024: 16). In these cases, the victims are deliberately targeted by reason of their religious identity or behaviour, constituting religious persecution, even though the persecution is not driven by religious motive or intolerance, but rather by the perceived threat posed by the victims' religiously inspired activism.

It is, of course, pragmatically true that in some instances, persecution may be both religiously motivated and directed by reason of religion. In such cases, religion operates both as the motivating catalyst for persecution (from the persecutor's perspective) and as the identifying element for victim selection (from the victim's standpoint), grounded in the persecutor's subjective religious truth-claim.

The significance that religion or belief may hold in a particular context of persecution – whether as catalyst, identifying element, or both – should neither be ignored nor become the sole focus of analysis. This is because religion, while often a salient factor, is rarely the only reason or basis for persecution.

With these differentiations, the ground is laid to review the best definitions of persecution known to us in various disciplines.[7]

2 Definitions outside theology

As a theological understanding of persecution should be communicable towards outside perspectives, it is appropriate to start broadly with non-theological uses of the term in psychology and definitions of sociological and legal nature.

2.1 Psychological perspectives on persecution

A psychological perspective on persecution considers the mental and emotional processes that can make persecution seem possible, acceptable, or even justified in certain contexts. Without claiming any subject-matter expertise, this section briefly highlights a few distorted individual or collective cognitive perceptions that may influence how persecution is understood or framed. Such distortions will be excluded from the discussion thereafter.

---

[7] Concerning generic criteria for a definition of persecution cf. Sauer (2021: 27-28), and Sauer & Nel (2025).

First, the persecuted and their descendants risk developing a victim mentality. This can lead to anomalies, such as a collective *historical persecution reaction complex*, as a consequence of past persecution among its survivors and their descendants (Cherepanov 2021), which can be observed, e.g. among Mennonites (Juhnke 2003) and Armenians (Karenian et al. 2010).

Second, groups perceiving a loss of collective privilege in society might develop a *persecution complex*, while in fact not being persecuted by any objective standards. This is criticised by those among their midst who demonstrate a higher level of differentiation (cf. Knippa 2015).

Third, psychiatry deals with the medical anomaly of individual *persecutory delusions*, a form of paranoia, consisting of a mental perception of being persecuted while in fact one is not (Preti & Cella 2010: 21).

The key point in surveying some of the categories of distortions above, is that, while the experience of persecution is deeply personal – and must be acknowledged and addressed through pastoral care – it should also correspond to some objective, lived reality. In this regard, the overview of cognitive misperceptions presented above is not intended to contribute directly to a conceptual definition of persecution, but rather to caution Christian theologians and missiologists against the potential pitfall of interpreting persecution through a lens that may be psychologically skewed or disconnected from actual circumstances.

2.2 Sociological definitions of persecution

In this section, we will successively analyse a definition of persecution in *general*, then a definition of *religious* persecution, and finally a definition of religious persecution of *Christians*.

The historian Charles Tieszen (2008b: 41) defines *persecution* in its most general and basic form as:

> "An unjust action of varying levels of hostility with one or more motivations directed at a specific individual or a specific group of individuals resulting in varying levels of harm as it is considered from the victim's perspective."[8]

Persecution is thereby understood as a spectrum of hostility towards an individual or group by another individual or group, based on differing "motivations" targeting the victim or victim group because of an attribute or characteristic of their identity, such as the victim's religious identity or political allegiances (2008b: 37-38). While Tieszen's understanding of the term

---

8 This definition is part of a theological Masters thesis, and at the time was the most developed, which led to its publication by the newly emerging IIRF.

"motivations" may be open to critique, an issue explored further later, it nonetheless clearly points to discriminatory treatment based on identity.

It is common to encounter persecution in the context of, and within the understanding of, discrimination (UN General Assembly 1946). Discrimination, in this context, should be understood as the unfair or illegitimate differentiation between groups of people based on attributes or characteristics that are central to their inherent human dignity. Religion or belief is one such characteristic of identity. Discriminatory treatment may be expressed through legal means (e.g., laws excluding religious minorities) or socio-political practices (e.g., refusal to hire someone because of their faith), and it may occur for a variety of reasons. What renders discrimination unfair is its effect: namely, the infringement of human dignity or the reinforcement of patterns of systemic disadvantage and inequality.

Religious persecution cannot occur without such discriminatory treatment of individuals or groups on the basis of their religion. The determining factor is the arbitrary and unjust impact of that discrimination on its victims.

Crucially, discriminatory treatment is not synonymous with intolerance or hatred. This means that religious persecution does not require a hateful mindset or refusal to accept the religious beliefs of others – although such attitudes are frequently present. Rather, religious persecution involves the arbitrary or discriminatory mistreatment of individuals or groups by reason of their religious identity, and it results in violations of fundamental human rights, which may range from moderate to severe depending on the context. Therefore, it can be concluded that the core elements of persecution relate to deliberate hostility directed arbitrarily at a specific person or group, resulting in a variety of harmful consequences (Tieszen 2008b: 41).

Within a hostile social environment, those involved or affected often have diverging views on the nature and legitimacy of their persecutory experience or conduct. Therefore, a sociological perspective considers two main perceptions: persecution experienced from the viewpoint of those persecuted, versus the perception of those who attempt to justify their persecutory conduct, i.e. the persecutor or antagonist's viewpoint.[9]

[9] One must beware of the language of persecutors. In their minds, they have rationales for persecution, such as protecting something important (e.g. the unity of the community) or imaginary threats (e.g. blasphemy). This leads to their prejudice against those whom they persecute (Nel 2020: 32-34). In effect, persecutors often do not perceive themselves as such, but instead regard their actions as those of 'protectionists.'

Tieszen (2008b: 41) contends that the victim's perspective is the most important, but of course this subjective perception must align with observable facts or circumstances.[10]

Tieszen (2008b: 40-43) adds qualifiers to his general definition to narrow it down to *religious persecution* specifically as:

> "An unjust action of varying levels of hostility directed at a believer or believers of a particular religion or belief system through systematic oppression or genocide, or through harassment or discrimination which may not necessarily limit these believers' ability to practise their faith, resulting in varying levels of harm as it is considered from the victim's perspective, each action having religion as its primary motivator."

There are several crucial additions to the definition: Firstly, the identification of those persecuted as believers; second, the exemplification of persecution scenarios, emphasising that persecution must not be conflated with the limiting of the ability of those believers to practise their faith (e.g. to have public worship); and third, the emphasis on religion[11] as the principal identifying characteristic and the underlying catalyst.

After establishing a general definition of persecution and a more specific one on religious persecution, Tieszen (2008b: 43-47) further proceeds to a sociological[12] definition of *religious persecution of Christians* as:

> "Any unjust action of mild to intense levels of hostility directed at Christians of varying levels of commitment resulting in varying levels of harm which may not necessarily prevent or limit these Christians' ability to practice

10 The need for objectifiable facts is also emphasised by Jung (2023: 25-26). However, while Tieszen contrasts the victim's perspective with that of the perpetrator, Jung appears to understand "victim's perspective" as the intersubjective variety among different victims in considering a situation as persecution, and therefore rightly calls for objective measurements of communal context. Tieszen himself, in hindsight considers it a pitfall of his definition that it can be abused to legitimate weak claims of persecution by people experiencing a loss of privileged position in their society (Email to W. Nel 19 March 2019).

11 See below for critical remarks on the precise determination of the role of religion in defining persecution.

12 While Tieszen's background reflections preparing this third level definition include Christian theological reflections, which is laudable, counter to his claim, this is not a "theological definition" but remains a sociological definition of religious persecution of Christians that includes theological considerations (Sauer 2021: 32 fn 32). Tieszen self-critically remarks in hindsight that the lack of robust biblical/theological grounding was a main shortcoming of his definition. Röthlisberger (2023: 20 fn 47) also deemed the attempt lacking theological depth and precision.

> their faith or appropriately propagate their faith as it is considered from the victim's perspective, each motivation having religion, namely the identification of its victims as 'Christian', as its primary motivator."

The added specifications for Christians are mainly parallel to those for believers of religions or beliefs. Further additions are the inclusive conception of Christians, encompassing any level of commitment, as well as the explicit mention of the ability to "appropriately propagate their faith" as a complement to the general practice of their faith. The latter means that, while Christians in a certain context might be able to exercise missionary activity, they could nevertheless simultaneously be suffering persecution. Thus, the ability to exercise missionary activity must not be made a criterion to exclude the presence of persecution.

While these definitions have been widely popularised by the inclusion of the second one into the internationally disseminated *Bad Urach Statement* (cf. Sauer 2025), upon closer scrutiny under a human rights lens, some terminology used by Tieszen is imprecise and at times ambiguous.[13] This particularly concerns the varying terminology used in trying to clarify the relation between religion and persecution. The component that we view critically in the second and third definition of Tieszen is the added requirement of both definitions that the persecutory action must have "religion as its primary *motivator*", or "the identification of its victims as 'Christians,' as its primary *motivator*".[14] The effect of including identification with a religion or the Christian faith as the "primary motivator" is that religious persecution must then, by definition, be religiously motivated. As a result, persecution that is directed at a religious or Christian group would not qualify as religious persecution under the second or third level of the definition if the persecutor's actions were driven by political, financial, or other ideological motives. This is because, under these definitions, the "primary motivator" of religious persecution must be "religion".

Our argument is that while the persecutor's motivation – religious or otherwise – may help explain *why* the group was targeted, the more crucial question is whether the individuals were targeted by reason of their,

---

13 Tieszen also remarks in hindsight that the definitions should have been better grounded in philosophical reflection. He regrets having flattened disparities and the intricacies of combining experiences of violently persecuted marginalised people with those of ridiculed people in otherwise privileged positions on the same scales. He consequently queries whether the key component of a definition of persecution should be context or privilege/marginalisation (Email to W. Nel, 19 March 2019).

14 Emphasis added.

actual or perceived, affiliation or identification with a religion or the Christian faith ("directed at"). We understand religious identity broadly. It encompasses the individual's inner conscience, sense of belonging and affiliation – both self-perceived and socially recognised, and the influence such a religious identity has on the person's choices, perceptions, and behaviour – including actions or inactions (cf. 1.2).

Therefore, we suggest the following revised sociological definition of *religious persecution*:

> An unjust and arbitrary measure[15] primarily directed at an adherent or group of adherents by reason of their deeply held existential convictions and related manifestations (or the absence thereof), the effects of which – whether arising from a single measure or the cumulative impact of multiple measures – result in varying degrees of fundamental rights violations and other harmful consequences, without necessarily restricting the ability of those targeted to practise their beliefs.

2.3 Legal dimensions of persecution

As a result of barbarous acts and the scourge of war which have outraged the conscience of mankind over the course of human existence, a legal framework emerged in the 20th century, recognising that "the inherent dignity and of the equal and inalienable rights of all members of the human family is the foundation of freedom, justice, and peace in the world".[16] While the notion of human rights has its roots in ancient moral and religious traditions, it has since been codified and has become a core element of international law and geo-political relations. Bielefeldt (2017: 51) explains:

> "... human rights represent the aspiration to empower human beings – on the basis of equal respect and equal concern for everyone's freedom – to develop and pursue their own specific life plans, to freely express their most diverse opinions and convictions, and to generally enjoy respect for their irreplaceable personal biographies, alone and in community with others."

---

15 Measures are defined in the Cambridge Dictionary as "a way of achieving something, or a method for dealing with a situation". The term "measure" is widely used in legal and human rights contexts to encompass a broad range of state or institutional conduct, including legislative instruments (such as laws and regulations), executive or administrative actions or omissions, as well as formal or informal policies and practices.

16 UN General Assembly, *Universal Declaration of Human Rights*, 10 December 1948, Resolution 217 A (III) (UDHR), Preamble par 1.

The protection of human rights is now recognised as an essential precondition for a life worthy of human dignity (Sepúlveda et al. 2004: 3), achieved through a combination of legal frameworks, institutions, and civil society efforts, supported by both international, regional, and domestic mechanisms. In the context of human rights protection, various branches of international law play important complementary roles from different perspectives. With regard to persecution, asylum law and refugee protection primarily seek to safeguard individuals and groups persecuted by their own governments, while international criminal law (ICL) establishes individual criminal responsibility for serious violations of fundamental rights arising from widespread or systematic persecution.

2.3.1 Religion and persecution in human rights law

An important conceptual clarification concerns the role of religion as a common denominator - both in discussions of religious freedom or FoRB within the human rights framework, and in the classification of a particular situation as *religious* persecution.

First, it should be noted that the pluralistic conceptualisation of FoRB in international human rights law (IHRL) implies that "religion" and the related "religious identity" encompass recognition and protection of a broad spectrum of deeply held or significant existential convictions or world-views, including sectarian and secular beliefs, as well as the right not to adhere to any religion or belief (Bielefeldt et al. 2016: 9).[17]

This broader understanding of religion and religious identity informs a more inclusive conceptualisation of religious persecution. It recognises that religious persecution extends beyond discrimination based solely on traditional religious beliefs to include the targeting of individuals based on any deeply held existential worldview, whether secular or sectarian, protected under international human rights law.[18] Accordingly, religious persecution

---

17 'Religion' is a protected ground in terms of the '*International Bill of Rights*' which includes the *Universal Declaration of Human Rights* (adopted in 1948) (UDHR), the *International Covenant on Civil and Political Rights* (ICCPR, 1966) with its two Optional Protocols and the *International Covenant on Economic, Social and Cultural Rights* (ICESCR, 1966); the UN General Assembly, *Declaration on the Elimination of All Forms of Intolerance and of Discrimination Based on Religion or Belief*, UNGA Res 36/55, 73rd plenary meeting, 25 November 1981 (*Religious Discrimination Declaration*); and in the context of persecution, art 7(1)(h) of the *Rome Statute*.

18 In *Campbell and Cosans v. United Kingdom* (1982, App. Nos. 7511/76, 7743/76, p. 13), the European Court of Human Rights affirmed that, for the purposes of the right

refers to a form of persecution in which a person's religious or belief identity, whatever that worldview may be, serves as the primary or predominant reason for their deliberate targeting. Where religion or belief can be identified as the principal basis for such persecution, religious persecution becomes clearly distinguishable from other grounds of persecution.

Second, the classification of a situation as religious persecution is not premised on the nature of the rights infringed. In other words, religious persecution is not classified as such due to the violation of an individual's right to FoRB. Persecution constitutes, first and foremost, "the violation of the right to equality in some serious fashion".[19] Consequently, the core element of persecution in international law is the *discriminatory* deprivation of any human rights and fundamental freedoms – including, but not limited to, FoRB – to which every individual is entitled, without distinction.[20]

As a result, discriminatory deprivation of fundamental rights is a *sui generis* element of religious persecution, conceptually distinguishable from impermissible infringements of FoRB.[21] However, the deprivation of religious freedom rights often acts as the proverbial canary in the coal mine, frequently serving as a forewarning of, or indicator of, impending religious persecution. Conversely, as an equality right, FoRB prohibits religious discrimination, and therefore the discriminatory nature of religious persecution inevitably constitutes a violation of the right to equality on the basis of religion or belief protected under international law.[22]

2.3.2 Asylum law and refugee protection

Asylum law and refugee protection primarily seek to protect individuals and groups of individuals from past or potential future human rights infringements suffered within their country. The focus is, under which

---

to FoRB, the notion of 'belief' is limited to convictions that exhibit "a certain level of cogency, seriousness, cohesion and importance."

19 *Prosecutor v Duško Tadić (Trial Judgement)*, Case No. IT-94-1-T, ICTY, 7 May 1997, par 697.

20 UN General Assembly, *Report of the International Law Commission on the work of its 48th session: resolution / adopted by the General Assembly*, 30 January 1997, A/RES/51/160. Par 11.

21 Article 18(3) of the ICCPR, interpreted in conjunction with UNHRC General Comment No. 22: The Right to Freedom of Thought, Conscience, and Religion in terms of Article 18 of the ICCPR (1993), clarifies the legal framework for permissible limitations on the right to freedom of religion or belief (FoRB).

22 UN General Assembly, *Declaration on the Elimination of All Forms of Intolerance and of Discrimination Based on Religion or Belief*, UNGA Res 36/55, 73rd plenary meeting, 25 November 1981 (*Religious Discrimination Declaration*). See also Bielefeldt et al. (2016) 311.

conditions a foreign state is obliged to grant asylum to a person from another state that claims (fear of) being persecuted, including for reasons of religion. The limiting interests lead to a high threshold for acknowledging persecution.

The *Refugee Convention of 1951* states that the term *refugee* shall apply to any person who:

> "... [O]wing to well founded fear of being persecuted for reasons of race, religion, nationality, membership of a particular social group or political opinion, is outside the country of his nationality and is unable or, owing to such fear, is unwilling to avail himself of the protection of that country; or who, not having a nationality and being outside the country of his former habitual residence as a result of such events, is unable or, owing to such fear, is unwilling to return to it."

Refugee status is determined based on a subjectively genuine fear of persecution, supported by an objectively reasonable possibility of persecution (UNHCR 2011: §39-41).

According to Hugo Storey (2013), the drafters of the Refugee Convention deliberately omitted a definition of the term persecution for fear of being too restrictive. Scott Rempell (2013: 52) quite convincingly proposes to define persecution for the purposes of asylum protection as "the illegitimate infliction of sufficiently severe harm". In this context, the core elements of persecution are manifestations of harm, severity, and an assessment regarding the legitimacy or permissibility of such harm. Importantly, the focus is on the nature and severity of harm, not on cataloguing specific persecutory acts or omissions.

The norms of recognising persecution in the context of asylum and refugee law are quite distinct, and constitute an example of a very narrow use of the term. Thus, one should avoid the pitfall of simply transferring these norms to the much broader discourse on advocacy for those suffering religious persecution, or from imposing it on inner-Christian and theological discussions of the phenomenon of persecution of Christians, as has at times been observed in some ecclesial contexts.

2.3.3 *International criminal law*

Religious discrimination and persecution remains "a major human rights issue of national and international concern, [accordingly] international prosecution systems, as provided by the International Criminal Court (ICC), are to be resorted to in pursuit of criminal accountability" (Van

Boven 2009: para. 22). Evidently, the concept of persecution lies at the natural intersection of IHRL – which recognises it as the severe denial of fundamental rights – and ICL, which acknowledges widespread or systematic persecution as a possible underlying inhumane act of crimes against humanity in terms of the Rome Statute of the ICC.[23]

Certain occurrences of religious persecution are, because of their scale, severity, and discriminatory effect, so heinous that they result in severe deprivations of fundamental human rights and may be justifiably categorised as crimes against humanity of religious persecution, with the potential to escalate into religious genocide or religicide.[24] Such occurrences denote a severe form of religion-based discrimination, characterised by serious violations of fundamental human rights, thereby satisfying the legal threshold for crimes against humanity. Therefore, a key definitional element of crimes against humanity of religious persecution is the requisite discriminatory criminal intent with which the perpetrator consciously and deliberately targets specific victims or a victim group, primarily by reason of their religious identity.

Legal academic Werner Nel (2020) proposes a taxonomy outlining the legal preconditions for establishing the ICC subject-matter jurisdiction over what he terms "grievous religious persecution" (crimes against humanity of religious persecution). The term is a severity-based expression that serves to distinguish particularly serious infringements of fundamental rights, which may amount to crimes against humanity of persecution under international law, from less acute or subsidiary forms of persecution encompassed within broader sociological and theological understandings of the concept.

Nel's taxonomy comprises two main components. The first is a systematic analysis of the distinctive definitional elements of the crime of religious persecution.

The second part of the taxonomy consists of a proposed definition of religious persecution as a crime against humanity in terms of the *Rome Statute* for the purposes of international criminal prosecution as:

---

23 Art 7(2)(g), read with Art 7(1)(h) of the Rome Statute (United Nations 1998), defines persecution as: the intentional and severe deprivation of fundamental rights contrary to international law by reason of the identity of the group or collectively ... on political, racial, national, ethnic, cultural, religious, gender, or other grounds that are universally recognised as impermissible under international law, in connection with any act referred to in this paragraph or any crime within the jurisdiction of the Court.

24 For a more detailed discussion of this topic, see Bennett, G. F., & White, J. (2022). *Religicide: Confronting the Roots of Anti-Religious Violence*. Post Hill Press.

> "The deliberate and unjustifiable persecutory conduct by a persecutor based on an explicit or implied policy of conscious and intentional discrimination against a particular civilian group, primarily targeted based on their religious identity (irrespective of the persecutor's motive), which act or its cumulative effect, resulted in the severe deprivation of the fundamental human rights of those persecuted, is connected to any jurisdictionally relevant inhumane act or core crime, and knowingly forms part of a widespread or systematic attack." (Nel 2020: 197)

It should be noted that the contextual focus of ICL confines the concept of religious persecution to particularly grave instances that meet the intensity threshold for crimes against humanity. This narrow construction significantly limits the conceptual scope, eclipsing the remainder of the scale of a wide-ranging phenomenology of persecution, and excluding less acute or subsidiary forms more commonly recognised within refugee protection frameworks or theological discourse.

While having the benefit of being based on international norms, none of the legal uses of the term persecution are meant to exhaustively cover all existential experiences of persecution. Nonetheless, a legal human-rights-based approach to defining persecution is particularly important for Christian entities engaged in advocacy efforts on behalf of those persecuted.

This is the broader framework in which more specific Christian reflections on persecution as a topic of theology and missiology take place.[25]

3 Theological terminology and definitions of persecution

The Lutheran theologian Michael Knippa (2015: 294) contends that it is not a task of the Christian church to *define* persecution, but to *discern* it. He considers it both difficult and counterproductive[26] to try to draw a precise

[25] Cf. Milán Mór Markovics (2024), who in his essay "An introduction to the theoretical framework of Christian persecution" points at further disciplines that produced theories on persecution (of Christians), such as socio-political theories (Conflict Theory, Resource Mobilisation Theory), Religious Market Theory, psychological and psycho-cultural theories (Scape Goat Theory, Social Identity Theory) and historical and contextual analysis. Among these, possibly diverging definitions of persecution might have been developed that are not covered in this article.

[26] Knippa is less clear about articulating why defining persecution would be counterproductive.

definition of persecution. The difficulty is seen in the fact that "persecution is not universal, uniform, or simplistic; it is rather particular, amorphous, and complex" (: 295). He declares the lack of "an absolutely precise, universally valid Christian definition of persecution" as a virtue to be maintained rather than a deficiency to be corrected (: 294). He rather emphasises discernment as the spiritual task of the church to always prayerfully and carefully discern what is, and what is not persecution in the specific times and locations to which God has called it. In this endeavour, according to him, the two extremes to be avoided, are (1) making the measure of persecution so extreme, as to rule it out of existence or consideration (against Moss 2013 and Kelhoffer 2011), and (2) conflating persecution with any Christian suffering.

We are aware of only few in-depth attempts to define persecution from a theological perspective. Therefore, this theological section will only consider exemplary attempts in Church historiography and NT exegesis.

3.1 Definition of persecutions of Christians in church historiography

In theological encyclopedia, the entries on *persecution* or *persecution of Christians* are most often dominated by a church history perspective and a descriptive approach, often remaining brief or vague about a definition. They usually speak of *persecutions* in the plural[27] to designate mass persecution campaigns directed against Christians, or related epochs.[28] The entry in *The Encyclopedia of Christianity* serves as an example. Kantzenbach (2005: 157) initially admits the difficulty of achieving a comprehensive definition: "We cannot give a single definition of what may be recalled and recounted as persecution for the faith, for it covers the whole period from the primitive Christian community right to the present day". He then, nevertheless, attempts a definition of *persecutions of Christians*:

> "Theologically we must realize that persecutions in the strict sense are violent measures designed to overthrow the Christian religion whether in institutional form or in the form of personal convictions. With their universal scope such measures take the form of laws, though popular movements have the same effect for those concerned. Experiences of the early Christians under the Roman Empire serve as both an example and a standard. Similar situations throughout history have kept those early experiences alive."

---

27 Theological encyclopedias in German most often use the plural *Christenverfolgungen* (TRE, RGG[4]).

28 This would be the third meaning of the term mentioned in the introduction (1.1).

The last phrases raise the issue of in how far the phenomenology of persecution in the first three centuries must be considered normative for a definition of persecution, or whether it becomes a straitjacket for a wider variety of phenomena in church history which is still open to the future.

A broader theological definition of *religious persecution* would also include Christians as persecutors (Kantzenbach 2005: 157), which covers both the persecution of Christian dissidents who are condemned as heretics, as well as persecution *by* Christians of Jews, adherents of non-Christian religions or atheists and agnostics.

Among the dictionaries of mission or missiology, few offer an entry on persecution,[29] and among those who do,[30] only one offers a definition – which is very general: “Suffering experienced by those whose opinion or belief is being attacked by another group” (Moreau 2000: 746).

3.2 Exegetical definitions of persecution of Christians

While the topic of persecution of the righteous and of the prophets of God is a theme deeply anchored in the whole biblical canon (Penner 2004),[31] we limit ourselves to New Testament perspectives here, as these focus more specifically on the persecution of *Christians*.

Chee-Chiew Lee examines the theology of *facing* persecution among NT authors, with an interest in empowering readers to appropriate the results for contemporary reflection (Lee 2022: 163-170). In her brief discussion of definitions, she refers to persecution of Christians in the New Testament as “the unjust treatment meted out to people due to their faith in Jesus Christ as their God, and their Lord and Saviour” and spells out various aspects (Lee 2022: 1-3). While most of these concur with Tieszen (2018a),[32] the following might go beyond his explorations: To call something persecution, it should occur over a reasonably long period of time. Persecution is more than mere opposition, and it must also be distinguished from conformity due to social pressure.

Daniel Röthlisberger (2021), in his published doctorate on support for and self-help of persecuted Christians in NT contexts, offers a broader

---

29 Negative result: Neill 1971, Müller 1987/1997, Bonk 2007.

30 Rzepkowski 1992: 104-105; Schirrmacher in Corrie 2007.

31 Penner cumulatively surveys all books in the biblical canon for their contribution to an understanding of discipleship and persecution but resists any systematisations.

32 She builds on the definitions in the *Cambridge English Dictionary* and by Scott Cunningham (1997), but considers some elements of definitions by Glenn M. Penner (2004) and James A. Kelhoffer (2010, 8) as too broad.

approach: He systematically surveys the semantics and phenomenology of persecution in the NT as a foundation for his study.[33] He summarises the extremely rich findings of manifestations and effects of persecution in ten key phrases (Röthlisberger 2021: 381-392; transl. CS; cf. Röthlisberger 2025), the following of which may provide more detail than the sociological definitions above, or move to dimensions beyond these:

> "(1) According to the NT, persecution can include verbal attacks in various forms, frequencies and intensities. [...] (3) Persecution in the NT can lead to temporary, repeated or permanent displacement through flight, expulsion, deportation or banishment. [...] (4) In the NT, persecution may involve social marginalisation and degradation, maximum economic or material losses and a variety of symptoms of deprivation. [...] (8) Impending or actual persecution can also lead believers in Christ to a clandestine Christian existence and to outward conformity with the non-Christian environment or to apostasy. [...] (10) Those affected by persecution interpret the attacks on their Christian existence as diabolically inspired interpersonal events, which have been repeatedly announced to them, and happen to them exclusively or partly because of their identity as Christians and especially their witness to Christ, and are ultimately directed against the person of Jesus as the Lord and Christ."

Based on these findings, Röthlisberger (2021: 19-20) posits that from a New Testament perspective, the persecution of Christians should be defined as

> "the action of individuals or collectives against believers in Christ, motivated mainly or in part by anti-Christian hostility. This action may vary in form, frequency and intensity, occur by law or illegally, differ in the effects intended, and may attack any dimension of human existence. Those affected interpret the events as diabolically inspired actions, which have been repeatedly announced, and happen to them exclusively or in part because of their identity as Christians and especially their witness to Christ. This is an integral part of discipleship and ultimately directed against the person of Jesus, the Lord and Christ."

The first half of this broad and comprehensive definition can also be regarded as sociological elements that build on the definition of Tieszen (2008b). The potential ambiguity surrounding the use of the term *motivated* is once again evident here. The second half provides the actual theological interpretation. By its nature, such a theological definition provides a

---

33 Cf. Sauer (2016: 126-143) for a number of frequently used terms in the NT for the issues of tribulation and persecution.

Christian "insider"-perspective. It uses its own concepts and categories, which are beyond the scope of sociology and law. Scholars of these disciplines would not see a metaphysical root component in the persecution of Christians in terms of a spiritual power struggle around the proclamation of Jesus as Lord and Christ (John 15,20), nor view it in terms of biblical prophecy or discipleship in the footsteps of Jesus (Matt 5,10-12).

Thus, a theological approach to defining and understanding persecution must not consider the (often narrow) definitions in secular disciplines as a straitjacket that it could not transcend. It bears emphasising that the persecution of Christians may, in certain contexts, be driven by socio-political, economic, or other contingent factors, rather than by direct opposition to the metaphysical or soteriological claims of Christian theology.

4 Divergences and commonalities in persecution definitions

Having examined definitions of persecution in various disciplines, analytical systematisation is called for. We will first distinguish broad and narrow uses of the term and then endeavour to isolate overarching definitional elements of persecution.

4.1 Broad and narrow uses of the term persecution

Broad and narrow uses of the term persecution could be observed (cf. Table 1). They can be distinguished in function, in representation of reality and perspective and have differing usefulness and limitations.

Table 1: Use of the term persecution

	broad	**narrow**
Function	umbrella term	specific phenomenon
Representation of reality	comprehensive	selective
Perspective	existential	mostly legal
Usefulness/limitations	not quantifiable/harder to prove	delimitable/quantifyable/can be proven

A broad use of the term employs *persecution* as an umbrella term in order to give a comprehensive representation of reality. The benefit is to cover everything. Thus, the sociological and theological perspectives examined above are interested in the full "existential dimension" of persecution. The limitation, however, is that if ridicule and sneering are included in the term at the low end of the scale, the fact is no longer quantifiable and harder to prove.

A narrow definition of *persecution*, on the other hand, is usually employed to focus on very specific phenomena, such as in the various applications of law. It therefore depicts a selective representation of reality. The benefit is that it can be more easily delimited and quantified (e.g. systematic state-driven intentional acts can be counted) and can be proven to fulfil certain predetermined narrow criteria.

4.2 Overarching definitional elements of religious persecution

Based on the above review, the following common definitional elements seem to be applicable to all contextual applications of the notion of *religious persecution* (cf. Nel 2020: 196-7):

- *Unjustifiability:* The harm or harmful consequences of persecution must not have been normatively or legally justified or otherwise permissible;
- *Persecutory conduct (actions or omissions)*: Manifestations of harm may be caused by various types of measures, or the effect of a discriminatory policy or ideology. "Measures" should be broadly understood to include actions, omissions, policies, and practices – whether by state or non-state actors, and whether institutional in nature or not;
- *Varying forms of harm*: Harm is the outcome-determinative factor that distinguishes discrimination and intolerance from persecution.[34] In instances of religious persecution, the discriminate harm inflicted on individuals or groups because of their delineated religious characteristics intensifies the overall harm suffered. Given its inherently discriminatory nature, persecution inevitably entails infringements of human rights to varying degrees, and may further give rise to additional forms of harm, including physical, psycho-

[34] From a Christian perspective, it must be acknowledged that some persecuted communities regard their suffering as an inevitable consequence of faithfulness to Christ, and therefore may not interpret it as 'harm' in the conventional sense. In such cases, the notion of harm is viewed less as a subjective experience and more as a socio-legal construct. Nonetheless, within restorative and transitional justice frameworks, recognising and engaging with the victim's experience of harm remains essential for achieving meaningful redress and healing.

logical, financial, or social consequences. The rights infringed in cases of persecution generally concern, inter alia, the rights to equality and non-discrimination, dignity, privacy, freedom and security of the person, and – particularly in cases of religious persecution – the right to freedom of religion or belief;

- *Deliberate targeting based on religion (discriminatory intent)*: At its very core, religious persecution reduces the individuality of the victim to a specific religious identity (broadly defined). Religious discriminatory intent implies that the harm was deliberately and arbitrarily inflicted on the victim or group because of their religious identity, or lack thereof. As mentioned, persecution by reason of religion is, where applicable, distinguishable from religiously motivated persecution, and may or may not stem from religious prejudice or hatred. The persecutor's motivations are not of definitional relevance, but are essential for understanding and countering persecution;
- *Primacy of religion*: The basis of the persecutor's discriminatory intent must primarily (not exclusively) relate to the victim's religious identity, whether based on objective criteria or in the mind of the persecutor;
- *Threshold of severity*: The persecutory measure – whether considered in isolation or through its cumulative effect – may give rise not only to different types of harm but also to varying degrees of severity in the harm or consequences suffered by the victim(s). Contextual understandings of persecution differ with respect to the required threshold of severity; in some frameworks, a minimum level of harm must be met before the measure qualifies as persecution under the applicable definitional criteria.

As can be expected, the specific theological interpretations of *persecution of Christians* cannot be found among the overarching definitional elements of *religious persecution*. Therefore, theologians and missiologists should avoid projecting Christian-specific interpretations of persecution or generalising from them when addressing the broader phenomenon of religious persecution affecting adherents of any religion or belief. However, the elements of discriminatory intent and primacy can be specifically delineated to speak to religious persecution directed at Christians.

The explorations of definitions of persecution in sociology, law and theology and the above definitional elements have provided us with the tools to proceed to critically examining definitions and terminological differentiations among various Christian entities.

5 Definitions of persecution among Christian agencies

The following analysis represents an exemplary sample of the variety of reflected approaches among international Christian role players.[35]

5.1 Open Doors World Watch List

Open Doors International's World Watch Research [ODI/WWR] 2024: 7) defines persecution of Christians in its World Watch List (WWL) methodology document as

> "any hostility experienced as a result of one's identification with Christ. This can include hostile attitudes, words and actions towards Christians."

This is, in fact, an adaptation of the biblical-theological definition developed by Ron Boyd-MacMillan (2006: 114) emphasising universal spiritual dynamics.[36] In his mind, such a definition "makes persecution a process that reflects the experience of the pursuit of Christ in us from the world and the devil" (2006: 115; cf. Bromiley 1995). Similar to Boyd-MacMillan, the WWL methodology statement continues to expand on *types* of persecution:

> "This broad definition includes (but is not limited to) restrictions, pressure, discrimination, opposition, disinformation, injustice, intimidation, mistreatment, marginalization, oppression, intolerance, infringement, violation, ostracism, hostilities, harassment, abuse, violence, ethnic cleansing and genocide." (ODI/WWR 2024: 7)

This statement includes the methodologically important distinction in the WWL between persecution by violent means and persecution through various forms of pressure (ODI/WWR 2024: 20-21). The explanation argues:

> "While this definition has its challenges because of its inclusiveness, such breadth is deemed necessary to cover the full range of hostility that is

---

35 In 2019 the authors conducted a survey among the member agencies of the *Religious Liberty Partnership* on the variety of terminology used to describe and differentiate the phenomena encountered. The compilation of results was shared with a number of leading experts for comment, but remained unpublished to date. Here, we select among the most influential or deeply reflected positions, also considering denominational variety.

36 This definitions additionally includes "hostile feelings."

experienced by Christians in all areas of life, rather than limit the term 'persecution' to more overt forms of persecution or extreme forms of suffering. [...] Also, to say that persecution has to be violent deliberately underestimates the implicit and indirect power of culture which has over time created a situation that squeezes Christians out of normal life in society." (ODI/WWR 2024: 7-8)

There are at least three debatable elements in this definition. The first is the focus on *hostility* as the overarching term instead of *harm*, which deliberately requires an antagonistic mental element, such as hatred or intolerance. The second is the inclusion of "attitudes" alongside words and actions, as depending on one's perspective, one can argue that attitudes that do not turn into actions do not cause any substantial harm. This might be countered by the argument that attitudes do not remain without effect and may e.g. manifest in body language that results in psychological harm. Third, attempting to provide an exhaustive list of the types of persecution is problematic, as it tends to be exclusionary. Just as murder is not defined by cataloguing every possible act that could result in death, persecution is more appropriately defined by reference to the deliberate and arbitrary harm it causes, rather than the specific forms it may take.

As a Christian ministry, serving Christians under pressure, and raising support among Christians, ODI, in line with Boyd-MacMillan (2006: Ch 5-6), explicitly opts for a Bible-based, holistic and comprehensive definition with theological character, aimed at communication among Christians.[37] When, however, developing the WWL as a major product of ODI, actually a legal human rights-based definition appears to dominate rather than the above overarching theological definition.[38]

5.2 Voice of the Martyrs Canada

The understanding of persecution within Voice of the Martyrs Canada (VOMC) is strongly shaped by its former CEO, the late Glenn Penner. It adopts a working legal definition of persecution as

[37] While the definition establishes a contrast between *the world* and Christians, the WWL actually covers both hostile attitudes, words and actions *towards* Christians, and *between* Christian groups (ODI/WWR 2024: 7-8).

[38] According to Anja Hoffmann (2017: 60), the WWL catalogue of questions demonstrates a high degree of conformity with the normative scope of FoRB as expressed in the General Comment 22 on the UN Civil Rights Covenant.

> "a situation where Christians are repetitively, persistently and systematically inflicted with grave or serious suffering or harm and deprived of (or significantly threatened with deprival of) their basic human rights because of a difference that comes from being a Christian that the persecutor will not tolerate." (Penner 2004: 63)

The numerous specifying elements (repetitivity, etc.) in fact lead to a narrow definition of persecution. According to VOMC (2005), and with reference to biblical scripture, *persecution* may range from mildly hostile to intensely hostile actions (cf. 6.4), and thus they argue that the use of the term must not be limited to certain levels of harm or hostility only. While VOMC recognises that, from a theological perspective, persecution includes certain forms of hostility and suffering intrinsic to the Christian experience of following Jesus, its organisational advocacy component poses the question: "At what point on this spectrum do we see our involvement as necessary?"

VOMC, in its public communication as an interdenominational Christian mission organisation, thus tends to emphasise a theological definition of persecution,[39] while the definitions Penner discusses in his theological work are rather legal or sociological.

5.3 Aid to the Church in Need: Religious Freedom in the World

Aid to the Church in Need (ACN), in its *Religious Freedom in the World Report* (ACN 2023), understands a violation of FoRB as a process, in which they distinguish four stages (cf. 6.2), one of which is persecution.

Rather than providing a precise definition of persecution, the report instead identifies and classifies the types of actions and behaviours that it considers to constitute persecution (Szymanski 2023):

> "This stage usually follows discrimination and includes more frequent and more cruel 'hate crimes'.[40] Acts of persecution and hate crimes are performed by a biased perpetrator operating under his own assumptions, who may or may not know the religious identity of the victim. [...] Persecution

---

39 A hallmark of VOMC and some other members of the family of organisations founded or inspired by Richard Wurmbrand is an emphasis on biblical teaching on persecution, which is at times more deeply developed than among some comparable other Christian organisations with a similar focus.

40 It appears problematic to us to mix legal categories. For hate crimes, the use of violence referred to below, is not a necessary element.

> might be an active programme or campaign to exterminate, drive away, or subjugate people based on membership of a religious group. [...] Acts of violence [...] may be perpetrated by single individuals. Acts of persecution are cumulative and need not be 'systematic' nor occur following a strategy.
>
> Both State and non-State actors may persecute any given group [...]
>
> Violence frequently accompanies persecution. Individuals belonging to minority groups may be subject to murder, expropriation and destruction of property, theft, deportation, exile, forced conversion, forced marriage, blasphemy accusations, etc. [...] In extreme cases 'persecution' may turn into genocide, particularly noticeable through the frequency and cruelty of the attacks."

The ANC report also provides an indicative list of acts most frequently associated with persecution, covering all crimes against humanity listed in Article 7 of the Rome Statute of the ICC.

The approach of ACN to persecution in this report is clearly narrowed down to the human rights framework, taking the categories of international crimes into consideration, while claiming to be equally based on Catholic social teaching. In the communication with its supporters, ACN employs Christian concepts and terminology, based on a Roman Catholic spirituality.

5.4 Roots of diversity in communication

All examples presented above demonstrate a considered and deliberately reflective use of the term. The definitions or understandings of persecution among the various Christian agencies range from broad to narrow, depending on whether their approach is more sociological/theological in nature or more grounded in legal-political advocacy. The agencies' choices also depended on their respective organisational mission, communication contexts and specific aims. In line with their respective organisational missions, some prioritise language that seeks to mobilise Christian solidarity, while others adopt an advocacy-oriented approach aimed at engaging broader societal or political audiences. Some focus solely on the plight of Christians, while others address it within the broader framework of advocacy of FoRB for all. Some combine several elements of this matrix of options, pursuing them simultaneously at varying degrees, at times in different departments of the same organisation. Some engage primarily in pragmatic action and education, while others, particularly those producing reports, aim to systematically measure either persecution or violations of religious freedom. For all of them, it is true that *persecution* is not the only term they are using.

6 Scales involving persecution

Due to specific thematic interests or concerns about the perceived overuse of the term persecution, some scholars and advocacy practitioners have proposed embedding it within a broader terminological scale to more clearly delimit its meaning, or alternatively, developing a scaling taxonomy that differentiates the various phenomena typically subsumed under this umbrella term. We start with examining scales that embed persecution as one phenomenon into a wider terminological framework.

6.1 Continuum of FoRB violations (Thames)

In the context of FoRB violations, Knox Thames (2009:11-12) recommends that advocacy efforts be aware of a continuum of five phenomena when describing a situation: persecution – repression – harassment – limitations – discrimination.

In Thames' view, religious persecution should be defined as "systematic, ongoing, and on account of religious or nonreligious beliefs". Ultimately, his understanding of persecution appears to be almost indivisibly linked with violations of the right to FoRB that are characterised by physical acts or the infliction of physical harm. All other phenomena listed are considered of lesser and decreasing severity and are distinguished from the stronger ones based on the methods used to enforce the violation of religious freedom.

While Thames' continuum appears useful for a human rights-based approach to religious freedom violations and restrictions, particularly in diplomacy and advocacy,[41] it should not be regarded as either a definitive academic articulation or practical scholarship of the concept of persecution. By conflating religious persecution as a sub-phenomenon of FoRB, this conceptualisation does not fully do justice to the complex interrelations between the two phenomena and neglects the profound existential nature of persecution.

---

41 In his recent book *Ending persecution*, Thames (2024) describes four types of persecutors, namely authoritarian regimes practicing government oppression, democracies implementing majoritarian rule, extremists closing civic space for religious pluralism, and terrorism in government that terrorises and maims those who fail to conform. However, such valuable differentiations do not seem to immediately contribute to a deeper understanding of above continuum of FoRB violations.

6.2 Escalation scale (ACN)

ACN's Report *Religious Freedom in the World* (ACN 2023) works on an ascending scale, somewhat similar to that mentioned above, adhering to terminology defined in international human rights law: intolerance - discrimination - persecution - genocide (Szymanski 2023).

Each term builds on the one before and escalates in terms of severity. Thus, there can be no discrimination without intolerance, there can be no genocide without persecution, etc.[42] Genocide is considered the ultimate or most extreme form of persecution.[43] The respective phenomena can potentially occur simultaneously. While the model may serve advocacy purposes well, it lacks the legal precision required for scholarly analysis, as it oversimplifies distinct legal categories by suggesting a linear progression from intolerance to discrimination, persecution, and ultimately genocide.

6.3 A typology of the pervasiveness of FoRB violations (Petersen & Marshall)

The scale by Marie Juul Petersen and Katherine Marshall[44] ranges from relatively limited patterns of intolerance and exclusion to systemic discrimination and outright restrictions, and culminates in severe forms of violations and persecution, and ultimately "religious cleansing" and genocide. Genocide is not listed as a separate category, but described as the "ultimate expression of persecution" (Peterson & Marshall 2019: 32).

The category "severe violations" is equated with "what some term persecution" (Petersen & Marshall 2019: 31) and denotes the following (32-33):

---

42 The definitions and what constitutes the passage to the next stage are described in detail. On persecution see 4.3.

43 This mirrors in some way Stanton (2023) who describes processes leading to state driven or supported discriminatory mass killings.

44 According to Petersen & Marshall (2019: 29) "the typology [...] and the terminology applied, is based primarily on the methodology outlined in the European Parliament Intergroup on FoRB & RT's [2018] report, developed by Gatti, Annicchino, Birdsall, Fabretti and Ventura (2018). Some terms are used in ways that are distinct from existing international agreed definitions and usages" (Cf. Gatti et al. 2019). "The methodology used by [ACN], developed by Marcela Szymanski with input from, among others, the former UN Special Rapporteur on FoRB, Heiner Bielefeldt, has also informed the typology" (Petersen & Marshall 2019: 94 fn30).

> "The state commits, sponsors, or tolerates religion-related acts of violence, or fails to prevent or respond to such acts. The state punishes the adoption, changing, or abandoning a religion or belief, blasphemy, religious insult and criticism, with death, forced labour, or longer imprisonment. The state systematically applies restrictions on individuals' or groups' freedom to manifest or practice their religion or belief. The state engages in systematic discrimination based on religion or belief against one or more groups or their individual members.
>
> Non-state actors systematically attack individuals or groups for adoption, changing, or abandoning a religion or belief, blasphemy, religious insult and criticism. Non-state actors systematically interfere with individuals' or groups' freedom to manifest or practice their religion or belief. Non-state actors engage in systematic discrimination based on religion or belief against one or more groups or their individual members."

As in the scales by Thames and ACN, persecution is narrowly delimited, in order to embed it with less severe phenomena termed with other labels. While nothing hinders theologians and missiologists from adopting such methods for empirical work, when doing so, they must not forget that such narrow use does not match the much broader existential significance of the term in Scripture.

Now, we turn to another type of scale that uses persecution as an umbrella term and differentiates its different levels by specific terms.

6.4 "Persecution scale" in biblical terms (Brobbel)

Floyd Brobbel, the current CEO of VOMC, in his book *Trouble on the way* (Brobbel 2021:18)[45], develops what he calls "The Persecution Scale", featuring varying degrees of hostile actions experienced in persecution: ridicule – harassment – discrimination – defamation – attack – arrest/imprisonment – torture – martyrdom.

Each term is briefly defined[46], linked to reports of experiences from biblical times, covering the life of Christ, the church, the righteous of the old covenant, and from contemporary Christians under pressure for their faith.

This scale serves the purpose of biblical education of the Christian church towards a multifaceted understanding of persecution. It stands out from other scales by not containing the term persecution, as it serves as a

[45] According to Brobbel (2021:18 fn1), the "Persecution Scale" was developed at VOMC utilising Glenn Penner's Persecution Blog and Tieszen (2008b).

[46] Definitions are taken from Funk & Wagnalls *Standard Desk Dictionary*, 1969.

terminological unfolding of this umbrella term. The terminology is formulated from the perspective of what happens to the victims. All terms can be accommodated in theological language, and most also in sociological terminology. The only exception is "martyrdom", if one considers this a theological interpretation from the perspective of the victim's community of a killing suffered, rather than a sociological term.

6.5 "Spectrum of persecution" (Anglican Consultative Council)

In various church communities, collective pastoral reflections have taken place on how to provide theological resources in times of persecution. *Out of the depths*, by the Anglian Consultative Council, is one of those publications. It presents a "spectrum of persecution" with some basic definitions of harassment - subjugation - persecution - martyrdom - annihilation - obliteration (Anglican Inter Faith Network [AIFN] 2016: 11-12).

The uniqueness of this scale is that persecution stands at the centre of the scale. Persecution is considered to take place when people "are physically and violently attacked, by individuals or the State". There are both terms for phenomena that are considered weaker or a prelude, and for other phenomena that are considered more extreme than persecution.[47] The choice of terminology, as with VOMC, is a mix of sociological terms with theological interpretations.

[47] The last two terms remind of the final stages of genocidal processes according to Stanton (2023).

6.6 Conclusions on scales

Table 2: Synopsis of various scales

Thames	**ACN**	**Petersen & Marshall**	**Brobbel**	**Anglican CC**
Continuum of FORB violations	**Escalation scale of religious freedom violations**	**Pervasiveness of FORB violations**	**Scale of persecution**	**Spectrum of persecution**
			ridicule (1)	
	intolerance (1)	intolerance and exclusion (1)		
harassment (3)			harassment (2)	harassment (1)
discrimination (1)	discrimination (2)	discrimination (2)	discrimination (3)	subjugation (2)
limitations (2)			defamation (4)	
			attack (5)	
repression (4)			arrest/imprisonment (6)	
persecution (5)	persecution (3)	severe violations (persecution) (3)		persecution (3)
			torture (7)	
			martyrdom (8)	martyrdom (4)
	genocide (4)	[genocide as ultimate expression of persecution – 4]*		annihilation (5)
				obliteration (6)

Legend: *The numbering refers to the order given by the authors. This table has used the longest scale as ordering principle.*
** This is not an explicit item of their scale but subsumed under persecution.*

It is no surprise that the scales examined are found to be competing, already based on the fact that the first three are concerned with violations of FORB, whereas the last two centre around the concept of persecution. Are they all mutually exclusive? Table 2 reflects an attempt to synchronise these scales around shared terminology or equivalent conceptual frameworks. They are shown to contain some identical terms or terms with conceptual overlap. The most frequent are discrimination, persecution, and genocide (or equivalents). However, there is no particular correspondence among the other terms interspersed between them.[48] Also, these terms are likely differently delimited by their respective proponents. Additionally, some terms are arranged in a different order.

All these and other attempts at differentiation of terminology and constructing scales are very welcome as they offer more differentiation than the single term *persecution* could. Each of these scales has a certain inner logic and specific frame of reference. Each applies different severity or intensity thresholds. Most focus on a section only of a broader reality, and their specific contextual understanding is therefore limited in application.

Furthermore, reality is more complex and often various persecution phenomena exist concurrently. We therefore conclude that a single linear scale would prove inadequate to exhaustively cover all possible forms of persecution, at least not for all different contextual uses.

7 Spectrums instead of scales?

Is there a way to view persecution phenomena in a multi-dimensional model, e.g. a pyramid with multiple facets (Figure 2), that exceeds the approach of scales (Figure 1)?

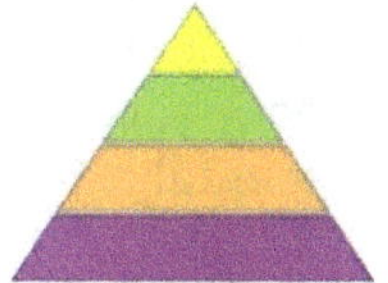

Figure 1

Figure 2

Spectrums of persecution could attempt to provide a description for a scattered spectrum of concurrent persecution phenomena. Some of the spectral dimensions that can be differentiated – without any claim to completeness – are described below. As FoRB infringements and persecution have a large degree of overlap, it appears legitimate to also make use of FoRB concepts that do not exclusively focus on persecution or might not cover all aspects of it.

48 Some of the terms in Brobbel's scale are found to be most difficult to match with those of the other scales. Such unequal terms found in the same lines in this table must not necessarily be considered synonymous or even overlapping.

Table 3: Overview of spectral aspects
Types of persecutory harm
Physical violence vs. pressure
Violations by state actors vs. abuses by non-state actors
Conscience (forum internum) and manifestations (forum externum)
Specific vs. negative discriminatory intent

7.1 Types of persecutory harm

Harm is at the core of persecution and implies actual harmful conduct (acts or omissions) or measures which has harmful consequences for the victims. As noted earlier, religious persecution is best defined in terms of the deliberate and arbitrary harmful consequences it inflicts, rather than by cataloguing the specific forms of persecutory conduct it may involve.

Rempell (2013: 9) notes that "creating a taxonomy of harm is essential to understanding persecution" and "[t]he extent of harm or prospective suffering cannot be accurately valuated without an understanding of the broad spectrum of harms that persecutors can inflict on their victims."

According to Rempell (2013: 10-13; 52; 24) the notion of *harm* may include physical harms, restraints and deprivations of privacy, resource and opportunity limitation, psychological harms, and infringements on human rights. These different forms of harm cannot be graded using the same scale of intensity.[49] The only common denominator between all these forms of harm is the existence of discrimination, considering that religious persecution attacks at least two fundamental aspects of being human.[50]

There are a number of complexities associated with persecutory harms. The conduct causing the harm may be criminal or non-criminal, physical or non-physical. In addition, a single act of persecution can encompass multiple identified categories of harm. For example, physical acts of violence, such as torture or sexual slavery, not only cause physical injuries but may also result in long-term psychological harm. Furthermore, the

[49] Therefore, the first important distinguishing feature of persecution is that not all persecutory conduct can be scaled as infringements of human rights.

[50] According to Luban (2004:116-7) these are, (1) the persecuted victim's individuality, given that persecution reduces a victim to a specific identity based on his or her membership in a religious group; and (2) the victim's ability to freely choose a religious identity and in terms thereof associate with others. However, according to Petri (2021: 19) religious behaviour rather than identity might be the discriminating trigger in some contexts.

perception of harm may differ individually, contextually or even geographically. For example, the deprivation of land will be more compounded for indigenous people or farmers. It should be noted that the harm suffered by a persecuted person may be compounded by intersecting forms of discrimination based on grounds such as religion and gender. In conclusion, types of persecutory harm cannot be comprehensively scaled on a single scale, such as those described above.

7.2 Physical violence vs. pressure

An important distinction lies in the nature of the persecutory conduct experienced, where physical actions and non-physical measures that result in pressure may overlap and have a complementary effect. Both aspects can be separately examined, but it is difficult to weigh them up against each other or to combine their effects on a unified scale. Contrary to popular belief, it is often the restrictive pressure that has the most detrimental impact on the individual or Church's religious freedom because "the degree of persecution can be so intense, and so all-pervasive, it actually results in fewer incidents of [physical acts of] persecution, since acts of public witness and defiance are so rare" (ODI/WWR 2024: 20).

7.3 Violations by state actors vs. abuses by non-state actors

Acts subsumed under a broad concept of persecution are committed either by states or state actors on the one hand, and non-state actors or entities on the other hand. In FoRB terminology, the respective acts by states or state actors are referred to as violations of FoRB, whereas those of non-state actors are referred to as abuses of FoRB or social hostility (Grim & Finke 2010). Quite frequently, there exists a combination of both.

Violations by state actors refer to measures employed by a *de facto* authority, which amount to a denial or deprivation of religious freedom, or other indivisible, interrelated and interdependent rights, which have an adverse effect on religious freedom. The former UN Special Rapporteur on FoRB, Heiner Bielefeldt (2017: 117-123), provided a "non-exhaustive typology" to identify widespread general patterns of systematic infringements of religious freedom committed by state agencies. Such measures may include criminal law sanctions, bureaucratic harassment and burdensome administrative stipulations, the imposition of an official religion or ideology, discriminatory structures in family law, violations in the context of the right of parents regarding religious education, and state-induced discrimination and stigmatisation.

The limitations inherent to this typology, particularly when focusing on "persecution" are, firstly that it does not cover acts that are random, isolated, or committed against a single victim without broader targeting. Second, it does not include all persecutory acts associated with or affecting religion or belief ('subsidiary forms of persecution').

Abuses of religious freedom by non-state actors include acts of religious hostility by private individuals, organisations or groups in society, which may manifest as social ostracism, religion-related armed conflict or terrorism, mob or sectarian violence, harassment for religious reasons or other religion-related intimidation or abuse. Such abuses are often perpetrated in circumstances that allow for impunity, where those in power are either unable or unwilling to respect and protect the rights of (all) their citizens.

7.4 Conscience (forum internum) and manifestations (forum externum)

The distinction between the degree of protection of the right to FoRB in the sectors of *forum internum* and *forum externum* can effectively also be regarded as a fundamental classification of severity of religious freedom violations (du Plessis & Nel 2021). However, the elements that make up those two forums respectively cannot easily be arranged on one scale of severity. Therefore, each of these forums can be considered to contain a broad spectrum of potential religious freedom violations.

The *forum internum* or the internal freedom to choose, have, change or keep a religious identity, enjoys the status of an absolute guarantee under international human rights law. In this regard, no derogation or limitation is ever permitted (United Nations Special Rapporteur on freedom of religion or belief 2023: 8ff; 175ff).[51] It may be argued that some forms of religious activities through worship, observance and practice may not necessarily require an external, public or communicative manifestation per se. Quiet meditation on issues of faith can qualify as worship, and the personal resolve to refrain from certain 'sinful' conduct can qualify as observance.

The *forum externum* or exercise of religious behaviour or manifestations consists of numerous elements as expounded in the relevant documents, which includes teaching, proselytising, publishing and importing religious materials, receiving religious personnel from abroad and other aspects of particular interest to the study of mission. These rights may, in certain circumstances, be limited or restricted in adherence to article 18(3) of the

---

51 See also *UNHRC General Comment No. 22* par 3 read with par 8.

International Convention on Civil and Political Rights (ICCPR), and further elaborated in UNHRC General Comment No. 22.

7.5 Specific vs. negative discriminatory intent

Persecution of a religious group or sub-group may be defined both in a positive manner based on the identity (e.g. Christian) or behaviour (e.g. proselytising) of the group targeted, or in a negative manner, i.e. any person from a non-acceptant or dissenting religion or belief (e.g. all non-Christians) or diverging behaviour (e.g. failure to register) (Lacabe 1998; Petri 2021: 19; 37). Consequently, a victim may be targeted because he or she has, or lacks, a specific religious identity or behaviour.

Such an understanding implies that Christians may experience religious persecution either (1) because of their Christian identity or behaviour (i.e. the persecutor specifically targeted Christians, or those with a particular behaviour), or (2) because they are not belonging to the particular religious persuasion of the persecutor or otherwise opposed or criticised the persecutor's religious identity (indirect or negative discriminatory intent) (Byron 2009: 229-230).

In instances where a persecutor specifically targeted Christians because of their Christian identity, there will usually be direct evidence or a religious discriminatory policy. However, in instances where a broad range of religious communities suffered as a result of a 'blanket' intent to persecute non-conforming religious groups, substantiating that Christians, specifically, were targeted, would require additional arbitrary persecutory treatment.

Consequently, the persecutor does not necessarily have to target a specific religious identity (e.g. Christians), but may target *any* religious identity (including Christians), which is dissimilar to his own (negative discriminatory intent). Conversely, it should not be overlooked that Christians may also persecute others if the victims are targeted because they either lack a Christian identity or a specific Christian denominational identity.

7.6 Analysis of spectrums

There is no claim to completeness of the spectral aspects presented; for example, further differentiation by gender or vulnerable groups could be incorporated. As the description of the five spectral aspects has shown, they each represent relevant but very different distinctions. Some spectral aspects lend themselves to a scale, others are not scalable at all, and again others only for sub-aspects. Among the different spectral aspects that are scalable, a synchronisation regarding intensity and severity in a joint model appears difficult. Thus, even a pyramid or some other geometrical multi-faceted figure does not appear to offer a sufficiently comprehensive model to combine all the spectral aspects mentioned.

However, Table 3 above may serve as a template for a multidimensional classification and differentiated analysis of individual cases of persecution.

Thus, complex approaches recognising the concurrent existence and the combined effect of various persecution phenomena, when trying to establish a comparative scale, usually only arrive at generic descriptors of severity, but not a neatly escalated list of phenomena. An example is the comparative scale of grades of severity in the context of the World Watch List of Open Doors (ODI/WWR 2024: 57). It measures persecution on a numerically defined scale of "extreme – very high – high – variable", offering descriptions of these scenarios.[52] As previously noted, perceptions of severity may vary subjectively among different Christian communities.

8 Conclusions

Although the words *persecute* and the act of *persecution* have come to acquire a broadly accepted meaning, a consensual definition has remained elusive. While distorted perspectives, such as persecutory delusion or self-justificatory rationales of persecutors, can more easily be excluded, the careless overuse of the term *persecution* has reduced its impact when describing an actual situation of persecution. Equally, one continuously needs to argue against a number of reductionist misperceptions of persecution.

In light of these challenges, some, like Petri (2021), have opted to discard the term persecution completely, examining the vulnerability of religious minorities instead, making use of the field of human security studies. Petri simultaneously seeks to overcome the limitation that *persecution* almost always implies an intentional action, which tends to eclipse structural and symbolic violence, including social injustice, which he empirically observes, particularly in the Latin American context.

For those who continue to make use of the term persecution, this survey of definitions of persecution has demonstrated quite a range of contextual understandings, which need to be interpreted on the basis of their

52 It also proposes an explanatory model on six stages in the gradual development of persecution, as an adaptation of the *Religious Economies Model* of B.J. Grim & R. Finke (2010: 68ff) in *The Price of Freedom Denied.*

presuppositions and particular purposes. While having the benefit of being based on international norms, none of the legal uses of the term persecution are meant to exhaustively cover all existential experiences of persecution. They rather represent quite narrow and specific contextual understandings, purposes, and a high threshold of severity of harm, which is generally limited to severe instances of religious persecution. One key advantage of approaching religious persecution through a legal lens, particularly within the framework of ICL is that it offers an objective standard for identifying acts of persecution and determining whether they may be objectively classified as *religious* persecution. This is especially valuable for those engaged in religious freedom advocacy on behalf of persecuted Christians, as it anchors their efforts in a recognised and authoritative legal framework. However, as Bielefeldt points out, "the language of law is not an existential language", and therefore, can never reach the inner existential dimension of a person's conscience.

Consequently, understanding the phenomenon of persecution cannot be a purely empirical exercise; it must remain attentive to its *existential dimension*, informed by sociological, philosophical, psychological, and theological perspectives. Viewed synchronously, it becomes evident that although each contextual use of persecution differs in certain respects, all contribute to a fuller understanding of the phenomenon. In particular, biblical terminology and a NT based definition offer a contextually significant interpretation for Christians and theologians compared to the secular approaches.

Whilst it may be possible to define persecution in each of its different contextual understandings, it seems unattainable to achieve a universal interdisciplinary understanding. Nonetheless, it seems possible to conclude that there are certain definitional elements common to all the contextual understandings of religious persecution. Unjustifiable discriminatory treatment persists as the core element of the notion of persecution.

On this basis, the operational use of definitions, scales, or spectrums of persecution was examined, mainly among selected Christian agencies. A certain range between legal and existential/theological emphasis was observed.

It seems imperative that scholarship on persecution demonstrate a working knowledge of the various contextual spectrums, conceptualisations, and applications of the term *persecution*. It is advisable to explicitly specify the contextual framework within which the term persecution is employed, and to clarify whether it is used in a broad or narrow sense. In this regard, it may be necessary to develop terminology (or build on existing terminology) that facilitates a better understanding of the varying contextual descriptions of the persecution phenomenon (spectrums), grades of severity (scales), and their rationale. An example of such a deliberately crafted term is *grievous religious persecution*, which functions as a context-specific variation of the term persecution, and its wording provides a clear indication of the required threshold of intensity.

It has also been noted that various authors, spanning sociological to theological disciplines, use terms related to motive – including motivation, motivated, and similar expressions – when defining religious persecution. Such terms should be used with caution, as the concept of motive carries a specific legal meaning that may differ from the intended usage, potentially leading to confusion.

In terms of the scales of persecution, it was shown that various institutions and authors have attempted to delineate a scale of persecution, some with great success. However, what these linear scales lack in conception is an appreciation of the spectrums of the persecution phenomenon. Thus, a single linear scale to cover all forms of persecution may not be possible. Therefore, the limitations of scales, when used, should be clearly acknowledged. However, the authors suggest that it may be possible to design a range of scales (as different facets of a pyramid), which consider each of the contextual thresholds discussed, and limit the forms of hostility and harm to an understanding relevant to that context.

To express such complex realities precisely, one needs nuanced language – for the sake of discriminated and persecuted Christians and for the sake of religious freedom of everybody everywhere. Our definitions, whichever we may choose, must never stand in the way of helping those who are vulnerable to human security threats and suffer discrimination and persecution.

9 References

Aid to the Church in Need. (2023). *Religious freedom in the world report 2023.* https://acninternational.org/work/religious-freedom-report/

Anglican Inter Faith Network. (2016). *Out of the depths: Hope in times of suffering: Theological resources in times of persecution.* Anglican Consultative Council.

Bielefeldt, H. (2013). Misperceptions of freedom of religion or belief. *Human Rights Quarterly*, 35(1), 33-68.

Bielefeldt, H. (2017). *Freedom of religion or belief: Thematic reports of the UN Special Rapporteur 2010-2016.* VKW.

Bielefeldt, H., Ghanea, N., & Wiener, M. (2016). *Freedom of religion or belief: An international law commentary.* Oxford University Press.

Boyd-MacMillan, R. (2006). *Faith that endures: The essential guide to the persecuted church.* Sovereign World; Revell.

Brobbel, F. A. (2021). *Trouble on the way: Persecution in the Christian life.* Genesis.
Byron, C. (2009). *War crimes and crimes against humanity.* Manchester University Press.
Bromiley, G. W. (1979). Persecute; persecution. In *ISBE*, Vol. 3 (pp. 771-774). Eerdmans.
Cherepanov, E. (2021). *Understanding the transgenerational legacy of totalitarian regimes: Paradoxes of cultural learning*. Routledge.
Du Plessis, G. A. & Nel, W. N. (2021). The dimensional elements of the right to freedom of religion or belief in the South African Constitution: An evaluation in light of relevant core international human rights instruments. *Journal for Juridical Science*, 46 (1): 25-56.
Gatti, M., et al. (2018). *Annual report annex,* European Parliament Intergroup on FoRB & RT.
Gatti, M., et al. (2019). Quantifying persecution: Developing an international law-based measurement of freedom of religion or belief. *The Review of Faith & International Affairs*, 17(2), 87-96.
Grim, B. & Finke, R. (2010). *The price of freedom denied: Religious persecution and conflict in the twenty-first century.* Cambridge University Press.
Guiora, A. N. (2009). *Freedom from religion: Rights and national security*. Oxford University Press.
Hoffmann, A. N. (2017). *Measuring freedom of religion: An analysis of religious freedom indexes* [Master's thesis in Human Rights, Universität Wien].
Juhnke, J. C. (2003). *Rightly remembering a martyr heritage. Mennonite Life*, 58(3). https://mla.bethelks.edu/ml-archive/2003Sept/
Jung, T. J. (2023). *Costly Kuyperianism: Neo-Calvinist public theology in a context of persecution with a focus on Pastor Wang Yi* [PhD]. Southeastern Baptist Theological Seminary.
Kantzenbach, F. W. (2005). Persecution of Christians. In E. Fahlbusch (Ed.), *The encyclopedia of Christianity.* Eerdmans; Brill.
Karenian, H., et al. (2010). Collective trauma transmission and traumatic reactions among descendants of Armenian refugees. *International Journal of Social Psychiatry*, 57, 327-337.
Kelhoffer, J. A. (2010). *Persecution, persuasion, and power: Readiness to withstand hardship as a corroboration of legitimacy in the New Testament.* Mohr Siebeck.
Kelhoffer, J. A. (2011). Withstanding persecution as a corroboration of legitimacy in the New Testament: Reflections on the resulting ethical and hermeneutical quandary. *Dialog: A Journal of Theology*, 50(2), 120-132.
Knippa, M. (2015). No "lions of gory mane": Persecution and loss of predominance in American Christianity. *Concordia Journal,* Fall, 293-306.
Lacabe, M. (1998). *The criminal procedures against Chilean and Argentinian repressors in Spain. Derechos Human Rights.* www.derechos.net [currently inaccessible]
Lee, C.-C. (2022). *When Christians face persecution: Theological perspectives from the New Testament*. Apollos.
Luban, D. (2004). A theory of crimes against humanity. *YJIL*, 29, 116-117.
Markovics, M. M. (2024). An introduction to the theoretical framework of Christian persecution. In J. Kaló, F. Petruska & L. Ujházi (Eds.), *Budapest Report on Christian Persecution 2022-2024* (pp. 34-46). L'Harmattan.
Moreau, A. S. (2000). Persecution. In A. S. Moreau (Ed.), *Evangelical dictionary of world missions* (pp. 746-7). Baker.
Moss, C. (2013). *The myth of Christian persecution*. Harper One.

Nel, W. N. (2020). *Grievous religious persecution: A conceptualization of crimes against humanity of religious persecution* (Religious Freedom Series 5). VKW.

Nel, W. N. (2023). Mind the misnomer: Juxtaposing discriminatory intent with motive in relation to grievous religious persecution. *Tydskrif vir die Suid-Afrikaanse Reg*, 3, 424-458, https://doi.org/10.47348/TSAR/2023/i3a3

Open Doors International / World Watch Research. (2024). *Complete World Watch List methodology* (revised October). https://www.opendoors.org/research-reports/wwl-documentation/complete-WWL-Methodology-October-2024

Penner, G. M. (2004). *In the shadow of the cross: A biblical theology of persecution and discipleship.* Living Sacrifice Books.

Petersen, M. J., & Marshall, K. (2019). *The international promotion of freedom of religion or belief: Sketching the contours of a common framework.* Danish Institute of Human Rights. https://www.humanrights.dk/sites/humanrights.dk/files/media/dokumenter/udgivelser/research/accessibility_checked_2020/rapport_internationalpromotion_updated.pdf

Petri, D. P. (2021). *The specific vulnerability of religious minorities* (Religious Freedom Series 6). VKW.

Preti, A. & Cella, M. (2010). *Paranoia in the 'normal' population.* Nova Science Publishers.

Refugee Convention of 1951. Article 1 A(2) of the United Nations General Assembly Resolution 429(V) of 14 December 1950, UN High Commissioner for Refugees (UNHCR), *Convention and protocol relating to the status of refugees.* https://www.unhcr.org/3b66c2aa10

Rempell, S. (2013). Defining persecution. *Utah Law Review*, 1, http://dx.doi.org/10.2139/ssrn.1941006

Röthlisberger, D. (2021). *Hilfe und Selbsthilfe für verfolgte Christen: Eine Studie zum neutestamentlichen Ethos.* Evangelische Verlagsanstalt.

Röthlisberger, D. (2025). Persecution in the New Testament: How semantic and phenomenological findings help to define "persecution". In R. Lilleaasen & C. Sauer (Eds.), *Religious Persecution.* VKW.

Sauer, C. (2016). Bedrängnis, Verfolgung und Mission: Begrifflichkeiten im Neuen Testament als Orientierungspunkte. In E. Werner et al. (Eds.), *Jahrbuch Bibelübersetzung 1* (pp. 126-143). VTR.

Sauer, C. (2025). Suffering, persecution and martyrdom: Revisiting the Bad Urach Statement. In R. Lilleaasen & C. Sauer (Eds.), *Religious Persecution.* VKW.

Sauer, C. & Nel, W. (2025). *Religious persecution: Definitions, scales, spectrums and language use reflected for the context of theology and missiology.* IIRF Reports. www.iirf.global

Sepúlveda, M., et al. (2004). *Human rights reference handbook* (3rd ed.). University for Peace.

Stanton, G. (2023). *The logic of the ten stages of genocide.* https://www.genocidewatch.com/tenstages

Storey, H. (2013). Persecution: Towards a working definition. In V. Chetail & C. Bauloz (Eds.), *Research Handbook on Migration and International Law* (pp. 459-518). Edward Elgar.

Szymanski, M. (2023). *Methodology and definitions.* [ACN Religious Freedom in the World Report] June 21. https://acninternational.org/religiousfreedomreport/executive-summary#methodology

Thames, H. K., Seiple, C., & Rowe, A. (2009). *International religious freedom advocacy: A guide to organizations, law and NGO's.* Baylor University Press.

Thames, H. K. (2024). *Ending persecution.* University of Notre Dame Press.
Tieszen, C. L. (2008a). Towards redefining persecution. *IJRF,* 1, 67-80.
Tieszen, C. L. (2008b). *Re-examining religious persecution: Constructing a framework for understanding persecution* (Religious Freedom Series 1). AcadSA; VKW.
UN General Assembly. (1946). *Resolution 103(I) Persecution and Discrimination,* 19 November 1946. https://digitallibrary.un.org/record/209880?v=pdf
UN High Commissioner for Refugees (UNHCR). (2011). *Handbook and guidelines on procedures and criteria for determining refugee status under the 1951 Convention and the 1967 Protocol relating to the status of refugees* (HCR/1P/4/ENG/REV. 3). UNHCR.
UN Human Rights Committee. (1993). *General comment No. 22: The right to freedom of thought, conscience and religion (Article 18),* U.N. Doc. CCPR/C/21/Rev.1/Add.4.
UN Special Rapporteur on freedom or religion or belief. (2023). *Rapporteur's Digest on FORB.* 2nd ed. https://www.ohchr.org/sites/default/files/Documents/Issues/Religion/RapporteursDigestFreedomReligionBelief.pdf
United Nations. (1998). *Rome Statute of the International Criminal Court* (A/CONF.183/9). https://www.icc-cpi.int/sites/default/files/RS-Eng.pdf
Van Boven, T. (2009). Racial and religious discrimination. In R. Wolfrum (Ed.), *Max Planck encyclopedia of public international law.* Oxford University Press.
Voice of the Martyrs Canada. (2025). *What is persecution?* https://vomcanada.com/whats-persecution.htm. Accessed 31 March 2025.

B. Biblical Studies

2 The zealous ones

Ambiguous models of faithfulness in the Hebrew Bible

Håkon Sunde Pedersen[1]

Abstract

In their zeal for YHWH, Phinehas, Elijah, and Jehu kill people perceived as threats to the exclusive worship of YHWH alone. While these figures and their zeal for YHWH seem overlooked in the *Bad Urach Statement*, they have been both praised and criticised as models of faithfulness to YHWH in other contexts. In this article, I devote attention to these characters and argue that the narratives about them cast a highly ambiguous light on them as models of faithfulness. Based on my reading, I suggest that those responsible for these narratives in their present form were perhaps more aware of the problem of zeal for YHWH and the act of killing in the name of YHWH than is often assumed. Hopefully, my reading of these narratives can be a constructive contribution to the further development of an evangelical theology of religious persecution.

Keywords: Religious persecution, zeal for YHWH, Phinehas, Elijah, Jehu.

1 Introduction

> "Elijah insisted upon the honor due the Father, but did not insist upon the honor due the son, as it is said: 'And he said, I have been very zealous for the Lord, the God of Hosts' (1 Kings 19:10). And thereupon what is said? 'And the Lord said unto him: Go return on thy way to the wilderness of Damascus; [...] Elisha the son of Shaphat of Abel-meholah shalt thou anoint to be prophet in thy room' (ibid., vv. 15-16). The expression 'in thy room,' used here, can have no purport other than: I am not pleased with your prophesying." (*Mekhilta de-Rabbi Ishmael*, 2004, Pisha I:17)

1 Håkon Sunde Pedersen (*1980), Associate Professor in Old Testament Studies, Fjellhaug International University College, hspedersen@fjellhaug.no, ORCID iD: 0009-0002-5534-8947.

In the Bad Urach Statement (2010, pp. 27-106), which aims to pave the way for an evangelical theology of religious persecution, it is emphasised that in the Hebrew Bible, "[c]onflict, persecution, and martyrdom were characteristic of all true prophets [of YHWH]" (p. 44). The prophets are seen as models of faithfulness, showing that "suffering, persecution and martyrdom have been the lot of God's people over and over again, all through Old Testament scriptures" (p. 44).

What is seemingly overlooked is that some prophets also demonstrated their faithfulness to YHWH by engaging in religious persecution, persecuting and killing worshippers of other gods themselves.[2] The prime example is Elijah, the zealous prophet of YHWH. While he certainly experienced persecution for his faithfulness to YHWH (1 Kings 19:2), his zeal for YHWH also led him to engage in religious persecution, as he "killed all the prophets [of Baal] with the sword." (1 Kings 19:1).

Contrary to the Bad Urach Statement, the rabbis quoted above were evidently aware of the duality in the story of Elijah and clearly viewed his zeal for YHWH as problematic. Employing their characteristic interpretative techniques,[3] they cast a shadow over Elijah's legacy: In his zeal for God, Elijah served only God (i.e. "the Father"), not his people (i.e. "the son"). This did not please God, and therefore, he was replaced by Elisha, says the rabbis.

According to Martin Hengel (1989, pp. 156-183), this criticism of Elijah reflects a hard-won admission among rabbis of the 2nd century AD The Jewish-Roman wars had ended, the tragic results were evident, and it was time for reckoning. In this context, some rabbis identified the praise and idealisation of zeal for YHWH – understood as "a passionate giving of oneself to God's cause" that manifests itself in an uncompromising and violent "readiness to avenge every form of sacrilege" (p. 177) – in certain branches of late second temple Judaism as a vital catalyst to the wars and the resulting tragedy for the people. In the aftermath of the wars, they saw the need to confront this phenomenon. They did so by launching an attack on the well-established role models of the Zealots, namely the zealous figures of the Hebrew Bible – that is, Phinehas, Elijah and Jehu. All three are explicitly characterised as zealous for YHWH (Num 25:10-13; 1 Kings 19:10-13;

---

2 For a similar tendency to overlook narratives in the Hebrew Bible that describe prophets of YHWH persecuting worshipers of other gods, see Penner (2004, pp. 11-84).

3 For helpful introductions to characteristic interpretative techniques of rabbinic exegesis, see, for instance, the following sources: Kraemer (1996); Kalmin (1996); Neusner (1996).

2 Kings 10:16) and well-known for killing people in the course of avenging activities considered to threaten the exclusive worship of YHWH alone (Num 25:7-8; 1 Kings 18:40; 2 Kings 9:14-10:28).

Criticising Phinehas, Elijah, and Jehu was no easy task. The praise of their zeal for YHWH had deep roots, especially the praising of Phinehas (cf. Ps 106:30; Sir 45:23; 1 Macc 2:26, 54). Yet, the rabbis did not shy away from the challenge. Instead of simply ignoring them, the rabbis developed creative and clever readings that challenged the notion of them as commendable role models.

However, the rabbis might not be without predecessors. I would suggest that those responsible for the present form of the narratives about Phinehas, Elijah, and Jehu in the Hebrew Bible may have had certain reservations about embracing the zealous ones as ideal models of faithfulness, as well. At least, in this article, I will argue that a literary-canonical reading of the present form of selected narratives about Phinehas, Elijah and Jehu casts a highly ambiguous light on them as such models. My focus will be on how these three characters and their zeal for YHWH are portrayed and presented in narratives where they figure as major characters. I follow the canonical-chronological order of the Hebrew Bible, starting with Phinehas, then Elijah, and finally Jehu.

Hopefully, my reading of these narratives can be a constructive contribution to the further development of an evangelical theology of religious persecution – a theology that not only overlooks but also attempts to seriously consider the issue of zeal for YHWH and biblical narratives about YHWH-believing persecutors.

2 Phinehas in Numbers 25 and Joshua 22

Phinehas, son of Eleazar and grandson of Aaron, appears in four different narratives in the Hebrew Bible (Num 25; 31; Josh 22; Judg 20-21).[4] The most interesting to us are the narratives in Num 25 and Josh 22. One notable aspect is that Phinehas features as a major character in these narratives. More importantly, Phinehas takes on vastly distinct roles in these two narratives. When read together in accordance with their placement in the Hebrew Bible, a highly ambiguous light is cast on the zealous Phinehas. Let me begin with a closer look at Num 25.

In Num 25 Phinehas bursts onto the scene as a man of action. Phinehas sees (ראה), rises (קום), grabs (לקח) a spear, and pierces (דקר) a man of Israel

4 Brief references to Phinehas can also be found in Ps 106:30 and in the genealogies of Exod 6:25; Num 3:32; 1 Chr 5:30 [6:4]; 6:35 [6:50]; 9:20; Ezra 7:5; 8:2.

and a Midianite woman (vv. 6-8). For this action, YHWH praises Phinehas: "Behold I grant him my covenant of peace [...] a covenant of perpetual priesthood, because he was zealous for his God" (vv. 12-13).

What exactly Phinehas saw that awakened his zeal for YHWH is not explicitly stated in the text. This question has elicited various answers. Does the couple represent a sexual, ethnic, or cultic problem for Phinehas?[5] The difficulty in answering this question is further complicated by the intrinsic complexity of Num 25,[6] which is commonly understood as a compilation of at least two originally distinct narratives (e.g., Ashley, 1993, pp. 514-515; Budd, 1984, pp. 275-279; Levine, 2000, pp. 279-281). A literary-canonical approach, however, must attempt to make sense of the text as it stands before the reader, and a basic plot seems clear enough.[7]

The narrative begins with the people of Israel committing fornication with the daughters of Moab and worshipping their gods (vv. 1-3), provoking YHWH's anger (vv. 4-5). The scene then shifts to Moses and the people weeping at the entrance of the tent of meeting. At this moment, a man of Israel, Zimri (cf. v. 14), brings a Midianite woman, Cozbi (cf. v. 15), into the camp, right in front of the grieving people (v. 6). Phinehas then takes action and kills the couple (vv. 7-8). As a result, the plague that has struck Israel and killed twenty-four thousand people ceases (v. 9).

Given this basic plot, Phinehas' killing of Zimri and Cozbi is ultimately connected to the people's worship of the gods of the Moabites. Barbara E. Organ (2001, pp. 205-209) substantiates this understanding by highlighting the frequent occurrence of cultic references in vv. 6-13 and argues convincingly that Phinehas somehow perceived the couple as a threat to the exclusive worship of YHWH alone.

What is noteworthy about Phinehas' zealous killing of Zimri and Cozbi is, first, its spontaneity. As Marko Marttila (2014, p. 13) points out: "There is no report about any divine intervention or any command from God to

5 For further discussion on what sparked Phinehas' zeal, see Reif (1971, pp. 200-206); Waters (2017, pp. 38-55); Monroe (2012, pp. 211-231).

6 In addition to the obscurity of certain Hebrew expressions, particularly אל הקבה (NRSV: "into the tent") and אל קבתה ("through the belly") in v. 8, three features complicate the unity of the narrative. First, there is a shift from Moab (v. 1) to Midian (vv. 6, 14-18). Second, there is a change from "Israel" (ישראל) and "people" (עם) in vv. 1-5 to "sons of Israel" (בני ישראל) and "congregation" (עדה) in vv. 6-18. Finally, three sentences are mentioned without clarifying the relationship between them (cf. vv. 4, 5, 9).

7 It is also worth noting that the events in Num 25 are referred to as a singular incident both at the end of Num 25 (cf. vv. 17-18) and elsewhere in the Hebrew Bible (cf. Num 31:16; Deut 4:3; Josh 22:17; Hos 9:10; Ps 106:28-31).

do this. It is a spontaneous and voluntary act by Phinehas [...]." Phinehas' killing is presented as an immediate response to what he sees and observes. Second, YHWH's response to Phinehas' killing is one of approval and acknowledgement. In addition to the promise of "a covenant of perpetual priesthood" (v. 13), YHWH identifies Phinehas zeal as his own – "in that he was zealous with my zeal" (בקנאו את קנאתי, v. 11) – and attributes an atoning effect to Phinehas act of killing (v. 13). Because of Phinehas zealous act, YHWH turned his wrath away from the people and refrained from making an end of them (v. 11).

A stronger form of acknowledgement is difficult to imagine, and we may conclude with Organ's (2001, pp. 209-210) brief and pithy statement: "Phinehas, the hero of the hour, saves the day for Yhwh" – and not least, we may add, for the people of Israel and Phinehas himself.

However, if we now turn our attention to Josh 22,[8] Phinehas takes on a radically different role. And as will be seen, what "saves the day" in Josh 22 is that Phinehas does not act as he did in Num 25.

The setting in Joshua 22 is that the tribes of Israel are returning to their respective territories after the conquest of the land of Canaan is complete (vv. 1-8). Reuben, Gad, and the half-tribe of Manasseh return to their land east of the Jordan. On their way home, they build an altar for YHWH by the Jordan (v. 10). When the other tribes of Israel hear about the altar,[9] they gather in Shiloh "to go to war" against Reuben, Gad, and the half-tribe of Manasseh (v. 12). The reason for this dramatic decision is that the other tribes of Israel see the building of an altar by the Jordan as an act of apostasy and unfaithfulness to YHWH, and consequently as something that threatens the whole of Israel (vv. 16-20).

For some reason, however, the strategy changes. Instead of immediate war, a delegation of tribal leaders is first sent to confront Reuben, Gad, and the half-tribe of Manasseh about their altar (vv. 13-14). Phinehas leads the delegation (v. 13), and with Phinehas at the head, the problem is resolved, and all of Israel is "saved from the hand of YHWH" (v. 31).

The parallels to the narrative in Num 25 are clear, and the incident at Peor is explicitly referenced for comparison, along with the Achan incident in Josh 7 (cf. Josh 22:17, 20). The comparison emphasises the seriousness of

---

8 Although Josh 22 may have undergone several stages of composition, it is well-established that Josh 22, in its present form, reads well as a unified narrative (cf. Dozemann, 2023, pp. 306-308).

9 The other tribes of Israel are variously referred to as "(families/clans of) Israel" (vv. 14, 21, 22), "sons of Israel" (vv. 9, 11-13), or "the congregation (of Israel)" (vv. 12, 16-18, 20, 30).

the situation in Josh 22. Due to someone's unfaithfulness to YHWH, all of Israel is threatened with extermination (cf. Num 25:11; Josh 7:12; 22:18, 20). But just as at Peor, Phinehas plays a key role in resolving the problem, and he does so without divine instructions on how to solve it.

However, Phinehas' contribution to solving the problem in Josh 22 is entirely different from his contribution in Num 25. Instead of drawing weapons, Phinehas first resorts to verbal confrontation with reprimands and warnings (Josh 22:16-20). Then, he proposes a peaceful solution by inviting Reuben, Gad, and the half-tribe of Manasseh to join the other tribes of Israel west of the Jordan: "Come over to YHWH's own land, where YHWH's tabernacle is, and take for yourselves a possession among us" (v. 19). Finally, Phinehas follows up the invitation by allowing the opposing party room to explain and defend themselves against the accusations. In short, the zealous man of action "has turned into a man of words, a diplomat" (Organ, 2001, p. 214).

This change "saves the day" in Josh 22. For this time, Phinehas – along with the tribes of Israel gathered at Shiloh – are mistaken about what they see. The altar built by Reuben, Gad and the half-tribe of Manasseh is not a sign of apostasy and unfaithfulness. On the contrary, they built the altar for the sake of future generations, as a witness that they too – that is, their descendants living east of the Jordan – belong to Israel and "have a portion in YHWH" (v. 27). After hearing the explanation from Reuben, Gad and the half-tribe of Manasseh, Phinehas realises he was mistaken and concludes that this time, it is not him, but "you [i.e., Reuben, Gad and the half-tribe of Manasseh] who have saved Israel from the hand of YHWH" (v. 31).[10]

The comparison between the two narratives of Num 25 and Josh 22, which Josh 22 explicitly invites, is telling. Despite YHWH's strong approval of Phinehas' actions in Num 25, Josh 22 subtly highlights the danger of the Phinehan zeal for YHWH: One can be mistaken about what one sees and interpret the situation incorrectly. Without directly criticising Phinehas in

---

10 The different interpretations of the altar in Josh 22 are disputed (cf. Soggin, 1972, pp. 212-215; Dozeman, 2023, pp. 310-313; Woudstra, 1981, pp. 319-325). However, it seems clear that they somehow concern the question of what it means to worship YHWH alone. In that regard, Josh 22 serves as a good example of the point made by Gerhard von Rad (1975, pp. 209-210) regarding the first commandment: The Hebrew Bible does not provide "any ready-made authentic and once-for-all valid understanding of the meaning and scope of the first commandment. Rather was she [Israel] obliged in every situation to ascertain afresh what Yahweh's will for the cult was the moment, for the situation in which she had to remain loyal to the first commandment was constantly changing."

Num 25, a literary-canonical reading suggests that Josh 22 serves as a warning against an uncritical idealisation of Phinehas in Num 25. While Phinehas' zeal for YHWH "saved the day" in Num 25, it would have been a disaster in Josh 22.

3 Elijah in I Kings 17-19

If Phinehas is the zealous priest, then Elijah of Tishbe in Gilead is the zealous prophet. Elijah emerges as a major character in the narratives in 1 Kings 17-19, 21, and 2 Kings 1-2.[11] Without any introduction, Elijah takes the stage in 1 Kings 17, confronting Ahab, the king of Israel, and announcing, "[T]here shall be neither dew nor rain these years, except by my word" (1 Kings 17:1). Ahab, thoroughly introduced in the preceding chapter (cf. 1 Kings 16:29-33), is a king who "did evil in the sight of YHWH, more than all who were before him" (16:30, cf. v. 33). Among Ahab's evils are his marriage to Jezebel, daughter of the Sidonian king Ethbaal, and his building of a temple for Baal in Samaria (1 Kings 16:31-32). Elijah's struggle against Ahab, Jezebel and the Baal cult in Israel permeates the narratives about him and forms the context for Elijah's zeal for YHWH. However, although the narratives naturally sympathise with Elijah in this struggle, his zeal for YHWH is not presented without a critical perspective.

As regards the narratives about Elijah in the Books of Kings, the narratives in 1 Kings 17-19 are of particular interest to us. These include the statements about Elijah's zeal for YHWH – in the form of a self-attestation: "I have been very zealous for YHWH, the God of hosts" (19:10, 14). There is also the Mount Carmel narrative, which, more than any other narrative, has contributed to the common praise of Elijah as one of the greatest prophets of the Hebrew Bible. As Jerome T. Walsh (1992, p. 465) says: Elijah is the "quintessential hero" among all prophets of the Hebrew Bible. H. H. Rowley (1960, p. 191) argues that Elijah "was the prophet who saved the Israelite faith in the greatest peril it had to face between the days of Moses and the Exile." Elijah did so – that is, "saved the Israelite faith" and gained his hero status – by his zeal for YHWH: "[W]ith his fiery zeal [...], [Elijah broke] the power of the Baal-worship, and [...] secured an acknowledgment of the authority of Jehovah over His people" (Keil & Delitzsch, 1965, p. 233). The prime example of how Elijah "[broke] the power of Baal-worship" is, of course, his duel against the prophets of Baal at Mount Carmel where he demonstrated that YHWH is God (1 Kings 18:36-39) and ensured that all the

11 Brief references to Elijah can be found in 2 Kings 3:11; 9:36; 10:10, 17 and Mal 3:23 [Eng. 4:5].

prophets of Baal were put to death (1 Kings 18:40).[12] On Mount Carmel, Elijah truly lives up to his name: YHWH is God (אליהו).

However, with the emergence of literary and narratological approaches to biblical narratives in the 1980s and 90s,[13] new light was shed on the portrayal of Elijah. Scholars began to see Elijah as a considerably more ambiguous figure than commonly assumed.[14] Consequently, new and more ambiguous light was also shed on Elijah's zeal for YHWH. To clarify the claim of ambiguity, let me highlight three observations in the narratives. The third and final observation is the most important to us, while the first two pave the way for the final observation and the conclusions drawn from it.

First, it is a general characteristic of the Elijah narratives that Elijah tends to draw attention to himself and often operates with striking independence in relation to YHWH. A good example is when Elijah enters the scene in 1 Kings 17:1. Elijah does not act as a messenger announcing "thus says YHWH" like other prophets of YHWH usually do. Instead, Elijah draws attention to himself and his own words: "[T]here shall be neither dew nor rain these years, except by my word." Other examples of Elijah drawing attention to himself include his insistence that he must get bread first, before the widow and her son (1 Kings 17:13), his repeated assertion that he is the only one left of YHWH's prophets (1 Kings 18:22; 19:10, 14), his prayer that it must be known to all that he is a servant of YHWH (1 Kings 18:36), and his lament that he is not better than others (1 Kings 19:4).

Elijah also seems inclined to act independently of divine instructions, as indicated by the occurrences of explicit affirmations of Elijah's acts and speeches, and the notable lack of such affirmations. In addition to the affirming testimony of the widow of Zarephath – "Now I know that you are a man of God, and that the word of YHWH in your mouth is truth" (17:24), – the typical phrase "according to the word of YHWH" appears in 1 Kings 17:5, 16 and 2 Kings 1:17. However, this phrase is absent in 1 Kings 18-19

12 Certainly, the praise of Elijah as one of the greatest prophets of the Old Testament is not only due to his fight against the Baal cult. Other important factors include the great and sometimes frightening miracles that followed him (cf. 1 Kings 17:6, 16, 21-23; 18:38; 2 Kings 1:9, 12; 2:11) and the many parallels identified between Elijah and Moses (see, for example, Gray, 1970, pp. 376-377; Wiseman, 1993, p. 45; DeVries, 2003, pp. 209-210).

13 The starting point for this trend in biblical scholarship is often dated to the publication of Alter (1981).

14 See especially Gregory (1990, pp. 91-152); Kissling (1996, pp. 113-147); Olley (1998, pp. 25-51); Glover (2006, pp. 449-462).

and 21, which does not seem coincidental.[15] It is only in 1 Kings 17 and 2 Kings 1 that Elijah follows YHWH's instruction to the letter (cf. 1 Kings 17:2-5, 8-10, 14-16; 2 Kings 1:3-7).

In the Mount Carmel narrative (1 Kings 18:16-40), Elijah follows no instructions from YHWH. Both the duel and the slaughter of the Baal prophets occur at Elijah's own initiative (cf. 18:21-24, 40). In 1 Kings 19, Elijah does not follow up on YHWH's instructions to anoint the triad: Hazael, Jehu and Elisha (cf. 19:15-21).[16] Finally, in 1 Kings 21, the words of judgment Elijah announces over Ahab (21:29-24) differ quite remarkably from "the word of YHWH that came to Elijah" (cf. 21:17-19). Hence, it does not seem coincidental that it is only in 1 Kings 17 and 2 Kings 1 that it is emphasised that Elijah acted "according to the word of YHWH." In sum, these features suggest that Elijah is consciously portrayed as a character who is somewhat occupied with himself and inclined to act independently of divine instructions.[17]

Second, it seems clear that, in its present form, 1 Kings 17-19 constitutes a narrative unity consisting of a series of more or less self-contained narratives – "a cycle of tales" (Cogan, 2000, p. 456). The narratives are connected in various ways, primarily through an overarching chronology. The initial announcement of drought by Elijah (17:1) sets the stage for Elijah's stay by the brook Cherith (17:2-6), his journey to Zarephath in Sidon (17:7-24), and finally, Ahab's and Obadiah's search for Elijah (18:1-14) culminating in the climactic duel on Mount Carmel (18:15-40). After the duel, the drought ends (18:41-46).

Elijah's slaughter of the Baal prophets at Mount Carmel sets the stage for a new series of events. Jezebel threatens Elijah's life (19:1-2), and Elijah flees in fear, first into the desert (19:3-7) and then to a cave on the mountain of God, Horeb, where he meets with YHWH (19:8-18). This means that

---

15 One could, of course, argue that the fire of YHWH in 18:38 serves to affirm the duel at Mount Carmel (cf. 18:36). However, it is noteworthy that there is no explicit divine instruction concerning the duel, which is quite unusual (see Olley, 1998, pp. 35-36). Additionally, regarding Elijah's killing of the Baal prophets, there is no instruction or affirmation, either explicit or implicit, in 1 Kings 18.

16 First, there is no reference to Hazael being anointed as king of Damascus in the Books of Kings. Second, Jehu is anointed as king of Israel by "a son of the prophets" sent by Elisha (2 Kings 9:1-10). Finally, there is no reference to Elisha being anointed as a prophet, although Elijah's act of casting his cloak upon Elisha (1 Kings 19:19) "is no doubt some kind of investiture" (Olley, 1998, p. 41).

17 For further observations supporting this understanding of the portrait of Elijah, see the references provided in footnote 14.

all the narratives in 1 Kings 17-19 seem to be connected into a whole, with the Horeb narrative (19:10-18) serving as the climactic conclusion.

Finally, when taken as a unity, interesting points of connection between individual narratives and characters within 1 Kings 17-19 come into view. As Neil Glover (2006, p. 458) notes: "Words are what the narrative uses to throw [narratives and] characters against each other." Most important to us in that respect is the connection established between the Obadiah narrative (18:1-14) and the Horeb narrative (19:8-18), and eventually between Obadiah and Elijah, through the use of the keyword "cave" (מערה) in 18:4, 13; 19:9, 13. In both narratives, one or more prophets of YHWH hide in caves because of Jezebel's persecution. However, the parallel is filled with tension and contrast.

The Obadiah narrative describes twice how Obadiah saved a hundred prophets of YHWH from Jezebel's deadly persecution by hiding them in caves (18:4, 13). Apparently, Obadiah did this at significant risk to his own life. As the chief of Ahab's household (18:3), Obadiah is evidently a close and trusted man to Ahab (cf. 18:5-6). Nevertheless, Obadiah dares to sabotage Jezebel's plan to exterminate all the prophets of YHWH. No explanation is given for Obadiah's heroic action, except for a statement that he was a man who revered YHWH greatly (18:3) and a subtle hint through his name. Obadiah means "servant of YHWH" (עבדיהו).

The contrast with Elijah is striking. Elijah is also a servant (עבד) of YHWH (cf. 18:36), but a zealous one (19:10, 14). Unlike Obadiah, who adapts to Ahab's and Jezebel's YHWH-hostile regime and serves YHWH from within, Elijah seeks confrontation and retaliates by slaughtering the prophets of Baal (18:40). The outcome of Elijah's zealous slaughtering, however, remains unclear. While the people of Israel at Mount Carmel confess that YHWH is God (18:39), at Mount Horeb Elijah laments that all of Israel has forsaken YHWH and that he is the only exception (19:10, 14). Apparently, the dramatic and spectacular event at Mount Carmel did not leave a lasting impression on the people. This may also be the point in the theophany (19:11-13)? YHWH is not in the dramatic and spectacular phenomena of wind, earthquake, and fire, but in "the sound of a low whisper" (19:12).

Be that as it may, the most important point for us to notice is the juxtaposition of two radically different models of faithfulness to YHWH in 1 Kings 17-19. While it may be tempting to argue that the narrative favours the Obadiah model over the Elijah model, it is at least clear that the Obadiah model is highly appreciated. This appreciation places the zeal model of Elijah in a strikingly ambiguous light.

4 Jehu in 2 Kings 9-10

Finally, there is also a zealous king. Jehu – king of the northern kingdom of Israel – appears as a main character in 2 Kings 9-10,[18] which reads well as a unified narrative.[19]

Jehu is an extraordinary character in the Books of Kings. He declares his zeal for YHWH (2 Kings 10:16) and is the only king of Israel to be assessed favourably: "You have done well in carrying out what is right in my eyes" (10:30). As confirmation of this positive assessment, Jehu is promised a dynasty: "Your sons of the fourth generation shall sit on the throne of Israel" (10:30).[20] Although this is not a promise of eternal validity like that given to Phinehas, Jehu established the longest-standing dynasty in Israel according to the Books of Kings.[21] Nevertheless, in Jehu's case as well, the presentation of his zeal for YHWH is marked by a certain ambiguity.

Jehu's positive assessment and promise are inextricably linked to his achievements. Jehu enters the scene as a warrior and one of the commanders of the army of Joram, king of Israel and son of Ahab (cf. 9:5, 7). Then, behind Joram's back, Jehu is anointed as the new king of Israel and organises a rebellion against Joram (9:1-16). After this, a slaughter unfolds in essentially three acts. First, Jehu strikes down the house of Ahab. Jehu kills Joram (9:21-26), Jezebel (9:30-37), seventy sons of Ahab in Samaria (10:1-10), "all who remained of the house of Ahab in Jezreel, all his great men and his close friends and his priests" (10:11), and finally, "all who remained to Ahab in Samaria" (10:17). Second, Jehu kills Ahaziah, the king of Judah (9:27-29), and his brothers (10:12-14). Finally, Jehu kills all the worshipers of Baal in Israel by luring them into the temple of Baal in Samaria and killing them there (10:18-28).

The first two acts are closely related and intertwined in various ways (cf. Quine, 2019, pp. 541-544). It is sufficient to note that Ahaziah and his

---

18 Brief references to Jehu can be found in genealogies (2 Kings 14:8; 2 Chr 25:7), typical introductory notices (2 Kings 12:1; 13:1), parallel passages (2 Kings 15:12; 2 Chr 22:7-9), and finally in the announcement of judgment in Hos 1:4.

19 For a thorough literary analysis of 2 Kings 9-10, see Robker (2012, pp. 18-69).

20 The Jehu dynasty includes the following kings: Jehu (2 Kings 9:1-10:36), Jehoahaz (1 Kings 13:1-9, 22-25), Joash/Jehoash (13:10-13, 22-25), Jeroboam II (2 Kings 14:23-29) and Zechariah (2 Kings 15:8-12).

21 According to the Books of Kings, there were two long-standing dynasties in the northern kingdom of Israel: The Omri dynasty, which reigned for almost fifty year (cf. 2 Kings 16:21, 29; 22:52; 2 Kings 3:1), and the Jehu dynasty, which reigned for more than hundred years (cf. 2 Kings 10:36; 13:1, 10; 14:23; 15:8).

brothers partially belonged to the house of Ahab through their mother Athaliah, who was the daughter of Ahab (cf. 2 Kings 8:18, 26; 11:1).

More importantly, there are no references to Jehu's zeal for YHWH before the introduction to his slaughter of the Baal worshipers in Samaria. It is only on his way to Samaria that Jehu invites a man named Jonadab to "come [...] and see my zeal for YHWH" (10:16).

Nevertheless, scholars often tend to lump together all of Jehu's killings and see them as expressions of his zeal for YHWH. A good example is the summary provided by Walter Brueggemann (2008, p. 28): "The many deaths in the royal family, plus the death of Baal worshipers in general (2 Kings 10:18-28) [...] constitute the way in which Jehu has 'done well.' He has gone very far in zeal for Yhwh, as far as one could go without reembracing the Jerusalem temple and king."

In 2 Kings 9-10, however, a strikingly clear distinction is made between Jehu's slaughter of the house of Ahab and his slaughter of the Baal worshipers.[22] To begin with, the former, the stories about Jehu's killing of the Ahabites are characterised and sewn together by the prophecy-fulfilment pattern typical of the Books of Kings.[23] Like a refrain, it is repeated again and again that Jehu's slaughter of the house of Ahab is in accordance with a prophetic word of YHWH (cf. 9:25-26, 36; 10:10, 37). The prophetic word most often referred to is "the word YHWH spoke by his servant Elijah of Tishbe" (9:34; cf. 10:10, 17). In addition to Elijah's prophecy, the Jehu narrative opens with a prophecy by an unidentified "son of the prophets" sent by Elisha (9:6-10). Like Elijah's prophecy, this prophecy announces judgment over the house of Ahab. It is formulaic in character and has several similarities with the prophecies announced against the houses of Jeroboam and Baasha (cf. 1 Kings 15:10-11; 16:3-4; 21:21-24). Notably, this prophecy, shaped as a commission to Jehu (cf. 2 Kings 9:6-7), only concerns the extermination of the house of Ahab (cf. 9:7-10). Nothing is said about the extermination of Baal worshipers. Interestingly, this corresponds with the evaluation of Jehu at the end of the Jehu narrative. The "good" (טוב)

---

22 There are notable connections between the slaughter of the Ahabites and the Baal worshipers. Firstly, in the Books of Kings, the house of Ahab is closely linked to the Baal cult (cf. 1 Kings 16:31-33; 18:19). The slaughter of the Baal worshipers occurs in the temple of Baal, which was built by Ahab in Samaria (cf. 1 Kings 16:32; 2 Kings 10:10-28). Secondly, Jehu justifies his killing of Joram by citing the idolatry of Joram's mother, Jezebel (cf. 2 Kings 9:22). Thirdly, Jehu's final blow to the house of Ahab happens in Samaria, just before the slaughter of the Baal worshipers (cf. 2 Kings 10:17).

23 For more on the prophecy-fulfilment pattern in the Books of Kings, see Rad (1975, pp. 339-344).

and "right" (ישר) carried out by Jehu is specified: "[Y]ou have dealt with the house of Ahab in accordance with all that was in my heart" (10:30). Thus, just like the commission prophecy, the evaluation oracle refers exclusively to the house of Ahab, not the zealous slaughter of the Baal worshipers in Samaria.

It is therefore not surprising that the prophecy-fulfilment pattern central to the stories about Jehu's killing of the Ahabites is absent from the story about Jehu's slaughter of the Baal worshipers. In fact, as T. R. Hobbs (1985, p. 132) points out: "Nothing in this story reflects favorably upon Jehu." Jehu's slaughter is presented as an act initiated by Jehu himself, and it goes without any marks of approval or acknowledgement. Rather, two observations seem to suggest the opposite. First, Jehu's killing of the Baal worshipers begins in a way suggesting that, ultimately, this is all about himself. The initial invitation to Jonadab to come and see his zeal for YHWH (10:16) suggests that Jehu is doing it for his own sake, not for YHWH's sake. Second, it is worth noting that for Jehu, the end seems to justify the means. To achieve his goal, Jehu resorts to deceit and falsehoods by proclaiming his devotion to Baal and inviting all Baal worshipers to a sacrificial feast for Baal (10:18-22). Along with the striking absence of positive evaluations of Jehu's zeal, these observations, I would argue, cast an ambiguous light also on Jehu's zeal for YHWH.

5 Conclusion

In their zeal for YHWH, the priest Phinehas, the prophet Elijah, and the king Jehu kill people perceived as threats to the exclusive worship of YHWH alone. While these figures and their zeal for YHWH seem overlooked in the Bad Urach Statement, they have been both praised and criticised as models of faithfulness to YHWH in other contexts.

Instead of ignoring them, I have devoted attention to them in this article. At the same time, through a literary-canonical reading, I have challenged tendencies to idealise them as models of faithfulness. As they appear to us in their present form, the narratives about Phinehas, Elijah, and Jehu seem to cast a highly ambiguous light on their zeal for YHWH. Although Phinehas, uniquely, is praised by YHWH for his zealous act in Num 25, Josh 22 serves as a clear corrective to an idealisation of the zealous Phinehas. Similarly, Obadiah serves as a corrective to an idealisation of the zealous Elijah in 1 Kings 17-19. Finally, it is somewhat unclear how Jehu's zeal for YHWH is actually valued in 2 Kings 9-10, but several observations in the narrative of Jehu suggest that Jehu demonstrates his zeal for YHWH primarily for his own sake. And to achieve this goal, all means seem to be justified. In sum, this casts a highly ambiguous light on all three zealous figures in the Hebrew Bible. In my view, this may not be accidental. Like rabbis of the 2nd century AD, those responsible for these narratives in their present form were perhaps more aware of the problem of zeal for YHWH and the act of killing in the name of YHWH than is often assumed.

6 References

Alter, R. (1981). *The Art of Biblical Narrative*. George Allen & Unwin.
Ashley, T. R. (1993). *The Book of Numbers*. NICOT. Eerdmans.
Bad Urach Statement. (2010). In C. Sauer & R. Howell (Eds.), *Suffering, Persecution and Martyrdom: Theological Reflections*. RFS 2. AcadSA.
Brueggemann, W. (2008). Stereotype and Nuance: The Dynasty of Jehu. *The Catholic Biblical Quarterly, 70*(1), 16-28.
Budd, P. J. (1984). *Numbers*. WBC 5. Word Books.
Cogan, M. (2000). *1 Kings*. AB 10. Doubleday.
DeVries, S. J. (2003). *1 Kings* (2nd ed). WBC 12. Thomas Nelson.
Dozeman, T. B. (2023). *Joshua 13-24*. AB 6C. Yale University Press.
Glover, N. (2006). Elijah versus Narrative of Elijah: The Contest between the Prophet and the Word. *Journal for the Study of the Old Testament, 30*(4), 449-462.
Gray, J. (1970). *I & II Kings* (2nd ed). OTL. SCM.
Gregory, R. (1990). Irony and the Unmasking of Elijah. In A. J. Hauser & R. Gregory (Eds.), *From Carmel to Horeb* (pp. 91-152). JSOTSup 85. Sheffield Academic.
Hengel, M. (1989). *The Zealots: Investigations into the Jewish Freedom Movement in the Period from Herod I until 70 A.D.* D. Smith (Trans.). T & T Clark.
Hobbs, T. R. (1985). *2 Kings*. WBC 13. Word Books.
Kalmin, R. (1996). Patterns and Developments in Rabbinic Midrash of Late Antiquity. In M. Sæbø (Ed.), *Hebrew Bible/Old Testament. The History of Its Interpretation I/1: Antiquity* (pp. 285-302). Vandenhoeck & Ruprecht.
Keil, C. F. & Delitzsch, F. (1965). *The Book of Kings*. Translated by James Martin. Eerdmans.
Kissling, P. J. (1996). *Reliable Characters in the Primary History: Profiles of Moses, Joshua, Elijah and Elisha*. JSOTSup 224. Sheffield Academic.
Kraemer, D. (1996). Scriptural Interpretation in Mishnah. In M. Sæbø (Ed.), *Hebrew Bible/Old Testament. The History of Its Interpretation I/1: Antiquity* (pp. 278-284). Vandenhoeck & Ruprecht.
Levine, B. A. (2000). *Numbers 21-36*. AB 4A. Doubleday.
Martilla, M. (2014). The Figure of Phinehas from Different Perspectives. *Journal of Ancient Judaism, 5*(1), 2-24.
Mekilta de-Rabbi Ishmael (2nd ed). (2004). J. Z. Lauterbach (Trans.). Jewish Publication Society.
Monroe, L. (2012). Phinehas' Zeal and the Death of Cozbi: Unearthing a Human Scapegoat Tradition in Numbers 25:1-18. *Vetus Testamentum, 62*(2), 211-231.
Neusner, J. (1996). The Hermeneutics of the Law in Rabbinic Judaism: Mishna, Midrash, Talmuds. In M. Sæbø (Ed.), *Hebrew Bible/Old Testament. The History of Its Interpretation I/1: Antiquity* (pp. 303-322). Vandenhoeck & Ruprecht.

Olley, J. W. (1998). YHWH and His Zealous Prophet: The Presentation of Elijah in 1 and 2 Kings. *Journal for the Study of the Old Testament, 23*(80), 25-51.
Organ, B. E. (2001). Pursuing Phinehas: A Synchronic Reading. *The Catholic Biblical Quarterly, 63*(2), 203-218.
Penner, G. M. (2004). *In the Shadow of the Cross: A Biblical Theology of Persecution and Discipleship.* Living Sacrifice Books.
Quine, C. (2019). Jehu's Slaughter of Juda's Royal Family at Beth-Eked (2 Kings 10:13-14): A Closer Look. *Zeitschrift für die alttestamentliche Wissenschaft, 131*(4), 537-548.
Rad, G. von. (1975). *Old Testament Theology* (vol. 1). D. M. G. Stalker (Trans.). SCM.
Reif, S. C. (1971). What Enraged Phinehas? A Study of Numbers 25:8. *Journal of Biblical Literature, 90*(2), 200-206.
Robker, J. M. (2012). *The Jehu Revolution: A Royal Tradition of the Northern Kingdom and Its Ramifications.* BZAW 435. De Gruyter.
Rowley, H. H. (1960). Elijah on Mount Carmel. *Bulletin of the John Rylands Library, 41*(1), 190-219.
Soggin, J. A. (1972). *Joshua.* OTL. R. A. Wilson (Trans.). SCM.
Walsh, J. T. (1992). Elijah. In D. E. Freedman (Ed.), *The Anchor Bible Dictionary* (vol. 2, pp. 463-466). Doubleday.
Waters, J. L. (2017). The Belly: Phinehas' Target in Numbers 25:8. *Conversations with the Biblical World, 37*, 38-55.
Wiseman, D. J. (1993). *1 & 2 Kings.* TOTC. InterVarsity.
Woudstra, M. H. (1981). *The Book of Joshua.* NICOT. Eerdmans.

3 The Maccabees' motives

What caused believers to maintain their identity in a time of crisis

Geert W. Lorein[1]

Abstract

This study is about the motives of the Maccabees (second century BC) in their conflict with the Hellenistic king Antiochus IV Epiphanes. After sketching the historical background, the sources and the reasons why Antiochus IV started his repression (against which he could expect some resistance) the reaction of the Jews is described: what exactly were the points that could not be accepted and the motives that prompted action? Specific kinds of action were undertaken, with different opinions within the group about the use of violence. Not only theological convictions, but also character traits and practical considerations played a role. Although the main motives were overall the same, varieties in viewpoints and expression existed within the movement.

Parallels between Hellenistic times and our own days present themselves at several points, but it will be left to the reader to transfer to any contemporary situation.

Keywords: Maccabees, Antiochus IV Epiphanes, Megillat Antiochus, religious motives, persecution, trust.

1 Introduction

1.1 Historical background

With the name 'Maccabees' we indicate a Jewish group in the second century BC, in the context of their conflict with the Hellenistic kings, i.e. the

[1] Geert W. Lorein (PhD Groningen University 1997) is part-time professor of Old Testament at the Evangelische Theologische Faculteit, Leuven, and has published mainly in the domains of later Old Testament and early Jewish texts and theology, as well as on the relationship between law, religion and society. Email: glorein@etf.edu, ORCID iD: 0009-0003-4825-6718.

successors of Alexander the Great. Due to his untimely death, his succession was not established well and his large empire broke down in different pieces, among which was also the Seleucid Empire. Antiochus IV Epiphanes, its eighth king, born probably in 212 and reigning from 175 to 164 BC (Mørkholm 1966: 38, 43, 192-193; Lorein 2001: 166-167), had a very specific relationship with Greek culture and for that reason initiated persecution of the Jews.[2] The family that played a specific role in the reaction to this persecution was the family that came to be known as the Maccabees,[3] whose name is now used to designate this entire episode in history.

1.2 Sources

The documents that we have at our disposal do not date from the very days of the Maccabees. This implies a certain distance, but the advantage is that this distance has brought a form of theological synthesis. Anyhow, they give a description of what can be understood of the Maccabees' motives to stand firm in persecution and to react.

These four sources are sympathetic to the Maccabees' reaction, albeit with some variation. We presume that these variant voices in the sources represent variant viewpoints among the Maccabees themselves.

1.2.1 II Maccabees

The *earliest* source is *Second* Maccabees, an abridgment of the much larger work of a certain Jason from Cyrene. What we have is this text of the Pharisaic abridger, writing in the year 124,[4] convinced of the need of the Maccabean uprising, but a bit disappointed about its outcome.[5] Generally, this document does not consider foreign rule as such to be a problem, but views

---

2 With the term 'Jews', we underline the religious aspect; the term 'Judeans' underlines the geographical belonging. In light of the subject matter of this study, it is obvious that 'Jews' will be used more frequently. To make a distinction between I Macc. ('Judeans') and II Macc. ('Jews'), as Schwartz (2013: 20-22) would do, is too complicated, and after all, considering the spirituality of the author of I Macc., incorrect.

3 Called after John Maccabee (Aram. מַקָּבָא, 'the hammer'; I Macc. 2:60; Flavius Josephus, *Antiquitates* XII 284).

4 Bunge (1971: 615): "aus den Pharisäern nahestehenden Kreisen, die zwar dem Tempel treu ergeben waren, aber dem herrschenden Hasmonäerhaus eher ablehnend gegenüberstanden"; for the dating, see his p. 616. With a completely different reasoning Doran (1981: 112) arrives at a slightly later date.

5 Boccaccini (1999: 28): "un sostenitore convinto ma disincantato della rivolta maccabaica".

the measures taken by Antiochus IV Epiphanes as inacceptable (Collins 2016: 200; Hezser 2013: 226; Schwartz 2013: 8; Schwartz 2008: 482). We can already say at this moment that this is the document in which motives are most frequently mentioned.

There are no traces of any other original language than Greek. It is deuterocanonical, i.e. only in second instance recognised as canonical by the Roman Catholic Church and not considered canonical in the Churches of the Reformation (Lorein 2014: 136).

1.2.2 I Maccabees

First Maccabees was written in 100 BC (Schwartz 2013: 27; Deines 2001: 479).[6] According to this document, foreign rule is the problem (I Macc. 1) and the Hasmonean dynasty – 'Hasmoneans' is the name of the Maccabees once they had come to full reign – (in a moderated form) the solution (I Macc. 14; Schwartz 2013: 18). First Maccabees is by far the longest text, but it contains fewer remarks about what the author considers to be motivating people's acts.

Jerome claimed to have found I Maccabees in Hebrew (Prol. in libro Regum 'galeatus' 55-56), but we have only the Greek version. It is deuterocanonical too.

1.2.3 IV Maccabees

At a larger distance from the events come IV Maccabees and Megillat Antiochos, but for theological considerations these sources remain interesting.

Fourth Maccabees was written in the second quarter of the first century AD, with II Maccabees in the author's mind, but apparently not in his sight (Dupont-Sommer 1939: 26-32). Typical is the Hellenistic packaging of this document. Its content, however, is fully Jewish. It is in connection with God's Law and holiness that the human spirit is able to strive for the Greek virtues.

Fourth Maccabees clearly has been written in Greek, in about the second quarter of the first century AD, as the Temple still existed and the text was accepted by Christians (Anderson 1985: 532-534). Antioch is often mentioned as place of origin, in relation with the commemoration of the

6 Le Moyne (1972: 73-75) mentions already their lax attitude regarding the Sabbath (I Macc. 2:32-38, 41; 9:34, 43-46), the importance of the priests (2:54; 12:6; 14:20, 41, 47), the absence of angels, supernatural deliverance, resurrection (2:51, 59-60; 9:20-22; this must be nuanced); Davidic expectation (14:14).

martyrs at that place, but Asia Minor has also been proposed (deSilva 2018: 395-397). It has come to us in some Septuagint manuscripts[7] – indeed, often some interesting books were added to the canonical ones (Stordalen 2001: 137) – and some manuscripts of Josephus, because IV Maccabees has been considered a work of Flavius Josephus (e.g. Jerome, *De viris illustribus* 13). It has been highly appreciated by a lot of Church Fathers (deSilva 2018: 420-422), but is nowhere considered canonical (Dörrie 1937: 45-48, 53-54).

1.2.4 Megillat Antiochus

A last document is the Megillat Antiochos, in German also called 'Hasmonäerbuch', to be situated in the second century AD (Van Staalduine-Sulman 2011; Vivian 1987: 163-164), possibly in Antioch, because of the traditions about the Maccabees in that city (Kasher 1981: 228-229).[8] It rewrites in Aramaic the first chapters of I Maccabees – so a kind of Targum –; theologically, however, it is more in line with II Maccabees. It shows little respect for historical reconstruction.

2 Antiochus IV's persecution

The first phase that must be discussed is the reason why Antiochus IV started his repressive policies, an initiative against which he could expect resistance. Some discussion has always existed about this issue.

We must take into account two ideological aspects: Antiochus' self-image (Lorein 2001: 163-165), with a choice for Greek and more specifically Athenian culture[9] and his hate for the Jews (Baran 2014: 58-59).

A complicating factor is that a portion of the Jewish people (and we are not informed about numbers) saw new possibilities in these developments for their careers as members of one big Hellenistic family (Baran 2014: 63, 65). I agree[10] with Bickerman's (1979: 88) remarks about Menelaos: "What could be more human, what could be more natural, than their [= "Menelaus and his partisans"] desire to force this tolerance

---

7 At least in A and א and the 8th/9th century Venetus manuscript; not in B (where I, II and III Macc. are lacking too [Dupont-Sommer 1939: 4]). It makes part of the Sankt Gallen Stift 12 manuscript (8th-9th century AD) (Brandt 2001: 262), but that is exceptional for medieval manuscripts.

8 Vivian 1987: 176: Jerusalem.

9 Baran 2014: 61 n. 23, for γέροντα Ἀθηναῖον as a gerousia member from Athens. Cf. Antiochus' support for the Zeus temple in Athens (Mørkholm 1966: 58).

10 Even if I do not agree in full with his historical reconstruction; cf. Lorein 2001: 166 n. 49.

also upon those of their coreligionists who were still unenlightened? That was the persecution of Epiphanes".

The outburst came by a false rumour that Antiochus IV had died (II Macc. 5:5) in Egypt, which led to an uprising and then the king's reaction to it (Lorein 2001: 158-159). It was followed, in the year 167 BC,[11] by the decree compelling everyone to adopt the Hellenistic worldview, including its polytheism.[12] Antiochus was hoping that by extirpating Jewish religion, his problem would be finished too.[13]

The desecration[14] of the Temple (I Macc. 1:41-50, 54; II Macc. 6:1-2) and the pagan offerings of pig meat on the Zeus altar (Lorein 2001: 166) were part of the same movement.

The whole country had to bear the consequences of these changes, and it is there that the persecution[15] starts.

3 The Jews' reaction and their motives

3.1 Generalities and variations

This was not left without reaction on the part of the Jews. The main question for this study is: what were their motives? What prompted their actions? As we can find these only by reading the texts,[16] we must reduce this to: 'How were the motives of the Maccabees perceived by people who were standing in their tradition?'.

---

11 All dates are based on Goldstein 1976: 161-174, not because we are sure he is right, but because he has a practical overview that is not idiosyncratic. Cf., however, Lorein 2001: 166-167.

12 I Macc. 1:41-42, which must be seen as historical (Lorein 2001).

13 In other regions, outside Judea, this edict did not create much troubles, and we do not hear of any. In other words, from this silence it cannot be concluded that the edict would be an invention (Gutberlet 1920: 24; Tcherikover 1959: 186-193, 198-201).

14 βδέλυγμα τῆς ἐρημώσεως.

15 I am aware of the definition problem of 'persecution' (see Sauer 2020) but I think the term can be applied to the situation with Antiochus IV Epiphanes (see Lorein 2001: 161-166).

16 But without the introductory parts; i.e. II Macc. 1-2 and IV Macc. 1:1-3:19. This comes up to 964 vv. or 60 pp. (Rahlfs) for I Maccabees; 487 vv. or 36 pp. (Rahlfs) for II Maccabees; 405 vv. or 23 pp. (Rahlfs) for IV Maccabees; and – much harder to compare but anyway it is by far the shortest document – 66 vv. or 10 pp. (https://opensiddur.org/readings-and-sourcetexts/mekorot/non-canonical/exoteric/extracanonical-megillot/megillat-antiokhus-critical-text-prepared-by-menahem-tsvi-kaddari-translated-by-john-reeves/) for Megillat Antiochos.

As far as differences occur between the four sources, it is obvious that *all* tendencies disliked the repression and persecution.[17] However, specific kinds of action were undertaken, with different opinions within the group about the use of violence, and probably also with different degrees of pride and nationalism. These differences were partly based on variation in viewpoints, but also on variation in the way that these viewpoints had to be *communicated*, and that aspect is depending rather on spirituality, that strange mix of character and theology, the living out of belief in what is considered a virtuous life.

I shall discuss the motives in categories, illustrated with some typical texts.

3.2 Theology in the strict sense: Who is God?

All Jews believed that there is only one God (II Macc. 7:37), who has created everything and who is sovereign.[18] God has installed a covenant – with instruction for the believers –, through which he wants to show his mercy. This implies that reverence is due to God (and that every form of dishonouring him must be avoided) and that he is able to intervene in a miraculous way. This worldview is common to all four sources.

Already at this first point we observe a difference in spirituality. The author of I Maccabees shares his belief in God with his colleagues, but in contrast to them, he does not mention the *word* 'God' at all (Blumenthal 2015: 696-697), completely in line with the keeping of distance towards him in intertestamental literature (Lorein 2022: 143-150).

3.3 Implications for believers

The author of I Maccabees emphasises the desire to stay in line with God's covenant, which is considered to be central for Israel's destiny (Choi 2021: 161).[19] I quote I Macc. 1:63:

> "And they chose rather to die so that they might not be defiled with food, or profane the holy covenant; and they did die."

---

17 Even those who joined Antiochus' policy, refrained themselves: see II Macc. 4:18-20 (Baran 2014: 71).

18 II Macc. 8:18 (Lorein 2022: 134-135); II Macc. 15:21 (Schmitz 2010: 75, 77: God is almighty and sovereign as main fundamental thoughts in II Maccabees).

19 I do not think that he is right when he says (p. 231) that "such zeal is compromised" when they decide to fight on the Sabbath (cf. infra, §33.3.2.2).

According to I Maccabees, the persecution was part of a disaster, and was not in itself fruitful (Janse 2012: 177). In II Maccabees we may see a self-chosen death with Eleazar; we will treat this story in some detail.

3.3.1 *Law & Covenant*

When we count the verses where God's Law is mentioned in II Maccabees, we must conclude that it is a very important theme for this author. Nevertheless, we should keep in mind that it is also a very important theme in I Maccabees (2:21, 26, 27, 29, 44, 48, 50, 58, 64, 67-68; 3:5; 10:14; 13:3, 47; 14:29) and in IV Maccabees and that the related theme of the Covenant is very important in I Maccabees and Megillat Antiochos. It may seem strange that 'Law' and 'Covenant' are so related, but we need to keep in mind that the word 'Law' (and we cannot translate the Greek νόμος [*nomos*] otherwise) is influenced semantically by the word it translates, the Hebrew תּוֹרָה (*tôrâ*), for which the basic meaning is 'instruction'. The Covenant is given by God, and so is his instruction (Lorein 2024: 27-28). With that background information, the combination does not surprise anymore.

In I Maccabees, the principle of keeping God's Law is the most frequently mentioned motive for their actions.

God's Law is also most important for the author of IV Maccabees. The observance of God's Law leads to peace, as is illustrated by IV Macc. 3:20:[20]

> "While[21] our fathers were having profound peace through their observance of the Law, and were prospering so that even Seleucus Nicanor,[22] the king of Asia, both set funds aside for them for their religious service and recognised their polity, ..."

Observing the Law does not lead necessarily to resistance to foreign governments. In the past it has led to שָׁלוֹם (*šālôm*). And in some cases, the Seleucid Empire had subsidised the Temple.[23] After all, Jews were willing to

---

20 A kind of parallel of II Macc. 3:7-34.

21 For this translation, see Den Dulk 2014: 136.

22 Seleucus Nicanor might be Seleucus IV Philopatôr (Anderson 1985: 548): born in 218, reigned from 187 to 175 (3 IX 175, to be precise: Mørkholm 1966: 43), descendent of Seleucus I Nicator (born in 358, reigned from 312 to 281). Nic*an*or is a doublet of Nic*at*or (Den Dulk 2014: 134-135), one of the several Nicanors mentioned in our sources. Because both Seleucus I and Seleucus IV have been benefactors of the Jerusalem Temple at some stage (Den Dulk 2014: 136-138; for Seleucus I, see Flavius Josephus, *Antiquitates* XII 119), a confusion of both figures might be possible.

23 Not structurally, anyhow: Aperghis (2004: 208) observes that the Seleucid Empire did not do so, differently from the Ptolemaic Empire.

participate in the life of the society, as long as this was compatible with their religious convictions (Baslez 2014: 85-90).[24]

3.3.2 *Need of symbols*

As a more specific command the *Sabbath* is mentioned, along with *purity laws* and the *Temple*. It is important to notice that within the same community, different weight was given to different symbols or outward manifestations.

3.3.2.1 Temple[25]

The Temple is a central item for II Maccabees, much more than in I Maccabees (I Macc. 2:7-8) and in IV Maccabees (IV Macc. 4:9). For II Maccabees, the holiness of the Temple is an important consideration for the people's willingness to fight. When the Temple is in danger, this fails God's honour. This is illustrated in II Macc. 15:17-18, but the theme has already figured earlier in II Maccabees (II Macc. 3:15-22; 8:2-4; 13:11, 14; 14:34-36). This chapter discusses the battle of 8 III 161 (Lorein 2003: 74), at Adasa; we have already arrived at the reign of the Seleucid king Demetrius I[26] and Judas Maccabaeus has just ended his speech:

> "Encouraged by the very beautiful words[27] of Judas, which had the power of moving to virtue and to stir souls of young people to act manly, they determined not to organise a strategy[28] but to set upon the foe nobly and, by fighting them with all behaviour of a good man, body to body, to decide the issue, since the city and the religion and the sanctuary were in danger. Indeed, it was of lesser weight for them what happened with wives and children, as well as brethren and relatives: their greatest and first fear was about the consecrated Temple." (II Macc. 15:17-18)

This is a clear indication that the group behind II Maccabees, the Pharisees, had not given up the straight relationship with the Temple. In this way they occupied a middle position: farther away from the Temple management

24 The term πολιτεύεσθαι can be found in II Macc. 6:1; 11:25; IV Macc. 4:23; 5:16.

25 The term ἅγια is best translated by 'religion' (I Macc. 13:3; 14:29, 43; II Macc. 15:17) (Abel 1949: 475; Doran 2012: 293).

26 Demetrius I Soter, 185-162-150 (Athas 2023: 302, 390, 414).

27 Or "fine arguments" (Doran 2012:293).

28 Cf. De Lang & Van der Lingen 1999: 8. A varia lectio exists (στρατοπεδεύεσθαι, 'to pitch camp') and a conjecture has been proposed (στραγγεύεσθαι, 'hesitate'): Nelis 1975: 286.

(Boccaccini 1999: 29) than the Sadducees, but still valuing the Temple, differently from the Essenes, who had actually given up all hopes about the Temple.

3.3.2.2 Sabbath

For the Sabbath command, a difference exists and probably here we arrive at the centre of the variance between I and II Maccabees. In the context of Antiochus' persecution, where being a blessing for society has become impossible (cf. Jer. 27-28) and with a thousand persons killed,[29] Mattathias concluded (I Macc. 2:40-41)[30] that completely keeping the Sabbath would imply that Jews would be killed and that their principal goal would not be reached:

> "'If we all do as our brethren have done and do not fight with the Gentiles for our lives and our ordinances, they will quickly destroy us from the earth.' On that day, they resolved after deliberation: 'Everyone who comes to us for war on the Sabbath day, let us fight against him; so that we may not all die as our brethren died in their hiding places'."

Suspending the Sabbath commandment *temporarily* would permit the Jews to keep once again, after the victory, *all* the commandments. It is important to note that the Pharisaic interpretation of the Sabbath laws was not the strictest possible: the Essenes were stricter.[31]

3.3.2.3 Purity

The motive of personal purity occurs in I Maccabees and Megillat Antiochos (I Macc. 4:43; 13:47, 50; 14:7; Meg. Ant. 61), but was especially important for II Maccabees.

A personal application of the laws can be seen in the purity that Eleazar, ninety years old (II Macc. 6:24), wanted to maintain, according to II Macc. 6:19, at the beginning of the persecution, in the year 167. He would rather die than to eat pork,[32] forbidden by Jewish law:

---

29 I Macc. 2:29-38. The fact is mentioned too in II Macc. 6:11, but without the number of casualties. The author of II Maccabees elaborates nine deaths; he has a different theology. Meg. Ant. 40, however, mentions "about about one thousand men and women were killed".

30 It is only in I Macc. 9:44 that the decision is applied.

31 See Jub. 50:6-13; CD x 14 – xi 18; 1QM ii 8-9. Cf. Lorein 2016: 313.

32 According to Baran 2014: 75, coming from the sacrifices to Zeus in the Jerusalem Temple.

"But he, welcoming death with renown[33] rather than life with defilement, went up to the drum out of his own choice."

Several solemn words of classical literature (Homer, Tragedies) are used in order to emphasise Eleazar's conscious choice to be a model for his fellow people (Doran 2012: 152). The drum is a torture instrument, probably "a fixed object to which one marches, a drum-shaped block on which Eleazar was tied and perhaps stretched" (Goldstein 1983: 286).[34]

In which sense is this a self-chosen death? It is rather presented as resistance against sin and the determination to stay with God's Law (and in that way being an example for the young people around him) (Mela 2022: 30-34, 44-47), than as a form of autonomous suicide.[35]

3.4 Trust in God

Trust in God, in general and in some specific forms, is a second motive occurring in all four documents.[36] When people trust in God, they have more room to act. In I Maccabees it is present, although less frequently formulated than in II Maccabees. We read from the letter to the Spartans (I Macc. 12:15a; cf. I Macc. 2:61; 3:18-19, 60), written during Jonathan's leadership,[37] probably in the summer of 143 BC:

"For we have the help from heaven that helps[38] us."

As often, God is not named but circumscribed, here by the word 'heaven' (Lorein 2022: 147). Trust in God is expressed here within an international relationship (Blumenthal 2015) – exactly in that kind of situation some people would act differently. It can be considered the Maccabees' battle cry (Nelis 1972: 214).[39]

---

33 Cf. Mela 2022: 43.

34 Cf. Heb. 11:35. Differently Abel 1949: 366-367 (strokes of the cane).

35 The same reasoning may be applied to II Macc. 7:7. On the other hand, II Macc. 14:37-46 is not completely parallel.

36 Even in – though less clear – Megillat Antiochos: see Meg. Ant. 42.

37 In the years 161-143 (Van der Woude 1983: 88).

38 The act. ptc. praes. βοηθοῦσαν indicating generality.

39 If Nelis is also right in surmising Prov. 21:31 as its source, this would be another example of Scripture places outside the Pentateuch playing a role for Sadducees.

3.4.1 Resurrection

We illustrate the motive of trust with II Macc. 7:23, the important chapter of the death of the seven brothers and their mother, who are commanded to eat pork around the beginning of the persecution, at the end of the year 167. This verse is important too for the motive of God's mercy and God's Law.

In the mother's speech (vv. 22-23), she considers her sons' life from the Creator's point of view and so wants to encourage her children while dying:[40]

> "Therefore then the Founder of the world who shaped[41] the becoming[42] of mankind and devised[43] the becoming of all,[44] restores[45] in mercy to you your spirit and your life, even as you now leave out yourselves for his laws' sake."

The word normally translated by 'Creator' is the word used in Hellenistic texts for kings who *founded* a city. In this way, Antiochus IV Epiphanes is called 'founder and benefactor of the city'.[46] By using the same expression, the author of II Maccabees makes clear that God is greater than the king. God has not just founded a city, but he is the Founder of the universe and of every human being. The one who has created is also able to give spirit and life back to the dead. Even if the mother's reasoning is not strictly speaking a logical necessity, it is clear that God is almighty and will be merciful towards those who have sacrificed their lives (Gutberlet 1927: 108-109). That forms a reason in the Maccabees' decision-making process to be more frightened by breaking the Law than by possible death.

---

40 Rather than 'encourage her children to die', as Schmitz (2010: 61) wants it.

41 Same verb as in Gen. 2:7.

42 The repetition of γένεσιν seems strange; should we conjecture γένος (cf. Nelis 1975: 171)?

43 Not 'to discover' (as Doran [2012: 160] rightly remarks). – In this way not only creation but also providence plays a role in the reasoning, with specific attention for every person (Gutberlet 1927: 109).

44 Rather than 'of all things', because everywhere in these verses is spoken of humankind, not of other parts of Creation. Differently Abel 1949: 377.

45 Present tense (as Gutberlet 1927: 109 rightly remarks).

46 OGIS 253, probably Babylon. Cf. Schmitz 2010: 67-68, 76-77; Mittag 2006: 205.
We find another instance of criticising Antiochus IV in II Macc. 12:22, a divine appearance where the word ἐπιφανείας occurs, instead of the non-composite φάν-, through which it was made clear who was the real God appearing in history (Schmitz 2012: 270-274, 276). She remarks (pp. 274-275) that God is not only seen in opposition to Antiochus IV Epiphanes but also somehow ("vorsichtig-kritische Haltung"; p. 275) to Judas Maccabeus.

Thus, from the perspective of the Creator who is not limited in his deeds,[47] death is not seen as the end. No intellectual obligation exists to doubt the corporeal resurrection of those who disregarded themselves for the sake of his laws (Yakim 2024: 220). God brings[48] them over the frontier of the end of this life. Just as the world has been created out of what was not, resurrection will follow after death (Schmitz 2010: 73-74).

In IV Maccabees we find a second speech by the mother (IV Macc. 18:8-19), recalling her own virtue and the lessons her husband taught[49] from 'the law and the prophets'[50] and stressing in this way the importance of the home as the primary locus of training (deSilva 2016: 530). The wife has an important role and is a good theologian. IV Macc. 18:17-19 read as follows:

> "[My husband] confirmed Ezekiel who was saying, 'Will these dry[51] bones live?' For he did not forget teaching you the song that Moses taught and that says, 'I will kill and will make to live. This is your life and the length of days.'"

The reference to different parts of the Old Testament makes clear the line of the resurrection thought in Old Testament times.[52]

This implies that the expression 'the law and the prophets' can be translated as 'instruction spoken in God's name'.

3.4.2 *Historical precedents*

The trust in God is illustrated by references to historical precedents, a third motive occurring in all four documents.[53] David, the Assyrian king Sanherib (fl. 705-681), the three young men in the fiery furnace and Daniel are most often cited.[54]

---

47 Deut. 32:39 and I Sam. 2:6; Yakim 2024: 220.

48 The form δίδωσιν is praes.

49 For the different teaching methods, see Steyn 2015: 285-286.

50 τὸν νόμον καὶ τοὺς προφήτας (IV Macc. 18:10).

51 The word ξηρὰ is taken from the verse preceding the quoted verse Ezek. 37:2.

52 Besides Ezek. 37:3 also the most important Deut. 32:39. For the importance of the *Canticum Mosis* in intertestamental literature, see Steyn 2015: 286-288; the LXX has exactly the same words: ἐγὼ ἀποκτενῶ καὶ ζῆν ποιήσω – it is combined with Deut. 30:20. Cf. Yakim 2024: 78-172.

53 And not at all a new one: see already Ex. 19:4.

54 David: I Macc. 2:57; 4:30; IV Macc. 18:15. Three young men: I Macc. 2:59; IV Macc. 13:9; 16:21; 18:12. Daniel: I Macc. 2:60; IV Macc. 16:21; 18:13. Sanherib: II Macc. 8:19; 15:22; I Macc. 7:41. Although in the narrative I Macc. 4:9 is parallel with II Macc. 8:19, it offers a different example. – We must note that, while IV Maccabees is using the same historical examples, the author applies them in an opposite way.

We read one example[55] from Mattathias' last exhortation in the year 166 to his sons – and to himself, through the example of Abraham (Schwartz 2022: 201):

> "Was not Abraham found faithful in temptation[56], and it was reckoned[57] to him as righteousness? Joseph, in the time of his distress, kept the commandment and became lord of Egypt. Phinehas, our father, for that he was zealous exceedingly, obtained the covenant of an everlasting priesthood. Joshua, for fulfilling the word, became a judge[58] in Israel. Caleb, for bearing witness in the congregation, obtained land (as) an heritage. David through his loyalty inherited the throne of a kingdom forever. Elijah, for that he was exceedingly zealous[59] for the Law, was taken up into heaven. Ananias, Azarias and Misael,[60] believing (in God), were saved from the flame. Daniel, for his singlemindedness, was delivered from the mouth of the lions." (I Macc. 2:52-60)

The list as such seems quite parallel to the list in Heb. 11, but a direct relationship should not be supposed.[61]

The reference to Phinehas,[62] especially as "our father", seems to connect the document with the Sadducees' strong relationship with the priesthood. However, this must be nuanced in light of the use of exactly the same list in IV Macc. 18:11-13.

Whereas in I Macc. 2:53 Joseph's attitude made him finally lord of Egypt, for IV Macc. 18:11 prison is the result of this same attitude; both facts are historically true, but their use in view of the author's message is quite different. While in I Maccabees victory (I Macc. 4:30) and eternal kingship (I Macc. 2:57) were awaiting David, IV Macc. 18:15 mentions afflictions. While in I Macc. 2:59-60 the salvation of the three young men in the oven and of Daniel in the lions' den is mentioned, IV Maccabees stops at mentioning the fire (IV Macc. 13:9; 16:21; 18:12) and the lions (IV Macc. 16:21; 18:13). Admittedly, Isa. 43:2 is mentioned too (with the words "Even though thou pass through the fire, the flame shall not hurt thee"), as well as the fact that men having died for God are living unto God (IV Macc. 16:25) – ultimately, there will be deliverance.

55 See also I Macc. 4:9 (parallel with II Macc. 8:19, but with a different example), 30; 7:41 (with the same example as in II Macc. 8:19; 15:22).

56 Exactly the same quality for Abraham in Sir. 44:20.

57 Passivum divinum; cf. Lorein 2022: 146.

58 According to Tilly 2015: 106, Joshua is never called a judge in the Bible. Choi (2021: 108) and Schwartz (2022: 201) provide arguments to consider him nevertheless as such.

59 This expression must have been inspired by the Hebrew absolute infinitive in I Kgs 19:10, 14 (קַנֹּא קִנֵּאתִי).

60 Hananiah, Azariah and Mishael in Dan. 1; in Dan. 3 they have their Babylonian names: Shadrach, Meshach and Abednego.

61 Contra Steyn 2015: 282.

62 See also I Macc. 2:26. For the Biblical story, see Num. 25:11-13.

Also in Sirach's *Laus Patrum* (Sir. 44-50), Phinehas is followed by Joshua, whose faithfulness brought him to military and civil leadership (Nelis 1972: 88-89) in Israel, a prefiguration of a Hasmonean leader[63] in his ideal form.

This chapter cannot be used as a basis for the combination of king and high priest by the Hasmoneans,[64] seeing that the list goes further.

For Elijah too, his zeal for the law is stressed. He was taken up – by God, presumably![65] – to heaven: a reference to life after death in I Maccabees.

In the references to the book of Daniel, miracles are mentioned – although the author of I Maccabees is known for not mentioning miracles for his own days (Le Moyne 1972: 75). Can we say: he believed miracles are possible but did not claim them for his own situation? Then it is an example of the tension between what members of a faith group say loudly and what they believe.

This remembrance of historical situations informs their trust that God will keep his covenant. The belief in the historical trustworthiness of these stories gave them a fundament to their actions in time of danger (Oswalt 2018: 165-166).

3.5 Specific guidance

Motives are not only found in ancient and internalised principles; it is also believed that God can give specific guidance in one's life towards specific actions. This guidance is sought for in all traditions. As always, II Maccabees is most open over it and thinks of Scripture, appearances, prayer, but also of concrete circumstances and human counsel.

3.5.1 Prayer

Prayer is the fourth motive occurring in all four documents.[66]

In II Maccabees, prayer is the most frequently mentioned device for guidance. It is mostly collective[67] and by men, but also by women (II Macc. 3:20),[68] and individually (II Macc. 15:21), e.g. by Judas Maccabaeus before

63 After all, the highlighting of Phinehas is less strategic, as high priests in principle should be descendants of him (Schwartz 2022: 201).

64 As Van der Kooij (2012: 43-47) suggests.

65 Blumenthal 2015: 704. Again a *passivum divinum*: cf. n. 57.

66 Even though it be only once in IV Maccabees: IV Macc. 12:20.

67 Even with a prayer meeting in II Macc. 8:29.

68 Within the Pharisaic tradition, women's prayers are mentioned too in Tob. 3:11-15; Jdt. 9:1.

defeating Nicanor,[69] five miles north of Jerusalem (Habicht 1979: 246; Nelis 1972: 152), on 8 III 161.[70] We quote II Macc. 15:21:

> "Maccabaeus, looking at the presence of the masses, the varied equipment of the weapons and the savageness of the beasts, holding up his hands to heaven, called upon the Lord, the worker of wonders, for he knew that it is not by weapons but as is decided by him, that he procures the victory for those who are worthy."

As soon as the elephants ('the beasts')[71] are seen, Judas Maccabaeus prays.[72]

Prayer plays also an important role in I Maccabees, mostly collectively (I Macc. 3:44, 50; 4:10; 7:36-37; 9:46), but individual prayer occurs too (I Macc. 4:30; 7:40-42; 11:71), more often than in II Maccabees, perhaps again due to a difference in spirituality, according to which they did not like prayer *meetings*.[73]

Prayer is also an important device in Megillat Antiochos with an interesting link (Meg. Ant. 51-52a):

> "They decreed a fast and sat on ashes to ask for mercy before the God of heaven.[74] Then a good advice fell in their heart."

The Maccabees had gathered in Mitzpeh Gilad, a place where in the past God had provided salvation (I Sam. 14) – another case of referring to historical examples – and they fasted.[75] Obtaining a good idea is immediately linked to their seeking God. God's answer can come in a fully human way.

3.5.2 Scripture

As far as Scripture is concerned, I Maccabees stays in line with Sadducean theology in its specific texts, consulting (I Macc. 3:48) the book of the Law,

---

69 See n. 22.

70 See §3.3.2.1.

71 Probably 'elephants', but that causes a historical problem (see Bengtson 1977: 482; Doran 2012: 294). However, even when some elephants had disappeared, other could appear again, the expertise still being at hand.

72 Συνιδών asyndetically at the same level as ἀνατείνας (Doran 2012: 294).

73 This makes that we cannot accept Schwartz' remark when he says that I Maccabees offers very few prayers and that in II Maccabees they are numerous, long and answered (Schwartz 2013: 24-25, and even stronger on p. 26).

74 This must have included prayer.

75 As in I Macc. 3:47.

apparently the Torah; but we have seen that it is not that clear, since I Maccabees does not limit itself to the Pentateuch for historical precedents.

II Macc. 15:9 presents clearly 'from the Law and the Prophets', as a *hendiadys* 'from the instruction spoken in the name of God', i.e. the whole of the Old Testament, in line with Pharisaic bibliology.

3.5.3 *Direct divine interventions*

Appearances are mentioned too as form of specific guidance. I Maccabees is quite reserved about supernatural appearances. This leads to a general remark about this source. Some commentators say that in I Maccabees nothing supernatural is mentioned (Schwartz 2013: 23), but we should not be too absolute in this matter: the author of I Maccabees has his spirituality too. Prayer is important and hope for prophecy is real. Arenhoevel (1967: 179, 181) says: "Gott wirkt in *1Makk* im Verborgenen, in *2Makk* ganz *offenbar*."; "Der Verf. von *1Makk* ist nüchtern und konkret. Er verbindet eine genaue Kenntnis seiner Gegenwart mit einem tiefen Verständnis der alten Traditionen" – which is a compliment. However, that political understanding exists not only in I Maccabees (I Macc. 2:40; 9:44), but also in the more spiritual II Maccabees (II Macc. 4:4, 6; 14:30). It seems that the Sadducean author of I Maccabees had a more cautious spirituality. Resurrection did not belong to their vocabulary – obviously so because it did not turn up in the Pentateuch (Puech 2006: 261)[76] – but rays of hope surface.[77]

3.6 General considerations

We arrive in the next category, that of general considerations – not typically Biblical, but common for the days of Hellenism. In this category, IV Maccabees is clearly at the forefront with its attention for piety (IV Macc. 5:18, 24, 31, 38; 6:22; 7:1, 18; 9:24, 29-30; 11:20; 13:26; 14:3; 15:1-2; 18:2), although virtues as singlemindedness[78] (I Macc. 2:37), righteous-

---

76 In this study, we shall not try to distinguish between immortality of the soul and the resurrection. Emmanuelle Main (1996: 431-432) points out that for the Sadducees something of the soul continued to exist in Sheol, but that anyhow a bodily resurrection was excluded; cf. Flavius Josephus, *Antiquitates* XVIII 16, I Macc. 2:58; our n. 48.

77 See §3.4.2.

78 The Greek word is ἁπλότης. Cf. Lorein & Van Staalduine-Sulman 2009: n. 141. Gutberlet 1920: 37, is less optimistic and opts for "ohne viel Überlegen".

ness[79] (I Macc. 2:29; 14:35) and innocence (I Macc. 2:37, 60) are mentioned also in I Maccabees.[80] One general virtue should be discussed, for its implications for attitudes towards the government.

We find this virtue of loyalty in the letter to the Spartans (I Macc. 12:11), with whom they had a treaty, written during Jonathan's leadership,[81] probably in the summer of 143 BC. Indeed, trusting God does not exclude this kind of human means (Gutberlet 1920: 208):

> "We therefore, on every occasion, without ceasing,[82] both at our feasts and on other convenient days, do remember you at the sacrifices which we offer, and in our prayers, as it is right and proper to remember brothers."

Sacrifices and prayers for pagan kings have always been possible: when the Jews were under Persian authority (Ezra 6:10) for the Persian king, under Seleucid authority (I Macc. 7:33) and under Roman authority (Flavius Josephus, *Contra Apionem* II 76-77; cf. Schürer & Doubles 1979: 311-312).

Together with more lofty motives, material interests can always play their role. That is simply human, and not necessarily to be blamed. The category of the interests is better filled in I Maccabees than in the other sources. The author is well aware of the importance of prosperity, e.g. in I Macc. 16:14, February 134, at the end of Simon's leadership (143-134 BC; Bickerman 1979: 8):

> "Now Simon was visiting the towns of the country, taking care for their needs."

3.7 Emotions

We arrive at a last category presenting emotions that are doubtful or even unacceptable in our eyes.[83] In this vein, 'murder with a cause' is met in Meg. Ant. 25:

---

79 For the motive of righteousness, it must be remarked that εὐσέβεια (especially in IV Maccabees but also in II Macc. 12:45) is often translated by 'righteousness' but that the translation 'piety' should be preferred, in order to avoid confusion with δικαιοσύνη (which does occur in IV Macc. 5:24).

80 In spite of the special relation between IV Maccabees and II Maccabees that is usually observed.

81 In the years 161-143 (see n. 37).

82 This must be read within the rules of the diplomatic document genre (Gutberlet 1920: 208).

83 Revenge has been mentioned in I Macc. 2:67; anger in I Macc. 2:24, 44; 10:74; II Macc. 10:35; Meg. Ant. 13.

> "My Lord, don't consider this as guilt because I killed him in the house of your sanctuary."

This is simply part of reality. It is not because we are speaking about faith and virtues, that everything would fall within that category.

4 Summary

4.1 Common motives

The importance of God's commandments, trust in him (faith), relatedness to the past and prayer[84] are important in all descriptions of the Maccabean period. In stressful circumstances, here are the ingredients that determine attitude and action.

4.2 Varieties

In spite of these constants, variety exists between the traditions.

II Maccabees is the most open about its motives. God as Creator, the holiness of his Name, his mercy, his commandments, the Sabbath, Jerusalem, the Temple, trust in God, faith in the resurrection, prayer, courage: the author is generously handing out his motives to his audience.

I Maccabees is specific in its soberness, more down to earth. That does not exclude spirituality – is even fed by spirituality –, but it leads to a different treatment of the question whether to fight on the Sabbath. Should this be called activism? That will depend on the definition of the word 'activism'. Can members of a faith community be blamed that they do not retreat from the world into the caves?

Although the group behind IV Maccabees is more than once following the theology of those behind II Maccabees, while differing from that of I Maccabees, IV Maccabees has a very specific philosophical flavour. This flavour, however, is not separating IV Maccabees from the general Jewish tradition,[85] as is already clear by the points in which it follows II Maccabees.

---

84 Although it is mentioned only once in IV Maccabees.

85 Or, as Vriezen & Van der Woude (2000: 459) puts it: "een jood in wie de theoloog het van de filosoof wint".

4.3 Conclusion

What was moving the Maccabees? Why did they do what they did? Other motives can be mentioned, even human considerations, interests and circumstances, but most important are the *awareness* of God asking something from believers and their *trust* in him, in coherence with what he is believed to have done in the past. His guidance is looked for, through Scripture and prayer. Differences between subgroups continue to exist, but this is where they stood, also in times of persecution. God is Creator and remains so beyond death; that changes the perspective on life and death in times of persecution and gives a motive to act in a specific way. God can be *trusted* in difficult times because in the course of history he has always taken care of his people.

5 References

Abel, F.-M. (1949). *Les livres des Maccabées*. Gabalda.

Anderson, H. (1985). 4 Maccabees. In J. H. Charlesworth (Ed.), *The Old Testament Pseudepigrapha II* (pp. 531-564). Doubleday.

Aperghis, G. G. (2004). *The Seleukid Royal Economy*. Cambridge UP.

Arenhoevel D. (1967). *Die Theokratie nach dem 1. und 2. Makkabäerbuch*. Grünewald.

Athas, G. (2023). *Bridging the Testaments*. Zondervan.

Baran, G. M. (2014). The Jewish Community and the Hellenistic Culture in the Light of the Books of the Maccabees. *Teologia i Człowiek* 25, 55-78.

Baslez, M.-F. (2014). 'Vivre en citoyen selon les coutumes ancestrales': Les enjeux du dossier documentaire conservé dans le deuxième livre des Maccabées. In M.-F. Baslez & O. Munnich (Eds.), *La mémoire des persécutions: Autour des livres des Maccabées* (pp. 77-90). Peeters.

Bengtson, H. (1977). *Griechische Geschichte: Von den Anfängen bis in die römische Kaiserzeit*. Beck. 5th edition.

Bickerman, E. (1979). *The God of the Maccabees: Studies on the Meaning and Origin of the Maccabean Revolt*. Brill.

Blumenthal, C. (2015). Der weitgehend verborgene Hauptakteur. Zur expliziten Rede von Gott in I Makk. *ZAW* 127, 696-715.

Boccaccini, G. (1999). Esiste una letteratura farisaica del secondo tempio? In R. Penna (Ed.), *Fariseismo e origini cristiane* (pp. 23-41). Dehoniane.

Bunge, J. G. (1971). *Untersuchungen zum zweiten Makkabäerbuch: Quellenkritische, literarische, chronologische und historische Untersuchungen zum zweiten Makkabäerbuch als Quelle syrisch-palästinensischer Geschichte*. Rheinische Friedrich-Wilhelms-Universität Bonn.

Brandt, P. (2001). *Endgestalten des Kanons: Das Arrangement der Schriften Israels in der jüdischen und christlichen Bibel*. Philo.

Choi, D. (2021). *The Use and Function of Scripture in 1 Maccabees*. T&T Clark.

Collins, J. J. (2016). Temple or Taxes? What Sparked the Maccabean Revolt? In J. J. Collins & J. G. Manning (Eds.), *Revolt and Resistance in the Ancient Classical World and the Near East: In the Crucible of Empire* (pp. 189-201). Brill.

Deines, R. (2001). The Pharisees Between 'Judaisms' and 'Common Judaism'. In D. A. Carson, P. T. O'Brien & M. A. Seifrid (Eds.), *Justification and Variegated Nomism I: The Complexities of Second Temple Judaism* (pp. 443-504). Mohr Siebeck.

de Lang, M. & van der Lingen, H. & S. (1999). *Nieuwe Bijbelvertaling. 2 Makkabeeën. Toelichting*. NBG.

den Dulk, M. (2014). Seleucus I Nicator in 4 Maccabees. *JBL* 133, 133-140.

deSilva, D. A. (2016). The Author of 4 Maccabees and Greco-Roman Paideia: Facets of the Formation of a Hellenistic Jewish Rhetor. *BBR* 26, 501-531.

deSilva, D. A. (2018). *Introducing the Apocrypha: Message, Context, and Significance*. Baker. 2nd edition.

Doran, R. (1981). *Temple Propaganda: The Purpose and Character of 2 Maccabees*. Catholic Biblical Association of America.

Doran, R. (2012). *2 Maccabees*. Fortress.

Dupont-Sommer, A. (1939). *Le quatrième livre des Machabées. Introduction, traduction et notes*. Champion.

Goldstein, J. A. (1976). *I Maccabees*. Doubleday.

Goldstein, J. A. (1983). *II Maccabees*. Doubleday.

Gutberlet, C. (1920). *Das erste Buch der Machabäer*. Aschendorff.

Gutberlet, C. (1927). *Das zweite Buch der Machabäer*. Aschendorff.

Habicht, C. (1979). *2. Makkabäerbuch*. Gütersloher Verlagshaus.

Hezser, C. (2013). Seduced by the Enemy or Wise Strategy? The Presentation of Non-Violence and Accommodation with Foreign Powers in Ancient Jewish Literary Sources. In R. Albertz & J. Wöhrle (Eds.), *Between Cooperation and Hostility: Multiple Identities in Ancient Judaism and the Interaction with Foreign Powers* (pp. 221-250). Vandenhoeck & Ruprecht.

Janse, S. (2012). Actio en Passio. De afwending van Gods toorn in 1 en 2 Makkabeeën. *NTT* 66, 173-188.

Kasher, A. (1981) The Historical Background of *Megillath Antiochus*. *Proceedings of the American Academy for Jewish Research* 48, 207-250.

Le Moyne, J. (1972). *Les Sadducéens*. Gabalda.

Lorein, G. W. (2001). Some Aspects of the Life and Death of Antiochus IV Epiphanes: A New Presentation of Old Viewpoints. *Ancient Society* 31, 157-171.

Lorein, G. W. (2003). *The Antichrist Theme in the Intertestamental Period*. T&T Clark.

Lorein, G. W. (2014). The Latin Versions of the Old Testament from Jerome to the *Editio Clementina*. In A. Houtman, E. van Staalduine-Sulman & H.-M. Kirn (Eds.), *A Jewish Targum in a Christian World* (pp. 125-145). Brill.

Lorein, G. W. (2016). Entwicklungen zwischen dem Alten und dem Neuen Testament. In H. J. Koorevaar & M.-J. Paul (Eds.), *Theologie des Alten Testaments: Die bleibende Botschaft der hebräischen Bibel* (pp. 301-323). Brunnen.

Lorein, G. W. (2022). Different Currents in Israel and Beyond: Knowing God in the Intertestamental Period. In: J. Kok, M. Webber & J. Otten, *On Knowing God: Interdisciplinary Theological Perspectives* (pp. 123-179). Gorgias.

Lorein, G. W. (2024). *Ezra-Nehemiah*. IVP.

Lorein, G. W. & van Staalduine-Sulman, E. (2009). CšD II, 4 – IV, 9: A Song of David for Each Day. *Henoch* 31, 387-410.

Main, E. (1996). Les Sadducéens et la résurrection des morts: Comparaison entre Mc 12, 18-27 et Lc 20, 27-38. *RevB* 103, 411-432.

Mela, F. (2022). Análisis narrativo del martirio de Eleazar (2 Mac 6,18-31). *Revista Bíblica* 84, 29-52.
Mittag, P. F. (2006). *Antiochus IV. Epiphanes: Eine politische Biographie*. Akademie.
Mørkholm, O. (1966). *Antiochus IV of Syria*. Gyldendal.
Nelis, J. T. (1972). *I Makkabeeën*. Romen.
Nelis, J. T. (1975). *II Makkabeeën*. Romen.
Oswalt, J. (2018). *Creatio ex nihilo*: Is It Biblical, and Does It Matter? *Trinity Journal* 39, 165-180.
Puech, É. (2006). Resurrection: The Bible and Qumran. In J. H. Charlesworth (Ed.), *The Bible and the Dead Sea Scrolls II: The Dead Sea Scrolls and the Qumran Community* (pp. 247-281). Baylor UP.
Sauer, C. (2020). 'Christenverfolgung': Eine Frage der Definition. In T. Schirrmacher & M. Warnecke (Eds.), *Jahrbuch Verfolgung und Diskriminierung von Christen 2020* (pp. 53-57). VKW.
Schmitz, B. (2010). Geschaffen aus dem Nichts? Die Funktion der Rede von der Schöpfung im Zweiten Makkabäerbuch. In T. Nicklas & K. Zamfir (Eds.), *Theologies of Creation in Early Judaism and Ancient Christianity* (pp. 61-79). De Gruyter.
Schmitz, B. (2012). Antiochus IV Epiphanes und der epiphane Gott: Gefühle, Emotionen und Affekte im Zweiten Makkabäerbuch. In R. Egger-Wenzel & J. Corley (Eds.), *Emotions from Ben Sira to Paul* (pp. 253-279). De Gruyter.
Schürer, E. & Doubles, M. C. (1979). *Priesthood and Temple Worship.* In G. Vermes et al. (Eds.), *The history of the Jewish people in the age of Jesus Christ II*. T&T Clark (pp. 237-313).
Schwartz, D. R. (2008). *2 Maccabees*. De Gruyter.
Schwartz, D. R. (2013). Judeans, Jews, and their Neighbors: Jewish Identity in the Second Temple Period. In R. Albertz & J. Wöhrle (Eds.), *Between Cooperation and Hostility: Multiple Identities in Ancient Judaism and the Interaction with Foreign Powers* (pp. 13-31). Vandenhoeck & Ruprecht.
Schwartz, D. R. (2022). *1 Maccabees*. Yale UP.
Steyn, G. J. (2015). The Maccabean Literature and Hebrews: Some Intertextual Observations. *Tydskrif vir Semitistiek* 24, 271-291.
Stordalen, T. (2001). Law or Prophecy? On the Order of the Canonical Books. *TTKi* 72, 131-150.
Tcherikover V. (tr. S. Applebaum) (1959). *Hellenistic Civilization and the Jews*. Jewish Publication Society of America & Magnes.
Tilly, M. (2015). *1 Makkabäer*. Herder.
van der Kooij, A. (2012). The Claim of Maccabean Leadership and the Use of Scripture. In B. Eckhardt (Ed.), *Jewish Identity and Politics between the Maccabees and Bar Kokhba: Groups, Normativity, and Rituals* (pp. 29-49). Brill.
van der Woude, A. S. (1983). Geschiedenis en godsdienst van het palestijnse Jodendom. In A. S. van der Woude (Ed.), *Bijbels Handboek IIB: Tussen Oude en Nieuwe Testament* (pp. 5-89). Kok.
van Staalduine-Sulman, E. (2011). Mag het een boekje meer zijn? *Theologisch Debat* 8/1, 34-40.
Vivian, A. (1987). La Megillat Antiochus: Una reinterpretazione dell'epopea maccabaica. In F. Parente (Ed.), *Aspetti della Storiografia ebraica* (pp. 163-195). Carucci.

Vriezen, T. C. & van der Woude, A. S. (2000). *Oudisraëlitische en vroegjoodse literatuur*. Kok. 10th edition.

Yakim, V. (2024). *The Power of God over Life and Death. The Reversal-of-Death Motifs in the Book of Daniel in Relation to Similar Motifs in the Hebrew Bible and in Second Temple Literature*. ETF Leuven.

4 Persecution in the New Testament

How semantic and phenomenological findings help to define "persecution"

Daniel Röthlisberger[1]

Abstract

Discourses surrounding the suffering of Christians frequently employ terms such as "discrimination," "persecution," and "martyrdom," yet these concepts often lack precise definitions and are used variably across ecclesiastical, secular, political, and academic contexts. This study addresses the ambiguity inherent in the term "persecution of Christians" by seeking a philologically and theologically grounded definition based on New Testament texts. Recognising that existing lexical and exegetical resources inadequately capture the complexity and phenomenological scope of persecution-related terminology, the study employs a systematic semantic and lexical analysis of key Greek word pairs – διωγμός/διώκω, θλῖψις/θλίβω, and πάθημα/πάσχω – using BibleWorks software. These terms are central to Jesus' teachings and the lived experience of early Christian communities. Through comprehensive lemma searches and semantic field studies, the research uncovers a broad and nuanced spectrum of meanings and manifestations of persecution within the New Testament. The findings contribute to a more accurate and contextually sensitive understanding of persecution of Christians, bridging philological, theological, and sociological approaches.

Keywords: Persecution of Christians, New Testament definition, semantic analysis, lexical field, phenomenology.

---

1 Dr. Daniel Röthlisberger (*1981) is a New Testament scholar and currently serving as a pastor in the Reformed Parish of St. Stephan, Switzerland. This essay is based on updated results of his doctoral dissertation on assistance and self-help for persecuted Christian (Röthlisberger 2021). E-mail: daniel.roethlisberger@posteo.com, ORCID iD: 0009-0007-3739-345X.

1 The problem, methodology and research question

Wherever the suffering of Christians[2] is discussed, there is often talk of "discrimination and persecution" or "oppressed and persecuted Christians". These and similar buzzwords are frequently encountered in discourses on human rights and religious freedom, as well as in academic and popular contexts. For example, at academic conferences, in the field of policy making, in publications or when aid organisations and other non-governmental organisations address circles of supporters or the public media.

However, the term "persecution of Christians" – here reduced to "persecution" for reasons of linguistic economy – is by no means clearly defined.[3] One major problem is that terms such as discrimination, affliction, persecution and martyrdom are used in different ways for different reasons, are sometimes used as merism[4] or are not used at all as terms foreign to the respective field. In addition, the terminology chosen varies depending on whether the phenomena in question are discussed in ecclesiastical, secular, official or political milieus.[5] Rhetorical and argumentative interests also determine the choice of words. Depending on the pragmatics, this can be emotional, factual, hyperbolic or euphemistic. It is to be welcomed that research is now collecting comparative and systematising data in this regard.[6] Sociological approaches to defining the persecution of Christians are now also common, combined with efforts to incorporate individual theological aspects of the topic. However, where this is done without the necessary systematics and philological depth of focus,[7] the extent to which such works actually reflect the findings of the New Testament may be critically questioned. Obviously, there is still a considerable need for clarification, especially with regard to a New Testament-based and thus exegetically-theologically and philologically responsible definition of the persecution of Christians.

For this reason, this study seeks a definition of "persecution" that is based on the New Testament and which is supported by systematically collected data on semantic and phenomenological findings. It should be noted here: Even in the New Testament, the simple term "persecution"

---

2 Essentially, this refers to the suffering that said people experience due to their Christian religious affiliation or the manifestations of their Christian existence.

3 See also Tieszen (2008: 17-35).

4 Referring to something by its polar extremes or by a list of its parts (GGNT § 295r), i.e. representing the whole range of anti-Christian experiences.

5 Cf. Sauer (2021: 2-11.378-84). See also Boyd-MacMillan (2006: 85-100).

6 Cf. Sauer (2014: 201-12, esp. 208f.).

7 E.g. Boyd-MacMillan (2006: 101-19); Tieszen (2008: 44-82); cf. Tieszen (2012: 43-49).

refers to an extremely complex issue that is difficult to grasp linguistically within the New Testament writings and therefore defies a simple definition. Lexical reference works such as Theologisches Wörterbuch zum Neuen Testament or Exegetisches Wörterbuch zum Neuen Testament largely fail to explain the range of meanings of central terms such as διωγμός/διώκω (persecution/to persecute), θλῖψις/θλίβω (affliction/to afflict) and πάθημα/πάσχω (suffering/to suffer) as well as their derivatives and compounds in more detail.[8] Phenomenological aspects are almost completely absent, let alone a systematic survey of the relevant material. The same applies to monographs and essays, which are often rather brief and eclectic with regard to the biblical findings.[9]

The present study on the semantic field and range of meanings of the collective term "persecution" was carried out, among other things, using BibleWorks software. As a starting point, the following three pairs of words were deemed suitable: διωγμός/διώκω, θλῖψις/θλίβω and πάθημα/πάσχω. With the exception of the word pair mentioned third, these common New Testament terms are used in all the Gospels to reflect fundamental statements of Jesus in relation to the experiential horizon of his followers.[10] They can therefore be considered central from a philological point of view. On this basis, the phenomenological spectrum of meanings of persecution can be explored in two combined steps. Firstly, a *lemma search* is carried out *for the entire New Testament* with regard to the aforementioned word pairs, with regard to the context, parallel passages and the use of the terms in other places.[11] In addition, a *semantic word field study* of the word pairs is carried out.[12] This results in extremely rich findings on manifestations and effects of persecution, which are presented and explained in more detail below in a structured way.

---

8 (1) *ThWNT*: Schlier (1957: 139-48); Oepke (1935: 232f.). Also not very productive: Michaelis (1954: 903-39). (2) *EWNT*: Knoch (1992: 816-19); Kremer (1992: 375-79, s. v. θλῖψις κτλ.); Kremer (1992: 120-24, s. v. πάσχω).

9 Cf. Hare (1967: 19-129) (Matt); Penner (2004: 161) and Pervo (1987: 14-17.43) (Acta); Pobee (1985: 1-12) (Paulines); Williams (2012: 299-326) (1 Pet); see also Schirrmacher (2011: 102ff.); Sauer (2016: 38-56); Boyd-MacMillan (2006: 101-19); Tieszen (2008: 44-82); Tieszen (2012: 43-49).

10 On the findings of the initial lemma search with regard to the Gospels and followers of Jesus: Röthlisberger (2021: 520, tabular overview). The terms παθήματα/πάσχω are not attested in the Gospel of John.

11 On the findings: Röthlisberger (2021: 520f., table).

12 The findings result in numerous terms, which in turn – according to the subsequent lemma query – are used in many places. The results, insofar as they reveal forms of persecution and related scriptural passages, are integrated on an ongoing basis.

2 On the findings: Documentation and interpretation

(1) ***According to the New Testament, persecution can include verbal attacks in various forms, frequencies and intensities.*** In our context, we encounter threats[13] and abusive words[14], false insinuations and the spreading of untruths and malicious lies about believers in Christ,[15] defamation/slander/demeaning words[16] and the incitement of the people[17], all of which may be once-off or repeated. Furthermore, there are prohibitions on speaking and commands of silence regarding the testimony of Christ or the preaching of Christ.[18] In forensic contexts, there are also denunciations, filing of complaints, laying of charges before authorities and judges[19] and false testimony from witnesses[20]. Verbal violence is aimed at shaming[21], derogation, public exposure

---

13 Acts 9:1 (ἀπειλή); cf. 4:29 (both); 4:17 (ἀπειλέω); 4:21 (προσαπειλέω).

14 Also scolding and derogatory words, words of abuse and insult: (1) Matt 5:11; Luke 6:22; Rom 15:3; 1 Pet 4:14 (all with ὀνειδίζω); (2) concerning Jesus: Matt 27:44 (cf. v. 41 and many more, each with ἐμπαίζω – to mock); Mark 15:32; (3) Heb 10:33 (ὀνειδισμός; cf. Heb 11:26; 13:13 [like Jesus]); (4) 1 Pet 2:23 in conjunction with v. 21 (λοιδορέω); cf. John 9:28 (Jesus); 1 Cor 4:12 (Paul); (5) 1 Pet 3:16; cf. Luke 6:28 (both ἐπηρεάζω).

15 Matt 5:11 (εἴπωσιν πᾶν πονηρὸν καθ' ὑμῶν [ψευδόμενοι]); 10:24f. (Beelzebub).

16 (1) 2 Tim 3:11 in connection with Acts 13:45 (βλασφημέω); cf. Acts 18:6 (Paul); 26:11 (believers in Christ); 1 Cor 10:30; 1 Tim 6:1; 1 Pet 4:4; 2 Pet 2:2.12; Jude 1:10; Rev 13:6; 16:9.11.21; (2) concerning Jesus: Matt 27:39; Mark 15:29 (in connection with shaking of the head); Luke 22:65; 23:39; (3) Rev 2:9 (βλασφημία); cf. 1 Tim 1:13 (a blasphemer, persecutor and perpetrator of violence – ὄντα βλάσφημον καὶ διώκτην καὶ ὑβριστήν); Rev 13:1.5f.; 17:3; (4) 1 Pet 2:12; 3:16 (both καταλαλέω); (5) Acts 24:5 (a plague [λοιμός]; an insurrectionist; leader [πρωτοστάτης] of the sect of the Nazarenes, LWND).

17 (1) 2 Tim 3:11 in conjunction with Acts 14:2 (ἐκάκωσαν τὰς ψυχὰς τῶν ἐθνῶν κατὰ τῶν ἀδελφῶν) and v. 19 (πείσαντες τοὺς ὄχλους; cf. 23:21; Luke 27:43); Acts 17:5-8 (ὀχλοποιέω; ταράσσω; cf. v. 13).

18 Without the context of the three word pairs in question: (1) Acts 4:17f. (λαλέω, φθέγγγομαι, διδάσκω); v. 20f. (λαλέω; cf. 4:29), 5:28 (παραγγέλλω, διδάσκω); 5:40 (παραγγέλλω, λαλέω); cf. 6:13 (all negated); (2) 1 Thess 2:16 (κωλύω, λαλέω); (3) On the request for boldness in preaching (παραρρησία): Röthlisberger (2021: 103ff.).

19 (1) Matt 10:17.19.21; 24:9; Mark 13:12; Luke 21:16 (all with παραδίδωμι); cf. Matt 10:34-36; Mark 13:12; Luke 12:51-53; Acts 17:5-8; 18:15; 19:38; 22:24.30; 23:28ff. (with ἐγκαλέω; ζήτημα; ἔγκλημα); 24:1f.8.13.19; 25:2.5.11.14-27 (with ἐμφανίζω; κατηγορέω; ἔγκλημα; αἰτία); 26:2f.7; 28:18ff.; (2) Concerning Jesus: Matt 20:18f.; Mark 3:19; Mark 15:1.10; Luke 22:4; John 6:71; Acts 3:13f. and many more. (3) In detail on apologies and appeals in investigative and judicial proceedings: Röthlisberger (2021: 331-402).

20 Acts 6:11ff. (without the context of the word pairs in question); cf. 21:27f.

21 1 Pet 4:14.16 (αἰσχύνομαι).

and embarrassment[22], silencing[23] and, in the case of complaints, denunciations and false statements, judicial conviction and punishment[24] of the person concerned. Mere contradiction, mere unwillingness to listen, and mere non-acceptance of the gospel, when they occur in the context of the proclamation of the gospel,[25] can hardly be considered verbal attacks and persecution.

(2) ***In the New Testament, persecution can lead to the search for believers in Christ, their arrest, imprisonment, as well as investigation and legal proceedings.*** The targeted search for believers in Christ,[26] their arrest and imprisonment,[27] as well as investigations and legal proceedings,[28] are well attested in the context of persecution. As an additional security measure, prisoners were bound at the hands and/or feet with shackles and chains or fixed to a wooden (foot) block.[29]

(3) ***Persecution in the New Testament can lead to temporary, repeated or permanent displacement through flight, expulsion, deportation or banishment.*** Thus, some believers in Christ are driven away, expelled,[30] or banished

---

22 Heb 10:33; 1 Cor 4:9f.13f. (to be a spectacle, to be despised, blasphemed and regarded as filth or scum).

23 Cf. fn 18.

24 Cf. fn 20.

25 Acts 13:45; 18:6; cf. Luke 21:15; Acts 4:14; 7:57 (albeit in connection with violence); 19:9; 28:19.22.

26 Acts 8:1-4; 11:19f.; cf. 17:5f. and fn 34. For further examples see Röthlisberger (2021: 279-299).

27 (1) Luke 21:12; (2) Acts 20:23; 22:4; 2 Cor 6:5; 11:23; Eph 3:13 in conjunction with v. 1, 4,1; 6,20; Phil 4,14; Col 1:24 in connection with 4:3.18; Heb 10,32-34; Rev 2,10; (3) Without the immediate context of the word pairs in question: cf. Matt 14,3.10; 25,31-46; John 21,18f.; Acts 4,3; 5,18-34; 9,2.14.21; 12:1.4-7; 16:23ff.; 21:11.13.27.33; 22:19; 23:18; 24:27; 25:14.27; 26:10; 28:17-23; 2 Cor 11:32; Phil 1:12; 2 Tim 1:8.16; 2:9; Phlm 1:1.9; Heb 11:36; 13:3; Rev 13:10 etc. (4) with ἀπολύω: e.g. Acts 4:21,23; 5:40; 16:35f.; 26:32; 28:18; Heb 13:23.

28 (1) Luke 21:12-15; cf. 11:19; (2) Acts 6:12 and 8:1-4 (persecution of the Jerusalem believers); cf. Matt 23:34; Mark 13:9-11 and many more. Tabular overview of the forensic contexts of Acta: Röthlisberger (2021: 515f.); cf. Kelhoffer (2010: 293-344). The extremely broad vocabulary on this issue forces us to limit ourselves largely to passages that use the selected word pairs.

29 (1) Acts 9:2.14.21; 22:5 (Paul as persecutor); cf. Acts 12:6f. (Peter); 16:24.26; 20:23; 21:11.13.33; 22:29; 23:29; 24:27; 26:29.31; 28:20; Eph 6:20; Phil 1:7.13f.17; Col 4:3.18; 2 Tim 1:16; 2:9; Phlm 1:10.13 (Paul suffering persecution); Heb 11:36.

30 2 Tim 3:11f. in conjunction with Acts 13:50; cf. Acts 16:37 (Paul); 7:58 (Stephen).

as punishment[31]. They are pursued from place to place[32] or, as is often the case, forced to flee[33]. Persecution may also necessitate hiding or going underground locally.[34]

(4) *In the New Testament, persecution may involve social marginalisation and degradation, maximum economic or material losses and a variety of symptoms of deprivation.* In addition to economic sanctions (Rev 13:16f.; cf. 2:14.20), these include the partial or total loss of possessions, social prestige and the loss of the previous – i.e. pre-conversion – social context,[35] which also includes exclusion from the Jewish religious community[36]. All of this can be associated with the loss of existential security, the need to rebuild an existence and the dependence on the support from fellow believers.[37] Various symptoms of deprivation, such as hunger, thirst, poor clothing, etc., also occur in connection with persecution.[38]

(5) *According to the New Testament, persecution may entail extreme psychological stress or may jeopardise the psychological well-being of those affected.* The New Testament, with regard to persecution, repeatedly speaks of fear, worry, existential hardship and anxiety,[39] feelings of unbearable stress,

---

31 Rev 1:9.

32 Matt 10:23; 23:34; cf. Acts 14:19; 26:11 and fn 33.

33 Matt 10:23; Acts 8:1ff.; 11:19ff. (flight of the Jerusalem believers); Acts 9:23ff.28-30 in conjunction with 2 Cor 11:32f. (flight of Paul from Damascus and Jerusalem); cf. 2 Tim 3:11f.; Heb 11:38. Persecution-like circumstances of Pauline travel movements also in: Acts 13:50f.; 14:2-7.19f.; 16:39f.; 17:5-10.13f.; 20:1.3; 22:18.21.

34 (1) Jesus: John 7:10; 8:59; (2) circle of apostles: Acts 8:1b; (3) Paul: Acts 17:6; 2 Cor 11:32f.; (4) disciples, negative connotation: John 20:10.19.26; (5) Old Testament examples: Heb 11:23 (Moses); 11:31; Jas 2:25f. (Israelite spies). In detail: Röthlisberger (2021: 304-319).

35 Mark 10:29f.; Heb 10:32-34; cf. Matt 5:39f.; 10:37; Luke 6:29; 12:51-53; 14:26; Phil 3:3-8 in conjunction with Acts 22:3-5; 26:4ff.; Rom 11:1; 2 Cor 11:22 (excellent pre-conversion reputation).

36 John 9:22.34; 12:42f.; 16:2; Luke 6:22.

37 (Implied) rebuilding of existence after expulsion/refuge: Acts 8:1ff.; 11:19ff. (Jerusalem believers); Rom 12:12ff. (Jewish Christians).

38 Rom 8:35f.; 1 Cor 4:11; Phil 4:10-18; Rev 7:13f. in conjunction with v. 16; cf. 2:9; 12:14 and 2 Cor 8:1f.; 11:27 as well as Matt 5:6; 25:31-46; Luke 6:21; Heb 11:37. In detail: Röthlisberger (2021: 147-213).

39 (1) Matt 10:19.26; 1 Pet 3:14; Rev 2:10 (φοβέω); 2 Cor 7:5; 1 Pet 3:14; (all with φόβος); cf. Matt 2:22; Luke 12:4f.11(.32); cf. John 14:1.27; 19:38; 20:19 (disciples); Acts 9:26; 18:9; 1 Cor 12:25f.; Heb 11:23.27; 13:6; (2) Rom 8:35; 2 Cor 4:8; 6:4; 12:10 (all with στενοχωρέομαι [to be distressed/constrained] or στενοχωρία [narrowness, embarrassment, distress, fear]); (3) 2 Cor 6:4; 12:10; 1 Thess 3:7; cf. 1 Cor 7:26 (all with

depression, discouragement, weakness, powerlessness and despair,[40] tears, grief and pain,[41] as well as shocks and trials[42]. Persecution also causes feelings of hatred and a desire for revenge on the part of those affected.[43]

(6) *Persecution in the New Testament may imply physical violence in various forms, frequencies and intensities, up to and including death.* Physical violence against believers in Christ is attested as a singular or repeated event: in the form of scourging blows,[44] punches/slaps,[45] blows with rods, sticks and whips,[46] and otherwise carried out beatings, among others on the head and mouth[47]. The animal fighting of believers in Christ (*damnatio ad bestias*)[48], which has been documented many times in church history, is also mentioned in the New Testament, albeit probably only in a figurative sense (1 Cor 15:32).[49] When Paul says that as a perpetrator of violence (1 Tim 1:13) he persecuted the faith in Christ to the death (ἄχρι θανάτου; Acts 22:4; cf. 9:1; 22:20; 26:10), and coercive measures were used to persuade those concerned to commit blasphemy (i.e. apostasy) (πολλάκις τιμωρῶν αὐτοὺς

ἀνάγκη – predicament, distress); (4) 1 Pet 5:7 (μέριμνα); cf. v. 10. (5) Acts 20:38 in conjunction with 19:22ff. (ὀδυνάω, affliction of third parties); (6) Cf. Matt 10:17; Mark 13:9.

40 (1) 2 Cor 1:8 (βαρέω; cf. 4:17; 5:4); 4:9 (καταβάλλω); Eph 3:13 in conjunction with 3:1 (ἐγκακέω); on the request for boldness in preaching: Röthlisberger (2021: 103ff.); (2) 2 Cor 11:23-33; esp. vv. 29f.; 12:9f.; cf. Heb 11:34 (all with ἀσθένεια; ἀσθενέω); cf. Matt 25:39.43f.; (3) 2 Cor 1:8 (despair of life); 4:8f. (both with ἐξαπορέω); (4) John 16:33; Acts 23:11 (θαρσέω); (5) 1 Pet 5:10 (6) Rev 2:2; 14:13; cf. 2 Cor 6:5; 11:23.27 (κόπος).

41 (1) Rev 7:13f.17; cf. 21:4 and Acts 20:19 (all with δάκρυον; 21:4 also with κραυγή [cries of anguish, lamentation]; πόνος [pain]); (2) John 16:6.20-22; Phil 2:27; 1 Pet 2:19 (all with λύπη).

42 1 Thess 3:1-8, esp. v. 5; Rev 2:10; cf. Acts 20:19; Heb 2:18; 4:15; 1 Pet 5:8f.; Rev 3:10. On the diabolical origin of the trials: Fn 73.

43 Matt 5,44; Rom 12,14.17.19. On the question of counter violence: Röthlisberger (2021: 403-439).

44 Matt 23:34; cf. Matt 10:17 (disciples); 20:19; Mark 10:34; Luke 18:33; John 19:1 (Jesus) (all with μαστιγόω) and Heb 11:35f. (with μάστιξ [scourging; cf. Acts 22:24f.]; τυμπανίζω [torture]; ἐμπαιγμός [mockery]).

45 1 Cor 11:4; 1 Pet 2:20 (all with κολαφίζω); cf. Matt 26:57; Mark 14:65 (Jesus).

46 2 Cor 6:5 (πληγή); Acts 16:22f. (with ῥαβδίζω; like 2 Cor 11:24f.); Acts 16:37; cf. 5:40; 22:19; Mark 13:9 (disciples); Luke 22:63; John 18:23 (Jesus) (all with δέρω).

47 Without context of the word pairs in question, with τύπτω: Luke 6:29 (disciple/cheek); Acts 18:17 (Sosthenes); 21:32 (Paul); 23:2f. (Paul/mouth); cf. Matt 27:30; Mark 15:19 (reed/head; regarding Jesus).

48 Cf. the list of capital punishments against early church Christians in: Bähnk (2001: 40f.); Allard (1907: 273-308) (each with references).

49 Schneider (1992: 366f.); BA, s. v. θάνατος; Mommsen (1899: 925-28); cf. Pobee (1985: 1f.).

ἠνάγκαζον βλασφημεῖν; 26:11, cf. 9:1; 22:19), this may also refer to mistreatment or torture.[50] Where the mob seizes Stephen by force (with συναρπάζω, Acts 6:12), throws itself on him and drives him to the place of stoning (with ὁρμάω; 7:58), and where the Christ-believers Gaius and Aristarchus are forcibly taken to the theatre (Acts 19:29; like 6:12), this is probably also accompanied by physical abuse. This must also be assumed when Paul is taken into Roman protective custody out of concern that the mob might tear him apart (with διασπάω; 23:10). The same applies where believers in Christ are dragged away captive, Jason and some brothers and sisters in the faith are dragged before the city rulers and Paul's lifeless body is dragged out of the city after stoning (all with σύρω, Acts 8:3; 14:19; 17:6). Physical abuse is attested with certainty when Paul is exposed to the anger of the people in Jerusalem (21:27-32). In addition, there are a whole series of unspecific terms that also suggest the use of physical or other violence.[51] It is clear from Acts 5:41 (with ἀτιμάζω) that corporal punishment – similar to verbal violence (see above) – is associated with insulting or degrading those affected.

According to the New Testament and Jesus' statement, persecution can also mean a violent death: In addition to murder plots[52], death threats[53] and numerous unspecified types of death[54], the texts document

50 Röthlisberger (2021: 281).

51 2 Cor 12:10 (dishonor, insult, mistreatment); 2 Tim 3:11f. in conjunction with Acts 14:5 (ὑβρίζω – mistreat, mock, insult); cf. Luke 18:32 (in connection with being spat upon); Acts 18:10 (κακόω); Gal 6:17 (presumably bearing the scars and wounds of Jesus; BA, s. v. στίγμα); 1 Thess 2:2 (in conjunction with προπάσχω [to suffer beforehand]; ὑβρίζω [to mistreat]); 1 Pet 3:13 (κακουχέω; like 11:37); 2 Cor 6:5 (ἀκαταστασία).

52 (1) with συμβουλεύω: Acts 9:23; cf. Matt 26:4; Joh 18:14 (Jesus); (2) with ἐπιβουλή: Acts 9:24; 20:3.19 (= unsuccessfully attempted attacks), 23:30 (3) others: 9:29; 23:12.15f. (ἐνέδρα); 23:20f.27; 25,3 (ἐ.); 2 Cor 11,26.32f.

53 Acts 21:31-33; 23:10; 27:42; 2 Cor 1:9f.; 11:23.26; Rev 2:10; cf. Acts 14:19; 2 Cor 4:12; Phil 1:20f.; 2:27.30; 2 Tim 4:17, and also Rom 8:35; 1 Cor 15:30.

54 (1) With ἀποκτείνω: Matt 23:34.37; 24:9; Luke 11:48f.; 1 Thess 2:15; cf. Matt 10:28; Luke 12:4f.; 13:34; John 12:10; 16:2; Acts 21:31; 23:12.14; 27:42; Rev 2:13; 6:11; 11:7; 13:15; cf. Acts 7:52; Rom 11:3; (2) with θανατόω: Matt 10:21; Luke 21:16; Rom 8:36; 2 Cor 6:9; cf. Mark 13:12; (3) Acts 9:1 (φόνος; cf. Heb 11:37; Rev 9:21); (3) with θάνατος: Acts 22:4; (Rom 8:38); 2 Cor 1:9f.; 4:11f.; 11:23; Rev 2:10f.; cf. Matt 10:21; Mark 13:12; 22:33; John 21:18f.; Acts 23:29; 25:11.25; 26:31; 28:18; Phil 1:20; 2:27.30; 3:10; Rev 12:11f.; 21:4; (4) with ἀναιρέω: Acts 26:10; cf. Matt 2:16; Acts 5:33; 9:23f.29; 23:15.21.27; 25:3; (5) with ἀποθνήσκω: 2 Cor 6:9; Phil 1:21; Rev 14:12f.; cf. 1 Cor 15:31f.; Rev 3:2; (6) other: Matt 16:21.24f.38; Mark 8:31.34ff.; Luke 9:22-27; cf. 17:25.33 (all cruciform discipleship) and John 15:20; see also Rev 17:6; 18:24.

crucifixion[55], stoning[56] and execution by the sword[57] as a possible deadly fate for believers in Christ. The brothers and disciples James and John Zebedee are promised violent death as "drinking the cup that Jesus drank"[58], and as "being baptised with the baptism with which Jesus was baptised"[59]. Paul's journey to Rome shows that the execution of Christians is also possible without an anti-Christian motive (Acts 27:42), whilst originally faith in Christ was the reason for imprisonment and transportation of the prisoner. In this case, persecution and imprisonment (caused by Jewish opponents) almost led to death for the sake of faith (from the victim's perspective), without this being intended by the (Roman) authorities or motivated by hostility against Christians. Moreover, Christian existence in persecution-related mortal danger is referred to as carrying the death of Jesus in the body.[60]

(7) ***Persecution in the New Testament can be sporadic or widespread, legal or unlawful, authorised or unauthorised by those in power.*** Where believers in Christ are persecuted, this may have been spontaneously decided by the perpetrators or planned beforehand. In the New Testament, we encounter both actions in which only individuals are affected, as well as large-scale and widespread actions directed against entire groups of people. Many of the examples cited so far clearly show whether the respective use of violence is within or outside the legal or official bands: physical violence is often an integral and lawful part of investigative and court proceedings and is therefore considered legitimate from the perpetrator's point of view as long as the briefed rights of those affected are not violated.[61] The view of

---

55 Matt 23:34 (σταυρόω); cf. 1 Cor 1:13 and fn 54/(6).

56 (1) Matt 23:37; cf. Luke 13:34; Acts 7:58f.; 1 Tim 3:11f. in conjunction with Acts 14:5 (all λιθοβολέω); (2) Acts 14:19,22; cf. 5:26; 2 Cor 11:25; Heb 11:37 (all λιθάζω). See also Acts 22:20ff.

57 Rom 8:35f.38 (μάχαιρα in conjunction with θανατόω; θάνατος). Without the context of the word pairs in question: Acts 12:2 (described as mistreatment, v. 1); Rev 13:10; 20:4 (πελεκίζω); cf. Matt 10:34; Rom 16:4; Heb 11:34.37 (also πρίζω – sawed in pieces) and Matt 14:10; Mark 6:16.27; Luke 9:9.

58 Mark 10:38f.; cf. Luke 12:50; Rev 16:6 (LWND).

59 Matt 20:22f.; Mark 10:38f.; cf. Matt 26:39; Mark 14:36; John 18:11 (LWND).

60 2 Cor 4:8-12 (ἐν παντὶ θλιβόμενοι ... διωκόμενοι ... πάντοτε τὴν νέκρωσιν τοῦ Ἰησοῦ ἐν τῷ σώματι περιφέροντες ... ἀεὶ ... εἰς θάνατον παραδιδόμεθα διὰ Ἰησοῦν); cf. Phil 3:10 (suffering as an assimilation to Jesus' death or as "being conformed through suffering, whether this leads to death or not", Michaelis 1954: 931, trans. D. R.).

61 A selective sample: (1) Non-legitimate authority: John 18:20; Acts 7:58-8:2 (Stephen, in detail: Röthlisberger 2021: 458ff.); cf. Acts 12:1f. (James; probably illegitimate); (2) Authorized authority: Matt 27:26-31; Luke 23:13-16.22 (Jesus); Acts 8:1ff.;

the victims is different: They know themselves to be innocently persecuted because of their Christianity and testimony of Christ (point 10), and that this would actually not deserve punishment.[62]

Fig. 1 Damnatio ad bestias (animal fighting), crucifixion and drowning of early church Christians under the Roman Emperor Traian. Copperplate engraving by Giovanni Battista Cavalieri, 16th century. © Prisard Collection (2025)

16:22f.37f.; 22:24-29 etc. (Paul); (3) With further references: Röthlisberger (2021: 148/fn 775).

62 Matt 5:10f.; Acts 25:7-19; 1 Pet 2:11-25; 3:12-17; 4:14-16 etc.; cf. Rom 13:1-7; Heb 13:18.

(8) ***Impending or actual persecution can also lead believers in Christ to a clandestine Christian existence and to outward conformity with the non-Christian environment or to apostasy.*** It is documented many times in the New Testament that persecution, distress and suffering can go hand in hand with the pressure to conform[63] to the non-Christian environment, to conceal ones faith[64] and with the risk of apostasy or actual apostasy[65]. On the other hand, there are numerous scriptural passages – listed here only as examples – that call for steadfastness[66], courage[67], joy and pleasure in persecution[68] or communicate such as a given.

(9) ***Persecution may also be described in general terms with reference to central aspects of the event and to the motives of the persecutors.*** In connection with the word pairs considered, some images are figuratively mentioned, such as a blaze of fire (πύρωσις, 1 Pet 4:12), battles (μάχαι, 2 Cor 7:5) and war against believers in Christ (ποιῆσαι πόλεμον, Rev 12:17; cf. 13:7; 20:7-9). It is likely that the focus is on essential aspects of the event of persecution, not least from the perspective of the experience and interpretation of those affected – the specific meanings are determined by the respective

---

63 Gal 2:12; 6:12; cf. 1 Pet 2:11f.; Rom 12:9-21; Rev 6:9-11.

64 Without referring to the three word pairs in question: John 7:13; 19:38; 20:19; cf. 3:2 and the Lord's words Matt 10:32f.; Mark 8:38; Luke 9:26; 12:8f.; cf. Matt 26:69-75 (Peter); 2 Tim 1:8; 2:12; 1 Pet 3:15; 1 John 2:23.

65 (1) Matt 13:21; Mark 4:17; 14:27.29; cf. Matt 11:6; 16:31.33; Luke 7:23; John 16:1f. (all with σκανδαλίζω) as well as Luke 8:13 etc.; (2) Acts 14:22; Rom 5:3; (8:35); 1 Thess 3:3-8; 2 Thess 1:4; 1 Pet 5:8-10; Rev 2:10 etc. (3) In detail, with references: Röthlisberger (2021), §§ 2.1; 2.4; 4.3.6; 5.3.3; 7.1.2.1.

66 (1) with ὑπομονή: Luke 21:19; Rom 5:3f.; 2 Cor 1:6; 6:4; 1 Thess 1:3 in conjunction with v. 6; 2 Thess 1:4ff.; 3:3; 2 Tim 3:10f.; Rev 1:9; 13:10; 14:12; cf. 2:2; (2) with ὑπομένω: Matt 10:22; Rom 12:12; 2 Tim 2:10,12; Heb 10:32; 1 Pet 2:19f.; cf. Mark 13:13; (3) with ἀνέχω: 1 Cor 4:12; 2 Thess 1:4; cf. Acts 18:14; (4) with τηρέω: John 15:20; cf. John 14:15.21.23f.; 15:10; 2 Tim 4:7; Rev 2:25f.; 3:8ff.; 12:17; 14:12; (5) with μένω: 2 Tim 3:14 in conjunction with v. 12; cf. Heb 10:34f.; (6) with ἀνθίστημι: 1 Pet 5:8f.; cf. Eph 6:13; (7) miscellaneous: Acts 14:22 (ἐμμμένω); Rev 2:10.13 (πιστός; cf. Heb 10:23; Rev 17:14); Rev 12:11 (νικάω); 1 Pet 5:8f. (στερεός); cf. Röthlisberger (2021: 71, esp. fn 325). The reference to suffering and standing firm in faith/in fellowship with the Lord also points to steadfastness in persecution, depending on the context: e.g. 1 Thess 2:14; 3:7f.; cf. 2 Tim 4:16-18, which also presupposes the steadfast testimony of Christ.

67 See the references listed above at point 5.

68 Acts 5:41; 2 Cor (6:4f.10; 7:4); 12:10; Rom 5:3; Phil 1:29 (gift); 1 Thess 1:6; 2 Thess 1:4f.; 1 Pet 3:14; 4:13f.16; Col 1:24; cf. Acts 16:25, Rom 8:17; Phil 2:17; Heb 10:37; Jas 1:12; 5:11 and the macarisms of Jesus: Matt 5:1-12; Luke 6:20-23.

context.[69] If, for example, there is a general report of malice experienced, of hatred and great anger, this is a judgment about the respective behaviour, but also an essential statement about the attitudes and motives of the persecutors towards the believers in Christ.[70] Where persecution is attributed to the horror and torment associated with the coming of the messianic era and possibly the eschatological rebirth of the world, persecution can also be spoken of as birth pangs.[71] Finally, the terms in question, διωγμός/διώκω, θλῖψις/θλίβω and πάθημα/πάσχω, can also occur individually or in pairs as rather indefinite collective terms – more concrete details only become apparent in a broader context.[72]

(10) *Those affected by persecution interpret the attacks on their Christian existence as diabolically inspired interpersonal events, which have been repeatedly announced to them, and happen to them exclusively or partly because of their identity as Christians and especially their witness to Christ, and are ultimately directed against the person of Jesus as the Lord and Christ.* Time and again, the New Testament writings reveal that they also assign a spiritual dimension to the inner-worldly, interpersonal persecution and see it as diabolically inspired.[73] They see the main reason for the persecution

---

69 In 1 Pet 4:12, as can be seen in the subordinate clause, it is about "the fiery heat for purification (of metals) as an image for the testing of believers through suffering" (Balz 1992: 486, trans. D. R.).

70 (1) Wickedness (lit. evil): Rom 12:17.21 (meant as the sum of corresponding behavior; Lattke 1992: 588); see also Rom 9:13 (about the persecutor Paul); 1 Pet 3:9; 2 Tim 3:11f.: 4:14; (2) Hatred: Matt 24:9; Luke 21:17; cf. Matt 10:22; Mark 13:13; Luke 6:22; John 15:18. Here as the "basic attitude of the enemies" (Giesen 1992: 1060, trans. D. R.). (3) Great anger: Rev 12:12 (said by the devil: ὁ διάβολος ... ἔχων θυμὸν μέγαν).

71 Matt 24:8; Mark 13:8 (BA, s. v. ὠδίν; Radl 1992: 1210).

72 Thus, for example, regarding (1) θλῖψις/θλίβω: Rom 5:3; 12:12; 1 Cor 1:4 (in all our tribulation); 2 Cor 4:17; 6:4-6 (tribulations in the midst of a series of specifics); 1 Thess 1:6; Rev 7:13f. (but see v. 16); cf. the references to localisable and datable events: 2 Cor 1:8; 7:4f.; 8:1f.; 1 Thess 3:3-8; (2) παθήματα/πάσχω: Acts 9:16 (blanket for all of Paul's negative experiences during his ministry as an apostle); Rom 8:18; Col 1:24 in conjunction with 4:3.18 (suffering coupled with afflictions, in the broader context: imprisonment); Phil 1:29f. (suffering of the Philippians as a struggle like that of Paul); 1 Tim 5:10; 1 Pet 5:9f. etc. (3) Cf. the special case of Acts 26:14.

73 (1) Luke 8,12f. along with Matt 13:21/Mark 4:17 (diabolically wrought persecution/testing; 1 Thess 3:1-8; 1 Pet 5:8f.; Rev 2:9f.13; 12:3ff.10-17; 13:7f.15-18; 20:4.7-9; cf. Matt 6:13; Luke 11:4 (Lord's Prayer); (2) Without the word pairs in question: Eph 6:10-17; 2 Thess 3:1-3; cf. Jas 4:7; (3) On the diabolic presence and power in the Passion events: Matt 26:41; Mark 14:38; (Gethsemane) Luke 22:3f.; John 13:2.27 (Judas); Luke 22:31-34 (Peter/disciples); 22:53f. (arrest of Jesus); cf. Matt 16:23; 8:31-33.

in their turning to Christ, in their being Christians or witnessing to Christ. Stereotypical phrases interpret such experiences as something that happens to believers in Christ "for the sake of Jesus" or "for Christ's sake",[74] "for the name of Christ" or "for the name of the Lord Jesus"[75] and "for the blood of the Lamb"[76]. Phrases such as "for the gospel"[77] or "for the sake of the word of God and for the sake of the testimony (of Jesus)"[78] emphasise the testimony of Christ more than the cause of violence and suffering. There is a very similar situation where Paul speaks of the gospel, which he knows he is called to preach: "For this cause"[79] he would suffer, and actually - according to the macro-context - as a prisoner awaiting the death sentence (2 Tim 4:9-22). Other phrases are also used in the context of persecution: Believers in Christ suffer "for the sake of righteousness", "on account of the conscience before God" and "for the sake of the kingdom of God",[80] have come close to death "for the sake of the work of Christ",[81] experience persecution "because of the life in Christ Jesus"[82] or seek to escape persecution that happens "for the sake of the cross"[83]. Paul endures his suffering as a prisoner who is bound like a criminal "for Christ's sake" and "for the sake of the elect".[84] Persecuted people not only believe in Christ, but also suffer "for his sake"

---

74 (1) 2 Cor 4:11 (διὰ Ἰησοῦν); (2) 2 Cor 12:10 (ὑπὲρ Χριστοῦ); cf. Phil 3:7f. (διὰ τὸν Χριστὸν ... διὰ τὸ ὑπερέχον τῆς γνώσεως Χριστοῦ Ἰησοῦ τοῦ κυρίου μου - for the sake of Christ ... for the unsurpassable greatness of the knowledge of Christ Jesus my Lord). The prepositions διά mentioned here and below in conjunction with accusative and ὑπέρ in conjunction with genitive can both be rendered with "for" or "for the sake of" (GGNT § 184f/r), the same applies to the improper preposition ἕνεκα/ἕνεκεν (GGNT § 185a).

75 1 Pet 4:14 (ἐν ὀνόματι Χριστοῦ); Acts 21:13 (ὑπὲρ τοῦ ὀνόματος τοῦ κυρίου Ἰησοῦ).

76 Rev 12:11 (διὰ τὸ αἷμα τοῦ ἀρνίου).

77 2 Tim 1:8 (τῷ εὐαγγελίῳ; as dative of advantage/of benefit: "for the gospel"; GGNT § 176a; NSS: 1125); here possibly referring to pagan and inner-Christian opposition.

78 Rev 1:9; 6:9 (διὰ τὸν λόγον τοῦ θεοῦ καὶ τὴν μαρτυρίαν ['Ιησοῦ]); 20:4 (διὰ τὴν μ. Ἰησοῦ καὶ διὰ τὸν λόγον τοῦ θεοῦ); cf. 12:11 (καὶ διὰ τὸν λόγον τῆς μ.).

79 2 Tim 1:10-12 (διὰ τοῦ εὐαγγελίου εἰς ὃ ἐτέθην ἐγὼ κῆρυξ καὶ ἀπόστολος καὶ διδάσκαλος, δι' ἣν αἰτίαν καὶ ταῦτα πάσχω).

80 (1) 1 Pet 3:14 (διὰ δικαιοσύνην); (2) 1 Pet 2:19f. (διὰ συνείδησιν θεοῦ); (3) 2 Thess 1:5 (τῆς βασιλείας τοῦ θεοῦ, ὑπὲρ ἧς καὶ πάσχετε).

81 Phil 2:30 (διὰ τὸ ἔργον Χριστοῦ); cf. Rom 16:4; Acts 15:26.

82 2 Tim 3:12 (οἱ θέλοντες εὐσεβῶς ζῆν ἐν Χριστῷ Ἰησοῦ).

83 Gal 6:12 (ἵνα τῷ σταυρῷ τοῦ Χριστοῦ μὴ διώκωνται).

84 Phil 1:13 (ἐν Χριστῷ - causal: for Christ's sake; NSS: 1070); 2 Tim 2:9f. (διὰ τοὺς ἐκλεκτούς).

and endure even the greatest insults "for the sake of his name".[85] They are "fools for Christ's sake", the reason for their persecution is the "offence of the cross".[86] Then afflictions, persecution and other adversities are associated with a Psalm saying that those affected are killed "for your sake" like sheep for the slaughter.[87] These phrases correspond to Jesus' statements that his followers must expect persecution "for the sake of the Son of Man"[88], "for my name's sake"[89], "for my sake"[90] and "for my sake and for the sake of the gospel"[91], but also "for the sake of justice"[92], "for the sake of the kingdom of God"[93] and "for the sake of the word of God"[94]. The fact that, from the perspective of the persecutors, other religious and then political, social, economic and emotional or personal motives may be decisive for the persecution,[95] is *secondary* for the perspective of those affected, especially as the persecution is accompanied by said anti-Christian motives according to the textual findings. What is striking is that the widely used expression of persecution, affliction or suffering "for the sake of faith" is not found anywhere (!) in the New Testament Scriptures.[96] It may be appropriate and serve to simplify the facts, but it is not based on the philological findings of the New Testament.

85 (1) Phil 1:29 (τὸ ὑπὲρ αὐτοῦ; cf. GGNT § 184r); (2) 1 Pet 4:16 (ὡς Χριστιανός); (3) Acts 5:41 (Οἱ μὲν ἐπορεύοντο χαίροντες ..., ὅτι κατηξιώθησαν ὑπὲρ τοῦ ὀνόματος ἀτιμασθῆναι).

86 (1) 1 Cor 4:10 (μωροὶ διὰ Χριστόν); (2) Gal 5:11 (τὸ σκάνδαλον τοῦ σταυροῦ).

87 Ps 44:22 (43:23 LXX, verbatim quoted in Rom 8:35 – with ἕνεκα σοῦ; cf. Dunn (1988: 505).

88 Luke 6:22 (ἕνεκα τοῦ υἱοῦ τοῦ ἀνθρώπου).

89 Matt 10:22; 24:9; Luke 21:17; John 15:21 (διὰ τὸ ὄνομά μου); Matt 19:29; Luke 21:12 (ἕνεκεν τοῦ ὀ. μου); cf. Acts 9:16 (ὑπὲρ τοῦ ὀνόματός μου); Rev 2:3 (διὰ τὸ ὄνομά μου).

90 Matt 5:11; 10:18.39; 16:25; Mark 13:9; Luke 9:24 (ἕνεκεν ἐμοῦ).

91 Mark 8:35 (ἕνεκεν ἐμοῦ καὶ τοῦ εὐαγγελίου); 10:29 (ἕνεκεν ἐμοῦ καὶ ἕνεκεν τοῦ ε.).

92 Matt 5:10 (ἕνεκεν δικαιοσύνης).

93 Luke 18:29 (ἕνεκεν τῆς βασιλείας τοῦ θεοῦ).

94 Matt 13:21 (διὰ τὸν λόγον).

95 Cf. the overview in Penner (2004: 162f.) (with references) and the contexts of the respective scriptural passages.

96 Even a computer-aided query with BibleWorks, which combined all forms of πίστις/πιστεύω with all forms of the prepositions in question here, διά and ὑνεκα/ἕνεκεν, as well as the improper preposition ἕνεκα/ἕνεκεν (with any word order and a possible word spacing of even 0-10 words between the search terms), did not produce any (!) results that could prove a phrase of persecution, suffering or affliction *for the sake of faith*. Passages such as Acts 14:22; 1 Thess 3:7; 2 Thess 1:10; Heb 6:12 and even passages such as 1 Thess 3:1 and 2 Thess 1:4ff. have a different meaning if one looks closely.

Speaking of persecution "for the sake of being a Christian" or the "testimony of Christ" is philologically justifiable.[97]

From a New Testament perspective, the spiritual dimension of persecution also includes the fact that the inner-worldly, interpersonal events are not only diabolically inspired (see above), but are aiming beyond the believers in Christ at the historical person of Jesus, proclaimed in the kerygma as the Messiah (Χριστός) and Lord (κύριος)[98]: *He* is *the actual target* of all persecution; as he is the "ultimate revelation of God"[99], the world's hatred directed at God means him.[100] This is the consensus of the New Testament writings and in particular Jesus' statements, according to which the persecution of his followers and the hatred of them is actually directed *at him.*[101] If God-fearers were already persecuted in Old Testament times and the prophets sent by God were killed,[102] this line continues in the fate of Jesus and his followers.[103] They know that they are connected to their Lord in a community of destiny; suffering for his sake was announced to them.[104] Persecution is therefore always something that comes as little surprise and

---

97 Sociological definitions can certainly speak of persecution e.g. "for the sake of faith" or of persecution "because of the Christian faith" or "because of Christian religious affiliation". However, they cannot claim to cover the New Testament or theological findings.

98 Luke 2:11.26; John 11:27; Acts 2:36; 10:36; 28:31; Rom 5:11.21; 8:39; Eph 3:8-11; Phil 2:5-11, esp. v. 11; 3:20; 2 Pet 1:11; Jude 1:25; Rev 11:15; cf. John 20:31; 1 John 1:2; 4:14 etc.

99 Schwöbel (2002: 9).

100 Schirrmacher (2011: 55.61).

101 Matt 10:22; 24:9; Mark 13:13; Luke 21:17; John 15:18ff.; Acts 9:4f.; 22:7f.; 26:14f.; cf. John 7:7; 17:14ff.; 1 John 3:13 and Rev 12:13 along with v. 17 (Schirrmacher 2011: 55.61, supplemented by the author with further references); cf. above the numerous references according to the scheme "for the sake of". The statement by Boyd-MacMillan (2006: 103) that Christians are not the actual *object*, but rather the *victim* of persecution, must be questioned: from a theological perspective, they are the object *and* victim of a persecution that is ultimately aimed at Jesus.

102 Cf. Schirrmacher (2011: 37f.43-46, with references).

103 Matt 5:12; 23:29-37; Luke 6:23; 11:47-51; 13:33f.; Acts 7:52-60; 1 Thess 2:14-16; cf. Matt 13:57; 17:12; Luke 18:31-33; Rom 11:3; Heb 1:1-3; 11:32-40; Jas 5:10f.; Rev 11:18; 16:6; 18:20.24; 22:9. On the murder of the prophets cf. Matt 23:31f.par; Acts 7:52; Heb 11:36f.; 1 Thess 2:15 see Schoeps (1943: 3-22).

104 References in fn 54/(6), to be supplemented here by the following passages with a reference to the announcement of suffering: (1) *Through Jesus himself*: Matt 5:10-12; 10:16-23.35f.; 23:34; 24:9f.; Mark 13:9-19; Luke 6:22f.; 11:49-51; 12:11f.51-53; 21:12-17; John 15:18-21; 16:1-4; Rev 2:10; (2) *Through third parties*: 9:22; 17:14f.; Acts 14:22; Rom 8:17; Phil 1:29; 1 Thess 1:6; 2:14f.; 3:4; 2 Tim 3:12; 1 Pet 2:19-21; 3:14; 4:12f.; 5:8-10 etc.

is consciously accepted by believers in Christ as an integral part of discipleship – in other words: following Jesus means following in suffering.[105]

3 "Persecution" according to a New Testament definition

The semantic and phenomenological findings on the New Testament, which have been systematically determined here for the first time ever, allow persecution of Christians to be defined as follows:

> "From a New Testament perspective, persecution of Christians is the action of individuals or collectives against believers in Christ, motivated mainly or in part by anti-Christian hostility. This action may vary in form, frequency and intensity, occur by law or illegally, differ in the effects intended, and may attack any dimension of human existence."[106]

The internal perspective of those affected, as these findings show, can then lead to supplementing the above definition with the following additional aspects:

> "Those affected interpret the events as diabolically inspired actions, which have been repeatedly announced, and happen to them exclusively or in part because of their identity as Christians and especially their witness to Christ. This is an integral part of discipleship and ultimately directed against the person of Jesus, the Lord and Christ."[107]

---

105 In the New Testament, believers in Christ/Christians must expect persecution at any time: Matt 5:10ff.44; 10:23; 23:34; Luke 11:49; 21:12; Acts 14:22; 1 Cor 4:9; 2 Cor 6:4f.; 11:24f.; Gal 4:29; 5:11; 6:12; Phil 1:29; 1 Thess 2:14; 2 Tim 3:12; Heb 10:32f.; 1 Pet 3:13-17; 4:12-19; I John 3:13; see also the example of Paul: Acts 9:16; 22:4; 9:4f.; 22:7f.; 26:14f.; 1 Cor 15:9; Gal 1:13.23; Phil 3:6. On Jesus' statements of persecution: Matt 5:10f.; 10:18.22.39; 13:21; 16:25; 19:29; 24:9; Mark 8:35; 10:29; 13:9; Luke 6:22; 18:29; 21:12,17; 22:39-46; John 15:21; cf. Acts 9:16; Rev 2:3. The following speaks of God's will regarding persecution: 1 Pet 2:20; 3:17; 4:(16.)19; cf. Luke 22:39-46 as well as Paul's imprisonment and journey to Rome (Acts 21-28; for details: Röthlisberger 2021: 180-190).

106 Röthlisberger (2021: 490).

107 Röthlisberger (2021: 490).

4 References

Allard, P. (1907). *Dix leçons sur le martyre.* (6th ed.). J. Gabalda (1921).

Bähnk, W. (2001). *Von der Notwendigkeit des Leidens: Die Theologie des Martyriums bei Tertullian.* (FKDG 78). Vandenhoeck & Ruprecht.

Balz, H. (1992). πύρωσις. In H. Balz & G. Schneider (Eds.), *Exegetisches Wörterbuch zum Neuen Testament.* (2nd ed., vol. 3, p. 486). W. Kohlhammer.

[BA] Bauer, W. (1988). *Griechisch-deutsches Wörterbuch zu den Schriften des Neuen Testaments und der frühchristlichen Literatur*, ed. by K. & B. Aland. (6th ed.). Walter de Gruyter.

Bible Works LLC (Ed.). (2013). *BibleWorks. Software for Biblical Exegesis and Research.* (CD-Rom, Version 9.0.12.718). Bible Works LLC.

- [LXX] (1) Brenton, L. C. L. (1851). *The Septuagint with Apocrypha.* S. Bagster.
- [LWND] (2) Louw, J. E. & Nida, E. A. (Eds.). *Greek-English Lexicon of the New Testament Based on Semantic Domains.* (2 vols., 2nd ed.). United Bible Societies.

Boyd-MacMillan, R. (2006). *Faith That Endures. The Essential Guide to the Persecuted Church.* Revell.

Dunn, J. D. G. (1988). *Romans 1-8.* (WBC 38A). Thomas Nelson.

Giesen, H. (1992). μισέω. In H. Balz & G. Schneider (Eds.), *Exegetisches Wörterbuch zum Neuen Testament.* (2nd ed., vol. 3, pp. 1060-62). W. Kohlhammer.

Hare, D. R. A. (1967). *The Theme of Jewish Persecution of Christians in the Gospel according to St Matthew.* (MSSNTS 6). Cambridge University Press.

[NSS] Haubeck, W. & von Siebenthal, H. (2007). *Neuer sprachlicher Schlüssel zum griechischen Neuen Testament. Matthäus bis Offenbarung.* (2nd ed.). Brunnen.

Kelhoffer, J. A. (2010). *Persecution, Persuasion and Power: Readiness to Withstand Hardship as a Corroboration of Legitimacy in the New Testament.* (WUNT 270). Mohr Siebeck.

Knoch, O. (1992). διώκω κτλ. In H. Balz & G. Schneider (Eds.), *Exegetisches Wörterbuch zum Neuen Testament.* (2nd ed., vol 1, pp. 816-19). W. Kohlhammer.

Kremer, J. (1992). θλῖψις κτλ. In H. Balz & G. Schneider (Eds.), *Exegetisches Wörterbuch zum Neuen Testament.* (2nd ed., vol. 2, pp. 375-79). W. Kohlhammer.

Kremer, J. (1992). πάσχω. In H. Balz & G. Schneider (Eds.), *Exegetisches Wörterbuch zum Neuen Testament.* (2nd ed., vol. 3, pp. 120-24). W. Kohlhammer.

Lattke, M. (1992). κακός. In H. Balz & G. Schneider (Eds.), *Exegetisches Wörterbuch zum Neuen Testament.* (2nd ed., vol. 2, pp. 587-89). W. Kohlhammer.

Michaelis, W. (1954). πάσχω κτλ. In G. Friedrich (Ed.), *Theologisches Wörterbuch zum Neuen Testament.* (vol. 5, pp. 903-39). W. Kohlhammer.

Mommsen, T. (1899). *Römisches Strafrecht.* Duncker & Humblot.

Oepke, A. (1935). διώκω. In G. Kittel (Ed.), *Theologisches Wörterbuch zum Neuen Testament.* (vol. 2, pp. 232f.). W. Kohlhammer.

Penner, G. M. (2004). *In the Shadow of the Cross: A Biblical Theology of Persecution and Discipleship.* Living Sacrifice Books.

Pervo, R. I. (1987). *Profit with Delight: The Literary Genre of the Acts of the Apostles.* Fortress.

Pobee, J. S. (1985). *Persecution and Martyrdom in the Theology of Paul.* (JSNTS 6). JSOT Press.

Radl, W. (1992). ὠδίν κτλ. In H. Balz & G. Schneider (Eds.), *Exegetisches Wörterbuch zum Neuen Testament.* (2nd ed., vol. 3, pp. 1209f.). W. Kohlhammer.

Röthlisberger, D. (2021). *Hilfe und Selbsthilfe für verfolgte Christen. Eine Studie zum neutestamentlichen Ethos.* Evangelische Verlagsanstalt.

Sauer, C. (2016). Bedrängnis, Verfolgung und Mission: Begrifflichkeiten im Neuen Testament als Orientierungspunkte. In T. Schirrmacher et al. (Eds.), *Jahrbuch Verfolgung und Diskriminierung von Christen heute 2016* (pp. 38-56). VKW.

Sauer, C. (2021). *Martyrium und Mission im Kontext. Analyse ausgewählte theologische Positionen aus der weltweiten Christenheit.* (MF.NF 37). Erlanger Verlag für Mission und Ökumene.

Sauer, C. (2014). Survey on language use regarding Discrimination, Persecution, Martyrdom. *IJRF* 7 (1/2), 201-212.

Schirrmacher, T. (2011). *Christenverfolgung geht uns alle an: Auf dem Weg zu einer Theologie des Martyriums. 70 biblisch-theologische Thesen.* (Studien zur Religionsfreiheit 19). VKW.

Schlier, H. (1957). θλίβω κτλ. In G. Kittel (Ed.), *Theologisches Wörterbuch zum Neuen Testament.* (vol. 3, pp. 139-48). W. Kohlhammer.

Schneider, G. (1992). θηριομαχέω. In H. Balz & G. Schneider (Eds.), *Exegetisches Wörterbuch zum Neuen Testament* (2nd ed., vol. 2, pp. 366f.). W. Kohlhammer.

Schoeps, H.-J. (1943). *Die jüdischen Prophetenmorde.* (SyBU 2). Wretman.

Schwöbel, C. (2002). *Gott in Beziehung. Studien zur Dogmatik.* Mohr Siebeck.

[GGNT] von Siebenthal, H. (2011). *Griechische Grammatik zum Neuen Testament. Neubearbeitung und Erweiterung der Grammatik Hoffmann/von Siebenthal.* Brunnen.

Tieszen, C. L. (2012). Redefining Persecution. In W. D. Taylor et al. (Eds.), *Sorrow and Blood: Christian Mission in Contexts of Suffering, Persecution and Martyrdom* (pp. 43-49). William Carey Library.

Tieszen, C. L. (2008). *Re-Examining Religious Persecution: Constructing a Theological Framework for Understanding Persecution.* (Religious Freedom Series 1). AcadSA/VKW.

Williams, T. B. (2012). *Persecution in 1 Peter: Differentiating and Contextualizing Early Christian Suffering.* (NT.S 145). Brill.

5 Neglected aspects of conflict in the inner-Jewish conflict accounts in Acts 9-19

Christoph Stenschke[1]

Abstract

The Book of Acts contains the first systematic account of some strands of the earliest Christian mission. At first sight, the book abounds with conflicts of various kinds and the suffering of Christ-believers that, on occasion, resulted from their missionary efforts. However, taking inspiration from some recent theorising about religious conflict, other aspects can also be detected in these accounts. Amid intensive missionary activities and, at times, serious conflicts, there are not only instances of de-escalation or resolution of conflict but also instances of relatively peaceful co-existence and even co-operation between Jews and Jewish Christ-followers in the Jewish diaspora. Such co-existence created or at least allowed for a climate that was conducive to transition and co-operation. The article seeks to identify some of these instances and analyse them in order to understand what factors enabled these more desirable forms of interactions between representatives of different convictions and practices, and at what points conflict arose and why.

Keywords: Religious conflict, Acts of the Apostles, de-escalation or resolution of religious conflict, interreligious co-existence and co-operation, early Christian mission, Paul, the apostle.

---

1 Christoph W. Stenschke (*1966) is Dozent at Biblisch-Theologische Akademie, Forum Wiedenest, Bergneustadt, Germany, Privatdozent at the Evangelisch-Theologische Fakultät, Universität Bonn, Germany and Professor extraordinarius at the Department of Biblical and Ancient Studies, College of Human Sciences, University of South Africa, Pretoria and at the Department of New Testament and Related Literature, Faculty of Theology and Religion, University of Pretoria, South Africa. Email: CStenschke@t-online.de, ORCID iD: 0000-0002-0009-8461. – This article had its origin in a presentation at the 2023 Fjellhaug Symposium on *Mission and Religious Freedom*, held at *Fjellhaug International University College* in Oslo, Norway, 20-21 September 2023. Many thanks to the organizers of the conference and for the careful reviewers of the original submission.

1 Introduction

Many readers of the Book of Acts love the so-called missionary journeys of Paul, the pre-eminent champion of the Gospel. They are fascinated by his preaching and the pace at which he founded congregations of Christ-followers among Jews and non-Jews. Others are no less fascinated with Luke's portrayal of the earliest community in Jerusalem, with its phenomenal growth and its nascent ministry to non-Jews. Yet, from the very beginning in Jerusalem, Acts also mentions conflict, sometimes moderate and other times fierce and even fatal for the Christ-believing protagonists.[2] Shortly after Pentecost, the apostles end up in prison; later, Stephen dies for his faithful and bold witness to Jesus. Readers are told that Saul would have to suffer much for the name of Jesus (Acts 9:16). Soon after his conversion/calling, he has to flee from Damascus and Jerusalem. This continues throughout his later journeys. From Acts 21 onwards, Paul is a prisoner. Acts ends with Paul in prison in Rome (28:16, 30-31). This portrayal is not surprising, as Jesus speaks of the cost of discipleship when training and commissioning his disciples (e.g., in Luke 6:22-23; 9:23-27; 12:11-12; 21:12-19).

Because of the selection of programmatic events from a period of over thirty years, including these instances of suffering, and perhaps also because of Paul's own emphasis on his suffering and ministry in the Spirit[3], the impression can easily arise that what eventually became Christianity caused conflicts of every kind and encountered violence of all sorts from the very beginning. This perception can easily align with the observation that, for a number of reasons, most of them sad and disturbing, religious conflict has become a dominant theme in religious studies in the past two decades.[4] This quest is part of a larger interdisciplinary interest in violence.[5]

The seeming prevalence of conflict in Acts easily prevents readers from seeing that there are also other aspects in the portrayal of the earliest Christ-followers and the conflicts in which they were involved than is apparent at first sight. In her survey of definitions, problems and theoretical approaches to religious conflict in antiquity, Wendy Mayer rightly observes that, in the recent discussion of religious conflict

---

2 See the summary in Keener (2012, 505) and Cunningham (1997).

3 See the summary in Wu (2023, 1020-1027).

4 For a convenient survey, see Mayer (2013, 1-19); on religion and violence in general, see Juergensmeyer, Kitts, & Jerryson (2013).

5 For a survey, see Gudehus & Christ (2013).

> "the *focus on violence* (one extreme of religious conflict) obscures broader questions about what occurs *before or apart from violence*: the mechanisms at play in how conflict originates in the first instance, how it manifests in its early stages, the phenomenon of splintering into sub-groups (sectarianism) within a religion, and precisely what factors are operative in *conflict escalation* and *de-escalation*."[6]

While Acts offers vivid portrayals of, at times, fierce religious conflict between different groups in changing constellations, in its reports of conflict and elsewhere, it also contains traces of *conflict de-escalation* and *conflict resolution* that must also be noted.

Mayer furthermore insists that the usual focus on religious *conflict* should not blind scholars to the "prevalence of evidence for actual religious co-existence and co-operation, as well as ... transition and assimilation" (Mayer 2013, 17). Following this reminder, we will also search for indications of *co-existence* and *co-operation*, as well as *transition* and *assimilation*, although at times more *e silentio* or in passing than by direct mention. This means that we also note when some people in the narrative do not take the measures or pursue a course of action that others readily take elsewhere in the narrative. Caution is needed when arguing *from silence*. When some course of action is not pursued by the Christ-believing protagonists or their opponents, it might indeed not have happened or has simply not been narrated. Thus, such observations carry less weight than direct statements.

As the "mechanisms involved in the resolution of religious conflict and the role of religion in reconciliation, for instance, prevalent in studies of contemporary religious conflict, are aspects rarely addressed" (Mayer 2013, 18), we focus here on these "broader questions" and probe the contribution of Acts regarding such instances of *de-escalation* or *resolution* of conflicts, the evidence for *co-existence* and *co-operation* as well as *transition* and *assimilation* between the parties involved in these conflicts.

---

6 Mayer (2013, 19), italics CS. Mayer's essay serves as the introduction to the collection of essays entitled *Religious Conflict from Early Christianity to the Rise of Islam*. Mayer's insights were formulated with the ancient context in view. When applying them to our quest, we are obviously limited by the amount of information that is available in ancient sources and by how these sources portray the instances of conflict they chose to address. In our case, we do hardly know what the opponents of the Christ-believers made of the events. Current conflicts or past conflicts that are much better documented (in particular, if different documents or witnesses from a variety of perspectives are available) allow for more nuanced theorising on religious conflict and for the application of different methods. Theoretical insights gleaned from current conflicts can serve as useful heuristic tools but will be limited in their applicability to ancient conflicts and usefulness.

With earlier research as a point of departure, we focus here as a case study on encounters in the Jewish Diaspora according to Acts 9-19.[7] For a fuller picture, one would need to consider the accounts of conflict with other conflict parties.

This quest will lead to a more comprehensive understanding of Luke's portrayals of conflict. A detailed and, in particular, nuanced portrayal of religious conflict is not the purpose of Acts. At first glance, the accounts of religious conflict are by-products of Luke's overall apologetic purpose. However, on closer examination, it becomes clear that these instances – and the way in which they are narrated – contribute in their own way to the purpose.

We concentrate on the *literary portrayal* of these conflicts. We cannot discuss the historical plausibility or validity of this portrayal,[8] nor its contribution to the reconstruction of early Christian history. As Luke does not give a comprehensive account of all that happened (whether out of material constraint, choice or due to a lack of information) and has a clear focus on certain protagonists (in our case, Saul/Paul), there is much that we simply do not know.[9] The fate of the "rank-and-file" Christ-believers in these conflicts is barely addressed.

In short, we will apply a number of insights from recent theorising on religious conflict to Acts in order to shed fresh light on the relationship between the earliest Christian missionaries and other Jews in a diaspora setting. We will search for traces of de-escalation or resolution, co-existence and co-operation, transition and assimilation[10] in the conflicts between these groups as they are narrated in Acts 9-19.

---

7 See my earlier studies of conflict constellations and accounts in Acts; Stenschke (2017a; 2017b; 2020, 2022).

8 Mayer (2013, 15) rightly points to the "perennial issue of the bias of the surviving sources, and the historical forces that led to the transmission of some and the suppression or dwindling into obscurity of others". For a recent survey of the issues and debate, see Keener (2012, 90-220). The historicity of the nature and extent of persecution in ancient Christianity is fiercely debated; see, for instance, the discussion in Moss (2013); Ployd (2023); Rebillard (2021) and Waldner (2024).

9 For instance, the early Jewish historian Josephus Flavius wrote the *seven*-volume historical monograph *Bellum Judaicum* to cover the first Jewish war (66-73 AD) and some of its pre-history (from 170 BCE onward).

10 Obviously, each of these terms would need further discussion and definition with regard to its meanings in the context of the study of religious conflicts in general and in antiquity in particular. In a survey article, a more general definition is permissible. After a detailed definition, each term could serve as a heuristic tool for a series of studies.

2 Traces of de-escalation or resolution, co-existence and co-operation, transition and assimilation in the accounts of conflict between Jewish Christian missionaries and other Jews

Even when the Christ-believing mission ventures beyond predominantly Jewish territories, the majority of instances of religious conflict concern different groups *within* early Judaism. We briefly summarise the portrayal of the events in Jerusalem, before the narrative moves to different diaspora settings. Acts 4-8:3 can be read as the beginning of an *intra*-religious conflict narrative tracing the painful and at times violent separation between various forms and representatives of early Judaism, one of them being the nascent Christ-believing movement. In view of the, at times, strained relationship between other groups in early Judaism (also reflected in Acts, see 23:6-10), it is not surprising that these developments include conflicts.

According to Acts 4-8:3, some Jewish Christ-followers and other Jews separate early on. This is caused by some Jews refusing to accept or at least tolerate the apostles' and Stephen's claims regarding Jesus and to repent. The religious leaders hold on to their negative assessment of Jesus and do not relinquish their claim to their leadership role. In the portrayal of Acts, this development is not the fault of the apostles, who are presented as faithfully fulfilling the commission that they had received from the risen Lord. There is no indication that the apostles are mistaken in doing so or could or should have acted otherwise. There are no traces of self-criticism or a reflection-in-hindsight by the author of Acts that the course of events could or should have been different.

In their proceedings against the apostles, the religious leaders act in isolation and in contrast to inhabitants of Jerusalem, many of whom become believers or, in the initial phase, hold the apostles in high esteem. Like the rejection of Jesus, the early separation between the Christ-followers and the Jewish establishment is presented as the fault of the Jewish leaders, not of the Jewish people as a whole.

Although they lead a community of their own with distinctive convictions and perhaps also practices, and act in ways that are unusual for their social status, the apostles and Stephen are portrayed as Jews acting firmly within Judaism. While the leaders consider and treat them as heretics and impostors who must be disciplined, they never question their Jewish identity or their belonging to the people of God. In contrast, the apostles indicate that belonging to the people of God depends on the stance taken vis-à-vis Jesus: those who refuse to listen to him will be rooted out from the people (Acts 3:23).

The portrait of the Jewish leadership is not entirely negative. While they refuse to repent and believe in Jesus, they – guided by a variety of motives (due to the popularity of the apostles, none of the enabling conditions available to them proves to be efficient) – de-escalate the conflict and eventually give in or, at least, do not take further measures against the apostles after beating them and charging them not to speak in the name of Jesus (Acts 5:40). The conflict does not run to its fatal end. The picture is different for the opponents of Stephen and the way they proceed against him (even though he is brought before the same Sanhedrin and his defence there results in his death). With his death, the narrative leaves Jerusalem, although it returns repeatedly to the city.

Acts indicates that more than the evaluation of Jesus was contested. Closely related to this contested domain, a number of other domains (such as access to space, the leadership of the people of God, public recognition or material interests) were directly or indirectly, deliberately or by chance, affected by this estimate and contested in this conflict. The early separation in Jerusalem was a complex issue.

Once the narrative ventures beyond Jerusalem, a number of conflicts between Christ-believers and other Jews in the diaspora emerge, from Saul's ministry in Damascus to his interactions in Ephesus.[11] We cannot analyse each instance in detail, but we do note some recurring features.

2.1 De-escalation and resolution of conflict?

2.1.1 On the side of the Jewish opponents

There is little direct evidence with regard to de-escalation and resolution of conflict on the side of the Jewish opponents. Nevertheless, some observations are possible. The opponents in Damascus apparently tolerate Saul's preaching in their synagogue "for many days" (Acts 9:23) before they eventually plot to kill him, because he "confounded the Jews who lived in Damascus by proving that Jesus was the Christ" (9:22).[12] The opponents in Antioch in Pisidia do not take action immediately but "began to contradict what was spoken by Paul, reviling him" (13:45), followed by a

11 For a detailed analysis, see Stenschke (2018).

12 Marguerat (2022, 379) comments: "Die Intensivierung der Missionstätigkeit des Saulus und sein Beharren 'eine Reihe von Tagen' lang erklären die heftige Reaktion, die sich gegen ihn richtet".

verbal response from the missionaries (13:46-47). Despite the interventions of the opponents,[13] there is time for the word of the Lord to spread throughout the whole region (13:49; see below on *co-existence*).

In some instances, the opponents use and exhaust all the enabling conditions available to them against the missionaries, going so far as to co-operate with non-Jews and instigating them against the Jewish Christ-following missionaries (see below).[14] In other cases, the opponents leave it at expelling the missionaries ("and drove them out of their district", 13:50). Other than in Lystra, no attempts are made to actually kill the missionaries (see the plans to do so in Iconium, 14:5; and of radical Jews in Jerusalem, 23:12-15). Only in two cases do the opponents follow the missionaries to other places and cause trouble there (14:19; 17:13). Otherwise, they confine their actions to their own places (perhaps out of moderation or in realistic estimation of their lack of resources or influence elsewhere). The anti-Jewish sentiments voiced against the missionaries in Philippi (16:20, "These men are Jews, and they are disturbing our city") could also erupt against other Jews.

2.1.2 On the side of the missionaries

The missionaries regularly leave the Jewish synagogues without further ado once opposition arises. They do not contest this space but go elsewhere: "And Paul left there and went to the house of a man named Titius Justus, a worshipper of God. His house was next to the synagogue" (Acts 18:7[15]; see also 19:9: "Paul withdrew from them and took the disciples with

---

13 According to Marguerat (2022, 519), the opponents discredit themselves "weil sie den Missionaren nichts anderes als Gewalt entgegenzusetzen haben". Eventually this is the case.

14 In Ephesus, the Jews seek to distance themselves in public from Paul and his companions only when the riot instigated by Demetrius gains momentum (Acts 19:33-34).

15 Marguerat (2022, 638) notes the highly symbolic significance of this move and writes with regard to the theological claim of Luke's note:

> "Kann man noch konkreter darauf hinweisen, dass, wenn die Sonderrolle Israels aufgehoben ist, die Missionare dennoch nicht auf die Verbindung zum Judentum verzichten? Die Wahl eines Ortes direkt neben der Synagoge beweist in den Augen des Erzählers, dass der ungewollte Bruch mit Israel nicht dazu führt, ihm den Rücken zu kehren, und noch weniger, es zu verfluchen. Der Streit verursacht eine Trennung der Körper, aber nicht der Herzen" (639).

For the opponents, this proximity was probably perceived as an act of provocation.

him, reasoning daily in the hall of Tyrannus"). There are no attempts to take over the building (whether the missionaries, together with their new adherents, could even have done so is difficult to determine). In all cases, the missionaries de-escalate the conflicts by withdrawing from a place to avoid further escalation (13:51), although they return later to re-visit the Christ-believers (14:21-23; 16:1-5; 18:23). In Thessalonica, Silas and Timothy can stay behind (17:15). These later, probably low-profile, visits of the Christ-followers seem not to cause problems.

As happens to Saul in Jerusalem (see above), in some cases, the endangered missionaries are sent off by local Christ-believers. Acts 17:10 notes: "The brothers immediately sent Paul and Silas away by night to Berea". "Then the brothers immediately sent Paul off on his way to the sea, but Silas and Timothy remained there" (Acts 17:14).[16] Paul is escorted all the way to Athens (17:15). This is done to avoid further escalation, to save Paul's life and to protect the local Christ-believers who have to, and apparently can, stay behind without major threat (however, their fate might simply not be Luke's focus; Paul's letters paint a different picture). In this manner of presentation, the missionaries from other places – and who are the active and public protagonists of the Gospel in word and deed – are the cause of conflict, not necessarily the local adherents to the new faith.

Other than the fierce interaction with the *Jewish* sorcerer Elymas in Paphos (Acts 13:4-12), there are no punitive miracles performed by the missionaries (see Rydryck 2024). However, even in Elymas' case, punishment is relatively mild: "... you will be blind and unable to see the sun *for a time*" (13:11).[17] Elsewhere, the missionaries pronounce severe warnings before they leave (13:46) and accentuate such warnings with accompanying gestures ("But they shook the dust from their feet against them and went to Iconium", 13:51, see Keener 2013, 2105-2106); "and he shook out his garments", 18:6), but do not take any direct actions against their opponents.

Throughout, the missionaries avoid measures that would endanger the Jewish communities in the diaspora (see Stenschke 2024, 82-85).

---

16 Marguerat (2022, 610): "Diesmal werden ohne Aufschub Sicherheitsmaßnahmen ergriffen". Marguerat's description of the Jewish activities as "eine Strafexpedition nach Beröa ... und wiegeln die Stadt auf" (610), raises the important issue of the language that interpreters use to summarise and interpret such accounts of conflict. While "agitating and stirring up the crowd" (17:13) is acceptable (even though less than inciting the (entire) city; a crowd of how many people is in mind? See 17:5), the notion of a "punitive expedition" is beyond the evidence and the means available to the opponents; see the adequate terminology in Keener, *Acts* (2014, 2563). Haacker (2019, 292), speaks of an "Eingreifen" and an "Intervention".

17 Acts 13:11, see Keener (2013, 2023-2024) and Stenschke (2023).

Nowhere in these conflicts with his fellow Jews does Paul make use of his privileges as a Roman citizen as he does in other conflicts (see Acts 16:35-39, 22:23-29; 23:27; 25:6-12). In contrast to their opponents, the missionaries never draw on the support of non-Jews against their fellow Jews or use slanderous accusations (see, e.g., Acts 17:6-7). This takes us to a further observation.

2.1.3 Resolving conflict through extension?

There are several instances when the Jewish opponents are portrayed as involving *non-Jews* in their conflicts with the missionaries or attempting to do so. They do so either by drawing on support from the crowds, local authorities or office bearers of the Roman Empire. In all but one case, they employ this strategy with favourable outcomes. In Antioch, some "Jews incited the devout women of high standing and the leading men of the city; stirred up persecution against Paul and Barnabas, and drove them out of their district" (Acts 13:50; see also 14:4-6 where it is not clear who took the initiative). In Lystra, Jews from Antioch and Iconium, "having persuaded the crowds, stoned Paul and dragged him out of the city, supposing that he was dead" (14:19). In Thessalonica, jealous Jews take some wicked men of the rabble, form a mob, set the city in uproar and attack the house of Jason, seeking to bring the missionaries out to the crowd (17:5, see also 17:6-9). In response, the local Christ-believers send Paul and Silas away by night to Berea (17:10; see the repetition of this course of action in Berea and its consequences, 17:13-14; earlier on, Paul was ushered off to Tarsus, 9:30). In Corinth, the Jews accuse Paul before Gallio, the Roman proconsul of Achaia (18:12-17).

At first sight, these are not instances of de-escalation and resolution of conflict – rather, the opposite seems to be the case; as they are extended, the conflicts intensify. However, one could also argue that once a stalemate in inner-Jewish conflicts is reached (that is, neither side can prevail against the other with the different enabling conditions available to them or opts not to employ all means available to them), the opponents seek to resolve the conflict by drawing on non-Jewish support. In all but one case (Corinth), the opponents succeed in disposing of the missionaries. In this way, and at least for the moment, their conflict with the missionaries is "resolved". The missionaries either leave of their own accord, are driven away by the authorities, or are sent on elsewhere by their converts.

However, the Corinth incident (Acts 18:12-17) indicates that this course of action can be perilous and backfire on those who pursue it. The proconsul refuses to get involved in the conflict ("But since it is a matter of questions about words and names and your own law, see to it yourselves", 18:15). Rather, he drives the Jewish opponents away from the tribunal, probably employing violent means in doing so. Worse than that, the crowds follow official violent action and "seize Sosthenes, the ruler of the synagogue [perhaps the representative of the opponents or considered to be in that role] and beat him in front of the tribunal". Also under these circumstances, the proconsul refuses to be involved and pays no attention to any of this" (18:17). The opponents are humiliated publicly while the missionary can stay many days longer (18:18).

With its several occurrences of this strategy, Acts covers its different potential results: The missionaries are driven away (Antioch) or flee on their own initiative (Iconium). Paul is stoned (his death is intended or at least accepted) and leaves of his own accord (Lystra). The local believers are brought before magistrates for their support of the missionaries and send the missionaries away immediately to avoid further escalation (Thessalonica and Berea). Acts also notes that this strategy can backfire on those who employ it, in particular when those who employ it themselves belong to a minority group (Corinth).

2.2 Co-existence and co-operation?

In view of the intensity of these conflicts and the suffering they caused for Paul and others, it is surprising to also find some instances or even longer periods of relative *co-existence* in Acts, perhaps caused less by deliberate choice than by circumstances. In Damascus, Saul "confounded the Jews who lived in Damascus by proving that Jesus was the Christ" (Acts 9:22). Only after "many days had passed" was there a plot to kill him (9:23-24). The missionaries get a second chance to preach in the synagogue of Pisidian Antioch before their opponents become active (13:43-44). Although the unbelieving Jews in Iconium "stirred up the non-Jews and poisoned their minds against the brothers" (14:2), the missionaries can "remain for a long time, speaking boldly for the Lord, who bore witness to the word of his grace, granting signs and wonders to be done by their hands" (14:3). Perhaps only due to Luke's focus on the exorcism, the missionaries' arrest and mistreatment and the conversion of the Philippian jailor, no conflict is mentioned with the Jewish community in Philippi (16:13, 16).[18] The

[18] Possibly this lack is related to the size of the small Jewish community meeting "at the riverside" (were there simply not enough men to offer resistance?), the mention of Lydia as a potential patron of the entire group and the Roman identity of Philippi, where Jews would better tread cautiously (see Acts 16:20). It is not clear

missionaries can minister there for many days (16:18). Paul can proclaim the Gospel on three Sabbath days in the Thessalonian synagogue (17:2-3). He also preaches in the Berean synagogue. His audience was "more noble than those in Thessalonica; they received the word with all eagerness, examining the Scriptures daily to see if these things were so" (17:11). Many Jews come to faith. Paul reasons in the Athenian synagogue with the Jews and the devout persons; no opposition is mentioned (17:17). Paul reasons in the Corinthian synagogue every Sabbath and tries to persuade Jews and Greeks (18:4). Once Silas and Timothy arrive from Macedonia, "Paul was occupied with the word, testifying to the Jews that the Christ was Jesus" (18:4).

After leaving the synagogue in Corinth, Paul continues his ministry in the immediate neighbourhood (see above). Even Crispus, the ruler of the synagogue, comes to faith together with his entire household (Acts 18:8). "And Paul stayed a year and six months, teaching the word of God among them" (18:11).[19] This period of "tolerance" continues until an opportune moment arises to instigate against Paul, that is, the inexperience of the newly arrived Roman proconsul. Once attempts to take Paul before the proconsul fail and backfire (18:12-17), there is some form of "truce". No further action is taken against Paul. So, "After this, Paul stayed many days longer ..." (18:18). There is some grudging co-existence as the opponents have exhausted their enabling conditions in this conflict. The portrayal of the conflict in Thessalonica and Corinth suggests that the course that the conflicts take is also dependent on the local situation and different enabling conditions (on what measure of non-Jewish support the opponents can count). What might have been an option in one instance is not possible or advisable in another instance.

After Paul reasons with the Jews in the synagogue of Ephesus (Acts 19:19), they ask him to stay for a longer period (19:20; see also the unhindered ministry of Apollos in Ephesus and in Achaia, 19:26, 28). After returning from Jerusalem (19:22-23), Paul enters "the synagogue [in Ephesus] and for three months speaks boldly, reasoning and persuading them about the kingdom of God" (19:8). Only after this period does opposition arise. Paul withdraws from the synagogue and continues his ministry

---

what status Paul as a Roman citizen, as an eloquent (the portrayal of Paul in Acts) Pharisee well trained in the Scriptures and their interpretation, and also with strong ties to Jerusalem would have had in this context. Is some of the violent opposition which Paul faces in Acts due to the fact that his opponents could not prevail against his persuasive powers otherwise? See Acts 6:10.

19 The length of time is astonishing in view of the fact that Crispus' coming to faith "may have both embarrassed the detractors and led to more conversions", Keener (2014, 2748), also see pp. 2748-2750.

elsewhere in Ephesus (19.9): "This continued for two years, so that all the residents of Asia heard the word of the Lord, both Jews and Greeks" (19:10; see also 19:17). There is no mention of further Jewish resistance (see, however, 21:27-29).[20]

In addition to genuine interest in the missionaries' proclamation or a more tolerant attitude, such instances of co-existence might also be due to the lack of enabling conditions on the side of the opponents or due to the realisation that the Jews as a religious minority were better off keeping a low profile, in particular in the anti-Jewish context of the Roman world. Whether some non-Jews also benefited from the extraordinary miracles of Paul in Ephesus is impossible to say for sure (Acts 19:11-12). If they did, open hostility to Paul, their benefactor, would not be wise.[21]

There is no instance of co-operation once conflict arises (prior to the conflict, Jews in the diaspora invite the missionaries to speak during a synagogue service, Acts 13:15, 42-44 – see also 17:2 – and might benefit from their miraculous power). The local Jews who accept the missionaries' message withdraw with them from their synagogues and form communities of their own ("... he withdrew from them and took the disciples with him", 19:9). In the portrayal of Acts, there is no hostility on their side against those who stay behind.

Two references explain the motives of some Jewish opponents. According to the *English Standard Version*, in both cases, the opponents act out of *jealousy* (Acts 13:45; 17:5), that is, out of moral flaw. However, the Greek word ζῆλος could also be translated as *zeal*. In this case, it would identify the motivation positively as pious concern and dedication to the Law/ancestral traditions (an ancient virtue) and a determination to preserve Jewish identity.[22] Thus, the opposition is not vicious. Keener opts for *jealousy* and writes with regard to the reasons:

> "The motive of jealousy in this case would not be difficult to understand. Outsiders – offering the entire local Gentile community faith on terms that would have seemed 'cheap' to traditional Jews who had laboured among them – would have appeared to treat lightly, in the name of and by means

---

20 Acts 19:33-34 suggests that the Jews of Ephesus had to be careful of resorting to public instigation; proceeding like in Thessalonica or Berea is apparently not an option (Acts 17:5-9, 13). Is their later attack on Paul in Jerusalem (21:27-28) related to their inability to intervene against him in their home city?

21 Whether and how Paul's "extraordinary miracles" (explicitly noted in Acts 19:11-12, including exorcisms) contributed to the reservation to intervene against him out of admiration or fear is difficult to determine.

22 See the detailed discussion in Schnabel (2008).

> of their synagogue, the traditional Jews' own years of work as a minority community. They probably viewed the newcomers as violating their hospitality, demanding conformity with new beliefs, and stirring trouble. The perspective one takes on the apostles' behaviour here will rest largely on one's Christology.
>
> More important, however, would have been the immediate attention of synagogue-attending Gentile sympathizers to the new teaching. God-fearers may have been of higher social status more often than were proselytes because persons of status had more to lose by full conversion. Their presence in the synagogues showed their attraction to Jewish ethics and monotheism and their willingness to question their own religious heritage. To be welcomed as first-class members of this faith without having to undergo circumcision and renounce their own ethnic identity must have been especially appealing to these sympathizers, helping to explain their rapid conversion to Christian faith."[23]

Yet, also with this understanding of the word ζῆλος, the opposition to the missionaries becomes comprehensible. While the author of Acts surely does not approve of their actions and clearly sides with the missionaries as they faithfully fulfil the commission of the risen Jesus (Acts 1:8), he displays some measure of empathy with these zealous Jews. The missionaries' opponents are not vilified (as, for instance, some of the authors' opponents are maligned in the Dead Sea Scrolls; see Wischmeyer, Scornaienchi 2011, 15-119). This would take us to the larger question of the stance that the author takes in his portrayal of conflict in Acts.

2.3 Transition and assimilation?

According to the portrayal in Acts, many Jews in the diaspora respond to the Gospel just as Jews did in Jerusalem. They adhere to the missionaries and become founding members of Christ-following congregations. For instance, "And some of them [from the audience in the synagogue of Thessalonica] were persuaded and joined Paul and Silas, as did a great many of

---

[23] (2013, 2094). Keener further notes that what appealed to non-Jews, could prove offensive to the synagogue's base constituents. While some non-Jewish sympathisers would be unwilling or unable to become full members of the synagogue, they might have been its benefactors. Their transfer of support (if the synagogue community itself rejected the apostolic message) would stir opposition (cf. Acts 13:45, 50; 17:12). Non-Jews who had already fully converted to Judaism might also not have approved of a "lower" standard for other non-Jews. "Possibly the higher-status members of the synagogue (13:15) or these high-status God-fearers were able to stir others with status against the outsiders (13:50)" (2094).

the devout Greeks ..." (Acts 17:4; see Jervell 1972, 41-74). In that sense there is *transition* from traditional forms of early Judaism in the diaspora to a variant of early Judaism that adheres to Jesus of Nazareth as God's Messiah. This transition leads to an *assimilation* of the convictions of the Jewish missionaries and their practices, to the extent that these differed from those of other diaspora Jews.[24]

Impressed by Paul's extraordinary miracles (Acts 19:11), some itinerant Jewish exorcists in magic-ridden Ephesus try to draw on the supernatural powers, so evidently available to Paul, and adjure evil spirits "by the Jesus whom Paul proclaims" (19:13).[25] This is an instance of *assimilation* of the practice of Paul despite the previous conflict (19:9, whether they were involved earlier on is not clear; "itinerant", περιερχομένων, perhaps characterises them as newcomers). Whether – and if so, in what way – other aspects of the Christ-believing missionary enterprise would have affected Jews in the diaspora or changed their practices and circumstances is not mentioned in Acts.

Paul's personal circumcision of Timothy, who "was the son of a Jewish woman who was a believer, but his father was a Greek" (Acts 16:1), was influenced by the presence of "the Jews who were in those places, for they all knew that his father was a Greek" (16:3). Despite the thoroughly Jewish portrayal of Paul in Acts, this act is motivated in the narrative by his desire to avoid irritation as "the Jews who were in those places all knew that his father was a Greek". Paul's action can be understood as an act of accommodation/assimilation to essential convictions of diaspora Judaism or as an attempt at de-escalation in view of existing (after all, the incident takes place in Lystra, see 14:19-23) or looming conflict. Whether Paul would have done so under other circumstances remains open.[26]

3 Summary and implications

Our study of these often-neglected aspects of the conflict accounts in Acts 9-19 has shown that these conflicts are portrayed in a nuanced manner. This concerns not only the different actors on both sides: Paul and his

---

24 Acts 19:34-35 mentions one instance where Jews attempt to deliberately distance themselves from the Jewish Christian missionaries, even though they are propagating Jewish monotheism to great effect.

25 See Marguerat (2022, 663-665): "Dass die jüdischen Exorzisten versuchen, die mit dem Namen Jesu verbundene Kraft zu ihren Gunsten zu gewinnen, wird durch den Zusatz ‚Jesus, den Paulus verkündigt' bestätigt. Ohne persönliche Beziehung zu Jesus halten sie sich an das, was sie gehört haben".

26 See Haacker (2019, 272) and Marguerat (2022, 580-581).

co-workers versus some Jews in different places in the Eastern Mediterranean world. The nuanced portrayal also concerns the different courses of these conflicts. On the one hand, there is fierce conflict, escalation of conflict to which both sides contribute, the use of verbal and physical violence, other illegitimate means, suffering and even the near martyrdom of some Christ-believing protagonists.[27] On the other hand, we also see – before, during and after conflict – on both sides[28] – attempts and instances of de-escalation and perhaps, in a few instances, even conflict resolution, which is a noble achievement rarely reached and much dependent on the ideal to be reached. There are situations and times of relative co-existence and perhaps even slight traces of co-operation, and transition and assimilation in one way or another, at least in some cases and for some conflicts/people. Their nature and extent vary, but traces of these other aspects of religious conflict appear in almost all the conflicts we examined.

Thus, the theorising about religious conflict to which we referred at the beginning of this study has led to a careful reading of these conflict accounts from the perspective of this particular analysis of religious conflict in antiquity and allowed us to see facets in the narrative that might otherwise have been missed. At the same time, our study confirms the validity and usefulness of Mayer's reflections on the nature of religious conflict. If they are noted at all, assessments of these other aspects (that is, how they are related to the more prominent aspects and to history) also depends on longstanding habits and traditions of reading Acts.

The community of faith, to whose canon of sacred writings the Book of Acts (including its accounts of religious conflict) belong, had different experiences of the nature and intensity of religious conflicts throughout its history. It was, to varying degrees, on the receiving end and (more or less directly) the giving end of the spectrum and everything in between. Even in the present time, Christians in different contexts will read and appreciate the accounts of Acts differently. For instance, they will mean something very different in areas where the Church is being persecuted[29] than in secular Western societies. What Christians might learn from studying these accounts from this perspective and in search of the neglected other aspects will also differ. As in the study of religious conflict in antiquity, so

---

[27] For the response of early Christ-believers, see Röthlisberger (2021).

[28] The focus of the narrative is on the missionaries and their behaviour in these conflicts.

[29] See, for instance, the annual "World Watch List" of Open Doors ministries, https://www.opendoors.org/en-US/persecution/countries (access 04/03/2025); see also Sauer (2021) and Schirrmacher (2007).

too today the focus on religious conflict and in particular on violence must not overshadow the potential and search for opportunities, however small they may be, of de-escalation and resolution of conflict, co-existence and co-operation, and assimilation and transition that Acts mentions and that also belong to the Christian heritage, although these aspects have at times been neglected.

Revisiting these conflicts in the earliest days of Christianity from this perspective can contribute to a nuanced dialogue about the earliest times in the relationship between Jews and Christians including its challenges, as well as debates about encounters between Christianity and other religions, be these in the context of Christian mission or interreligious dialogue of various kinds.

4 References

Cunningham, S. (1997). *"Through Many Tribulations": The Theology of Persecution in Acts* (JSNT.SS 142). Sheffield Academic Press.

Gudehus, G., & Christ, M. (Eds.). (2013). *Gewalt: Ein interdisziplinäres Handbuch.* J. B. Metzler.

Haacker, K. (2019). *Die Apostelgeschichte* (ThKNT 5). Kohlhammer.

Jervell, J. (1972). The Divided People of God. The Restoration of Israel and Salvation for the Gentiles, In J. Jervell, *Luke and the People of God. A New Look at Luke-Acts* (pp. 41-74). Augsburg Fortress.

Juergensmeyer, M., Kitts, M. & Jerryson, M. (Eds.). (2013). *The Oxford Handbook of Religion and Violence.* Oxford University Press.

Keener, C. S. (2012). *Acts. An Exegetical Commentary I: Introduction and Acts 1:1 – 2:47.* Baker.

Keener, C. S. (2013). *Acts. An Exegetical Commentary II: Acts 3:1 – 14:28.* Baker.

Keener, C. S. (2014) *Acts. An Exegetical Commentary III: Acts 15:1 – 23:35.* Baker.

Marguerat, D. (2022). *Die Apostelgeschichte* (KEK 3). Vandenhoeck & Ruprecht.

Mayer, W. (2013). Religious Conflict: Definitions, Problems and Theoretical Approaches. In W. Mayer & B. Neil (Eds.), *Religious Conflict from Early Christianity to the Rise of Islam* (AKG 121) (pp. 1-19). De Gruyter.

Moss, C. (2013). *The Myth of Persecution: How Early Christians Invented a Story of Martyrdom.* Harper.

Ployd, A. (2023). *Augustine, Martyrdom, and Classical Rhetoric.* Oxford University Press.

Rebillard, E. (2021). *The Early Martyr Narratives: Neither Authentic Accounts nor Forgeries* (Divinations: Rereading Late Ancient Religion) University of Pennsylvania Press.

Röthlisberger, D. (2021). *Hilfe und Selbsthilfe für verfolgte Christen: Eine Studie zum neutestamentlichen Ethos.* Evangelische Verlagsanstalt.

Rydryck, M. (2024). *Die Wunder an den Widersachern: Wunderhermeneutik am Beispiel der Strafwunder im lukanischen Doppelwerk* (WUNT II.612). Mohr Siebeck.

Sauer, C. (2021). *Martyrium und Mission im Kontext: Analyse ausgewählter theologischer Positionen aus der weltweiten Christenheit* (MWF.NF 37). Erlanger Verlag für Mission und Ökumene.

Schirrmacher, T. (2007). "Persecution". In L. Corrie et al. (Eds.), *Dictionary of Mission Theology: Evangelical Foundations* (IVP Reference Collection), (pp. 286-289). IVP.

Schnabel, E. J. (2008). Jewish Opposition to Christians in Asia Minor in the First Century, *BBR* 18, 233-270.

Stenschke, C. W. (2017a). The Conflicts of Acts 1-8:3 in View of Recent Research on Religious Conflict in Antiquity. Part One: Theoretical Issues and Contested Domains, *EJT* 26, 15-31.

Stenschke, C. W. (2017b). The Conflict of Acts 1-8:3 in View of Recent Research on Religious Conflict in Antiquity. Part Two: Enabling Conditions and Other Factors, *EJT* 26, 114-134.

Stenschke, C. W. (2018). Contested Domains in the Conflicts Between the Early Christian Mission and Diaspora Judaism according to the Book of Acts. In W. Mayer & C. de Wet (Eds.), *Reconceiving Religious Conflict: New Views from the Formative Centuries of Christianity* (Routledge Studies in the Early Christian World), (pp. 139-181). Routledge.

Stenschke, C. W. (2020). 'When they heard this, they were silenced' (Acts 11:18): Some Inner-Christian Conflicts and Their Resolution in Acts 6-15:35, *JGAR* 4, 69-89.

Stenschke, C. W. (2022). Contested Domains and Enabling Conditions in the Conflicts between the early Christian Mission and non-Jews according to the Book of Acts, *Neot.* 56, 129-163.

Stenschke, C. W. (2023). 'Then Peter, Filled with the Holy Spirit ...' (Acts 4:8): References to the Holy Spirit in the Context of Accounts of Conflict in the Book of Acts, *EstBíb* 81, 365-386.

Stenschke, C. W. (2024). Emissary to Jews in the Diaspora and to Some Non-Jews, Champion of Jewish Monotheism and Circumspect of Diaspora Judaism: Paul of Tarsus in the Book of Acts, *NTS* 70, 72-87.

Waldner, K. (2024). *Die Erfindung des Martyriums: Wahrheit, Recht und religiöse Identität in Hellenismus und Kaiserzeit* (STAC). Mohr Siebeck.

Wischmeyer, O., & Scornaienchi, L. (Eds.). (2011). *Polemik in der frühchristlichen Literatur: Texte und Kontexte* (BZNW 170). de Gruyter.

Wu, S. F. (2023). Suffering. In *DPL*, 2nd ed., (pp. 1020-1027).

6 Longing for Christ's appearing

Persecution and Christian existence in the Pastoral Epistles

Håkon Leite[1]

Abstract

By calling Timothy to suffer for the gospel (2 Tim 1:8, 2:3), Paul is embracing persecution in the Pastoral Epistles as a part of Christian existence. This article discusses how Paul's positive attitude towards persecution fits the view of Christian existence in the Pastoral Epistles. It argues that the view known as "christliche Bürgerlichkeit" does not sufficiently explain Paul's embracing attitude towards persecution. In contrast to a diminished view of the imminent second coming of Christ, which the "christliche Bürgerlichkeit" entails, persecution in the Pastoral Epistles should be understood in view of the tension between the present age and the age to come. This tension also has impact on how Paul views the role of persecution in mission.

Keywords: Persecution, Pastoral Epistles, eschatology, Christian existence, "christliche Bürgerlichkeit".

1 Introduction[2]

"Indeed, all who want to live a godly life in Christ Jesus, will be persecuted" (2 Tim 3:12).[3] To Paul, persecution was an inseparable part of Christian existence. Persecution, according to Paul, is not just an unpleasant outcome of following Christ, it is treated as part of a sacred calling (2 Tim 1:8, 2:3,

1 Håkon Leite, Assistant Professor Fjellhaug International University College, hleite@fjellhaug.no, ORCID iD: 0009-0006-9672-4637.

2 I am grateful to the two anonymous peer reviewers, my colleagues Sverre Bøe and Harald Aarbakke and the editors of this anthology for constructive feedback and help to organize my thoughts for this article.

3 I have consulted NA28 for the Greek and unless otherwise indicated, the English translation is from the NRSVUE. The title is drawn from 2 Tim 4:8: "[...] all who have longed for his appearing".

4:5). How does Paul's attitude towards persecution fit into the view of Christian existence expressed in the Pastoral Epistles? That is the question I will explore in this article.

In opposition to a commonly discussed view, called "christliche Bürgerlichkeit", my thesis in this article is that Paul's attitude towards persecution in the Pastoral Epistles is better explained by the eschatological tension of the present age and the age to come. This also has implications for how he understands the role of persecution in mission.

To explore this question, I will first discuss the instances of persecution in the Pastoral Epistles, to see what Paul had in mind when speaking about persecution. Then, I will present and critique the model of Christian existence called "christliche Bürgerlichkeit". I will then discuss how Paul's attitude towards persecution fits into the view of Christian existence in the Pastoral Epistles and how this shapes his view of persecution in mission.

Scholars disagree on the degree to which the Pastoral Epistles should be treated together as a corpus or as three individual letters. The shared commonalities cannot be overlooked, but it is also necessary to take into account the distinctives in each individual letter. My emphasis in this article will be on 2 Timothy, since it contains more material on persecution than the other two of the Pastoral Epistles. 1 Timothy contains one explicit mention of persecution (1 Tim 1:13), and the letter to Titus none. Due to their close relationship with 2 Timothy, they will provide a broader theological context, in which 2 Timothy belongs.

Due to the letters' content and vocabulary etc. most scholars regard these letters as "deutero-Pauline".[4] Although my arguments will have implications for authorship, they do not depend on a certain view.[5] In this article, my intention is to explore how the attitude towards persecution fits the larger theological framework of the letters. Whether my findings fit the letters that are widely accepted as Pauline or not is a separate issue. Since the author of the Pastoral Epistles calls himself "Paul", I will refer to the author by that name.[6]

---

4 For a helpful summary of arguments for and against Pauline authorship, see (Carson & Moo, 2005, pp. 555-568).

5 If my observations are correct, the content of the Pastoral Epistles are more in alignment with the eschatological tension in the so-called "authentic Pauline letters".

6 N. T. Wright (2003, p. 267) is right in pointing out in brackets that if is the case that the Pastoral Epistles are not written Paul, "[...] they are clearly by someone, or more than one person, who thought they should belong closely with his work and thought."

2 Persecution in the Pastoral Letters

I will use a simple working definition of persecution, provided by James Kelhoffer for this article. He uses "persecution" and "unjust suffering" as "[...] any undeserved penalty or punishment – whether real, imagined, anticipated, or exaggerated – that is said to be incurred in the course of the Christian life" (Kelhoffer, 2010, p. 8). The words "penalty" and "punishment" imply intentionality from a personal agent, which distinguishes this kind of suffering from suffering in general. Although the suffering that is highlighted in the Pastoral Epistles is related to persecution, not all suffering in these letters can be labelled as such. Trophimus' sickness (2 Tim 4:20) is an example of such exception, as Craig L. Blomberg (2018, pp. 472-473) rightfully points out.

The instances of persecution in the Pastoral Epistles include imprisonment. Paul is referring to himself as Christ's "prisoner" (2 Tim 1:8), he mentions his "chain" (2 Tim 1:16) and talks about "being chained like a criminal" (2 Tim 2:9). His imprisonment is explicitly related to his engagement with the gospel (2 Tim 2:9).

Persecution in the Pastoral Epistles also includes violence. When speaking about his own past as a persecutor of the church, Paul is referring to himself as "a man of violence" (1 Tim 1:13). There are few indications in the Pastoral Epistles of what the violence against Christians specifically involved.[7] The perhaps clearest indication is 2 Tim 4:6 which I take to refer to Paul's expecting execution. Paul mentions that Alexander the coppersmith did him "great harm" (2 Tim 4:14), but whether the harm he is referring to is violence or not is hard to determine from the expression. Whether the harm belongs to the category of "persecution" is not entirely clear either, although it is implied by the general context of the letter and the following verse (2 Tim 4:15) which states that Alexander at least was attacking Paul's teachings verbally and thereby linking the "great harm" to Alexander's opposition to the Christian message.

Just a few verses later, Paul says he was "rescued from the lion's mouth" (2 Tim 4:17). Taken literally, it could mean that Christians were thrown to the lions (*damnatio ad bestias*). Taken figuratively, which is a

7 The Acts of the Apostles add a few details to that, saying Paul was "dragging off both men and women" to commit them to prison (Acts 8:3). The verb here translated "dragging" (greek = *suron*) occurs two other times in Acts. In Acts 17:6 Jason and some fellow Christians are being "dragged [...] before the city authorities", but in Acts 14:19, Paul is the one being "dragged". Paul's role has been reversed.

more probable reading, it is echoing Psalm 22:22.[8] We find similar usage in 1 Peter 5:8 which compares the devil to "a roaring lion". This suggest that the "lion" Paul had in mind was not a physical animal, but a spiritual enemy.

The social dimension of persecution is expressed by the instances of people turning away from Paul. He speaks of "all who are in Asia" and names specific people (2 Tim 1:15). The surrounding verses speak about suffering for the gospel and not to be ashamed of the gospel, nor Paul's chains (1:8-14 and 1:16). This implies that the people who left Paul (v. 15) did so to avoid the shame of being associated with the gospel.[9]

Paul frequently writes about doctrinal error and false teachers in the Pastoral Epistles.[10] He makes the point that these false teachings are from "deceitful spirits and teachings of demons" (1 Tim 4:1). Although spiritual resistance is not in and of itself persecution, it draws attention to the spiritual battle going on and is a crucial aspect of the resistance he is facing.

To sum up, the Pastoral Epistles contain different instances of persecution. This brief overview shows that persecution involved imprisonment, violence, social distancing and the underlying spiritual opposition is also present.

3 Persecution and "christliche Bürgerlichkeit"

3.1 "Die christliche Bürgerlichkeit" explained

How do the occurrences of persecution in the letters fit into the view of Christian existence expressed in the letters? We will start by discussing a view of Christian existence that has been widely held among scholars. Martin Dibelius and Hans Conzelmann' commentary on the Pastoral Epistles, have argued that the Pastoral Epistles reflect a code of conduct often referred to as "christliche Bürgerlichkeit" (Dibelius & Conzelmann, 1972, p. 39-41). According to this interpretation, the first generation of Christians expected Christ to return within their own lifetime. But since the second coming did not occur, the later generation of Christians (among whom the author of the Pastoral Epistles is to be regarded) needed to adjust their

8 Philip H. Towner (2007, pp. 910-912) makes some interesting observations about this.

9 See also 2 Tim 4:16.

10 See 1 Tim 1:3-11, 19-20, 4:1-7, 5:8, 15, 6:3-5, 10, 2 Tim 14-18, 23-26, 3:1-9, 4:3-4, Tit 1:19-16, 3:9-11.

expectations of the second coming of Christ and find a way to relate to the present world.[11] As Philip H. Towner, who has critiqued this view, explains: "[...] what began as the enthusiastic expectancy of Christ's imminent return turned gradually to disappointment, or at least sober realism, as it dawned on the Church that a considerable delay of the Parousia was probable" (Towner, 1989, p. 11).[12]

According to Dibelius and Conzelmann (1972, p. 38) "[t]he author of the Pastorals seeks to build the possibility of a life in this world, although on the basis of Christian principles. He wishes to become part of the world. Thus, for him, the peace of a secure life is a goal of the Christian." Dibelius and Conzelmann therefore claim there is a conflict between the historical Paul and the author of the Pastoral Epistles. While the author of the Pastoral Epistles seeks a peaceful life, the historical Paul "joyfully affirmed (in 2 Cor 6:4-10) the suffering of this existence as part of citizenship in the other kingdom" (Dibelius & Conzelmann, 1972, p. 39).

The biblical material[13] that is used to support this is for instance 1 Tim 2:1-2 where Paul is urging Timothy to pray for everyone, including "kings and all who are in high positions, so that we may live a quiet and peaceable life in all godliness and dignity" (1 Tim 2:2; Dibelius & Conzelmann, 1972, pp. 38-39). Paul's exhortation "to be subject to rulers and authorities, to be obedient" (Tit 3:1) can also be taken to support this idea. Much attention has been drawn to the concept of "godliness" (= *eusebeia*) (Dibelius & Conzelmann, 1972, p. 39). This term is not found in any other Pauline letters, than the Pastoral Epistles. This term was often used in a Roman context expressing the proper attitude towards Roman government.[14] The emphasis in the Pastoral Epistles on church government (see Tit 1:5-9 and 1 Tim 3.1-13) are also used to support the idea of a diminished view of the imminent second coming of Christ. James D. G. Dunn (2006, p. 384) says that "[i]ncreasing institutionalization is the clearest mark of early Catholicism [...]". Since they

---

11 The diminished expectancy of the *parousia* is one of the characteristics of a related concept called "early catholicism". See (Downs, 2005, p. 642). James D. G. Dunn (2006, p. 376) includes three main characteristics of the "early catholicism" or "Frühkatholizismus": "The fading of the parousia hope", "Increasing institutionalization" and "Crystallization of the faith into set forms".

12 James D. G. Dunn (2006, p. 377) writes that "early catholicism" at least partly can be defined as "a reaction consequent upon the failure of the parousia hope."

13 See Dibelius & Conzelmann, 1972, pp. 39-41 for their treatment on "The ideal of Good Christian Citizenship".

14 T. Christopher Hoklotubbe (2017, p. 105) explains Roman pietas as "the faithful disposition to fulfil one's obligations to deities, the emperor, fatherland, and family".

did not expect the imminent second coming of Christ, they might as well take the time to build a long-lasting church government.

3.2 Evaluation

3.2.1 *Conforming or contextualizing?*

To this article, there are mainly two questions that need to be addressed concerning the "christliche Bürgerlichkeit". First, does Paul seek conformity to the world in the Pastoral Epistles? Or to put it more sharply, is Paul compromising to the world to avoid persecution?

Dibelius and Conzelmann are right in pointing out that the Pastoral Epistles reflect an attempt to find a way to deal with the external world. T. Christopher Hoklotubbe (2017, p. 104) highlights the challenges Christians were facing from the surrounding culture, which included "[...] social ostracism, exclusion, imprisonment, and even execution on account of elite Roman prejudicial stereotypes." He writes, that the rhetorical use of piety (= *eusebeia*) in the Pastoral Epistles serves as an "apologetic appeal" (Hoklotubbe, 2017, p. 145) to show outsiders that "[...] Christians are neither dangerous nor foreign anarchists" (Hoklotubbe, 2017, p. 146), but civilized and loyal subjects under Roman rule. Hoklotubbe points to the fact that the terminology in the Pastoral Epistles is corresponding to the terminology in the culture for expressing loyalty to the political authorities. Hoklotubbe's findings at least demonstrate that the Pastoral Epistles are an attempt to deal with potential external threats of persecution. He explains:

> "It is not the case that the audiences of the Pastorals would have been led to think that by embodying such virtues as piety they might be perceived to be actual Roman or Ephesian *citizens*. Rather, through their embodiment of pious principles and practices, early Christians may have sought to be perceived as civilized and loyal enough subjects according to Greco-Roman sensibilities and tolerance." (Hoklotubbe, 2017, p. 147)

Hoklotubbe's observations suggest that the Christian community took into consideration potential external threats and was trying to avoid (at least) unnecessary persecution. One could therefore argue that the Pastoral Epistles to some degree reflect an attempt to seek conformity and peace with the world. However, an overemphasis on this point, does not explain Paul's embracing attitude towards persecution. Paul's explicit exhortations to suffer for the gospel (2 Tim 1:8, 2 Tim 2:3), which includes imprisonment, social ostracism and execution, are clearly not an expression of conformity.

Dibelius and Conzelmann's (1972, p. 38) claim that "[...] the peace of a secure life is a *goal* of the Christian"[15] seems to be an overstatement and leaves too little room for the persecution Paul is admonishing Timothy to embrace.

One tendency among scholars, according to James J. Wainwright (1993, pp. 211-212), has been to read into the *eusebeia* its Hellenistic meaning. Wainwright rightly points out that the term must be interpreted by the usage in the Pastoral Epistles and states:

> "It does not primarily reflect the secular connotation of Greek literature, nor is it the chief virtue of a new, socially accommodation ethic. Instead, the Christian community adapted the word *eusebeia*, and changed certain aspects of its meaning to reflect Christian experience, behaviour, and doctrine." (Wainwright, 1993, p. 223)

The clearest example that *eusebeia* does not necessarily entail conformity, is the fact that practicing *eusebeia*, according to 2 Tim 3:12, is ensuring persecution, not protecting against it (Wainwright, 1993, p. 222).[16]

The Pastoral Epistles also contain examples of Paul challenging the existing norms of the time. David W. Pao (2014, p. 751) observers that calling Timothy to not let anyone despise him because of his age (1 Tim 4:12) goes against the grain of the cultural norms.[17] The context suggests that this exhortation is grounded in "the example that points back to Paul (and the gospel he preaches) and the hope that points forward to a reality that remains to be fully revealed" (Pao, 2014, pp. 751-753). These observations challenge the idea that Paul is simply seeking conformity "for the sake of survival" (Pao, 2014, p. 754). Paul does not simply go with the grain of the societal norms of the time but seeking to transform them (Pao, 2014, p. 755).

To sum up, the Pastoral Epistles certainly contain evidence of attempts to relate to the world, to live in peace and obedience and are signalling high held virtues in society like *eusebeia* to avoid persecution. A more nuanced view also needs to take into account Paul's embracing attitude towards persecution and the fact that *eusebeia* in Paul's usage not necessarily equals that of the Roman culture.

---

15 Italics mine.

16 Hoklotubbe (2017, p. 52) also seems to be aware of this.

17 He also makes the case that Paul does the same by calling Timothy to honour the widows in 1 Tim 5:3 (Pao, 2014, pp. 753-754). He further notes: "Both groups lie outside the center of the power structure in ancient societies, but both are not to be deprived of their proper honor and dignity" (Pao, 2014, p. 754).

3.2.2 *The delay of the second coming of Christ?*

The second point that needs to be addressed is accuracy of the alleged diminished view of Christ's second coming, which is the overarching eschatological framework for the "christliche Bürgerlichkeit".

One argument for the diminished view of the second coming of Christ or decreasing apocalyptic nature of the letters, is the emphasis on church structure in the Pastoral Epistles (Downs, 2005, p. 646). But a decreased apocalyptic expectation does not necessarily follow from an increased institutionalization. David J. Downs (2005, pp. 647-651) points to the fact that the Qumran community was highly structured but also highly apocalyptic. This demonstrates that a decreased expectation of the second coming of Christ is a *non sequitur*.

This argument can be taken a step further. G. K. Beale (2011, p. 819) observes that a time tribulation according to Dan 12:1-3, will occur before the resurrection. The Pastoral Epistles' references to "the last days"[18] suggest that end times tribulations are the proper eschatological backdrop for understanding the ecclesiastical structures in the same letters. Institutionalization does not stand in opposition to eschatological expectations. On the contrary, it is a protection against false teaching, deception and persecution expected in the last days (Beale, 2011, pp. 819-822). He writes: "[...] the office of elder is not a response to occasional or temporarily unique conditions but rather owes its existence to the ongoing, uninterrupted eschatological tribulation of false teaching and deception" (Beale, 2011, p. 822).

A closer look at the Pastoral Epistles, shows that the Pastoral Epistles *do* contain evidence of an eschatological tension. Matthew Y. Emerson points to eschatological terms and themes in the Pastoral Epistles like false teaching, time, "mystery", final salvation and judgement and tribulation to demonstrate that these letters are more loaded with eschatology than what is recognized by others (Emerson, 2015, pp. 92-94).[19]

To borrow from Craig L. Blomberg's words, the charge that the second coming in the Pastoral Epistles is delayed is "overblown" (Blomberg, 2018, p. 488).[20] I will elaborate on this point in the next section where I discuss

---

18 He is referring to 1 Tim 4:1-3; 2 Tim 3:1 (cf. 3.2-9). (Beale, 2011, p. 820).

19 He is also pointing out that Frances Young and Philip H. Towner have demonstrated that eschatological terms in the Pastoral Epistles have been ignored (Emerson, 2015, p. 84 n. 5 and 6).

20 The whole quotation is: "We saw with Luke-Acts that this charge is overblown, although there are a few tendencies in this direction. The same is true for the Pastorals."

the eschatological framework in the Pastoral Epistles, in which persecution should be understood.

4 Longing for his appearing: Persecution and eschatology

4.1 The opponents' over-realized eschatology

Paul's view of Christian existence, of which persecution is an inseparable part, is tied to his view of eschatology. Here, I will discuss the eschatological framework that undergirds Paul's attitude towards persecution. The letters reflect two underlying and contrasting views of eschatology framing the Christian life. On the one hand, we glimpse an over-realized eschatology, represented by Paul's antagonists.[21]

Their theology is most explicitly stated in 2 Tim 2:18 "saying resurrection already has occurred". There are different views with regards to how to pin down the details to this false teaching[22], but the adverb "already" (*ede*) is at least implying the belief that there will be no future resurrection. and thereby implying an over-realized eschatology. Philip H. Towner (1989, p. 32) explains: "As far as broader implications go, their resurrection doctrine reveals a shift in their thinking about salvation from realization in the future to realization in the present. For them the Eschaton had arrived in fuller form." An over-realized eschatology

---

[21] See for instance Skarsaune (1994, p. 9) and Towner (1987, pp. 29-33). Jerry L. Sumney (1999, pp. 253-302) argues that only Paul's opponents in 2 Timothy reflect an over-realized eschatology and that this must not be read into the other Pastoral Epistles. Although I appreciate his effort to read the letters individually, I am not convinced of the sharp distinction between these letters. Philip H. Towner represents an approach that differs greatly from Sumney's. He sees enough similarities between the Pastoral Epistles and 1 Corinthians that he extends the discussion to also include that letter (Towner, 1989, pp. 29-36). Scholars disagree on the identity of the false teachers (Towner, 1987, pp. 98-99). There is also disagreement regarding the significance of the false teachers for interpreting the letters. Towner regards false teaching as essential for interpreting the letters, while Christopher R. Hutson (2019, p. 13) disagrees with Towner. Hutson (2019, p. 14) writes: "References to false doctrines are vague, because correcting false doctrine is not what the PE are about." As the following discussion reveals, I agree with the view that Paul's opponents in the Pastoral Epistles teach an over-realized eschatology, but to pin down the exact identity of the false teachers lies outside the scope of this article.

[22] For more details, see (Marshall, 1999, pp. 751-754).

leaves the Christian hope in the present age, which is hard, if not impossible, to reconcile with being persecuted.[23]

4.2 Paul's eschatology of two ages

As a contrast to the over-realized eschatology, the Pastoral Epistles are frequently distinguishing between two ages – this age and the age to come (1 Tim 4:8, 6:12-19, 2 Tim 4:8). Although one must distinguish between these two ages, one cannot separate them. As George Eldon Ladd (1993, p. 596) puts it: "Because of what God has done in Jesus' historic mission, the contrast between the two ages does not remain intact."

The overlapping of the ages is not a predominate theme in the Pastoral Epistles, but there are a few passages that demonstrate or at least indicate this point. Paul encourages Timothy to "take hold of the eternal life" (1 Tim 6:12) in the present. The future "life to come" is attainable in the present.

Another, perhaps even clearer example is that according to the letters, believers have already received the Spirit (2 Tim 1:7, Tit 3:5-6). Receiving the Spirit is a sign of the coming of the eschaton (Joel 2:28-29).[24] Simultaneously, Paul further exhorts Timothy to "[...] join with me in suffering for the gospel, in the power of God" (2 Tim 1:8). Although experiencing the Spirit and suffering belong to two fundamentally different "ages", they are happening at the same time. While living in the present age filled with suffering, Christians experience the age to come by virtue of being filled with the Spirit.

These two eschatological frameworks are crucial for how to approach persecution. For the false teachers who teach an over-realized eschatology, all they can live for has already been realized in the present. Since there are no more resurrection to hope for, the life they live in the present is all there is.

Paul, however, has a completely different approach to suffering in the present world. Because he believes in the life to come, he admonishes Timothy to live *in* the present world and *for* the next. This involves living modestly and being content with food and clothing (1 Tim 6:8), for "we can take

---

23 I. Howard Marshall (1997, p. 50), referring to 2 Tim 2:18 and 1 Corinthians, accurately comments on the over-realized eschatology: "This must have been a view that required looking at the world through rose-colored spectacles and ignoring the suffering and evil still around. It is hard to see how people reconciled the evidence of their senses with a belief that the end had fully come."

24 Gordon Fee (1997, p. 169) explains that "the coming of the Spirit" is a "sure evidence that the future had already been set in motion."

nothing out of [the world]" (1 Tim 6:7). It also includes not striving for wealth in the present age (1 Tim 6:9-10, 17), "not to [...] set their hopes on the uncertainty of riches but rather on God" (1 Tim 6:17), not to exaggerate "physical training", but rather "[t]rain yourself in godliness, for, while physical training is of some value, godliness is valuable in every way, holding promise for both the present life and the life to come" (1 Tim 4:8).

The application for persecution, is that Christians can face persecution and suffering in this present age, for they have a hope of a future resurrection. This explains why Paul can encourage Timothy to suffer with him (2 Tim 2:3). Paul continues by drawing the attention to Christ's resurrection: "Remember Jesus Christ, raised from the dead, a descendant of David – that is my gospel, for which I suffer hardship, even to the point of being chained like a criminal" (2 Tim 2:8-9a). He can suffer in this age for the gospel that promises him life in the age to come. The hope for the Christian is in the resurrection, not the present age. The Christian "will reign with him" (1 Tim 2:12) and be rewarded with "the crown of righteousness" (2 Tim 4:8). This means suffering in the present age does not conflict with the Christian hope. Rather, it is making it even more precious.

The fundamental difference between these two eschatological frameworks and their significance for persecution, might be illustrated by the example of Paul and Demas. Paul is experiencing struggles and hardships in the present life (2 Tim 4:6-7), for he is longing for (*agapekosin*) "the appearing" (2 Tim 4:8) of the Lord, i.e. the age to come. Demas, on the other hand, has left Paul and his suffering lifestyle, because he is in love (*agapesas)* with "this present world" (2 Tim 4:10), and implicitly not the age to come.

The distinction between these two groups can be further developed by comparing Paul to Alexander the coppersmith, mentioned a few verses later. On the one hand, God will reward (*apodosei*) the suffering Paul with "the crown of righteousness" (2 Tim 4:8). On the other hand, God will "pay [Alexander] back (= *apodosei*) for his deeds". This portrays for us a pattern of "eschatological reversal" – the persecuted will be rewarded and the persecutors judged.

5 Fight the good fight: Persecution and mission

5.1 The present age as a struggle

The implication of the not fully realized eschaton that we have discussed, is not just that persecution is to be expected in the present world, but also that life in the present world still is a struggle to be fought, like in 1 Tim

6:12: "Fight the good fight of the faith." In some places, this fight imagery is drawn from warfare (2 Tim 2:3), in other places it seems to be more drawn from athletics (2 Tim 4:7). In other places, like in 1 Tim 6:12, there is an ambiguity and disagreement among scholars whether the image is drawn from athletics or warfare. The common denominator, in any case, is the struggle (Knight, 1992, p. 263; Marshall, 1999, p. 659).

The fight or struggle entails at least two elements. Firstly, it entails actively fighting (1 Tim 1:18, 6:12, 2 Tim 2:3, 7), which means service for spreading the gospel, what we could summarize in the word "mission". Paul also qualifies "the fight" with the attribute "good" (1 Tim 6:12, 2 Tim 4:7). In so doing, he is implicitly making a contrast between the fight Timothy ought to fight and the "bad one", represented by his antagonists who are "craving for controversy and disputes about words" (1 Tim 6:4). The contrast is also made between his own past as a violent persecutor (1 Tim 1:13) and the good fight he exhorts Timothy to join in (1 Tim 1:18).

Secondly, fighting a battle involves suffering. Paul exhorts Timothy not only to take part in the suffering, but to suffer "like a good soldier of Christ Jesus" (2 Tim 2:3). Despite his innocence, when Timothy suffers, he is not to regard himself primarily as a victim, but as a soldier fighting for a greater cause.[25] Timothy should regard suffering as an inseparable part of his call for the gospel. Paul is frequently treating suffering and service side by side, as if they are two sides of the same coin. He is exhorting Timothy to "endure suffering" as well as to "do the work of an evangelist, carry out your ministry fully" (2 Tim 4:5) and according to Paul, "a godly life" necessitates being "persecuted" (2 Tim 3:12). Paul is giving the call to service for the gospel as the main reason for his sufferings (2 Tim 1:11-12, 2:8-9). Serving God and suffer evil are to sides of the same coin. As James Kelhoffer (2010, p. 88) puts it: "[S]uffering is not optional".

This gives persecution a purpose, and explains why Paul is not only suffering, but suffering *for* the gospel (2 Tim 1:11-12, 2:8-9). He can, therefore, "endure everything for the sake of the elect, so that they may also obtain the salvation that is in Christ Jesus, with, eternal glory" (2 Tim 2:10). And he invites Timothy the embrace this call and "join with me in suffering for the gospel" (2 Tim 1:8) and "[s]hare in suffering like a good soldier of Christ Jesus" (2 Tim 2:3). Paul's primary calling is to be an apostle and spread the gospel. But since suffering is an integrated part of spreading the gospel and fighting the good fight, suffering becomes a part of his calling.

25 Glenn Penner (2004, p. 220) accurately states that "[t]he Persecuted Church, ultimately, is not a Church of Victims!"

5.2 Suffering as offering to God

That suffering is a service to God is further underscored by 2 Tim 4:6 where Paul says he is "being poured out as libation" (2 Tim 4:6). Although there has been some disagreement among scholars, I take the view that Paul is here referring to his own death.[26] The only other occurrence of the word *spendomai* is in Philippians 2:17 where it takes the same or a similar meaning. In the OT it is frequently used for a drink offering – both for Yahweh (Exod 25:22, 2 Sam 23:16, Hos 9:4), but also foreign deities (Jer 7:18, 19:13, Ezek 20:28). Although the term *spendomai* was also used in the Hellenistic world (Collins, 2002, p. 273), it is more likely referring to the Jewish liturgical custom from the OT (Kelly, 1963, p. 208), the point being that Paul was serving God by suffering. Or as I. Howard Marshall (1999, p. 806) explains "His life blood will be poured out as a sacrifice for the sake of the gospel." This might explain what Paul had in mind when speaking of "[...] completing what is lacking in Christ's afflictions for the sake of his body, that is, the church" (Col 1:24). The fundamental difference between the death of Christ and the death of Paul is what the death accomplishes. Christ's death is soteriological in nature. He died as "a ransom for all" (1 Tim 2:6) to accomplish salvation. Paul's suffering, and eventually death, however, is about bringing this salvation to the people. He is, therefore, enduring "[...] everything for the sake of the elect, so that they may also obtain salvation [...]" (2 Tim 2:10).

6 Conclusion

Persecution and Christian existence go hand in hand in the Pastoral Epistles, but how do they fit together? In this article, I have argued that the "christliche Bürgerlichkeit" model of Christian existence is inadequate to explain Paul's attitude towards persecution in the Pastoral Epistles. Dibelius and Conzelmann are right in pointing out that there are clear tendencies in the Pastoral Epistles to find a way to relate to the non-Christian world. Christians are indeed taught to live in peace, live with *eusebeia* and not to bring shame on the gospel. But an overemphasis on this point leaves the reader with the impression that Christians are to avoid all sorts of confrontation. Being persecuted is part of practicing *eusebeia* (2 Tim 3:12) and the view that the Pastoral Epistles contain a diminished view of the *parousia* has challenges.

---

[26] For different views regarding the meaning of this expression, see (Hutson, 2019, p. 200; Marshall, 1999, pp. 805-806; Twomey, 2009, p. 176). Paul seems certain that he soon will die as a martyr (Knight, 1992, p. 456).

The underlying eschatological framework in the letters is key for understanding how followers of Christ deal with persecution. The over-realized eschatology of Paul's antagonists leaves little if any room for experiencing persecution. Persecution is hard to reconcile with the view that the final hope has already been realized. Paul on the other hand frequently refers to two ages – the present age and the age to come. There are clear indications in the letters for saying that the age to come has broken into the present age. This gives the follower of Christ an eschatological framework for making sense out of persecution and therefore possible to reconcile with Christian existence.

Further, I have discussed how this theological framework shapes how the relationship between persecution and mission. Paul's use of warfare metaphor of fighting the good fight and suffer like a soldier presupposes "an already but not yet" view of eschatology. To fight and to suffer are two sides of the same coin. This places persecution in the category of calling. Paul does not only give Timothy a theological framework for understanding for the occurrence of persecution. He also provides him a greater purpose for it. Timothy is called to suffer *for* the gospel. This might provide further background for saying that he is "being poured out as libation" (2 Tim 4:6). When suffering for the gospel, suffering is a service to God.

7 References

Beale, G. K. (2011). *A New Testament biblical theology: The unfolding of the Old Testament in the New*. Baker Academic.

Blomberg, C. L. (2018). *A New Testament theology*. Baylor University Press.

Carson, D. A., & Moo, D. J. (2005). *An introduction to the New Testament* (2nd ed). Zondervan.

Collins, R. F. (2002). *1 & 2 Timothy and Titus: A commentary*. Westminster John Knox Press.

Dibelius, M., & Conzelmann, H. (1972). *The Pastoral Epistles: A commentary* (H. Koester, Ed.; P. Buttolph & A. Yarbro, Trans.). Fortress Press.

Downs, D. J. (2005). 'Early Catholicism' and apocalypticism in the Pastoral Epistles. *The Catholic Biblical Quarterly*, *67*, 641-661.

Dunn, J. D. G. (2006). *Unity and diversity in the New Testament: An inquiry into the character of earliest Christianity* (3rd ed.). SCM.

Emerson, M. Y. (2015). Paul's eschatological outlook in the Pastoral Epistles. *Criswell Theological Review*, *12*(2), 83-98.

Fee, G. D. (1997). Paul's conversion as key to his understanding of the Spirit. In R. N. Longenecker (Ed.), *The road from Damascus: The impact of Paul's conversion on his life, thought, and ministry* (pp. 166-183). W. B. Eerdmans.

Hoklotubbe, T. C. (2017). *Civilized Piety: The rhetoric of pietas in the Pastoral Epistles and the Roman Empire*. Baylor University Press.

Hutson, C. R. (2019). *First and second Timothy and Titus*. Baker Academic.
Kelhoffer, J. A. (2010). *Persecution, persuasion, and power: Readiness to withstand hardship as a corroboration of legitimacy in the New Testament*. Mohr Siebeck.
Kelly, J. N. D. (1963). *A commentary on the Pastoral Epistles: I Timothy, II Timothy, Titus*. Black.
Knight, G. W. (1992). *The Pastoral Epistles: A commentary on the Greek text*. W. B. Eerdmans; Paternoster.
Ladd, G. E. (1993). *A theology of the New Testament* (Rev. ed). Eerdmans.
Marshall, I. H. (1997). A new understanding of the present and the future: Paul and eschatology. In R. N. Longenecker (Ed.), *The road from Damascus: The impact of Paul's conversion on his life, thought, and ministry* (pp. 43-61). W. B. Eerdmans.
Marshall, I. H. (with Towner, P. H.). (1999). *A critical and exegetical commentary on the Pastoral Epistles*. T & T Clark.
Pao, D. W. (2014). Let no one despise your youth: Church and the world in the Pastoral Epistles. *Journal of the Evangelical Theological Society*, *57*(4), 743-755.
Penner, G. M. (2004). *In the shadow of the cross: A biblical theology of persecution and discipleship*. Living Sacrifice Books.
Skarsaune, O. (1994). Heresy and the Pastoral Epistles. *Themelios*, *20*(1), 9-14.
Sumney, J. L. (1999). *'Servants of Satan', 'false brothers' and other opponents of Paul*. Sheffield Academic Press.
Towner, P. H. (1987). Gnosis and realized eschatology in Ephesus (of the Pastoral Epistles) and the Corinthian enthusiasm. *Journal for the Study of the New Testament*, *10*(31), 95-124.
Towner, P. H. (1989). *The goal of our instruction: The structure of theology and ethics in the Pastoral Epistles*. JSOT Press.
Towner, P. H. (2007). 1-2 Timothy and Titus. In G. K. Beale & D. A. Carson (Eds.), *Commentary on the New Testament use of the Old Testament* (pp. 891-918). Baker Academic; Apollos.
Twomey, J. (2009). *The Pastoral Epistles through the centuries*. Wiley-Blackwell.
Wainwright, J. J. (1993). Eusebeia: Syncretism or conservative contextualization? *Evangelical Quarterly: An International Review of Bible and Theology*, *65*(3), 211-224.
Wright, N. T. (2003). *The resurrection of the son of God*. Fortress Press.

C. Church History and Systematic Theology

7 On dealing with persecution of Christians in the course of church history

Exemplary explorations on piety, faith praxis, theology and historiography

Klaus Wetzel[1]

Abstract

Throughout church history, churches have dealt with the experience of persecution in different ways. This article uses examples from three periods of church history (antiquity, the Reformation and Pietism) to show the far-reaching consequences for piety, religious practice and theology, and particularly in church historiography. We find the development of the veneration of relics, the esteem in which Tertullian held persecution, the typologisation in Eusebius of Caesarea and the application of the act-and-consequence scheme by Lactantius. As a result of the theology of the Christian empire, the church itself becomes a persecutor, later through the Inquisition and in the face of the Reformation. The Reformation reacted with collections of martyrdom accounts and a theology of suffering. The Anabaptists are robbed of their missionary impetus by persecution. While separatist Pietism was unable to find a viable response to the situation of persecution, it was precisely the spiritual heritage of a church wiped out by persecution, the Moravian Brethren Unity – conveyed by Comenius – that, in cooperation with mainline Protestant Pietism, brought about a spiritual awakening in the Herrnhut Moravian Church with a great impact.

Keywords: Church history, historiography, persecution, Eusebius, Tertullian, Lactantius, Reformation, Anabaptists, Pietism, Gottfried Arnold, Comenius, Moravian Church.

---

1 Klaus Wetzel (*1952) was a missionary with WEC International in Indonesia (1987-1993), and split his time from 1994 to 2017 between being a Protestant pastor and a lecturer at Akademie für Weltmission in Korntal, Germany (European School of Culture and Theology in cooperation with Columbia International University). He focuses on theology of mission, church and mission history. Email: klaus.wetzel@t-online.de.

1 Introduction[2]

The experience of persecution poses a challenge to Christian existence.[3] This article deals with the question of how dealing with this challenge has shaped piety, theology, in particular church historiography, and church practice, including the willingness to engage in world mission.

To this end, several examples from three epochs of church history are dealt with: the veneration of relics, the theological approaches of Tertullian, Eusebius and Lactantius, as well as the emergence of the state church from antiquity. From the Reformation period, the contrary developments of the Roman Catholic Inquisition and the Reformation, as well as Anabaptism, are analysed. From the modern era, the experiences of the Moravian Brethren Unity, the historiographical approach of Gottfried Arnold, the paradigm shift of Pietism and the awakening of the Moravian Church to world mission, which resulted from the interaction of the spiritual heritage of the Unity of the Brethren and Pietism, are discussed.

It is evident that a church history approach to the topic of persecution is only possible if the challenge of persecution of Christians by other Christians is included.

2 Early Church: Effects of the persecution of Christians in faith practice and theology

2.1 The emergence of the veneration of relics as a reaction to the experience of persecution

The challenge of persecutions has accompanied the Church since New Testament times (Röthlisberger 2025). Very early on, the Church met this challenge with the development of the veneration of relics, which first appears in the sources in connection with the martyrdom of Polycarp of Smyrna. Polycarp of Smyrna was still in touch with the apostolic period. He is described as a disciple of the apostle John. In response to his martyrdom, his community began to venerate his gravesite and honour his mortal remains. This way of dealing with the memory of Polycarp's martyrdom can be understood as a reasoned response to the crucial experience of the

---

2 The essay was written in German and translated by Barbara Felgendreher with the assistance of DeepL.com and Christof Sauer. All translations of citations into English are the responsibility of these translators.

3 On the various aspects of the topic see: Schirrmacher 2017; Sauer 2017; Reiche 2019; Sookhdeo 2019; Kattnig 2021; Röthlisberger 2025; Open Doors 2025.

martyrdom of one of the leading figures of the church in Smyrna. The account of Polycarp's martyrdom (probably in 155 AD; Ritter 1987, 39-40), and the practice of commemorating the anniversaries of his martyrdom at his burial place described therein, are regarded in church historiography as the beginning of the practice of venerating relics, which still plays an important role in the religious practice of the Roman Catholic Church today (Angenendt 1997, 35; Markschies 2006, 116).

After the Constantinian shift, as the construction of the first large cathedrals began, the connection between the liturgy and the veneration of relics emerged: "At the place where the transubstantiation of the holy gifts takes place, the relics of the first martyrs were buried in the so-called Confessio under the simple mensa, a few steps below the altar" (Sas-Zaloziecky 1963, 422). The church father Ambrose was the first to introduce the burial of relics in the altar into the Western church (Gemeinhardt 2013, 415). "The close connection between altar and martyr relics eventually resulted in churches and cities that did not have a saint's gravesite, endeavouring to obtain relics for their church and altar. Canon 7 of the Second Council of Nicaea (787) finally stipulated that every altar must contain a relic" (Binsfeld 2006, 154; cf. Moeller 1987, 71).

Arnold Angenendt emphasises the theological considerations that justify the veneration of relics in the Roman Catholic Church. The martyrs, who through their death gave an unrivalled testimony to their faith (and later the saints through their way of life and their testimony of faith) continue to carry the power of life in Christ even after their death (Angenendt 1997, 112.115). The attribution of the instrument of execution as an attribute, as can be found in the case of various martyrs, is characteristic of the way in which the veneration of martyrs dealt with the borderline experience of martyrdom.[4]

2.2 "The blood of the martyrs is the seed of the Church": Tertullian's optimistic view of the impact of martyrdom

A further case of processing the experience that fellow Christians are suffering as a testimony to their faith can be observed with Tertullian. Here it is of theological nature. The amazing experience that many Christians who died as martyrs in public executions, went to their deaths with

4 S. Keller 1979, e.g. Euphemia – sword, Eustachius – taurus, Florian – millstone, Castulus – spade, Kilian – sword, Lawrence – fire grate, Lucy – dagger, Valentine – sword.

confidence despite the horrors, moved and comforted not only many Christians. For many non-Christians, this perception was a testimony to the power of the Christian faith and an impetus to come to terms with the offer of the Christian faith for themselves. The executions of Christians, which were intended as a deterrent, sometimes achieved the opposite and contributed to the spread of the gospel. While on the one hand some "mocked the religion of loving one's enemies, renouncing violence and forgiveness ..., steadfastness and uncompromising behaviour were also admired and led to baptisms" (Möller/Ammerich 2014, 29). Tertullian's famous statement, "The blood of the martyrs is the seed of the Church", is to be understood in this sense (cf. Aland 1990, 135).

The refusal of Christian confessors to sacrifice to pagan deities became the decisive criterion in the persecutions. "According to Tertullian, refusal to sacrifice was regarded by Christians as the lex propria Christianorum [characteristic law/characteristic of Christians] ..., according to Lactantius as the primus gradus [first/highest level] of Christianity" (Girardet 2006, 75; cf. Girardet 2007b, 235).

It is difficult to say whether Tertullian's call to even seek martyrdom had anything to do with his increasing dissatisfaction with the Church's great willingness to compromise, which he considered as excessive. Eventually, Tertullian left the Church and joined the Montanists. The fundamental question is whether Tertullian's one-sided view of the fruitfulness of martyrdom is not far too optimistic. After all, church history has repeatedly witnessed that churches do not emerge from persecution stronger, but weaker, or even perish as a result of persecution, such as the Church in North Africa or Nubia (Brandl 2012; cf. Jenkins 2008; Orth 2016).

2.3 Eusebius and Lactantius: Theological evaluation of the overcoming of persecution in the Roman Empire by the theologians of the Constantinian shift

The experience of persecutions in the Roman Empire was deeply engraved in the memory of the growing church. This applies in particular to the empire-wide persecutions under Emperor Decius (249-251) and the great Diocletian persecution at the turn to the 4th century. This was not just about the threat of physical annihilation. The persecutions also meant the extensive destruction of the written memories and traditions of the church. This is why any tradition on the history of the early church up to 180 is almost completely missing (cf. Hengel 1979, 12; Hengel 2008, 338).

Against the backdrop of the experience of Diocletian's persecution, the complete reversal of circumstances through the Constantinian shift appeared to Christian contemporaries as a miracle wrought by God.[5] This becomes evident through the historiographical work of Christian theologians and writers.

Eusebius of Caesarea, who was also an advisor to Emperor Constantine and thus not only an eyewitness but also an agent, emphasises the miraculous nature of the turn of events in the 10th book of his Church History, which he understands as God's intervention (Eusebius 1989, 410-441). Eusebius' theological and historiographical treatment of the persecutions has had a long and lasting history of impact, which is based in particular on a concise typologisation. According to Eusebius, the number of ten persecutions of Christians in the first three centuries of the Church corresponds to the ten Egyptian plagues of the Old Testament. Eduardo Hoornaert states that "the image that Christianity carries with it through the centuries of the 'era of persecution' in contrast to the 'Christian times' (christiana tempora) is primarily formed by him [Eusebius]" (Hoornaert 1987, 19). In doing so, Eusebius characterised Christian thinking about history: "he breaks with the historical function of 'fate' (fatum), which was so typical of Greek historiography, and replaces it with the rationality of providence, that is, divine reason, which governs the world" (Hoornaert 1987, 19). In doing so, Eusebius follows a guiding thesis:

> "His central idea becomes tangible in the contrast so clearly constructed between the victory in the person of Constantine and the difficulties in the time before this emperor. The picture of the persecutions, as Eusebius draws it, is highly symbolic and is based on a comparison with the ten plagues of Egypt. Just as there were ten plagues, there were also ten persecutions. Constantine is depicted as a liberator, a kind of Moses." (Hoornaert 1987, 20).

In this way, "an imperial theology or historical theology that was completely new for that time unfolds" (Hoornaert 1987, 20; cf. Brennecke 2006, 563). Eusebius is convinced of the "truth of his own conception of the present culmination point of human history" (Wallace-Hadrill 1982, 539). Eusebius describes the mood of the Christians after the Constantinian shift:

> "Sing to the Lord a new song, for marvellous things he has done! ... After those terrible and gloomy spectacles and reports, we have been honoured to now see and praisingly proclaim things that many truly righteous and God's witnesses on earth before us have desired to see and not seen and desired to hear and not heard. ... All men were delivered from the reign of terror of tyrants;

5 On Constantine and the Constantinian shift cf. Brandt 2006; Fiedrowicz/Krieger/Weber 2007; Girardet 2007a; Schlange-Schöningen 2007.

> and redeemed from former sufferings, some confessed in this way, others in that, that the only true God is he who fought for the pious. But above all, we who had placed our hope in the Christ of God were filled with inexpressible joy." (quoted in Aland 1990, 160; Eusebius 1989, 411-412)

The Christian writer *Lactantius*, whom Constantine had called to Trier in 314/315 to educate his son Crispus (Heinz 2003, 290; Clauss 2005, 35) and who, like Eusebius, was therefore also at the centre of events, explores the question of God's actions in the context of the persecutions even further. In his apologetic work *On the death of the persecutors (De mortibus persecutorum)* (Wlosok 1990, 371), Lactantius consistently applies the act-and-consequence scheme to the fate of the persecutors. All persecutors had to suffer their deserved fate as God's punishment. Lactantius was convinced "that religion must not be forced, but presupposes free will" (Fiedrowicz 2007, 24). In the various explanations, we find an underlying understanding of a battle between God and Satan for the souls of men, which leads to a powerful victory of God through the end of the persecutions.

One might wonder whether the triumphalism of Eusebius and the satisfaction of Lactantius did not promote a development through which the church, after her creed had become the state religion, became a persecutor herself.

2.4 The paradigm of the imperial church and persecution by the Christian state

Beginning with the Constantinian shift, and then very clearly with the declaration of the orthodox Catholic creed as the only permitted religion (*religio licita*) in the Roman Empire by Emperor Theodosius I in 381 (Gemeinhardt 2007, 126; König 2007, 66), the question of the Church's attitude to the matter of persecution took a remarkable turn.

Already for Constantine I, the uniformity of the Christian faith in his empire was of paramount importance. The emperor considered himself responsible for ensuring that the true God was worshipped in the right way throughout the empire (cf. Bringmann 2007, 125; Clauss 2005, 77). With the introduction of the state church by Theodosius I in 381 at the latest, the unity and orthodoxy of the church also became a political and constitutional issue and a matter of national interest. From then on, the idea of the Christian empire characterised the church history of Europe until the 19th century.

A remarkable consequence of the idea of the Christian empire is that the ruler not only considers himself responsible for the uniformity and orthodoxy of the church. He also sees himself as responsible to enforce uniformity and orthodoxy against non-Christian subjects and Christian subjects of a different confession, if necessary, by violence. This meant that the Christian empire, in turn, could now become a persecutor in the field of religious creeds. Alan Kreider states: "Emperor Theodosius I ... choose violence" (Kreider 2007, 127).

For many theologians, a theological argument became important in this context. Since the question of orthodoxy is about the eternal salvation of people, we repeatedly find the argument that since the salvation of the people concerned is at stake, even coercion and violence can be theologically justifiable in order to force non-Christians and heretical Christians to the right creed. We find such an attitude with the "father of orthodoxy", the church father Athanasius (Tetz 1979, 333-349). For his part, Athanasius himself had suffered persecution for his uncompromising attitude and was twice banished from Alexandria to Trier (Heinz 2003, 291; Brandt 2001, 37; Vogt 2007, 137).

The church father Augustine was actually of the opinion that the word of the gospel should be convincing, i.e. a decision in favour of the Christian faith should be made voluntarily and without coercion (Angenendt 2007, 236). Through his confrontation with Donatism, however, Augustine came to the conclusion that it can be right to use coercion for the sake of the salvation of the souls of the people concerned (cf. Speigl 2002, 37). His interpretation of Luke 14:23 is famous in this context: "compelle intrare" – "force them to enter".

3 Two opposing paradigms at the turn of the modern era: Inquisition and Reformation

3.1 The enforcement of the Iberian paradigm by the Inquisition

At the turn to the modern era, two opposing developments emerged in Christianity: the Iberian state church and the Reformation.

Spain, which had just been united by Ferdinand II of Aragon and Isabella I of Castile, once again resolutely developed the concept of a unified Christian empire. There was to be *one* empire, *one* language, Castellano, and *one* faith, Roman Catholicism. According to the will of Isabella I and Ferdinand II, the united Spain was to be, above all, religiously unified (Ruiz 2003, 137). In Spain at the end of the 15th century, a programmatic decision of far-reaching significance was made. Based on the idea of the Christian empire, characterised by dogmatic Catholicism, the "Catholic kings" – a title awarded to them by Pope Alexander VI in 1496 for their services to Roman Catholicism (Ruiz 2003, 137) – decided that there could only be *one* religious confession in their kingdom, the Roman Catholic one. This decision manifested itself above all in the introduction of the Inquisition, through which this uniformity was monitored and guaranteed by the state and the church (Marboe 2006, 288-302; Angenendt 2007, 276-283). Guillermo Cook calls the Spain of this era "fanatically intolerant" (Cook 1994, 43).

The Inquisition was authorised to carry out coercive measures to enforce this concept. Portugal adopted this understanding (Meyers Großes Taschenlexikon 6 1998, Emanuel I, 50). The concept of the Christian empire, as it had developed among the Iberian powers, now unfolded its impact on world history in connection with the papacy's claim to ecclesiastical and secular world domination, as established by Pope Boniface VIII in his bull *Unam sanctam* in 1302 (Kaufhold 2013, 118; Haller 1965, 133-134). In the bull *Unam sanctam*, Boniface VIII described obedience to the pope as essential for salvation (Benrath/Lenzenweger 1988, 199).

When, in 1492, the year in which the Spanish *reconquista* was completed (Marboe 2006, 273-278), Christopher Columbus 'discovered' new territories on his voyage westwards across the Atlantic, this immediately called the papacy into action (Eggensperger/Engel 1991; Hubers 2009). In the Treaty of Tordesillas (1494), Pope Alexander handed over the territories yet to be discovered to the patronage of Spain and Portugal under the condition that they assume responsibility for the Christianisation of the indigenous population (Ohm 1961, 97, 98; Gensichen 1976, 2). This gave rise to the concept of the patronage mission.

It is thanks to a decision with far-reaching consequences that the Christianisation of the population of Latin America *did not* become a state-political undertaking based primarily on coercive measures. The concept of the Inquisition was therefore not applied to missionary work in Latin America, thus taking a decisive step away from the application of the theology of the Christian empire concerning this missionary work.

In the pioneering phase of the patronage mission, Emperor Charles V and his former teacher, Pope Hadrian VI, decided in 1521 that the mission in Latin America should be carried out neither by the state nor by the Church as a whole, but by the mendicant orders of the Franciscans, Dominicans and Augustinians (Franzen/Bäumer 1974, 289; Sievernich 2009, 75; Prien 2007, 109). These orders had just undergone an inner renewal and were once again recalling their founding narrative, in which the peaceful proclamation of the Christian message played a central role. These orders carried out their mission in Latin America with religious motivation only.

As a result, the Christianisation of Latin America through the patronage mission essentially had the character of evangelisation; it, therefore, did not primarily have the character of a forced Christianisation (cf. Cárdenas 1992; Fernández 1992).

3.2 The Reformation: freedom of conscience in matters of faith

25 years after Roman Catholicism set out to Christianise non-European territories through the patronage mission, an opposing paradigm began to unfold in Christendom: the Reformation. The standard of truth was not church tradition and the authority of the church office, but the word of God. Martin Luther fought for the freedom of conscience in matters of faith (Stupperich 1980, 20-25; Noormann 2006, 69-71). Coercion on the part of the church or the Christian state with regard to the listener's response to the proclamation of the Gospel was out of the question for Luther.

Luther's confession earned him persecution from the Roman Church, the ecclesiastical and the imperial ban, from which his sovereigns granted him protection (Pesch 2013, 474). Fundamentally, the Roman Church threatened Luther and his followers, and then also the newly established Protestant churches, with persecution, as was later manifested in many cases during the Counter-Reformation. The actions of Emperor Charles V in the Holy Roman Empire of the German Nation, who as King Carlos Primero was also the ruler of the Spanish Empire, demonstrate the same concept of uniformity of the Christian empire that had led to the introduction of the Inquisition in Spain.

The establishment of Protestant churches did not initially lead to a replacement of the concept of the state church in the mainstream of the Reformation movement. However, as a long-term consequence not only for Protestantism, but even for Christianity as a whole, the concept of religious freedom was inherent to this movement, as the movement of the baptised in the Reformation period showed, which completely broke away from state influence. Later, the concept of religious freedom initially developed primarily in Anglo-Saxon Protestantism (Schirrmacher 2010).

3.3 Protestant church historiography dealing with the topic of persecution

The young Protestantism and the newly emerging Protestant churches experienced themselves as communities persecuted by the Roman Catholic Church, with an "intra-Christian" persecution. The confrontation with this situation of persecution led the emerging Protestant church historiography to develop two concepts. The first was that of witnesses to the truth.

3.3.1 *The concept of "witnesses to the truth"*

After the Reformation, Protestant church historiography elaborated its criticism of the Roman Catholic Church. It paralleled the emergence of Islam with the clearly manifesting position of power of the papacy in the Western Church. Protestant historiography of the Reformation period saw both as God's punishment for the church's apostasy from the New Testament standard, which was considered to have become manifest around the year 600. It spoke of the appearance of the "double Antichrist", the inner and outer one (Benrath 1984b, 101). A high point in the development of the power of the inner Antichrist, i.e. the papacy, was its claim to world domination, as Pope Boniface VIII had unsurpassably expressed in his bull *Unam Sanctam* in 1302 (Mokrosch/Walz 1989, 156-158).

In the context of this understanding of the spiritual decline of the church around the year 600, the pressing question arose for Protestant church historiography as to where the true church had been between around 600 and the Reformation. The Protestant historiography of the Reformation century answered this question with the concept of the "witnesses of truth" according to Hebrews 11; these were considered to have existed more or less hidden at all times in church history. The witnesses to the truth were persecuted in the period between 600 and the Reformation by the church that had fallen away from the true faith (Benrath 1984b, 102).

3.3.2 *The Protestant books of martyrs as a result of dealing with the situation of persecution*

Protestant church historiography of the Reformation period (Benrath 1984a) not only addressed the question of where the true church had been before the Reformation. It also sought to theologically classify the experience that the churches of the Reformation were persecuted by the Roman Catholic Church.[6] Protestant historiography developed the instrument of

---

[6] The experience of persecution accompanied Protestantism in Europe for more than two centuries. The Counter-Reformation in particular brought a peak in the persecution and suppression of Protestantism. Individual episodes of persecution extended beyond the end of the 17th century (Huguenots, Waldensians) into the first half of the 18th century (Salzburg exiles). For a geographical overview, see

books of martyrs for this purpose, in which it combined the concept of witnesses to the truth in the Middle Ages with the portrayal of Protestant martyrs. "The history of the Reformation here became the history of martyrdom" (Benrath 1984b, 104).

The Strasbourg theologian Ludwig Rabus wrote the first Protestant book of martyrs, which begins with Abel and moves on to the Protestant martyrs of his time via the persecuted in the Old and New Testaments and Hus and Savonarola as typical "witnesses to the truth" (Benrath 1984b, 104).

Jean Crespin in Geneva developed a theology of suffering in his *Book of Martyrs*: "Suffering and being persecuted" are "a principal characteristic of the Church of all times" (Benrath 1984b, 104). It is an end-time battle against Satan and the Antichrist willed by God, in which the persecuted have God on their side.

John Foxe emphasises "the Reformation as a divine work", but "the persecution of the church as the punishment of the divine educator for the sin of the church or as the painful intervention of the divine physician to heal its infirmities" (Benrath 1984b, 105).

In the second half of the 16th century, the understanding of church history as the history of martyrdom was at the forefront in Protestantism. The Protestant historiography of the Reformation century was therefore decisively characterised by the experience of persecution. The effects of this characterisation were far-reaching, as Gustav Adolf Benrath points out. Not only Protestant historiography, but also Protestant theology as a whole was characterised by an apocalyptic, end-time mood due to the books of martyrs and the theology of suffering. Particularly because of the experience of persecution, people located themselves in the last times before the return of Jesus Christ – with their end-time afflictions and catastrophes.[7] The Protestant theology of the Reformation century was

---

the map 'Gegenreformation und Ansiedlung Glaubensvertriebener 1525-1732' in: *Westermanns Großer Atlas zur Weltgeschichte* 1969, 105 I; cf. also 'Katholiken, Protestanten und die verfemten Übrigen – Konfessionen in Mitteleuropa bis 1618' and 'Innere Konsolidierung und äußere Erfolge – Katholische Reform und Gegenreformation [1555-1648]' in: Rudolf/Oswalt 2006, 84,85 and 86,87; 'Zeitalter der Glaubensspaltung/Deutsches Reich II 1555-1618' in: Kinder/Hilgemann 2004, 250.251.

7 In a complementary manner, so to speak, Roman Catholicism posed the question of how to understand the loss of around a quarter of its followers as a result of the Reformation. In response, Roman Catholic theologians developed the compensation theory (Koschorke 1994, 15). God would make up for what Catholicism had lost in Europe as a result of the Reformation through the gains overseas; indeed, the growth overseas would ultimately far exceed the losses (Sievernich 2009, 122).

therefore characterised by a pessimistic world view that had no positive expectations for the future of the church, i.e. it did neither expect Protestantism to grow nor to spread to other parts of the world.

The burden of the persecution of the Protestant churches during the Reformation and beyond weighs heavily. This can be shown by the example of lacking willingness to engage in world mission. It is striking that – despite numerous Roman Catholic examples – Protestantism did not embark on any lasting endeavours in world mission in the first two centuries of its history. The main reason for this probably lies in the pessimistic orientation of Protestant theology. The fixation on an eschatological-apocalyptic world view prevented the kind of activity facing the world with anticipation that world mission would have represented. The main reason for this negative theological orientation, however, lies in the strong effectiveness of the theological processing of the experience of persecution through the books of martyrs and through the theology of persecution and suffering.

3.4 The Anabaptist experience of persecution and its negative effects

While the main streams of Protestantism were not directly confronted with persecution everywhere, this was, however, entirely true of the Anabaptist movement (cf. Lichdi 1983, 25-28). It faced persecution not only from the Roman Catholic Church, but also from the newly established Protestant churches. The Anabaptists were "concerned with the kingdom of God, which they saw as being realised neither in the Christianisation by the state church (Catholic) nor invisibly in the hearts of the people (Reformation). Rather, they called people to follow Jesus and gathered them into visible kingdom-of-God-communities" (Ott 1996, 31). The Anabaptists were committed to complete separation from the state, as already expressed in the Schleitheim Confession (Lichdi 1983, 36-41), and to the consistent missionary orientation of their communities: "As early as 1527, on the occasion of the assembly in Augsburg that became known as the Martyrs' Synod, missionaries were sent out in twos and threes" (Ott 1996, 31).

For the Anabaptists too, the experience of persecution proved to be an obstacle to their commitment to mission. In their case, there was a preexisting effective missionary commitment which, however, was destroyed by persecution. The Anabaptists were the only branch of Protestantism that

The compensation theory thus represents the processing of the loss resulting in a positive expectation.

was missionary from the outset – and was aware of the high costs of this commitment. David Bosch points out that the Anabaptists affirmed the commitment to mission:

> "One reason why the Anabaptists subscribed to the 'mandate' of the 'Great Commission' and the Reformers did not may be found in their contradictory readings of the realities of their time. ... The Anabaptists ... pushed aside with consistent logic every other manifestation of Christianity to date; the entire world, including Catholic and Protestant church leaders and rulers, consisted exclusively of pagans ... All of Christianity was apostate. ... In their understanding, there was no difference between the mission in 'Christian' Europe and mission among non-Christians. The reformers, however, could not really bring themselves to such a view." (Bosch 1993, 247)

In the Protestant churches, the experience of persecution indirectly hindered the emergence of an active engagement for world mission in the first two centuries after the Reformation. With regard to the Anabaptists, we can see how the persecutions led directly to the extinction of the strong missionary impulse that had already developed among them. The ongoing discrimination, persecution, expulsion and displacement to remote areas ultimately destroyed their willingness to engage in missionary work and led them into reserved introversion. Bernhard Ott quotes Wolfgang Schäufele:

> "'The persecution had achieved its main purpose when Anabaptism died out in certain areas at the beginning of the 17th century and the missionary fervour had dwindled in all wings of the movement by the middle of the 17th century. It was replaced by the traditional piety of the quiet ones.' When the great era of world mission dawned towards the end of the 18th century, the Mennonites in any case had long ceased to be missionary-minded. They were not among the pioneers of the newly emerging missionary movement." (Ott 1996, 33)

Just as persecution destroyed entire churches such as the North African or the Nubian Church, in the case of the Anabaptists persecution destroyed their world-facing missionary commitment.

4 Examples of Pietist approaches to persecution

Continental European Pietism was triggered by Philipp Jakob Spener's initiative. Spener not only developed his principles in his programmatic treatise *Pia Desideria* (Spener 1964). With the *Collegia Pietatis*, Spener also founded communities that organised their life of faith according to these principles. Many of these Bible discussion groups remained connected to the Protestant church. Others turned theologically to separatism or were forced into separation by the rejection they experienced in large parts of the churches.

4.1 Gottfried Arnold's church-historical treatment of the subject of persecution

Gottfried Arnold was a theologian influenced by separatist Pietism. At the turn of the 17th and 18th centuries, he took up the approach of the Protestant books of martyrs of the 16th century, which at the time was still entirely characterised by confessional thinking, combined it with the theological approaches of the Anabaptists, shaped by the experience of persecution, and applied it to the experiences of the separatist Pietists. In his *Kurzgefaßte Kirchenhistorie* (*Abridged History of the Church*, Leipzig 1697), Arnold takes up the theology of martyrdom. The title of the first paragraph of each of the five chapters of the account of church history makes this clear: "The external state of Christianity ... Because it has mostly been eager and pious in persecutions/ safe and cool-headed in good days" (Reminder to the reader; first page). The persecution caused spiritual fervour, while the pleasant times caused the spiritual life to grow cold. Like Tertullian, Arnold sees a spiritual blessing in the experience of persecution.

Arnold's *Unparteiische Kirchen- und Ketzerhistorie* (Non-partisan history of the church and heretics, Frankfurt a. M. 1699) is a monumental design that grew out of intensive study of the sources. Here Arnold radicalises even further the approach of the books of martyrs, in particular Crespin's theology of suffering, but also the concept of witnesses to the truth now without a positive aspect, as in the *Kurzgefaßte Kirchenhistorie* (*Abridged History of the Church)*: Throughout the history of the Church, the true Church can only be found among the true believers who were persecuted by the mainline Church and labelled as heretics by the latter. According to Arnold, the visible church is never the true church.[8] Although Arnold calls his great work "impartial", his position is entirely centred on one side. The members of the true church can always be recognised by the fact that they are persecuted. Without persecution, there is no membership of the true church.

8 On Arnold's *Kurzgefaßte Kirchenhistorie* and his *Unparteiische Kirchen- und Ketzerhistorie*, see Wetzel 1984, 175-209; 468-471.

The extent to which the topic of the persecuted church has moved and continues to move Christianity and the public is clear from the fact that Arnold's *Unparteiische Kirchen- und Ketzerhistorie* is considered one of the most influential, if not the most influential work on church history in Protestant theology. To this day, a correspondingly radical approach characterised by the concept of decay can be found in church historiography, like that of Baptists, for example in Günther S. Wegener's *Die Kirche lebt: Der Weg der Christen durch zwei Jahrtausende* (Wegener 1978).

4.2 Synthesis of Moravian legacy and Pietism's positive expectations: the Herrnhut Mission

4.2.1 John Amos Comenius' concept of pilgrimage: Overcoming the trauma of the persecution

The situation of the adherents of the Unity of Brethren (Unitas Fratrum), which had been founded in Bohemia and Moravia in pre-Reformation times in 1457, had become increasingly difficult since the Counter-Reformation. The Thirty Years' War then brought about the persecution and expulsion of the Moravian Brethren and the destruction of the Unity of Brethren.

John Amos Comenius (Jan Ámos Komenský), the last bishop of the Unity of Brethren, experienced and witnessed the persecution and destruction of his church. Comenius' theology and pedagogy represent a response to and a processing of the experience of persecution. In his work *The Labyrinth of the World and the Paradise of the Heart* (1623), Comenius defines Christian existence as a pilgrimage:

> "The main character, Pilgrim, like Comenius, journeyed through the world seeking to make sense of the confusion, difficulty, and deception that he encountered in language, religion, politics, and relationships. After much searching, Pilgrim discovered peace and contentment not in the circumstances of life but in fidelity to the Divine." (Stroope 2005, 204)

Mike W. Stroope states: "The pilgrim identity became a mode by which Comenius and the Brethren existed in a hostile world and remained faithful in their witness to Christ" (Stroope 2005, 204). Comenius' faith in Christ gave him the strength to transform the bitter experiences of persecution into positive impulses. Comenius is known for his pioneering work in education (Glenn 2016; Dent 2021).

Only seemingly paradoxical, for Comenius the experience of persecution meant a commitment to world mission. Comenius compared the persecution of the Unity of Brethren with the persecution of the early church in Jerusalem: "He reminded them that 'the dispersion of the Apostolic church at Jerusalem was very sad, and yet it was nothing but the dissemination of the Gospel among other nations'" (Stroope 2005, 206). Comenius was convinced "that evangelisation was an unavoidable responsibility of the church. The true church would exist as the instrument of world missions" (Stroope 2005, 205). Comenius was convinced that "the purpose of life on earth is to prepare for life in heaven" (Dent 2021, 8).

Comenius, who had to spend the last years of his life in exile in the Netherlands, "lamented the demise of his beloved church and yet at the same time expressed faith in its vitality, but only as a seed that might yet come to full fruition" (Stroope 2005, 207). While Comenius does seem to take up Tertullian's statement, he does so without its radicalism and combined with a consoling, compassionate, hopeful attitude, i.e. in a pastoral manner.

4.2.2 Pietism's hope for better times for the church instead of pessimism

In the first two centuries after the Reformation, Protestantism found it difficult to be cosmopolitan and optimistic about the future. The main reasons for this pessimistic world view were the direct and indirect effects of the persecutions that parts of Protestantism had suffered and in some cases continued to suffer, and their description in the books of martyrs and in the theology of suffering.

How could Protestantism gain a positive expectation of the future and turn towards the world, for example in diaconal work, in the field of science and not least in its commitment to world mission?

I have chosen the example of world mission. In my opinion, the decisive impetus came from theological sources, or more precisely from a new exegetical approach. Philipp Jakob Spener, who is regarded as the "father of Pietism", read the biblical prophecies about the time before the return of Jesus Christ from a new perspective. Spener did not contradict the exegesis that reckoned with apocalyptic end-time calamities before the return of Jesus Christ, and thus with the great persecution of the Church. But Spener stated that, according to the exegetical findings, "better times" could still be expected for the Church *before* these end-time catastrophes (Spener 1964, 45-46; Beyreuther 1978, 95; Reinhard/Schneider 1989, 59,60). This "hope for better times" for the Church became the decisive impulse for an optimistic new beginning of Protestantism (cf. Hornig 1988, 98.99; Delgado 2003, 110). Spener set out his theology of hope for better times for the Church in his programmatic work *Pia Desideria* (Spener 1964).

One of the important expectations that developed in the growing Pietist movement was the hope that many people around the world would turn to the Christian faith. This allowed the concept of world mission to gain new ground in Protestantism.

4.2.3 The world mission of Pietism as a result of overcoming a pessimistic world view shaped by the experience of persecution

The dawn of Protestant world mission is linked to the leading figure of the second generation of Pietism, August Hermann Francke (Beyreuther 1978). Francke's work combined the fundamental conviction that all people should experience conversion to Jesus Christ (cf. de Boor 1983, 316; Peschke 2007, 42-61, esp. 46,47) with a strong commitment to diaconal and educational work, including the "invention" of education in realia, craftsmanship and, for the first time, practical bedside training in medical studies. It is logical that the missionary spirituality of Francke's work in Halle led to the first permanent endeavour of Protestant world mission, the Danish-Halle Mission in Tranquebar in South India from 1706 (Brecht 1993; Jeyaraj 1996; Jeyaraj 2000).

While the Danish-Halle Mission was the first exemplary endeavour that paved the way for the cause of world mission in Protestantism (Brecht 1993, 529; cf. Walls 1996, 80), the third generation of Pietism developed a much more comprehensive commitment to world mission with the Herrnhut Mission, namely the first globally effective endeavour of Protestant world mission (cf. Zinzendorf 1979; Beck 1981; Zimmerling 1985, 42-44; Kane 1971, 79-81; Meyer 1995, 34-40). The Moravian missionary movement cannot be understood without its prehistory. In addition to its roots in Spener's and Halle's Pietism, the legacy of the Moravian Unity of Brethren should be mentioned first and foremost.

Count Nikolaus Ludwig von Zinzendorf, the leader of the Moravian Church, descended from an aristocratic family originally from Lower Austria, who had been forced to leave their homeland due to their commitment to Protestantism around six decades before Herrnhut was founded (Beck 1981, 29). In addition to the Pietist heritage – Zinzendorf had been a student of Francke[9] – the heritage of the Moravian Unity of Brethren played a decisive role in the founding and orientation of Herrnhut.

Comenius, who was the last bishop of the Unity of Brethren, had shown its persecuted followers the way to Protestant Europe. They brought with

---

[9] Rosenkranz 1977, 172; Zimmerling, 1985, 30; on Zinzendorf see Beyreuther 1978, 177-288; von Zinzendorf 1979.

them not only their experience of overcoming persecution, but also their missionary spirituality, as Mike W. Stroope notes:

> "The ensuing worldwide mission effort of the Moravians is part of Comenius' legacy. The Brethren who arrived on Zinzendorf's estate had a certain missionary consciousness, having the reformation spirit of Jan Hus, a spirit of the suffering and discipline learned as Brethren, and the convictions and example of John Comenius. What Comenius wrote and practiced was in full view of the intimate family of the Brethren, and his writings provided hope and encouragement to the exiled church. The Brethren arrived at Herrnhut as a pilgrim people. They were schooled in suffering, which defined their allegiance, and in universality, which opened before them the possibility of world-wide missions." (Stroope 2005, 207)

One of these Moravian exiles was Christian David (1691-1751) (Beyreuther 1958, 51), who encouraged many other members of the Unity of Brethren to emigrate to Herrnhut (Beck 1981, 21). Christian David built up a network of supporters by travelling extensively and was ultimately one of the first three missionaries to Greenland to be sent from Herrnhut.

Thus, part of the nature of the Moravian Church and of the missionary movement it brought into being, was the consciousness of being spiritually characterized by the experience of a persecuted church. This influence was reflected in the realisation that following Jesus Christ can require sacrifice. This applies in particular to the great willingness to sacrifice whatever was required for service in world mission. The focus was not on persecution, but on the uncertainty of travelling and, above all, the threat posed by tropical diseases.

Overcoming the experience of persecution in a positive way through Moravian-Herrnhut spirituality was a crucial impetus for the emergence of the exemplary Herrnhut missionary movement, alongside the theological heritage of Pietism with its expectation of better times for the church.

5 Summary

This survey of examples from three epochs of church history makes it clear that the spiritual and theological processing of the experience of persecution has far-reaching consequences. Thus, one may ask whether the psychologically comprehensible development of the veneration of relics does not represent an approximation of Christian religious practice to animistic concepts.

Tertullian's one-sidedly positive view of martyrdom cannot be upheld on the basis of church history's experience that churches can perish. On the other hand, Tertullian's statement "The blood of the martyrs is the seed of the Church" is a lasting challenge to look for where God has allowed such fruit of martyrdom to grow.

Eusebius' triumphalism and Lactantius' satisfaction harbour the danger of self-confidence and arrogance to the extent that the Church could see itself justified in persecuting dissenters.

The pseudo-theological argument that such persecutions were about the salvation of the souls of the people concerned falls apart when faced with the biblical truth that faith in Christ can only be voluntary. Of course, this also applies to the understanding of the Inquisition, which, however, presents itself above all as an instrument of power.

Without the perception of the persecution of the followers of the Reformation by the Roman Church, neither the situation of the emerging Protestant churches nor the theological processing in the books of martyrs and in the theology of suffering can be understood, which resulted in the pessimistic orientation of Protestant theology in its first two centuries, and prevented, for example, a commitment to world mission.

The Anabaptists' experiences with persecution are even more depressing. In their case, persecution not only marginalised a spiritual movement, but even destroyed their pro-active, missionary awakening.

Arnold makes persecution the main theme of the church historiography of separatist Pietism. The radicalism of his approach is similar to that of Tertullian, with the difference that Arnold cannot link the suffering of persecution to a positive expectation; Arnold's approach thus leads to an *aporia*.

Comenius is quite different; he shows a very impressive spiritual approach to the experience of persecution. Comenius adapts Tertullian's approach, but without its one-sidedness. As the last bishop of a dying church, the Moravian Unity of Brethren, he nevertheless conveyed a positive expectation of the future to its scattered followers, which was to bear fruit later.

Remarkably, in the mainstream of Pietism, a new exegetical approach led to the overcoming of pessimistic expectations of the future and released forces that now, for the first time in Protestantism, led to a lasting world missionary endeavour.

When the spiritual legacy of Comenius and the Pietist awakening in the Moravian Church were brought together, the obstacles, i.e. the negative conclusions from the experience of persecution, were finally removed or turned into positives, and the first globally effective Protestant missionary endeavour, the Moravian Mission from Herrnhut, could begin.

It therefore depends on how the Church deals with persecution in its spirituality, religious practice, theology and historiography.

6 References

Aland, K. (1990). *Die Frühzeit der Kirche in Lebensbildern.* 5th rev. ed., Brunnen.
Angenendt, A. (1997). *Heilige und Reliquien.* 2nd ed., C. H. Beck.
Angenendt, A. (2007). *Toleranz und Gewalt.* 3rd ed., Aschendorff.
Arnold, G. (1697). *Kurtz gefaßte Kirchen=Historie des Alten und Neuen Testaments.* Leipzig.
Arnold, G. (1699). *Unparteyische Kirchen= und Ketzer=Historie / von Anfang des Neuen Testaments biß auff das Jahr CHristi 1688.* Frankfurt a. M.
Beck, H. (1981). *Brüder in vielen Völkern.* Ev.-luth. Mission.
Benrath, G. A. & Lenzenweger, J. (1988). Geschichte der abendländischen Kirche im späten Mittelalter. In R. Kottje & B. Moeller (Eds.), *Ökumenische Kirchengeschichte* Vol 2: *Mittelalter und Reformation.* Sect. VII. (pp. 195-274). 4th ed., Grünewald; Chr. Kaiser.
Benrath, G. A. (1984a). Geschichte/Geschichtsschreibung/Geschichtsphilosophie VII. Reformation und Neuzeit VII/1 16. bis 18. Jahrhundert. *TRE* 12, 630-643.
Benrath, G. A. (1984b). Das Verständnis der Kirchengeschichte in der Reformationszeit. In L. Grenzmann & K. Stackmann (Ed.). *Literatur und Laienbildung im Spätmittelalter und in der Reformationszeit* (pp. 97-109). Metzler.
Beyreuther, E. (1958). David, I. Christian. *RGG* 3rd ed. vol. II, 51.
Beyreuther, E. (1978). *Geschichte des Pietismus.* J. F. Steinkopf.
Binsfeld, A. (2006). *Vivas in Deo: Die Graffiti der frühchristlichen Kirchenanlage in Trier.* Die Trierer Domgrabung, vol 5. Selbstverlag des Bischöflichen Dom- und Diözesanmuseums.
Bosch, D. J. (1993). *Transforming Mission.* Orbis.
Brandl, B. (2012). *Wenn Kirchen sterben.* VTR; VKW.
Brandt, H. (2001). *Das Ende der Antike.* C. H. Beck.
Brandt, H. (2006). *Konstantin der Große.* C. H. Beck.
Brecht, M. (1993). August Hermann Francke und der Hallische Pietismus. In M. Brecht (Ed.), *Der Pietismus vom 17. bis zum frühen 18. Jahrhundert* (pp. 440-539). V&R.
Brennecke, H. C. (2006). Constantin und die Idee eines Imperium Christianum. In F. Schweitzer (Ed.). *Religion, Politik und Gewalt* (pp. 561-576). Gütersloher.
Bringmann, K. (2007). Die Konstantinische Wende: Zum Verhältnis von politischer und religiöser Motivation. In H. Schlange-Schöningen (Ed.). *Konstantin und das Christentum* (pp. 109-132). WBG.
Cárdenas, E. (1992). Das königliche Patronat und Vikariat in den überseeischen Besitzungen Spaniens. In M. Sievernich et al. (Ed.). *Conquista und Evangelisation* (pp. 147-166). Grünewald.
Clauss, M. (2005). *Konstantin der Große und seine Zeit.* C. H. Beck.
Cook, G. (1994). Protestant Mission and Evangelization in Latin America. In G. Cook (Ed.), *New Face of the Church in Latin America* (pp. 41-55). Orbis.
de Boor, F. (1983). Francke, August Hermann. *TRE* 11, 312-320.
Delgado, M. (2003). Missionstheologische und anthropologische Gemeinsamkeiten und Unterschiede zwischen Katholiken und Protestanten im Entdeckungszeitalter. *zmr,* 87(2): 93-111.
Dent, R. A. (2021). John Amos Comenius: Inciting the Millenium through Educational Reform. *Religions,* 12: 1012.
Eggensperger, T., & Engel, U. (1991). *Bartolomé de las Casas.* Grünewald.

Ethnographie und Herrnhuter Mission: Völkerkundemuseum Herrnhut. 2003. Staatliches Museum für Völkerkunde.

Eusebius von Cäsarea (1989). H. Kraft (Ed.). *Kirchengeschichte.* 3rd ed., WBG.

Fernández, I. P. (1992). Die „Goldene Zeit" der ersten Missionierung Amerikas: Zum Werk des Bartolomé de las Casas. In M. Sievernich et al. (Ed.), *Conquista und Evangelisation:* (pp. 99-118). Grünewald.

Fiedrowicz, M., Krieger, G., & Weber, W. (Eds.) (2007). *Konstantin der Große.* 2nd ed., Paulinus.

Fiedrowicz, M. (2007). „Freiwillig um Unsterblichkeit kämpfen": Christliche Einflüsse in der Religionspolitik Kaiser Konstantins. In M. Fiedrowicz et al. (Eds.). *Konstantin der Große* (pp. 11-30), 2nd ed., Paulinus.

Franzen, A., & Bäumer, R. (1974). *Papstgeschichte.* Herder.

Geißler, H. (1957). Comenius, Joh. Amos (1592-1670). *RGG*3, vol. I, 1853-1854.

Gemeinhardt, P. (2007). *Das lateinische Christentum und die antike pagane Bildung.* Mohr/ Siebeck.

Gemeinhardt, P. (2013). Volksfrömmigkeit in der spätantiken Hagiographie: Potential und Grenzen eines umstrittenen Konzepts. *ZTHK* 110: 410-438.

Gensichen, H.-W. (1976). *Missionsgeschichte der neueren Zeit.* Die Kirche in ihrer Geschichte, vol. IV T. 3rd ed., V&R.

Girardet, K. M. (2006). Konstantin und das Christentum: die Jahre der Entscheidung 310-314. In J. Engemann (Ed.). *Konstantin der Große* (pp. 69-81). Rheinisches Landesmuseum.

Girardet, K. M. (2007a). *Die Konstantinische Wende.* 2nd ed., WBG.

Girardet, K. M. (2007b). Konstantin – Wegbereiter des Christentums als Weltreligion. In A. Demandt & J. Engemann (Ed.). *Konstantin der Große: Ausstellungskatalog* (pp. 232-242). Philipp von Zabern.

Glenn, J. (2016). Toward a Contextual Theological Reading of John Amos Comenius. *International Journal of Christianity & Education*, 20(3): 186-198.

Haller, J. (1965). *Das Papsttum: Idee und Wirklichkeit.* V *Der Einsturz.* rowohlts deutsche enzyklopädie.

Heinen, H. (1996). *Frühchristliches Trier.* Paulinus.

Heinz, A. (2003). Das gottesdienstliche Leben der Trierer Kirche in der Spätantike und in merowingischer Zeit. In H. Heinz, H. H. Anton, & W. Weber (Eds.). *Im Umbruch der Kulturen.* Geschichte des Bistums Trier, vol 1 (pp. 285-322). Paulinus.

Hengel, M. (1979). *Zur urchristlichen Geschichtsschreibung.* Calwer = M. Hengel (2008). *Studien zum Urchristentum.* Kleine Schriften VI. C.-J. Thornton (Ed.) (pp. 1-104). Mohr/Siebeck.

Hengel, M. (2008). Überlegungen zu einer Geschichte des frühesten Christentums im 1. und 2. Jahrhundert. In M. Hengel. *Studien zum Urchristentum.* Kleine Schriften VI. C.-J. Thornton (Ed.) (pp. 313-352). Mohr/Siebeck.

Heussi, K. (1981). *Kompendium der Kirchengeschichte.* 16th ed., Mohr.

Hoornaert, E. (1987). *Die Anfänge der Kirche in der Erinnerung des christlichen Volkes.* Patmos.

Hornig, G. (1988). Der Pietismus. In G. A. Benrath et al. *Die Lehrentwicklung im Rahmen der Ökumenizität.* Handbuch der Dogmen- und Theologiegeschichte, vol 3, Ungekürzte Studienausgabe (pp. 97-105). V&R.

Hubers, J. (2009). „It is a Strange Thing": The Millennial Blindness of Christopher Columbus. *Missiology* 37(3): 333-353.

Jedin, H., Latourette, K. S., & Martin, J. (1988). *Atlas zur Kirchengeschichte.* 3rd ed. of updated new ed., Herder.

Jenkins, P. (2008). *The Lost History of Christianity.* HarperOne.

Jeyaraj, D. (1996). *Inkulturation in Tranquebar: Der Beitrag der frühen dänisch-halleschen Mission zum Werden einer indisch-einheimischen Kirche (1706-1730).* Erlanger.

Jeyaraj, D. (2000). Halle-Danish (Tranquebar) Mission and Western Protestant Missionary Tradition. *zmr* 84(1): 3-28.

Kane, J. H. (1971). *A Global View of Christian Missions.* Baker.

Kattnig, M. (2021). Die weltweite Religionsfreiheit ist massiv bedroht. *Die Welt,* 21 April.

Kaufhold, M. (2013). *Europas Werte: Wie wir zu unseren Vorstellungen von richtig und falsch kamen.* F. Schöningh.

Keller, H. L. (1979). *Reclams Lexikon der Heiligen und der biblischen Gestalten.* 4th ed., Reclam.

Kinder, H., & Hilgemann, W. (2004). *dtv-Atlas zur Weltgeschichte,* Vol I *Von den Anfängen bis zur Französischen Revolution.* 37th ed., DTV.

König, I. (2007). *Die Spätantike.* Geschichte Kompakt. WBG.

Koschorke, K. (1994). Konfessionelle Spaltung und weltweite Ausbreitung des Christentums im Zeitalter der Reformation. *ZThK* 91(1): 10-24.

Kreider, A. (2007). Violence and Mission in the Fourth and Fifth Centuries. *IBMR,* 31(3): 125-133.

Kurten, P. (1985). *Umkehr zum lebendigen Gott: die Bekehrungstheologie August Hermann Franckes als Beitrag zur Erneuerung des Glaubens.* Schöningh.

Lichdi, D. G. (1983). *Über Zürich und Witmarsum nach Addis Abeba: Die Mennoniten in Geschichte und Gegenwart.* Agape.

Mainstream of Civilization. (1994). Stanley Chodorow et al. *The Mainstream of Civilization,* 6th ed., Thomson Learning.

Marboe, R. A. (2006). *Von Burgos nach Cuzco: Das Werden Spaniens 530-1530.* Magnus.

Markschies, C. (2006). *Das antike Christentum.* C. H. Beck.

Meyer, D. (1995). Zinzendorf und Herrnhut. In M. Brecht & K. Deppermann (Eds.), *Der Pietismus im achtzehnten Jahrhundert* (pp. 3-106). V&R.

Militzer, K. (2005). *Die Geschichte des Deutschen Ordens.* Kohlhammer.

Moeller, B. (1987). *Geschichte des Christentums in Grundzügen.* V&R.

Möller, L., & Ammerich, H. (2014). *Einführung in das Studium der Kirchengeschichte.* WBG.

Mokrosch, R., & Walz, H. (1989). *Kirchen- und Theologiegeschichte in Quellen.* Vol. II. Mittelalter. 3rd ed., Neukirchener.

Neill, S. (1990). *Geschichte der christlichen Mission.* 2nd augmented ed., Ev.-luth. Mission.

Noormann, H. (2006). *Kirchengeschichte.* Calwer.

Ohm, T. (1961). *Wichtige Daten der Missionsgeschichte: Eine Zeittafel.* 2nd expanded and revised ed., Aschendorff.

Open Doors (2025). *Gesichter der Verfolgung: Weltverfolgungsindex 2025.*

Orth, S. (2016). Zur Zukunft der Christen im Nahen Osten: Werden sie zerrieben? *Herder Korrespondenz* (4): 22-25.

Ott, B. (1996). *Missionarische Gemeinde werden: Der Weg der Evangelischen Täufergemeinden.* ETG.

Pesch, O. H. (2013). Martin Luther im katholischen Urteil. In Reformationsgeschichtliche Sozietät der Martin-Luther-Universität Halle-Wittenberg (Ed.). *Spurenlese: Kulturelle Wirkungen der Reformation* (pp. 449-483). EVA.

Peschke, E. (2007). *Die Theologie August Hermann Franckes.* Linea.

Prien, H.-J. (2007). *Das Christentum in Lateinamerika*. Kirchengeschichte in Einzeldarstellungen IV/6. EVA.
Pro, J., & Rivero, M. (2006). *Breve Atlas de Historia de Espana*. 2nd ed., Alianza Editorial.
Reiche, S. (2019). Gegen Christenverfolgung ist Appeasement nutzlos. *Die Welt*, 16 January.
Reinhardt, R., & Schneider, H. (1989). Geschichte der europäischen Kirchen in der frühen Neuzeit (1648-1803). In R. Kottje, B. Moeller (Eds.), *Ökumenische Kirchengeschichte 3: Neuzeit* (pp. 3-99). Grünewald; Chr. Kaiser.
Richebächer, W. (2011). Edinburgh 1910: Mission zwischen Machbarkeitsideal und ökumenisch-dialogischer Neuorientierung. *ZMiss* 37(4): 349-363.
Riley-Smith. (1990). Kreuzzüge. *TRE* 20, 1-10.
Ritter, A. M. (1987). *Kirchen- und Theologiegeschichte in Quellen*. Vol. I. Alte Kirche. 4th ed., Neukirchener.
Rosenkranz, G. (1977). *Die christliche Mission: Geschichte und Theologie*. Chr. Kaiser.
Röthlisberger, D. (2025). Verfolgung im Neuen Testament. In R. Lilleaasen & C. Sauer (Eds.), *Religious persecution*. VKW.
Rudolf, H. U., & Oswalt, V. (2006). *TaschenAtlas Deutsche Geschichte*. 2nd ed., Klett.
Rudolf, H. U., & Oswalt, V. (2010). *TaschenAtlas Weltgeschichte*. 6th updated ed., Klett.
Ruiz, E. M., et al. (2003). *Atlas Histórico de Espana I*. Ediciones Istmo.
Sas-Zaloziecky, W. (1963). *Die altchristliche Kunst*. Ullstein Kunstgeschichte 7. Ullstein.
Sauer, C. (2017). Kann man Märtyrer zählen und wenn ja, wie? In E. Spohn (Ed.). *Gottes Handeln in der Geschichte* (pp. 85-113). VTR.
Schirrmacher, T. (2010). Eine evangelikale Sicht des Verhältnisses von Religionsfreiheit und Mission. In F. Walldorf, L. Käser, B. Brandl (Eds.), *Mission und Reflexion im Kontext* (pp. 322-340) VTR; VKW.
Schirrmacher, Thomas. (2017). Hinterfragenswerte Statistiken zu Religionsfreiheit und Christenverfolgung. In E. Spohn (Ed.). *Gottes Handeln in der Geschichte* (pp. 114-132). VTR.
Schlange-Schöningen, H. (Ed.).(2007). *Konstantin und das Christentum*. WBG.
Sievernich, M. (2009). *Die christliche Mission: Geschichte und Gegenwart*. WBG.
Sookhdeo, P. (2019). *Hated without reason. The remarkable story of Christian persecution over the centuries*. Isaac Publishing.
Speigl, J. (2002). Zur apologetischen und antihäretischen Ausrichtung des Religionsbegriffes Augustins. *ZMR* 86(1): 26-43.
Spener, P. J. (1964). *Pia Desideria*. Ed. K. Aland. 3rd ed., De Gruyter.
Stroope, M. W. (2005). The Legacy of John Amos Comenius. *IBMR*, 29(4): 204-208.
Stupperich, R. (1980). *Die Reformation in Deutschland*. 2nd rev. ed., Gütersloher.
Tetz, M. (1979). Athanasius von Alexandrien. *TRE* 4, 333-349.
Vogt, H. J. (2007). Konstantin und die Konzilien. In M. Fiedrowicz, G. Krieger, W. Weber (Eds.), *Konstantin der Große* (pp. 97-137). 2nd ed., Paulinus.
Wallace-Hadrill, D. S. (1982). Eusebius von Caesarea. *TRE* 10, 537-543.
Walls, A. F. (1996). *The Missionary Movement in Christian History*. Clark.
Wegener, G. S. (1978). *Die Kirche lebt: Der Weg der Christen durch zwei Jahrtausende*. 3rd ed., Oncken.
Westermanns Großer Atlas zur Weltgeschichte. (1969). Westermann.
Wettach, T. (1975). Pietismus und Mission. *Lexikon zur Weltmission*, 437-438.
Wetzel, K. (1983). *Theologische Kirchengeschichtsschreibung im deutschen Protestantismus 1660-1760* [PhD Mainz]. Brunnen.

Wlosok, A. (1990). Lactantius, L. Caelius Firmianus (ca. 250-325). *TRE* 20, 370-374.
Zeeden, E. W. (Ed.). (1995). *Großer Historischer Weltatlas Zweiter Teil Mittelalter Erläuterungen.* 2nd ed., Bayerischer Schulbuch-Verlag.
Zimmerling, P. (1985). *Pioniere der Mission im älteren Pietismus.* Brunnen.
Zinzendorf, N. L. von. (1979). *Texte zur Mission.* Ed. H. Bintz. Wittig.

8 Reform movements within the Ethiopian Orthodox Tewahedo Church

Religious freedom at stake?

Finn Aa. Rønne[1]

Abstract

Over the past five decades, various reform movements have emerged within the Ethiopian Orthodox Tewahedo Church (EOTC), an institution with roots tracing back to the fourth century, which served as the national church of Ethiopia until relatively recently. Some movements have ultimately been expelled from the EOTC, while others persist as distinct groups within the church, often operating clandestinely. This is mainly because these renewal movements have faced opposition and suppression from influential factions within the church. Consequently, these movements raise pertinent questions regarding religious freedom. To fully comprehend the reform movements, one must consider them in relation to, firstly, the historically entrenched EOTC, viewed as a vital representation of Ethiopian identity, serving as a custodian of the nation's diverse cultural and historical legacy, and secondly, the Protestant churches that have significantly influenced the country's modern development.

Keywords: Ethiopia, the Ethiopian Orthodox Tewahedo Church, reform movements, Protestant churches, persecution, state-church.

1 "The Way of Life Reformation Movement"

One of my students at the Ethiopian Graduate School of Theology was the first to introduce me to a reform movement, known locally as Tähadiso, within the Ethiopian Orthodox Tewahedo Church (EOTC).[2]

---

1 Finn Aasebø Rønne, Dr. theol., is professor at Dansk Bibel-Institut in Copenhagen, Fjellhaug International University College – Copenhagen, and Ethiopian Graduate School of Theology, Addis Ababa. Email: finn@dbi.edu, ORCID iD: 0009-0003-2135-7738.

2 This article is primarily based on course papers authored by various students at the Ethiopian Graduate School of Theology, all of which are appropriately referenced

The EOTC is recognised as one of the Oriental Orthodox churches, a group of Christian churches distinct from the Eastern Orthodox and Roman Catholic churches. The EOTC historically served as the national church of Ethiopia, maintaining a close relationship with the state for centuries until approximately 50 years ago. Today, it comprises about 40-45% of the Ethiopian population (Prunier & Ficquet, 2015, p. 123), making it the largest church in the country. The church sees itself as a custodian and representative of Ethiopia's rich cultural and historical heritage. Grasping this historical context, which is deeply woven into centuries of tradition and influence, is crucial for understanding the circumstances surrounding current reform movements within the church.

After what could be called an evangelical experience or a reformation discovery, my EGST student pioneered one of many Tähadiso movements within the EOTC over the past three decades. This movement is known as Finote Hiwot Mahibere Medahniyalem (FHMM), or the Way of Life and Saviour of the World Fellowship (Tsion Seyoum, 2018).[3]

The fellowship and its ministry target Ethiopian Orthodox monks, priests, teachers, and deacons. Their initiatives include offering training, distributing Bibles, and working to establish small, reformed churches within the larger church structure (Tsion Seyoum, 2018, p. 5). They provide three types of training: one for newcomers that covers fundamental truths about salvation, a discipleship training as a follow-up, and leadership training aimed at equipping church leaders. The leadership training takes place at Finote Hiwot Tesfa Tehadiso Bible School, an accredited institution. In 2018, FHMM had 14 full-time and over 60 volunteer ministers (Tsion Seyoum, 2018, p. 6). They had established 21 small churches within the EOTC. By focusing on the development of leaders, the fellowship aims

---

in the bibliography. Additionally, it draws significantly from Seblewengel Daniel's doctoral thesis: *Perception and identity: A study of the relationship between the Ethiopian Orthodox Church and evangelical churches in Ethiopia* (Seblewengel Daniel, 2019). Specific citations are only provided where particular information is taken from a given source. The students' academic papers were submitted as assignments for a historical methods course that I instruct. For their research, the students and Dr. Seblewengel gathered data from interviews, unpublished theses, as well as various documents, newspapers, magazines, and literature in Amharic – resources that are typically not readily accessible to Western scholars. As I lacked direct access to the oral sources they employed, I do not refer directly to them in the article. I extend my gratitude to my students and to Seblewengel Daniel for their invaluable contributions to this article.

3 Information regarding FHMM is also acquired through personal acquaintance with the founder and visits to their headquarter in Addis Ababa.

for them to influence regular church members, thus fostering the spread of reformation principles throughout the church.

Figure 1: Wallpainting within the headquarter of Finote Hiwot Mahibere Medahniyalem. Private photo

The reference to Jeremiah 6:16 on a painting within the headquarter of FHMM articulates their objective: "This is what the Lord says: 'Stand at the crossroads and look; ask for the ancient paths, ask where the good way is, and walk in it, and you will find rest for your souls.'" This invocation of ancient paths signifies their desire for a substantive reformation, explicitly aiming to redirect the church towards what they perceive as *original* Christianity, as delineated in the Bible (Tsion Seyoum, 2018, p. 2). The same holds true for most other Tähadiso movements. They seek to revive Christianity in its original form, before the subsequent alterations implemented within the EOTC *tradition*. Consequently, their efforts are directed towards challenging certain practices and beliefs they view as divergent from biblical teachings. In particular, they criticise the roles of angels, saints, and the Virgin Mary as mediators and intercessors between humanity and God, as well as the reverence and veneration they receive (Tsion Seyoum, 2018, p. 11). Additionally, they seek to eliminate practices they classify as occult within specific segments of the EOTC. Nonetheless, they explicitly state in the 'Rules and Regulations of the Finote Hiwot Mahibere Medahniyalem' that their intention is not to transform the EOTC into a Protestant denomination, but rather to effectuate reform that preserves its historical, cultural, and identity framework (The Finote Hiwot Mahibere Medahniyalem, n.d.; Tsion Seyoum, 2018, p. 14).

2 The Tähadiso movements

2.1 A presentation

The records of the EOTC from 2016 document the presence of 28 distinct Tähadiso movements (Tsion Seyoum, 2018, p. 14). Among these, eight had been excommunicated by 2016, while the remaining twenty continued to operate within the church's structure. Notably, FHMM is included among the latter group, indicating that the EOTC leadership is aware of its existence and potentially some of its activities. Furthermore, the records indicate a rise in the number of movements affiliated with the EOTC, suggesting that from the church's perspective, this phenomenon represents an escalating concern.

In this article, I will examine the Tähadiso movements in view of the opposition they have faced from significant factions within the EOTC. These movements have been notably underrepresented in scholarly discourse,[4] thus necessitating increased attention in future studies. However, the primary focus of this article will be on elements pertinent to the context of religious freedom and persecution. The article does not primarily aim to describe and classify the specific measures implemented by the EOTC regarding the Tähadiso movements. Instead, it will concentrate on the contextual framework surrounding these actions and the pertinent questions that arise in relation to religious freedom.

The Tähadiso movements and their contextual circumstances must be interpreted through a dual lens: firstly, the enduring influence of the EOTC, which is intricately woven into the fabric of Ethiopian society and culture; and secondly, the impact of Protestant churches, which have significantly contributed to the modern development of the nation.

In addition to FHMM, two movements are particularly noteworthy and warrant specialised analysis. The most prominent among these is *Amanuel Hibret Bete Kerestian*, also known as Amanuel United Church, which is currently classified within the Protestant denominations (Henok Afework, 2016,

[4] An essential exception pertains to the doctoral thesis of Seblewengel Daniel (Seblewengel Daniel, 2019).

pp. 14-17). However, it emerged as a conventional Tähadiso movement affiliated with the Saint Mary Orthodox Church in the central Ethiopian town of Nazareth/Adama. This movement began when a group of textile factory workers initiated a Bible study group within the factory's premises. Following this, they sought and received permission from the local leader of the Saint Mary Church to transition their Bible study group into the church itself. As time progressed, the group's membership increased substantially, and their gatherings began to feature characteristic charismatic practices, including speaking in tongues, healing, and exorcism. This development incited significant resistance from church leaders, ultimately compelling the group to separate from the local congregation. They subsequently established a fellowship, referred to as mahibere,[5] while still under the auspices of the EOTC and named Amanuel Menfesawi Mahibere or Amanuel Spiritual Fellowship. The influence of this movement subsequently expanded throughout other regions of Ethiopia, eventually leading to its recognition as an independent church entity, Amanuel Hibret Bete Kerestian.

Haimanota Abaew, also known as The Faith of the Fathers, was established in the late 1950s with the explicit aim of educating young Ethiopian Orthodox Christians and protecting them from Protestant teachings (Henok Afework, 2016, pp. 9-12; Seblewengel Daniel, 2019). This initiative proved particularly effective among university students. The curriculum emphasised the study of the church fathers and the Bible, aiming to preserve Orthodox traditions for the emerging generation. Initially, Haimanota Abaew resembled Mahibere Kidusan, presented below (Tibebe Eshete, 2009, pp. 58-59); however, due to ecumenical engagements abroad, it gradually shifted its focus to align more closely with the Tähadiso movements. Additionally, its worship style evolved, incorporating modern musical instruments. As a result, the EOTC leadership ultimately imposed a ban on

---

5 The Tähadiso movements frequently employ the term 'mahibere' in their name while concurrently functioning within the EOTC. This term bears considerable historical implications and has been utilised by various groups to confer legitimacy within both ecclesiastical and public spheres. In the constitution of the Ethiopian Imperial government enacted in 1955, Protestant churches were officially registered under the designation of Mahibere. Donald Levine describes Mahibere as "a type of formal association which has sprung up in Addis Ababa ... Becoming popular for the first time in 1960. ... the name is taken from Orthodox fraternal association" (Levine, 2014, p. 279). Worku Demeke explains that Mahibere in Ethiopia has "a very wide ranging meaning. ... Any group of people associated for a certain purpose" (Worku Demeke, 2011, p. 284). And in the broader Ethiopian social and cultural setup, Mahibere "... favors the attainment of greater values ... being deeply rooted in the culture, having love as its foundation and creating an atmosphere that can handle every discussion" (Worku Demeke, 2011).

the movement, despite its efforts to uphold numerous Ethiopian Orthodox traditions, such as the observance of fasting days.

2.2 A counter-reformation movement

In contrast to the Tähadiso movements that are the focus of this article, another significant movement operates within the EOTC: *Mahibere Kidusan*, also known as the Association of the Saints (Henok Afework, 2016, pp. 13-15; Seblewengel Daniel, 2019, pp. 369). Established in the 1980s, the organisation initially focused on supporting the religious education provided by the EOTC congregations.

The identity and position of Mahbere Kidusan within the EOTC is characterized by complexity and ambivalence. This group functions not only as a robust counter-reform movement but also occupies a distinct role within the contemporary religious and political landscape of the EOTC. It possesses aspirations that are notably distinct from those of other factions within the church. Furthermore, while maintaining close affiliations with the national leadership of the EOTC, it does not receive full support or ownership from the leading synod of the church (Prunier & Ficquet, 2015, p. 84). Mahbere Kidusan also extends its activities to Ethiopian Orthodox congregations abroad.

Supporters of Mahibere Kidusan primarily advocate for *traditional* Ethiopian Orthodox beliefs and practices, contrasting with the Tähadiso movements that emphasise a return to what they consider the *original* Ethiopian Orthodox Christianity. This includes a strong emphasis on the intermediary roles and intercession of angels, saints, and the Virgin Mary, as well as the importance of fasting on specific days and during designated periods.

The group is deeply aware of Ethiopia's rich cultural and historical heritage and recognises the pivotal role of the EOTC in its preservation. Members express a commitment to contributing to this endeavour, as evidenced by Mahibere Kidusan's proactive stance in the ongoing discussions and challenges posed by the Tähadiso movements.

In summary, Mahibere Kidusan is situated at the vanguard of initiatives aimed at preserving and promoting traditional beliefs and practices within the Ethiopian Orthodox framework. As an integral component of these initiatives, they engage proactively in countering the Tähadiso movements.

2.3 Roots of modern Tähadiso movements

The narratives associated with, and narrating about, various religious movements demonstrate a historical lineage traceable to earlier Tähadiso movements within the EOTC (Genaye Eshetu, 2021, pp. 3). Movements such as FHMM and Amanuel Hibret Bete Kerestian perceive themselves as both a continuation and an inheritor of the legacy embodied by the Deqiqe Estifanos, a reform movement that emerged in the 15th century (Seblewengel Daniel, 2019, pp. 351), as well as a Bible-reader movement from the 19th century, which are acknowledged as foundational influences upon one of the major Protestant churches in Ethiopia, The Ethiopian Evangelical Church Mekane Yesus.

Deqiqe Estifanos represents a monastic movement initiated by the renowned monk Estifanos (Genaye Eshetu, 2021; Taddesse Tamrat, 1966). The adherents of this movement notably refused to prostrate themselves before the cross, the icon of Madonna and Child, or the king, which contrasts starkly with the customary practices of devout members of the EOTC. They asserted that such acts of veneration were appropriate solely for the Trinity (Genaye Eshetu, 2021, p. 9). Furthermore, the movement explicitly rejected the mediating roles of saints and the Virgin Mary in spiritual matters. This stance did not align with the beliefs of the established church hierarchy, prompting growing concern among the palace and senior clergy as interest in the movement intensified. The monks' steadfast adherence to their principles ultimately led to severe repercussions, as the ruling authority enacted brutal measures against them. Their refusal to accord what was deemed appropriate honour to the Virgin Mary earned them the label of Tsere Maryam, effectively branding them as enemies of Mary. This pejorative designation has been consistently associated with Tähadiso movements throughout history. Nevertheless, the primary source of contention for Deqiqe Estifanos appeared to be their refusal to extend similar respect to the king himself (Genaye Eshetu, 2021, pp. 10, 15).

Deqiqe Estifanos' principal adversary was King Zar'a-Yaeqob, who, paradoxically, is recognised as one of the foremost reformists in the history of the EOTC, both politically and religiously (Henok Afework, 2016, p. 4). A fundamental aspect of his reform agenda was the establishment of a close relationship between the state and the church. This positioned him as an advocate of religious nationalism, promoting a heightened sense of both national and spiritual identity among Ethiopians. Zar'a-Yaeqob aimed to leverage Ethiopian Orthodox Christianity, viewed as a relatively cohesive entity, to unify the diverse populations within his realm, thereby strengthening both the kingdom and his authority as monarch. For this initiative to thrive, he needed to garner the clergy's allegiance while maintaining a degree of uniformity in church life and theology, aligned with established traditions. In this context, the Deqiqe Estifanos presented a significant challenge, leading to their persecution by Zar'a-Yaeqob and senior church officials, who accused them of propagating an alien or imported faith (Genaye Eshetu, 2021, p. 15; Henok Afework, 2016, p. 8).

Mahibere Kidusan aligns closely with Zar'a-Yaeqob's perspectives and objectives, embracing his approach to reformation (Henok Afework, 2016, p. 18). This contrasts with the Tähadiso movements, which are regarded as successors to Deqiqe Estifanos.

2.4 Church, state, and resistance

In the case of Zar'a-Yaeqob, we observe a significant illustration of the intricate relationship between church and state that has characterised extensive segments of Ethiopian history, until the Ethiopian Revolution of 1974. The introduction of Christianity to Ethiopia in the 4th century positioned it as a court religion; consequently, Ethiopian kings and emperors have historically played crucial roles in the administration and life of the church (Henok Afework, 2016, p. 5). Much like Zar'a-Yaeqob, these monarchs utilised Ethiopian Orthodox Christianity as a means to articulate Ethiopian identity, fostering unity among their subjects, consolidating state stability, and fortifying their own positions of power. Conversely, the church benefited from state patronage, which facilitated the expansion of its missionary endeavours, provided protection, and conferred upon it a privileged status within the societal framework.

This has often been accompanied by strong resistance to foreign missions and non-Orthodox churches. Given the EOTC and Ethiopian Orthodox Christianity's role in relation to the Ethiopian state and ruler, a rival church was viewed as a threat to the state. It is essential to recognise that opposition against and subsequent suppression of the other religious groups stemmed from this resistance.

The dynamics described herein extend to the relationship between the Ethiopian authorities and the EOTC on one side, and Protestant missions and churches on the other, particularly during the 20th century. This is applicable to mainline Protestant churches since the onset of the century, and notably to the Pentecostal groups that emerged in the 1960s. The interaction was notably pronounced during the restoration period following the Italian occupation, a time characterised by heightened religious nationalism and an emerging sense of national and religious identity across Ethiopia, echoing the era of Zar'a-Yaeqob. Consequently, this frequently resulted in opposition against Protestant Christians and the subsequent suppression, which manifested in the form of imprisonments and the destruction of churches and private property. The events discussed persisted until the Ethiopian Revolution of 1974, significantly impacting Pentecostal groups from the 1960s. Furthermore, throughout the Marxist regime from 1974 to 1991, churches encountered challenging conditions; however, distinct circumstances were evident during this period, warranting their exclusion from the analysis presented in this article.

In contemporary Ethiopia, there is a clear separation between the state and the church. Consequently, the government does not leverage Ethiopian Orthodox Christianity as a mechanism for national unity. Nevertheless, as previously discussed, the EOTC considers itself a custodian and representative of Ethiopia's extensive cultural and historical heritage. Therefore, for the EOTC, adherence to Ethiopian Orthodox Christianity serves as a means of articulating and preserving a distinct Ethiopian identity in the present day.

This context is crucial for understanding the reaction of the EOTC towards the Tähadiso movements.

2.5 EOTC reaction against the Tähadiso movements

It is evident that a substantial segment of the governing factions within the EOTC opposes the goals and initiatives associated with the Tähadiso movements. These factions perceive these movements as a significant threat, prompting them to employ various strategies to counteract their influence.

The EOTC perceives these movements as instruments of the Protestant churches, which seek to expand their influence while undermining the EOTC by transforming it into a Protestant Church (Tsion Seyoum, 2018, p. 7). In a publication by Mahibere Kidusan titled "Ye Tehadiso Menafikan Zemecha: The Mission of Heretical Reformers," this purported strategy of the Tähadiso movements is articulated through three distinct approaches and stages (Mahibere Kidusan, 2011): The initial phase spans from the introduction of Protestant Christianity until 1958, characterised by the assertion that Protestant Christianity represents the singular true faith. The subsequent phase, from 1958 to 1998, involves a strategy focused on discrediting the EOTC as a false religion. The final phase, which spans from 1998 to the present, aims to reform the church internally. Proponents of this phase argue that the *ancient* EOTC embodied the *original* faith, which has historically subsequently incorporated specific heretical teachings, thus necessitating a reformation to return to its foundational beliefs.

This demonstrates, firstly, that the EOTC possesses precise knowledge of the current views and objectives of present-day Tähadiso movements regarding reforming the EOTC from within, but not, as we have seen, about transforming it into a Protestant church. However, the described reformation strategy is not new. It was the declared aim of earlier reform movements, such as the Bible-reader movements, which were foundational for the Ethiopian Evangelical Church Mekane Yesus. Similarly, some of the early Protestant missions that came to Ethiopia sought not to establish a distinct Protestant church but to reform the EOTC from within by returning to its original biblical roots and the heritage of the early Church.

Secondly, the presentation in the book indicates that ETOC's perspective on the Tähadiso movements is influenced by its historical relations with foreign missions. Notably, the text references only Protestant churches, omitting Catholic ones. This omission is understandable, given that Protestant missions and churches have exerted a significantly greater influence in Ethiopia compared to their Catholic counterparts. However, from a broader historical context, the attempts by the Catholic Church, albeit briefly successful, to assert dominance over the Ethiopian Church also fostered a deep-seated aversion and resistance within both the Ethiopian state and the Church towards foreign powers and religious institutions (Sofanit T. Abebe, 2014).

The Protestant churches were regarded as a notable threat to the EOTC throughout the last century. The EOTC has experienced a significant loss of membership to these Protestant denominations. The ability of Protestant churches to attract an extensive number of new adherents is primarily attributed to their provision of modern educational and healthcare services. This capability has been underpinned mainly by resources sourced from Western missions, which the EOTC has historically lacked access to (Getatchew Haile et al., 1998). Similarly, documentation originating from the EOTC indicates concerns regarding the Tähadiso movements, which are believed to possess economic resources that they leverage to draw in followers (Tsion Seyoum, 2018, p. 8).

Nonetheless, the opposition to the Tähadiso movements from the EOTC is significantly driven by theological considerations, mirroring issues present in the Protestant denominations. Both the Tähadiso movements and Protestant churches refute the mediating roles of saints and the Virgin Mary, along with the associated duty to venerate them specifically. Consequently, both groups are labelled as "Tsere Maryam," or adversaries of Mary. This rejection also extends to the dismissal of numerous rules for Christians upheld by the EOTC, particularly regarding the observance of fasting periods.

Furthermore, within the context of Ethiopian Orthodox Christianity, the relationship between religious beliefs and practices exhibits significant differences when compared to those commonly observed in Western contexts. In the West, a clear distinction between belief and practice is prevalent, which contrasts with the situation observed in the Ethiopian context.[6] Consequently, the theologically motivated reactions encompass specific practices that diverge markedly from those prevalent in the EOTC. As a result, there is a notably stronger resistance to Tähadiso movements within the EOTC that adopt Pentecostal practices, compared to the responses elicited by Protestant churches with more traditional and liturgical worship styles. In this context, the use of modern musical instruments for church hymns, rather than the traditional ecclesiastical instruments characteristic of the EOTC, emerges as a contentious issue.

And behind the various motivations for the EOTC's opposition to the Tähadiso movements lies the perception that the EOTC serves as a crucial representation of Ethiopian identity, acting as a custodian of the nation's rich cultural and historical heritage. Consequently, opposing the Tähadiso movements is regarded as imperative for the preservation of Ethiopian identity, history, and culture.

It is crucial to consider this when evaluating the measures implemented by the EOTC in response to the Tähadiso movement.

3 Counter reformation – religious freedom at stake?

3.1 Counter-reformation

Motivated by the perspective described above, prominent factions within the EOTC, supported by Mahibere Kidusan, have implemented several initiatives that can be characterised as a 'counter-reformation' (Henok Afework, 2016, p. 15).

The primary and notable measure taken to counter the Tähadiso Movements was the formal rejection of these movements by the church's national leadership. Significantly, this action also served as an official acknowledgement of the presence of a critical faction within the church. The revelation of such a substantial movement challenging the church on specific issues implicitly acknowledges the existence of particular internal challenges.

Simultaneously, it constitutes a vital component in the campaign against the Tähadiso Movements, aimed at raising awareness among lay members regarding the movements and the threats they pose to the church (Tsion Seyoum, 2018, p. 12). In this regard, a somewhat contentious educational initiative has been launched to inform the general public

[6] This also suggests that the distinction between *forum internum* and *forum externum* (Sauer & Nel, 2025) is less significant in an Ethiopian context.

about matters of particular significance concerning the Tähadiso Movements. The church has developed a variety of publications and diverse audiovisual materials to facilitate this effort.

Another strategy to combat the Tähadiso movements involves publicly identifying and condemning associations, preachers, singers, and notable church officials perceived to have a direct or indirect connection to these movements. This approach aims to restrict these individuals from holding official positions and even from participating in church congregations. Social media has served as the principal medium for engaging with the community of believers concerning these initiatives.

The EOTC maintains a comprehensive system of Sunday schools that function as auxiliary assemblies within local parish churches, complementing conventional worship services. These educational sessions emphasise the essential components of preaching, instruction, and hymnody, thereby fostering community engagement and participation. The Tähadiso Movements have effectively leveraged these educational frameworks to extend their outreach to wider audiences. Likewise, these structures have also been utilised during the Counter-Reformation.

3.2 The Tähadiso perspective

A significant aspect of the narratives surrounding the Tähadiso movements is the adversity they face from powerful factions within the EOTC. Mahibere Kidusan is reported to play an active role in this context (Henok Afework, 2016, p. 15). Consequently, the movements draw parallels to the historical experiences of Deqiqe Estifanos and Zar'a-Yaeqob.

The challenges have allegedly escalated into systematic persecutions, which are attributed to either expelling the movements from the EOTC or necessitating a more covert operation within the Church (Henok Afework, 2016, pp. 16-17). For instance, the founder of FHMM mentioned earlier has both a civil name and a church name, known as a kiristina sem. However, he primarily utilises his kiristina sem in his professional and teaching roles within the EOTC, specifically as a Memhir Hadiss, a recognised teacher within the church. This distinction helps him separate from his civil identity, ensuring he is not perceived as the same individual, such as being enrolled as a student at the Evangelical Ethiopian Graduate School of Theology.

Moreover, the pioneer of FHMM reveals cases of individuals who have faced ostracism from their families or social circles or have been dismissed from their employment due to their association with FHMM. In response to these challenges, FHMM has initiated an aid program to support those in need (Tsion Seyoum, 2018, p. 7).

The exclusion from the social community experienced by members of various Tähadiso movements (Haniel Kurema Hassen, 2024, p. 11) may also result in being ostracised from significant social groups, such as burial associations ('Edir'), or being denied burial rights in the local cemetery (Hailu Chaklu, 2024, p. 9; Solomon Mekonnen, 2020, p. 16). Instances have even occurred in which marriages were dissolved as a consequence of one spouse's participation in a Tähadiso movement.

Finally, there have also been reports of more brutal and violent persecutions (Alemu Shimalo, 2022, p. 11). It involves imprisonment (Abraham Mamecha, 2023, p. 10) and torture, for example beating (Haniel Kurema Hassen, 2024, p. 9), mutilation (Hailu Chaklu, 2024, p. 6), and cutting with knives (Thomas Alemu, 2024, p. 10).

Additionally, Mahibere Kidusan and various factions within the EOTC that oppose the Tähadiso movements reportedly maintain connections with influential social groups and local police forces (Israel Sisay, 2022, p. 9). There are allegations that they might leverage their influence to persecute proponents of the reform movements, leading to instances of individuals mysteriously disappearing (Andarge Tesera, 2018).

3.3 Religious freedom at stake?

An important question is whether any of these measures constitutes a violation of religious freedom. Determining this is not a straightforward task.

The leadership of the EOTC, as an autonomous organisation, possesses the authority to employ legal measures to counteract actions perceived by a majority of its constituents as inconsistent with their theological beliefs and ecclesiastical practices. This stance is particularly understandable when considering that they perceive the Tähadiso movement as a significant threat to the fundamental existence of the EOTC, viewing the movement's objective as an attempt to transform the EOTC into a Protestant denomination, thereby undermining its traditional foundations.

At the same time, the Tähadiso movements currently enjoy comprehensive freedom to advocate for their cause, both in theory and in practice, outside the EOTC – but even among its members. This level of freedom was unattainable prior to 1974, during which there existed a close relationship between the EOTC and the Ethiopian state. However, present-day Ethiopia upholds the principle of religious freedom, as enshrined in the constitution, whereby no Ethiopian citizen is mandated to be a member of the EOTC. Notably, the current Ethiopian Prime Minister identifies as Pentecostal.

A key question is whether supporters of the Tähadiso movements, as members of the EOTC, possess legal rights to share their critical perspectives during internal discussions and persuade others to join their cause. Additionally, can they effectively exercise this right in practice?

However, should we expect – or even demand – that they enjoy this right and freedom? What constitutes the standard of religious freedom in this context? Who is responsible for determining this standard?

Simultaneously, in regions of Ethiopia where the EOTC is predominant, particularly in rural and remote areas, the practical expression of freedom may be significantly constrained within tightly knit local communities. In such contexts, considerable social pressure is often exerted on individuals to engage in the practices associated with the local Ethiopian Orthodox Church.

The story of FHMM highlights the close ties between influential and hostile factions within the EOTC and local authorities. This closeness raises concerns that actions taken against the Tähadiso movements could blur the lines and escalate into violence, particularly given the aggressive stance that authorities in Ethiopia can adopt towards civilians.

On the other hand, it is somewhat surprising that it is even possible for FHMM and the other Tähadiso movements to carry out such large-scale activities, especially considering the hostility from influential circles within the EOTC. Why haven't they excommunicated FHMM along with the other movements? This could be attributed to a combination of the vastness of the church and the often very unorganised manner in which it operates. For example, the EOTC literature, such as Ye Tehadiso Menafikan Zemecha, points to Tsiwa Mahiberats – special gatherings in honour of the saints, attended by many EOTC members – as a setting where the Tähadiso movements typically operate and recruit supporters (Mahibere Kidusan, 2011). Thus, it is known to the EOTC leaders. Still, they admit being unable to address the issue due to the extensive reach of Tsiwa Mahiberats and the very disorganised nature of their operations (Tsion Seyoum, 2018, p. 8). The same holds true for the network of Sunday schools that both the Tähadiso Movements and the 'counter-reformation' are utilising.

4 Conclusion

This article analyses the relationship between the EOTC and various reform movements that have emerged within this church over the past three decades. It particularly emphasises the opposition these movements have encountered from the EOTC.

In the context of religious freedom and persecution, this serves as a salient example of intra-church conflict. Given that the opposition to the Tähadiso movements from the EOTC is significantly influenced by theological factors, the persecution within this context may be characterised as both *religiously motivated persecution*, which pertains to the perpetrator's motives or intentions rooted in religious beliefs, and *religious persecution*, which focuses on the perpetrator's discriminatory intent primarily directed at victims due to their religious identity or the absence thereof (Sauer & Nel, 2025).

Consequently, this study contributes to a missiological perspective regarding religious freedom and persecution, particularly within an ecumenical context. Pertaining to the historical background of the Tädadiso movements, this took on a concrete expression in relation to the abuses endured by Pentecostal groups at the hands of the Ethiopian state and the EOTC during the 1960s. Notably, two Norwegian missionaries affiliated with the Norwegian Lutheran Mission gathered evidence of these persecutions, which was subsequently presented to the World Council of Churches for consideration, allowing for dialogue with the EOTC, which also held representation within this international ecumenical organisation.

Sauer and Nel (2025) also assert that it is essential to distinguish between the intention to discriminate on religious grounds and religiously motivated persecution. Even if the persecutor's motivations are not of definitional relevance, they are crucial for understanding and countering persecution. This applies to both religious motivations and all other reasons and motives behind discrimination on religious grounds. In light of this, the contextual framework surrounding the relationship between the EOTC and the Tähadiso movement, along with the actions undertaken by the EOTC, is particularly pertinent. The opposition to the Tähadiso movements from the EOTC is significantly motivated by religious considerations. Nonetheless, numerous other factors are influential: the perception of imbalanced competition due to disparities in access to economic resources, the apprehension of a fundamental transformation of the church into a divergent church tradition, and the paramount desire to safeguard the unique Ethiopian identity, history, and culture. Considering this contributes to a comprehensive understanding of the EOTC's perspective, which is indispensable for mitigating the reported abuses and advocating for religious freedom within Ethiopian society.

5 References[7]

Abbreviation: EGST = Ethiopian Graduate School of Theology

5.1 Sources

5.1.1 Oral sources

Andarge Tesera. (2018). [Interview by F. Aa. Rønne]. FAaR.
Andarge Tesera. (2018b, January 12). [Interview by Tsion Seyoum]. FAaR.

5.1.2 Written sources

The Finote Hiwot Mahibere Medahniyalem. (n.d.). *Rules and Regulations of the Finote Hiwot Mahibere Medahniyalem.*

5.2 Unpublished papers (Course papers)

Abel Ayele. (2025). *The Beginning of Zetseat Apostolic Reformation Church in Addis Ababa Ethiopia In 2004 GC*. EGST.
Abraham Mamecha. (2023). *The Relationship Between Evangelical and Ethiopian Orthodox Church (EOC)*. EGST.
Aemere Ashebir. (2014). *The Relationships between African States and Western Missionaries in Africa in the Nineteenth Century. The Relationship Between Emperor Tewodros and Foreign Missionaries*. EGST.
Alemu Shimalo. (2022). *The History and Emergence of Ethiopian Renewal Church (1984-1996) from Ethiopian Orthodox Tewahdo Church (EOTC)*. EGST.
Amaha Bekele. (2021). *The Reformation Movement in Ethiopian Orthodox Tewahdo Church that has resulted in Establishing the Ethiopian Emanuel United Church*. EGST.
Amanuel Genene. (2025). *The Role of Cultural and Historical Significance in the Return of Reformation Members to the Ethiopian Orthodox Tewahedo Church*. EGST.
Asayehegn Legesse. (2020). *Why the Ethiopian Orthodox Church Persecuted the Emerging Evangelical Groups In Western Wellega: A Case in Boji in the 1930's*. EGST.
Daniel Abebe. (2016). *Was the Objective(s) of the Amanuel Renewal Movement succeeded: If not why? If Yes How?* EGST.
Deribe Hibebo. (2018). *The unsuccessfulness of church planting strategy of the Ethiopian Addis Kidan Baptist Church*. EGST.
Elias Lemma Haile. (2018). *The Internal External factors for the Exodus of "MEDHANEALEM MAHBER" from Ethiopian Orthodox Tewahdo Church*. EGST.
Fanos Workalemahu. (2014). *The 'Reformation Movement' of Dekike Estifanos*. EGST.

[7] According to common rules for Ethiopian names, the proper name and the father's name are rendered in that order in the references, overruling the reference style that otherwise applies to Western names.

Genaye Eshetu. (2021). *Comparative Analysis of the Dekike Estifanos and Bible Readers Movement as an Indigenous Rise of the Evangelical Christianity in Ethiopia*. EGST.

Hailu Chaklu. (2024). *Transition of Mahibere Ahaw ministry to an independent Church out of the EOTC*. EGST.

Haniel Kurema Hassen. (2024). *The Emergence of Addis Ababa Emmanuel United Church from Debre Mihret Kidus Michael Church*. EGST.

Henok Afework. (2016). *Comparing Reformation History in Ethiopian Church Between 15th and 20th century*. EGST.

Israel Sisay. (2022). *The Establishment of Ethiopian Emanuel United Church: Case study on the history of Nazret Amanuel Reformation movement*. EGST.

Mahder Eshetu. (2022). *The Distinction between the Ethiopian Evangelicals and Ethiopian Orthodox Church on their View of Aba Estifanos Movement*. EGST.

Melesse Degefa. (2019). *Comparative study of Addis Renewal Church and Ethiopia Medihanialem Renewal Church on their: Doctrine, church tradition, church management, church growth in Addis Ababa, Ethiopia, from 1991 to 2019*. EGST.

Mesfin Kassa. (2016). *The Fire that Quenched for the Time Being at the Beginning of Its Ignition in Ethiopian Church History from 1412-1529*. EGST.

Paulos Fekadu. (2014). *The Italian Occupation and the Establishment of the Ethiopian Patriarchy*. EGST.

Seblewongel Alemu. (2018). *The separation of Emmanuel United Church from Ethiopian Orthodox Tewahdo Church: The case of Mexico Emmanuel United Church*. EGST.

Seifu Desta. (2025). *The Main Cause For The Separation Of Bethania Reformation Church From EOTC And Its Origin*. EGST.

Sofanit T. Abebe. (2014). *Catholicism in Seventeenth Century Ethiopia: Reasons for the Failure of Emperor Susənyos to Catholicize the Empire*. EGST.

Solomon Mekonnen. (2020). *The Dispute between Reformation Movement and the Ethiopia Orthodox Tewahedo Church in Tigray (1991 -2020)* . EGST.

Thomas Alemu. (2024). *Historiography Writing of Ye Huletegnaw Bet Kibir Tehadiso Church*. EGST.

Tsion Seyoum. (2018). *An Undertaking in the EOTC: The Finote Hiwot Mahibere Medihanialem*. EGST.

Yared Temesgen. (n.d.). *Contextual Approach to Evangelize the Evangelized: A Reconstruction of Mission Model Through the Lenses of Qes Badima Yalew*. EGST.

Zewdu Mamo. (2023). *The Survival Mystery of the Lalibela Full Gospel Church under Persecution in the Historical Heritage of the Lalibela Monastery*. EGST.

5.3 Published

Arén, G. (1978). *Evangelical pioneers in Ethiopia: Origins of the Evangelical Church Mekane Yesus*. EFS-förl.; The Evangelical Church Mekane Yesus.

Binns, J. (2020). *The Orthodox Church of Ethiopia: A history*. T & T Clark.

Casalini, C., Choi, E. H., & Ayenachew A. Woldegiyorgis (Eds.). (2021). *Education beyond Europe: Models and traditions before modernities*. Brill.

Dirshaye Menberu. (2005). Estifanos. In *Dictionary of African Christian Biography*. https://dacb.org/stories/ethiopia/estifanos/

Getatchew Haile. (1983). The Cause of the Ǝsṭifanosites: A Fundamentalist Sect in the Church of Ethiopia. *Paideuma, 29*, 93-119. JSTOR.

Getatchew Haile, Lande, A., Rubenson, S. (Eds.). (1998). *The missionary factor in Ethiopia: Papers from a Symposium on the Impact of European Missions on Ethiopian Society, Lund University, August 1996*. Symposium on the Impact of European Missions on Ethiopian Society, Frankfurt am Main; New York. P. Lang.

Getatchew Haile. (2016). *Deqiqa Estifanos: Behigg Amlak*. Getatchew Haile Publishers.

Levine, D. N. (2014). *Wax and gold: Tradition and innovation in Ethiopian culture* (Repr.). Univ. of Chicago Press.

Mahibere Kidusan. (2011). *Ye Tehadiso Menafikan Zemecha: The Mission of Heretical Reformers*. The Ethiopian Orthodox Tewahido Church.

Meron Zeleke & Kiya Gezahegne. (2017). Tähadiso Movement a Myth or Reality?: Inter-Ethiopian Orthodox Tewahdo Church Rivalries. *Journal for the Study of the Religions of Africa and Its Diaspora*, *3*(1), 36-45.

Prunier, G., & Ficquet, É. (Eds.). (2015). *Understanding Contemporary Ethiopia: Monarchy, Revolution and the Legacy of Meles Zenawi*. C. Hurst and Company (Publishers) Limited.

Sauer, C., & Nel, W. (2025). Religious persecution: Definitions, scales, spectrums reflected for the context of theology and missiology. In R. Lilleaasen & C. Sauer (Eds.), *Religious persecution*. VKW.

Seblewengel Daniel. (2019). *Perception and identity: A study of the relationship between the Ethiopian Orthodox Church and evangelical churches in Ethiopia*. Langham Monographs.

Taddesse Tamrat. (1966). Some Notes on the Fifteenth Century Stephanite «Heresy» in the Ethiopian Church. *Rassegna Di Studi Etiopici*, *22*, 103-115. JSTOR.

Taddesse Tamrat. (2009). *Church and State in Ethiopia 1270-1527*. Tsehai Publ.

Tibebe Eshete. (2009). *The evangelical movement in Ethiopia: Resistance and resilience*. Baylor University Press.

Worku Demeke. (2011). A Religious Association Yasewa Mahebar. *Ethiopian Review of Cultures*, *2011*(14), 283-299.

9 Suffering, persecution and martyrdom

Revisiting the Bad Urach Statement

Christof Sauer[1]

Abstract

The evangelical consensus statement on suffering, persecution and martyrdom emanated from a global expert consultation in Bad Urach, Germany, in 2009. Fifteen years later, this essay reviews its impact and briefly reminds of its origin and nature. The Bad Urach Statement is generally appreciated by numerous missiologists and has impacted some major Christian statements. It continues to be cited, as well as ignored or – more seldom – criticised. More than half of its specific content has been referred to in various works. The essay closes with desiderata and suggestions for a future upgrading of the statement.

Keywords: Suffering, persecution, martyrdom, theology, consensus, evangelical.

1 Introduction

The recent review by Brent Hamoud (2024) of *Suffering, persecution and martyrdom* (Sauer & Howell 2010) aroused my interest. Much of it deals with the leading feature of that volume, the *Bad Urach Statement* (BUS), subtitled "Towards an evangelical theology of suffering, persecution and martyrdom for the global church in mission". Hamoud (2024, 8) comes to the conclusion:

1 Christof Sauer (*1963) is part time Professor II at Fjellhaug International University College, and Consultant for its Research Project "Religious Freedom and Religious Persecution"; resident in Germany. Email: ChristofSauer@icloud.com, ORCID iD: 0000-0002-4976-7574. – Readers interested in more details and particularly the genesis of the Bad Urach Statement are referred to a more extensive research manuscript on which this essay is based (Sauer 2025). I wish to thank all colleagues – too numerous to mention – who authorised references to email correspondence, responded to my evaluation of their positions, and particularly made suggestions on which aspects of my recollections and analysis might be of greatest interest to readers.

> "The statement itself is a meaningful accomplishment, ... a thorough document that offers something of substance while also proving widely acceptable to members of the global Church body. ... Overall, it is an achievement in establishing grounds for approaching the challenges (and opportunities) of suffering, persecution, and martyrdom in a way that is productive, faithful, and relevant to a diverse Christian community."

This review triggered my resolve as the principal drafter to revisit the Bad Urach Statement 15 years after its initial publication. The purpose of this essay is to critically examine the impact of the statement: Who refers to the BUS?[2] What aspects are picked up or developed further in the meantime?[3] It is also appropriate to ask whether the BUS still fulfils its purpose of providing a theological framework for theologising on suffering for Christ, persecution and martyrdom (henceforth abbreviated SPM) with an emphasis on the mission of the church.

First the genesis and structure of the statement are clarified, then its reception, followed by an analysis of specific content and concluding suggestions.

2 Roots and origins of the Bad Urach Statement

As the subtitle indicates, the BUS emanates from within the evangelical movement. More specifically, the organiser was the International Institute for Religious Freedom (IIRF, at the time "of the World Evangelical Alliance" [WEA]) founded by Schirrmacher and Sauer in 2005. The consultation was also sponsored by Commissions of the WEA on Religious Liberty and Theology, as well as the Theological Working Group of the Lausanne Movement (for World Evangelization). This cooperation is considered of high symbolic value in the foreword by Schirrmacher and Yogarajah (Sauer & Howell 2010, 12). The emergence of the study process for the BUS was an "outcome of numerous discussions with key role players" I conducted at the WEA General Assembly and its Mission Commission Consultation in 2008 in Pattaya, Thailand (Sauer 2009, 88).

---

2 Extensive searches were conducted on 15 May 2025 (queries: BUS, suffering-persecution-martyrdom, Sauer & Howell) on Google Scholar, Google Books, Google, ProQuest (Dissertations), Academia, WorldCat, IxTheo, Open Access Theological Library (query: persec*). All results were verified in the respective publications. In addition, all citation links for publications on the BUS by Sauer were checked. Villanueva (2017) and Zaki (2022; quoting Sauer & Howelll 2010) could not be accessed.

3 Thus, this survey might be considered a "scoping review", which is appropriate for a little explored field.

2.1 Rationales and role players

The rationales for the BUS are a combination of those stated in the publication itself, the purposes of the institution that took the lead in organising it, and rationales connected to the biographies of its editors.

The BUS itself identifies three challenges arising from the scope of contemporary persecution of Christians around the globe, namely (1) remembering the persecuted, (2) understanding the complexities of persecution, and (3) transforming the lives of the rest of the global body of Christ through the spiritual insights of persecuted Christians (BUS 1.1). Thus, it sees "an urgent need for a deeper evangelical understanding of the theology of the cross with regard to suffering, persecution and martyrdom for Christ and its relevance for the global church in mission" (BUS 1.1).

This fits among the stated aims of the IIRF, one of which is "working towards ... the study of pastoral issues relating to those who are affected" by restrictions of religious freedom (IIRF 2008, 11).

The editorial group of the BUS consisted of Dr. Richard Howell, Prof. Dr. Bernhard Reitsma, and Prof. Dr. mult. Thomas Schirrmacher, beside myself as the chair. I was at the time engaged in post-doctoral research in the field of missiology on how Christians of various traditions around the globe are reacting theologically to SPM, and started building a network of researchers who had contributed to the topic. Based on research and publications starting in my student days (Sauer 1989; 1991; 1994; 1996; 2005; 2010e) I had already called for such a consultation in 1989.

Dr. Richard Howell of New Delhi, India, at the time General Secretary of the Asia Evangelical Alliance acted as a co-convener and co-editor of the consultation compendium. Prof. Dr. Bernhard Reitsma,[4] a Dutch theologian, attended as a general advisor and had already presented a dissertation that interprets the theology of suffering in Romans 8 (Reitsma 1997; cf. Reitsma 2012).

Prof. Dr. mult. Thomas Schirrmacher,[5] a German theologian and human rights expert, had earlier published "70 biblical-theological theses" on a theology of martyrdom (Schirrmacher 1999a; 1999b) and as a director of the IIRF was decisively involved in guiding the consultation initiative.

---

4 See his CV at https://feet-europe.org/posts/2020-bernard-reitsma-featured-author-ejt.

5 See his CV at https://en.wikipedia.org/wiki/Thomas_Schirrmacher and https://thomasschirrmacher.net/bio/biography/ (retrieved 24 April 2025).

2.2 The Bad Urach Consultation 2009 and its publications

The consultation held in September 2009 aimed at

> "bringing the various evangelical theologies from various contexts of either suffering for Christ, persecution for Christ or Christian martyrdom into fuller dialogue; scrutinising and building upon previous consultations and statements; learning the best from theologies of other Christian traditions on the topic; developing a synthesis of evangelical approaches to the topic; and describing remaining differences of opinion." (*IJRF* 2009, 164)

Unfortunately, only few women could be identified at the time who had developed theological expertise on the topic and even fewer were able to attend.

Before the consultation the experts exchanged their most important research insights, and based on the feedback received, I sketched a first draft of a statement. During the consultation this was discussed, and in the course of 2010 augmented and revised by the editorial team, corrected and approved by the participants.

There are two resulting documents which need to be distinguished: The extensive *Bad Urach Statement* was initially published in 2010 as a PDF online and in the consultation compendium (Sauer, ed. 2010a) and later separately as a small book (Sauer, ed. 2010b). It was disseminated globally in printed and digital form, among others at the Lausanne Congress in Cape Town 2010 and is still freely available online today.[6] The *Bad Urach Call*, constitutes a short popularised summary of the BUS and due to its brevity has been included in numerous collections.[7]

In retrospect, I wonder whether the title "Bad Urach Statement", with its difficult to pronounce place name, is an obstacle to the promotion of the document and its content. Might reversing subtitle and title draw more attention?

3 The architecture of the statement

The BUS consists of five parts, namely (1) an introduction, (2) the main part with a "theological consensus and disagreements", (3) a short apologetic part "overcoming current misconceptions and distorted terminology", (4) extensive theological reflections on "practical application [in]

6 https://iirf.global/publications/books/bad-urach-statement/

7 Cf. Taylor, van der Meer and Reimer (2012, 499-502), Johnson et al. (2017, 49-53); German translation "Bad Urach Erklärung" (2010, 28-33).

responding" to SPM, and (5) a very short conclusion, list of signatories and references.

The *introduction* frames SPM as contemporary challenges, set in a wider context of theological interpretation of human suffering, human rights and religious freedom, and offers theological working definitions on suffering for Christ, persecution (following Tieszen 2008 a+b), and martyrdom (following Wespetal 2005 and Schirrmacher 2001).

The core of the BUS, presents *Theological consensus and agreements.* It is divided into 11 subsections, named "aspects" (cf. Table 1), all cutting across the three topics of SPM. Some of these aspects combine multiple related topics under one term.

Table 1: Aspects in the BUS theological framework

#	Aspect	Section title
1	epistemological	The drama of God's history with the world
2	typological	Old Testament models of faithfulness
3	christological	Christ, the suffering servant
4	mimetic	Discipleship: Following in the footsteps of Christ
5	antagonistic	Super-human conflict
6	soteriological	God's salvation and comfort
7	ecclesiological	The body of Christ
8	missiological	God's mission for the church
9	eschatological	The victory of the kingdom of God
10	doxological	The honor of God and his martyrs
11	ethical	Christian ethics of suffering, persecution and martyrdom

This second part consists mainly of a systematic presentation of contents of scripture, based on the foundational role of scripture and the assumption that this is the most likely basis to achieve some degree of consensus across a wide range of contexts. Where available, this is supplemented by systematic theological and ethical reflections by the contributors and in the sources used which gained some degree of consensus.

The short apologetic third part, *Overcoming current misconceptions and distorted terminology*, is summarised from Tieszen (2008 a+b) and Wespetal (2005).

The extensive fourth part on *Practical application* focuses on theological reflection of pastoral and ethical issues concerning a proper Christian response to SPM. Some sections mirror theological foundations in Part 2, now with a praxis focus. While its first four aspects are more of a foundational nature, including individual responses to persecution, the remaining four aspects deal with the collective level, addressing the responsibilities of leadership in church, mission and Christian networks, as well as in theological education and missionary training.

The short *Conclusion* of the BUS finally makes some suggestions on how the BUS could be put to fruitful use.

4 The impact of the BUS

The 66 hits on Google Scholar for *Bad Urach Statement* appear few compared to other major Christian statements. However, they witness a substantive quoting of the BUS in scholarly texts. This section examines general appreciation and promotion, reception in other statements, outstanding engagement with the BUS, and critical reception, silence and ignorance.

4.1 General appreciation and promotion

Richard Howell remarks in retrospect:

> "The Bad Urach Consultation gave the Evangelical Alliance a firm theological and practical foundation for engaging with urgent issues of religious freedom, suffering, and persecution – equipping them to respond with clarity, courage, and compassion in an increasingly challenging world."[8]

Numerous independent statements also appreciate the impact and helpfulness of the BUS. It has been acknowledged among missiologists as "important" (Engelsviken 2020, 6), "extensive" (Payne 2020, 61) and "comprehensive" (Kipfer 2017a, 5).[9] Donald LeRoy Stults (2021, 26), when "looking at persecution and suffering theologically", gives prime place to the BUS, calling it "a foundational document for all who desire to think theologically about suffering and persecution". In most major anthologies considering contemporary persecution of Christians theologically or missiologically since then, the BUS is acknowledged.[10]

---

[8] Private email to author, 27 April 2025.

[9] Engelsviken (2020, 6), Payne (2020, 61), Kipfer (2017a, 5); Chiang et al. (2012, 510) call it "an exceptional resource".

[10] E.g. Taylor et al. (2012), Gravaas et al. (2015), Ireland & Raven (2020), Theocharous (2024).

The BUS was naturally propagated through publications of its editorial team and the other Bad Urach Consultation participants.[11] I made known the contents of the BUS in numerous conference lectures and publications globally – publishing at least 19 contributions that wholly or selectively are based on the BUS.[12] When engaging with theological educators in Asia in a context of oral or illiterate communicators, I developed the illustration of a radiant flower growing out of dirty soil to illustrate core statements of the BUS (Illustration 1).

Illustration 1: Symbolic sketch

4.2 Reception in other Christian statements

The most significant and planned literary impact of the BUS has been on the *Cape Town Commitment* (CTC) 2010 of the Lausanne Movement for World Evangelization. The drafting processes of the CTC and the BUS actually occurred in part simultaneously and were interwoven.

As the editor of the BUS, I received a preliminary draft of Part One of the CTC with the opportunity to give input: This played out on topics such as the Holy Spirit assisting witnesses on trial (CTC I,5), the antagonistic aspect in loving one's enemies (CTC I, 7D; II, B2-D – cf. BUS 2.5;

11 Other members of the editorial group of the BUS, due to different roles, showed little literary engagement with the BUS. Schirrmacher focuses more on securing the funding for widely disseminating the BUS (cf. 2.4 above) and making it known via multiple media releases (Cf. Schirrmacher's Blog: https://thomasschirrmacher.net/?s=urach [e.g. 4 October 2010] and *Bonner Querschnitte/Bonn Profiles* [BQ 118, 147, 153, 159, 489, 490] https://bonn-profiles.net/pdf-archiv/). Several other signatories mentioned the BUS in later publications (Hölzl 2014, 157; Hölzl 2025; Reimer 2012; van der Meer 2011, 155).

12 E.g. summaries: Sauer 2010c; 2010d; 2013b; 2013c; 2014a; specific aspects: Sauer 2013d; 2015a; 2016; 2014b; Sauer & Handayani 2015; transcending BUS: Sauer 2013a; 2021.

2.5.2; 4.2), love calling for solidarity in suffering with the body of Christ (CTC I, 9C – BUS 2.7).

In addition, I could – on invitation – submit specific text modules for Part Two of the CTC, on the topics of suffering for the gospel (CTC II, C2 – BUS 2.6.3; 2.8.1; 2.8.3; 2.8.4; 4.7.3), religious freedom (CTC II, C6 – BUS 1.5.2), and ethical mission, most of which were taken from the substance of the BUS, and included (cf. Sauer 2013a, 83-86; Sauer 2011). Thus, the BUS helped shape some aspects of the CTC as an important mission document of its time.[13]

Soon thereafter, another statement, Christian witness in a multi-religious world, was issued, which also evidences mutual influence with the BUS. This joint statement was released in 2011 after a five-year discussion process by the Vatican, the World Council of Churches and the WEA. While – more importantly – the statement is a major advance in ecumenical understanding, its very succinct contents also have an overlap in several instances with concerns about persecution and religious freedom as voiced in the BUS.[14] Thomas Schirrmacher was the one building the bridge, as he was involved in both statements.

A third, broadly ecumenical statement shows clear influences in theology, tone, commitments, and calls from the BUS and the Bad Urach Call, and may be read with these in the background. The short *Consultation Message* on *Discrimination, persecution, martyrdom: Following Christ together* of the Global Christian Forum (Tirana, Albania, 2015) emerged from the interactions of high level leaders and representatives of various Church traditions gathered to listen to, learn from and stand with discriminated and persecuted Churches and Christians in the world today (von Beek & Miller 2018, 241-244; Johnson et al., 2017, 95-97).[15]

Thus, the BUS has impacted three significant global Christian statements.

---

13 In turn, the draft of the theological foundations of the CTC influenced some phrasing of the BUS. For example, the emphasis on love in the CTC inspired some sections of the BUS, which were not fully completed at that time.

14 Three instances can be identified among the three categories of 'bases', 'principles' and 'recommendations': Base 5: commission to witness despite prohibitions etc.; Principle 6: "Rejection of violence"; Principle 7: "Freedom of religion and belief". In return, the section in the BUS on ethical mission (BUS 2.11.2. "Doing no harm and avoiding unethical means") was influenced by those very ecumenical conversations which had been ongoing since 2006.

15 Schirrmacher and Sauer were members of the planning group of this consultation, and Sauer was the scribe of the group drafting the statement.

4.3 Outstanding engagement with the BUS

Moving to the world of academia, among 14 qualification treatises engaging with the BUS, six authors do so most substantially. Starting with doctoral dissertations, Wolfgang Häde, in his theological interpretation of the accusations against Christians in Turkey, places a strong emphasis on the christological aspect (Häde 2017, 193) while also covering others.[16] He goes far beyond the BUS, making recommendations for appropriate responses by those falsely accused (Häde 2017, 197-260).

Věra Miláčková (2022, 47.63-67) makes repeated reference to "avoiding persecution" by fleeing, when developing a fourfold model of theological perspectives on fleeing persecution.[17] Steven Veach (2021) extensively uses the BUS as a basis for preparing the American Church for persecution by appropriate training.[18] Werner Nicholaas Nel (2020, 35.31-32.40), in a doctorate in law references the BUS as an authority in his discussion of definitions of suffering, persecution and martyrdom in the context of religious epistemology.

Below the PhD level, Brent L. Kipfer (2017a; 2017b) in his Dmin thesis amply quotes from the BUS verbatim and basically summarises its theological core for the sake of examining Christian leadership in a context of persecution.[19] Several other authors use the theological aspects in the BUS as a heuristic grid and benchmark for their empirical research results.[20] Joel Hofer has repeatedly used it, both in examining the interrelations of conversion and persecution in a missiological Masters thesis (Hofer 2020)[21] and in a BA dissertation on pastoral training in contexts of pressure (Hofer 2018).[22] He considers the BUS a helpful grid for covering all essential topics in a theological training program.

Most other such works only refer to the BUS briefly[23] or indirectly via Sauer (2013c)[24]. Beyond that, there are certainly others, who in similar and

16 Also cf. Häde 2025, 70.

17 Cf. Miláčková & Veverková 2022a; 2022b.

18 In some instances, it is hard for the reader to make a direct connection between his statements and the contents of the BUS.

19 Some of this is mirrored in Kipfer 2019.

20 Cf. essays by Belibi (2025) on Sunday school material and Kirkholm (2025) on sermons.

21 Multiple essays emanated from this (Hofer 2021, Hofer & Sauer 2023, Hofer 2025).

22 Also in an unpublished seminary paper on the interpretation of sermons about persecution.

23 Dombong 2017; Laagland Winder 2018, 1.19-21; Johnson 2025, 20.56; Hölzl 2025, 10.38.169.219.229. – Steven Taylor et al. (2023) refer six times to the BUS in Korean.

24 Audi 2016, fn393; Reddy 2017, 31.46-47; Nayak 2021, 27-30.140-145; Marshall 2021, 23.24.46.

less accessible, unpublished works and essays, have engaged with the BUS, particularly in the field of missiology. All works mentioned above and many others, which refer to the BUS briefly only, are considered in the analytical section 5 (cf. Table 3).

In addition, the BUS is used as a resource text and teaching material. I myself used it in theological and missiological courses taught from 2010 to 2022; likely also the late Roy Stults (Wesleyan University, Oklahoma). Beyond that, other lecturers picked it up too, such as Ron Boyd-MacMillan (Fuller Theological Seminary and Pakistan), Wolfgang Häde (CIU Korntal), Martin Heißwolf (Stuttgart), Anna Hampton (online),[25] Jelle Creemers and Tatiana Kopaleishvili (ETF Leuven), T. Jarred Jung (East Asia Theological Seminary Singapore), and Mansour Borji (online[26] in Farsi).[27]

4.4 Critical reception, silence and ignorance

Beyond the affirmative reception, the BUS and the consultation compendium (Sauer & Howell 2010) in which it is reproduced have also received critical review and analysis by a few. We consider these chronologically, before briefly touching on relevant works that are silent about the BUS or ignore it.

Christoffer H. Grundmann (2014, 284) passes a critical verdict on the consultation compendium, which could be read to possibly also include the BUS, as he does not explicitly exclude it:

> "No doubt, this volume is a compact source of information about thinking on these topics in evangelical circles. But it also documents – regrettably – the almost complete shunning of discourse with theology at large, and current missiology in particular, on similar topics, thus making it a somewhat awkward collection of well-intended texts by likeminded people – to the detriment of the cause."

Joel Hofer (2018, 54-55), in his very thorough examination of the BUS, points to some possible shortcomings or missing parts. He suggests the possible deepening of the OT references (such as Psalms and Lamentations)

---

25 Master Class on Shrewdness 2025. https://theologyofrisk.com/masterclass-description; Reference to the BUS is also expected in her forthcoming book *Facing persecution*.

26 Preparing for persecution. https://articleeighteen.com/resources/training/p4p/

27 In future: Ruth Sutcliffe. She also announces that she will be citing the BUS quite a bit in a broader forthcoming book (Emails to author 23 April and 6 June 2025).

and the use of OT characters. He rightly misses lament as a legitimate biblical reaction to persecution (cf. Sauer & Handayani 2015), and the aspect of forgiveness (cf. Howell 2009). He further suggests a more intensive dealing with spiritual realities of demons and dark powers, as well as with the danger of heresies and misguided practices from which contexts of persecution are not spared.

Joel Edwards refers to the BUS as an example of a globally existing "cautious attitude towards deeper engagement in FoRB [freedom of religion or belief]" even among Christian organisations which have expertise in religious liberty (Edwards 2019, 258). He claims that the BUS "made no significant reference to FoRB" (however cf. BUS 1.3; 1.5.2).

Brent Hamoud (2024, 10-12) reviews the BUS as part of Sauer & Howell (2010) and thus it is not always possible to disentangle whether his comments apply to the essays only or to the BUS as well. He misses considerations about the experiences of families, children and communities. He misses the aspect of despair paired with hopefulness. The primarily ideas-based approach feels "detached from human realities and experiences" to him, and he demands empirical research and more stories. He lauds the book for being "helpful in setting parameters of suffering, persecution and martyrdom to clarify what it is and (just as important) what it is not". However, he feels, an opportunity has been missed to attempt solidarity building with other persecuted religious groups due to the "primary focus on theological explanations". Likewise, he thinks that "too little attention is brought to the need for activism and advocacy on behalf of victims of persecution". In his opinion "in many cases the source of the problem is systems, and these need systematic engagement across various levels of cultures and societies".

Regarding his own Middle Eastern context, he finds the arguments "highly relevant": "The way this text offers clarity and a practical framework for the discussion, particularly the Bad Urach Call, is very useful and should be used to communicate what is being experienced in the region". However, it would have had greater relevance if it discussed Islam and abusive political systems: "The failure of theology to consider structural socio-political problems in the region (or elsewhere) is apparent", and thus he opines "this book does not move beyond the traditional theological discourse to address socio-political topics".

Despite his contextually focused criticism, Hamoud concludes "this book sets clear grounded truths that should shape the way we understand suffering, persecution and martyrdom". He highlights the emphasis on the sovereignty of God, the Christocentric outlook, "hopefulness through the pain", and faithful devotion to scriptural truths.

There are indeed few who have taken the trouble to critically and constructively engage with the content of the BUS in view of shortcomings or possible improvement. Based on a broad literature review, one can also note that the BUS has not been cited in some significant dissertations even though their authors were inspired by it.[28] Other more ministry-oriented qualification work sometimes only refers to secondary literature based on the BUS, without proceeding to the original source.[29] There is also a major research project[30] and some professional literature on persecution[31] which ignores the BUS even though it would have been relevant. Nevertheless, they all contribute in some way to the call in the BUS (4.8.2), for "in-depth study of the persecution of the church throughout history."

5 Analysis of overall engagement

This section analyses which content of the BUS receives particular attention in the literature, the geographical origins of these authors, and the chronological distribution of these references.

Some authors find it more convenient to only refer to the short Bad Urach Call[32], but much more frequently the BUS itself is cited. The focus of this systematic analysis is therefore on the BUS.[33]

When statistically evaluating the citations, it becomes apparent that these are unequally spread and some aspects of the BUS are more considered than others (Table 2). The theological core (part 2) with its 11 aspects is most frequently referred to, with several (sub)aspects being cited mul-

---

28 Cf. Graf (2012) participated in Bad Urach but was too close to submission; Goss (2015) participated in the process but wrote in a secular context outside theology; Sutcliffe (2024) was informed by the BUS but advised by examiners to remove contemporary perspectives; Röthlisberger (2021) makes use of essays in Sauer & Howell (2010) but does not cite the BUS.

29 Particularly Sauer (2013c) has been frequently cited, such as by Crudup (2018, 35), Schone (2018), and Ollis (2020).

30 Philpott & Shah (2018) do not include theological perspectives.

31 E.g. IJRTL 2015, Brobbel 2021, and Hampton 2023.

32 E.g. Brink 2013, 4.

33 Cf. Sauer 2025, Table 3 for an exhaustive overview of the detailed analysis. Authors who simply summarise the theological core of the BUS are excluded from this analysis, as well as those who make summary statements that cannot be allocated to a specific section, e.g. Akano (2023, 72). Among those who make comprehensive use of the BUS, or use it as a heuristic grid or benchmark, Belibi (2025) and Kirkholm (2025) have only been selectively noted in Tables 3 and 4.

tiple times (Table 3). This is followed by the introduction,[34] where a substantial number of citations refer to contextualising statements on "contemporary challenges"[35] which are not at the core of the BUS. The most frequently quoted item is the definition of persecution.[36] The BUS thus popularised the definition by Tieszen. The various other definitions are also cited.[37] Practical applications also cumulatively found attention depending on the varied interests of the authors (Table 4). An analysis of the density of citation[38] shows that it decreases progressively section by section (Table 2).[39]

Table 2: Statistics of BUS use				
Section	**Content**	**pp.**	**Citations**	**Density**
1	Introduction	13	24	1,8
2	Theology	25	32	1,3
3	Corrections	5	4	0,8
4	Practical application	27	15	0,6
	Totals	**70**	**75**	**1,1**

34 Cited aspects from BUS 1.2 not separately noted below are: learning from persecuted (Marshall 2021), need for comprehensive systematic theology (Häde 2017, 15), criticism of theology of glory and success (Reddy 2019, 31).

35 Magnitude of persecution (Vyssotskaia 2012, 112; Vyssotskaia & Subedi 2021, 325; Asumang 2017, 53; Hölzl 2025, 169.219); challenge of remembrance, understanding and transformation (Hölzl 2025, 229); forces causing persecution (Budhathoki 2020, 179); critical view of Western culture (Veach 2021); learning from persecuted (Kipfer 2017a, 5-6).

36 Various authors pick up the definition of persecution from BUS 1.6.2, e.g. Stults 2021, 28; Hof 2011; Dombong 2017. For some this is their only reference to the BUS: Falako 2019, 441; Abba 2022, 31; Jung (2023, 24-25; critical of subjectivism of victim's perspective). The more thorough authors usually go straight to the more detailed original in Tieszen (2008a+b) clearly referenced in the BUS, e.g. Nel (2020, 115; differentiation from deprivations of religious freedom); Botha & Nel 2021, 144; Hampton 2023, 8-9.16.

37 Human suffering (Nel 2020,35); human rights (Engelsviken 2020, 6.12.13); religious freedom (CTC II, C6; theological rationales for FORB – Engelsviken 2020, 13; freedom of choice in religious matters = natural right – Nel 2020, 328); suffering for Christ (distinction of suffering because of or by the world or for the world – Niemandt 2019, 95 f); martyrdom (Nel 2020, 115; Johnson 2025, 20).

38 Citations divided by page numbers of respective parts.

39 The rather short BUS section (3) on "overcoming misconceptions" is commended by Hamoud (2024, 8) for correcting harmful claims. Others emphasise the indictment of the Western church for its lack of attention to persecution (Stults 2021: 29; Marshall 2021, 46; Filho & Amado 2012, 359).

Table 3: Engagement with the theological core	
BUS section	**Content**
2. Theological consensus and disagreement	Dialogical character (Hamoud 2024, 8); Use as a grid (Hofer 2020; Belibi 2025; Kirkholm 2025); selective grid (Nayak 2021)
2.1 Epistemological aspect	Persecution as part of God's plan of salvation (Häde 2017, 192-196)
2.3 Christological aspect	Summary (Nayak 2021, 27.143*); Jesus as *martys* (Johnson 2025, 56)
2.3.1 Suffering and persecution in the ministry of Christ	Normativity of Christ for Christian interpretation of SPM (Reddy 2019, 31.46; Nayak 2021, 18*); Persecution in the life of Christ (Reddy 2019, 46-47)
2.4 Mimetic aspect	(discipleship)
2.4.1 The uniqueness of the cross of Christ	Jesus' death as a pattern to follow (Nayak 2021, 17.143*)
2.4.2 The cross of Christ as a pattern of ministry	Kenotic spirituality for missional leadership (Niemandt 2019, 95*); Discipleship on the way of the cross (Tizon 2023, 120; Nayak 2021, 27*); Call for theology of the cross (Dombong 2017)
2.5 Antagonistic aspect	Loving one's enemies (CTC I, 7D; II, B2-D)
2.5.3 Hatred of the world against Christ	Demonological aspect (Häde 2017, 193; Häde 2025, 70); Hostile attitudes to evangelism (Hölzl 2025, 169)
2.6 Soteriological aspect	
2.6.3 Salvation or destruction of the persecutors	Suffering for the gospel (CTC II, C2)
2.6.4 Completing the suffering of Christ	Paul's apostolic suffering being instrumental (Nayak 2021, 28.145; John 2023, 132*)
2.7 Ecclesiological aspect	Solidarity with the persecuted (Sauer 2015a; 2016); Relation of SPM to body of Christ (Nayak 2021, 28.140*); Love calling for solidarity in suffering with the body of Christ (CTC I, 9C)
2.8 Missiological aspect	Suffering for the gospel (CTC II, C2); Relation of SPM to mission (Nayak 2021, 28.143*)
2.8.1 Suffering is a mode of missionary involvement	Suffering and weakness as mode of mission; martyrdom as the most radical form of witness (Niemandt 2019, 95*);

	Suffering unavoidable but not the aim to pursue (Adt 2020, 38)
2.8.4 God can use suffering, persecution and martyrdom to advance his mission	Caution against triumphalistic use of Tertullian's saying (Knippa 2015, 303, fn 31); Regarding the multiplication of the church (Nayak 2021, 145; John 2023, 132 heavily misquoting Sauer 2013c)
2.9 Eschatological aspects	Sauer 2014b
2.10 Doxological aspects	Sauer & Handayani 2015
Legend: ** = quoted from from Sauer 2013c*	

Table 4: Engagement with practical applications	
BUS section	**Content**
4. Practical application: responding to suffering, persecution and martyrdom	
4.1 Christian responses to suffering for Christ	
4.1.1 Perseverance	Assurance that Christ will keep the believers safe in suffering and that they will persevere in faith (Verster 2019, 4-5)
4.1.4 Hope	Laagland-Winder 2018, 1.19-21
4.2 Christian responses to persecution	Sauer 2013d
4.2.1 Avoiding persecution	Theology of fleeing (Miláčková 2022, 47.63-67)
4.2.2 Enduring persecution	Dombong 2017, Reddy 2017, 31.46-47 from Sauer 2013c
4.2.4 Solidarity with the persecuted	Sauer 2015a; 2016
4.3.1 Accepting martyrdom as a grace from God	Bonhoeffer quote (Dombong 2017)
4.4.4 Intercessory prayer for the persecuted	Hibolin 2024
4.5.1 Integration into worship, teaching and counseling	Sunday school material (Belibi 2025); sermons (Kirkholm 2025)

4.6 Practical application for Christian networks and the church	Challenge of capacity building (Kipfer 2017a, 5-6); recommendations which BUS echoes from Asia (Kipfer 2017a, 271)
4.7 Practical applications for mission 4.7.3 Awareness	 Suffering for the gospel (CTC II, C2)
4.8 Practical applications for theological education	Kipfer 2017a, 5-6
4.8.2 Domains to be included [in theol. curricula]	Self-defence as a Christian response to persecution (Jakada 2020, 23)

The geographical origins of the approximately 60 authors[40] captured in this essay and referring to the BUS, are widely scattered, with a clear predominance of Europe, North America and Africa (cf. Table 5). About half of the contributions stem from US-American, German or Nigerian authors.[41]

Table 5: Geographical spread of authors referencing the BUS

#	**Region**	**Comment**
23	Europe	incl. 9 from Germany
17	North America	incl. 15 from US
10	Africa	incl. 5 from Nigeria, 4 from South Africa
5	Asia	
2	Latin America	
1	Middle East	
4	Global	Compendia and anthologies
62	**Total**	

One of the questions posed at the outset was, whether the BUS still fulfils its purpose. This could in part be answered by examining the chronological spread of the references to the BUS. The interesting result is, that since 2017, the references to the BUS by independent authors have markedly increased and remained quite steady compared to the previous

40 My own publications are not included in this analysis.

41 This picture, however, might be slanted by the use of heuristic tools that are more effective for North America and the English speaking world, and the lack of search in other languages such as Spanish or Chinese.

years. Thus, despite my own almost completely ceasing publication of articles emanating from the BUS after 2016, the total annual output of works citing the BUS has remained steady throughout, with an annual average of around 5 works and a peak of 9 in 2021. Thus, it appears safe to say, that the BUS is still attracting the same degree of attention in academia.

Table 6: Chronological spread of reference to the BUS

Year	2010	11	12	13	14	15	16	17	18	19	2020	21	22	23	24	25
Ref	0	2	5	2	2	2	1	6	2	5	6	8	4	6	4	6+
Sauer	5	1	1	4	2	3	2					1				1
Sum	5	3	6	6	4	5	3	6	2	5	6	9	4	6	4	7+

6 Desiderata

This section focuses on what was left to be desired. On the one hand, it will ask "To which sections of the BUS could no references be found?" On the other hand, it will summarise the elements or perspectives the critics missed in the BUS.

From the core Part 2 of the BUS, the one aspect that appears completely neglected in the reception is the typological aspect, referring to OT models of faithfulness (2.2). The doxological aspect (2.10) seems to be little referenced, except by myself. The ethical aspects (2.11) are not referred to except for "not pursuing persecution". Among the BUS reflections on practical applications, three appear most neglected among the references to the BUS: general Christian responses (4.1) by the individual or the local church, practical applications for mission (4.7), and theological education (4.8). Otherwise, the neglect is limited to specific sub-aspects as listed in Table 7. This poses the challenge to make the BUS, and particularly its neglected aspects better known.

Obviously, the much more far-reaching question, namely which recommendations of the BUS remain to be implemented in praxis, is a broad field which is beyond the scope of this article. But it appears safe to say, that most recommendations for church, mission and theological education still await broad implementation, and, towards this end, more academic dissemination.

Table 7: Neglected aspects of the BUS
(2. Theological consensus and disagreements)
2.2 Old Testament models of faithfulness (typological aspects) 2.2.1. Suffering for faithfulness and obedience to God 2.2.2. Martyrdom of the prophets of God
2.6.1. The seriousness of confessing Christ [soteriological aspects] 2.6.2. Trinitarian divine and angelic assistance
2.9.1. Resurrection power [eschatological aspects] 2.9.3. Expectation of the returning Lord – as bridegroom, judge and king
2.10 The honor of God and his martyrs (doxological aspects)[b)] 2.10.1. God is honored by his witnesses 2.10.2. God honors those suffering and martyred for his sake 2.10.3. God promises heavenly reward
2.11 Christian ethics of suffering, persecution and martyrdom (ethical aspects) 2.11.1. Pursuit of holiness and not of persecution[a)] 2.11.2. Doing no harm and avoiding unethical means 2.11.3. Loyal citizenship and primary allegiance to God
(4. Practical application: responding to SPM)
4.1 Christian response to suffering for Christ[a)] Love, faith, joy, peace, patience, kindness, goodness, faithfulness, gentleness, self-control
4.3.2. Rightly remembering martyrs
4.4 Practical applications for the individual Christian[a)] 4.4.1. The practice of an 'evangelical spirituality' 4.4.2. Nurturing a loving relationship with Christ
4.5 Practical applications for the local church[a)] 4.5.1. Integration into worship, teaching and counseling[a)] 4.5.3. Transitioning to situations of lesser persecution
4.7 Practical applications for mission[a)]
(4.8 Practical applications for theological education) 4.8.1. The place of the topic in theological curricula 4.8.3. Steps for implementation
Legend: *Rows in brackets only provide structure, they are not wholly neglected.* *a) Several subtopics of this section have been neglected, but not all.* *b) Beyond the contributions of Sauer, this topic seems neglected.*

Beyond the challenge of making better know what is already in the BUS, there are particular characteristics and aspects of the BUS, that should be improved according to its critics (cf. section 4.4 above). The following additional issues could be considered in a potential future upgrading of the BUS.

In general, a more intensive interaction with scholarly works in general and with related fields, such as theological interpretations of vulnerability, suffering and illness could sharpen some aspects (cf. Grundmann). This would likely be a mammoth undertaking. However, a new generation of scholars might be ready for it. More scholarly works have been published in the meantime that promise usefulness for contemporary applications.

An upgrading of the BUS could also include new elements such as structural injustice and its prophetic denouncement, as well as more attention to communal realities (cf. Hamoud). References to the OT characters[42] and scriptures, such as Psalms and Lamentations could be deepened. Lament should be included as a legitimate biblical reaction to persecution. The aspect of forgiveness could be strengthened; possibly also the questions of how to deal with spiritual realities of demons and dark powers, and the danger of heresies and misguided practices from which contexts of persecution are not spared (cf. Hofer 2018, 54-55). More attention could also be given to the different expressions of persecution for women and men, as well as for children and other multiply vulnerable groups, and whether these require different or additional theological interpretations and practical Christian responses.

According to Sauer and Nel (2025) the definition of persecution based on Tieszen might need further fine-tuning. I also maintain that the doxological aspect could be made more dominant as the overall frame, and not only the theological culmination point (Sauer 2013a). This could be used as a lens for revisiting the BUS.

Beyond the voices above, one might ask, whether the BUS would have a different tone if more women had participated in its drafting. All this could be attempted with a potential future upgrading of the BUS.

7 Summary and conclusion

This essay has analysed the reception of the Bad Urach statement and elucidated its origins and nature. The rationales for the BUS lie in contemporary challenges of persecution of Christians, calling for a deeper theological understanding of suffering for Christ, persecution and martyrdom.

Does the BUS achieve the aim to provide a "benchmark and stepping stone for future reflection on the topic" (BUS 1.2) or is Knippa (2015, 303 fn18) right in claiming that it has "not received much attention in the church at large". If "the church at large" emphasises the roughly three

42 Cf. Pedersen (2025) on persecution of others by OT prophets.

quarters of global Christianity not affiliated with or represented by the World Evangelical Alliance, no evidence to the contrary to Knippa's claim can be produced. If the BUS, however, is considered as an attempt of influencing mainly evangelical theology and missiology, including theological education and missionary training and practice, it can be concluded: (1) The BUS has contributed to shaping three major Christian statements of the time; (2) It continuously gains a significant hearing among some evangelical missiologists as well as mission practitioners in various parts of the world; (3) However, there is still a long way for its theological stance to be said to generally shape evangelical theology at large or for its recommendations to be broadly implemented.

Maybe it is indeed time to revisit the Bad Urach Statement thoroughly. It should also be made better known and available outside academic circles. It should be applied to better practically serve Christians under pressure for their faith. As a mission director wrote to me: "More can be done with the Bad Urach Statement".

8 References

Abba, W. K. (2022). A systematic persecution of Christians and the Church in Northern Nigeria. *JORAS*, 11, 30-44.

Adt, M. (2020). *Scope and limits of missionary activities.* [MA Human Rights]. University Erlangen-Nürnberg.

Akano, B. I. (2023). Disciple-making movement as an effective operational model for Christian missions amid insecurity. *Missionalia*, 51(1), 70+.

Asumang, A. (2017). Bearing witness nicodemously: A Christomorphic assessment of crypto-discipleship in John 7. *Conspectus*, 24, 1-63.

Audi, M. (2016). *World Christianity in crisis: Glocalization, re-transmission, and Boko Haram's challenge to Nigerian Baptists (2000-2012).* [PhD]. Southwestern Baptist Theological Seminary (published by LAP, 2019).

Bad Urach Erklärung: Unser Aufruf an die Gemeinde: Zum Verständnis von Leiden, Verfolgung und Martyrium für die weltweite Gemeinde in ihrer Mission. *Märtyrer 2010: Das Jahrbuch zur Christenverfolgung heute,* 15, 28-33. [German translation of Bad Urach Call]

Belibi, T. (2025). Challenging stories for children: Addressing persecuted Christians in Sunday school. In R. Lilleaasen & C. Sauer (Eds.), *Religious persecution*. VKW.

Botha, C. & Nel, W. N. (2021). The role of religious identity in determining the "mode of persecution" for crimes against humanity [Afrikaans]. *Tydskrif vir Geesteswetenskappe*, 61(1), 128-154.

Brink, E. R., et al. (2013). "Blessed are the persecuted": Planning multiethnic worship, highlighting resources from the suffering church. Calvin University, Symposium on Worship Archive. 7. https://digitalcommons.calvin.edu/cgi/viewcontent.cgi?article=1321&context=uni-cicw-symposium

Brobbel, F. A. (2021). *Trouble on the way: Persecution in the Christian life.* Genesis.

Budhathoki, R. K. (2020). The accused Church in Nepal: reasons and response. *JAET*, 24(2), 177-197.
Chiang, S., Chiang, R., & O'Connell, B. F. (2012). Select annotated bibliography on persecution, suffering and martyrdom. In B. Taylor et al. (Eds.), *Sorrow and Blood* (pp. 503-512). WCL.
Crudup, N. L. (2018). *The religious persecution of Christians* [Dmin]. Liberty University.
Dombong, J. N. (2017). *The impact on and the response of the ECWA to the violent activities of Boko Haram in Northern Nigeria* [MTh Missiology]. Stellenbosch University.
Edwards, J. N. P. (2019). *An exploration into Christian engagement in freedom of religion or belief* [Doctor of Theology and Ministry]. Durham University.
Engelsviken, T. (2020). Misjon og religionsfrihet – samsvar eller spenning? *Dansk Tidsskrift for Teologi og Kirke*, 1, 5-34.
Falako, F. O. (2019). "You will be arrested, persecuted and killed": Nigerian realities and the question of attitude to organized persecution. *Humanities and Social Sciences Review*, 09(01), 441-448.
Filho, P. M. & Amado, M. (2012). Preparing both church and local missionaries: Global South: A view from Brazil. In B. Taylor et al. (Eds.), *Sorrow and Blood* (pp. 357-361). WCL.
Goss, G. (2015). *Participatory action research on emerging practice in psychological interventions for survivors of religious persecution* [Doctor of Social Work]. Capella University.
Graf, E. (2012). *Durch Leiden geprägt: Die gegenwärtigen Leidenserfahrungen der indischen Nethanja-Kirche mit einem Blick auf die paulinischen Gemeinden* [PhD]. TU Dortmund (2012). LIT.
Gravaas, H. A., et al. (Eds.). (2015). *Freedom of Belief and Christian Mission*. (Regnum Edinburgh Centenary Series, 28). Regnum; Wipf & Stock.
Grundmann, C. (2014). Book review of C. Sauer & R. Howell (Eds.)(2010), Suffering, persecution and martyrdom. *Mission Studies*, 31, 281-309.
Häde, W. (2017). *Anschuldigungen und Antwort des Glaubens: Wahrnehmung von Christen in türkischen Tageszeitungen und Maßstäbe für eine christliche Reaktion*. Lit.
Häde, W. (2025). Understanding origins of discrimination and reflecting on Christian responses: A case study on Turkey. *IJRF*, 18(1), 65-75.
Hamoud, B. (2024). South Africa (and Germany): Suffering, persecution and martyrdom: Theological reflections. In M. Theocharous (Ed.), *Suffering and persecution*. (Rethinking the church in the 21st century), (pp. 7-14). Langham.
Hampton, A. (2023). *Facing fear: The journey to mature courage in risk and persecution*. WCL.
Hibolin, A. (2024). *Solidaritet och enhet i förbön för förföljda kristna: En fenomenologisk undersökning av förbön som liturgisk handling i en förföljelsekontext* [BA]. Lund University. [Solidarity and unity in intercession for persecuted Christians: A phenomenological examination of intercession as a liturgical act in a context of persecution].
Hof, E. (2011). Violence, hatred and marginalization: incorporating the perspective of persecution in missiology. https://www.academia.edu/1688950/Violence_hatred_and_marginalization_incorporating_the_perspective_of_persecution_in_missiology
Hofer, J. (2018). *Pastorenschulung im Kontext von Bedrängnis Implementierung theologischer Kerninhalte zum Thema ‚Verfolgung' am Beispiel vom Bad Urach Statement und der Open-Doors-Schulung „Theology of Persecution and Discipleship"* [BA]. STH Basel.

Hofer, J. (2020). *Zusammenhänge von Konversion und Verfolgung. Eine missiologische Untersuchung ausgehend von der Regnum Edinburgh Centenary Series.* [MTh]. STH Basel.

Hofer, J. (2021). Christliche Erfahrungen von Konversion und Verfolgung: Eine theologische Einordnung der Zusammenhänge. *Evangelische Missiologie*, 37(2), 88-102.

Hofer, J. (2025). Interrelations between conversion and persecution, In R. Lilleaasen & C. Sauer (Eds.), *Religious persecution*. VKW.

Hofer, J. & Sauer, C. (2023). Zusammenhänge von Konversion und Verfolgung: Vorschlag einer Typologie. *ZMR*, 107(3-4), 356-371.

Hölzl, M. J. (2014). Religious monopoly and the loss of religious freedom in Christendom. *IJRF* 7(1/2), 157-174. - Simultaneously published as: The Era of Constantine. In H. A. Gravaas et al. (Eds.) (2015), *Freedom of belief and Christian mission* (pp. 79-92). Regnum.

Hölzl, M. J. (2025). *Nonconformist anticipations of post-Christendom mission: Exemplified in John Bunyan and John Wesley* [PhD]. University of Manchester.

Howell, R. (2009). Christian suffering and martyrdom: An opportunity for forgiveness and reconciliation. *IJRF* 2(2), 13-27. – Reprinted 2010 In C. Sauer & R. Howell (Eds.), *Suffering, persecution and martyrdom – theological reflections* (pp. 343-356). AcadSA; VKW.

International Institute for Religious Freedom (IIRF) (2008). Introducing the International Institute for Religious Freedom. *IJRF*, 1, 11-12.

Ireland, J. M. & Raven M. L. K. (Eds.) (2020). *Practicing hope: Missions and global crises.* (EMS 28). WCL.

Jakada, Y. T. (2024). *Through the flames: Early Christian responses to persecution and implications for Christians in Northern Nigeria* [PhD, Asbury Theological Seminar 2020]. Pickwick.

John, W. (2023). *South Karnataka Riots between 1998-2008: Its impact on Christians then and now* [Dmin]. Asbury.

Johnson, L. S. (2025). *Martyrs and riskers: Examining the definition of Christian martyrdom and proposing a new term to honor Christians faithful unto death for Jesus's sake.* [PhD]. Southeastern Baptist Theological Seminary.

Johnson, T. K., Schirrmacher, T. & Sauer, C. (Eds.) (2017). *Global Declarations on Freedom of Religion or Belief and Human Rights.* (The WEA Global Issues Series, 18). VKW.

Jung, T. J. (2023). *Costly Kuyperianism: Neo-Calvinist public theology in a context of persecution with a focus on Pastor Wang Yi* [PhD]. Southeastern Baptist Theological Seminary.

Kipfer, B. L. (2017a). *Persecuted and thriving: Meserete Kristos Church leadership during the Ethiopian revolution (1974-1991).* [D. Min]. Gordon-Conwell Theological Seminary.

Kipfer, B. L. (2017b). Thriving under persecution: Meserete Kristos Church leadership during the Ethiopian revolution (1974-1991). *Mennonite Quarterly Review*, 91: 297-369. [Condensed D. Min.]

Kipfer, B. L. (2019). Overlooked Mentors: What can persecuted Christians teach us about leadership? *Journal of Global Christianity*, 5(1) 16-33. - (also in French, Spanish, Arabic, Chinese)

Kirkholm, K. K. (2025). "If the world hates you": Persecution in sermons. In R. Lilleaasen & C. Sauer (Eds.), *Religious persecution*. VKW.

Knippa, M. (2015). No "lions of gory mane": Persecution and loss of predominance in American Christianity. *Concordia Journal*, Fall, 293-306.

Laagland Winder, P. (2018). *Discussing persecution and hope: Perspectives of Christian faith-based organizations supporting persecuted Christians and leaders of persecuted communities.* [MA Theology]. ETF Leuven.

Marshall, J. L. (2021). *The relationship between contemporary evangelical church leadership and church discipleship formation.* [D. Ed]. Liberty University.

Miláčková, V. (2022). *Practical-theological aspects of fleeing as a result of religious persecution of Christians from Iraq and Egypt* [PhD]. Charles University Prague.

Miláčková, V. & Veverková, K. (2022a). Theology of fleeing from persecution. *Egyháztörténeti Szemle [Church History Review]*, 23(2), 124-139. [= (2025). A theology of fleeing from persecution. In R. Lilleaasen & C. Sauer (Eds.), *Religious persecution.* VKW.]

Miláčková, V. & Veverková, K. (2022b). Theologie der Flucht vor Verfolgung. *Historia Ecclesiastica,* 13(1), 184-196.

Nayak, L. K. (2021). *Kandhamal riot 2008: Its impact on current and future Christian community* [Dmin]. Asbury.

Nel, W. (2020). *Grievous religious persecution: A conceptualization of crimes against humanity of religious persecution.* VKW.

Niemandt, N. (2019). *Missional leadership.* AOSIS.

Ollis, J. (2020). *An examination of the global refugee crisis – How have we hurt? How can we help? – With special emphasis on enhancing resilience in the Somali population resettled in Columbus, Ohio* [Dmin]. George Fox University.

Pedersen, H. S. (2025). The zealous ones: Ambiguous models of faithfulness in the Hebrew Bible. In R. Lilleaasen & C. Sauer (Eds.), *Religious persecution.* VKW.

Philpott, D. & Shah, T. S. (2018). *Under Caesar's sword: How Christians respond to persecution.* Cambridge University Press.

Reddy, J. C. (2019). *The knowledge of end-time prophetic scriptures prepares believers at Northcliffe Baptist Church to expect religious persecution* [Dmin]. Liberty University.

Reimer, R. (2012). Christian responses to suffering, persecution and martyrdom. In W. D. Taylor et al. (Eds.), *Sorrow and Blood* (pp. 23-30). WCL.

Reitsma, B. J. G. (1997). *Geest en schepping: een bijbels theologische bijdrage aan de systematische doordenking van de verhouding van de Geest van God tot de geschapen werkelijkheid.* [PhD Leiden]. Boekencentrum.

Reitsma, B. J. G. (2012). Health, wealth and prosperity: A biblical-theological reflection. In C. van der Kooi, E. van Staalduine-Sulman, A. W. Zwiep (Eds.), *Evangelical theology in transition* (pp. 164-181). VU University Press.

Röthlisberger, D. (2021). *Hilfe und Selbsthilfe für verfolgte Christen: Eine Studie zum neutestamentlichen Ethos.* Evangelische Verlagsanstalt.

Sauer, C. (1989). *The Lausanne Movement and the pathway of the cross: A study of the relevance of suffering, persecution and martyrdom for Christ's sake in the publications of the Lausanne Committee for World Evangelization, and an attempt toward 'a theology of the pathway of the cross that leads to glory'.* Privately printed.

Sauer, C. (1991). *Mission und Martyrium: Die Bedeutung Karl Hartensteins für die evangelikale Suche nach einer Theologie des Martyriums* [MTh equivalent thesis, Tübingen University]. Privately printed.

Sauer, C. (1994). *Mission und Martyrium. Studien zu Karl Hartenstein und zur Lausanner Bewegung.* VKW.

Sauer, C. (1996). Die Bedeutung von Leiden und Martyrium für die Mission nach Karl Hartenstein. In F. Lamparter (Ed.), *Ein Leben in weltweitem Horizont. Beiträge zum 100. Geburtstag von Karl Hartenstein* (pp. 96-111). VKW.

Sauer, C. (2005). Appendix 1: Terminology and definitions of suffering, persecution and martyrdom; Appendix 2: Six New Testament aspects of martyrdom. In P. Sookhdeo (Ed.), *The Persecuted Church.* (Lausanne Occasional Paper 32) (pp. 69-70) – Also published in D. Claydon (Ed.), (2005). *A New Vision, A New Heart, A Renewed Call. 2004 Forum - LOP Compendium*. WCL.

Sauer, C. (2009). Between advocacy and readiness to suffer: Religious liberty and persecution of Christians as topics at the World Evangelical Alliance General Assembly and its Mission Commission Consultation 2008. *IJRF*, 2(1), 73-91.

Sauer, C. (2010c). Mission in bold humility. *IJRF*, 3(1), 65-79.

Sauer, C. (2010d). Suffering and Persecution as a mode of evangelism. *The South African Baptist Journal of Theology*, 19, 63-73.

Sauer, C. (2010e). Towards a theology of "mission under the cross": a contribution from Germany by Karl Hartenstein. In C. Sauer and R. Howell (Eds.), *Suffering, persecution and martyrdom - theological reflections* (pp. 257-285). AcadSA; VKW.

Sauer, C. (2011). International Institute for Religious Freedom welcomes Cape Town Commitment: Sauer commends The Lausanne Movement for timely statement. *Bonner Querschnitte* 05 (159), https://bonner-querschnitte.de/wp-content/uploads/BQs/BQ0159eng.pdf

Sauer, C. (2013a). *Martyrium und Mission im Kontext: Ausgewählte theologische Positionen aus der weltweiten Christenheit* [Habilitation]. Protestant University Wuppertal.

Sauer, C. (2013b). Suffering, persecution and martyrdom in the witnessing church. In: B. Nicholls (Ed.), *Light for our Path: the authority meaning and mission of Scripture for our world* (pp. 238-250). Asia Theological Association.

Sauer, C. (2013c). Theology of persecution and martyrdom; an example in globalizing theology. *ERT*, 37(3), 267-274.

Sauer, C. (2013d). 'To flee or not to flee': Responses to persecution and the issue of relocation. *Missionalia*, 40(1/2), 53-65.

Sauer, C. (2014a). A theology of persecution and martyrdom: An example in globalizing theology. In G. L. Heath & S. M. Studebaker (Eds.). *The globalization of Christianity: Implications for Christian ministry and theology* (pp. 143-153). McMaster Divinity College Press; Pickwick Publications.

Sauer, C. (2014b). Ist Martyrium das Ende? – Wie die Wahrnehmung von Bedrängnis, Verfolgung und Martyrium die Zukunftserwartung beeinflusst. In H. Afflerbach et al. (Eds.), *Reich Gottes - Veränderung - Zukunft: Theologie des Reiches Gottes im Horizont der Eschatologie.* (GBFE Jahrbuch 2014) (pp. 215-235). epubli.

Sauer, C. (2015a). Christian solidarity in the face of discrimination and persecution. In H. A. Gravaas et al. (Eds.), *Freedom of Belief and Christian Mission* (pp. 452-64). Regnum.

Sauer, C. (2015b). Persecution and martyrdom in scripture and today. In B. Nicholls (Ed). *Love God, love your neighbor: Our Christian engagement with contemporary Islam*, Barnabas Fund.

Sauer, C. (2016). Christliche Solidarität angesichts von Diskriminierung und Verfolgung. In T. Schirrmacher et al. (Eds.), *Jahrbuch Verfolgung und Diskriminierung von Christen heute 2016* (pp. 57-71). VKW.

Sauer, C. (2021). *Martyrium und Mission im Kontext: Analyse ausgewählter theologischer Positionen aus der weltweiten Christenheit.* (MF.NF, 37), Erlanger Verlag für Mission und Ökumene. – (revised and updated version of major part of post-doc habilitation thesis completed in 2013).

Sauer, C. (2025). Suffering, persecution and martyrdom: Revisiting and re-introducing the Bad Urach Statement: A research documentation. (IIRF Reports). www.iirf.global [forthcoming].

Sauer, C. (Ed.) (2010a). The Bad Urach Statement: Towards an evangelical theology of suffering, persecution and martyrdom for the global church in mission. In C. Sauer & R. Howell (Eds.), *Suffering, persecution and martyrdom: Theological reflections* (pp. 27-106). AcadSA; VKW.

Sauer, C. (Ed.) (2010b). *Bad Urach Statement: Towards an evangelical theology of suffering, persecution and martyrdom for the global church in mission.* (The WEA Global Issues Series, 9). VKW. (2nd ed 2013)

Sauer, C., & Handayani, D. M. (2015). A doxological framework for interpreting discrimination, persecution and martyrdom. In H. A. Gravaas et al. (Eds.), *Freedom of belief and Christian mission* (pp. 47-57). Regnum.

Sauer, C., & Howell, R. (Eds.) (2010). *Suffering, persecution and martyrdom: Theological reflections.* AcadSA; VKW.

Sauer, C., & Nel, W. (2025). Religious persecution: Definitions, scales, spectrums reflected for the context of theology and missiology, In R. Lilleaasen & C. Sauer (Eds.), *Religious persecution*. VKW.

Schirrmacher, T. (1999a). *Christenverfolgung geht uns alle an: Auf dem Weg zu einer Theologie des Martyriums.* idea; VKW (2001², 2011).

Schirrmacher, T. (1999b). *The persecution of Christians concerns us all: Towards a theology of martyrdom: 70 biblical-theological theses written for the German Evangelical Alliance and its Religious Liberty Commission.* VKW/RVB (2001; 2008²; 2018).

Schone, B. M. (2018). *Persecution and the Church: Why continual study of the persecuted Church matters* [MDiv]. Wisconsin Lutheran Seminary.

Stults, D. L. (2021). Looking at persecution and suffering theologically: Initial thoughts. *IJRF* 14(1/2), 25-37.

Sutcliffe, R. (2024). *Blessed victors: Theology of persecution in the Third Century Church.* T&T Clark.

Taylor, S., et al. (2023). 고난과 하나님의 선교: 선교적 해석학으로 본 고난의 의미 [*Suffering and God's mission: The meaning of suffering from a missionary hermeneutic perspective*]. ebook IVP South Korea/Institute for Missional Theology.

Taylor, W. D., et al. (Eds.) (2012), *Sorrow and blood: Christian mission in contexts of suffering, persecution and martyrdom.* WCL.

The global witness of the reformed faith (2015). *Unio Cum Christo: International Journal of Reformed Theology and Life* 1(1-2).

The Lausanne Movement (2011). *The Cape Town Commitment: A confession of faith and a call to action.* https://lausanne.org/statement/ctcommitment

Theocharous, M. (Ed.) (2024). *Suffering and persecution.* (Rethinking the church in the 21st century) (pp. 7-14). Langham.

Tieszen, C. L. (2008a). Towards redefining persecution. *IJRF*, (1)67-80.

Tieszen, C. L. (2008b). *Re-examining religious persecution: Constructing a framework for understanding persecution* (Religious Freedom Series, 1). AcadSA Publishing; VKW.

Tizon, A. (2023). *Christ among the classes: The rich, the poor, and the mission of the church.* Orbis.

Van der Meer, A. (2011). Book review of Sauer & Howell (2010), Suffering, persecution and martyrdom. *IJRF* 4(1), 155-6.

Veach, S. (2021). *In preparation of apostasia: Persecution against American Christians within an Enochian worldview as informed by a philosophy of death* [DTh]. Forge Theological Seminary.

Verster, P. (2019). The perseverance of the saints, persecution and mission, and its implications for Reformed churches. *In die Skriflig*, 53(3), a2446. https://doi.org/ 10.4102/ ids.v53i3.2446

Villanueva, F. G. (2017). *It's ok to be not ok: Preaching the lament Psalms.* Langham.

von Beek, H. & Miller L. on behalf of Global Christian Forum (Eds.) (2018). *Discrimination, persecution, martyrdom: Following Christ together. Report of the global consultation, Tirana, Albania 2-4 November 2015.* VKW. – (Consultation message, pp. 241-244) [previously in Johnson et al. (2017), Global declarations (pp. 57-62). VKW]

Vyssotskaia, A. (2012). Theological education in the context of persecution and economic hardship: Focus on TEE in Central Asia. *IJRF* 5(2): 111-122.

Vyssotskaia, A. & Subedi, T. (2021). Chapter 12 – TEE as a tool for providing theological education to churches facing persecution and poverty. In D. Burke et al. (Eds.), *TEE for the 21st century: Tools to equip and empower God's people for his mission*. Langham.

Wespethal, T. (2023). *Martyrdom and the furtherance of God's plan: The value of dying for the Christian faith*. Kindle edition. Amazon.

World Council of Churches, Pontifical Council for Interreligious Dialogue, World Evangelical Alliance (2011). *Christian witness in a multi-religious world: Recommendations for conduct.* https://www.worldevangelicals.org/pdf/1106Christian_Witness_in_a_Multi-Religious_World.pdf

Zaki, A. E. (2022). *As those with hope: Crisis preaching in the Protestant Church of Egypt during and post the Arab Spring* [PhD]. Fuller.

10 From Good Friday to Resurrection

The Holy Saturday of the persecuted church

Sara Afshari[1]

Abstract

This essay develops a theology of persecution through the lens of Holy Saturday, the silent day between crucifixion and resurrection. It argues that the persecuted church dwells not only in Good Friday's suffering or Easter's hope, but in the in-between space of fear, abandonment, and sacred waiting. Grounded in the story of the Episcopal Church in Kerman, Iran, the essay frames persecution through three interwoven narratives: the disciples' fear and disorientation, Christ's descent into abandonment, and the Triune God's shared suffering. Holy Saturday is revealed as a theological space where faith endures in silence, identity is tested, and hope is gestated in obscurity. This descent is not defeat, but sacred solidarity with Christ. The essay invites the global church into deeper empathy – not through triumphalist narratives, but by dwelling with the persecuted in their silence, waiting, and wounds, where the seeds of resurrection are quietly sown.

Keywords: Theology of Holy Saturday, persecution and suffering, Iranian Christianity, sacred waiting, resilience, theology of descent.

1 Introduction: A theology hidden in the silence between

Persecution is not new to the Christian story. From the early church to the present, Christians have faced arrest, torture, isolation, exile, and even martyrdom (Sauer & Howell, 2010). Yet, Christian theology has often struggled to articulate a framework that accounts not only for the visible

1 Dr. Sara Afshari is originally from Iran. She is a Research Tutor at Oxford Centre for Mission Studies. She received her PhD from Edinburgh University in Media Religion and Culture. She is co-founder and former Executive Director of SAT-7 PARS, a Christian television channel in Farsi/Persian language. Email: safshari@ocms.ac.uk, ORCID iD: 0000-0003-4850-0306.

pain of Good Friday or the hope of Easter Sunday but for the long, uncertain silence in between. That silence – Holy Saturday – has remained theologically under-explored, even though it may best reflect the lived experience of the persecuted church today.

This essay proposes a theological reading of persecution through the lens of Holy Saturday. It invites us to consider what happens when the church is no longer shouting in victory or crying out in defeat, but waiting in fear and uncertainty. It is in this silence, in the tomb, that the persecuted church is not absent from the story of Christ, but deeply embedded in it.

Drawing from the lived experience of the Episcopal Church in Kerman, Iran (St Andreas), and grounded in biblical and theological reflection, this essay introduces a framework of descent. Here, descent does not mean theological collapse, but sacred solidarity with Christ, who also descended. Holy Saturday is more than a historical day between events – it is a theological space in which the persecuted church learns to wait, grieve, endure, and trust. It is here that faith is stripped bare, identity is questioned, and theology emerges not in declarations, but in whispers, tears, and prayers.

This framework connects three interwoven stories: The disciples in hiding, caught between hope and despair, embody the existential questions of the persecuted church: Who are we now? Christ in descent, bearing the full weight of sin, abandonment, and silence, becomes the theological and spiritual centre of persecuted endurance. The Triune God – Father grieving, Son descending, and Spirit hovering (Balthasar, 1988, 16-18) – remains mysteriously and painfully present throughout, calling the global church into solidarity.

These stories converge to form a theology of persecution rooted in communal endurance, sacred waiting, and divine descent. The silence of Holy Saturday does not deny the pain of persecution; it gathers it into the heart of God. The descent of Christ into death does not bypass suffering but enters into it fully, affirming that God is not only with us on the mountaintop but also in the grave.

This essay does not seek to finalise a theology of persecution but to begin a conversation. Much more is needed to build a comprehensive theological framework of Holy Saturday as it relates to persecution. What follows is a sketch – a scaffold upon which future theological, pastoral, and ecclesial work can be constructed. The intent is not to resolve mystery but to dwell in it – to say that in the silence between Friday and Sunday, the church still breathes, still prays, and still belongs to Christ.

The outline of this chapter is as follows: I begin by introducing the story of the Kerman church as a lived case study. I then frame the concept of persecution through the lens of Holy Saturday, exploring how silence and suffering become theologically significant. The next section reflects on the experience of the disciples on Holy Saturday, offering insight into fear, disorientation, and identity crisis within persecuted communities. This is followed by a theological exploration of Christ's descent, focusing on his solidarity with human suffering and his redemptive presence even in divine absence. A brief theological reflection on the Triune God follows, emphasising communal suffering as an expression of divine love. The essay concludes with a sketch toward a communal theology of persecution, inviting further theological engagement.

2 Kerman Church: A wounded body and a living theology

This theological framework – rooted in Holy Saturday as a theology of descent framed within the broader arc of Good Friday, Holy Saturday, and Easter Sunday – was not developed in abstraction. It emerged from my own lived experience as part of the wounded yet sacred body of the Episcopal Church in Kerman, Iran. In this essay, I use the Kerman Church as a living example of the theological framework for the persecuted church that I am proposing. Therefore, it is important to begin by telling a brief story of the church before proceeding with the theological reflection. All personal names have been changed to protect individual identities, except for two cases where names are used with the express permission of those individuals.

The aim here is not to recount the full institutional history of the Episcopal Church Kerman, St. Andrew's, which was established by the Church Mission Society (CMS) in the early 20th century (Dehqani-Tafti, 1990, 18). After the 1979 revolution and the establishment of the Islamic Republic, the Episcopal Church in Iran came under increasing surveillance. The pastor of the Kerman church was arrested in 1980 (see Dehqani-Tafti, 1990, 19). He was released later, after a few months in prison. Eventually, all church members – including the pastor and his family – left. This marked the end of the CMS missionary chapter in Kerman. The framework that this essay involve is from 1988-2012.

The only faithful person who remained and kept the light of the church on was Daniel. A new chapter began with three young men from Muslim backgrounds who desired to convert to Christianity and were discipled by Daniel. A few months later, a friend and I joined them. With six of us, we reopened the church. After three months, five of us were baptised by Bishop Iraj Mottahedeh, who lived in Esfahan and visited Kerman every 3-4 months.

Our newly revived church had no pastor and no experienced Christian leaders. Daniel, though deeply faithful, had no theological training. We developed our own Bible study methods, our own preaching and worship styles – though we continued using the Episcopal church's liturgy translated into Farsi. We also developed our own methods of evangelism and discipleship. After seven months, twenty-five people had been baptised, and the church had grown rapidly – especially among university students and local youth. On Sundays and Fridays, the church was packed.

But soon, the Islamic Intelligence Services took notice and considered our community a threat to national security. The persecution began. Our church compound was raided at least twice a month. Every week, one or two of us were arrested and imprisoned. Most of our families rejected us. All we had was the church and each other.

During these years, the uncertainty of the future, the fear, loneliness, and isolation were sometimes more difficult to endure than imprisonment itself. Reconstructing our identity as Christians – both individually and communally – became an immense spiritual challenge. In one Bible study, one of us, frustrated and jokingly, said, "I think we need to change the name of our church." "To what?" we asked. He replied, "To the Islamic Church of St. Andrew."[2]

Despite the pressure, the church was respected by some local Muslims. After two years of repeated arrests and releases, the Revolutionary Guard Corps unofficially closed the church. We began meeting in Daniel's home. Then Daniel and his wife were arrested. We moved to public parks – until we were stopped there too. We gathered early on Friday mornings in the mountains – again we were stopped. Eventually, we began a chain of continuous prayer across the city.

But the exhaustion, the descent, the fear, and the isolation became too much for many of us. Some left the city; some fled the country. Some, under duress, gave up Christianity entirely. When our church was closed, we wept. We wept for the loneliness of the church. When the authorities came to gather testimonies against us from our neighbours and nearby shop-

---

2 The logic behind this ironic suggestion was that, due to the lack of access to Christian theological resources, many of our interpretations of the Bible were influenced – directly or indirectly – by Islamic sources or Islamic cultural frameworks. Without trained pastors or theological guidance, our community often navigated Scripture using the only conceptual tools readily available to us: those rooted in the dominant religious worldview around us and in our education system. This statement, though made in jest, reflected a deeper frustration about our theological isolation and the contextual challenges we faced in constructing a faithful Christian identity.

keepers, not one gave a negative statement.[3] One man even said, "I wish my children were like them." That was the testimony of the church in Kerman.

Like many others, I was arrested multiple times and interrogated by Iran's intelligence services. The interrogations were not just about me – they were about the Church. We were accused of evangelism, foreign collusion, and betraying the culture of our homeland. In those cold and dark rooms, in humiliation and pressure, we experienced something paradoxical: the weight of hostility, yes – but also, strangely, the nearness of God. In pain, there was clarity – carrying our cross was part of the package of following Christ.

But the heavier burden was not the torture or the arrest – it was the waiting, uncertainty, fear and the guilt of dining Christ under pressure. The long, uncertain silence of Holy Saturday – many times we felt the resurrection Sunday may never arrive.

The Kerman Church was closed, reduced, stripped, wounded – and finally its sanctuary bulldozed to the ground in 2012. But it never ceased to be the Church. In her long season of Holy Saturday, she taught us to see the resurrection light even while still in the darkness.

This is where my theology of Holy Saturday – of descent, of silence, of waiting, and, finally, of resurrection hope – began to emerge. A theology not of triumph. Not loud. But real. This is a theology for church under persecution.

3 A theology hidden in silence

Defining persecution is already a complex task, but it becomes even more challenging when religion is involved. Religious persecution is often entangled with political motives and interpretations – sometimes by the persecutors themselves, and sometimes by advocates seeking to raise awareness. This is not surprising, given that in both historical and contemporary contexts, religion has increasingly become a tool in political agendas, used

[3] We learned of this after two of our members were released from detention. As they approached the church gate, several neighbouring shopkeepers greeted them warmly and shared what had occurred in their absence. The shopkeepers recounted how, when the authorities came to gather accusations against the church, no one offered negative testimony. Instead, the neighbours had spoken well of the church, with one man reportedly saying, "I wish my children were like them." This affirmation from the local community, despite the climate of fear and surveillance, became a powerful witness to the church's quiet integrity and its impact beyond its walls.

by politicians and lobbyists alike (Hertzke, 2012, 107-108; Grim & Finke, 2011, 61). How, then, should we define religious persecution? While this essay does not aim to resolve that question in full, a working definition is necessary in order to build a coherent theological framework.

Persecution, within this theological framework that is grounded in Holy Saturday, is best understood not merely as physical violence or political repression directed at Christians (Grim & Finke, 2011, 70-73), but as a sustained, sacred descent into marginalisation, fear, and uncertainty experienced collectively by the Church as the Body of Christ. It includes not only the visible suffering of martyrdom but also the silent wounds of those who are silenced, surveilled, and emotionally or socially exiled.

This definition draws upon biblical theology (e.g., Glenn Penner's *In the shadow of the cross*), which connects suffering and persecution directly to the vocation of discipleship and the cross-shaped life. It also resonates with Strauss' notion of internalised persecution (Strauss, 1988, 23-25) and hiddenness in the life of thought and faith under totalitarian conditions, suggesting that persecution can be a form of theological pressure that reshapes identity, not just endangers life.

In this framework the concept of martyrdom also changes to include those who have gone through suffering (imprisonment, torturing and loss) yet remain alive but silenced. I provide a few examples throughout this essay mainly from the Kerman Church.[4] In fact, it was both the blood of martyrs who died and the blood of martyrs who stayed alive, who have become and are becoming the seeds of the church in difficult contexts (Afshari, 2021a, 415-416). In this light, martyrdom is not only the spilling of blood but the silencing of the voice, the erasure of presence, and the carrying of pain in obscurity.

Thus, religious persecution for this essay is defined as follow: A communal experience of sacred descent, often prolonged, where suffering, silence, and marginalisation are borne not just by individuals, but by the Church as a body, awaiting the hope of resurrection (Afshari, 2021b, 295).

This theology does not glorify suffering, but it recognises it from three key perspectives. First, as a site of redemption – where the Church's wounds bear witness to Christ's redemptive suffering, while also crying out for justice, healing, and hope. Second, as a season marked by invisible faithfulness – where the Church endures in silence, obscurity, and vulnerability. Third, as a space of uncertain vocation – where believers live with fear and trembling, unsure of what lies ahead, yet holding fast to God's presence.

---

4 The anecdotes from the Kerman church are set as indented blocks.

Christian theology has often celebrated the incarnation and glorification or cross and the resurrection as primary poles of the redemptive narrative (Wright, 2003, 75). Yet nestled between cross and resurrection is Holy Saturday, a day of profound silence, theological mystery, and spiritual and identity uncertainty. Holy Saturday is a bridge between despair and hope, between fear and faith, between abandonment and restoration. It is a space of silence, waiting and unknowing – a sacred threshold where grief has not yet given way to joy, yet knowing that the seeds of resurrection are already buried in the soil of suffering (Dau, 2012, 116). The day started with half an hour of stillness in heaven (Revelation 8:1). Yet much happened after that muted half-hour – both in heaven and on earth – in the journey of Christ's descent, in the anticipation of the Father and the Holy Spirit, and in the pain and abandonment of Christ, as well as in the uncertain lives of Jesus' disciples. The disciples hid in fear, shame, and confusion. This in-between day – theologically rich, spiritually profound, and ecclesiology significant, holds deep resonance for the persecuted church today.

Theologically, Holy Saturday reveals a God who does not bypass suffering, but enters fully into the silence of death and abandonment (Balthasar, 1988, 67; Ratzinger, 1986, 13-24). Christ does not merely die; he descends. The descent into hell (1 Peter 3:19) may not be a spectacle of triumph as some of the Church Fathers such as Augustine insisted but a continuation of divine solidarity with broken humanity. In this descent, as Balthasar (1990, 91-92) advocates, the crucified one also becomes the forsaken one, and yet, even in abandonment, remains united with the Father in trust: "Into your hands I commit my spirit". Spiritually, Holy Saturday is a space of radical trust – where uncertainty and marginalisation persist but so does the prayer despite God's silence, and faith is refined not by sight, but by waiting in the marginal time. It is the spirituality of not knowing, of dwelling in mystery, and of worship without answers. Ecclesially, this day models the church not as a victorious institution, but as a wounded body: hidden, scattered, yet still bound together by the Spirit as I witnessed in the Kerman church. In this space, the persecuted church finds its likeness – not only in suffering and abandonment, but in the holy endurance of waiting: "Do not hold on to me, for I have not yet ascended to the Father" (John 20:17). The Kerman Church did not only endure Good Friday moments of arrest and violence; it lived and is living in the Holy Saturday of silencing, fear, unknowing and now in exile. It seemed that their Good Friday and Holy Saturday were in a loop yet they believed in the Resurrection Sunday. They knew that to celebrate Resurrection Sunday they had to go through their own Good Friday and uncertain Saturday.

> When a group of Iranian Christians who were dubbing Christian programs into Farsi were arrested, all their equipment was confiscated. Upon their release, they had nothing left to return to. When someone contacted them to express sympathy, their dubbing manager responded, "Sister, please don't feel sorry for us. What we are going through is not even half a drop of what Jesus endured for us." Though they eventually left Iran, it was not their Good Friday – the moment of arrest and loss – that drove them out, but the weight of their prolonged Holy Saturday: the season of waiting, uncertainty, and silence that followed (Ascott, 2021, 148-154). Though they left, the light of the church's endurance continues to shine throughout Iran. This silent endurance has become a witness more profound than words.

Holy Saturday calls the Church not to rush toward resurrection, but to dwell in the space where healing begins in the dark and the Gospel is preached without words – where the Spirit hovers over the chaos (Genesis 1:2), and God again whispers, "Let there be light."

4 The Holy Saturday

Tietje (2018, 23-25) presents Holy Saturday as a theological space of God's silence, abandonment, and presence-in-absence. He proposes that Christ's descent into hell is not merely a doctrinal curiosity, but a pastoral anchor for those suffering. Jesus' cry of abandonment on Good Friday ("My God, my God, why have you forsaken me?") reaches its full weight on Holy Saturday – when Christ, having died, descends to hell. The question which can be raised here is: Did the divine let go of Jesus on his descent to "hell"? It is difficult to answer this question since the Bible is silent here. Church Fathers such as Augustine, though they do not speak much about Holy Saturday, interpreted Christ's descent as a continuation of his mission to extend the good news to those who died and to liberate the dead.

Contrary to this view, Balthasar (1988, 23-24) and Ratzinger (1986, 117) argue that Christ went to hell (*sheol*) while being forsaken by God the Father. Both emphasise that Christ continued suffering in the land of the dead, because the humanity of Christ must endure utmost human suffering and brokenness. Balthasar also states that even in utter God-forsakenness, the Spirit of Love persists, knitting together the forsaken Son and the grieving Father. This Trinitarian suffering – Father, Son, and Spirit – together with the disciples' feelings of abandonment, fear and uncertainty are held up as the theological lens through which we can understand the Church's experience of persecution. Just as Christ endures the depths of hell, just as the disciples go through fear and uncertainty, so too does the persecuted Church dwell in "Saturday" – a place of loneliness, unresolved trauma, and waiting, yet not without the hidden presence of God. Together with the disciples we have three stories that parallel what happened on Holy Saturday.

The act of descent happens twice, once in the incarnation (John 1:14), in which Christ descends with his full divine power, so he become the second Adam – fully human and fully Divine. His descent to the land of dead after his death on the Cross is the second one. However, at the second time the divine abandoned him ("why have you forsaken me?") – in his journey to hell or *sheol*, he faces dehumanisation and brokenness. Tietje (2018, 29) argues that Holy Saturday is not a pause between events but a theological space of descent, a place where Christ experiences dehumanisation. His descent is not only linked to God's redemption of the world but also the ultimate form of divine solidarity with suffering humanity, especially those abandoned, tortured, or silenced.

Theologically, Holy Saturday is as communal space and solidarity, where the suffering and pain of abandonment and isolation do not cancel hope (Tietje, 2018, 37), and persecution is not the absence of God, but the site of divine descent and divine solidarity with broken humanity. For persecuted communities like the Episcopal Church in Kerman, Holy Saturday offers a sacred framework for understanding their suffering not only as trial but as a participation, together with Christ's disciples, in Christ's redeeming journey through death, silence, and finally, resurrection. This synthesis offers a powerful theological foundation: the persecuted Church embodies Holy Saturday living in the void between promise and fulfilment, yet bearing in its wounds the seeds of resurrection – this can be referenced to the Road to Emmaus story in Luke 24:13-35.

Holy Saturday as a theological framework also provides a guide to explore identity confusion, divine silence, and hope in exile by engaging three interwoven stories – the disciples' despair, Christ's descent, and the Triune God's suffering and solidarity.

5 The story of the disciples: Fear, disorientation, and disappearance

After Jesus' crucifixion, the disciples fled, they hid, they mourned. It was a moment of collapse, confusion and identity crisis. The community that had followed Jesus for three years now found itself leaderless, uncertain, and in fear for their lives and pushed underground (Emerson, 2019, 75). They faced the existential questions of loneliness and fear: "The doors were locked where the disciples were, for fear of the Jews" (John 20:19); of uncertainty and confusion: "We had hoped he was the one to redeem Israel" (Luke 24:21); of disoriented identity: With Jesus gone, their vocation – fishers of men, heralds of the Kingdom – was suspended. In this section I will explore three episodes: witnessing the burial of Jesus, disciples in hiding and the women with spices.

5.1 Witnessing the burial of Jesus

In the Gospel narratives, those who witnessed the burial of Jesus – Joseph of Arimathea, Nicodemus, Mary Magdalene, and other women – occupy a liminal space: the place between devastation and resurrection hope (Emerson, 2019, 89). They are not passive onlookers of death; they are witnesses to a sacred act of love and defeat, loss and loyalty. Their witness marks a theological paradox of moment: even in death, even in defeat, Christ is not abandoned. The liminal space and the moment of witnessing the burial parallel the experience of Christian communities suffering persecution today. The persecuted Christian – whether in Iran, India, Nigeria, or elsewhere – are not simply the victims of a hostile regime or violent group. They become living witnesses to the reality that faith can endure when stripped of all earthly support. Like those who remained with Jesus when most fled, persecuted believers remain present in the moment of Christ's "burial" – a moment of silencing, of descent, of apparent defeat.

In Greek, the word "*martyria*" (witness) shares its root with "martyrdom" (Wespetal, 2010, 232). Witnessing is not only to "see," but to testify – to affirm publicly what one believes privately, even in suffering. To witness the burial of Christ was to say: "This is the one we followed; even in his death, we will not leave him." In contexts of persecution, this theology of presence is enacted when believers refuse to deny Christ, even when the community is scattered, leaders are arrested, and churches are shut down. Their faithful endurance says: "He may be in the tomb – but he is still Lord." Witnessing, then, is not a passive observance but a participatory theological act. It is a protest against the erasure of faith and a confession of God's sovereignty in the face of state or societal power.

To bear witness to Christ's burial is not only the task of the persecuted; it is also the responsibility of the global Body of Christ. When the global church listens, mourns, prays, and advocates alongside the persecuted, it becomes Joseph of Arimathea – offering dignity in death, refusing to let the testimony of faith be buried without reverence (Schirrmacher, 2008, 65-68).

But the global church often prefers the triumph of Easter Sunday without dwelling too long at the sealed tomb. A theology of Holy Saturday, however, calls the wider church to linger in that space – between martyrdom and miracle, between persecution and liberation. It is here that solidarity is forged, as the global church takes seriously the suffering of its members, not as anomalies but as central to the gospel witness.

The local society also witnesses persecution. In the story of the Kerman church, for example, the neighbours of the church gave positive testimonies about them when security forces sought accusations. This "witness of the outside" echoes the centurion's confession at the cross: "Surely this man was the Son of God" (Mark 15:39). Even those outside the faith, when confronted with genuine suffering endured with grace, recognise something holy (Johnson, 2012, 31.34.35).

This is a critical space for theological imagination. The persecuted church becomes salt and light not only in proclamation, but in posture – faith under fire, love under loss. Their very endurance becomes a form of evangelism not born of strategy, but of sanctity.

> After the closing of the church, the Iranian Ministry of Intelligence and Security (MOIS) sent a threatening letter to Maryam's father, one of leaders of the church, demanding that she surrender. Her family pleaded with her to comply, and the next day, Maryam reported to the authorities. She endured a full day of interrogation while blindfolded, questioned by three officials. Very soon, the questions became theological. The interrogator asked: "do you believe Jesus Christ is the Son of God?" At the end of the session, the lead interrogator told her, "The way you engaged with and answered my questions has moved me. To tell you the truth, before your arrival, we had already sentenced you to eight months in prison. But your responses have changed my mind. I'm going to release you instead. What you've found in Christ seems deeply precious to you. If you are truly a Christian, I encourage you to stay true to it."

As in the story of Maryam, even persecutors become unintended witnesses. The burial scene in the Gospels includes the placement of guards at the tomb – meant to suppress resurrection hope, but ironically securing the credibility of the resurrection itself (Matt. 27:62-66). In a similar way, persecutors often become accidental midwives of testimony. Their attempts to extinguish faith frequently amplify it (see Dau, 2012, 126-127).

In many cases, as in the Iranian context, the intelligence officers who interrogated believers became curious. Some even respected the quiet, unyielding dignity of those they imprisoned. The persecutors may never convert – but they cannot "unsee" what they've seen. As in Acts, Saul the persecutor becomes Saul/Paul the apostle because of what he witnessed in Stephen's martyrdom.

Finally, to witness the burial of Christ is to witness that even in silence, faith speaks. The tomb of Christ is not just a symbol of death, but a site of hope and liberation incubated in darkness (Sobrino, 1993, 193-198). For the persecuted church, their silent witness – often buried from the world's attention – is not mute. It is loud in heaven. The witness of global believers, local societies, and even persecutors themselves weaves together a tapestry of testimony: that Christ is not absent in persecution, but present in descent. And that the witness of the buried is never buried forever – for resurrection always draws near. In this light, to witness persecution is to stand beside the tomb – not just in mourning, but in reverence, expecting glory to break forth from the silence.

5.2 Disciples in hiding

Holy Saturday is also the space in which the disciples found themselves in hiding, wrestling with fear, shame, and identity confusion. After the crucifixion, the disciples scattered. John's Gospel tells us they locked themselves behind closed doors "for fear of the Jews" (John 20:19). Their fear was existential – an instinct to survive. For persecuted Christians today, particularly in places like Iran, North Korea, or parts of Nigeria, hiding is not cowardice but survival. It is the first instinct of a community that has witnessed brutality. Their fear, like that of the disciples, is a response to very real threats. However, there is more in the concept of hiding.

> When Daroush was released from prison, church members asked how he was. He answered with tears in his eyes, "I denounced Him." Maryam embraced him and said, "I was ashamed to confess to you that I too denied Him during my previous arrest. But you are brave – for you have confessed it."

The disciples too abandoned Jesus, and some, like Peter, even denied him. So they hide from shame. Shame of denial and abandonment. Peter's triple denial of Christ (Luke 22:54-62) stands as one of the most humanising scenes in the Passion narratives. Here we find the leader of the apostles broken by shame (Emerson, 2019, 86.101).

Many Christians under persecution may relate deeply to the story of Peter – those who are forced to recant their faith publicly, not out of rejection of Christ, but out of unbearable pressure. Peter's story reminds us that failure under persecution is not the end; it is a station on the journey of grace. Unfortunately, the accounts of crypto-Christians have not been well documented. Their story might help us to shed a light in the concept of church survival in persecution (Afshari, 2021a, 416).

The disciples also hide from uncertainty. The Road to Emmaus is the exodus of the disillusioned. Luke 24 tells the story of two disciples on the road to Emmaus. They had left Jerusalem, disillusioned, saying "we had hoped he was the one to redeem Israel" (Luke 24:21). Their walking away was a kind of migration – a departure from danger, but also from disillusionment. Many Christians in hostile contexts must flee not just their homes but their certainties. The Emmaus story suggests that Christ walks with the disillusioned, even when they do not recognise him.

> Andreas was arrested and imprisoned numerous times. He endured brutal torture. Eventually, he was forced to flee Iran. When someone later asked him how he felt about leaving, he quietly replied, "I feel I did not finish my race, so I don't know who I am anymore without my calling", referencing the words of Paul in 2 Timothy 4:7.

Holy Saturday creates a theological vacuum. The one they had followed, trusted, and proclaimed was now dead. Who were they now? For persecuted Christians, this mirrors a deep crisis: who are we without a visible church, without pastoral leadership, without community recognition? Andreas was called to serve the Kerman church, and the church as he knew it no longer exists and he is in exile.

5.3 The women with the spices: Persistent love

> Reza came from a devout Muslim family deeply rooted in Sufi tradition. When his father failed to convince him to return to Islam, he called upon a prominent Sufi leader, hoping he could persuade Reza. The sheikh arrived with three respected Sufi scholars. After a long and intense theological discussion, the Sufi leader looked at Reza and said, "Son, where you have reached is what we long for. I cannot in good conscience encourage you to return to Islam."

The story of the women with the spices fits within the framework of Holy Saturday descent by embodying a theology rooted in faithful presence and communal care amid uncertainty. Their quiet, courageous act becomes a model for the persecuted church, showing that even in silence and fear, theology can emerge from the grassroots – where love, witness, and endurance carry the seeds of resurrection hope. By preparing Jesus' body for burial, they bore witness to Christ's dignity even in death. For persecuted communities, this suggests that theology must emerge from within – from their shared acts of endurance, lament, hope, witness and from engaging with context and culture.

These experiences of the persecuted church belong to the theology of Holy Saturday. For the first travellers (converts) in the faith like the congregation in Kerman, it meant living on the boundary between yesterday and tomorrow. As a fully convert church, the congregation of Kerman church did not have much communal memory of a Christian past and they didn't have trained church leaders to teach them. Instead, they looked back to the Bible and traced the uncertain footsteps of the disciples themselves. Their spiritual anchor was not tradition but testimonies. That is how they formed their Bible studies.

The Eucharist celebrations were nostalgic events, though they did not happened often, only every three months. Participating in the Eucharist was not from a place of ecclesial safety, but from the shadow of Holy Saturday – a place marked by fear, shame, failure, and deep uncertainty. It is because under pressure, many of us failed Christ. Yet as Lewis (1994, 44) reminded us, such failure is "less of the weak than of the wrong". Though weak and vulnerable, the church felt that in the Eucharist Christ stood in solidarity with them, even on the dark side of abandonment and shame. In the participation of the Eucharist, Christ planted the seeds of hope – not a triumphant hope, but an enduring, suffering hope that takes root in the soil of silence and humiliation. The Eucharist reminds us that the persecuted church lives between yesterday's collapse and tomorrow's promise. Its descent into uncertainty becomes not the end, but the beginning of something deeper. Like Christ, the church enters the tomb not to be extinguished, but to be sown.

Holy Saturday teaches the church that even in hiding, the church is not lost. Even in shame, it is not abandoned. Even in the grip of uncertainty, it is not without divine direction. The church that waits in the grave of persecution is still the church of Christ – and from that grave, the stone will one day be rolled away. The church must therefore develop and embrace a theology of Holy Saturday – a theology where the seeds of hope are quietly planted, and the roots are growing deeper, where descent becomes preparation for resurrection. This is not the job of seminaries alone, nor of survivors alone, but the sacred calling of the whole Church: to nurture hope in silence, to witness in waiting, and to become the womb of resurrection.

6 The story of Christ: Descent, abandonment, and endurance

The Gospels offer two simultaneous narratives of persecution: the event of suffering and the event of faith. Both must be held together. The former speaks to external realities – imprisonment, torture, harassment. The latter unfolds inwardly – in trust, despair, hope, and waiting. Together, they illuminate the nature of Christ's descent: both as an historical moment and a theological event (Penner, 2004, 85-89).

The Apostles' Creed affirms that Christ "descended into hell." This descent – while theologically rich – has often remained in the shadows of Christian reflection. Yet for the persecuted church, it is precisely here, in the silence and forsakenness of Holy Saturday, that the story of Christ most resonates.

Christ's Passion does not end with the crucifixion; nor does it leap directly to resurrection. Between death and new life lies the grave – a space of descent, uncertainty and silence (Balthasar, 1988, 26). There is no clear contrast between Good Friday and Easter Sunday, no simple binary of death and life. Rather, the entire Triduum – Good Friday, Holy Saturday, and Easter Sunday – forms a continuous, indivisible movement of God's redemptive action (Moltmann, 1972, 229). Acts 2:23-24 speaks to this: "This Jesus, whom you crucified and killed ... God raised him up." The grave – Holy Saturday – is thus not an intermission, but an integral act in the divine drama (Vahoozer, 2005, 124).

6.1 Descent and silence: The heart of the gospel

The silence of Holy Saturday is not void but reverberates with the agony of divine abandonment. It echoes through Holy Saturday as the incarnate Son experiences not only human death but the terrifying absence of the Father. Hans Urs von Balthasar insists that Christ's descent into hell was not a symbolic triumph but a radical entry into godforsakenness. This is not the silence of absence – but the silence of God suffering with and for the world. (Balthasar, 1988, 92 & Emerson, 2019, 115).

This descent into hell represents the deepest point of Christ's solidarity with human pain. In contrast to the incarnation – where the Word became flesh in power and humility – Holy Saturday is the descent of broken flesh: dehumanised, betrayed, crushed. Christ no longer descends as the God-Man, but as the broken image of humanity, stripped of all strength. In him, sin is not only punished but carried. As such, sin itself becomes a burden that opens the possibility of redemption and healing.

This is the heart of Holy Saturday theology: the seeds of victory lie not outside the grave, but within it. "The only flower of victory," as Lewis (1994, 49) puts it, "germinates in the darkness of a tomb." Hope is not an escape from suffering, but its mysterious fulfilment. Resurrection cannot come without descent. Salvation cannot bypass forsakenness.

The angel's question – "Why do you seek the living among the dead?" – is not a denial of the grave's importance. Rather, it affirms that the grave is precisely where the Lord of life has been. Christ remains forever the Living One who was dead (Rev. 1:18). In his descent, he sanctified the silence. He made the darkness part of the Gospel. His forsakenness makes possible our healing.

In persecution, the church must not reduce its story to mere victimhood or pragmatic evangelism. To understand persecution theologically is to see in it a descent like Christ's – one filled with pain and mystery, but also the possibility of communal transformation. As Moltmann (1972, 229) has written, "God weeps with us so that we may one day laugh with Him".

The persecuted church carries the sin, suffering, and abandonment of its context – not to be destroyed by it, but to hold open the possibility of redemption. In this light, the Kerman church did not simply endure persecution. It descended – into silence, loneliness, and fear. The community felt abandoned and forsaken. The worship scattered. The building was destroyed. Yet like Christ in the grave, their faith held the ember of hope. They did not know when resurrection would come. But they believed – like Christ commending his spirit to the Father (Luke 23:46) – that even in silence, God's redemptive story continued.

6.2 The story of healing in descent

Theology often avoids Holy Saturday because it is difficult: it does not promise answers. But precisely because it holds space for "unknowing," it speaks powerfully to persecuted Christians. When Christians like those in Kerman feel they are living in a "long Saturday" – a space where they are neither fully crushed nor yet delivered – they are not outside the Gospel story. They are inside it, deeply embedded in the descent of Christ.

If Christ's descent into hell was not a defeat but the dark soil in which resurrection was planted, then the persecuted Church must understand its own suffering not as divine abandonment, but as a sacramental participation in the redeeming suffering of God. The Church is not outside the grave – it is with Christ in the tomb, waiting. And in that waiting, light is coming.

This means the persecuted Church is not merely surviving. It is bearing light. It becomes, in its silence and endurance, a voice of grace to the world. Like the Spirit hovering over the chaos in Genesis, the Church waits – not in despair, but in creative readiness for God's new act.

Moreover, echoing Balthasar's (1988, 88) argument, if Christ bore the sin of the world, then sin becomes something carried, not just punished. It becomes a wound to be healed, not merely a transgression to be paid. In this, I would also argue that the persecuted church shares something of Christ's vocation – not only to suffer, but to carry the wounds of their society, to absorb its violence and the sin of their persecutors, and in doing so, to hold open the possibility of healing.

7 The story of the Triune God: Divine suffering and the church's redemptive pain

If Christ's descent into death reflects the depth of divine solidarity, then it must be read through the lens of the Trinity. Holy Saturday is not only the day of Christ's abandonment; it is the moment of Trinitarian pain. The Father, in permitting the abandonment, does not remain unmoved. The Spirit, in witnessing the separation of Son from Father, grieves and bears the agony. As Basil the Great said, "The Spirit suffers with those who suffer." This is not divine division, but divine communion in grief. The cross and the tomb do not divide the Trinity; they reveal the mutual love that is willing to suffer for the redemption of the world (Ratzinger, 1986, 13-24; Emerson, 2019, 105).

In this image, the Church emerges as both child and mother. As a child, the Church suffers. It is the Son – broken, rejected, carrying sin not its own. As a mother, the Church watches – like the Father – helplessly, as its members are tortured, scattered, or lost. In the Spirit, the Church groans – carrying within it the suffering of all its members, even when they are silent. The Kerman church is an example of such suffering. When believers were imprisoned, the rest of the church suffered deeply – not just emotionally, but theologically. The absence of community members echoed the Father's silence. The confusion and paralysis reflected the Spirit's groaning. The church endured not just persecution from without, but a deep rupture from within.

> One night, the Islamic Revolutionary Guard Corps raided our church and arrested several members. Only three remained. They stayed overnight at the church to pray, seated beneath the open sky, surrounded by silence and stars. One of them said: "If someone kills us here tonight, no one would know what happened." Another responded softly, "But Christ would know."

As the church mothers its children through exile, loss, and displacement, it too becomes a suffering parent – like the God who watched his Son descend and who entrusted the Spirit to carry that sorrow across eternity. At the heart of the Triune God's story is its communal nature. It is not only

Christ suffering but the triune God. This is what makes the Holy Saturday theological framework distinct. Persecution is often cast as an individual story of heroism or endurance. But in reality, it is borne by the whole body. The disciples hid together. The women prepared anointing oils together. Peter gathered the others. In Kerman, it was Daniel's faithfulness, Andreas' courage, Nady's perseverance and many more who kept the church alive through daily acts of presence, prayer and care., As Augustine in his book *The Trinity* (book 6) describes, the Holy Spirit is the bond of love and peace between Father and Son. In the persecuted church, the Spirit becomes the bond of shared endurance – uniting scattered members, bearing their silence, and groaning toward resurrection.

In all three stories – the disciples, Christ, and the Triune God – there is a thread of ecclesial and redemptive depth in a shared suffering. The disciples' fear was not private – it was communal. Christ's suffering was not solitary – it carried the pain of the world. The Triune God's silence was not apathy – it was a shared heartbreak. All three stories come together in the early morning of resurrection Sunday. So too, persecuted churches suffer not as scattered individuals, but as members of one wounded body. Even those who migrate, some of them carry the spiritual memory of that body. Their witness does not end when they leave their homeland. Their displacement became part of the Church's wider witness – a Holy Saturday movement from the centre to the margins. This is how we must understand persecution: as a communal participation in Christ's descent and in Eucharist, a bearing of wounds that may one day become signs of healing, and a calling to wait together.

8 Conclusion: Waiting together in the silence of God

This essay has offered a theological framework rooted in Holy Saturday as a space for the persecuted church – a space not of triumph, but of sacred waiting. Drawing from the lived witness of the Kerman church and the biblical narratives of the disciples, Christ, and the Triune God, the chapter sought to articulate a theology of Holy Saturday, of descent, absence, and enduring hope. It is a framework not meant to provide closure, but to open new theological conversations – ones that are often left out of the discourse. If our theology cannot hold space for the long, uncertain Saturday, then it cannot speak truthfully to the reality of persecution. A theology that moves too quickly from crucifixion to resurrection risks leaving behind those who dwell in the in-between. It was argued that the story of the disciples reflects the identity questions and fear faced by the persecuted church; the story of Christ's descent offers a model of redemptive suffering and deep solidarity; and the story of the Triune God calls the global church to stand in solidarity and prayer with persecuted churches. Together, these three strands form a trinitarian theology of persecution – not as an isolated episode, but as a communal vocation. Persecution is not a tool for church growth nor a romanticised spiritual battle; it is a crucible in which the church's identity is clarified, its hope tested, and its endurance refined.

Holy Saturday is the theological space between Good Friday's trauma and Easter Sunday's glory. In this silence, God's deepest solidarity with suffering is unveiled. As Romans 6:3-4 reminds us, through baptism into Christ's death, the persecuted are buried – not forgotten. Holy Saturday becomes the existential terrain for Christian witness, not in triumph but in descent. Here, the healing of nations begins – not in Christian power, but in Christ's humility.

The Church is called not only to understand this space but to inhabit it. This is the Trinitarian rhythm of suffering and redemption: the Father grieves, the Son descends, and the Spirit hovers – binding pain to promise, silence to renewal. The chapter also reminded us that for the persecuted Church Holy Saturday is a sanctuary of lament and a seedbed of hope. As the Spirit once hovered over chaos in Genesis 1:2, so too the Spirit hovers now – waiting to speak again, "Let there be light." This is the hidden voice of resurrection. Adding to this is the fact that the resurrection was not immediately recognised. Jesus was mistaken for a gardener. Thomas doubted. The women returned first with spices, not with songs. Resurrection never erases Holy Saturday – it moves through it.

However, many cannot bear the length of this Saturday. Migration is often born not of fear, but of exhaustion. And those who receive such exiles must go beyond hospitality. They must honour the wounded memory of communities like the church in Kerman. They must learn to walk gently with those whose resurrection is still unfolding. The persecuted church's resurrection may not be seen in numbers or buildings, but in quiet fidelity. It may be found in an old believer who refuses to forget, or a refugee who prays in their mother tongue. In countries like Iran, where state violence continues, the very survival and slow flourishing of faith is itself a resurrection. This chapter has merely opened a conversation. Much more theological work is needed. But perhaps this is how all resurrection begins: in silence, in small lights, and in the stubborn, collective act of waiting. Let us, then, wait with the Church in Kerman. Let us light candles for the exiles. Let us tend to the wounds of the Body. And let us believe, with trembling, that Sunday is coming, even if the dawn remains unseen.

9 References

Afshari, S. (2021a). Hidden Christians/churches in the Middle East. In M. Raheb, M. Riedel & M. Lamport (Eds.), *Christianity in the Middle East* (pp. 414-425). Rowman & Littlefield.

Afshari, S. (2021b). Marginalization and negotiation of boundaries: The case of the Armenian Church in Iran. *Mission Studies,* 38(2), 278-296. DOI: 10.1163/15733831-12341794

Ascott, T. (2021). *Dare to believe: Stories of faith from the Middle East.* Wipf & Stock.

Augustine of Hippo. (1990). *The Trinity* (E. Hill, Trans.; J. E. Rotelle, Ed.; Book 6). New City Press.

Balthasar, H. U. von. (1988). *Theo-Drama: Theological dramatic theory.* Vol. 5: The Last Act. (G. Harrison, trans.). Ignatius Press.

Balthasar, H. U. von. (1990). *Mysterium paschale: The mystery of Easter.* (A. Nichols, trans.). T&T Clark.

Dau, I. M. (2012). The problem of evil and suffering. In W. D. Taylor et al. (Eds.), *Sorrow and blood* (pp. 113-130). WCL.

Dehqani-Tafti, H. (1990). *The unexplained.* Hodder & Stoughton.

Emerson, M. J. (2019). *He descended to the dead: An evangelical theology of Holy Saturday.* IVP.

Gravaas, H. A., et al. (Eds.). (2015). *Freedom of belief and Christian mission.* Regnum.

Grim, B., & Finke, R. (2011). *The price of freedom denied.* Cambridge University Press.

Hertzke, A. D. (Ed.). (2013). *The future of religious freedom.* Oxford University Press.

Johnson, T. M. (2012). The demographics of martyrdom. In W. D. Taylor et al. (Eds.), *Sorrow and blood* (pp. 31-36). WCL.

Lewis, A. E. (2003). *Between cross and resurrection: A theology of Holy Saturday.* Wm. B. Eerdmans.

Miller, D. A. (2015). Power, personalities and politics: The growth of Iranian Christianity since 1979. *Mission Studies,* 32(1), 66-86.

Moltmann, J. (1972). The "Crucified God": A trinitarian theology of the cross. *Interpretation: A Journal of Bible and Theology,* 26(3), 278-299.

Penner, G. M. (2004). *In the shadow of the cross: A biblical theology of persecution and discipleship.* Living Sacrifice Books.

Ratzinger, J. (1984). *Behold the pierced one: An approach to a spiritual Christianity.* (G. Harrison, trans.). Ignatius Press.

Sauer, C., & Howell, R. (Eds.). (2010). *Suffering, persecution and martyrdom.* VKW; AcadSA.

Schirrmacher, T. (2008). *The persecution of Christians concerns us all.* VKW.

Sobrino, J. (1993). *Jesus the liberator: A historical-theological view.* Orbis.

Strauss, L. (1988). *Persecution and the art of writing.* University of Chicago Press.

Taylor, W. D., Van der Meer, A., & Reimer, R. (Eds.). (2012). *Sorrow and blood: Christian mission in contexts of suffering, persecution, and martyrdom.* William Carey Publishing.

Tietje, A. D. (2018). *Toward a pastoral theology of Holy Saturday: Providing spiritual care for war wounded souls.* Wipf & Stock.

Vanhoozer, K. J. (2005). *The drama of doctrine: A canonical-linguistic approach to Christian theology.* Westminster John Knox Press.

Wespetal, T. J. (2010). Martyrdom and the furtherance of God's plan. In C. Sauer & R. Howell (Eds.), *Suffering, persecution and martyrdom* (pp. 231-256). VKW.

Wright, N. T. (2003). *The resurrection of the son of God.* SPCK.

11 A theology of fleeing from persecution

Věra Miláčková[1] *& Kamila Veverková*[2]

Abstract

This article ponders the theological reasoning behind fleeing from religious persecution. It emerged as a reaction to questions raised about the legitimacy and purpose behind the fleeing of Christians from the Middle East. We compared the types of fleeing and reasons behind it mentioned in the Bible with stories of persecuted, fleeing Christians from Iraq and Egypt, drawing from it four different theological approaches – the 'Salvation at stake' approach, the Altruistic/common sense approach, Hearing God's voice approach, and an Opportunistic Approach. Our aim is to provide for the persecuted as well as those ministering to them the opportunity to navigate different reasoning options the persecuted take when considering fleeing.

Keywords: Religious persecution of Christians, Middle East, theology of fleeing, typology of fleeing, fleeing in the Bible, persecuted Christians.

1 Introduction[3]

The migration[4] wave to Europe from the Middle East during and after the war against ISIS raised many questions about the legitimacy and purpose

---

1 Věra Miláčková studied Cultural anthropology of the Middle East. She holds a PhD in theology and works in the realm of FORB in the MENA region. Email: milackovavm@gmail.com, ORCID iD: 0009-0004-8654-9631.

2 Kamila Veverková studied theology, international relations, and Asian studies. She is a Doctor of Theology. She is an assistant professor of historical theology and church history at Hussite Theological Faculty at Charles University in Prague. Email: kamila.veverkova@gmail.com, ORCID iD: 0000-0003-4336-4376.

3 This article was first published as Miláčková, V. & Veverková, K. (2022). Theology of fleeing from persecution. *Egyháztörténeti Szemle [Church History Review]*, 23(2), 124-139.

4 This article presents topical findings of Miláčková's dissertation which was written with the support of GA UK 108119 – Persecution of Christians in the Middle East and Their Migration.

behind the fleeing of Christians. In this article, we focus on a narrow subgroup of Christians from Iraq and Egypt who fled as a result of religious persecution,[5] aiming our attention at their reasoning behind fleeing and then drawing from it theological approaches.

In this article, we first focus on what the Bible has to say about fleeing from persecution, and then we present the research design and the conclusions of the field research among persecuted Christians from Iraq and Egypt and based on the interviews. Finally, we offer four systematic-theological approaches that represent motivations behind fleeing from persecution among the researched group.

We hope that the conclusions will help to further the knowledge of the afflicted as well as those ministering to persecuted Christians.

2 Fleeing in the Bible

The foundational premise of this article is that the Bible is a word of God. He is sovereign and relational and communicates through various intermediaries as well as directly with individual believers and the Bible should be for Christians a guide for life. Yet, does the Bible offer normative guidelines about when to flee, or does it allow for individual decision-making? The importance of understanding the biblical message is crucial and pressing for many contemporary Christians who face the decision to stay or flee and seek guidance in the Holy Book.

What does the Bible say about fleeing? What typology can we see in the biblical texts? In the Old and New Testaments, we find many reasons behind fleeing. A central theme uniting the various narratives of fleeing is to escape from severe physical danger, punishment or death. The most frequent reasons were: a) famine in the land (e.g., Noemi and her family fleeing to Moab (Ruth 1), Abram fleeing to Egypt (Gen 12)); b) escaping physical danger (e.g., Moses fleeing to Midian (Ex 2), David fleeing from Keilah (1 Sam 23)); c) seeking a better future (e.g., Noemi/Ruth returning to the land of Judah (Ruth 1)); d) escaping dictatorial paranoia (e.g., David escaping from the furious king Saul (1 Sam 20-21, 27) and his son Absalom

5 We use Tieszen's theological definition of persecution as working definition for this article. "Any unjust action of mild to intense levels of hostility directed at Christians of varying levels of commitment resulting in varying levels of harm which may not necessarily prevent or limit these Christians' ability to practice their faith or appropriately propagate their faith as it is considered from the victim's perspective, each motivation having religion, namely the identification of its victims as 'Christian,' as its primary motivator" (Tieszen 2008: 47).

(2 Sam 15), Jesus's parents fleeing before Herod (Matt 2), and the nation of Israel fleeing Egypt (Ex 12-14) which was at the same time clearly a case of e) religious persecution. Other examples of fleeing motivated by threats against one's life include Elijah fleeing from the wrath of Jezebel (1 Kings 19) and the prophet Uriah fleeing to Egypt before king Jehoiakim (Jer 26). Paul fled from Damascus (Acts 10) and, with his co-preacher Barnabas, fled from Iconium to Lystra and Derbe (Acts 14). Even Jesus himself fled when his life was threatened on several occasions (e.g., in Jerusalem (John 8 and 10), in Nazareth (Luke 4), and in John 7, where we read that he purposefully avoided Judea because he knew that certain Jewish leaders wanted to kill him).

In the examples mentioned above, we can see that the Biblical narratives give rather blunt accounts of the true motives behind fleeing. Furthermore, they point out guiding principles for staying or fleeing. Upon what did the individuals in these narratives base their decision? There are several different motivations. First, we find God's direct intervention in people's lives through dreams and prophecies. These interventions spoke directly into their situation and instructed the concerned person/people about the coming danger and their task to leave. The concerned people then had to choose whether to stay or leave. Submission to God's will was their choice: if they obeyed, they survived.

The second type of decision making was built on a personal relationship with God, on knowing his will and hearing his voice. In some texts we read about the importance of timing. This is obvious in Jesus' case, for he knew that his time to die had not come yet (John 2:4, 7:6; 30).

The third type of decision was built on a "common sense" of the concerned person or people around them. For example, Naomi, or even the families of Joseph's brothers, were in danger of starving to death, and the only way to avoid this fate was to migrate/flee into a country where food was abundant. In these two cases, we do not see any divine guidance or that they sought God's guidance while making a decision about staying or fleeing.

These three main approaches rescued the concerned people from death through fleeing for a given time and situation.[6] The Biblical texts do not imply or assume that God was displeased with people who fled based on a common sense decision; likewise, we do not see a divine abandonment

---

6 There are also other cases in which preventative steps saved Israelites from a disaster. That happened during the reign of Hezekiah (2 Chronicles 29-30) when persecution was avoided because they returned to God and followed his will, or again through the faith and action of Esther and Mordecai.

of those who flee. God often used their exile to shape them and transform them for whatever he had for them in the future. In most cases, the times of exile were only temporary. The return to the homeland was then either initiated based on God's direct guidance or on common sense.

Even though some biblical characters (e.g. Jesus, Paul, Peter) were rescued for a given time in a given situation, in some cases, later at another time and in a different situation, they did not flee, but submitted themselves to persecution, and many died.

In sum, we identified three different reasoning types behind decision-making about fleeing, yet we cannot see any normative approach through those texts that a believer must certainly follow (Andrews, 2018, p. 35). However, the examples show the importance of personal knowledge about God, recognition of his voice and the willingness to obey his command. Decision-making about fleeing from persecution, as shown in those biblical passages, is highly relational, personal, and situational. The uniting theme in these examples is fulfilling God's will and/or protecting one's life.

Having had the three reasoning types behind fleeing that we discovered in the Bible in mind, we designed our field research aiming to explore what led the persecuted Christians (either believers of Christian background (BCBs) or believers of Muslim background (BMBs) from Iraq and Egypt to flee, and how they argued their decision-making about fleeing.

3 Methodology

The research was designed as an adapted grounded theory research using semi-structured interviews and convenience sampling for choosing participants.

This research topic was security-wise and emotionally very sensitive; therefore, extremely high confidentiality measures were taken to protect the participants as well as the interviewer. The targeted participants were contacted either by the researcher in person in refugee camps in Lebanon or through different gatekeepers (church and humanitarian workers) in Egypt, Lebanon, and the Czech Republic. The participants, who are supposed to be believers of Christian background (BCBs) or believers of Muslim background (BMBs), come from Egypt, Iraq, and Syria, and had to flee their home(country) because of being persecuted for their Christian faith. The faith aspect must have been the main reason for persecution. The current physical location of the person during the time of the interview wasn't important.

The pilot research took place in the summer of 2018 in Lebanon. As a result of this time, the research sample and research instrument (questionnaire) were adjusted. The pilot showed that it is practically impossible to find Syrian BMBs or BCBs who fled because of being religiously persecuted; they fled because of the atrocities of war. Therefore, we limited the research to Egyptians and Iraqis. Yet, the four contacted Egyptian BCBs who fled because of religious persecution refused to give an interview due to fear for their families in Egypt being targeted (persecuted) by the police. After identifying suitable participants, about half rejected the interview due to fear for their or their families' security. Also, we excluded from the research Christians whose stories indicated economic or political reasoning behind fleeing.

The study was conducted due to COVID travel restrictions, partially in person in Lebanon, Egypt, and Czechia and partially synchronously online. The research took place in three phases between 2019 and 2021. The research sample includes 16 participants, 11 men and 5 women. Not all wanted to mention their age, but it was obvious that there were two main age groups represented. The young adults were between 20 and 30 years old, and participants in their forties; only one participant was older. Half of the participants were single, two were divorced, and six were married. Eight participants were from Egypt and eight from Iraq; four were of Christian background and 12 of Muslim background, of which four were of Salafi background, two of Shia, and one of Sufi background. The research sample includes different forms and intensities of persecution (from fear of future harm, threats, incarceration, physical attacks and killing a family member). At the time of the interview, the participants were in Egypt (3), Lebanon (8), Czechia (2), the Netherlands (1), Greece (1), and France (1). Out of the 16 participants, three fled within their home country, and 13 fled abroad.

4 Typology of fleeing

The field research suggests the following: 1) All interview participants saw fleeing as the only option for survival and to live out their Christian faith. 2) There isn't one type of fleeing but two types depending on the purpose of the flight. We call them the immediate and subsequent types.

The *immediate type* of fleeing from persecution is instinctive. The believers felt imminent danger, therefore, they wanted to save their lives. The goal of the immediate flight was to reach physical safety. They did not have much time to think about it and choose the "most suitable and best" destination. They just fled. After evaluating their situation and type of persecution, some ran to another city within their country, or some fled abroad. Previous contacts and the possibility of entering another country also played a role in deciding where to flee. Since their flight was in a rush, they usually fled without anything (e.g. money, personal documents). Depending on the situation of the persecuted believer, multiple immediate moves might have occurred. They fled from one place to another, and when they faced persecution in that city also, they fled to another one.

The *subsequent type* of move has another goal. It is a move to pursue happiness.[7] This flight means that persecuted believers were already physically safe, yet the hardship of life, lack of opportunities, and the desire for a better life, accompanied by an opportunity to travel to a better (meaning religiously safer and economically more developed) country, made them move again. This is not a flight out of danger, but a planned move.

All of the interview participants underwent the immediate type of flight, fearing for their own lives. Only a few at the moment of the interview or when we met some of them again have done the subsequent type of move. Those who moved again were located either in Lebanon or in Iraqi Kurdistan. They were looking for opportunities to move to another place and start again. When an opportunity came up, they moved to another place.

Based on the field research, we have identified four types of motivations behind fleeing from religious persecution. Three are related to fleeing itself, and the fourth one is implied as it stands in opposition to fleeing.

1. The first category can be called altruistic as the people who fled did it for the sake of their family members, or because they had to preserve their (own) life, some adding that this was in order to take care of their family and to continue Christian ministry. This category of decision-making was identified for both the immediate as well as the subsequent type of move with interviewees who had a family and were responsible for it. Single or divorced ones argued with protecting one's lives.
2. The second category has been identified only as a reason for the subsequent type of move. It is 'decision-making based on direct guidance by God, by hearing His voice, and abiding by it. Yet, none of them directly mentioned God's guidance while fleeing from the immediate danger. However, the interviewees repeatedly mentioned the importance of seeking God's will, guidance, and protection through prayer. They attributed to God and his will the fact that a way opened up for them during the persecution and that they were able to escape and save their lives. This type of "indirect" guidance has been apparent regarding the immediate type of flight.

7 The term and concept are taken from the US Declaration of Independence.

3. The third approach can be called an opportunistic approach and it was identified with the subsequent type of move. With the move, people sought their personal and family interests and well-being, claiming that the reason for their flight was religious persecution. Such an approach was labelled by a number of BMBs as disgraceful, for people who move for this reason "make Christ's sacrifice cheap".
4. We identified one more type of action related to persecution: Christians refused to flee and decided to stay and endure persecution regardless of the cost. They either felt called to stay in their area to continue the ministry, or were so old, weak, or rooted to their area (Iraqi BCBs) that they had no more strength and courage to move. Since these people didn't flee, we didn't include them in the field research.

Among the interviewees, there were people who repeatedly refused to move abroad as a subsequent move, or they returned back to their countries because they were convinced that the Lord had called them to minister there.

In sum, the field research suggests that the altruistic approach is the main argument behind the immediate type of fleeing, while for the subsequent move, it is common that obedience to a personal calling of God or family/self-interest play a more significant role.

5 Theological perspectives on fleeing

In this section, we interpret these four identified types of thinking theologically, building on various authors and theologians throughout history.[8]

5.1 'Salvation at stake' approach

This approach views fleeing as a negative or even forbidden option in light of salvation. Christians professing this approach do not see flight as an alternative, because they see fleeing as denying their Lord and by doing so, they would lose their own salvation.

---

8 We do not place demand on presenting an exhaustive overview of possible theological interpretations, we want to re-open the discussion about escaping from religious persecution and to give the afflicted followers of Christ a possibility to navigate themselves in the possible interpretations hoping that they would search their own hearts and seek God's will in the process.

At the beginning of the 3rd century major religious persecution came against Christians through the decrees of Caesar Decius and later Valerian. Many refused to deny Christ by fleeing from persecution. Those who stayed were often severely tortured, and many were martyred.[9] For many church leaders of that time, fleeing was viewed as denying Christ (apostasy); therefore, one's salvation was at stake. One representative of this approach was Tertullian, who believed that nothing happens without God's will and that "persecution is worthy of God" and that "it ought not to be avoided, because it is good" (Tertullian, n.d.). "Tertullian viewed flight as, at best, a poor alternative to standing firm and at worst, as apostasy." For Tertullian, fleeing from persecution was unacceptable, for it only showed human fear, weakness, and cowardice, which is not what the Lord calls his followers to embody (Sutcliffe, 2018, p. 139; Tertullian, n.d.). Enduring persecution until the end was viewed as giving back to God and a guarantee of entering heaven (Sutcliffe, 2018, p. 142).

Not all bishops and church leaders from the 3rd century viewed Tertullian's hardline approach as the only option for a believer. Cyprian and Origen, for example, fled first themselves, yet later in life they argued against and encouraged withstanding persecution till the end and they themselves underwent torture (and Cyprian was martyred) (Sutcliffe, 2018, pp. 148-160).

Since the clergy was to set an example, martyrdom became the fate of many bishops of that time. These martyrs set the precedent for the coming generations. Those who fled or otherwise avoided persecution were viewed as apostates and as such were doomed for eternity. Martyrdom had become a standard virtue and expectation of a Christian's lifestyle. However, "rushing" to death or voluntary martyrdom was discouraged[10] and viewed as heretical and unorthodox (Middleton, 2006, pp. 24-25).

This approach to fleeing can also be viewed as preconventional using Kohlberg's scale of moral development[11], insofar as it is the external

---

9 Christians could have avoided persecution either by bribing Roman officials or sacrificing to Roman Gods (Lane 1996: 23-30).

10 Schirrmacher sees a tendency to seek after martyrdom during the 2nd century, and compares it with certain similar aspects of slavery, such as that if one can be set free, it is better and wiser to do so. Jesus understood the circumstances behind persecution, therefore he told his disciples that they should be "as shrewd as snakes and as innocent as doves" (Matthew 10:16) (Schirrmacher 2018: 59-61).

11 Kohlberg has come up with six stages of moral development divided into six stages where the stage one meant the lowest level of moral development and level six the highest level. Stage one is also called (obedience and punishment) and is to be observed at children till the age of nine. In this stage rules are viewed as absolute

authority figures, the church fathers, the bishops, the exegetes who say what is true about fleeing and salvation, what is right or wrong. The believer's thinking and behaviour follow a pattern of obedience and punishment, for if one would flee, he would lose his salvation.

5.2 Altruistic/common sense approach

The second approach views decision-making about fleeing from persecution as an act made out of respect, love, and responsibility to others and oneself. I list four reasons that argue for fleeing rather than enduring persecution: not to be guilty of one's own death, to continue God's work, to protect the body of Christ, and for the benefit of the neighbour.

It was already the early church fathers who pondered the question of if and under which conditions it is permissible for a Christian to escape from persecution and so to prevent one's death or forced denial of Christ.[12] The first argumentation that supports fleeing is that Jesus requires us to take care of ourselves. Therefore, one should protect himself and if possible avoid death in order not to make oneself and the murderers abettors of evil. According to Clemens, if one stays unnecessarily in persecution that would lead to death, he would be guilty and an abettor of one's own death (Sutcliffe, 2018, p. 147). The second theological position considers that one may preserve oneself through flight in order to benefit other Christians and continuation of God's work (Sauer, 2012, p. 67). Unnecessary martyrdom would be viewed as selfish and inconsiderate (Sutcliffe, 2018, p. 151). The third reason encouraging fleeing is for the good of the entrusted believers. To protect the flock, the bishop or church leader should avoid drawing "negative attention to the whole Christian community" and spare them so violence.[13] That should happen in order to serve the interest of the church, and only under the guidance of the Holy Spirit (Sauer, 2012, p. 68).

The three above mentioned argumentations provide a relational caring aspect for others. Even though the first one focuses the most on the person itself, it still takes into consideration the others (the persecutors) in a way that believers should not submit themselves unnecessarily to death and so

---

and therefore must be obeyed. If not, punishment will follow (Cherry n.d.; Zhang and Zhao 2017).

12 One issue was to escape the persecution and/or so deny Christ, yet the bigger issue was under what conditions may these Christians return back to church (the Donatist schism).

13 Cyprian fled from Carthage for prominent people of his time "were more likely to be targeted" (Sutcliffe 2018: pp. 154-155).

cause the persecutors to commit a sin by killing them. The other two argumentations see the protection of one's life as a means to benefit the community of other believers. The relational caring aspect for others is obvious.

The Old and New Testaments present God as a loving and caring God full of compassion.[14] Those attributes God seeks also for the world and expects that his followers will extend these relational values to the people they are living with. God calls us to care for our neighbours, the "particular others"[15], those near to us, family members and other people God put in our lives. The example of the Good Samaritan in Lk 10:29-39 extends these particular others to anyone around us who needs help, even an enemy.

The Ethics of Care theory which stresses "the compelling moral salience of attending to and meeting the needs of the particular others for whom we take responsibility" corresponds with this biblical notion (Held, 2006, p. 10). Moral emotions such as sympathy and empathy for others aren't viewed in this theory as egoistic emotions, but rather – if cultivated – as guides of what morality recommends in a sense of what would be the best moral action on behalf of the particular others (Held, 2006, pp. 10-11).

Relating this mandate of care with decision-making about fleeing from persecution comes out very naturally. Fleeing from persecution in order to protect and preserve the particular others should be of the highest moral calling (if the particular others cannot handle persecution anymore). This approach proves a certain level of sacrifice for the responsible one, for he/she is not to "further their own individual interests; their interests are intertwined with the persons they care for" (Held, 2006, p. 12). That is especially true if fleeing wouldn't be a personal choice for the responsible one, but that they would do it for the benefit of others.

5.3 Hearing God's voice approach

This approach is based on a biblical premise that God is a communicating God and the followers of Jesus, his sheep, hear his voice (John 10:27). This implies a rather intimate relationship with God, his knowledge, a certain level of spiritual sensitivity or even maturity and willingness to listen to God's voice and then submit to his will.[16]

---

14 For example: Ex 34:6-7, Ps 86:15, Ps 89:14, Mica 6:8, Lk 6:36, Mark 12:28, Mat 22:39.

15 Held uses this term in her book to refer to those who need our care; may it be children, family members, friends, etc. (Held 2006).

16 Recognition of God's voice is a highly subjective process and as Kierkegaard aptly mentions growing in faith can be learned only over a long period of time. Therefore, the word of God to a believer is (into some extend) unverifiable by

God's direct word brought to the believer through the Holy Spirit is the decisive aspect[17] for a persecuted believer on the issue of fleeing or staying (Andrews, 2018, pp. 33-41). It is the Holy Spirit who blows where he wills, somewhat unpredictable, unbound, who can "suspend" ethics (meaning independent morality) yet always acts in unity with the Father and the Son (Ellul, 1969, pp. 213-214). In Kierkegaard's words, it is the paradox of faith in which "the individual determines his relation to the universal [the world] by his relation to the absolute [God]." That relationship may be unintelligible to the outer world (Kierkegaard, 1941, Chapter Problem II). It is the believer's personal relationship with God from which flows the certainty about God's will for one's life that overrides other reasons for decision-making, such as love and concern for family members/neighbours, church doctrine or personal desires without compunctions. A believer's submission to God's voice comes from loving and respecting Him.[18] This means that God may ask some believers to persevere in enduring persecution, and for some to move away from it. Their response should honour his request.

In this approach, we can see a connection with the ethics of care theory. It is the fact that one acts/cares (sacrificially) for the good or on behalf of the particular others that links this approach with the theory. The believer acts out of love and the desire to please God, not as a result of duty and an order.[19]

5.4 Opportunistic approach

By this term, we mean an individual's decision-making based solely on what the person views as most suitable. This approach does not have much theological support, unless one considers the approach (often pejoratively dubbed 'the prosperity gospel or wealth and health gospel') representing

---

the outsiders for only the one who heard God's voice knows if he heard well and acts accordingly in faith (Kierkegaard 1941: Preface). Acts 16:6-25 emphasizes that apostle Paul's ministry had been guided and led by the Holy Spirit.

17 This was the case of Cyprian who fled being prompted by the Holy Spirit (Sutcliffe 2018: 153-155).

18 In footnote 20, Ellul remarks that God respects individual's decisions, seeing him as ethically responsible, yet God awaits one's "free decision of willing obedience in love" without manipulating the human or "spiritual automation" that would certain acts view as "holy" because commanded by the Holy Spirit (Ellul 1969: 213).

19 In Acts 16:6-25 we can read how the apostle Paul's ministry was guided and led by the Holy Spirit and that Paul submitted to God's guidance out of relationship and trust that that is the best and wisest decision.

the view that God wants us to be successful and do well (Coleman, 2000, p. 28; Wilkinson, 2013). This approach encourages Christians to take steps that will lead them on a path of fulfilment of their desires and needs, including moving for a better future.[20]

The majority of theologians and churches adhere to a view that even though one should take into consideration one's own well-being and that of others, well-being and protection of one's own life should not be the "supreme good". One should not flee out of fear or cowardice or emigrate in order to find a more secure, peaceful and prosperous life (Accad, 2014; Sauer, 2012, p. 68).

Theology of fleeing and staying plays an important role in personal decision-making. Based on the above-mentioned approaches, the question is not whether fleeing from persecution is right or wrong so much as which reasons guide the decision. Were persecuted Christians seeking God's will for their lives regarding staying and fleeing? Were they honest and obedient in the process? These questions cannot be answered by anyone else but them, yet one thing is clear: "When persecution arises, careful consideration must be given to determine whether or not remaining in a situation of suffering is necessary in order to accomplish the will of God" (Sauer, 2012, p. 68).

6 Summary

In this article we presented our research findings about how Christians (BMBs and BCBs) from Iraq and Egypt reason their decision about fleeing from religious persecution, and then we suggested theological interpretations that explain their reasoning. Doing so, we aim to provide for the afflicted as well as those ministering to them the opportunity to navigate different reasoning options while considering staying or fleeing.

While comparing the biblical stories with the field research, we conclude that there are many similarities when it comes to reasoning behind fleeing – the physical survival, the wellbeing of the family, obedience to God's calling, or the desire to have a better life. From these reasons, we concluded four approaches that guide believers in making a decision. First, it is the fear that fleeing would mean the denial of Christ and therefore one will lose salvation; second, the best interest of the particular others must be the highest motivation for fleeing. The third theology expects

[20] The prosperity gospel approach generally avoids the topic of persecution and suffering (as well as the persecuted and suffering church) for it collides with their general approach focused on health and wealth.

deep personal knowledge of God's voice, which will become the decisive argument for staying or fleeing from persecution. The fourth theology is related to pursuing happiness.

7 References

Accad, M. (2014, March 31). *When the State Starts Crumbling: A Theology of Staying*. Good Faith Media. https://goodfaithmedia.org/when-the-state-starts-crumbling-a-theology-of-staying-cms-21663/

Andrews, J. (Ed.). (2018). *The Church in Disorienting Times: Leading Prophetically through Adversity*. Langham Global Library.

Cherry, K. (n.d.). *Levels of Developing Morality in Kohlberg's Theories*. Verywell Mind. Retrieved September 13, 2021, from https://www.verywellmind.com/kohlbergs-theory-of-moral-development-2795071

Coleman, S. (2000). *The Globalisation of Charismatic Christianity: Spreading the Gospel of Prosperity*. Cambridge University Press.

Ellul, J. (1969). *To Will & To Do*. Pilgrim Press.

Held, V. (2006). *The Ethics of Care: Personal, Political, and Global*. Oxford University Press.

Kierkegaard, S. (1941). *Fear and Trembling* (W. Lowrie, Trans.). Religion Online. Retrieved September 20, 2021, from https://www.religion-online.org/book/fear-and-trembling/

Lane, T. (1996). *Dějiny křesťanského myšlení* (J. Bartoň, Trans.). Návrat domů. – [Engl. orig.: The Lion Book of Christian thought, 1992].

Middleton, P. (2006). *Radical martyrdom and cosmic conflict in early Christianity*. T & T Clark.

Sauer, C. (Ed.). (2012). *Bad Urach Statement: Towards an evangelical theology of suffering, persecution and martyrdom for the global church mission*. VKW.

Schirrmacher, T. (2018). *The Persecution of Christians Concerns Us All: Towards a Theology of Martyrdom* (3rd ed.). VKW.

Sutcliffe, R. (2018). To Flee or Not to Flee? Matthew 10:23 and Third Century Flight in Persecution. *Scrinium, 14*(1), 133-160. https://doi.org/10.1163/18177565-00141P10

Tertullian. (n.d.). *De Fuga in Persecutione* (Thelwall, Trans.). Retrieved August 25, 2021, from https://www.newadvent.org/fathers/0409.htm

Tieszen, C. L. (2008). *Re-examining religious persecution: Constructing a theological framework for understanding persecution*. VKW; AcadSA.

Wilkinson, B. (2013). *The Prayer of Jabez: Breaking through to the Blessed Life*.

Zhang, Q., & Zhao, H. (2017). An Analytical Overview of Kohlberg's Theory of Moral Development in College Moral Education in Mainland China. *Open Journal of Social Sciences, 05*, 151-160. https://doi.org/10.4236/jss.2017.58012

D. Practical Theology

12 Pastor, mentor and prophet

Development in theology and practice of pastors working with religiously persecuted

Henrik Nymann Eriksen[1]

Abstract

This article explores the pastoral role of Danish pastors in relation to Christian converts facing persecution upon repatriation to their Muslim homelands, based on interviews with pastors and Christian leaders. The pastoral role encompasses three key figures: pastor, mentor, and prophet. As pastors, ministers provide care through presence, prayer, blessings, Biblical teaching and practical assistance which aligns with traditional Lutheran pastoral duties but also expands upon them. The mentor role enlarges traditional ministry by offering discipleship and helping converts navigate their relationships with their Muslim backgrounds and the associated risks of persecution. The leadership aspect balances between the authoritarian styles of imams and a more anti-authoritarian Danish approach, necessitating a consideration of contextualisation and counter-cultural elements. Finally, the prophetic role involves advocating for vulnerable refugees before authorities, exemplifying public theology and prompting critical self-reflection among several interviewees.

Keywords: Pastoral role, public theology, converts, persecution, discipleship, leadership style.

1 Introduction

This article examines the role of Danish pastors in relation to Christian refugees, particularly from Iran and Afghanistan, who face persecution[2]

---

[1] Henrik Nymann Eriksen (1965), Rector at Dansk Bibel Institut and General Manager of Fjellhaug International University College campus Copenhagen, hne@dbi.edu, ORCID iD: 0009-0007-1293-7246.

[2] In the introductory chapter of this anthology, Sauer and Nel provide a thorough discussion on different definitions of 'religious persecution'. The present

upon repatriation due to their conversion from Islam.[3] The period primarily covers the 2010s. The main question addressed is: How have Danish pastors lived out their pastoral role towards Christian refugees with a strong narrative of persecution linked to their situation? The article explores the experiences of pastors and Christian leaders regarding their role toward migrants in Denmark. The study is thereby limited both in terms of the migrants' perspective on the role of pastors and the potential role of pastors toward repatriated refugees after they have left Denmark. Both themes are relevant but must be addressed in other studies.

2 Research context

Since the onset of the refugee crisis in 2015 several academic and popular contributions have been published concerning the church's role in relation to refugees and converts in Denmark. Early contributions include thematic issues in the journal *Ny Mission* (Mogensen 2016a and 2016b), which discuss the church's response to the refugee crisis and the relationship between migration and mission. Sara Afshari's (2018) systematic work on the new Farsi-speaking group in the Danish church provides a current picture of the situation for Farsi-speaking Christians in Denmark and their needs. Studies edited by M. J. Petersen and S. B. Jensen (2019) discuss the risk of religious persecution on repatriation as a factor in asylum cases. A 2022 contribution applies public theology to the Danish refugee situation (M. S. Mogensen and N. N. Eriksen, 2022). However, there has yet to be a study focusing on the pastoral role of Danish pastors and Christian leaders towards refugees who feel threatened by persecution upon repatriation. This article aims to initiate a discussion on this aspect.

3 Theoretical perspectives

Two theoretical perspectives will be used in the analysis: pastoral theology focused on the pastoral role in Lutheran theology and public theology.

---

chapter operates with a broad definition offered by *World Watch Research*: "Any hostility experienced as a result of one's identification with Christ. This can include hostile attitudes, words and actions towards Christians" (World Watch Research 2024 p. 3).

3 All Danish texts from literature and interviews are translated by the author helped by AI.

3.1 Pastoral theology

The pastoral role towards converts can be seen as an application of existing pastoral practice in a new field that calls for both adaptation and additions. To identify these new elements, we will reflect the pastoral practice of informants against a traditional Lutheran understanding of the pastoral role, as expressed by C. F. W. Walther (1987). Walther emphasises the pastoral role as a service with God's word, instituted by God, and which always holds relevance in the church, including in encounters with persecuted converts in the 21st century. This pastoral service is not indicative of a "more holy state" like the Levitical priesthood (Walther, 1987, p. 198) but rather a "ministry of service." The pastoral role is public and has the authority "to preach the gospel and administer the holy sacraments" (Walther, 1987, p. 213). The pastoral office is assigned a special and defining role compared to other ministries in the church: "The pastoral ministry is the highest office in the church and from it stem all other offices in the church" (Walther, 1987, p. 289). This view of the pastoral role implies that the congregation must recognise and obey their pastor insofar as God's word is preached. Walther (1987, p. 303) explicitly states this obedience to the pastor's authority: "To the ministry there is due respect as well as unconditional obedience when the pastor uses God's Word." However, reservations are also made regarding tyrannical use of the office's power. Walter is chosen as a clear representative of the traditional Lutheran understanding of the pastoral office.

In addition to Walther, it is relevant to incorporate elements from the ordination ritual for pastors in the Lutheran Church of Denmark. The bishop mentions that new pastors should preach God's word based on the Bible with a view towards repentance, mercy towards the suffering, Christian brotherhood, love for one's neighbour and obedience to authority. Moreover, pastors are to administer the sacraments, teach, guide the confused, comfort the fearful and admonish gently. The pastoral vow also adds that the pastor shall "oppose the misuse of the holy means of grace" (Ritualbog, 1994, p. 149).

Another representative of a Lutheran perspective on the contemporary adaptation of the pastoral role, is O. Skjevesland: "The church simply needs pastors with a range of qualities, and these should primarily work together to renew the proclamation of the gospel" (Skjevesland, 1998, p. 107).

Skjevesland chooses "the interpreter" as a metaphor for a renewed pastoral role. As an interpreter, the pastor has three functions:

1. Preaching and teaching Scripture and the church's tradition.
2. Leadership, which primarily occurs through communication.
3. A role model aimed at shaping an authentic life of faith (Skjevesland, 1997, p. 301).

The pastor's authority is partly linked to the office itself (formal authority) and partly to personal authenticity and competence. Skjevesland summarizes: "The pastor is tasked with (...) exercising reflective pastoral leadership. That is the expectation of the congregation" (Skjevesland, 1998, p. 118).

3.2 Public theology

Public theology is broadly defined by Lodberg and Nissen (2022, p. 20) as "theological engagement in word and/or action regarding issues affecting all citizens of society". A principal justification refers to Danish theologian Regin Prenter, who during World War II justified the church's active role against injustice by stating that the gospel impacts not just a particular religious and spiritual part of life but speaks into all aspects of existence. With reference to Kim and Day, Lodberg and Nissen (2022, pp. 17-18) identify six characteristics of public theology:

4. *Incarnational* – following Christ's example, theology must dwell and take shape in the concrete contexts and issues people face.
5. *Multiple Publics* – awareness that the public sphere is not a singular concept.
6. *Interdisciplinarity* – theology must listen to other disciplines when addressing concrete challenges.
7. *Dialogical* – theology's conversation in the public sphere also involves listening and learning.
8. *Global Perspective* – many themes have international implications.
9. *Performative* – public theology engages in concrete activities.

Lodberg and Nissen's presentation of public theology contains elements that can inform pastors' involvement in the challenges faced by persecuted refugees in the public sphere. Another theologian, Miroslav Volf (2022), understands public theology through the lens of Christianity as a prophetic religion, contrasting it with mystery religions. The prophetic type advocates for active transformation of the world while others encourage the soul's flight upward to God (Volf, 2022, p. 26). Volf advocates for Christian engagement in all dimensions of culture to contribute to the common good through wisdom. In Christian terms, wisdom involves a comprehensive understanding of the good life God created us for, practical advice on how to live that good life and wisdom as a person, Jesus Christ. The Christian and the church contribute their wisdom in a secularized and/or multireligious society by "everyone speaking in the public sphere with their own religious voice" (Volf, 2022, p. 193). Thus, it is about being present in the public sphere with integrity to contribute Christian wisdom to the common good. Public theology provides a language to reflect on some of the dimensions present in the pastoral role towards converts.

4 Method

The material for this article is derived from six semi-structured qualitative interviews with Danish pastors and Christian leaders who have had a pastoral role towards converts primarily from Islam, who have sought asylum in Denmark and fear religiously motivated persecution upon repatriation.[4] Most informants are from the Lutheran Church, with one having a background in the Pentecostal Church. The interviews lasted approximately 90 minutes.

The interviews were semi-structured, allowing open questions for informants to describe how they exercised their pastoral role, what they found significant, and how they reflected on it in hindsight (Kvale 1997). Supplementary questions ensured that relevant themes were addressed, and the interviewer received answers to specific points of interest. However, the individual informant's assessment of significance guided the conversation's focus.

In post-interview analysis, the material was examined using Thematic Analysis, where an abductive approach combines a deductive top-down coding of predetermined themes with an inductive ground-up coding that remains open to emerging themes (Thomson 2022). The approach is phenomenological and explores informants' experiences and subsequent reflections without drawing normative conclusions (Justesen & Mik-Meyer 2010). Thus, various perspectives are allowed to stand on their own and in dialogue or potential conflict with one another.

4 The main questions have been: In what situations have you served as a pastor to refugees who felt threatened by persecution? How have you ministered to them? How have you related to their situation of persecution? What role has discipleship played? What has your role been in relation to their case with the authorities? How do you evaluate your own role as a pastor? What advice would you give to other pastors who come into contact with persecuted refugees?

5 Findings

The following findings are grouped into three main themes that have played a significant role for some or all informants.

5.1 Pastoral care

Under this heading, four subthemes are articulated: Presence, Prayer and blessing, the Bible and practical help.

Presence: Presence is frequently noted by several as an important pastoral activity. The most mentioned element of presence is that the pastor must listen: "I have listened to their story. I have not corrected them when they have told me about their risk" (Informant 1). This listening conversation often revolves around the converts' experience of uncertainty regarding repatriation to their Muslim homeland: "We sit and talk together, and the person tells how he feels about possibly being sent out of the country soon" (Informant 3). Language barriers can be so significant that only a few meaningful words can be exchanged. One informant reflects on almost wordless presence with an inmate as an incarnational and sacramental presence: "There is such an incarnational presence ... There are seven words we can communicate with, right? And I listen a bit and say a short prayer in silence. Yes, it is an incredible presence. It is sacramental" (Informant 5). Presence can also involve friendly hospitality inviting someone to visit one's private home, for example, during one of the Christian holidays: "He needs a friend" (Informant 4). In certain situations, some informants have gone to great lengths to show presence in critical circumstances. This includes a case of church asylum, where the pastor not only opened the church doors but also moved into the church himself: "So he lives up there next to the organ on the pulpit, and he sleeps up there at night. I also slept up there for three weeks" (Informant 1). A tense situation could also be in the Ellebæk prison where an inmate awaited imminent repatriation to Afghanistan: "It is like visiting a death cell. He is completely frozen. He was facing expulsion to a country where it was known he would be persecuted. I visited him every week. We shared the sense of powerlessness[5]" (Informant 5).

Prayer and Blessing: Prayer is a significant element in pastoral care: "Many want prayer. Because it is hopeless. Not for everyone, but for most" (Informant 5). Intercession was an articulated need that called for immediate response: "They are people under great pressure. They come and sit

5 The Danish word "afmagt" also includes "despair" and "hopelessness".

in the service. And they cry and ask for you to lay hands on them and pray for them and give them over into God's hands" (Informant 1). They do not need so much practical advice as they need caring intercession (Informant 3). It is noted by several informants that the Aaronitic blessing holds great significance as something that they, as pastors, can concretely offer those who fear persecution: "And when I say pray it should perhaps be added that the invocation of the blessing at the end is something I have become aware of actually holds great significance for many Iranians. So we must, of course, conclude the personal intercession with the Aaronitic blessing with the laying on of hands" (Informant 1).

The Bible: Comfort and encouragement from specific biblical verses play a role in the pastors' assistance to persecuted converts. A biblical verse that appeared several times in the interviews is Jesus' words to Pilate (John 19:11). One informant recounts an early experience where this biblical verse became significant: "It is the evening before the rejection, I am with him, and he is really scared. Then there is a Bible verse that we share which becomes decisive in a way. It is Jesus standing before Pilate and saying to him: 'You have no power at all unless it has been given to you by my heavenly Father.' What that means is like saying: This is not you against the Refugee Board. Your heavenly Father also plays a part in the game. You must believe that. He has a way in this and through this – and then boldly, or at least courageously, show up tomorrow. And he did, I believe" (Informant 1,). In a meeting with a small group of rejected asylum seekers one informant describes how he is with them in a cell in Ellebæk prison, and how the Bible plays an important role in keeping their spirits up: "The uncertainty about the future was terrible. I come and sit there. We have the Bible, we read a piece, we find a piece; it is not always well chosen, but we read a piece. We read" (Informant 5). Biblical texts about hope have naturally been a central focus in preaching. In the "Bording Bible Café," where rejected asylum seekers from the Kaershovedgaard detention center attended, systematic Bible teaching has been conducted weekly over several years: "Generally, it is Bible teaching. Very often it has been texts that focus on hope, but also a simple introduction to the Christian faith, and that they learn to know the Bible" (Informant 6). In several places, the Danish congregation's service was translated into English and Farsi if necessary so that converts could understand the sermon.

Practical help: Many refugees find themselves in situations where they need practical assistance to handle their circumstances, such as transportation, finances and correspondence with authorities. On this practical and apolitical level informants agree on helping as much as possible. One informant expresses that there are limits to how much help can be provided: "It is a huge challenge in the Iranian church. Everyone has a case going on. It is clear that the stronger a relationship becomes, the more you cannot disregard the care for their worries. But there is a great sense of powerlessness. In reality ... we cannot. Where we can help we should help" (Informant 2).

5.2 Discipleship

Many of the converts who obtained asylum in Denmark in the 2010s have subsequently not maintained their active connection to the church. The picture is complex but several informants articulate this observation and raise the question of how the training for discipleship has been conducted. One expresses the matter as follows: "In a way, we have succeeded in evangelisation, but we have not succeeded in 'making disciples'" (Informant 4).

Baptismal instruction: The path to discipleship begins with baptismal instruction. The desire for baptism was for many refugees in the 2010s coinciding with the desire to obtain asylum in Denmark. For many, both desires were seemingly genuine, but for some the desire for baptism was solely linked to an improved possibility for asylum. This impacted the baptismal instruction: "During this period, we had the practice that you come six months to church on Sundays. Then you have a conversation, and then the baptismal training lasts six months. And then a conversation with the pastor, and then you are baptised" (Informant 1). Several informants expressed experiences with asylum seekers who, for pro forma reasons, wanted to be baptised but ended up becoming believers (Informant 3). After baptism, there has been an opportunity to continue in the church community. In relation to Iranians and Afghans, there have been Farsi-speaking communities and services with interpretation in several places. The general pattern appears to be that most baptised individuals remained part of the church community as long as they were asylum seekers. However, after obtaining residency permits and relocation to another part of the country many of them no longer attend church.

Discipleship training: There is a shared understanding among informants of the importance of continued training in discipleship but also a realistic assessment of the resources available to facilitate this (Informant 3). At the same time, one informant emphasises discipleship as fundamentally important in the training of converts from Islam: "Paul talks about bearing the scars of Jesus or sharing in Christ's sufferings, and that resonates completely in the Iranian environment. I have just read that, yes, of course, caution and wisdom regarding persecution. Yes, but also trust in God, and then it is about becoming a disciple of Jesus. That is the focus, isn't it?" (Informant 2). The same informant believes that the church seems to have forgotten something fundamental about discipleship that needs to be rediscovered: "I think it is a craft that the church has lost. How do we do it? We must follow Jesus. However, this following is often connected to my learning from others, and I have been quite conscious of that. One must engage in companionship with people, as new believers need to learn from others and practice faith collectively." (Informant 2). The deep relationship with God as the loving Father is the innermost core of discipleship. It is also here that the motivation to endure persecution is found: "Yes, a rooting in God's grace. I just think it is about getting a view of God as a loving judge who has paid the price for me so that I can experience forgiveness. If He does that, then He is my Father, He is my protector. And then I can stand for Him and pay the price" (Informant 2). The same informant has been involved in developing a discipleship program called "Safar": "Many times, I just met once a week with a person, and then we conceptualised it into a tool we call Safar which is actually 30 steps you go through. We say in our network that as soon as someone surrenders to Jesus, we must start with discipleship" (Informant 2). A significant element of discipleship is being a witness; one states: "All discipleship must involve equipping and encouraging people to be witnesses. Otherwise, we fail" (Informant 2). Others are more cautious about not putting pressure on converts to witness as it is associated with risk (Informant 3).

Leadership role: An Iranian pastor perceives himself as an older brother to his congregation: "I am like an older brother to them; I also know they are scared, and they carry anxious hearts. So often, I hold their hands ..." (Informant 3). Another emphasises the necessity of being more directive in pastoral leadership towards converts if the task is to be satisfactorily solved: "I think we make a huge mistake by being too little directive in our leadership towards these people. You need to be directive. They are used to imams, and we should not be like the imams, but we have to take it upon ourselves to be clear and explicit" (Informant 2). Another pastor fears taking on the imam role in relation to converts and emphasises servant leadership instead: "They are so used to not being allowed to ask questions. Pastor's role and imam's role? No, for heaven's sake, we should not have that power as pastors" (Informant 6).

Approach to Islam: The relationship to Islam is a significant element in discipleship for a converted Muslim. This is vital on a deeper level concerning the freedom of the gospel: "So when I speak about discipleship there are some cultural issues that also play a role, but the whole area around relationships and authenticity, sincerity and especially forgiveness is just absent in Islam" (Informant 2). Another recommends converts to be cautious about speaking negatively about Islam. He advocates for a respectful attitude towards the religion they have left: "I always tell converts that they should be polite regarding the religion they have left. They should not go around speaking poorly of it because we have so much good in Christ; we do not need to elevate ourselves by bringing the other down" (Informant 3).

Approach to persecution: On a practical level, repatriated converts are advised to maintain a low profile towards authorities but to preach and witness privately to their family and acquaintances: "Most know that they should keep a low profile if they are sent back to Iran. But they have also all received some strength, a ballast that makes it so that even if they may not say at the airport that they have become Christians, because it is foolish to say that to the authorities, they start seeking out other Christians and also preaching to their families" (Informant 3). In relation to converts in Denmark an Iranian pastor realistically emphasises that persecution is part of the package of becoming a Christian: "We tell them that Christianity is not always a bed of roses, and that is all part of a package that we as Christians want to be a part of. For if God is God in times of joy then He is also God in times of sorrow. So we often talk about that. But we also admire our siblings in Iran for the way they hold church in homes, in basement rooms or when they distribute Bibles to the taxi driver or the garbage collector" (Informant 3). He does not believe that they exaggerate the risk of persecution, but he has a sober view of it. Another pastor states: "In my work as a pastor, I have not really engaged in a proper risk assessment. I have left that to the authorities. I have listened to their story. I have not corrected them when they have mentioned their risk. I would also say that as time has passed on my picture has also become somewhat more nuanced" (Informant 1). The same pastor expresses concern that the persecution narrative in the Farsi-speaking part of the congregation was not sufficiently nuanced (Informant 1). However, it is not only upon repatriation but also in asylum centres that converts may risk persecution: "There are Chechens, Syrians and Palestinians in the asylum centres. They can be terrible to converts. In that way, it still costs something. I have talked to several who have been beaten in the asylum centers or have been verbally abused" (Informant 3). The same informant advises converts who feel pressured in the asylum centers to politely and quietly acknowledge their faith in Jesus if asked but not to proclaim it aggressively.

5.3 Contact with authorities and public engagement

Contact with authorities: One informant reflects on a dual approach to the persecution of Christians: "You can say that there is, in a way, a built-in theological dilemma regarding persecution which consists on one side of seeing the description of persecution as a condition for Christians in their new situation. And then you can say that the task is to dare to say: Take it upon yourselves. You should not seek to avoid it. You should not seek protection from it. That would be the radical approach. And then on the other side we must stand up for them. They are our brothers and sisters, and they are under threat, and therefore they need protection" (Informant 1). This advocacy for converts concerning various authorities played a greater or lesser role for the interviewed pastors.

One pastor, who has closely followed many asylum seekers, believes that one cannot sharply separate spiritual assistance from practical action regarding the authorities: "My attitude is that you cannot have completely watertight compartments between spiritual guidance and practical action" (Informant 1). Another Christian leader has somewhat assumed a lawyers role: "I am not a pastor. I am not a lawyer. But still, some use me as both their pastor and lawyer" (Informant 4). Others have not gone as far in their involvement. The leader of an Iranian congregation describes the modest help they can provide: "We do not have time, and we do not have resources for that. I have read a letter. Another has just called the lawyer. That is what we have done. But we do not have a dedicated team for that" (Informant 3).

Some informants have also stood up for converts in language schools, asylum centers and prisons if they felt the conditions were unreasonable or if the new Christians were subjected to pressure or persecution from other residents or inmates. One informant describes this as his prophetic service: "It is the prophetic. Back to the Old Testament prophets. They say that the poor are being oppressed. Their rights are suppressed. That is how I best understand myself. That is what I rest most in" (Informant 5). Others have taken a lower profile but encouraged converts to contact the management at the asylum centers if they experience fanatical Muslims: "If someone experiences at the asylum center that there are some fanatical Muslims I encourage them to contact the office and report it to the authorities at the asylum center and not just let themselves be intimidated by them" (Informant 3).

Church asylum: On several occasions, converts sought church asylum after being denied by the Refugee Board. Initially, this happened quite anarchically, but later it became more regulated with contact with the police and other authorities. A pastor who had church asylum in his church in Copenhagen several times recounts the first time he granted church asylum to a rejected convert: "He seeks church asylum. So, he goes into the church, stays there one Sunday after the service and doesn't want to leave the church again; he is allowed to stay. During the church asylum he decides to go on a hunger strike. Today, I would not have allowed a hunger strike in the church. I did back then. And he is on the news in the evening. It ends up with his case being reopened, and he is granted asylum" (Informant 1). Subsequently, the pastor reflects: "I should have said that if you want to go on a hunger strike, then you must leave the church. A hunger strike is to instrumentalise your death in the ultimate instance: 'I will die from not eating anything, or you must give me what I want.' And I do not think that is an appropriate means for a Christian community" (Informant 1).

Public and media: A pastor recounts a convert who was seriously injured in a fight at an asylum center because he was a Christian. The case developed and ended up in a nationwide news outlet: "That is when I contacted Jyllands-Posten, and it became quite a large feature with pictures and stories, etc. And afterwards, it turned out that the story about that school fight had two sides. And there was probably an unnecessary provocation on his part. So, one can say that there were real threats at the asylum centers, but it was also instrumentalised. However, when I look back, I do not regret standing up for NN. I do not. I think it was right. What he was subjected to was persecution of the worst kind. And it was not recognised by the Red Cross. I thought it was good that we did that. And it was good that we had that process. One could say that the involvement of the media afterwards, in hindsight, was not helpful" (Informant 1).

Reflection on practice: A pastor critically considers his practice in connection with a specific case of church asylum: "One could say that the risk of persecution would not be present with the lack of ecclesiastical practice he has subsequently had. Therefore, there is also an element in which, as a pastor, I have contributed to putting pressure on the asylum authorities or creating the opportunity for him to put pressure on the asylum authorities in a way that in hindsight leads one to ask oneself: 'Have I actually contributed to having a functioning asylum system that people can trust, or have I done the opposite?'" (Informant 1).

An informant who previously went to great lengths for converts to ensure their residence permits is now unwilling to engage in the same way: "Ten years ago, I had a motto that said if someone converted and received a rejection I would put myself on the field in front of the airplane. Gradually, I say that I will not lay myself out on the field for anyone at all. And that is because there are too many asylum seekers who have received approval and have stopped coming to church" (Informant 4).

The strong narrative of persecution was a driving force in relation to cases at the Refugee Board and also played a significant role in church circles. One informant cannot follow the negative assessment of the Refugee Board: “There was, in parts of the church, a strongly critical approach to the Refugee Board. But they have their sources which are carefully selected. It was believed that they do not really know what it is about. But my experience is that there has been a very large receptiveness when I have been in dialogue with the authorities” (Informant 1). Pastors’ efforts to assist refugees with asylum sometimes succeeded very well. One pastor reflects somewhat skeptically on his own success: “In fact, I would say that looking back, I can become unsure whether I have succeeded a bit too well in asserting my influence. A legal member of the Refugee Board said to me: ‘The best, most effective example of lobbying I have ever encountered is what you did regarding converts in the Refugee Board. It has helped change something.’ He said it as a compliment” (Informant 1). However, in hindsight, the pastor expresses a certain distance from his earlier political role in relation to blindly adopting the narratives of converts concerning the risk of persecution (Informant 1).

The three overarching themes around which these findings are grouped give rise to the consideration of whether a specific pastoral figure can be assigned as a title for each of them. For the first main theme the figure of the *pastor* is natural as the role lies in the immediate extension of the classical pastoral role. The second main theme concerning discipleship could be grouped under designations such as “leader” or “older brother” as one informant referred to himself. Instead, the figure of a *mentor* is chosen which is not mentioned in the interviews but rather gathers elements associated with the pastoral role under the theme of discipleship, including the personal one-to-one relationship. The third main theme is the relationship with the authorities. Here, it concerns being the converts’ defender against unfair treatment. One informant calls himself their “lawyer,” while another uses the term “prophet”, referring to the biblical prophets’ call against injustice. We choose the *prophet* as the third figure because it is precisely as a Christian pastor that he steps forward as the defender of the converts. Therefore, in the following we will gather the analysis of the pastoral role towards persecuted converts in these three figures: Pastor, Mentor, and Prophet.

6 Discussion

6.1 Pastor

Care for new Christians who experience an urgent risk of persecution is a prominent feature of the pastoral role among informants, encapsulated in the Pastor figure. It is remarkable, though perhaps not surprising, that *concrete presence* plays a significant role in the pastors' practice. Presence is understood as active listening both to the converts' faith and life stories and to their fears for the future. Sometimes, presence can be a silent presence where the pastor joins the sense of powerlessness of the convert's situation. At times, pastors have gone to great lengths to meet the need for presence which one describes as the need to have a friend. Particularly one informant emphasizes the incarnational and sacramental nature of presence. In this lies a hint to Jesus' words that where two or three are gathered in His name, He is present (Matt 18:20). Considering how significant presence is in the pastoral role towards persecuted Christians, it is noteworthy how little this element features in Walther's description of the pastoral office. The ordination ritual does not mention presence directly but it is indirectly expressed in the pastor's obligation to preach "mercy towards all who suffer, Christian brotherhood and love for one's neighbor," as well as the command to guide the confused and comfort the fearful (Ritualbog, p. 145). The dimension of presence must thus be considered an extension and unfolding of a theme that receives limited or no attention in a classical Lutheran understanding of pastoral care.

Intercession and blessing also emerge as significant parts of the pastor's role. There is a clear need for this element, but it seemingly plays no role for Walther and can only be indirectly linked to the ordination ritual. Therefore, there is in this intercessory service a pastoral emphasis that is new in relation to the traditional description of the Lutheran pastoral role. It is a dimension of the pastoral role that presses forward as a need in encounters with persecuted Christians. Alongside intercession, the personal invocation of the blessing is mentioned. The Aaronitic blessing is part of the liturgy of the Lutheran Sunday service, but the need of personal blessing, including laying hands on the converts, neither Walther nor the ordination ritual gives help. Skjevesland mentions, among several models, the pastor as the administrator of rites, but likewise does not mention anything about the personal, targeted aspect of the Aaronitic blessing (Skjevesland 1998). It is a significant new element in the pastor's role as a pastor to bless fearful converts individually with the laying on of hands.

The Bible is used in several ways in the pastoral role towards converts. Firstly, biblical texts play a central role in preaching during services and Christian teaching. This use of the Bible is important both for building a theological understanding of what Christianity is and for the converts personally benefiting from the Bible in their new faith journey, especially the texts of hope. This use of the Bible as a pastoral tool aligns perfectly with Walther's emphasis on the pastoral office as a service with God's word. It is also in immediate continuation of the bishop's words at the ordination of pastors: "Therefore, I now lay upon you the duty: To preach God's word correctly as it is found in the prophetic and apostolic scriptures" (Ritualbog, p. 144). This also corresponds to Skjevesland's description of the pastor as an interpreter through preaching and teaching (Skjevesland, 1997). Following this, the Bible is also used in line with classical Lutheran spiritual care as preaching for the individual. This can be words of comfort in a tense, unsafe situation or in the face of a bleak future. This individual use of the Bible for comfort corresponds to the ordination ritual's mention of "comforting the fearful" (Ritualbog, p. 145). The strong emphasis in a classical Lutheran understanding of the service with God's word is thus significantly accentuated in the informants' use of the Bible toward persecuted converts.

Practical help has been a natural and necessary part of the pastoral role for all informants when it comes to needs that press in here and now. On this level, it does not concern "political" contact with the authorities but rather practical matters such as transportation, translating letters, etc. This practical help has emerged as a necessary part of the effort towards converted refugees. Care has sometimes been extensive. In his principled description of the pastoral office Walther does not mention this side, but in the ordination ritual, it speaks of "mercy towards all who suffer, Christian brotherhood and love for one's neighbor." Thus, this diaconal dimension lies in clear extension of the classical Lutheran pastoral role.

The *Pastor* figure towards persecuted converts thus encompasses a care for individuals that is both entirely in line with a classical Lutheran pastoral role and also contains elements that are both an expansion of the classical role and add something new, though without being in conflict with a Lutheran understanding of the pastoral role. Walter, as a representative of a strong traditional Lutheran position, seems to be too narrow in his approach to give serious help to the pastoral need, except for the ministry with the Word. The ordination ritual and Skjevesland have a broader perspective, but not enough to give much help for the new elements in the pastoral role toward persecuted Christians.

6.2 Mentor

The pastoral role in discipleship training towards converts can be summarised under the designation Mentor. One informant used the term "older brother" in relation to his role towards converts which encompasses several of the same elements. There is consensus on the importance of training in discipleship for an independent and mature Christian faith and practice, although the emphasis may vary. Some informants express that the reason many converts become passive regarding church involvement after obtaining residency permits may be due to a lack of discipleship training: "In a way, we have succeeded in evangelisation, but we have not succeeded in making disciples" (Informant 4).

Baptismal training has often been thorough and can reasonably be seen as a discipleship training course. The rejection of pro forma baptism fulfils the words of the pastoral vow to "oppose the misuse of the holy means of grace" (Ritualbog, p. 149). However, it has typically involved group teaching rather than individual teaching which one informant highlights as an essential element for discipleship training to succeed. Personal faith development can be hindered by a very collective Iranian culture which is the backdrop for the emphasis of the Safar material on pair-based processes in discipleship training. Training in the form of preaching and Bible teaching is entirely in line with a classical Lutheran understanding of the pastor as "the servant of the Word" (Ritualbog, p. 144, and 149), while the individual mentor or older brother role is absent in both Walther and in the ordination ritual.[6] This, along with the issue of resources, may contribute to the apparent lack of a targeted place for it among Lutheran folk church pastors.

The pastor, as a *leader* for converts, also leans towards the mentor role. Iranian and Afghan converts have grown up with the authoritarian spiritual leadership of the imam which affects their experience of church leaders. Some informants have experienced it as a challenge that Iranian leaders, in their opinion, acted too authoritatively and reminded them of imams in their leadership. In reaction to this, one informant emphasises that the pastor should practice servant leadership which excludes the imam's authoritarian role. Conversely, a leader from an Iranian congregation emphasises that we have a problem with converts from the Middle East regarding our anti-authoritarian leadership style because they simply do not take it seriously. Therefore, the pastor, in his role as a mentor for converts, must dare to be more directive but without being authoritarian and imam-like. It is suggested that a too weak leadership role may influence how seriously converts take the necessity of being an active part of the church community after obtaining asylum. This directive leadership style is supported by Walther's (1987, p. 303) emphasis on obedience to the pastor. In Walther's case, however, it concerns a view of office while the

6 One element in Skjevesland's description of the minister as an interpreter does, however, point toward discipleship training – namely, that the minister should 'be able to shape an authentic life of faith with a modeling intention' (Skjevesland 1997, p. 301).

informant's appeal to be more directive is culturally grounded. Thus, there appears to be a continuum regarding the pastor's leadership style between authoritarian imam-like leadership and anti-authoritarian cautious leadership. Where informants position themselves on this continuum is either determined by a countercultural stance because the gospel demands that the leader be a servant, or by a contextually accommodating approach because effective leadership requires that the pastor be more directive. Skjevesland (1998, p. 126) puts this issue into perspective in his discussion of the minister as a leader, noting that the congregation expects a reflective pastoral leadership. Furthermore, he describes this leadership as the exercise of a 'non-dominating authority,' distancing himself from both clericalism and anti-clericalism.

Contrary to what one might expect, the direct *threat of persecution* is not often articulated in preaching and teaching but it is nonetheless present as a backdrop. Pastors recommend the converts to keep a low profile especially regarding authorities in their home country. Some emphasise the importance of *witness* for non-believers as part of discipleship with the associated risks while others are cautious about pressuring converts to witness. This also applies in asylum centers where converts may meet resistance. The persecution issue does not play a role in the classical Lutheran pastoral role, so practice in this field is new.

Regarding the *Muslim background*, deep cultural elements in Islam that differ greatly from the gospel are emphasized where discipleship entails a deeper understanding of especially God's grace and God as a loving Father. This represents a fundamental break from the Muslim background. Some converts think very negatively about Islam, but an Iranian pastor urges politeness and respect in discussing their previous religion, partly to avoid unnecessary opposition and partly to show respect for what they come from even though they are now happy to have chosen a different path. Just as in the matter of leadership, there seems to be a continuum here between discussing the relationship to Islam solely as a break and emphasising continuity with their previous faith.

The pastor as a *Mentor* encompasses several elements and thus plays a significant role in the training for discipleship. Although a traditional Lutheran pastoral role does not provide help for discipleship training, Skjevesland has contributions to the pastor as a role model and leader.

6.3 Prophet

One pastor refers to his role as a defender of converts against various authorities as his prophetic service. This alludes to the protest of the biblical prophets, who spoke against injustice and the oppression of the weakest in society Another informant states that he has been the converts' lawyer. Not all informants have had this direct contact with authorities as part of their pastoral role towards converts, but for some it has been a significant element. The designation of prophetic service corresponds to Volf's (2022, pp. 26-30) discussion of Christianity as a prophetic religion that seeks to make a difference for the common good in the world which is the goal of public theology.

Lodberg and Nissen's (2022, pp. 17-18) six characteristics of public theology correspond on several points to the prophetic element in the pastoral role towards converts. The *incarnational* element is expressed in the empathy for the persecuted Christians' situation which serves as the starting point for addressing authorities on their behalf. In subsequent reflections, several express that their empathy at times became too one-dimensional regarding the seriousness of the persecution risk which may have weakened the actual contribution to the common good by counteracting the authorities' decisions. The second characteristic of public theology is the idea of *multiple publics* which is expressed in contact with a variety of different public authorities, such as the Refugee Board, authorities at asylum centers, language schools and prisons as well as the public media. The third characteristic is *interdisciplinarity* which in the case of asylum seekers especially involves the inclusion of legal competence. Public theology is fourthly *dialogical* which is manifested in the dialogues pastors have with for example the jurists of the Refugee Board and the leaders of asylum centers where, by listening, they also learn that some cases are more complex than initially assumed. The fifth characteristic of public theology is a *global perspective*, which, in relation to asylum-seeking converts, is very concrete in their fear of repatriation to Iran or Afghanistan. Although some pastors later question how realistic the risk of heavy persecution may have been in Iran, the global perspective is constantly present in their role towards this group. Public theology is also *performative* as its last characteristic. This has been expressed in several ways including the form of church asylum, media coverage and services for persecuted asylum seekers. An element of critical self-reflection is also tied to this performative side. This is particularly due to considerations regarding the suitability of means for the Christian church. This especially concerns hunger strikes but also the use of media to exert unreasonable pressure on the authorities. However, this critical reflection does not imply a total rejection of performative activities as part of pastors' prophetic service.

Thus, public theology provides a language for the *prophetic* element in the pastoral role towards persecuted Christians. This is a new element in relation to the traditional Lutheran pastoral role.

7 Concluding remarks

We began this article by asking: How have pastors in Denmark lived out their pastoral role towards Christian refugees with a strong narrative of persecution linked to their situation? The answer is multifaceted as none of the informants has had an identical practice. However, three pastoral figures emerge as responses to the study, namely pastor, mentor, and prophet. As a *pastor*, the pastoral role has been unfolded both as a classical Lutheran ministry with God's word but with supplementary elements such as presence, intercession and practical support. The *mentor* figure is particularly tied to discipleship training. For some informants the lack of discipleship training may explain why many converts are not active in the church after obtaining residency permits. Another element tied to the mentor role is the question of leadership style towards converts where the pastor must position himself on a scale between authoritarian and anti-authoritarian. The pastor as a *prophet* is a new element in relation to the classical pastoral role but is also a concrete example of public theology. Not all informants have included this element in their pastoral role, but some have, which has subsequently led to critical self-reflection, especially due to a potentially one-dimensional picture of the risk of persecution, combined with performative actions that have challenged the authorities' case handling. Overall, the three figures stand as relevant elements in pastoral care for persecuted Christians.

8 References

Afshari, S. (2018). *A strategy for integration of Farsi speaking newcomers into the Danish church.* The Council on International Relations of the Evangelical Lutheran Church in Denmark.

Justesen, L. & Mik-Meyer, N. (2010). *Kvalitative metoder i organisations- og ledelsesstudier.* Hans Reitzels Forlag.

Kvale, S. (1997). *InterView,* Hans Reitzels Forlag.

Lodberg, P., & Nissen, U.(2022). Hvad er offentligheds teologi? In Jørgensen et al. (Eds.), *Offentlighedsteologi – En introduktion* (pp.13-34). Eksistensen.

Mogensen, M. S. (2016). Jeg var fremmed og I tog jer af mig. Flygtningekrisen og kirkens svar. *Ny Mission* 30.

Mogensen, M. S. (2016). Migration og mission. *Ny Mission* 31.

Mogensen, M. S. & Eriksen, N. N. (2022). Kirke og migration. In Jørgensen et al. (Eds.), *Offentlighedsteologi – En introduktion* (pp. 129-143). Eksistensen.

Petersen, M. J., & Jensen, S. B. (Eds.) (2019). *Faith in the system? Religion in the (Danish) asylum system.* Aalborg Universitetsforlag.

Ritualbog (1994). *Gudstjenesteordning for Den Danske Folkekirke.* Det Kgl. Vajsenhus' Forlag.

Safar. *One-to-one Discipelship* (2025, June, 24). Safar. https://www.safar.org.

Skjevesland, O. (1997). Den pastorale identitet. Perspektiver på presteutdannelsen i dag. *Tidsskrift for Teologi og kirke,* 4, 291-303.

Skjevesland, O. (1998). *Morgendagens menighed: Ledelse og livsform*. Verbum.

Thompson, J. (2022). A Guide to Abductive Thematic Analysis. *The Qualitative Report* Vol. 27(5) How To Article 17.

Volf, M. (2022). *Offentlighedsteologi: En offentlig tro. Hvordan kristne skal bidrage til det fælles bedste?* Forlaget Semper.

Walther, C. F. W. (1987). *Church and Ministry.* The Lutheran Church of Missouri Synod (1875/1987).

World Watch Research / Open Doors International. (2024). *Short version of World Watch List* (revised October).

13 Followership in the context of persecution

Preliminary explorations

Robert Lilleaasen[1]

Abstract

This article examines the dynamics of followership within Christian congregations facing religious persecution. Integrating perspectives from ecclesiology, leadership theory, and studies on persecution, this analysis explores how persecution affects the leader–follower relationship and the broader leadership process. Drawing on Chaleff's model of courageous followership and theories of crisis and extreme context leadership, the article highlights the increasing significance of followers under pressure. It argues that persecution intensifies the need for shared leadership, courageous support, and constructive challenge from followers. The article also emphasises the importance of theological and cultural preparation for persecution, suggesting that congregations must foster resilient leadership structures. Ultimately, it contributes to the emerging field of research at the intersection of followership and religious persecution, calling for further empirical and theological investigation into the role of followers in sustaining church identity and mission under duress.

Keywords: Followership, persecution, courageous followership, crisis leadership.

1 Introduction

This article investigates followership in the church in the context of persecution. It seeks to integrate perspectives on the persecuted church and the follower-leader relationship. The aim of this article is to enhance the understanding of followership, particularly the specific challenges and opportunities followers encounter in a leader-follower relationship while

1 Robert Lilleaasen (* 1981), Associate Professor, Fjellhaug International University College, rlilleaasen@fjellhaug.no, ORCID iD: 0009-0006-7638-6896.

involved in the leadership process within churches facing persecution. Followership and follower perspectives on the leadership process are receiving more research attention (Northouse, 2021, p. 353). Likewise, research on religious persecution is garnering increased attention from various disciplines. However, to my knowledge, there has been little to no research combining these fields. This article serves as an exploratory introduction to an area that requires further examination in the future.

The article's main question is: How is followership in the church affected by religious persecution? It is a theoretical discussion of followership in churches and how the leadership process is affected by religious persecution. As a preliminary step in this area of research, the article consults existing studies on persecution, church leadership, leadership in challenging circumstances, and followership to identify characteristics of followership within the context of persecution. Three sub-questions have guided the article: What characterises religious persecution? How does persecution impact the church and its leadership process? What characterises followership in the church?

The article's central terms are *followership* and *religious persecution*. Followership is closely connected to leadership, and together, these two constitute the leadership process. If either is missing, there will be no leadership or followership. Therefore, leadership is understood as a "process that is co-created in social and relational interaction between people" (Uhl-Bien et al., 2014, p. 83). Followership, then, "is the characteristics, behaviors and processes of individuals acting in relation to leaders. [...] For a construct to qualify as followership it must be conceptualized and operationalized: (a) in relation to leaders or the leadership process, and/ or (b) in contexts in which individuals identify themselves in follower positions (e.g., subordinates) or as having follower identities" (Uhl-Bien et al., 2014, p. 96). In leadership theory followers are defined as "individuals who adopt the leader's goals temporally (e.g., following someone's direction to a restaurant) or structurally (e.g., accepting the authority of a parent, manager or president) and freely accept the influence of leaders" (Bastardoz & Van Vugt, 2019, p. 82). The leadership process is shaped by its context. Kellerman (2012, p. xxi) argues that context is equally as important as followers and leaders, whereas Carsten et al. (2010, p. 546) argue that context influences how one socially constructs roles (leaders and followers) and how these individuals enact such roles. In this article, the context is the church in the context of religious persecution.

The second central term in the article is *religious persecution*. The Oxford Dictionary of English defines persecution as a noun that refers to hostility and ill-treatment, especially because of race or political or religious beliefs.

Based on a lexical definition of persecution, Tieszen (2011, p. 41) has argued that a definition of persecution "must consider elements of unjust action; a spectrum of hostility ranging from mild to intense; the motivation behind persecution; and the resulting effect of harm". These elements, argues Tieszen, must be considered from the victim's perspective. It is the motivation behind the persecution that qualifies persecution as religious. Tieszen's (2011, p. 48) understanding of religious persecution of Christians serves as the point of departure: "Any unjust action of varying levels of hostility perpetrated primarily on the basis of religion and directed at Christians, resulting in varying levels of harm as it is considered from the victim's perspective."

2 Religious persecution

The first sub-question is: What characterises religious persecution? Building on the aforementioned definition, this section will address the following themes: unjust action, the spectrum of hostility, the motivation behind persecution, and the results from the victims' perspective.

2.1 Unjust action and spectrum of hostility

Tieszen (2011, p. 38) asserts that persecution must be understood as an action rather than just hateful attitudes. Perpetrators must act on their negative sentiments for persecution to occur. Nel (2020, p. 56) expands this perspective by discussing persecutory conduct as both active and passive (omissions). An example of omission can be found in government officials who fail to act against social hostility towards specific groups. Nel (2020, p. 56) emphasises that the actions constituting persecution must be intentional and voluntary, aligning with Tieszen's (2011, p.38) association of persecution with unjust actions, defined in the Oxford Dictionary as behaviour not aligned with moral righteousness.[2]

The second part of Tieszen's definition addresses the spectrum of hostility. Petersen and Marshall (2019, pp. 29-32) developed a typology reflecting varying degrees of Freedom of Religion or Belief (FoRB) violations, categorising them from intolerance to severe persecution. According to

[2] For more on the complexity of persecution see The Pew Research Center's two indexes: the Government Restriction Index and the Social Hostilities Index (Pew Research Center, 2018, p. 49) and the introductory chapter of this anthology where, Sauer and Nel (2025) provide a thorough discussion on different definitions of *religious persecution*.

Petersen and Marshall, only severe hostilities directly equate to persecution, while Tieszen (2011, p. 39) suggests that even mild hostilities should be recognised as such. Nel (2020, p. 48) contends that discrimination is central to understanding persecution and becomes persecution when it inflicts consequential harm. The spectrum reveals a continuum of both discrimination and the intensity of harm inflicted.

Another significant aspect of understanding persecution is the differentiation among victims based on their level of commitment to their faith. Marshall (1998, p. 4) identifies varying levels of identification with Christianity: census Christians, member Christians, practising Christians, and committed believers.[3] Both Tieszen and Nel reference Marshall to underscore the relationship between persecution and commitment. Nel (2020, pp. 37-38), applying the term "faithful follower" to committed believers, argues that "groups will experience suffering for their beliefs [...] to a different extent based on the varying levels of commitment." "Those who are truly committed to their conviction, the 'faithful followers', will encounter religious persecution on every level of intensity and harm, and will undergo more systematic suffering based on their religious identity than the preceding groups" (Nel, 2020, p. 38). Tieszen (2011, pp. 45-46) argues that less committed Christians pose less of a threat to the perpetrator and may avoid certain types of persecution.[4] These distinctions are relevant to the study of the leader-follower relationship in the church. Both because leaders most likely belong to the committed believers' group, but also in a relationship with differences in followership behaviour.

2.2 Persecutors and victims

The final part of Tieszen's definition relates to the two groups involved in persecution: the persecutors and the victims. Regarding the persecutors, the question is what causes the hostility and what motivates the persecuting behaviour. Marshall's (1998, p. 4) identification of a relationship between persecution and commitment suggests that persecution is motivated by the threat (genuine or imagined) a person or a group represent. Nel (2020, p. 37) points out that this relationship between commitment and persecution is also relevant to the persecutors. A person with a strong commitment to a cause (religious or ideological) is more likely to participate in

3 Marshall (1998, p. 4) also notes the fifth category of "crypto Christians", referring to Christians who believe but, out of fear, keep the faith hidden from others.

4 See also Petri (2021, pp. 38 and 87) on vulnerability as a result of deviant social behaviour.

discriminating behaviour.[5] In terms of motivation for persecution or discriminatory behaviour, the abovementioned spectrums display a wide range of motivations. Commenting on this, Tieszen (2011, p. 39) argues that persecution rarely has a single motivation, and usually, there is an overlap of motivations.[6]

Tieszen (2011, p. 41) maintains that the victims' perceptions of persecution and discrimination are the most important. From a victim's perspective, something could be considered persecutory, even if this was not the intent. There could be a variety of motives that did not intend to discriminate but still had persecuting results. Hence, argues Tieszen (2011, p. 40), it is not the motive but the result of an action that is the issue. That said, individuals' feelings and perceptions of a situation may be interpreted as persecution where there is no justified cause. A compulsive and subjective fixation on persecution, explains Nel (2020, p. 32), could lead to "persecutory delusion". Some ecclesial traditions see persecution as a sign of the church; others consider "suffering for the sake of Christ" a "privilege which accentuates the Christian virtues of dependency on, and vulnerability in, Christ" (Nel, 2020, p. 36). An intensified perception of persecution, whether it is in the mind of an individual or a larger group or community, calls for truthful and sober interpretive voices in the leadership process.

2.3 Summary

Based on the first sub-question, religious persecution is characterised as a will-controlled and unjust action or non-action in situations where there is a legal duty to act. The term "persecution" refers to a spectrum of hostility and a variety of intensities of harm; a common denominator is discrimination and consequential harm. The variation in hostility and harm relates to commitment, indicating that changes in follower behaviour influence the intensity of discrimination. Also relevant to follower behaviour is the need for a truthful and sober interpretation of the context in ecclesial traditions where persecution serves as a sign of the church.

---

5 Nel (2020, p. 38) notes that in the context of intra-religious persecution, individuals with a lack of commitment may be targets of persecution from the most committed.

6 Bielefeldt and Wiener (2020, p. 134) highlight three patterns of motives: the enforcement of religious truth or purity claims, the defence of a religiously defined national identity, and the control obsessions of authoritarian governments.

3 Persecution and the leadership process

The second sub-question asks: How does persecution impact the church and its leadership process? This section will deal with the following themes: church and congregational leadership, the impact of persecution and responses to persecution, and leadership in extreme contexts.

This article's basic assumption is that leadership is context-dependent. The investigation is motivated by the implications of persecution for the leadership process in general and followership in particular. Therefore, there are two contexts that we need to consider in this investigation, i.e. church and persecution. In theological literature, this relationship between context (church) and leadership is recognised both in studies on congregational leadership and in studies on the church. Skjevesland (1998, p. 23), in his book on leadership in the church, argued that before we can discuss church leadership, we must establish an ecclesiology.[7] Skjevesland maintains that ecclesiology and ecclesial structures influence the leadership process. A similar argument is expressed in Dulles's (2002) book on church models. Following his introduction of the various models, Dulles (2002, p. 154) outlines how the characteristics of these models shape or actualise different perspectives of leadership. Correspondingly, Skjevesland (1998, p. 108) argues that different ecclesiology implies different pastoral images and pastoral role expectations. Neither Dulles nor Skjevesland mentions the persecuted or suffering church and the pastoral images or perspectives on leadership such a church actualises.

Given the basic assumption that leadership is context-dependent, we must keep in mind that context is not all. In an introduction to the close relationship between congregational and generic leadership, Sirris and Askeland (2021b, p. 47) refer to Peter Drucker, who argues that only 10 percent of leadership is context-specific. We may question the empirical accuracy of this number. However, it serves as a reminder that a persecuted church is more than a persecuted church; suffering and persecution are only part of the church's identity. Moreover, investigating what characterises followership in the church in the context of religious persecution must include insights from generic theory on followership and the leadership process.

How we understand and describe the church depends on our perspective. A basic understanding of the church differentiates between a sociological and a theological perspective. Hegstad (2013, p. 17) maintains that these

7 More recently, Niemandt (2019, p. 11) has developed this argument in connection with the missional church.

two perspectives are brought together in Matthew 18:20: "For where two or three are gathered in my name, I am there among them."[8] In its most basic form, the church is an empirical fellowship of people combined with a statement on divine presence. It is this theological statement that distinguishes the church from other fellowships, and it is from this understanding that its purpose is derived. Carroll (2011, p. 7) argues the church "finds its identity and purpose in the story of Jesus Christ and the broader context of the story of the people of Israel." Building on this understanding, and with a reference to Karl Barth, Carroll (2011, p. 7) argues further that "the history of the church from its earliest days is the history of the effort of its leaders and members to discover what it means to be Christ's body at particular times and places and in the face of widely differing challenges." The particular challenge in focus is that of persecution; the ecclesiological task for leaders and followers is that of discovering what it means to be the body of Christ and the people of God in the face of persecution.[9]

According to Carroll (2011, p. 92), the primary task of church leadership "is that of preserving the congregation's identity as Christ's body, but doing so in a way that is also appropriate in its particular culture and context." Drawing on the insights of sociologist Philip Selznick, Carroll (2011, p. 93) outlines church leadership in connection with the three tasks: *meaning interpretation, community formation*, and *empowering and supporting the congregation's public ministry*. Meaning interpretation refers to the pastoral practices in preaching, liturgy, teaching, and counselling aimed at equipping and forming the congregation and its members as disciples of Christ. Community formation, explains Carroll (2011, p. 100), points to the pastoral responsibility "to shape the congregation as a community of belonging," to build structures and relationships that provide nurture and support. Empowering public ministry refers to the relationship between church and civil society and the pastors' task to help equip the congregation and its members for "their everyday roles in family life, work, civic affairs and leisure activities" (Carroll, 2011, p. 105). Given Carroll's introduction to congregational leadership, the specific task of leadership in this article could be described as empowering and preserving under pressure and persecution.

8 Volf (1998, p. 135) calls Matthew 18:20 "the church definition," arguing that it has been important in ecclesiological thinking since quite early in church history.

9 In some ecclesial traditions, persecution is more than a challenge to handle; it is understood as characteristic of the church. Martin Luther, in his 1539 treatise *On the Councils of the Church,* names suffering and carrying the cross as followers of Christ as the seventh sign of the Church.

3.1 Impact of persecution

The impact of persecution on the church depends both on the severity and character of the persecution and the theology and characteristics of the church. Based on empirical studies, Kipfer (2019, pp. 17-18) has outlined the impact in two categories: positive and negative ministry outcomes. First, he lists the following reported positive ministry outcomes in environments of persecution: *Personal spiritual growth and heightened commitment to Christ; exceptional corporate vitality; miraculous answer to prayer; revelation of God's grace and power as believers show love to persecutors; interest and respect from people as they see believers' courage and witness for Christ; reduced nominalism; expression of love and care shared between suffering believers, and/or numerical growth.* Kipfer's (2019, pp. 18-19) second category outlines reported negative consequences of persecution: *Emotional, physical, and spiritual pain; believers denying faith to escape suffering; disempowering fear; reduced integrity for Christians who hide their faith and make moral compromises to survive; privatisation of faith; evangelism stifled; mistrust between individuals and groups of believers; local churches isolated; churches becoming closed subcultures marked by legalism, defensiveness, and suspicion toward change; weakened confidence in the gospel; loss of effective witness; violence and religious conflict; death of congregations.* Although Kipfer includes some positive outcomes following persecution, the persecutors' intention is to harm the church and individual Christians. The reported outcome of persecution listed by Kipfer shows that the church is affected negatively on an individual level, on the fellowship and relationship between believers, and persecution negatively affects the congregational ministry in the world. This means persecution represents a significant threat to the church and a challenge for the congregational leadership.

In terms of how persecution impacts congregational leadership, Kipfer (2019, p. 19) acknowledges that the need for creative and committed leadership is acute. He also points out that leaders are often targeted to weaken or eliminate their influence. While many remain faithful, Kipfer (2019, p. 19) lists the following negative consequences of persecution on congregational leadership: Leaders *cease giving leadership due to apostasy, fear, exile or death; are hindered by physical and emotional results of persecution, including injury, lack of sleep, debilitating fear, paranoia and post-traumatic stress disorder; compromise their faith and call, undermining their moral authority and followers' trust; conform to persecutors' demands, such as limiting preaching to "safe" topics; imitate dysfunctional leadership norms; experience insecurity and tension in their marriage and families; feel regret, guilt and shame when their responses to persecution are not as loving and faith-filled as they would like them to be.* This list of negative consequences on leadership serves to highlight the importance of supporting those with leadership responsibility. Moreover, the negative impact of persecution on the congregation and the congregational leadership could motivate us to rethink our understanding of leadership. In connection with this list, Kipfer (2019, p. 19) points out that "persecution does not, in and of itself, transform Christian leaders into super-saints or spiritual heroes." What I find particularly interesting in this quote is the underlying premise that leadership is focused on the traits and behaviour of the individual leader. Given the grievous consequences of persecution for the congregation, this is a demanding and vulnerable approach to leadership.

Nel (2020, p. 205) discusses leadership in the context of persecution as a Christian response to persecution.[10] According to Nel, the "persecuted Christian community's response to persecution is based on their theology of suffering, church, and culture, which is cultivated by an expectation of persecution and a determination to rejoice in suffering." The response then falls into three main categories: survival strategies, association with sympathisers, and strategies of confrontation. Most Christian communities, argues Nel (2020, p. 205), "adopt survival strategies such as going underground, flight, and behavioural respect for repressive regimes." Nel categorises these strategies as the least proactive form of opposition but, at the same time, strategies that involve creativity, determination, and courage. The second most common strategies, "association with sympathisers", refer to Christian communities that "seek to strengthen their resilience and secure their religious freedom by developing ties with other actors" (Nel, 2020, p. 206). The least common response is strategies of confrontation. These strategies, explains Nel (2020, p. 206), "serve to bear witness to the faith, expose (publicise) and end injustice, mobilise others to oppose injustice, and engage positively with the aim of replacing oppression with religious pluralism." Each of these strategies aims to preserve the congregational identity under pressure. The strategies are descriptive, not assessing best practices but offering an empirical-based summary of how congregations deal with pressure and persecution. Together with the outline of the impact of persecution, these common strategies provide a basis for discussing the leadership process and followership in the church.

3.2 Crisis leadership and leadership in extreme contexts

To my knowledge, religious persecution is not discussed in generic research on leadership. In the search for insights from leadership theories

---

10 His observations draw on Boyd-MacMillian (2006) and Philpott and Shah (2018).

that might inform research on the leadership process (leadership and followership) in the context of persecution, I searched for leadership theories that covered situations with a similar impact on the leadership process. This led me to theories on "crisis leadership" and "leadership in extreme contexts."[11] Crisis leadership is the first approach to leadership relevant to the context of persecution. Collins et al. (2023, p. 2) define an organisational crisis as "a rare, abnormal, or infrequent event" that "poses a significant threat to the organization's long-term health and viability" and has "the potential to result in a profoundly negative impact on stakeholders." Based on this understanding, Collins et al. (2023, p. 2) define crisis leadership as "the influencing process that occurs between a leader and stakeholders (internal and external) in the context of organizational crises, as opposed to run-of-the-mill business challenges, over the various stages of the crisis lifecycle." Drawing on the Coombs and Holladay (1996, p. 284) crisis typology, Collins et al. distinguish between four crisis types and crisis leadership types. Given the context of persecution, the type relevant to this study is leadership in the context of external-intentional crisis. This crisis type is transferable to a church organisation in situations where someone outside the church takes action that intentionally or knowingly harms the church. Collins et al. (2023, p. 7) explain that "leaders studied in the context of external-intentional crisis were seen to support and ultimately empower their followers to successfully navigate the crisis." Moreover, the researchers argue that leadership in this kind of context is "extremely difficult because both leaders and followers may feel highly fearful about their future". Effective crisis leaders in this type of crisis, Collins et al. (2023, p. 14) name "saints", providing "followers with comfort, support and hope for the future".[12]

Leadership in extreme contexts is the second approach to leadership relevant to the context of persecution. Hannah et al. (2009, p. 898) define extreme contexts "as an environment where one or more extreme events[13]

---

11 Other leadership theories can offer valuable insights into the leadership process for Christians under pressure. Further research could investigate more generic theories (e.g. Adaptive-, Servant-, and Authentic-leadership).

12 All four leadership types are designated with faith-related terms: sinners, spokespersons, shepherds, and saints (Collins et al., 2023, p. 5). One could include the external-unintentional crisis in relation to the abovementioned possibility of a persecuting result of an action without discriminatory intent. Effective leaders in this crisis, named Shepherds, contribute with sensemaking and the protection of followers.

13 Extreme events, Hannah et al. (2009, p. 898) explain, "must 1) have the potential to cause massive physical, psychological, or material consequences that occur in

are occurring or are likely to occur that may exceed the organization's capacity to prevent and result in an extensive and intolerable magnitude of physical, psychological, or material consequences to – or in close physical or psycho-social proximity to – organization members." Based on this understanding, Hannah et al. (2009, p. 899) have developed a model for leadership in extreme contexts. The focal construct of the model is the "level of extremity", which in the context of persecution relates to the abovementioned spectrum of hostility. According to the model, the level of extremity is based on five primarily contextual dimensions and organisational factors that serve to either attenuate or intensify the extremity experienced.

In addition, Hannah et al. distinguish between the four types of organisations: Trauma, Critical action, High reliability, and Naïve.[14] The researchers point out that leaders and followers experience the extreme context (persecution) embedded in the organisational context (church), respectively, the intra-organisational and extra-organisational context. The church would normally fit the description of a naïve-organisation. These organisations "suffer from a lack of training and resources to respond to such events", with leaders that often fail to prepare for such events (Hannah et al., 2009, p. 901). However, some churches will have similarities with trauma organisations because "their leaders and followers have extensive exposure to how individuals and the group functions under extreme conditions" (Hannah et al., 2009, p. 900). Over time, some churches have experienced that pressure and hostility are the norm.[15]

The first dimension of extreme contexts is the location in time. Hannah et al. (2009, p. 902) argue that "leadership vary over the stages of preparation, response and recovery from an extreme event." Prior to an event of persecution, leadership is connected to possibility thinking and a cognitive shift to better realise potential threats. During extreme events, such as persecution, leadership draws on the trust built prior to the situation,

---

physical or psycho-social proximity to organisation members, 2) the consequences of which are thought unbearable by those organization members, and 3) are such that they may exceed the organization's capacity to prevent those extreme events from actually taking place."

See also Hällgren et al. (2018) Extreme context typology that distinguishes between risky, emergency and disruptive contexts.

14 Examples of Critical action organisations are military combat units, whereas High-reliability organisations are police and fire operations (Hannah et al., 2009, pp. 900-901).

15 On persecution as the normal situation to some churches, see Tieszen (2011, p. 26) or Hampton (2023).

how the leader addresses the followers' expectations and concerns, and how the leaders keep followers focused on the goals. Hannah et al. (2009, p. 903) also maintain that "shared forms of leadership may become critical to sustaining effective performance in sustained extreme contexts, allowing different leaders to emerge while others recover." Post-event, "people need opportunity to reflect in a supportive environment if they are to learn from hardship, requiring leadership that is emphatic and individually considerate and that offers sufficient levels of psychological safety to process events" (Hannah et al., 2009, p. 905).

The next two dimensions of extreme contexts are the potential magnitude of consequences and the probability of the consequence occurring. Hannah et al. (2009, p. 906) argue that followers reassess their leaders based on the magnitude and probability of the consequences, suggesting that the factors followers value in a leader may change. The form of threat is a fourth dimension of extreme contexts. Potential consequences could be physical, psychological or material. Hannah et al. (2009, p. 908) argue that "each form of threat also likely requires a different leadership response."

The fifth dimension is physical, social and psychological proximity. Physical distance refers to who is at risk. From research on persecution, we know that leaders share the risk with their followers and, in many cases, are more at risk compared to other believers (Kipfer, 2019, p. 19; Petri, 2021, p. 107). The psychosocial distance between leaders and followers translates into levels of trust and cohesion. A strong sense of identification with the leader and group results in greater feelings of belonging but may also reduce followers' willingness to question leaders' directions (Hannah et al., 2009, p. 907). Psychological proximity in extreme contexts relates to group structure and functioning. In extreme contexts, people expect and desire someone to be in charge and establish some level of perceived control. Hannah et al. (2009, p. 908) maintain that "heightened sense of vulnerability may provide the spark for leaders to control followers in support of their visions, leading to potentially dangerous situations if those leaders are inept". In view of this, Hannah et al. (2009, p. 908) suggest leadership should "be organized as a shared process".

3.3 Summary

The second sub-question explores how persecution affects the church and its leadership process. Consequently, it draws on the findings from the first research question concerning the characteristics of persecution. This question has been examined from three perspectives. From the ecclesiology and church leadership viewpoint, the ecclesiological task for leaders and followers involves uncovering what it means to be the body of Christ in the face of persecution. Furthermore, congregational leadership pertains to empowering and sustaining the community under pressure. From the perspective of persecution's impact on the church, although there may be potential positive outcomes from persecution, the reported outcomes indicate that believers and the fellowship are adversely affected. Leaders, in particular, are at risk of being targeted in an attempt to undermine or eliminate their influence. From the standpoint of generic leadership theories, we observe that leadership expectations vary depending on the type of crisis and organisation. Given the complexity of leadership in these contexts, shared forms of leadership are emphasised. Lastly, we note that in risk situations, people anticipate and seek leadership, which may lead to negative or unhealthy leadership scenarios.

4 Followership in the church

The third sub-question asks: What characterises followership in the church? The first part of this section introduces characteristics of followers and followership in local congregations. In the second part, I will introduce a theoretical perspective on followership. This perspective highlights features of followership relevant to the leadership process in the context of persecution.

Lilleaasen (2023, p. 554) argues that followership in local congregations is characterised by volunteerism, a spectrum of affiliation, and value consciousness that includes theological convictions. "To have a follower position in relation to someone with a leading position in a local congregation is for most people a voluntary relationship" (Lilleaasen, 2023, p. 551). Unlike followership in workplaces, followership in the church is not motivated by salary. Instead, like in other volunteering arenas, followership in the church is motivated by learning, values, and social relations (Wollebæk et al., 2015, p. 87). The importance of values is further highlighted by the church's commitment and focus on values and norms (Sirris & Askeland, 2021b, p. 47) and congregational leadership as value-conscious (Sirris & Askeland, 2021a). Based on this description of the leadership process in congregations, Lilleaasen (2023, p. 551) describes "followership in local congregations as value-conscious followership." Above, the church and church leadership were described in connection with a theological statement of divine presence. This theological understanding of the church also relates to the follower–leader relationship. Carroll (2011, p. 33) points out that in church, God is believed to be the ultimate source of authority, and a "leader is granted authority to lead because she or he is believed to represent, interpret, and exemplify the group's core values and beliefs and thus to contribute to their realization."

Another feature of being a follower in the church relates to affiliation. Among individuals affiliated with the church, some have a close relationship with congregational leaders, while others have little or no contact with the church and its leaders. This spectrum of affiliation can be outlined in different ways. Råmunddal (2017) has identified three theological features of congregational affiliation. Based on the New Testament, he distinguishes between identity, affiliation, and participation. The basic feature is identity, which refers to discipleship and identification with Jesus as Lord. The term affiliation refers to the individual believers' connection to the people of God and to the local congregation. Participation refers to ministry in the local congregation. In the abovementioned research on persecution, we have seen that the level of commitment is connected to the level of harassment (Marshall, 1998, p. 4; Tieszen, 2011, p. 45). Nel (2020, p. 37) distinguishes between census believers, parishioners, habitual believers and faithful followers. We observe a similar distinction based on engagement in generic research on followership. Kellerman (2008) distinguishes between five levels of engagement, whereas Carsten et al. (2010, p. 546) distinguish between the three levels passive, active, and proactive.

4.1 Theoretical perspectives on followership

In research on followership and the leadership process, Uhl-Bien et al. (2014, p. 97) distinguish between role-based and constructionist approaches. The constructionist-based approach to followership "focuses on the interpersonal process and one person's attempt to influence and the other person's response to these influence attempts" (Northouse, 2021, p. 354). The basic assumption is that leadership only occurs when someone follows. This approach, explained by Uhl-Bien et al. (2014, p. 99), allows investigation of 'non-following' "when someone's leading attempts are not responded to with following behaviour."

The role-based perspective on followership and leadership focuses on how individuals construe and enact their role (leader or follower) and how their behaviours affect the leadership process outcomes. Seeing followership as a role occupied by individuals in formal or informal positions, the role-based approach studies followership in the context of hierarchical systems (Northouse, 2021, p. 354; Uhl-Bien et al., 2014, p. 90). Research on the follower role has developed typologies, grouping followers according to type or style.

A typology relevant to the above-outlined context of persecution is Chaleff's model of courageous followership. The model has five dimensions of courage; these are courage to support the leader, assume responsibility, constructively challenge the leader, participate in any transformation needed, and take a moral stand (Chaleff, 2008, p. 72). The typology distinguishes between four styles of followership, which are based on a matrix of high and low support and challenge. The styles of followership are: Resource, Individualist, Implementer, and Partner. The *partner*, which is high on support and challenge, is the ideal follower, giving "vigorous support to a leader but is also willing to question the leader's behavior or politics" (Chaleff, 2009, p. 40). The *implementer* is high on support and low on challenge, the *individualist* is low on support and high on challenge, whereas the *resource* is low on both support and challenge (Chaleff, 2008, p. 74).

4.2 Summary

The third sub-question presents followership from two perspectives. Firstly, followership within the church is characterised by volunteerism, a range of affiliations, and a commitment to values. Secondly, drawing from the first two research questions regarding persecution and its impact on the leadership process within the church, Chaleff's model of courageous followership is deemed relevant for the concluding discussion on the characteristics of followership in the church in the context of religious persecution.

5 Discussion

The courage to assume responsibility is, according to Chaleff (2009, p. 37), the first and, to some extent, the basic dimension of courageous followership. In his introduction to this dimension, he maintains that before a person can assume responsibility for an organisation, "we must assume responsibility for ourselves". This pertains to an individual's self-identification as a follower and an evaluation of their followership style. The courageous follower, argues Chaleff (2009, p. 12), serves a purpose, not a leader. This aligns with the aforementioned value-conscious followership in congregations and the theological understanding that authority has its ultimate source in God. Value-consciousness and purpose-consciousness help followers discover what it means to be the body of Christ in the situation and to negotiate follower behaviour given the congregation's strategy in response to persecution and pressure (Nel, 2020, p. 205).

Volunteerism, as a characteristic of followership in congregations, involves taking on responsibilities. From a social science perspective, assuming responsibility in the church is voluntary. However, theologically, for many Christians, responsibility in the church is an obligation. Failing to take on such responsibility would compromise their identity as followers of Christ. In the context of pressure or persecution, we have observed that increased commitment can increase the potential for suffering. Therefor, to assume responsibility in the church in the context of pressure or persecution is to assume an increased potential of hostility and harm. That said, drawing on the insight from Extreme Context Theory, assuming responsibility enables the follower to participate in the leadership process, influencing the attenuating and intensifying factors that potentially influence the level of harm (Hannah et al., 2009, p. 902), and attenuating the negative ministry outcomes and stimulate the positive ministry outcomes identified by Kipfer (2019, p. 18).

The second dimension in Chaleff's model is the courage to support and serve the leader. The Extreme Context Theory displays that in difficult times, "people expect, if not desire, someone to be in charge" (Hannah et al., 2009, p. 908). There is an increased need for leadership among believers under pressure and in congregations in the context of persecution. At the same time, research on religious persecution suggests that leaders are targeted to weaken their influence (Kipfer, 2019, p. 19). Both perspectives highlight the importance of supporting leaders. The constructionist-based approach to followership shows that leadership is created when someone's leadership attempts are met with followership behaviour (Uhl-Bien et al., 2014, p. 89). By taking on a followership role and meeting leadership attempts with followership behaviour, the follower supports the leader and co-creates the leadership needed. Similarly, Carroll (2011, p. 28) has described this relational aspect of congregational leadership in relation to the concepts of authority and legitimacy. According to Carroll (2011, p. 28), legitimacy as a leader is, to some extent, "based more informally on a congregation or community's tacit agreement that a pastor has won the right to lead either by virtue of her or his religious authenticity grounded in a sense of call from God, or by demonstrated competence, or both."

Courage to challenge the leader is the third dimension. Chaleff (2009, p. 39) describes courage to support and courage to challenge as the two critical dimensions in the model. A leader who, in a context of persecution, effectively embodies the fellowship's values and mission requires support. Conversely, a leader who struggles to do so should receive constructive feedback and encouragement to refine or adjust their approach to leadership. Among the abovementioned negative outcomes of religious persecution are the temptation to cease leadership or to compromise faith and call, there is also a risk that pressure leads to dysfunctional leadership (Kipfer, 2019, p. 19). The list of negative leadership outcomes following religious persecution highlights the importance of followers with the courage to offer both support and challenge. That said, Extreme Context Theory displays that in difficult times, followers tend to be more supportive and less critical of their leaders (Hannah et al., 2009, p. 907). This decrease in critical internal voices makes congregations under pressure more vulnerable both to external pressure and to weakened internal mechanisms for addressing the pressure. In addition, the voice of the courageous follower is also needed in a context of what Nel (2020, p. 32) calls "persecutory delusion".

The fourth dimension, the courage to participate in transformation, is a continuation of the courage to challenge. When the congregation suffer from weakened or dysfunctional leadership, the courageous follower is both "helping a leader with the process of personal transformation" and participates in structural and organisational transformation (Chaleff, 2009, p. 7). Given the two observations, persecution demands exceptional leadership but "does not, in and of itself, transform Christian leaders into super saints or spiritual heroes." (Kipfer, 2019, p. 19). A potential way forward is connected to the followers and an understanding of the leadership process that distinguishes between the leader as a person and leadership as a process (Uhl-Bien et al., 2014, p. 88). This aligns with Hannah et al. (2009, p. 908), which suggests leadership in difficult contexts should "be organized as a shared process."

In Chaleff's (2009, p. 118) presentation of the dimension "courage to participate in transformation", he argues that "the role of courageous followers is to preempt that crisis by engaging the leader in transformation before the storm." This aligns with research on religious persecution, which argues that the response to persecution is influenced by a church's theology of suffering and its culture (Nel, 2020, p. 205). It also aligns with Extreme Context Theory, which posits that leadership prior to an event is crucial to an organisation's ability to cope (Hannah et al., 2009, p. 902). For followers, participating in transformation also includes contributing to creating a congregational culture and nurturing a theology that prepares the congregation and its leaders for pressure and discrimination.

The fifth and final dimension is the courage to take a moral stand. Chaleff (2009, p. 151) maintains that "although moral action does not always require leaving a group or organization, it always implies the potential of leaving". In the context of persecution, leaving the congregation is particularly problematic, as this could mean the pressure or persecution is working. However, when the courageous follower stops following, it is not motivated by the pressure itself but by unhealthy developments in the congregation and/or dysfunctional leadership. It is described as courage to take a moral stand because it is a value-conscious decision. In a congregational context, followership is ultimately connected to discipleship and identification with Christ (Råmunddal, 2017). The relationship between followers and leaders concludes when it ceases to fulfil this fundamental purpose.

6 Concluding remarks

This article presents a theoretical discussion on how followership in the church is affected by religious persecution. The theoretical perspectives consulted include religious persecution, congregational leadership, crisis leadership, extreme context leadership, and followership.

Based on the analysis provided in the article, I maintain that as the pressure on the church and its leaders intensifies, the role and behaviour of followers become increasingly significant. This heightened significance of followership is evident in the theories on religious persecution and leadership in difficult situations, suggesting that congregations should prepare for pressure and discrimination by organising leadership as a shared process. Leaders in this context are targeted and vulnerable, and the congregation and its leadership are more susceptible to dysfunctional leadership. When the church experiences persecution, it becomes increasingly challenging for followers to pose critical questions and challenge leadership; yet, this is more essential than ever. The pressure on leadership, coupled with its accompanying vulnerability, calls for a recognition of leadership as co-created with followers, and this situation increases the leader's need for courageous followership. The courageous follower offers both challenge and support, with support manifesting in following behaviour. Finally, the increasing significance of followers also entails a greater risk of harm and hostility towards them.

7 References

Bastardoz, N., & Van Vugt, M. (2019). The nature of followership: Evolutionary analysis and review. *The Leadership Quarterly*, *30*(1), 81-95. https://doi.org/10.1016/j.leaqua.2018.09.004

Carroll, J. W. (2011). *As One with Authority* (2nd ed.). Wipf & Stock.

Carsten, M. K., et al. (2010). Exploring social constructions of followership: A qualitative study. *The Leadership Quarterly*, *21*(3), 543-562. https://doi.org/10.1016/j.leaqua.2010.03.015

Chaleff, I. (2008). Creating new ways of following. In R. E. Riggio, I. Chaleff, & J. Lipman-Blumen (Eds.), *The Art of Followership: How Great Followers Create Great Leaders and Organizations* (pp. 67-87). Jossey-Bass.

Chaleff, I. (2009). *The Courageous Follower: Standing Up to and for Our Leaders* (3rd ed). Berrett-Koehler.

Collins, M. D., et al. (2023). Traversing the storm: An interdisciplinary review of crisis leadership. *The Leadership Quarterly*, *34*(1), 101661. https://doi.org/10.1016/j.leaqua.2022.101661

Coombs, W. T., & Holladay, S. J. (1996). Communication and Attributions in a Crisis: An Experimental Study in Crisis Communication. *Journal of Public Relations Research*, *8*(4), 279-295. https://doi.org/10.1207/s1532754xjprr0804_04

Dulles, A. (2002). *Models of the church*. Image Books / Doubleday.

Hannah, S. T., et al. (2009). A framework for examining leadership in extreme contexts. *The Leadership Quarterly*, *20*(6), 897-919. https://doi.org/10.1016/j.leaqua.2009.09.006

Hegstad, H. (2013). *The real church: An ecclesiology of the visible*. Pickwick.

Kellerman, B. (2008). *Followership: How Followers Are Creating Change and Changing Leaders*. Harvard Business Review Press.

Kellerman, B. (2012). *The End of Leadership*. Harper Business.

Kipfer, B. L. (2019). Overlooked Mentors: What can persecuted Christians teach us about leadership? *Journal of Global Christianity*, *5*(1), 16-33.

Lilleaasen, R. (2023). Church Followership and Power. *Scandinavian Journal for Leadership and Theology*, *10*, 545-559. https://doi.org/10.53311/sjlt.v10.94

Marshall, P. A. (1998). Persecution of Christians in the Contemporary World. *IBMR*, *22*(1), 2-8.

Nel, W. N. (2020). *Grievous Religious Persecution*. Wipf & Stock.

Northouse, P. G. (2021). *Leadership: Theory and Practice* (9th ed.). SAGE.

Petersen, M. J., & Marshall, K. (2019). *The international promotion of freedom of religion or belief: Sketching the contours of a common framework*. Danish Institute of Human Rights.

Petri, D. P. (2021). *The Specific Vulnerability of Religious Minorities*. VKW.

Pew Research Center. (2018). *Being Christian in Western Europe*.

Råmunddal, L. (2017). Homo Ecclesiae. Om å være et menighetstilhørende menneske i en individualistisk orientert kultur. In A. H. Balsnes (Ed.), *Hva er nå et menneske? Tverrfaglige bidrag*. Cappelen Damm Akademisk.

Sauer, C., & Nel, W. (2025). Religious persecution: Definitions, scales, spectrums reflected for the context of theology and missiology, In R. Lilleaasen & C. Sauer (Eds.), *Religious persecution*. VKW.

Sirris, S., & Askeland, H. (Eds.). (2021a). *Kirkelig organisering og ledelse*. Cappelen Damm Akademisk/NOASP. https://doi.org/10.23865/noasp.129

Sirris, S., & Askeland, H. (2021b). Kirken som organisme og organisasjon. Ekklesiologiske og organisasjonsteoretiske perspektiver på kirken som felleskap. In *Kirkelig organisering og ledelse* (pp. 35-57). Cappelen Damm Akademisk/NOASP. https://doi.org/10.23865/noasp.129.ch2

Skjevesland, O. (1998). *Morgendagens menighet: Ledelse og livsform*. Verbum.

Tieszen, C. L. (2011). *Re-examining religious persecution: Constructing a theological framework for understanding persecution* (2nd ed.). VKW.

Uhl-Bien, M., et al. (2014). Followership theory: A review and research agenda. *The Leadership Quarterly*, *25*(1), 83-104. https://doi.org/10.1016/j.leaqua.2013.11.007

Wollebæk, D., Sætrang, S., & Fladmoe, A. (2015). *Betingelser for frivillig innsats motivasjon og kontekst*. Senter for forskning på sivilsamfunn og frivillig sektor.

14 Challenging stories for children

Addressing persecuted Christians in Sunday school

Tonje Belibi[1]

Abstract

This article investigates how persecuted Christians are portrayed in Norwegian Sunday school materials for children aged 3-9. It analyses three curricula – *Ordets liturgi for barn* (Catholic), *Sprell Levende* (Evangelical Lutheran), and *Awana* (adapted for the Norwegian Evangelical Lutheran context) – through the lens of theological perspectives on persecution and selected theories of child development, including Fowler's stages of faith. The study finds that while persecuted Christians are addressed in all three, the depth and frequency vary. *Awana* presents the most direct and vivid depictions of persecution, often linking it to mission and discipleship. In contrast, *Sprell Levende* and *Ordets liturgi for barn* tend to adapt or omit more difficult content, often emphasizing God's love and comfort. The article also considers how these approaches align with children's emotional and cognitive development. This research highlights the importance of integrating difficult biblical stories to foster a sustainable faith and awareness of global Christian suffering.

Keywords: Faith education, child development psychology, persecution, Bad Urach Statement, Sunday school.

1 Introduction

Christian faith education seeks to provide children with a sound understanding of the living God and to equip them for a life of discipleship (Kirkerådet, 2010, pp. 4-5). Research in Norway has demonstrated that the church can create safe spaces for children to grow in faith, even when they carry vulnerabilities or burdens (Engedal, 2015; Engedal et al., 2013). Moreover, scholars argue that children should not be shielded from more

[1] Tonje Belibi (*1991), Assistant Professor, Fjellhaug International University College, tbelibi@fjellhaug.no, ORCID iD: 0009-0002-9956-5855.

challenging biblical narratives, as these stories are essential for fostering meaningful engagement with faith (Saxegaard, 2009, pp. 88-89, 2010, pp. 70-71). However, the question of when and how to introduce such topics remains, given the varying maturity levels of children. This article addresses a gap in current research by examining how Christian faith education presents persecuted Christians.

According to research from the International Institute for Religious Freedom (IIRF), "By any definition of persecution, the worldwide Body of Christ can count many millions of Christians experiencing persecution today" (Sauer, 2012, p. 11). The IIRF further notes that these persecuted believers "are not remembered, prayed for and assisted" as they ought to be by the global church (Sauer, 2012, p. 11). The Lausanne Covenant – still affirmed by many Christians today – underscores the importance of being informed about, praying for, and advocating on behalf of the persecuted. It reminds believers that Jesus warned all his followers that they would face persecution for his sake (*The Lausanne Covenant*, 1974, Clause 13).

Building on the existing research – or lack thereof – on Christian faith education in Norway, this article aims to examine how persecuted Christians are represented in Sunday school curricula in Norway today, and whether these findings relate to theories of children's psychological development. This leads to the following research question:

> How are persecuted Christians portrayed in the Sunday school materials "Ordets liturgi for barn", "Sprell Levende", and "Awana", considering selected psychological development theories for children aged 3-9?

2 Theory

2.1 Theoretical insights into persecuted Christians

To address my research question, it was first necessary to define and elaborate on the concept of persecuted Christians.

The term *persecution* lacks a universally accepted legal or international definition. Some interpret it as the experience of conditions that contradict the protections outlined in Article 18 of the Universal Declaration of Human Rights, which guarantees freedom of thought, conscience, and religion (Open Doors org, 2024; United Nations, 2024, Article 18). This study does not attempt to catalogue all forms of opposition individuals may encounter, nor does it examine religious hostility across all faith traditions. Rather, it focuses specifically on persecuted Christians, who currently represent the largest group affected by religion-based hostility worldwide

(Crawford, 2024). For this purpose, I adopt Tieszen's definition of persecution as "any unjust action of varying levels of hostility perpetrated primarily on the basis of religion and directed at Christians, resulting in varying levels of harm as it is considered from the victim's perspective" (Tieszen, 2008, p. 46). This definition also underpins the theoretical framework drawn from the *Bad Urach Statement – Towards an Evangelical Theology of Suffering, Persecution and Martyrdom for the Global Church in Mission* (Sauer & Howell, 2010, pp. 27-106). Tieszen's victim-centred approach provides a conceptual bridge to the Bad Urach Statement (BUS), which offers a structured evangelical framework for interpreting suffering and persecution in a church context.

The BUS emanates from a consultation in the city of Bad Urach, Germany, in 2009, led by Dr. Richard Howell and Dr. Christof Sauer from *the International Institute for Religious Freedom*. It presents a coherent evangelical theology of persecuted Christians and seeks to give churches advice on this subject. More than 24 participants with different views agreed on the statement that presents eleven ways to perceive theology on Christians who experience suffering, persecution and martyrdom.

The BUS was selected for this study due to its theological depth and practical relevance. Developed through international evangelical collaboration, it provides a structured framework for interpreting persecuted Christians and helps churches understand persecution through shared theological language.

These eleven aspects served as analytical categories for identifying how persecuted Christians are represented in the material and to what extent each aspect is discernible. They are briefly outlined below (see Sauer & Howell, 2010 for further explanation of each):

1. The drama of God's history with the world (epistemological aspects)
2. Old Testament models of faithfulness (typological aspects)
3. Christ, the suffering servant (Christological aspects)
4. Discipleship: Following in the footsteps of Christ (mimetic aspects)
5. Super-human conflict (antagonistic aspects)
6. God's salvation and comfort (soteriological aspects)
7. The body of Christ (ecclesiological aspects)
8. God's mission for the church (missiological aspects)
9. The victory of the kingdom of God (eschatological aspects)
10. The honour of God and his martyrs (doxological aspects)
11. Christian ethics of suffering, persecution and martyrdom (ethical aspects) (Sauer & Howell, 2010, pp. 43-69).

2.2 Integrating child development psychology with faith education

From an evangelical perspective, understanding child development is essential to ensure that faith formation is age-appropriate, spiritually nurturing, and theologically sound. This perspective also informs the methodological foundation of this study. Before presenting the method used to obtain my results, it is necessary to include selected theories on children's developmental psychology and faith education that inform the research question. Given the abundance of theories available, I will focus on three key aspects.

The Institute for Church and Childhood (IKO) in Norway has developed relevant approaches to faith education, including guidance on how to present Bible stories and which narratives to select (Gunleiksrud, 2011). An important aspect of biblical education for children is helping them recognise their own experiences within the narratives. Limiting exposure to only simple texts may reduce the Bible's relevance, as more complex and challenging stories are equally important for fostering meaningful engagement with faith (Skippervold, 2011, pp. 22-27). In my findings, I explore how this is put into practice through the inclusion of 'difficult stories' in Sunday school materials.[2]

How much should children be taught from an early age? According to a deacon and hospital chaplain at St. Olav's Hospital in Trondheim, writing in the IKO publication *Children Need Hope,* it is generally better to tell children the truth than to leave them uncertain, as guessing can lead to unnecessary fear and confusion. However, each child is different, and it remains essential to adapt difficult messages to the child's personality and level of understanding (Hirsch & Røen, 2012, pp. 24-25). In my analysis, I examine whether and how this principle is reflected in the materials studied.

To connect child development theory with faith education, I draw on James Fowler's well-known stages of faith, based on 359 interviews and first published in 1981.[3] Fowler outlines seven stages of faith development,

---

[2] By 'difficult stories,' I mean those that depict violence or murder involving characters often seen as heroes by children reading the Bible, or accounts of brutality against innocent people – such as Herod's massacre of the two-year-olds in Bethlehem (Matthew 2:16-18).

[3] While newer models – such as Kiesling's (2024) developmental approach – offer valuable insights, Fowler's framework remains widely used in both academic and practical contexts. Despite critiques of its generality and empirical limitations (see, e.g., Parker, 2010), its relevance to the age group studied makes it a suitable choice for this research.

each reflecting different aspects of religious understanding and maturity (Fowler, 2004, pp. 408-410; Tetzchner, 2019, pp. 315-316, 381-382).

This study focuses on the stages Fowler identifies as *Intuitive-Projective Faith* (ages 3-7) and *Mythical-Literal Faith* (ages 7-12) (Fowler, 1991, pp. 24-25). In the first stage, children project their thoughts and feelings onto their surroundings. Their perspective is egocentric, shaped by imagination, and often includes first encounters with complex topics such as death (Fowler, 1981, pp. 123, 133). If children at this stage can grasp the concept of death, are they also ready to learn about the realities faced by persecuted Christians?

The second stage, *Mythical-Literal Faith*, is marked by a tension between lived experience and imagination. Children interpret Bible stories and moral teachings literally and develop a strong sense of justice (Evenshaug & Hallen, 2001, p. 362; Fowler, 1981, pp. 135-137, 149). This raises a key pedagogical question: Do the materials encourage children at this stage to engage with the injustices faced by persecuted Christians?

3 Method

This study focuses on Sunday school materials used over a selected period, examining the content presented to children during regular church attendance. My own experiences with various Sunday school materials in Norway have informed and supported the development of this study.

The method I used was document analysis. I examined materials from both churches and organisations involved in faith education. The first step was to contact various congregations to identify which Sunday school materials they used. Many did not have their own resources but relied on interdenominational materials, which I was able to access. I aimed to include a broad range of denominations and ultimately focused on four, based on recommendations and their willingness to participate. As age ranges varied across the materials, I limited the study to content aimed at children aged 3-9.[4]

The next step involved analysing the four sets of materials provided by the final respondents, all of which were used in Sunday school settings. These included:

4 Documents intended for Christian schools, children's Bible study groups, and youth ministries were excluded. Some respondents also shared extensive material for teenagers, which may be explored in future research.

1. *Ordets liturgi for barn*, developed by the Roman Catholic Church for children aged 3-9
2. *Sprell Levende*, produced by the Norwegian Sunday School Association and used across various denominations, for ages 3-9
3. *Awana*, originally from the US and adapted for Norwegian use, covering ages 2-19
4. *Jesus hele livet*, developed by Pentecostal churches for ages 0-19.[5]

Lastly, I organised the findings as presented in part 4 and integrated insights from child development theory in the results.

3.1 Overview of the material

3.1.1 Ordets liturgi for barn

The material used in Roman Catholic Sunday schools is referred to as both *Evangelieforklaring* (*Explanation of the Gospel*) and *Ordets liturgi for barn* (OLFB; *Liturgy of the Word for Children*). Aimed at children aged 3-9, OLFB serves as an alternative to the sermon during High Mass for families with children (Personal communication with the Catechetical Centre's Advisor, C. Cselenyi, 20 April 2021; Oslo katolske bispedømme, 2021). It follows the liturgical calendar, and weekly materials are made available online for Sunday school teachers. The limited time allocated for Catholic Sunday school restricts the depth of teaching compared to other materials. Nonetheless, it is valuable to examine how the Bible and the lives of the saints are presented within this short format. I reviewed the lectionaries for 2021, 2022, and 2023 (Oslo katolske bispedømme, 2021).[6]

OLFB differs from the other materials in that it includes stories from church history. Relevant information about saints was therefore included in my analysis. Additionally, OLFB is the only material that consistently follows the same Bible texts as the main congregation each Sunday. Although OLFB is Roman Catholic, applying the BUS allows for cross-denominational insights and highlights shared theological themes related to persecuted Christians. These will be explored further in the analysis.

---

[5] A preliminary version of this research was presented at the 2021 *Symposium on Religious Freedom and Forced Faith*. As OLFB materials were incomplete at the time, the article has since been expanded. All translations from Norwegian to English are mine.

[6] The material published from January to September 2021 was reviewed during spring 2021, while the remaining content was examined in autumn 2024.

3.1.2 Sprell Levende

Sprell Levende (Vibrantly Alive) is an interdenominational resource developed by the Norwegian Sunday School Association (NSSA), based on Evangelical Lutheran theology. It targets children aged 3-9.[7] NSSA has published *Sprell Levende* annually since 2006, with major revisions in 2012 and 2022. The latest edition appeared after my data collection and analysis were completed (Søndagsskolen Norge, 2016, pp. 10-11, 42-43, 2024).

To gather relevant material, I reviewed the *Sprell Levende* archive from 2006-2020 and requested specific texts from editor Søren Nielsen that aligned with my research focus (S. Nielsen, personal communication, 20 January 2020). Some stories I expected to find – such as the stoning of Stephen or the three friends in the fiery furnace – were not included. The primary analysis focuses on the material identified as most relevant to the study.

At the time of research, *Sprell Levende* was the only curriculum with accessible theoretical foundations, which made it difficult to explicitly compare how child development psychology was addressed across all the materials.

3.1.3 Awana

Awana is an international, non-profit ministry for children, active in many countries (Awana, 2021). In Norway, *Awana* was adapted to the Norwegian Evangelical Lutheran context in 2016 by Indremisjonsforbundet (Norwegian Inner Mission) in a collaboration with Frikirken (the Evangelical Lutheran Free Church of Norway). It is now used across several denominations in Norway (Awana Norge, 2021b).[8]

The materials were received digitally, enabling a thorough review of the relevant texts covering my age group. I also consulted with faith education advisor Bjarte Vesetvik, who shared his views on which texts were most relevant to my research (B. Vesetvik, personal communication, 21 April 2021). Although the Awana programme spans ages 2-19, I focused on the age-specific materials for 3-9-year-olds: *Puggles* (ages 2-3), *Cubbies* (ages 3-5), and *Sparks* (ages 6-9). Each group is supported by a leader handbook outlining weekly topics, which served as the primary sources for my analysis (Awana Norge, 2021a).

---

7 When I began my research, the material covered ages 3-10, but this was later adjusted to 3-9.

8 Including Misjonssambandet, Normisjon, Misjonskirken, Pinsebevegelsen, Baptistsamfunnet, Den norske kirke, ImF and Frikirken.

3.1.4 Jesus hele livet

Jesus hele livet (*Jesus throughout life*), developed by the Pentecostal church, offered a more limited scope of material compared to the other curricula. Due to space constraints and the relatively few relevant findings it yielded, I ultimately chose to exclude this material from the final analysis.

4 Findings in the Sunday school material

To explore how persecuted Christians are represented, the findings are organised according to the persecution theory outlined earlier. A summary table is provided, with selected examples discussed in the analysis. Due to word limits, only a sample is included. Insights from child development theory are also integrated.

Aspects/Material	OLFB	Sprell Levende	Awana	Sum
Epistemological	2			2
Typological		1	3	4
Christological		1	3	4
Mimetic	2	2		4
Antagonistic				0
Soteriological	1	3	3	7
Ecclesiological		1		1
Missiological	1		7	8
Eschatological	1		3	4
Doxological	2	1	3	6
Ethical	2	2	4	8
Sum	**11**	**11**	**26**	**48**

Table 1: Findings from the aspects of persecution theory

Overall, the Sunday school materials portray persecution not as something to be sought, but as a reality believers may face while remaining loyal citizens who ultimately obey God (cf. Acts 4:12, *ethical aspects*). The *missiological aspects* – persecution as part of God's mission – are especially prominent in *Awana*. The *soteriological* and *doxological aspects* are also evident, with persecution shown as a source of divine comfort and a way to honour God. However, little attention is given to persecution as sharing in Christ's suffering, and the *antagonistic aspects* – the cosmic struggle between good and evil – are entirely absent. These findings raise the question of how such portrayals align with children's psychological development.

4.1 Ordets liturgi for barn

The Roman Catholic Sunday school material, *Ordets liturgi for barn* (OLFB), highlights the relevance of John 15:1-8 for persecuted Christians. It suggests that Jesus' warning about unfruitful branches being cut off refers to those concealing their faith during persecution. This is linked to contemporary Christian responsibility: to follow Christ and accept the consequences (Oslo katolske biskedømme, 2021a). On St Olav's Day (29 July), the material includes age-appropriate content: younger children are encouraged to sing about God's protection, while older children learn about martyrdom and the story of Saint Olav (Oslo katolske biskedømme, 2021c).

The leader's notes for All Saints' Day (2021 and 2022) focus on the Beatitudes, emphasising the call to holiness and obedience to Jesus. They also mention those who suffered for Christ, affirming that "their suffering is not in vain." Saints commemorated on this day are described as peacemakers, some of whom endured pain or death for their faith. The text states: "Some had to suffer and endure pain because they believed in Jesus, and some didn't like that. Others were brave and dared to speak out against something that was wrong. Some were killed because of it. Today, we thank God for all who said yes to what God asked them to help with" (Oslo katolske biskedømme, 2021b, 2022b). This reflects the *doxological*, *mimetic*, and *ethical aspects* of the BUS.

OLFB does not always follow the same lectionary texts as the main congregation. For example, on 13 November 2022 (Luke 21:5-19), the leader's guide explains the decision to omit the Gospel reading:

> "In this text, Jesus uses strong words. He tells us that we will be betrayed by parents and siblings, and that some of us may even be killed. He warns us that being a Christian in this world can be tough, but those who persevere and testify to what they believe is true will receive eternal life in heaven. This is not a text suitable for young children, as it primarily belongs to the faith life of adults: understanding the seriousness of life and reading the signs of the times. The other readings are also warnings and are not suitable for the Liturgy of the Word for children. Young children first need to become familiar with God's safety, care, and love before they can understand any of this." (Oslo katolske biskedømme, 2022a)

This aligns with Fowler's theory of faith development, which suggests such themes are more appropriate for later stages of maturity. However, the material does not specify when children are considered ready to engage with more complex theological concepts. Instead of the Gospel reading, the story of the Russian widow Varenka is used (Oslo katolske biskedømme, 2022a).[9]

On 30 December 2022, "The Holy Family" Sunday, the Gospel text (Matthew 2:13-15, 19-23) is used to introduce martyrdom. A red tablecloth symbolises the blood of martyrs, and children are told: "In today's reading, you will hear about some very small children who died for Jesus. They were completely innocent, but they had to die when Herod decided that all children under two years old should be killed because he was afraid that the baby Jesus would become a greater king than him" (Oslo katolske biskedømme, 2022c). While the story briefly acknowledges the massacre, the focus remains on Jesus' escape, reflecting the *epistemological aspects* of the BUS.

In the OLFB material for 29 January 2023, the Gospel reading is again the Beatitudes (Matthew 5:1-12a). In the storytelling section titled "Other aspects to consider", the leader is advised: "it's important to help the children understand that Jesus does not think it's good for people to suffer or be in pain. Experiencing pain, being poor, and being persecuted are not things that are positive in themselves, and Jesus does not desire this for people" (Oslo katolske biskedømme, 2023). This clarification of the role of persecution aligns with the *ethical aspects* of the BUS, which states that "A Christian should not aspire after persecution or provoke it" (Sauer & Howell, 2010, p. 68).

4.2 Sprell Levende

From autumn 2006 to spring 2021, the Bible stories in *Sprell Levende* that addressed persecuted Christians were scheduled for Sundays in autumn 2014 and autumn 2018 (Bergsjø et al., 2014; Manvik et al., 2018).[10] These periods included the stories of "Daniel in the Lion's Den", "Saul at Damascus", "Paul's First Missionary Journey" and "Paul and Silas in Jail." In these documents, persecuted Christians are addressed either within the biblical narrative itself or both in the story and in its application to the present day. Three of the four documents reference the organisation Open Doors, and both the children and the leader are encouraged to pray for persecuted Christians. In the last two documents, it is emphasized that children

---

[9] Similar substitutions occur on 3 September 2023 (Matthew 16:21-27) and 26 November 2023 (Matthew 25:31-46), where texts are deemed too difficult and postponed "until a later stage" (Oslo katolske biskedømme, 2023c, 2023b).

[10] From the *Sprell Levende* material I had access to – spanning a 15-year period – I selected the documents in which the presentation of persecuted Christians within the Bible stories was clearly evident.

should be told that Christians face resistance; however, since their imaginations can amplify these stories, adults need to be cautious and adapt the content to suit the child's age (Manvik et al., 2018, p. 84). This aligns with the faith education theory discussed earlier and acknowledges the formative role of children's imagination.

The "Daniel in the Lion's Den" document included an additional story from Open Doors about Salwa and Fatima – two persecuted children fleeing with their Christian mothers from a violent father opposed to their secret faith. The message behind the story is to teach children that they have brothers and sisters in the world who cannot openly express their beliefs. The children are then led in a prayer of gratitude for Norwegian freedom and intercession for persecuted Christians (Bergsjø et al., 2014, pp. 98-116, 302).

When these materials are analysed through the lens of the persecution theory, the *doxological aspects* are evident in the introduction to the story of Daniel, where suffering for Christ is portrayed as an honour. As the story is drawn from an Old Testament prophet, the *typological aspects* are also relevant. The verse from Acts 4:19 – "we must obey God rather than men" – is included in the material as a question posed to the children, asking whether there are situations in which one must obey God over people. This introduces the *ethical aspects*, which underscores God's authority above human rules, institutions, and expectations. In the story of Salwa and Fatima, the *soteriological* and *Christological aspects* are also present, as their mother comforts them with truths about God's love and Jesus' atoning death, highlighting divine presence and strength in suffering.

The four Bible stories identified in these documents are all intended to be told in a vivid and realistic manner. They may be dramatised, illustrated with posters, or visualised using props such as sweets. The storytelling includes many concrete and sensory details – from Daniel being thrown into a den of hungry lions, to Saul nearly being stoned, and Paul suffering in a cold, dark prison (Bergsjø et al., 2014, pp. 97-119; Manvik et al., 2018, pp. 53-110).[11]

In the material on Saul in Damascus, the statement "Persecuting the Christians is persecuting Jesus himself. The Christians are Jesus' body in the world (...)" (Manvik et al., 2018, p. 54) reflects the *ecclesiological aspects*

---

11 During Sunday school sessions, children in *Sprell Levende* are first sitting together before being divided into two age groups, each with tailored activities: *Gullivergjengen* (ages 3-5) and *Agentklubben* (ages 6-9) (Søndagsskolen Norge, 2024). The theme of persecuted Christians was predominantly discernible during the plenary session.

as defined in the BUS. This is the only explicit reference to the *ecclesiological aspects* found in all the material I reviewed. As a storytelling method, the leader is encouraged to take on the role of Saul and express his intense hatred for Christians. The script notes that he intended to imprison them, though it does not elaborate on what this would have meant for the Christians themselves. During the reflective segment, the leader is invited to guide the children in considering how Paul's life was radically transformed – how God redirected his path to serve a completely new purpose. As a former persecutor who was saved, this narrative clearly illustrates the *soteriological aspects* (Manvik et al., 2018, pp. 54-67).

The material for Paul and Silas in prison (Acts 16:16-40) engages with multiple aspects of persecution. It offers guidance to leaders on how the story might be presented to children and what the pedagogical aim should be:

> "Complaining is a good trait in children! We must dare to enter the incomprehensible and painful alongside the children and ask: God, where are you? If children do not experience that we can talk to Him about the painful things as well, atheistic spaces will be created in their lives, spaces where God does not exist. And if God is not relevant when we need Him the most, faith becomes less sustainable." (Manvik et al., 2018, p. 95)

This aligns with the faith education theory outlined earlier, which advocates including difficult Bible stories to present a more realistic image of God, one that supports a more resilient and enduring faith. Although the leader is encouraged to validate children's complaints, one version of the story highlights that Paul and Silas did not complain, even though they had every reason to. Here, both the *mimetic* and *soteriological aspects* become visible. The *mimetic aspects* are also reflected in the line: "They were sitting [in prison] because those in power in the country didn't like that they were telling others about Jesus and healing people. They hadn't done anything wrong" (Manvik et al., 2018, pp. 97-104). This is a clear example of how the leader is encouraged to explain the persecution of Paul and Silas in a way that children can understand and relate to.

4.3 Awana

The theme of persecuted Christians is explored in greater depth and more frequently in *Awana* than in any of the other Sunday school materials examined. Within the *Sparks* programme, designed for children aged 6-9, persecuted Christians are mentioned repeatedly across two of the four handbooks (Djupvik, 2019, 2020a, 2020b, 2021). Even the material intended for 3- to 5-year-olds includes direct and unfiltered narratives such as "the three friends in the fiery oven" and "Paul and Silas in prison." These stories encourage children to reflect on trusting in God's love regardless of their circumstances, emphasising that faithfulness does not guarantee protection from hardship. Rather, God promises to support believers through trials and offers the hope of heaven (Djupvik, 2018, pp. 84, 212-217).

The story of "the friends in the fiery oven," as presented to 3- to 5-year-olds, reflects several theological aspects of persecution: *typological*, *eschatological*, *soteriological*, and *ethical*. In the account of "Paul and Silas in prison," the narrative highlights the wisdom and hope that can be drawn from enduring suffering. Paul and Silas, despite their circumstances, worshipped and shared the gospel with fellow prisoners – a reminder that believers are never alone (Djupvik, 2018, pp. 216-217). This story illustrates the *missiological*, *soteriological*, and *doxological aspects* of persecution.

One particularly illustrative example from the *Sparks* program in *Awana* is the story of Stephen's testimony and martyrdom in Acts 6:8-7:60. The leader's guide acknowledges the emotional weight of the narrative: "This can be a challenging story to share with the children at Sparks. It is a frightening event – a man is stoned to death because he tells the truth about God" (Djupvik, 2021, p. 30). Rather than focusing on the violence of the stoning, the material encourages leaders to emphasise the peace Stephen experienced – and the peace children can also find in frightening situations. By helping children relate to fear and pointing to Jesus' constant presence, the material underscores that, although Stephen died, he was received by Jesus and would be with him forever (Djupvik, 2021, pp. 30-32). This presentation of persecution reflects both the *eschatological* and *soteriological aspects* of the BUS.

In addition to the theological aspects of persecution, one *Sparks* text includes a family activity involving prayer for countries where Christians are persecuted, using resources from Open Doors (Djupvik, 2019, p. 113). Another suggests organising a gathering focused on persecuted Christians with a similar emphasis (Djupvik, 2021, p. 82). These are two of eight references to Open Doors or persecuted Christians in *Sparks*, though they do not include explicit theological reflection.

A general perspective on persecuted Christians within *Awana* is captured in the following statement from the *Sparks* material, addressed to leaders:

> "Many people are persecuted for their faith around the world. Many have been imprisoned and tortured, and many have had to flee. And not everyone has experienced God intervening so radically when they were in danger. No, many Christians have died as martyrs." (Djupvik, 2019, p. 110)

This honest and serious approach to the topic of persecuted Christians is also evident elsewhere in the *Awana* material. Even the youngest children are introduced to these themes through storytelling and role-play. For instance, in a lesson for 3- to 5-year-olds about Paul and Silas, children are asked to imagine being in a cold, dark, and smelly prison cell, hurting after being beaten. Leaders are encouraged to ask how that might feel. The material then suggests acting out the moment when the jailer places Paul or Silas in wooden stocks. However, it also includes a note of caution, reminding leaders to be especially sensitive, as some children might know someone who is in prison (Djupvik, 2018, pp. 212-217). While the content is slightly adapted to suit young children's emotional development, how it is received ultimately depends on the attentiveness and discretion of the leader.

Awana leaders are generally encouraged to present a realistic image of God – one who does not promise a life free from hardship. Instead, the emphasis is on God's faithfulness and care, regardless of circumstances. This message is consistently conveyed through many of the more challenging stories included in the *Awana* material (Djupvik, 2018, p. 84, 2019, pp. 106, 120).

5 Conclusion

This study sets out to examine how persecuted Christians are portrayed in selected Sunday school materials and whether these portrayals align with theories of children's psychological development. While the materials reviewed did not explicitly integrate developmental psychology, they appear to be implicitly shaped by it. However, the theoretical foundations behind this influence were not clearly articulated or consistently accessible. Although I found occasional references outside the materials themselves, these were limited and varied across curricula. In my view, this underscores the need for more transparent and robust incorporation of developmental psychology into future curriculum design.

Persecuted Christians are not entirely absent from the curricula but appear infrequently throughout the church year. OLFB, despite its limited scope, frequently references persecuted Christians and incorporates various aspects of persecution theory, though none are particularly emphasized. *Sprell Levende*, with the most extensive archive, covers a wide range of biblical texts but omits some challenging stories, possibly due to concerns about age-appropriateness. The *soteriological aspects* – emphasizing God's comfort in suffering – are most prominent in this material.

Awana has twice as many results as *Sprell Levende* on the persecution aspects, despite having a smaller material bank. In *Awana*, the stories are often presented more directly from the biblical text, which makes them feel more dramatic and realistic than in the other materials reviewed. As a result, *Awana* appears to be more proactive than the others in presenting the situation of persecuted Christians to children aged 3 to 9 during regular Sunday school sessions. This is often done with a missiological focus, highlighting how persecution can lead to the spread of the Gospel.

Only *Sprell Levende* explicitly warns against leaving too much to children's imagination, which could lead to fear. Fowler's stages of faith were not clearly reflected in any of the materials. Although both *Sprell Levende* and *Awana* divide children into two age groups, the content does not appear significantly differentiated in terms of emotional readiness. This suggests that age separation may focus more on cognitive or physical development than on emotional receptiveness.

Notably, all aspects of persecution theory were represented in the materials except the *antagonistic aspects*. This absence may reflect an editorial decision to shield children from the concept of a cosmic struggle between good and evil.

As developmental theory offers only a blurred line regarding when children should be introduced to difficult stories, it is not possible to determine a universally appropriate age group. Children's maturity varies significantly, and what may be suitable for one child might not be for another.

This study highlights a gap in research concerning the portrayal of persecuted Christians in faith education, particularly within Sunday school materials. By addressing this gap, the aim has been to illuminate the current landscape and raise awareness of what each curriculum includes – and perhaps omits.

For future research, it would be valuable to explore how Sunday school leaders communicate stories of persecuted Christians and how they are received by children in real-time settings. Such a study could offer important insights into the pedagogical dynamics at play and further inform curriculum development.

6 References

Awana. (2021, August 24). *Awana About*. https://www.awana.org/about/

Awana Norge. (2021a). *Awana*. https://www.awana.no/

Awana Norge. (2021b). *Om – Awana*. https://www.awana.no/om/

Bergsjø, E., et al. (Eds.). (2014). *Sprell Levende Veiledninger Høstpakken 2014*. Søndagsskolen Norge.

Crawford, S. M. and S. (2024, March 5). *Harassment of religious groups returned to peak level in 2021.* Pew Research Center. https://www.pewresearch.org/religion/2024/03/05/harassment-of-religious-groups-returned-to-peak-level-in-2021/

Djupvik, J. S. (Ed.). (2018). *Cubbies Honningkrukke undervisningsplaner.* Awana Norge, Indremisjonsforbundet.

Djupvik, J. S. (Ed.). (2019). *Hvem trenger jeg å kjenne fra Bibelen 2.* Awana Norge, Indremisjonsforbundet.

Djupvik, J. S. (Ed.). (2020a). *Hvem trenger jeg å kjenne fra Bibelen 1.* Awana Norge, Indremisjonsforbundet.

Djupvik, J. S. (Ed.). (2020b). *Hvem trenger jeg å kjenne fra Bibelen 3.* Awana Norge, Indremisjonsforbundet.

Djupvik, J. S. (Ed.). (2021). *Hvem trenger jeg å kjenne fra Bibelen 4.* Awana Norge, Indremisjonsforbundet.

Engedal, L. G. (2015). *Trosopplæring for alle?* IKO-Forlaget AS.

Engedal, L. G., & Persson, B. L., & Torp, E. (2013). *Trygge rom: Trosopplæring i møte med sårbare og overgrepsutsatte barn og unge.* Verbum.

Evenshaug, O., & Hallen, D. (2001). *Barne- og ungdomspsykologi 4.utgave.* Gyldendal akademisk.

Fjellhaug International University College. (2021). *Religious Freedom and Forced Faith - Symposium 2021.* Fjellhaug. https://fih.fjellhaug.no/en/research/religious-freedom-and-forced-faith-symposium-2021

Fowler, J. W. (1981). *Stages of faith: The psychology of human development and the quest for meaning.* Harper & Row.

Fowler, J. W. (1991). The Vocation of Faith Developmental Theory. In *Stages of Faith and Religious Development: Implications for Church, Education, and Society* (pp. 19-36). Crossroad Pub Co.

Fowler, J. W. (2004). Faith Development at 30: Naming the Challenges of Faith in a New Millennium. *Religious Education, 99*(4), 405-421.

Gunleiksrud, K. (2011). *Bibelfortellinger Metode og formidling.* IKO-Forlaget AS.

Hirsch, A., & Røen, I. (2012). Å snakke med barn i sorg og krise. In A. Ramsfjell & S. Sagberg (Eds.), *Livstolkning og livsmestring* (pp. 23-34). IKO-Forlaget AS.

Kirkerådet. (2010). *Gud gir – vi deler: Plan for trosopplæring i Den norske kirke.* Den norske kirke, Kirkerådet.

Manvik, K. K., et al. (Eds.). (2018). *Sprell Levende Veiledninger Høstpakken 2018.* Søndagsskolen Norge.

Open Doors org. (2024). *World Watch List methodology.* Open Doors. https://www.opendoors.org.za/world-watch-list-methodology/

Oslo katolske biskedømme. (2021a). *Bli lys! 5. Søndag i påsketiden.* Ordets liturgi for barn for år 2021. https://blilys.no/wp-content/uploads/evforklar/B_5s_psktid.pdf

Oslo katolske biskedømme. (2021b). *Bli Lys! Allehelgensdag.* Ordets liturgi for barn for år 2021. https://blilys.no/wp-content/uploads/evforklar/ABC_Allehelgensdag.pdf

Oslo katolske biskedømme. (2021c). *Bli lys! Olav den hellige (29.juli).* Ordets liturgi for barn for år 2021. https://blilys.no/wp-content/uploads/evforklar/Hellig_Olav_Olsok.pdf

Oslo katolske biskedømme. (2022a). *Bli Lys! 33. Søndag i det alminnelige kirkeår C.* Ordets liturgi for barn for år 2023. https://blilys.no/wp-content/uploads/evforklar/C33_sondag.pdf

Oslo katolske biskedømme. (2022b). *Bli Lys! Allehelgensdag*. Ordets liturgi for barn for år 2022. https://blilys.no/wp-content/uploads/evforklar/ABC_Allehelgensdag.pdf

Oslo katolske biskedømme. (2022c). *Bli Lys! Den hellige familie – År A*. Ordets liturgi for barn for år 2022. https://blilys.no/wp-content/uploads/evforklar/A_hellige_familie.pdf

Oslo katolske biskedømme. (2023). *Bli Lys! 4. Søndag i det alminnelige kirkeår – År A*. Ordets liturgi for barn for år 2023. https://blilys.no/wp-content/uploads/evforklar/A4_sondag.pdf

Oslo katolske bispedømme, Kateketisk senter. (2021). *Bli Lys!*

Sauer, C. (Ed.). (2012). *Bad Urach Statement: Towards an evangelical theology of suffering*. VKW.

Sauer, C., & Howell, R. (Eds.). (2010). *Suffering, persecution and martyrdom: Theological reflections*. VKW, AcadSA.

Saxegaard, K. M. (2009). *Når Gud angrer – Nesten: Gammeltestamentlige fortellinger fremstilt i norske barnebibler. Prismet*, 2, 78-90.

Saxegaard, K. M. (2010). Bibelhermeneutikk for barn. *Tidsskrift for Praktisk Teologi*, *27*(1), Article 1.

Skippervold, P. (2011). Bibelen. Naturlig og nær. Uforståelig og fremmed. In *Bibelfortellinger Metode og formidling* (pp. 20-27). IKO-Forlaget AS.

Søndagsskolen Norge. (2016). *Sprell Levende håndbok* (2nd ed.). Norsk søndagsskoleforbund.

Søndagsskolen Norge. (2024). *Sprell Levende*. Søndagsskolen. https://sondagsskolen.no/frivillige/sprell-levende/

Tetzchner, S. von. (2019). *Barne- og ungdomspsykologi*. Gyldendal akademisk.

The Lausanne Covenant. (1974). Lausanne Movement. https://lausanne.org/content/covenant/lausanne-covenant

Tieszen, C. L. (2008). *Re-examining Religious Persecution: Constructing a Theological Framework for Understanding Persecution*. VKW.

United Nations. (2024). *Universal Declaration of Human Rights*. UDHR; United Nations. https://www.un.org/en/about-us/universal-declaration-of-human-rights

15 "If the world hates you"

On persecution in sermons

Knut Kåre Kirkholm[1]

Abstract

This article examines how persecution is preached about in Norwegian Lutheran Evangelical congregations through an analysis of twelve sermons delivered between 2019 and 2021. The study highlights the representation of certain theological aspects of persecution and discusses potential explanations for the choices made by the preachers, in particular the selection of lectionary texts and the preachers' own contexts. Additionally, the study notes a connection between persecution and the 'inner cross,' reflecting Lutheran theological tradition. The findings suggest that some theological aspects of persecution might be challenging for preachers to highlight in a context with little or no pressure. The article calls for further research to address these homiletical challenges. In addition, the study reveals that preachers tend to describe persecution in a too simplistic way by focusing only on the extremes – discrimination 'at home' and violent persecution 'out there'. This approach risks overlooking the complexities between these extremes.

Keywords: Homiletics, persecution, Bad Urach Statement, 'inner cross'.

1 Introduction

The Christian Church has faced persecution throughout its history. The Bible addresses this (e.g., Matt 5:11-12; John 15:18-21; 2 Tim 3:12; 1 Pet 4:12), and it is reflected in liturgical readings and commemorations, such as St. Stephen's Day on 26 December. Various organisations track Persecution of Christians globally, highlighting its ongoing relevance.[2]

---

1 Knut Kåre Kirkholm (*1982), Dean of Studies and Associate Professor Fjellhaug International University College, kkirkholm@fjellhaug.no, ORCID iD: 0009-0009-8711-4572.

2 Open Doors is probably the best known among these organisations, with their annual "World Watch List". Based on the parameters of Open Doors, more than 365 million Christians suffer high levels of persecution and discrimination for their

In this article, I examine how persecution is preached in a selection of Norwegian congregations. I do this by analysing sermons sent to me by pastors and preachers. Since the sermon has been and remains a central arena for shaping and communicating theology, it is interesting to find out how a topic like persecution is preached.

This article aims to provide new knowledge about this, and my research question is as follows: What kind of theology of persecution is conveyed through preaching in a selection of sermons delivered in Norwegian Lutheran Evangelical congregations?

In recent times, several empirical studies of Christian preaching have been conducted, and this research project situates itself within this branch of homiletics. There are, as far as I'm aware, very few recent studies of congregational preaching on persecution and martyrdom, but recently, J. Sergius Halvorsen has provided an analysis of Father Boules George's address after the tragic Palm Sunday bombings on 9 April 2017. This sermon is preached in a very different context than my sermons and offers insights into how the church responded to a horrible act of violent persecution (Halvorsen, 2024). In a 2022 dissertation from Fuller, Anne Emile Zaki analysed the preaching in the Protestant Church of Egypt during and after the Arab Spring (Zaki 2022).

The topic of preaching about persecution is also briefly discussed, with some recommendations, in Christof Sauer's book *Martyrium und Mission im Kontext* (2021, pp. 397-398). Of Norwegian publications, Egil Morland's study of sermons delivered during World War II, in a situation where religious freedom was limited by the Nazis, comes closest to my topic (Morland 2016).

2 Material and methodological considerations

Material: The sermon manuscripts were collected from congregations belonging to the Evangelical branch of Norwegian Lutheranism. The congregations belong to churches or mission organisations that are members of NORME (Norwegian Council for Mission and Evangelization), which is the

faith. For more information about the methodology behind the "World Watch List", see "Complete World Watch List Methodology" (Open Doors International, 2024). It is important to be sober minded towards statistics of this type and many factors influence on the results. This consideration applies to both preachers who speak about persecution and researchers who write articles. See Sauer (2021, pp. 163-167) for an account and assessment of the most common statistics on persecution of Christians.

Norwegian representative both in the European Evangelical Alliance and the Lausanne Movement.

I did not include sermons from the Church of Norway, which was the largest Lutheran mainstream denomination and state church until 2012, since the churches and mission organisations under the NORME umbrella often consider themselves somewhat independent from the Church of Norway, even though they share the Lutheran faith. The churches and organisations in question are the Evangelical Lutheran Free Church of Norway (Frikirken), the Evangelical Lutheran Church (DELK), Normisjon, and the Norwegian Lutheran Mission. There are a few other mission organisations under the NORME umbrella, but they do not have independent congregations.

My selected churches and organisations are theologically more conservative than the Church of Norway and maintain a closer connection to the global Evangelical mission movement. It is primarily this connection – rather than theological differences – that motivated the exclusion of the Church of Norway from this project. Many congregations invite advocacy organisations such as Open Doors Norway and the Stefanus Alliance (formerly known as the Mission Behind the Iron Curtain, or The Norwegian Mission to the East). I deliberately omitted sermons delivered by representatives from these organisations, as I was primarily interested in "regular" preaching.

I collected my sermons in the autumn of 2021, following two distinct approaches. For the mission organisations – Normisjon and the Norwegian Lutheran Mission – as well as the Evangelical Lutheran Free Church of Norway (Frikirken), I contacted pastors directly, since most of the congregations in major cities had websites with accessible contact information. In contrast, for the Evangelical Lutheran Church (ELC), I reached out through the national leader, as their website did not provide direct contact details for local pastors. Since then, the websites of all these churches and organisations have been updated, and the collection process would likely be easier today. I received material from approximately 25% of the congregations and pastors that were contacted.[3]

In my letter, I provided a brief description of the project, stating that my preliminary research topic was: What do pastors preach about persecution, with an emphasis on the kind of theology the preaching conveys to the congregants. I asked them to submit manuscripts no older than three years and encouraged them to provide links to any available recordings of the sermon. Unfortunately, nobody could offer such links.

---

3 Since I went via the national leader to collect sermons from DELK pastors, I cannot offer exact numbers.

As a general observation from the data collection process, it is worth noting that most respondents to my inquiry expressed regret, stating that they had not addressed the topic in their sermons. This could indicate that persecution is seldom addressed in sermons. However, several individuals mentioned in their feedback that they regularly host visits from organisations such as Open Doors or similar organisations.

In total, I received twelve sermons that were delivered during the congregations' Sunday services between 2019 and 2021.

The preachers themselves chose which sermons to submit. Since the sermons represent a selection, they should be regarded as snapshots. The strength of this approach is that the selected sermons are those that the preachers believe best reflect their message on persecution. The weakness, however, is that the researcher must rely on the preachers' judgment and has no means to verify whether other sermons might have been more suitable.

A significant weakness in my material is that all sermons were delivered by men. This is, to some extent, explained by the fact that many Evangelical congregations, for theological reasons, do not permit women to serve as pastors or priests. Women are allowed to preach, but for practical reasons, I contacted the pastors, which led to this unfortunate omission that I should have foreseen. Future research could explore whether men and women preach differently or if women offer unique perspectives.

This raises questions about representativeness; however, based on how these organisations and churches present their theological profiles, there is good reason to believe that the sermons are representative in terms of content.

The twelve sermons are presented below in chronological order according to the liturgical year. The first two are thematic sermons, while the others are expositional, based on the scripture readings in the lectionary.[4]

- Sermon 1: Thematic sermon on the persecuted church
- Sermon 2: Thematic sermon on the International Day of Prayer for the Persecuted Church
- Sermon 3: Second Sunday of Advent (Luke 21:25-36)
- Sermon 4: St. Stephens Day/December 26 (John 16:1-4)
- Sermon 5: St. Stephens Day/December 26 (Acts 6:8-15, 51-60)
- Sermon 6: Fourth Sunday after Trinity (Matthew 16:24-27)

[4] Most Lutheran churches and independent organizations in Norway use the same lectionary, which is printed in the most common Norwegian translations of the Bible.

- Sermon 7: Fourth Sunday after Trinity (Matthew 16:24-27)
- Sermon 8: Fourth Sunday after Trinity (Matthew 16:24-27)
- Sermon 9: Sixteenth Sunday after Trinity (Matthew 5:10-11)
- Sermon 10: Sixteenth Sunday after Trinity (Matthew 5:10-12)
- Sermon 11: Sixteenth Sunday after Trinity (Matthew 5:10-11)
- Sermon 12: All Saints' Day (Matthew 5:1-12)[5]

Methodological Considerations: To analyse the sermons, I applied thematic analysis to identify common themes in my material.[6] Since I analyse sermon manuscripts, some hermeneutical considerations are also relevant. Firstly, most of the sermons are expositions of the designated lectionary text, which means that the content of the biblical text determines the content of the sermon. Consequently, findings from my analysis could equally be due to the scripture reading rather than any other factor; therefore, I must be cautious not to draw overly firm conclusions regarding the motives of the preachers.

Secondly, I have applied the eleven theological aspects of persecution presented in the Bad Urach Statement.[7] This raises the issue of distinguishing between inductive and deductive approaches. On the one hand, I have taken an inductive hermeneutic approach and read the sermon manuscripts, allowing the contents to guide my results. At the same time, however, I have been influenced by the categories developed in the Bad Urach Statement, and thus my analysis risks being too influenced by preconceived themes and categories I expect to find in my material. In my analysis, I tried to resolve this tension by first analysing my material independently and then aligning my results with the categories in the Bad Urach Statement.

Thirdly, since I analyse sermon manuscripts and not the preaching event, important communicative features such as body language, facial expressions, and pauses are not included in the analysis.

Overall, these methodological considerations aim to ensure that my findings remain as objective and reflective of the material as possible while acknowledging the inherent complexities involved in the analysis.

---

5 Quotations from the sermons are translated from Norwegian with the help of AI (Microsoft Copilot).

6 I have followed a step-by-step guide provided in a Norwegian book on research methodology. The guide is based on the process description developed by Virginia Braun and Victoria Clarke (Rafoss, Johannesen & Rasmussen, 2018, p. 282). The four steps were: preparation, coding, categorizing, and reporting.

7 See the theory chapter below for a presentation of the *Bad Urach Statement*.

3 Theory

When analysing and discussing the sermons, I use the homiletical triangle as a frame of reference. In its simplest form, it expresses preaching as a conversation between the biblical passage, the preacher, and the listening congregation. In addition to the three poles of the triangle, I have considered the persecuted, to whom both the preacher and the listening congregation need to relate.

To discuss my findings, I draw on the theological aspects outlined in the Bad Urach Statement. This document was written during a consultation in Bad Urach, Germany, organised by The International Institute for Religious Freedom, with Dr. Richard Howell and Dr. Christof Sauer leading the consultation. The statement seeks to summarise the most essential elements that a theology of persecution and martyrdom should encompass, providing the church with practical guidance. The categories or aspects in the statement are broad, and the aim was to establish as comprehensive a theological foundation for discussing persecution and martyrdom as possible.

The eleven aspects of persecution are as follows:

1. *Epistemological aspects*: The Bible presents us with a worldview where the church exists in a state of struggle and persecution, while being certain of the comfort and rest that awaits.
2. *Typological aspects*: The Old Testament (OT) contains stories about prophets and others who suffered for their faith. These serve as models for the sufferings of both Christ and the church.
3. *Christological aspects*: Both in his life and, not least, on the cross, Christ had to suffer. This serves as an example for his disciples. Suffering believers have always drawn strength from this to endure their own sufferings.
4. *Mimetic aspects*: Jesus' disciples must expect to suffer in the same way as their master. By following in the footsteps of Christ, the church must also expect to suffer, and Jesus' suffering serves as a model.
5. *Antagonistic aspects*: In the world, the church encounters opposition both socially and politically. This opposition can be theologically explained through the cosmic battle in heaven (Ephesians 6:11-12). Although Satan has already been defeated on the cross, he continues to fight and remains a spiritual force to be reckoned with. The offence of the cross means that the church must contend with opposition rooted in satanic forces.
6. *Soteriological aspects*: It is necessary to confess Christ to be saved (Matthew 10:32-33), and this confession can lead to persecution.

The consolation is that God and his angels come to the believer's aid and provide help to endure. God is also the one who can call the persecutor to repentance, often accomplished through the testimony presented by the suffering of the persecuted.

7. *Ecclesiological aspects*: The believer who suffers is a member of the body of Christ, which is the church. This fellowship transcends history, geographical distance, and confessional dividing lines. The New Testament (NT) shows that persecution and martyrdom often serve to build up and strengthen the church.
8. *Missiological aspects*: Suffering goes hand in hand with the mission of the church to make disciples, and its bold witness of Christ often leads to persecution. At the same time, God uses persecution, suffering, and martyrdom to promote his missionary work in the world. Both the NT and church history attest to this.
9. *Eschatological aspects*: Creation awaits its redemption and the day when everything will be put right. The resurrection of Christ is the foundation for this hope. The final judgement will be held over evil, and on that day, God's church, including the martyrs, will receive their crowns of victory.
10. *Doxological aspects*: God is honoured through the bold witness of the persecuted church, and God has promised honour and an eternal crown of victory to those who suffer for his name. Believers consider it a privilege to suffer for Christ (cf. Philippians 1:29).
11. *Ethical aspects*: The reality of persecution and suffering raises important ethical questions. The church is not called to seek persecution but to grow in holiness. Christians who commit criminal acts must expect to be punished as others. Christians should not persecute others, nor speak falsely about their persecutors. Believers are called to live as loyal citizens while maintaining the principle that one must obey God rather than humans (cf. Acts 4:12).

These eleven aspects arise from an attempt to systematize the biblical material without distinguishing between frequency and importance. Therefore, simply counting instances is insufficient; however, these aspects assist in differentiating and categorising the biblical material, which is the purpose of my analysis.

4 How persecution is defined in the sermons

Before moving to the theological analysis of the sermons, I would like to offer a brief discussion about how persecution is defined in the sermons.

When reading the material, it struck me that the preachers operate with rather simplistic categories, distinguishing between violence and murder 'out there' and everyday animosity and derogatory speech 'here at home'.

The preachers bring violent persecution to the forefront when speaking about the situation of Christians outside of Norway, referring to it as 'something that takes place in countries far away' (sermon 9). Drawing on media stories, the preacher in sermon 9 states: 'the open persecution that our brothers and sisters around the world are facing'. In sermon 10, the preacher adds: 'We immediately think about Christians who live in countries where Christianity is banned. This could be in totalitarian states or in some Muslim or Hindu countries where being Christian is forbidden.' Some sermons also draw historical lines, referencing and comparing examples of violent persecution of Christians in the early church.

When discussing the situation in Norway – the context in which the listeners find themselves – the preachers primarily focus on what can be termed experiences of animosity and intolerance, and they avoid the word 'persecution' altogether. These experiences are exemplified by 'scornful looks and ignoring' or the negative media attention that conservative Christians receive in connection with discussions about homosexuality and same-sex marriage. One preacher mentions a growing scepticism towards Christians, which has recently been documented in certain surveys, such as in the context of job applications.

They are aware that this kind of animosity can be difficult and painful; as expressed in sermon 6: 'We become strangers in our own country.' However, it is worth noting that many of the preachers focus more on the privileged situation for Christians in Norway. The preacher in sermon 10 points out that Christians in Norway have much to be grateful for, as they do not face harsh persecution, while in sermon 1, the preacher draws a contrast between Norway and Syria: 'We don't need to be afraid, like Christians in Syria, of enemies throwing a bomb into the room while we are gathered for worship.'

Given the realities of this world, it is no great surprise that the description of the situation in Norway does not mention violence and martyrdom. However, what makes the preaching somewhat one-sided is that all examples are drawn from the extremes. When persecution is presented in such a simplified manner, one might question whether there is a risk of overlooking or losing the language to address what lies between everyday challenges and open acts of violence.

Thus, if we ask how competent the preachers are on the topic of persecution, the answer would be that they show little awareness of how complex the reality is; one could easily criticise them for generalizations and oversimplifications that might affect their listeners' understanding of the broader issues surrounding persecution.

5 Theology of persecution conveyed in the sermons

In this section of my paper, I use subheadings to categorise my findings, conducting my analysis with reference to the theological aspects of the Bad Urach Statement and the homiletical triangle. To provide the reader with an overview of the main theological tendencies in my material, I have included a table that aligns the theological statements and inferences within the sermons with the categories outlined in the Bad Urach Statement. This table does not, of course, present findings that are not expressed in the Bad Urach Statement.

Table 1: Aspect of a theology of persecution in sermons

Aspects/ Sermons	S1	S2	S3	S4	S5	S6	S7	S8	S9	S10	S11	S12	Sum
Epistemo-logical	1	1	1	1	1	1	4	1	1	3	1	1	17
Typo-logical					1					2	2		5
Christo-logical	1	1		1	1	2				1	1		8
Mimetic	2	3		4		5	6	2	1	6	2	1	32
Antago-nistic	2	3	2	8		1	3	1	2	3	1		26
Soterio-logical	1		1	1	3	2	5		1		1		15
Ecclesio-logical	4	1	1		3	1	1		2	1		1	15
Missio-logical	2	1			1	1	2			1			8
Eschato-logical		1	4		1	2	3		1		2	3	17
Doxo-logical	1	2		1		2	2		1	2	1	2	14
Ethical		1		1			1		1	1			5

To briefly summarise these alignments, we notice that all sermons presuppose that the Christian church exists in a context where animosity and persecution can be expected (epistemological aspects). To be saved, one must believe in Christ. Believers will experience hardship (soteriological aspects). Furthermore, there is much emphasis on the fact that Jesus' sufferings point to the church's situation in the world (mimetic aspects) and that persecution is a result of antagonistic forces in the world (antagonistic aspects). Based on such a description, most sermons encourage solidarity with the persecuted church (ecclesiological aspects). Finally, as noted earlier, most sermons highlight the eschatological hope found in Christ, which is also reflected in this table (eschatological aspects), usually at the end of the sermons.

5.1 A normal situation for a Christian

When discussing persecution, the preachers assume that we live in a fallen world, awaiting the day when Jesus returns to set everything right. In the meantime, the church must anticipate hatred and opposition (epistemological aspects).

Having read Matthew 5:10-12, one preacher claims: "The verses we have read affirm that being a Christian will entail persecution. They describe a situation that is normal for a Christian" (sermon 10).[8] Later, the same preacher adds that persecution and opposition can be taken as "signs that you belong to Jesus." Disciples of Jesus must expect suffering because that is the cost of following in Jesus' footsteps. Persecution language, in other words, serves to solidify the Christian identity of the listeners.

Several examples are given in the sermons, and as mentioned above, they are presented rather simplistically. Interestingly, very few examples are drawn from the Bible (typological aspects), with the example of Jesus (Christological and mimetic aspects) being an exception. Sermons 10-11 mention some precursors from the Old Testament, which can be explained by the fact that the content of both sermons references Matthew 5:12, which refers to the persecution of the prophets of old.

The Bible readings are also a probable explanation for the emphasis on Jesus' example. References to persecution and hardship "for my sake" are found in both Matthew 16:25 (text in sermons 6-8) and Matthew 5:11 (text in sermons 9-12). Therefore, expressions such as "for Jesus' sake" or "because of Jesus" appear frequently in my material and are often developed into reflections on the world's animosity towards a holy life and the fruits of sanctification, a theme I will return to.

Most examples, however, are taken from current media stories rather than the Bible, and in some of the sermons, the preachers also refer to

---

8 The same thing is expressed by the preacher in sermon 11: "The normal situation for the church in this world is to live in tribulation".

Christian brothers and sisters with whom many in the congregation feel a strong link, as these are active members of sister churches or organisations. By using such stories as a point of contact, the preachers attempt to give flesh and blood to the abstract term "persecution." My main concern regarding the use of current examples is that the preachers' choice of the most dramatic instances may oversimplify the nuanced discussion of persecution.

5.2 Subject to "hostile powers"

Having stated that persecution is a normal situation for Christians, the preachers in my material discuss the forces behind persecution (antagonistic aspects). Many preachers use abstract expressions like "the dark forces" (sermon 1 and sermon 5), "the forces around us" (sermon 7), "the world that is hostile to God" (sermon 4), "society's attitudes and lifestyle" (sermon 8), and "the spirit that reigns in the world" (sermon 10). However, human agents are also mentioned, ranging from "sceptical employers" (sermon 6) to "totalitarian states" and "Muslim or Hindu countries" (sermon 10).

In other words, an enmity between "the world" and the church is assumed, but the conflict is primarily political or ideological, with hardly any references to the devil or texts like Ephesians 6:12. Only one preacher (sermon 2) directly refers to the devil as the driving force behind the resistance that "the world" offers. The word "world" is understood as "the attitude of the hostile world," and the preacher goes on to say that there is "no doubt that the devil is successful in dragging people into the fight against those who believe in Jesus."

This observation came as a surprise to me. One possible explanation is that the devil is not mentioned in any of the lectionary texts used by the preachers, except in sermons 1 and 2. For that reason, it is not surprising that the spiritual dimension is underrepresented. It is also not surprising that the only sermon that explicitly mentions the devil as the driving antagonistic force is topical (sermon 2).

It should be added that expressions like "the dark forces" (sermon 1 and sermon 5), "the forces around us" (sermon 7), and "the spirit that reigns in the world" (sermon 10) are likely intended to convey the notion that these forces belong to the spiritual sphere. Therefore, I do not believe there is reason to think that the preachers reject this aspect of why persecution occurs.

One interesting observation found in two of the sermons is that the preacher, when contrasting the situation in Norway with that of the persecuted, suggests that the struggle is different in our context. Thus, sermon 3 distinguishes between "persecution" and "seduction," saying that Christians in the West are "more exposed to seductions," while Christians in other parts of the world "are persecuted for their faith." Similarly, the preacher in sermon 5 states: "We stand on a different kind of front line, where the battle is fought with completely different means. Not with swords and torture. We are not threatened away from Jesus, but we are enticed to doubt the word of God."

The persecutors are seldom spoken about in the sermons, and when they are mentioned, it is done in an impersonal way, such as "the world," "they," "IS," or similar. The focus is on the persecuted Christians.

Surprisingly, none of the sermons emphasise Jesus' words about loving our enemies and his command to "pray for those who persecute you" (Matthew 5:44). One might have expected that at least sermons 9-12, which were based on Matthew 5:10-12, would make such a connection. However, sermon 2 and sermons 4-5 indirectly make this connection by referring to people who pray for their persecutors.

If I had conducted a qualitative interview with the preachers, it would have been interesting to ask about their views on the lack of references to Jesus' command to love our enemies. Perhaps their reticence is a result of both the preacher and the congregation being distant from experiencing violent persecution and therefore finding it difficult to directly state that Christians who face severe violence must forgive and pray for their persecutors.

5.3 Sanctification and a transformed life

The fact that confessing Christ can lead to persecution (soteriological aspects) is assumed in my material but not further developed or discussed. Within the framework of soteriology, sanctification and a transformed life play significant roles in many of the sermons. In sermon 6, the preacher refers to 1 Peter 4:3-4, noting that the letter's recipients are alienated and despised because they live a different and more moral life than their compatriots. The preacher then links this alienation with persecution "for Jesus' sake." Similarly, the preacher in sermon 10 states: "This new life will be noticed by the world around, and the spirit that reigns in the world will not like it."

The emphasis on sanctification is expressed interestingly in sermon 7,[9] where the preacher discusses Christian suffering in a way that reflects the

9 But is also developed, however with less emphasis and clarity, in sermon 2 and the other sermons on Matthew 16:24-27 (sermon 6 and sermon 8).

Lutheran emphasis on the struggle between the Old Man and the New Man. This motif is echoed in Luther's Small Catechism, which speaks of "daily contrition and repentance," and in an old, much-quoted liturgical prayer in the Church of Norway, where we find the expression: "You raise us for your kingdom through cross and tribulation." In a Lutheran context, this expression encompasses both the outward persecution Christians may face as well as the inner spiritual struggle (Anfechtung), which plays a significant role in Lutheran theology.

In sermon 7, this aspect of a Christian's suffering is mentioned several times. The preacher states that "the human will is a battlefield between good and evil," and later follows with the paragraph:

> "To take up one's cross; a cryptic way of speaking for modern people. For the disciples, it was different. They had seen many crosses carried along the road to scorn and ridicule. And who were the ones carrying such crosses? Rebels, of course. Those who threatened the peace and order of the land were made to carry their own cross to the place of execution. Was this what Jesus was preparing them for? Preparing us for?
>
> We are such rebels. To follow Jesus is to be on a journey where the goal is that our rebellion against God should die."

As he continues, this is linked to the importance of not going with the flow. Facing resistance is connected to taking up the cross, as taking up one's cross also means standing out from the crowd.

It is understandable that this aspect of the inner struggle of Christian suffering is not included in the Bad Urach Statement, as it does not pertain to the physical resistance Christians may experience. However, it is interesting to note how naturally some preachers transition between outward persecution and inner spiritual struggle.

I would suggest that an important explanation for this shift is the Lutheran emphasis on the cross, understood as "all kinds of trials and evil from the devil, the world, and the flesh" (Luther 1966, p. 164). This is the seventh mark of the true church in Luther's treatise "On the Councils and the Church." The cross is described as a means of sanctification, and both inner and outer suffering and adversity are used so that Christians may become "like their head, Christ" (Luther 1966, p. 164). This aligns well with the ecclesiological aspect in the Bad Urach Statement, where suffering and the purification of the church are linked. The difference is that the preachers in my material mention the inner cross in connection with the sanctification of the individual. It also makes sense to assume that the rarity of direct persecution for Norwegian Christians makes the concept of "the inner cross" seem like a more plausible application of themes from Matthew 5:16 and John 16.

5.4 The prophetic task of speaking up against oppressors

One notable omission in the sermons is that none of the preachers mention any advocacy measures that the congregants might undertake. There is no exhortation to political activism on behalf of the oppressed. Even though they refer to concrete instances of severe persecution and emphasise that the persecuted are brothers and sisters in Christ, they do not address what actions, beyond prayer, the congregants might offer to support those who are persecuted.

This plays into a recurring debate in Norwegian Lutheranism about whether sermons should address current political issues and discussions.[10] In general, the branch of Norwegian Lutheranism from which my sermons are collected is more reluctant to speak directly to political issues than the Church of Norway. In Christian newspapers like Dagen and Vårt Land, which focus on faith issues and commentary on church matters, it is not uncommon to read criticism against the Church of Norway for being more devoted to politics than to the preaching of the gospel.

This might explain why the sermons I have analysed do not mention any political work or advocacy measures available to them. However, it is equally likely that the omission results from the strong connection drawn between persecution and sanctification, causing political issues to recede into the background.

5.5 Church strengthened and growing

The notion that suffering can help purify, strengthen, and even grow the church is discussed in several sermons (ecclesiological and missiological aspects) (cf. Sauer 2012, pp. 40-46). The sermon that develops this point in the most detail is sermon 1, where the preacher quotes from the book *Andens folk* (People of the Spirit) by the Swedish theologian Peter Halldorf:

---

10 This is reflected in the above-mentioned dissertation about sermons delivered during World War II, where Egil Morland discusses to which degree a prophetic voice was raised against the nazi regime in Norway and whether the analysed sermons reflect the first use of the Law (the civil use). Morland gives a positive answer, even though he admits that "There are several instances where priests appeared more willing to address their words" (Morland 2016, p. 343). Interestingly this prompted a response from professor Torleif Austad who thinks Morland is too positive in his assessment. He follows up on this by pointing out that a discussion about what he calls "social ethical preaching" is necessary in our time (Austad 2015, 70).

> "Resistance is a fire that tests faith. The trial is allowed so that only what is genuine remains. Thus, the church grows from within, increasingly refined in its character. The progress of the Gospel is tied to persecution and suffering. Too much goodwill from society contributes to secondary interests taking over the church's agenda." (Halldorf 2018, p. 210 – my translation)

This point is exemplified by church growth in Syria amid persecution and opposition. It is interesting to note that the preacher uses a quote and an example to express the role suffering and persecution play in growing and strengthening the church; this could have been stated directly. The reason for this choice is not clear; it may be due to a pedagogical consideration to give more weight and life to the statement vis-à-vis the listeners, or it could be a feeling that it is more appropriate to express it indirectly.

Given the congregations' involvement in the Norwegian mission movement, I was somewhat surprised that so little is said about God using suffering and persecution to spread the Gospel. Two sermons cite Tertullian's famous words that "the blood of the martyrs is the seed of the church" (sermon 5 and sermon 10), but this point is not elaborated upon beyond this brief reference.

One could question whether the preachers' reticence on this point relates to the distinction they make between the horrible sufferings "out there" and the everyday problems we experience "here at home" and consider whether there is a sense that we lack the right to speak on these matters given our privileged situation.

That said, it is worth noting that a couple of the preachers do make their audience aware that persecution may have the opposite effect. Opposition and pressure may lead a Christian to fall or take offence at Jesus (sermon 4). Furthermore, persecution can have devastating consequences for Christian fellowship, as it "creates a culture of fear," the preacher in sermon 4 continues. This could have been followed by an encouragement to support and pray for those Christians, but that was not done.

In most of the sermons, the preachers emphasise the bonds of Christian brotherhood. Christians who are violently persecuted are repeatedly referred to as "our brothers and sisters," and the congregation is reminded that "we" – the congregants – have a responsibility to remember the persecuted in prayer. In sermon 1, this solidarity is expressed in the following way: "It dawned on me: She is not a woman in a faraway land. She is my sister!" A similar sentiment is found in sermon 9, where the preacher talks about immigrants known to the congregation who have come to Norway, converted to Christianity, and then been sent back to their homeland, where they were killed: "In October, two members of our denomination – converts – were killed because they are Christians."

5.6 Hope in suffering

It is my impression that the preachers aim to provide a word of comfort to those who suffer for their faith in Christ.[11] Therefore, most of the sermons emphasise the eschatological hope shared by all Christians; the preachers underline the promises of redemption and final victory (eschatological aspects). Christians who stand firm in persecution bear witness to this hope. Sermon 3 articulates this sentiment: "Perhaps there is no one like the persecuted who can give us a reminder that we have a living hope ahead."

This same point is clear in sermon 12, where the preacher refers to the "great multitude in white robes" (cf. Revelation 7:9-17), indicating that they have "passed through death and have entered into the rest of God, where he comforts and provides for them, and they respond with praise and thanksgiving." The preacher applies this to his audience, stating that the point is "to give us something to look forward to with joy and expectation, so that we endure and maintain faith in Jesus when life gets difficult."

Sermon 3 also relates eschatological hope to God's judgment on the forces behind all opposition and persecution: "All the forces of destruction will be exposed to ridicule and mockery, not only the devil and all his demons, but also all the powers in the world that have allowed themselves to be used as instruments in his hand." This is followed by a point that emphasises the hope of a new creation and a new heaven and earth.

5.7 Glorification of suffering

In chapter 5.4, I mentioned that little is found in my material about the role persecution plays in strengthening and growing the church. In addition to the possible reasons mentioned above, the preachers may be hesitant to glorify or elevate persecution. In my material, I did not find any statements that glorified persecution as something Christians should long for and actively seek (ethical aspects). In the two sermons that explicitly address this question, the preachers encourage the congregation to pray for the persecuted

11 In her dissertation about preaching hope in a crisis Zaki offers a typology of preachers/pulpits. The position I have found in my sermons fits well with what Zaki labels "the comforting approach", that is the preacher who primarily seeks to offer God's comfort to the sufferers (Zaki 2022, pp. 2-3).

and stand in solidarity with them. Thus, the persecuted are neither portrayed as helpless victims nor as superhuman faith heroes. Instead, they are presented as fellow Christians who require help and support.

Even though persecution is not glorified, several instances exist where the preachers emphasise that suffering for Christ is considered a privilege in the Bible (doxological aspects). I believe the main explanation for this is that four sermons are based on Matthew 5:10-12 (sermons 9-12), where the disciples are pronounced blessed if they suffer for Christ's sake, along with three sermons from Matthew 16:24-27 (sermons 6-8), where Jesus speaks of finding life by losing it for his sake.

Another example is found in sermon 4, where the preacher quotes Philippians 1:29, which states that "it has been granted to you that, for the sake of Christ, you should not only believe in him, but also suffer for his sake."[12] The preacher interprets this phrase as follows: "Yes, they should regard the suffering itself as a gift, just as they received the gift of believing in Jesus." In sermon 2, the preacher also quotes Philippians 1:29 and asks rhetorically: "Do you view suffering in this way? That it is a grace, a proof of honour to suffer for Jesus?"

6 Conclusion and outlook

In this article, through an analysis of twelve sermons, I have shown how the interplay between the preacher, the biblical text, and the congregation influences the presentation of different theological aspects of persecution and the weight they are given. I indicate that both the preacher and the congregation, in a context with little or no pressure for their faith, may find it challenging to discuss the privilege of being persecuted for the sake of Christ or how persecution might strengthen and grow the church. The same applies to Jesus' words about praying for the persecutors.

This perceived reluctance raises interesting questions about identifying and addressing homiletical challenges in such a context. Most preachers face the challenge of balancing fidelity to the scriptural text with the context of their congregation while not neglecting the situation of those who are persecuted. This article identifies and discusses some of these issues; however, further work is needed.

As an aside, I also note that the preachers describe persecution in an overly simplistic and unnuanced manner by only addressing the extremes – discrimination "at home" and violent or deadly persecution "out there."

---

12 It is worth noting that in Norwegian bibles the expression "it has been granted to you" (χαρίζομαι) is translated with "you have been given the grace".

I criticise this approach and point out that such simplification can cause us to overlook what lies between the extremes.

7 References

Austad, T. (2015). Henrik Seips forkynnelse under okkupasjonen 1940-1945. En kommentar til Egil Morlands doktoravhandling. *Tidsskrift for praktisk teologi 32/2.* https://doi.org/10.48626/tpt.v32i2.5181

Halldorf, P. (2008). *Åndens folk.* Luther forlag.

Halvorsen, J. S. (2024). Preaching the Impossible in the Face of the Unthinkable: Nonviolence, Love, and Thanksgiving in a Coptic Easter Sermon. *Religions, 15*(4), 455. https://doi.org/10.3390/rel15040455

Luther, M. (1966). On the Councils and the Church. In E. W. Gritsch (Ed.), *Church and Ministry III* (Luther's Works Volume 41). Fortress Press.

Morland, E. (2016). *Motstand og forkynnelse: På prekestolen under andre verdenskrig.* Portal Akademisk. – A slightly modified version of his Dr. Philos. dissertation: Morland, E. (2014). *Forkynnelsen i en kampsituasjon: en analyse av Henrik Aubert Seips prekener 1940-45.* University of Bergen.

Open Doors International. (2024). *Complete World Watch List Methodology.* Open Doors International / World Watch Research. https://www.opendoors.org/research-reports/wwl-documentation/complete-WWL-Methodology-October-2024

Pileberg, S. (2019, 5. november). *Norske bedrifter velger bort religiøse jobbsøkere.* Universitetet i Oslo, Institutt for sosiologi og samfunnsgeografi (ISS). https://www.sv.uio.no/iss/forskning/aktuelt/aktuelle-saker/2019/velger-bort-religiose-jobbsokere.html

Sauer, C. (Ed.). (2012). Bad *Urach Statement: Towards an evangelical theology of suffering, persecution and martyrdom for the global church in mission.* VKW.

Sauer, C. (2021). *Martyrium und Mission im Kontext.* Erlanger Verlag.

Sauer, C. (2021). Wie viele Christen werden verfolgt? *Jahrbuch Verfolgung und Diskriminierung von Christen 2021.* 163-167. https://iirf.global/wp-content/uploads/Jahrbuch/cv_2021_web.pdf

Zaki, A. E. (2022). *As Those with Hope: Crisis Preaching in the Protestant Church of Egypt During and Post-The Arab Spring.* [PhD dissertation]. Fuller Theological Seminary.

E. Missiology and Religious Studies

16 Interrelations between conversion and persecution

Proposal for a typology

Joel Hofer[1]

Abstract

Conversion to Christianity and persecution of Christians as separate topics are the subject of numerous studies. In many contexts, converts are the most intensely persecuted group among Christians. A look at the mission history of older and more recent times shows that conversion and persecution are connected in many complex ways. This raises the question: What are potential interrelations between conversion and persecution? To find answers to this question, the *Regnum Edinburgh Centenary Series (RECS)*, one of the most comprehensive missiological series of the 21st century, was examined. The different aspects that emerge in the contributions of the series can be unfolded in five thematic groups: 1) conversion as a trigger for persecution, 2) persecution and conversion as reciprocal influences, 3) anti-conversion motives as reasons for persecution, 4) pro-conversion actors as victims and supporters, 5) other groups between conversion and persecution. In exploring these groups of topics, a nuanced and wide-ranging picture of the many dynamics between conversion and persecution emerges.

Keywords: Conversion, persecution, religious freedom, interrelations, conversion opponents, pro-conversion actors.

---

[1] Joel Hofer is a PhD researcher in the field of missiology and religious studies. Email: hofer.joel@protonmail.com, ORCID iD: 0009-0006-2216-4390. This chapter is an adapted English version of a previously published journal article, cf. Hofer, J., & Sauer, C. (2023). Zusammenhänge von Konversion und Verfolgung: Vorschlag einer Typologie. *Zeitschrift für Missionswissenschaft und Religionswissenschaft*, 107(3-4), pp. 356-370. It summarizes a missiological typology that was tentatively developed in Hofer's master's thesis.

1 Introduction

In several contexts, there is a reported growth of both conversions to Christianity *and* persecution of Christians (Johnson, 2014; Johnson & Zurlo, 2020). According to *World Watch Research,* the research department of *Open Doors*, in many cases, converts are affected more severely by persecution than other Christian groups (World Watch Research, 2024). This raises the question about *potential interrelations between conversion and persecution.*

The two topics of 'conversion' and 'persecution' are discussed in the literature from a perspective of human rights (Bielefeldt, 2017, pp. 108; Bielefeldt & Wiener, 2020), sociology (Meral, 2006; L. Rambo & Farhadian, 2014), theology (Penner, 2004; Sauer, 2013) and missiology (Gravaas et al., 2015). They are predominantly treated as independent issues, e.g. concerning conversion processes (L. R. Rambo, 1993; Strähler, 2021), conversion motives (Maurer, 1999) or persecution of Christians in different religious contexts, such as Muslim (Häde, 2017; Philpott, 2019; Schirrmacher, 2010), Hindu (Barua, 2015; Vandevelde, 2011) or Buddhist contexts (Finucane & Feener, 2014; Fischer, 2018). Some researchers have addressed individual links between conversion and persecution (Enstedt et al., 2020; Marshall & Shea, 2011). However, a more in-depth systematic examination of potential interrelations between conversion and persecution is still lacking.

Sauer (2017) has addressed the question of these connections by analysing two missiological collections of essays (Gravaas et al., 2015; Taylor et al., 2012) on the basis of a human rights typology (Bielefeldt, 2017). Given his limited source base and the legally oriented typology he chose, it can be assumed that an investigation of a broader source base with the aim of a missiologically oriented typology could lead to additional perspectives.[2]

The author of this chapter has elsewhere provided a biblical-theological categorisation of potential interrelations between conversion and persecution (Hofer, 2021). In terms of content, the present chapter goes beyond both Sauer (2017) and Hofer (2021) by attempting a more comprehensive missiological typology based on the extensive source base of the 35 volumes of the *Regnum Edinburgh Centenary Series* (2009-2016).

---

[2] Section 8 provides a comparison between Bielefeldt's human rights typology and the tentative missiological typology developed in this chapter.

2 A better understanding of potential interrelations between conversion and persecution

The aim of this chapter is to better understand the complex and sometimes reciprocal dynamics between conversion and persecution on a global scale. To this end, this chapter attempts to weave the diverse and contextually different interrelations into a multifaceted typology.

Although conversions take place between different religions and world views, the focus here is on conversions to *Christianity* and the persecution of *Christians*. It is acknowledged, however, that followers of various religions around the world experience persecution or discrimination as well (Bielefeldt & Wiener, 2020).

From this perspective, 'conversion' is understood as "leaving [one's own] former religion or ideological grouping to become a Christian" (Veerman, 2015, p. 145). 'Persecution' of Christians is understood in a broad sense as "any hostility experienced as a result of one's identification with Christ. This can include hostile attitudes, words and actions towards Christians." (World Watch Research, 2024, p. 4)[3]

The content of this chapter is mainly[4] based on the *Regnum Edinburgh Centenary Series* (RECS), which, with 35 volumes, can probably be viewed as one of the most comprehensive missiological series of the 21st century so far. It was compiled in ecumenical breadth by an international team of around 500 missiologists and published between 2009 and 2016.[5] Many of the 874 contributions address various links between conversion and persecution. Volume 28 on religious freedom and Christian mission contains a particularly large number of references that are of interest to the aforementioned issue (Gravaas et al., 2015).

In preparing the master's thesis on which this chapter is based, the author analysed the entire series (RECS), using an electronic keyword search,[6] and developed a tentative categorisation of different relationships

---

3 In the introductory chapter of this anthology, Sauer and Nel provide a thorough discussion on different definitions of 'religious persecution'. The present chapter operates with a broad definition offered by *World Watch Research*, also because it seems that much of the source material used for this chapter (RECS) entails narratives which build on such broad definition (cf. Veerman, 2015).

4 At some places, the contents of the main literature source used for this chapter (RECS) are complemented by referring to additional, mostly more recent, literature.

5 Cf. https://www.regnumbooks.net/collections/edinburgh-centenary (accessed 28 April 2025).

6 The advanced search function of the Adobe Acrobat Reader application for viewing and editing PDF documents was used for the analysis. In a first analysis run,

between conversion and persecution on this basis.[7] The different aspects that appear in the contributions to the series (RECS) can be categorised into five thematic groups: 1) conversion as a trigger for persecution, 2) persecution and conversion as reciprocal influences, 3) anti-conversion motives as reasons for persecution, 4) pro-conversion actors as victims and supporters, 5) other groups between conversion and persecution. In dealing with these thematic groups, a differentiated and wide-ranging picture of numerous dynamics between conversion and persecution emerges.

3 Conversion as a trigger for persecution

Conversions rarely remain without effect: often, a conversion not only changes the religious life of the convert, but in many places also triggers hostility from outside, which can be directed both against the convert and against other Christians. Conversion is not only a *turning towards* the Christian faith, but also a *turning away* from another religion or ideology. This turning away from the prevailing 'system' and the turn to the Christian faith is often met with resistance from the non-Christian religions or ideological groupings that have been abandoned, especially if the religion or ideology is radicalised (Veerman, 2015, pp. 145). While conversion to the dominant non-Christian system would not be a problem, conversion *away from* the system can be a thorn in the side (Premawardhana, 2011, p. 269). According to *World Watch Research,* one of the main motives for this resistance is the fear of the existing non-Christian system losing power (World Watch Research, 2024, pp. 8).

all those results were displayed that contained at least two terms from the word fields of the keyword combination 'persecution' and 'conversion' within a range of 1000 words (approximately one DIN A4 page). The respective keyword roots 'conver' and 'persec' were used as search terms. A supplementary secondary investigation was carried out with synonymous terms in the same semantic environment as well as on the basis of a diagonal reading of the 28th volume mentioned above. This is important because different terms were used for similar issues depending on the article and author. Even if the RECS contributions analysed did not explicitly aim to discuss the connections between conversion and persecution, the analysis revealed a differentiated, broad picture of acceptable connections. The footnotes in this chapter refer to representative passages in individual volumes without citing all 35 volumes. However, it became clear in the detailed report on the results of the master's thesis that almost all 35 volumes contain references between conversion and persecution that are relevant to the research question.

7 To analyse the content of the results from the keyword search, Hofer used principles of a Grounded Theory approach according to Strauss and Corbin (2008).

Conversion is often not only the starting point of persecution in the lives of individual converts, but also in the experience of larger Christian groups within a majority non-Christian environment: Christians in countries with a certain Christian population (e.g. foreign Christians or Christians within traditional churches) may be able to live for a long time without persecution, even though they are in a non-Christian context. However, as soon as large numbers of people convert from a non-Christian religion or ideology, persecution often begins. This usually affects converts first. The more the number of converts grows, the more other Christians can also be affected by persecution (Veerman, 2015, p. 147). It can also be observed that often the more people convert, the more missionary activities by other (e.g. foreign) Christians are perceived as a threat by non-Christian majorities. Therefore, after the initial persecution of converts, other Christians who pursue missionary activities are often persecuted in the next step. If the Christian movement continues to grow, anyone who is identified with the Christian faith is likely to be persecuted (Veerman, 2015, p. 147).

This suggests that, chronologically, conversions to Christianity in a majority non-Christian environment often form the starting point of persecution of Christians within a particular context, while the converts themselves are often the first group to be persecuted, before other Christian groups.

4 Persecution and conversion as reciprocal influences

Conversions and persecution can influence each other: conversions may have an influence on persecution and, conversely, persecution may also influence conversions.

4.1 Negative influences of conversions on persecution

From the perspective of the convert, conversion can have both negative and positive effects on persecution. A negative influence of conversion from the converts' perspective is that it can *reinforce persecution*. This can have a negative impact on various areas of a convert's life: in their private life, in their family life, in their social environment, at national levels and in church life, according to Veerman (2015, p. 131). Various other sources also confirm each of these aspects.

The *private lives* of converts can be affected by violations of their right to freedom of thought and conscience. In some contexts, conversion as an individual decision is prohibited (Josua, 2015, p. 209). In addition, personal life can be restricted, for example, by prohibiting meetings with other Christians (Josua, 2015, p. 205).

The *family life* of a convert is also often challenged. In many cases, the persecution begins within the convert's own family, even if there is no pressure from the state (Sered & Ben-David, 2015, p. 216). Family and religious identity are closely linked in many contexts (Sered & Ben-David, 2015, p. 216). A conversion can lead, for instance, to banishment from the family or loss of inheritance (Veerman, 2015, p. 145). In some cases, however, the initially tense relationship between converts and their respective families can relax again after some time (Strähler, 2021).

Converts are also sometimes disadvantaged in their *social environment*. Converts sometimes experience exclusion from social services, harassment or social incitement against them (Veerman, 2015, p. 145; Vysotskaya, 2015, p. 316).

In several contexts, converts face challenges regarding the *state* in which they live, including rights, laws, national administration, and public life, among other issues. Converts may lose their jobs because of their conversion, be excluded from public services or be officially sentenced, imprisoned or sometimes even killed by state legal bodies (Jørgensen, 2015, p. 115; Veerman, 2015, p. 145). Another particular challenge is the fact that in some Muslim majority countries, it is not possible to change religious identity on identity documents after converting to Christianity. This means that often a convert remains a Muslim on paper after converting (Andrews, 2020; Josua, 2015, p. 210).

The *church life* of converts can also be affected: This applies in particular to the restriction of meetings, communal life, public statements and the use of premises (Veerman, 2015, p. 132). In some countries, such as Iran, the gathering of Christians in congregations or house groups is seen as a major threat to state order (Josua, 2015, p. 192). In some regions, e.g. in the Middle East, churches are sometimes sanctioned for accepting converts (Josua, 2015, p. 205).

An examination of the *gender-specific* effects of conversion reveals that while women are particularly vulnerable to persecution following their conversion – for example, in the form of sexual violence or forced marriage – converted men also suffer significantly from negative consequences, such as physical violence or economic disadvantage. Consequently, distinct persecution dynamics can be observed for male and female converts (Miller et al., 2023).

The analysis of the sources has confirmed that in many places, conversion can lead to persecution in private life, family, social environment, at the national level and in church life, sometimes combined with physical violence.

4.2 Positive influences of conversions on persecution

However, there are also exceptions in which a conversion has no negative influence on the convert and can have a *positive* effect: The *conversion of a person in power*, for example, has the potential to reduce the persecution of other Christians, as becomes evident in view of the two statesmen Emperor Constantine and King Tiridates in Armenia in the 4th century AD. Before the conversion of the Roman Emperor Constantine, Christians were oppressed in many places. After his conversion, Christianity became not only a tolerated but even a favoured religion (Hölzl, 2015; Jongeneel, 2015, p. 435).

In addition, conversion may represent a liberation for *social minorities* from previous persecution emanating from society. Due to their minority status, some religious or ethnic minorities, such as Indian Dalits in the 20th century, were persecuted by representatives of other social groups. Their conversion to the Christian faith sometimes put an end to this persecution, either temporarily or even completely (Victor, 2014, p. 150).

4.3 Negative influences of persecution on conversions

Conversely, persecution can also have an influence on conversions, either negatively or positively. On the negative side, the pressure of persecution may *prevent interested people from* even considering the option of 'conversion', from taking the step to convert or from living out their newfound faith after conversion. While in some Muslim-dominated contexts, conversions from Christianity to Islam are viewed favourably by the government and society, Muslims are deterred from becoming Christians by the negative treatment of Christians sometimes occurring, as the history of Christian mission in Egypt, for example, shows (Wahba, 2013, p. 257).

Persecution sometimes also has the effect of causing converts to reverse their conversion *(reconversion)*. Although the two terms and phenomena 'deconversion' and 'reconversion' are related, they must be distinguished from each other: 'deconversion' refers to the abandonment of religious, usually acquired, convictions that one previously held. In contrast, 'reconversion' is the conscious return to beliefs or the forced resumption of traditions that one had *before* the conversion to a different faith. Reconversion, therefore, involves both the abandonment of a newly acquired belief and the re-acceptance of the previous belief (Popp-Baier, 2003).

Persecution can lead to both deconversion and reconversion. Persecution is sometimes used as a deliberate strategy by persecutors to influence converts to reconvert, as can be seen in India. According to Arles, radical Hindu groups have developed reconversion programmes to bring former Hindus who have converted to Islam or Christianity back to Hinduism. As Arles reports, these so-called 'Ghar Waapsi' programmes ('homecoming' programmes) use a mixture of enticement and persecution: Converts are challenged to return to Hinduism. They are told that their conversion to Christianity was the result of deception and coercion on the part of the Christians. The pressure on converts and Christians in general, which is exerted through attacks on churches and anti-conversion laws, leads some converts to return to Hinduism (Arles, 2015, p. 326). In Islamic countries today, many converts are also pressured to return to Islam (Vysotskaya, 2015, p. 316).

4.4 Positive influences of persecution on conversions

Persecution may also have the opposite effect of encouraging further conversions. *Disappointment about the violence against people of other faiths* in the name of their own worldview or religious formation sometimes leads followers of the persecuting group to become Christians too. Additionally, the *witness of Christian love* in persecution situations towards their fellow human beings and the *faithfulness* of Christians in their faith can provide the impetus for the conversion of others. The Romanian town of Toflea can be mentioned as an example of this: Once notorious for drugs, violence and alcoholism, it has become widely known for numerous conversions and baptisms, as well as large Christian congregations. In the 1990s, some residents of the town converted to Christianity. After their conversion, they were persecuted by their fellow citizens. However, through the testimony of their positively changed lives and their love for their persecutors, many more residents converted. In 2015, the town was 80-90% Christian (Wachsmuth, 2016, p. 556).

In addition, *migration due to persecution* often leads to further conversions in new places. The initial spread of the Christian faith and the conversions that accompanied it were primarily fueled by persecution-related migration at the very beginning of the Christian Church. Persecution from the Jewish authorities and the subsequent Roman persecution brought the Christian faith to places such as North Africa, where there had previously been no Christians (Walls, 2014, p. 23).

Persecution can also have a positive influence in that it reduces potential conversions due to *impure motives*: In China, for example, conversions usually only take place after careful consideration of the costs (Chan, 2015, p. 293).

Furthermore, persecution of Christians (including converts) can contribute to a *strengthening of faith*. This is reported, for example, by the churches in the Soviet Union during the communist oppression in the 20th century (Kool, 2016, p. 35) as well as by Christians under more recent persecution (Yang, 2014, p. 156).

4.5 Conversion-neutral persecution

The term 'conversion-neutral' is coined to describe dynamics where persecution seems to have no (thus, 'neutral') effects on conversions. In some regions, despite persecution, an increasing number of conversions could be observed in the early 21st century, such as in China (Chan, 2015, pp. 291), Burma (Storaker, 2015, p. 336) or Central Asia (Vysotskaya, 2015, p. 316). The same phenomenon can be observed in the 20th century: in Angola, for example, the number of Christians continued to grow steadily towards the end of the century despite persecution by the Marxist government (van der Meer, 2013, p. 93). While there were around one million Christians in China at the beginning of the communist persecution in 1949, their number grew to possibly 90 million during the decades of oppression (Barrett & Johnson, 2001, p. 231).

It can be concluded from this that, in some cases, persecution probably has no influence on conversions (which one could also denote as '*conversion-neutral persecution*'), which means that numerous people are not deterred from converting despite persecution (Wahba, 2013, p. 258).

It is difficult to say whether the number of converts in these contexts would perhaps be even higher if there had been *no* persecution (Chan, 2015, p. 293). It has already been shown that persecution can also have an inhibiting effect. The opposite cannot be said with certainty: the observation of a correlation between increasing persecution and rising conversion figures in various contexts is not a compelling indication of a causal relationship between the two (Jørgensen, 2015, p. 118).

5 Anti-conversion motives as reasons for persecution

A look at different contexts around the world shows that there are various driving forces that rise up against conversion and the Christian faith in general. According to Veerman (2015) and *World Watch Research* (2024), these driving forces are different world views or ideologies,[8] and the per-

[8] The following distinction between different driving forces is based on a classification drawn up by *World Watch Research* (2024, p. 10).

secution of converts (and Christians in general) is primarily carried out to preserve the power of a system or the honour of the family.

5.1 Driving forces behind the persecution of converts

Under the driving force *of Islamic oppression*, converts from Islam are often persecuted and sometimes even killed with the accusation of apostasy (Josua, 2015; Schirrmacher, 2020).[9] In the context of *religiously motivated nationalism*, converts, for example from Buddhism or Hinduism, are seen as a weakening of the respective nation and a danger to it (Arles, 2015). One example of this is Burma, where Christian converts are perceived as a disruption to the close links between Buddhism and Burmese culture. Buddhist authorities propagate this link as part of a 'Burmanisation process' with slogans such as "One race, one language, one religion" and "To be Myanmar is to be Buddhist" (Storaker, 2015, pp. 333).[10] Converts *from traditional ethnic groups* sometimes suffer persecution because they have left indigenous religions and world views, and certain ethnic groups see their existence jeopardised by the conversion (Petri, 2020). Converts who leave *criminal groups* are sometimes punished with persecution or death. Leaving a criminal organisation, such as the Colombian guerrillas, often carries great danger, as the defector is seen as a potential traitor to internal secrets (Veerman, 2015, p. 148). For *dictatorial regimes*, converts often represent a threatening opposition, as can be seen in various examples from the past (e.g. Ethiopia) and the present (e.g. Eritrea) (Eshete, 2015, p. 251; Mekonnen & Tronvoll, 2015, p. 265). In *communist systems* such as Cuba or North Korea, converts are sometimes persecuted as 'counter-revolutionaries' (Peters, 2015, p. 297; Petri, 2020, p. 169).

In the past, persecution of converts also took place *within* Christianity, based on denominational protectionism: such *intra-Christian persecution* was sometimes carried out by dominant and powerful churches against converts to other Christian denominations or denominations under the accusation of heresy or betrayal of national identity. In some countries, this manifested itself in such a way that a single Christian denomination saw itself as the only legitimate expression of Christianity and often instrumentalised state power to assert its claims. Often, the 'persecuting' denomination was the dominant majority denomination within a country,

---

9 Evans (2005, p. 167) offers a nuanced framework with a scale of potential reactions to apostasy.

10 Here Storaker uses quotes from two NGO reports (Chin Human Rights Organization (2012, p. 6); Rogers (2007, p. 13).

such as the Catholic Church in Latin American countries during the persecution of converts in the 19th and 20th centuries (Paredes, 2010, p. 114).[11]

A look at the aforementioned driving forces shows that the persecution of converts can be interpreted as a struggle for absolute power.

5.2 Reinforcing factors for the persecution of converts

In some countries, the persecution of converts, which is already rooted in society, is *reinforced by the state.* Apostasy laws or anti-conversion laws often create the legal basis for this persecution. A distinction must be made between these two types of law: *Apostasy laws* are mainly found in strict Muslim majority countries such as Pakistan, Saudi Arabia or Yemen and are directed against *converts* with the prohibition of apostasy and its punishment, sometimes also including the death penalty (Schirrmacher, 2020). *Anti-conversion laws,* on the other hand, ostensibly prohibit means such as enticement, deception or coercion to influence a person to convert. These laws are mainly used in the Hindu context and are not primarily directed against the converts themselves, but against *pro-conversion actors* (especially evangelizing Christians and churches) to prevent conversions in general. Such laws are subsequently misused in many ways for mostly false accusations (Arles, 2015). The Indian model is being imitated in Buddhist countries such as Burma and Sri Lanka (Premawardhana, 2011, p. 268). The example of Brazil shows how conversion is also argued against and hindered in other ways: To protect indigenous religions and ethnic groups, any 'proselytising' activity is prohibited there *(indigenous protectionism)* (Carvalho & dos Santos, 2015, p. 398).

Furthermore, where *religious and national identity* are closely intertwined, conversion is sometimes also seen as a betrayal of one's own culture and nation. In some Asian countries, conversions to Christianity are interpreted as a defection to Western powers. In part, these interpretations are influenced by previous negative experiences under 'Christian' colonial powers and associated Western missionary movements (Simorangkir, 2010, p. 23). Even if a convert remains loyal to his culture and state, his conversion is often interpreted negatively (Premawardhana, 2011, p. 268). *Disinformation and agitation* act as reinforcing means of persecuting converts. Turkish newspapers, for example, have portrayed that converts have allegedly

11 In this paragraph, which discusses past intra-Christian persecution of converts, the term 'convert' is understood in a wider sense than introduced at the beginning of this chapter, thus denoting any person who changes ('converts') from one Christian denomination to another.

fallen victim to the seductive skills of missionaries, who in turn are regarded as one of the greatest dangers for Turkey (Häde, 2015, p. 207).

However, anti-conversion motives are not only found among state or religious figures: In contexts characterised by shame and honour, converts may experience persecution from *their own families* who wish to preserve their family honour. The family members of a convert may put pressure on the convert to restore the family's honour within the society (Sered & Ben-David, 2015, p. 216).

It becomes clear that numerous anti-conversion forces, often fuelled by reinforcing factors, can lead to the persecution of converts.

6 Pro-conversion actors as victims of persecution and supporters of converts

Most conversions involve pro-conversion actors in one way or another: These are Christians who are actively involved in encouraging other people to embrace the Christian faith. The category 'pro-conversion actors' includes individuals or groups, such as foreign and local missionaries, converts propagating their faith or Christians and churches. Two different roles can be observed for pro-conversion actors in the context of conversion and persecution: Their commitment *pro* ('for') conversion often makes them *victims* of persecution, together with the converts themselves.[12] They also have a significant role as *supporters of* the converts in their persecution.

Pro-conversion actors may suffer persecution because they encourage people to convert and because they support converts even after their conversion. The persecution of pro-conversion activists has a deterrent effect in many places: precisely *because* the pressure on churches is so great, in several contexts churches are hesitant to accept converts (Sered & Ben-David, 2015, p. 216).

Pro-conversion actors often act as *supporters* of converts under persecution in various ways: Through *sensitive missionary work*, they can avoid additional 'avoidable' persecution of converts. Negative experiences of insensitive missionary work in the past and present reinforce a hostile atti-

---

12 In this section, the term 'victim' is used from the perspective of pro-conversion actors who experience persecution. Depending on the perspective chosen, it would also be conceivable to attribute the role of 'victim' to other actors. A Muslim religious community, for example, could also be seen as a 'victim' of the missionary activities of regarded Christians, e.g. when individual Muslims turn their backs on Islam and become Christians.

tude towards Christian mission and conversion in some places. Pro-conversion actors have a responsibility in this regard to promote a culturally sensitive contextualisation of the Christian faith. The way in which pro-conversion actors speak publicly about the respective non-Christian religion can also influence whether additional 'avoidable' persecution of converts occurs.

In addition, pro-conversion actors can support converts by *informing them about potential persecution* before their conversion. After conversion, they can sensitise converts *to avoid persecution* by not unnecessarily distancing themselves from their ancestral culture. Experience shows that sometimes converts are tempted to overzealously break with their own culture and distance themselves from their previous environment (Lalnghakthuami, 2016, p. 148). Even after their conversion, converts continue to need *support of various kinds* from pro-conversion actors, especially if they suffer persecution. This includes encouragement and counselling, theological training, practical help, integration into Christian communities, and even asylum support for converts who have fled.

7 Other groups between conversion and persecution

The previous sections have already discussed three groups of people, namely converts themselves, pro-conversion actors, and persecutors with anti-conversion motives. In addition, two further groups should be mentioned, which are sometimes more, sometimes less significant in the context of conversion and persecution: The relatives of converts as well as churches, which may remain uninvolved in conversions. Lastly, it is worth looking at converted former persecutors.[13]

7.1 Family members of converts

In some cases, not only are converts themselves affected by persecution, but sometimes also *their own family*, even if they have not converted (Ekka, 2011, p. 147). The family members of converts often suffer twice as a result of the conversion: on the one hand, the conversion of one member can bring *shame* on the family. Secondly, a conversion can lead to the *persecution* of the entire family (Sered & Ben-David, 2015, p. 216). To avoid their own persecution and to restore the family's honour, it can happen that the family members themselves become persecutors and turn

[13] Converted former persecutors can be viewed as a combination of the two particular groups 'converts' and 'persecutors'.

against the convert in their own family. However, the initially tense relationship between converts and their own family may sometimes relax again after a while (Strähler, 2021, p. 68).

7.2 Churches not involved in conversions

Some churches are not involved in advocating conversion or accepting converts, for theological[14] or political reasons. In contexts where Christian churches have a minority status, the *political* motivation to maintain toleration by non-Christian authorities and to secure their existence can probably be seen as a significant factor for a reserved attitude towards activities which promote conversion or the acceptance of converts. Nevertheless, in such contexts, conversion can also lead to persecution of the churches that are not involved.

7.3 Converted former persecutors

Occasionally, conversions happen even among persecutors. In some cases, persecutors convert through the testimony of martyrs who have previously suffered persecution (Jongeneel, 2015, p. 439). If a *former persecutor* converts, he often faces persecution himself as a result (Veerman, 2015, p. 145). The prime example of a converted persecutor is the apostle Paul: he was one of the strictest religious Jews and persecuted Christians in the belief that he was doing the right thing. After his encounter with Jesus Christ in his conversion, the readiness to suffer for his newfound faith grew in him (Lee, 2013, p. 204).

8 Comparison between missiological and human rights typology

In closing, the tentative missiological typology presented in this chapter is briefly compared to Bielefeldt's legal framework in relation to links between conversion and persecution. From a *human rights perspective*, Bielefeldt (2017, p. 109) identifies four aspects: 1) the right to change faith and its challenges, 2) the right not to be forced to change faith and associated

---

[14] The theological debate in some churches, especially in secularised Western countries, about the appropriateness of conversion-oriented missionary efforts, e.g. towards Muslims, cannot be discussed further here. It would need to be analysed further in which cases a rejection of mission may have *theological* reasons, and in which cases it may have *political* reasons.

threats, 3) the right to seek to convert others through non-coercive persuasion and its challenges, and 4) the rights of the child and its parents.

The comparison of this human rights perspective with the typology developed in this chapter from a *missiological perspective* shows that while some aspects are present in both frameworks, albeit using different formulations, other aspects are found in only one of the two frameworks. The missiological typology developed here offers a more detailed structure based on personal and correlation dynamics, thus offering reflections on aspects such as reciprocal influences between conversion and persecution, the role of pro-conversion actors as supporters in persecution, the conversion of persecutors, and the role of churches uninvolved in conversion. The human rights perspective, on the other hand, offers more insights on aspects such as the role of children, parents and relatives in general.

9 Suggestions for further research

The categorization of dynamics between conversion and persecution presented in this chapter is *tentative* and thus needs to be further adapted and developed, based on further research. The examination of further missiological literature, including literature in other languages, would presumably provide additional insights into the interrelations between conversion and persecution. In addition, a different, less person-centred perspective on the topic could shed further light on yet uncovered issues. Specific relevant topics appear to have received little attention in research so far and therefore require more intensive investigation: The potential influence of the conversion type on persecution,[15] the role of converts' relatives in the midst of persecution, the role of churches in receiving and accompanying converts,[16] the conversion of persecutors, and the relationship between theological and political reasons for a reserved attitude towards mission (and conversion) by some churches, to a name a few. A theological reflection on the links between conversion, persecution and Christian discipleship also seems necessary.[17]

Overall, it became clear that conversion and persecution can be regarded as two fundamental categories of Christian theology, which are closely intertwined. They are of fundamental importance in both the early Church and contemporary global Christianity.

---

15 Such research could build on Strähler (2021).

16 Such research could build on D. A. Miller (2020).

17 Such research could build on Penner (2004), Sauer (2013) and Hofer (2021).

1) Conversion as a trigger for persecution				
2) Reciprocal influences				
Potential influence of conversion on persecution:		Potential influence of persecution on conversion:		'Conversion-neutral' persecution
Negative*	Positive*	Negative*	Positive*	
Reinforcing persecution	Reducing persecution: ☐ Conversion of a power figure ☐ Conversion as liberation from persecution	☐ Preventing conversion ☐ Reconversion	Reinforcing further conversions: ☐ Disappointment over violence in own religion ☐ Testimony of love of the persecuted ☐ Testimony of loyalty of the persecuted ☐ Migration due to persecution	
			Preventing conversions for dishonest motives	
			Strengthening the faith after conversion	
3) Anti-conversion motives				
Drivers of persecution:		Other reinforcing factors:		
☐ Islamic oppression ☐ Religiously motivated nationalism ☐ Denominational protectionism ☐ Ethno-religiously based hostilities ☐ Organised crime ☐ Dictatorial paranoia ☐ Communist oppression		☐ Apostasy laws and anti-conversion laws ☐ Intertwined national and religious identities ☐ Disinformation and agitation against converts ☐ Pursuit of preserving family honour		
4) Pro-conversion actors				
Victims of persecution:		Supporters of converts in persecution:		
☐ Because of encouragement to conversion ☐ Because of support after conversion		☐ Sensitive mission work to avoid unnecessary persecution of converts ☐ Preparing converts for coming persecution ☐ Raising convert's awareness for possible avoidance of persecution ☐ Supporting converts in persecution		
5) Other players				
☐ Converts' relatives ☐ Churches not involved in conversions ☐ Converted (former) persecutors				

* The terms 'negative' and 'positive' are used from the perspective of converts/Christians.

10 References

Andrews, J. (2020). *Identity Crisis: Religious Registration in the Middle East*. Gilead.

Arles, S. (2015). India: Religious Polarisation in a Hindu Context. In H. A. Gravaas, et al. (Eds.), *RECS: Vol. 28. Freedom of Belief and Christian Mission* (pp. 320-330). Regnum.

Barrett, D. B., & Johnson, T. M. (2001). *World Christian Trends, AD 30 – AD 2200: Interpreting the Annual Christian Megacensus*. William Carey Library.

Barua, A. (2015). *Debating 'Conversion' in Hinduism and Christianity*. Routledge.

Bielefeldt, H. (2017). *Freedom of Religion or Belief: Thematic Reports of the UN Special Rapporteur 2010-2016* (2nd ed.). VKW.

Bielefeldt, H., & Wiener, M. (2020). *Religious Freedom Under Scrutiny*. University of Pennsylvania Press.

Carvalho, F. A. L., & dos Santos, U. S. (2015). Religious Freedom in Brazil and Latin America. In H. A. Gravaas et al. (Eds.), *RECS: Vol. 28. Freedom of Belief and Christian Mission* (pp. 395-410). Regnum.

Chan, K. (2015). Religious Freedom and Christian Mission. In H. A. Gravaas et al. (Eds.), *RECS: Vol. 28. Freedom of Belief and Christian Mission* (pp. 283-294). Regnum.

Chin Human Rights Organization. (2012). *Threats to Our Existence: Persecution of Ethnic Chin Christians in Burma.*

Ekka, J. N. (2011). Christianity and Tribal Religion in Jharkhand (India). In M. N. Behera (Ed.), *RECS: Vol. 8. Interfaith Relations after One Hundred Years: Christian Mission among Other Faiths* (pp. 142-162). Regnum.

Enstedt, D., Larsson, G., & Mantsinen, T. T. (Eds.). (2020). *Handbook of Leaving Religion*. Brill.

Eshete, T. (2015). Marxism and Religion: The Paradox of Church Growth in Ethiopia, 1974-1991. In H. A. Gravaas et al. (Eds.), *RECS: Vol. 28. Freedom of Belief and Christian Mission* (pp. 242-258). Regnum.

Evans, Edward (2005). 'Coming to Faith' in Pakistan. In D. Greenlee (Ed.), *From the Straight Path to the Narrow Way* (pp. 167-186). Authentic / OM Books India.

Finucane, J., & Feener, R. M. (Eds.). (2014). *Proselytizing and the Limits of Religious Pluralism in Contemporary Asia*. Springer.

Fischer, M. G. (2018). Anti-Conversion Laws and the International Response. *Penn State Journal of Law & International Affairs*, *6*(1), 1-69.

Gravaas, H. A., Sauer, C., Engelsviken, T., Kamil, M., & Jørgensen, K. (Eds.). (2015). *RECS: Vol. 28. Freedom of Belief and Christian Mission*. Regnum.

Häde, W. (2015). *Anschuldigungen und Antwort des Glaubens: Wahrnehmung von Christen in türkischen Tageszeitungen und Maßstäbe für eine christliche Reaktion*. LIT.

Häde, W. (2017). Strengthening the Identity of Converts from Islam in the Face of Verbal Assaults: A Study with the Background of Turkish Society. *Mission Studies*, *34*(3), 392-408.

Hofer, J. (2021). Christliche Erfahrungen von Konversion und Verfolgung: Eine theologische Einordnung der Zusammenhänge. *Evangelische Missiologie*, *37*(2), 88-102.

Hofer, J., & Sauer, C. (2023). Zusammenhänge von Konversion und Verfolgung: Vorschlag einer Typologie. *Zeitschrift für Missionswissenschaft und Religionswissenschaft*, 107(3-4), 356-370.

Hölzl, M. J. (2015). The Era of Constantine. In H. A. Gravaas et al. (Eds.), *RECS: Vol. 28. Freedom of Belief and Christian Mission* (pp. 79-92). Regnum.

Johnson, T. M. (2014). Demographics of Religious Conversion. In L. Rambo & C. E. Farhadian (Eds.), *The Oxford Handbook of Religious Conversion* (pp. 48-64). Oxford University Press.

Johnson, T. M., & Zurlo, G. A. (2020). *World Christian Encyclopedia* (3rd ed.). Edinburgh University Press.

Jongeneel, J. A. (2015). Do Christian Witness and Mission Provoke Persecution? In H. A. Gravaas et al. (Eds.), *RECS: Vol. 28. Freedom of Belief and Christian Mission* (pp. 430-443). Regnum.

Jørgensen, K. (2015). Christians in a Minority Situation. In H. A. Gravaas et al. (Eds.), *RECS: Vol. 28. Freedom of Belief and Christian Mission* (pp. 114-126). Regnum.

Josua, H. (2015). The Middle East: A Region without a Christian Future? In H. A. Gravaas et al. (Eds.), *RECS: Vol 28. Freedom of Belief and Christian Mission* (pp. 190-213). Regnum.

Kool, A.-M. (2016). Revolutions in European Mission: 'What Has Been Achieved in 25 Years of East European Mission?'. In C. Constantineanu et al. (Eds.), *RECS: Vol. 34. Mission in Central and Eastern Europe: Realities, Perspectives, Trends* (pp. 30-55). Regnum.

Lalnghakthuami. (2016). Mission and Power with Special Reference to Mizoram. In M. Ngursangzeli & M. Biehl (Eds.), *RECS: Vol. 31. Witnessing to Christ in North-East India* (pp. 145-153). Regnum.

Lee, C. (2013). Spirituality and Christian Mission: The Journey of Youngnak Presbyterian Church, Seoul, Orea. In W. Ma & K. R. Ross (Eds.), *RECS: Vol. 14. Mission Spirituality and Authentic Discipleship* (pp. 203-208). Regnum.

Marshall, P., & Shea, N. (2011). *Silenced: How Apostasy and Blasphemy Codes are Choking Freedom Worldwide*. Oxford University Press.

Maurer, A. (1999). *In Search of a New Life: Conversion Motives of Christians and Muslims* [DTh dissertation]. University of South Africa, Pretoria.

Mekonnen, D. R., & Tronvoll, K. (2015). Freedom of Belief and the Church in Eritrea. In H. A. Gravaas et al. (Eds.), *RECS: Vol. 28. Freedom of Belief and Christian Mission* (pp. 259-269). Regnum.

Meral, Z. (2006). Conversion and Apostasy: A Sociological Perspective. *Evangelical Missions Quarterly*, *42:4*, 508-513.

Miller, D. A. (2020). *I Will Give Them an Everlasting Name: Pastoral Care for Christ's Converts from Islam* [Kindle version]. Regnum.

Miller, E. L., et al. (2023). *The 2023 Gender Report: A Web of Forces*. Open Doors International. https://www.opendoors.org/en-US/research-reports/gender-persecution/The_2023_Gender_Report.pdf

Paredes, T. (2010). Holistic Mission in Latin America. In B. Woolnough, W. Ma, & B. E. Woolnough (Eds.), *RECS: Vol. 5. Holistic Mission: God's Plan for God's People* (pp. 102-116). Regnum.

Penner, G. M. (2004). *In the Shadow of the Cross: A Biblical Theology of Persecution and Discipleship*. Living Sacrifice Books.

Peters, T. A. (2015). Beset from Within, Beleaguered from Without: North Korea's Catacombs in an Era of Extermination. In H. A. Gravaas et al. (Eds.), *RECS: Vol. 28. Freedom of Belief and Christian Mission* (pp. 295-308). Regnum.

Petri, D. (2020). *The Specific Vulnerability of Religious Minorities* (PhD Dissertation, Vrije Universiteit Amsterdam).

Philpott, D. (2019). *Religious Freedom in Islam: The Fate of a Universal Human Right in the Muslim World Today*. Oxford University Press.

Popp-Baier, U. (2003). Konversionsforschung als Thema gegenwärtiger Religionspsychologie. In C. Henning & E. Nestler (Eds.), *Einblicke: Vol. 4. Konversion: Zur Aktualität eines Jahrhundertthemas* (pp. 95-115). Peter Lang.

Premawardhana, S. (2011). A Christian Ecumenical Exploration of Identity Dynamics. In M. N. Behera (Ed.), *RECS: Vol. 8. Interfaith Relations after One Hundred Years: Christian Mission among Other Faiths* (pp. 261-271). Regnum.

Rambo, L., & Farhadian, C. E. (Eds.). (2014). *The Oxford Handbook of Religious Conversion*. Oxford University Press.

Rambo, L. R. (1993). *Understanding Religious Conversion*. Yale University Press.

Rogers, B. (2007). *Carrying the Cross: The Military Regime's Campaign of Restriction, Discrimination and Persecution against Christians in Burma*. Christian Solidarity Worldwide.

Sauer, C. (Ed.). (2013). *Bad Urach Statement: Towards an Evangelical Theology of Suffering, Persecution and Martyrdom for the Global Church in Mission*. VKW.

Sauer, C. (2017). Contemporary Thinking on Conversion and Persecution: A Survey of Recent Missiological Compendia. *Mission Studies, 34*(3), 295-308.

Schirrmacher, C. (2010). Defection from Islam: A Disturbing Human Rights Dilemma. *IJRF, 3*(2), 13-38.

Schirrmacher, C. (2020). Leaving Islam. In D. Enstedt, G. Larsson, & T. T. Mantsinen (Eds.), *Handbook of Leaving Religion* (pp. 81-95). Brill.

Sered, D., & Ben-David, Y. (2015). Case Study: Israel and Messianic Jews. In H. A. Gravaas et al. (Eds.), *RECS: Vol. 28. Freedom of Belief and Christian Mission* (pp. 214-226). Regnum.

Simorangkir, M. (2010). Theological Foundation of Mission: An Asian Perspective. In C. Währisch-Oblau & F. Mwombeki (Eds.), *RECS: Vol. 4. Mission Continues: Global Impulses for the 21st Century* (pp. 18-27). Regnum.

Storaker, K. (2015). Mission and Persecution – Parallel Stories: The State of Religious Minorities in Burma. In H. A. Gravaas et al. (Eds.), *RECS: Vol. 28. Freedom of Belief and Christian Mission* (pp. 331-343). Regnum.

Strähler, R. (2021). *Einfach und komplex zugleich: Konversionsprozesse und ihre Beurteilung*. Evangelische Verlagsanstalt.

Strauss, A., & Corbin, J. (2008). *Basics of Qualitative Research: Techniques and Procedures for Developing Grounded Theory* (3rd ed.). Sage.

Taylor, W. D., van der Meer, A., & Reimer, R. (Eds.). (2012). *Sorrow and Blood: Christian Mission in Contexts of Suffering, Persecution, and Martyrdom*. William Carey Library.

van der Meer, A. L. (2013). The Bible in Mission: Evangelical/pentecostal View. In P. Hoggarth et al. (Eds.), *RECS: Vol. 18. Bible in Mission* (pp. 93-105). Regnum.

Vandevelde, I. (2011). Reconversion to Hinduism: A Hindu Nationalist Reaction Against Conversion to Christianity and Islam. *South Asia: Journal of South Asian Studies, 34*(1), 31-50.

Veerman, F. (2015). Religious Persecution and Violence in the 21st Century. In H. A. Gravaas et al. (Eds.), *RECS: Vol. 28. Freedom of Belief and Christian Mission* (pp. 127-148). Regnum.

Victor, B. K. (2014). Revisiting the Missional Engagement at Parkal: A Recovery of the Role of the Dalit Christian Community. In P. Rajkumar, J. P. Dayam, & I. P.

Asheervadham (Eds.), *RECS: Vol. 19. Mission at and from the Margins: Patterns, Protagonists and Perspectives* (pp. 142-159). Regnum.

Vysotskaya, A. (2015). Is the Silk Road still Open? Central Asia: Christian Mission under Growing Restrictions on Religious Freedom. In H. A. Gravaas et al. (Eds.), *RECS: Vol. 28. Freedom of Belief and Christian Mission* (pp. 309-319). Regnum.

Wachsmuth, M. (2016). Roma Christianity in Central and Eastern Europe: Challenges, Opportunities for Mission, Modes of Appropriation and Social Significance. In C. Constantineanu et al. (Eds.), *RECS: Vol. 34. Mission in Central and Eastern Europe: Realities, Perspectives, Trends* (pp. 544-568). Regnum.

Wahba, T. (2013). Reconciliation in Egypt: The Absent Ministry. In R. J. Schreiter & K. Jørgensen (Eds.), *RECS: Vol. 16. Mission as Ministry of Reconciliation* (pp. 252-260). Regnum.

Walls, A. F. (2014). Mission and Migration: The Diaspora Factor in Christian History. In C. H. Im & A. Yong (Eds.), *RECS: Vol. 23. Global Diasporas and Mission* (pp. 19-37). Regnum.

World Watch Research. (October 2024). *Complete World Watch List Methodology (Revised).* https://www.opendoors.org/research-reports/wwl-documentation/complete-WWL-Methodology-October-2024

Yang, J. H. (2014). Immigrants in the USA: A Missional Opportunity. In C. H. Im & A. Yong (Eds.), *RECS: Vol. 23. Global Diasporas and Mission* (pp. 148-157). Regnum.

17 "Making Christianity Chinese"

"Sinicisation" in the tension between political and theological interpretation

Meiken Buchholz[1]

Abstract

"Sinicisation of religion" is a widely used term for contextualisation in China. The term means basically "making religious faith Chinese" and, in a broad sense, can apply to any form of contextualised Christian faith in China. At the same time, it is a political term. Since 2015, "sinicisation of religions" is the ruling principle of religious policy in the People's Republic of China and the official umbrella organisation of Protestant churches in China (Three-Self Patriotic Movement). Using Bevans' contextualisation-models as analytical tools, this article discusses red lines beyond which the sinicisation-concept turns from a *theological* blueprint of a contextualised Chinese Christianity to a *political* guideline of religious policy.

Keywords: China, Sinicisation, Three-Self Patriotic Movement, religious policy, contextualisation.

1 Introduction

In 2020, the official umbrella organization of Protestant churches in China, the Three-Self Patriotic Movement (TSPM) celebrated the 70th anniversary of its first beginnings.[2] On this occasion, its national chairman, Rev.

---

1 Meiken Buchholz is Associate Professor at Fjellhaug International University College (Norway) and Gießen School of Theology (FTH, Germany). As a long-time lecturer at China Lutheran Seminary (Taiwan), she has a particular research interest in churches in the Chinese cultural area. Email: buchholz@fthgiessen.de, ORCID iD: 0000-0003-1706-5145.

2 The adoption of the Christian Manifesto by leading personalities of the church in the PRC on September 23, 1950, is regarded as the beginning of the Three-Self Patriotic Movement as a movement (Gänßbauer, 2004, pp. 113-115). The new catechism published by a committee of the TSPM in 2023 explicitly names this date as a day of remembrance for the whole church (Friemann, 2024, p. 226). This event

Xu Xiaohong, repeatedly called his audience "to hold on to the guiding principle of sinicisation." (Three-Self, 2020).[3] To "sinicise" (*zhongguo hua*) Christian faith – that is "to make s.th. Chinese"[4] – seems an appropriate theological goal for a church that wants to be faithful to its calling to witness to the Gospel in China.

What makes the matter complex is the fact that the term 'sinicisation' also has a historical background as a political and administrative concept (Introvigne, 2020, pp. 16-17; Yang, 2021, pp. 17-31). Since 2015, President Xi has emphatically propagated it as the guiding principle of current religious policy (Madsen, 2021, p.1; Vermander, 2019, pp. 3-4). Therefore, on the one hand, discussing the sinicisation of Christian faith never happens in a vacuum; the political background must always be taken into account. It is rightly pointed out that, due to its ambiguity, the term sinicisation can easily be used to enforce political goals in the church (Yang, 2021, pp. 36-38).

On the other hand, however, we must not let issues of state-church relations dominate research to such an extent that we lose sight of Christians as *religious* actors who make their choices because of *theological* convictions. Lee and Chow have recently pointed out this methodological danger in their "Methodological Reflections on the Study of Chinese Christianities" (Lee and Chow, 2021, pp. 113-114). The current discourse in the TSPM continues a theological concern that has been present from the beginning and which it claims is a significant contribution to the understanding of contextualization by the global church (Ting, 2004, pp. 346, 180-181, 188-189).

This article takes seriously the self-understanding of the TSPM's sinicisation concept as a *theological* quest and describes it as a contextualisation model with specific characteristics. It is argued that evaluating the TSPM's sinicisation concept as a theological model of contextualisation

---

is not to be confused with the founding of the TSPM as an organization in 1954 (Gänßbauer, 2004, p. 117).

3 All quotations from this source are the author's translations.

4 The Chinese term *zhongguo hua* is usually translated as "to sinicise". Recently, Yang Fenggang highlighted the fact that the Chinese term refers to "China" (*zhongguo*) as a national and political entity, while the English term "sinicisation" refers to the wider concept of Chinese culture and language ("sina", in Chinese: *han*) and the corresponding translation would be *han hua*. Therefore, Yang prefers to translate *zhongguo hua* as "Chinafication" (Yang, 2021, p. 16). I agree with Yang that "Chinafication" would help to draw attention to the central concern of its usage in political campaigns, namely "political domination" (p. 16). However, the term *zhongguo hua* and its translation 'sinicisation' have a history in other contexts, that also resonate in the discussion. These would be lost by introducing different translations.

reveals the red line beyond which the *theological* quest for contextualisation turns into an instrument of *political* control by religious policy.

2 Delimitation and methodology

2.1 Current state of research

In this short overview, I limit myself, first, to recent research about sinicising religion as a political concept, and second, to sociology of religion research that has sinicising Christianity as its major topic and was done after the term "entered the official discourse" in 2015 (Chang, 2018, p. 41). The overview does not intend to be comprehensive.

Concerning sinicising religion as a political concept, several authors have described in detail, how it developed into the dominant paradigm of the PRC's contemporary religious policy and strengthens the party's influence on religions (Chang, 2018, pp. 37-39; Fällman, 2021, pp. 109-113; Yang, 2021, pp. 17-18, 31-37). Others discuss its background in religious studies (Yang, 2021, pp. 18-30); which implication it has for religious practice and the study of religions (Vermander, 2019); and how it has been translated into concrete measures (Masláková & Satorová, 2019, pp. 5-10; Chang, 2018, pp. 41-44).

In recent sociology of religion research on sinicisation of Christianity, we can distinguish between two approaches which Madsen in his recent volume on sinicisation of religion in general distinguishes as sinicisation "from above" and "from below" (Madsen, 2021). On the one hand, we find empirical and historical case studies that understand sinicisation as a purely descriptive term referring to the emergence of groups of Chinese who identify as Christians – at any time and place (sinicisation from below). A prominent example is the volume "Sinicizing Christianity" published by Zheng Yangwen in 2017, containing case studies from the 18th to the 21st century (Madsen, 2017, p. 326). A further example is Cao Nanlan's investigation of Chinese diaspora churches entitled "A Sinicized World Religion?" (Cao, 2019). Scholars who take this approach emphasise the variety of forms in which sinicisation takes place and prefer to speak of 'Chinese Christianities' in the plural.

On the other hand, some sociologists of religion in the PRC design sinicisation as a normative concept (sinicisation from above). Through historical research, they construct a specifically Chinese religious culture to which each religion must conform in order to be authentically Chinese (Zhang, 2015[5]; Vermander, 2019, p. 7; cf. Yang, 2021, pp. 29-30).

5 Zhang Zhigang of Beijing University is an important representative of this approach.

Both approaches to sinicisation can be found in discourses in the TSPM. The descriptive usage and the plural understanding of sinicisation have their parallel in the pragmatic way many pastors interpret the term (cf. Harmsel, 2021, pp. 63-67). The normative understanding of sinicisation is held by circles with great influence on politics and influences the discourse at the TSPM leadership level.

2.2 Delimitation

Building on these findings, the focus of this article is on sinicisation as the TSPM's theological model of contextualising Christianity in China. As mentioned above, there is a rich variety of contextualized Christian faith in China today, and even within TSPM, preaching and belief at the grassroots differ considerably from the official concept of sinicisation (Harmsel, 2021). Within the scope of this article, it is not possible to address the negative effects of the sinicisation policy on various religious communities at the grassroots. However, this is not to deny or gloss over them.

The reason why this article focuses on texts by TSPM leadership is not because they are representative of most Christians in the PRC, but because here the distinction between political and theological sinicisation is particularly precarious. Since the research interest is the TSPM, neither Catholic Christians nor the situation in Hongkong are taken into regard. In addition to English and German literature, individual Chinese-language documents are included as primary literature.

First, the historical and political background of the TSPM and the closely related China Christian Council (CCC) is briefly introduced (chap. 3). It follows a description of the theological development in the TSPM and CCC. Here I show that it is possible to understand sinicisation as a theologically motivated model of contextualization when it is seen within the larger framework of the history and theology of the TSPM (chap. 4). Subsequently, I analyse the characteristics of this kind of contextualisation model, focusing on the relationship between theological and political-contextual factors. For this I, refer to Bevans' "models of contextual theology" (Bevans, 2002) which can still be considered a widely recognized standard (chap. 5).[6] The conclusion (chap. 6) evaluates sinicisation

6 Bevans' categorisation of models of contextualisation takes little account of newer research on grassroots movements (particularly indigenous Pentecostal movements) as local theologies (for China cf., e.g., Kao, 2013, Yang et al., 2017, Cao, 2012). However, this lack does not diminish its value for the analysis of TSPM-style contextualisation, since it is not related to this kind of grassroots movements.

as a model of contextualization between theological and political premisses, and identifies the red line beyond which a *theological* model of contextualisation turns into a *political* control instrument.

3 The political framework of sinicising Christianity

The post-Mao era brought a new approach to religion in the PRC. China's Communist Party (CCP) accepted the historical fact that religions will continue to exist under Communist rule and introduced a policy of cooperation instead of abolition by force (Dunch, 2008, p. 161).[7] The fundamentals of this approach were outlined by the CCP's Central Committee in 1982 in 'Document 19' and are relevant to this day.

The document legalizes religious activities only within the "patriotic religious associations" that had been established by the CCP's Religious Affairs Bureau for each of the five acknowledged religions (Taoism, Buddhism, Islam, Protestantism, and Catholicism) (Schak, 2011, p. 72).[8] These associations had already been founded in the 1950s, but were closed during the Cultural Revolution when all religious activities were prohibited. They were re-established from 1979 onward.

One of them is the Three-Self Patriotic Movement of Protestant Churches in China (TSPM). In 1980, on the initiative of the church's leadership, it was supplemented by the China Christian Council (CCC) whose work focuses on (re)building church life. Both organizations form parallel structures from the national to the local level, with the respective offices often being held by the same person (Gänßbauer, 2004, pp. 130-131).

For different reasons, many churches reject obligatory registration within the TSPM (Reny 2018, pp. 58-60). These are the so-called 'unregistered churches' or 'house churches' which exist without legal status and are exposed to punitive measures by the local Public Security Bureaus.

Concerning the task of the patriotic religious organizations (of all religions) Document 19 states:

> "The basic task of these patriotic religious organizations is to assist the Party and the government to implement the policy of freedom of religious belief, to help the broad mass of religious believers and persons in religious circles

[7] Though the focus of this article is on Protestant Christianity, we must keep in mind, that all laws and regulations of religious affairs were formulated with regard to all religions.

[8] In China, Confucianism is not regarded as religion but as moral philosophy. For historical reasons, Protestantism and Catholicism are dealt with as two different religions.

to continually raise their patriotic and socialist consciousness." (MacInnis, 1989, p. 19)

Granting of religious freedom is closely tied to the sociopolitical goals of the Chinese Communist Party (CCP). Since the 1990s, the CCP has taken a "functionalist stance" on religion and "is not interested in what religion means to the religious believers but, instead, in what it can achieve for its goal to accomplish national unity and social stability" (Tsai, 2017, p. 326, cf. Vermander, 2019, pp. 7-8; Fällman, 2021, pp. 104-107). The resulting religious regulations contained some ambiguous wording that gave religious life a certain space of freedom in which Christian churches flourished inside and outside the TSPM (Dunch, 2008, pp. 171-173; Fällman, 2021, pp. 104).

As part of President Xi's general concern for strengthening CCP's control over society, these pockets of freedom have been restricted. Since 2017, 'sinicisation of religion' has been officially established as the key principle of religious policy. Xi's preference for the term 'sinicisation' is in line with his general tendency to replace "the dominant prominence of the language of Chinese Communism with the language of Chinese nationalism" (Lewis, 2021, paragraph 10). Sinicisation is part of "Xi Jinping's Thoughts on Socialism with Chinese Characteristics for a New Era" that have been incorporated into the CCP's normative ideology and the PRC's constitution (Vermander, 2019, pp. 1-3; Chang, 2018, p.30 and 39).[9] These normative 'Chinese characteristics' constitute the standard for CCP-style sinicisation. However, they remain rather vague, making only general references to socialist values and Chinese culture (Masláková and Satorová, 2019, p. 7), and leave "right of interpretation" to the CCP (Fällman, 2021, p. 105). Accordingly, Madsen describes Xi's concept of sinicisation as "the vision of a powerful centralized state tightly controlling a homogeneous culture" (Madsen, 2021, p. 13).

To put the sinicisation of religion into practice, a revised edition of the 'Regulations on Religious Affairs' became effective in 2018 (Wenzel-Teuber, 2017, pp. 140-141, Madsen, 2021, pp. 7-8). These regulations provide an instrument of "extant bureaucratic oversight" (Chang, 2018, p. 42) to ensure the proper ideological attitude of clergy and religious believers and are constantly supplemented by further detailed regulations.[10] Through

9 Through the decision of the 19th Congress of the CCP in 2017 'Xi Jinping's Thought' have become part of the CCP's constitution and its normative ideology. In 2018, it was added to the preamble to the PRC's constitution. This gives Xi an authority that no other PRC president has had apart from Mao.

10 The 2018 regulations demanded patriotic *behaviour*, e.g., the raising of the national flag at religious buildings (Vermander, 2019, pp. 4-5). The 'Regulations for the

these legal documents, "sinicization became enshrined in the legislation and thus made mandatory" for all religious believers (Maslákova and Satorová, 2019, p. 7).

4 The theological framework of the TSPM's understanding of contextualisation

In this section, I consider sinicisation as a term for a theological task that the church derives from her own nature. I show that sinicisation as a form of contextualisation corresponds to a concern that has been part of TSPM-identity from the outset. Texts by Bishop Ting (*Ding Guangxun*, 1915-2012) are used as illustrations. Having had different leading positions for several decades in the TSPM, CCC, and its most important theological seminary, he has shaped the church's normative theological thinking at the leadership level (Ting, 2004, pp. 11-14).

In the following, I refer to texts recounting the historical developments and merits of the TSPM. They represent an influential theological narrative that gives sinicisation its theological meaning.[11] In the second part, I draw in addition on three texts dealing explicitly with the topic of contextualization.[12]

4.1 The history of TSPM as a history of contextualisation

Ting divides the history of the TSPM into three parts (Ting, 2004, pp. 342-344), starting with the emergence of the Three-Self principle in 1950. According to Ting, the very name of the movement (Three-Self) points to the need for indigenization in the form of decolonization. It takes up the three principles of self-governance, self-support, and self-propagation. Chinese Christians developed the meaning of 'Three-Self' beyond a missionary strategy and discussed it "from the perspective of the nature of the church" (Ting, 2004, p. 178). Ting stresses the historical significance of the "Three-Self road" for the church in China "to establish itself as the Body

administration of religious personnel' which came into force in January 2021, aim at intensified government control over religious personnel's patriotic *conviction*, cf. Feith et al., 2020, p. 192.

11 These texts are one article from the year 1982 reflecting the continuous need for the Three-Self Movement after its re-establishment (Ting, 2004, 178-194) and two articles on the occasion of the 50th anniversary of the beginnings of Three-Self Patriotic Movement in 1980 (Ting, 2004, pp. 342-345 and 345-349).

12 "Theology and Context" (Ting 2004, pp. 122-129), "Unchanging Faith, Evolving Theology" (pp. 448-451), and "Theology Adapting to a Changing Culture" (pp. 451-456).

of Christ" in its socio-political context (Ting, 2004, p. 180) and for the global church to show by the example of China "how the gospel takes root in all cultures" (Ting, 2004, pp. 188-189). In this context, Ting explicitly regards the concerns of the TSPM as part of the international theological discourse on contextual theology (Ting, 2004, pp. 180-181 and 346).

For Ting the second part of the story begins with the founding of the China Christian Council (CCC) in 1980. After the TSPM had begun "to create conditions for running the church well," by cutting all links to its imperialist past, the CCC was founded to serve "as a body to run the church well," (Ting, 2004, p. 347) in other words, to manage the internal church affairs of a contextualised Chinese church for the good of the church.

According to Ting, the "most crucial step in running the church well" is the "solid construction of theological thinking in the Chinese Church". Therefore, the third step of the story is marked by "advocating theological reconstruction"(Ting, 2004, p. 347). Here, Ting refers to the Theological Construction Movement (TCM),[13] which he propagated more strongly since 1998 (cf. Gänßbauer, 2004, p. 146; Brandner, 2004, pp. 200-201). Ting underlines that TSPM, CCC, and TCM are "three interconnected periods of one single movement, each period naturally leading to the next," and all serving the implementation of a well-run contextualised church for the Chinese socialist society (Ting, 2004, pp, 344-345).

4.2 The Theological Construction Movement as fulfilment of contextualisation

The concern of the Theological Construction Movement (TCM) must be seen in the context of the political developments of the 1980s. The new religious policy of the 1980s and the reestablishment of the TSPM offered Chinese Christians the opportunity to be part of 'the people'. In Ting's opinion, this offer requires in return a theology that breaks down theological barriers

[13] For a short introduction into the goals of the Theological Construction Movement, see Brandner, 2004, pp. 201-206. – The movement includes theologians before and alongside Ting, whose particular influence rests on his position. The Chinese term for 'theological construction', *shenxue sixiang jianshe,* literally means "building up theological thinking." Early translations established the translation 'theological reconstruction.' Fällman rightly points to the problem that the translation 'reconstruction' can be misleading since *jianshe* implies the construction process of something which has not yet come into existence rather than the remodelling of an existing theology (Fällman, 2010, p. 962). Newer publications use the more precise translation 'theological construction' and the acronym TCM (Theological Construction Movement) (e.g., Vala, 2018).

between Christians and 'the people' and guides Christians to actively contribute to the socialist society and welfare of China (cf. Ting, 2004, p. 186). In other words, for Ting, contextualisation is always contextualisation into the socialist society of the PRC.

In a speech which was published under the heading "Theology and Context", Ting introduces TCM as a form of contextualisation of the Christian faith to the social and political changes in the "ever progressing society" of China (Ting, 2004, p. 126).[14] He starts with the distinction between "basic Christian faith", viz. "basic creeds of Christian faith" (e.g., the Trinity, the Incarnation, the resurrection of Christ) that "do not change"; and "theological thinking" that must change in order "to assist believers to understand and continue to maintain their faith in the new era, to help them continue to be loyal to their basic faith" (pp. 122-123). The fact that this distinction is also found in both other texts (pp. 448 and 454) indicates that it is an important hermeneutic premise of Ting's contextualisation and the TCM.

The "construction of theological thinking" demanded by Ting has become a normative concept within TSPM's official theological discourse (Dunch, 2008, p. 173). In 2012, a "team for the propagation of the construction of theological thinking" set up a five-year plan for the period 2013 – 2017 to implement Theological Construction at the grassroots (Wenzel-Teuber, 2012, p. 141). It is noteworthy that the name of the following five-year plan was changed to "Five-year Working Plan for Promoting the Sinicization of Christianity in our Country (2018-2022)" (Three-Self, 2018, Stated aims; hereinafter referred to as the 'Five-year Plan for Sinicisation'). This indicates that sinicisation has become the predominant term while Theological Construction is regarded as one of its important goals (Wielander, 2021, p. 297). It should be noted that the term sinicisation was used long before in the TSPM. E.g., Ting applied 'sinicisation' as the Chinese equivalent of 'indigenisation' as early as the 1980s (Wen, 2020, p. 167).[15] Now, however, it is becoming the predominant term, parallel to the political development that demands five-year sinicisation plans from all religious associations.

The "Five-year Working Plan for Promoting the Sinicization" from 2018 starts with Ting's distinction, differentiating between "fundamental

---

14 Cf. the detailed presentation of theological (re)construction as process of indigenization by Duan Qi, who also elaborates on the contributions of other theologians in the TSPM (Duan, 2013).

15 From a linguistic point of view, it should be noted that in Chinese it seems quite natural to specify 'indigenisation' [*bentu hua*; literally "to make s.th. indigenous"] with reference to China as 'sinicisation' [*zhongguo hua*; literally "to make s.th. Chinese"].

beliefs" and the "elaboration on the church's doctrine and rules [that] will meet requirements ... of contemporary China" (Three-Self, 2018, chap. 1, §1). This demonstrates that sinicisation appears as a continuation of the TCM's model of contextualisation.

Similarly, in the speech on the occasion of the 70th anniversary of the TSPM's foundation held by its chairman Xu in 2020 (Three-Self, 2020), sinicisation is presented as the overarching goal which fulfils all objectives of the TSPM, with particular reference to Theological Construction, stating: "To realize the sinicisation of Christianity is the wish and request of Chinese Christians for generations" (Three-Self, 2020, §2). Accordingly, Wen's review of twenty years of the TCM concludes "[...] we should see that the ultimate goal of Theological Reconstruction, as Bishop Ting began to consider in the 1950s, is to realize the localization of Christianity, that is, Sinicization" (Wen 2020, p. 166).[16]

Regarding our topic, we can conclude: In the documents of the TSPM, sinicisation is presented in line with a theological quest for contextualization that has always been part of the TSPM's self-understanding and theology. When sinicisation is viewed in this larger context, it can be interpreted with good reason as a theological contextualization model.

To analyse the specific characteristics of this model of contextualisation, particularly the relationship between theology and political context, I compare it below to Bevan's models of contextualisation.

5 Evaluating the TSPM's concept of Sinicisation as a model of contextualisation

According to Bevans, "contextualisation of theology" means "the attempt to understand Christian faith in terms of a particular context" (Bevans, 2002, p. 3). Contextual theology, therefore, takes seriously that Christian theology has "*three* sources or *loci theologici*: scripture, tradition, and present human experience - or context" (p. 4).[17] Bevans differentiates between six models of contextualisation which differ in the weighting of the sources. The models are not mutually exclusive but provide complementary "ideal types" that "disclose actual features in the matter under investigation." (p. 30). In the following, I will refer to two models which help

16 See also Zhang 2015: Conveying a very positive picture of CCP's religious policy, Zhang regards sinicisation of Christianity as the historical mission of the TSPM, "whereby Christianity will truly meld into the Chinese nation, culture and society." (Zhang, 2015, p. 394).

17 Italics in the original.

analyse the TSPM's sinicisation model as a way of contextualising Christian faith to a Chinese context.

5.1 Sinicising Christianity and the praxis model of contextualisation

Ting's emphasis on social change and the underlying dynamic concept of culture make TCM-style sinicisation akin to Bevans' 'praxis model' of contextualisation (Bevans, 2002, p. 70). It is characterized by an understanding of culture, in which "cultural and social change" are "constitutive for culture itself." (p. 74). Contextualisation is understood as an ongoing process of reinterpreting the Gospel for concrete situations in a constantly changing reality (p. 76). It takes its name from the fundamental conviction that "theology finds its fulfilment not in mere 'right thinking' (*ortho-doxy*), but in 'right acting' (*ortho-praxy*)" (p. 72).[18] In other words, the aim of contextualisation according to a praxis model is not only to understand and theologically reflect historical processes but to become active subjects of historical processes initiated by God (p. 73).

The theological correspondence between Bevans' praxis model and Bishop Ting's understanding of contextualisation becomes particularly obvious in Wen Ge's article about Ting's "historical mission" (Wen, 2020). According to Wen, the sources of Ting's theology are, firstly, "theological realism", i.e., solidarity with the "realities of our own national conflicts" (Wen, 2020, p. 155); secondly, Liberation Theology that regards God's kingdom as being present in the world and not limited to the church (p. 156); and thirdly, a sociological view of the church as a subsystem of society (p. 157). Consequently, Wen identifies "Theology of History" as the "focal point" of Ting's TCM (p. 166), i.e. a theology that assumes that "its main task is to explore the theological significance of history" (p. 163) and "that people inside and outside the church are all within this process of God's continuous creation, redemption and sanctification" (p. 163). That is why, according to Wen, the historical mission of TCM is "a Sinicized Church" as a church that takes part in "God's continuous creative work and witness to God's kingdom" in China's socialist society (p. 169). Wen's article reveals the close affinity of TCM's contextual theology to Liberation Theology, the most prominent example of the praxis model (Bevans, 2002, p. 70).

Ting's "Theology of History" emerged clearly in his opening address to the third National Chinese Christian Conference in 1980,[19] a text that is not

---

18 Italics in the original.

19 "The Church after the Cultural Revolution" (Ting, 2004, pp. 242-259).

included in Wen's analysis. The way, how Ting presents the historical development of the theology and structure of the TSPM is entirely in line with the praxis model's hermeneutic principle, described by Bevans, viz. "to locate God and cooperate with God in God's work of healing, reconciling, liberating." (Bevans, 2002, p. 75). The historic accomplishment of the TSPM is, according to Ting, "making Chinese Christians patriotic Christians", through conveying a new view "for the achievements of socialist new China" (Ting, 2004, p. 247). Moreover, TSPM has created a structure that corresponds to this historical situation by organising the church as part of the China's society, thus, "has cleansed the church and enabled the light of the gospel to shine forth" (pp. 248-249). Ting concluded, "opposition to the TSPM not only showed a lack of patriotism but in a sense also negated the cause of the gospel and therefore was harmful to the cause of Christianity" (p. 250). This is tantamount to claiming that faithfulness to the principles of the TSPM is the necessary historical legitimisation for true Chinese Christianity. Consequently, Ting proposes the establishment of a "Three-Self Patriotic Chinese Church Movement" that unites all Christians, "who uphold patriotism and the Three-Self principle." (p. 255). This refers to the CCC founded at this National Conference (Gänßbauer, 2004, pp. 130-131).

In the TSPM's Five-year Plan for Sinicisation from the year 2018 we find the same ideal of a Chinese church with the consciousness of living in a historical 'new era', motivated by loyalty to socialist new China, and contributing to the nation's modernization, e.g. in the following paragraph:

> "In this historical period when socialism with Chinese characteristics has entered a new era, promoting the Sinicization of Christianity, consistently strengthening its [the church's] political awareness in recognition of contemporary China, consciously integrating into its culture and adapting to society, establishing a bloodline linked with the Chinese nation, ..., making its due contribution to [...] the Chinese dream of a great rejuvenation of the Chinese nation have all become a consensus of Chinese Christians." (Three-Self, 2018, chap 1, §1)

We see a prominent feature that runs from Ting's and the TCM's outline of a contextual theology to the TSPM's present sinicisation model: This model of contextualisation reinforces existing power structures – both CCP's rule and TSPM/CCC's administrative sovereignty. It leaves no room for the idea of the church as a prophetic voice confronting power structures.[20]

---

20 Cautious references to the prophetic role of the church have been found by Kuo in the "Christian Textbook of Patriotism", published in 2006 (Kuo, 2011, pp. 1051-1052).

TSPM leadership continues to use TCM for the consolidation of power structures, implementing its contextual theology from above through five-year plans. The TSPM's Five- year Plan for Sinicisation from 2018 explicitly states that "the Sinicization of Christianity is not only an objective requirement for the development of the church in China itself but also an ardent expectation of the Communist Party of the government" (Three Self, 2018, chap 1, § 1).

At this point, TCM and TSPM-style sinicisation break with Bevans' praxis model. The top-down method of sinicisation stands in stark contrast to the importance of "basic ecclesial communities" and "bible-sharing groups" as sites of an emerging theology, which Bevans sees as "an important presupposition of the praxis model" of contextualisation (Bevans, 2002 p. 75).

We can conclude that the contextual theology which is implied by the TSPM's notion of sinicisation is characterized by the same dynamic notion of culture, emphasis on socio-political change, and orthopraxy which are typical of a praxis model of contextualisation. The enthusiastic expectations regarding socialism make it akin to Liberation Theology, the most prominent example of the praxis model. However, the consolidation of power structures distinguishes TSPM's sinicisation from Bevan's praxis model which is fundamentally critical of power and oppressive structures (Bevans, 2002, p. 73). For a deeper analysis of this aspect of sinicisation we must turn to another model of contextualisation.

5.2 Sinicising Christianity and the anthropological model

According to Bevans, "[...] the primary concern of the anthropological model is the establishment or preservation of cultural identity by a person of Christian faith" (Bevans, 2002, p. 54). At the centre of its concept of culture is "the web of human relationships and meanings that make up human culture and in which God is present, offering life, healing, and wholeness" (p. 55).

The importance of the "web of human relationships" for Ting and TCM becomes clear from their understanding of cultural identity: Firstly, Christian Chinese identity is defined as a collective identity, viz. as the identity of the TSPM. And secondly, cultural identity and national identity coincide in one.[21]

21 Brandner, too, indicates the proximity of the TCM to the anthropological model, when he states that "on the level of theology the Chinese church can be seen as standing in a theological tradition which underlies the harmony between culture and faith" (Brandner, 2004, p.204).

In his 1982 speech on the "The Three Self's Contribution to Christianity in China," Ting created a narrative about God's mission, drawing a direct line from the New Testament to the historical mission of the TSPM in socialist China. The same narrative is found in a later text by Ting about TCM. Here, he reasoned that the Chinese church is "significant for world church history as a sort of breakthrough", in two regards: geographically, because it makes Christianity "indigenous on a large scale" in an Asian nation; and historically, because it roots the Christian church in "this new thing called socialism" (Ting, 2004, p. 181). Regarding TCM, Ting states, "Our success has strengthened the faith many people in China and in the world have in Christ and in the Church. Our failure would be their loss" (p. 181).

Consequently, Ting claimed that the individual Christian finds the fulfilment of his or her Chinese identity only in accordance with the TSPM as part of the CCC:

> "The Three-Self Committee and the China Christian Council are [...] the scaffold of the building in the construction process. We, too, each one of us, are but the numerous bamboo poles or steel tubes which form the closely grouped scaffolding. [...] let us find our tiny, individual task and meaning in the building up of this work of Christ – the Chinese Church." (p. 194)

In 2020, the same narrative pervaded the speech by chairman Xu of the TSPM on occasion of its 70th anniversary. In the beginning, TSPM is lauded as a church that left behind its connections to foreign forces and became an active part of China's socialist society (Three Self, 2020, § 1-4). The speech continues with "Deepen the construction of theological thinking and lay a foundation for the theoretical support for the sinicisation of Christianity" (§ 5). The final paragraph emphasises the global significance of the TSPM and its task as a witness to the global church by "sharing China's policy of freedom of religion and testifying the progress and development of the Chinese church and society" (§ 6).

According to Bevans, the anthropological model attends to "God's hidden presence [...] manifested in the ordinary structures" and enables healthy religious experiences of wholeness, healing, and relationship (Bevans, 2002, p. 55). Correspondingly, Ting regarded the CCP's post-Mao religious policy as a God-given opportunity to promote a contextual theology that can heal the relationship between the Christian faith and Chinese society and thereby enables Christians loyal to the PRC to have an undivided identity (Ting, 2004, p. 348). TCM thus claims to free Chinese Christians from a life of inner conflict.

After the traumatic experiences of the Cultural Revolution, Ting saw in the TSPM an opportunity to heal the broken relationship of Christians with the communist state and to regain patriotism as a moral value for Christians:

> "We Christians see more clearly today than before that the Christian faith does not demand from us that we negate or look down to our nationality [...] We are born Chinese not by our choice, nor our parents', it is God who so ordains." (Ting, 2004, p. 248)

Ting interpreted "to be born Chinese" as God's calling to create a patriotic church. This is the 'human experience' which, according to Bevans, is one of the three sources of any contextual theology (Bible, tradition, and human experience; Bevans, 2002, p. 4). Compare the following statement by Ting:

> "We must obey the God who reveals himself through the Bible. We must absorb the fine traditions and the solemn lessons of church history [in Bevans' words: tradition]. And we must allow the Holy Spirit to show us a path which others have not walked before but which is appropriate for China [in Bevans' words: human experience]." (Ting, 2004, p. 253)

Already in the early 1980s, Ting affirmed the positive value of cultural identity and tradition as parts of the created world (p. 182). He referred to Christ's incarnation as evidence that "bodily and material life, intellectual development, and the social political sphere, ethics and morality are all included within the realm of God's love and concern," and interpreted Christ's incarnation as his patriotic identification with his people (p. 182).

Here we can see that next to socialism, Chinese patriotism is the guiding moral principle of TSPM's theology. Patriotism guides the church to "make a clear distinction between right and wrong," and contribute "to the welfare of the people" (p. 184).

The fundamental importance of Chinese patriotism as a moral authority for a Chinese church has been emphasised by the TSPM leadership to this day. A prominent example is the Christian Textbook of Patriotism which was introduced in 2006 as part of the obligatory curriculum at all theological seminaries of the TSPM (Kuo, 2011, pp. 1042-1043). It reaffirms the conviction that "everyone must love their country" and thus implies – according to Vala – that patriotism is "more 'fundamental' than religious faith, which is a choice" (Vala, 2013, p. 63). In the TSPM's Five-year plan for Sinicisation the whole year of 2017 is dedicated to the aim "to make patriotism the due righteousness [*yi*] of Christians" (Three-Self 2018, XXX).

In 2020, on the occasion of the TSPM's 70th anniversary, the chairman of the TSPM reaffirmed patriotism as "the national heart and national soul of the Chinese people" which is inextricably linked to full confidence in the rule of the Chinese Communist Party (Three-Self, 2020, chap.2, §1).

It is worth noting that Bevans states as a "major danger" of the anthropological model of contextualisation "that it easily falls prey to a cultural romanticism" manifesting itself in "a lack of critical thinking about the particular culture in question." As a result, such a kind of contextualisation "rather than opening a culture to its greatest potential, functions as a conservative force and actually works against the good of culture" (Bevans, 2002, p. 60).

One question about the TSPM's contextualisation model, then, is whether its narrative presents such a romanticization. In any case, it leaves no room for critical thinking. This weakness is reinforced by a patriotism that confirms existing power structures.

The consolidation of power structures – specifically of CCP rule – runs through from Ting's patriotic model of contextualisation to the current sinicisation model of the TSPM (cf. Vala, 2018, p. 87). E.g., the opening paragraph of the speech of the chairman of the TSPM on its 70th anniversary in 2020 reads:

> "In these 70 years, the Chinese church under God's guidance has held high the flag of patriotism from the beginning to the end and achieved great success in full unity with the Party. Presently [...] is the crucial era in which the Chinese Church is eagerly pushing forward the process of Sinicization of the Christian Church and adapting to the socialist society." (Three-Self, 2020; §1)

6 Conclusion

Taking seriously the TSPM's claim that its program of sinicising Christianity is more than a political concept, the article has shown that the sinicisation concept of the TSPM can be regarded as a *theological* model of contextualisation when it is interpreted on the backdrop of the TSPM history and theology.

The comparison with Bevans' models of contextualisation made it possible to describe more precisely the characteristics of sinicisation as a way of theological contextualisation: On one hand, the political-historical framework of TSPM-style sinicisation creates close proximity to the praxis model described by Bevans, particularly Theology of Liberation. They share the same ideological foundations, enthusiasm for socialism, and critique of Western imperialism and hegemony. On the other hand, the sinicisation model's emphasis on Chinese patriotism is entirely in line with

Bevans' anthropological model. As a result, sinicisation-style contextualisation loses the critical potential which is typical of the praxis model and instead has a power-consolidating effect. These two characteristics can be found from Bishop Ting to today's TSPM.

This "double face" of sinicisation corresponds perfectly with the contemporary political context. On one hand, CCP's ideology and the praxis model share an understanding of culture that focuses on political and societal issues. On the other hand, the idealized era of revolution has become history. Communist ideals and heroes have become part of China's cultural heritage on par with traditional Confucian virtues. The 'socialist core values' which are part of Xi's China Dream list equality, freedom, and justice side by side with harmony and civility (Chen, 2021, pp. 46-47; Buchholz, 2020, p. 30; Quan, 2018, pp. 1-6). President Xi is not interested in a revolutionary overthrow of power structures. To consolidate the historical authority of the CCP, he instead emphasises Chinese patriotism and portrays his era as fulfilment of the thousand-year history of the Chinese people.

From a theological perspective, the TSPM project of sinicising Christianity can be interpreted as a form of contextualisation. It endeavours to proclaim the Christian message on the horizon of the prevailing patriotic narrative. The fact that the sinicisation model of contextualisation is politically influenced and leaves little room for criticism of existing power structures should be critically discussed in the theological discourse. But it is in itself no reason to reject it as *one* possible form of contextual theology in the current context. After all, all contextual theology presupposes that reality is always "interpreted from our own particular horizon and in our particular thought forms" (Bevans, 2002, p. 4). Accordingly, it can be concluded that the TSPM model of sinicising Christianity answers to the interpretation of reality in the "particular horizon" of Chinese patriotism, and in the "particular thought forms" of a socialist society and thus is one form of contextualisation of Christianity in China.

However, it becomes problematic when this model of contextualisation claims a monopoly for its historic-cultural context. Such a claim can neither be justified theologically nor empirically. *Empirically*, there are many 'Christianities' in China and therefore many ways of sinicisation (Madsen, 2017, p. 326; Yang, 2021, pp. 36-37). The peculiarity of the TSPM's sinicisation marks at the same time its limitation: It is a top-down construction, in response to a corresponding top-down interpretation of society.

A *theological* justification for a monopoly of this model of sinicisation is already excluded by its own hermeneutical premise, namely Ting's principal distinction between unchanging "basic faith" and changing "theological thinking". According to this approach, all forms of theological thinking

– including TSPM's model of sinicisation – can only be relative and provisional (Brandner, 2004, p. 205).

Whenever unique validity of the TSPM model of sinicisation is claimed – whether by the TSPM or the CCP – the claim is not based on theological arguments. It has been shown that such claims always refer to ideological and structural arguments, based on the premises of Chinese socialism and patriotism. Conversely, we can conclude regarding the TSPM model of sinicisation: Whenever it claims to be the only legitimate model of a truly contextualised Chinese church, it leaves the theological discourse and reduces itself to a political concept and administrative provision. This is the red line beyond which the TSPM' s sinicisation concept turns from a *theological* model of a contextualised Chinese Christianity to a *political* control instrument of religious policy.

7 References

Bevans, S. B. (2002). *Models of Contextual Theology* (2nd ed.). Orbis.

Brandner, T. (2004). Jianshe Theology. Reflections About the Process of Theological Reconstruction in China. *International Review of Mission, 93*(2), 199-208.

Buchholz, M. (2020). *Talking About Christian Faith in Chinese Moral Language. A Comparative Study of Chinese Narrative Ethics from Teachers' Desks and Preachers' Pulpits in Beijing at the Beginning of the 21st Century.* Projekt Verlag.

Cao, N. (2012). Elite Christianity and Spiritual Nationalism. *Chinese Sociological Review, 45*(2), 27-47. https://doi.org/10.2753/CSA2162-05554502

Cao, N. (2019). A Sinicized World Religion? Chinese Christianity at the Contemporary Moment of Globalization. *Religions, 10*(8), 459. https://doi.org/10.3390/rel10080459

Chang, K.-M. (2018). New Wine in Old Bottles: Sinicization and State Regulation of Religion in China. *China Perspectives, 1-2*, 37-44. https://doi.org/10.4000/chinaperspectives.7636

Chen, Y. (2021). 'Official Confucianism' as Newly Sanctioned by the Chinese Communist Party. In R. Madsen (Ed.), *The Sinicization of Chinese Religions: From Above and Below* (pp. 44-63). Brill.

Dessein, B. (2017). Religion and the Nation: Confucian and New Confucian Religious Nationalism. In C.-T. Kuo (Ed.), *Religion and Nationalism in Chinese Societies* (pp. 199-231). Amsterdam University Press.

Duan, Q. (2013). The Reconstruction of Chinese Christian Theology. In Zhuo Xinping (Ed.), *Christianity: Religious Studies in Contemporary China Collection Vol. 3* (pp. 31-61). Brill.

Dunch, R. (2008). Christianity and 'Adaptation to Socialism'. In M. Y. Yang (Ed.), *Chinese Religiosities: Afflictions of Modernity and State Formation* (pp. 155-178). University of California Press.

Fällman, F. (2010). Useful Opium? 'Adapted religion' and 'harmony' in contemporary China. *Journal of Contemporary China, 19*(67), 949-969. https://doi.org/10.1080/10670564.2010.508594

Fällman, F. (2021). Reducing the Burden of Religious Activities: On Propaganda, Social Action, and the Role of Christian Churches in Civil Society. In S.-H. Chan & J. W. Johnson (Eds.), *Citizens of Two Kingdoms: Civil Society and Christian Religion in Greater China* (pp. 102-126). Brill.

Feith, K., Friemann, I., & Wenzel-Teuber, K. (2020). *China Heute, 39*(4), 191-197.

Friemann, I. (2024). Neuer Katechismus der offiziellen protestantischen Kirche China: Eine Einführung mit Textbeispielen und Vergleichen zum Katechismus aus dem Jahr 1983. *China Heute, 43*(4), 220-229.

Gänßbauer, M. (2004). *Parteistaat und Protestantische Kirche: Religionspolitik im nachmaoistischen China.* Lembeck.

Harmsel, W. (2021). *The Registered Church in China: Flourishing in a Challenging Environment.* Pickwick Publications.

Introvigne, M. (2020). *Inside The Church of Almighty God: The Most Persecuted Religious Movement in China.* Oxford University Press.

Kao, C.-Y. (2013). The House-Church Identity and Preservation of Pentecostal-Style Protestantism in China. In F. K. G. Lim (Ed.), *Christianity in Contemporary China: Socio-cultural Perspectives* (pp. 207-219). Routledge.

Kuo, C.-T. (2011). Chinese Religious Reform: The Christian Patriotic Education Campaign. *Asia Survey, 51*(6), 1042-1064.

Kuo, C.-T. (2017). Introduction: Religion, State and Religious Nationalism in Chinese Societies. In C.-T. Kuo (Ed.), *Religion and Nationalism in Chinese Societies* (pp. 13-49). Amsterdam University Press.

Lee, T.-H. J. & Chow, C. C.-S. (2021). Methodological Reflection on the Study of Chinese Christianities. In M. T. Frederiks & D. Nagy (Eds.), *World Christianity: Methodological Considerations* (pp. 113-134). Brill.

Lewis, S. W. (2021, July 19). Centenary Propaganda and Chinese Socialism with Xi Jinping Characteristics. *Issue Brief No. 07.19.21.* Rice University's Baker Institute for Public Policy. https://doi.org/10.25613/4SW8-7R17

MacInnis, D. E. (1989). *Religion in China Today: Policy and Practice.* Orbis.

Madsen, R. (2017). Epilogue: Multiple Sinicizations of Multiple Christianities. In Y. Zheng (Ed.), *Sinicizing Christianity* (pp. 219-326). Brill.

Madsen, R. (2021). Introduction. In R. Madsen (Ed.), *The Sinicization of Chinese Religions, From Above and Below* (pp. 1-15). Brill.

Masláková, M., & Satorová, A. (2019). The Catholic Church in Contemporary China: How Does the New Regulation on Religious Affairs Influence the Catholic Church? *Religions, 10*(7), 446. https://doi.org/10.3390/rel10070446

Quan, S. (2018, May 1). How China's Socialist Core Value Propaganda Portrays China as a Serious Society. *The Palouse Review.* Washington State University. https://palousereview.wsu.edu/spring-2018-edition/

Reny, M.-E. (2018). *Authoritarian Containment: Public Security Bureaus and Protestant House Churches in Urban China.* Oxford University Press.

Schak, D. (2011). Protestantism in China: A Dilemma for the Party-State. *Journal of Current Chinese Affairs, 40*(2), 71-106.

Three-Self Patriotic Movement. (2018). Protestant Five-Year Plan for Chinese Christianity (2018-2022). *UCANews.* https://www.ucanews.com/news/protestant-five-year-plan-for-chinese-christianity/82107

Three-Self Patriotic Movement. (2020). *Jianchi zhongguohua fang xiang, hongyang aiguo aijiao chuantong, banhao xinshidaide chongguo jiaohui* [Hold on to the Guiding Principle of Sinicization, Enhance the Tradition of 'Loving the Country, Loving the Faith,' Run Well a Modern Chinese Church]. The Protestant Church in China. http://www.ccctspm.org/newsinfo/13806

Ting, K.-H. (2004). *God is Love: Collected Writings of Bishop K. H. Ting.* Cook Communications Ministries International.

Tsai, Y.-Z. (2017). 'We Are Good Citizens': Tension between Protestants and the State in Contemporary China. In C.-T. Kuo (Ed.), *Religion and Nationalism in Chinese Societies* (pp. 309-344). Amsterdam University Press.

Vala, C. T. (2013). Protestant Reactions to the Nationalism Agenda in Contemporary China. In F. K. G. Lim (Ed.), *Christianity in Contemporary China: Socio-cultural Perspectives* (pp. 59-77). Routledge.

Vala, C. T. (2018). *The Politics of Protestant Churches and the Party-State in China: God Above Party?* Routledge.

Vermander, B. (2019). Sinicizing Religions, Sinicizing Religious Studies. *Religions, 10*(2), 137. https://doi.org/10.3390/rel10020137

Wen, G. (2020). Reviewing K. H. Ting's Historical Mission: Theological Reconstruction. *Chinese Theological Review, 30*, 152-170.

Wenzel-Teuber, K. (2017). Stimmen zur Revision der "Vorschriften für religiöse Angelegenheiten" und Hinweise auf wichtige Veränderungen. *China Heute, 36*(3), 140-143.

Wenzel-Teuber, K. (2016). Chronik zu Religion und Kirche in China 23. März bis 28. Juni 2016. *China Heute, 35*(2), 75-82.

Wenzel-Teuber, K. (2012). Protestantische Gremien leiten neue Phase im "Aufbau des theologischen Denkens" ein. *China Heute, 31*(3), 141.

White Paper. (2018, April 4). *China's Policies and Practices on Protecting Freedom of Religious Belief.* https://english.www.gov.cn/archive/white_paper/2018/04/04/content_281476100999028.htm

Wickeri, Ph. L. (2007). *Reconstructing Christianity in China: K. H. Ting and the Chinese Church.* Orbis.

Wielander, G. (2021). Rejecting the Civil Society Paradigm: Chinese Christian Values and China's Hegemonic Discourse. In S.-H. Chan & J. W. Johnson (Eds.), *Citizens of Two Kingdoms: Civil Society and Christian Religion in Greater China* (pp. 285-310). Brill.

Yan, K. Sh. C. (2018). When the Gospel Meets the China Dream: Religious Freedom and the Golden Rule. *International Bulletin of Mission Research, 42*(3), 212-219. https://doi.org/10.1177/2396939317747149

Yang, F. (2021). Sinicization or Chinafication? Cultural Assimilation vs. Political Domestication of Christianity in China and Beyond. In R. Madsen (Ed.), *The Sinicization of Chinese Religions. From Above and Below* (pp. 16-43). Brill.

Yang, F., Tong, J. K. C, and Anderson A. H. (2017). *Global Chinese Pentecostal and Charismatic Christianity*. Brill.

Yang, F. (2017). Pentecostals and Charismatics among Chinese Christians: An Introduction. In F. Yang, J. K. C. Tong, & A. H. Anderson (Eds.), *Global Chinese Pentecostal and Charismatic Christianity* (pp. 1-13). Brill.

Zhang, Zh. (2015). Three-fold Thinking on the Sinicization of Christianity. *Evangelische Theologie, 75*(5), 385-394.

Zheng, Y. (Ed.). (2017). *Sinicizing Christianity*. Brill.

18 Between freedom and conformity

Negotiating the situation of religious minorities in Tunisia

Frank-Ole Thoresen[1]

Abstract

This article examines the intricate landscape of religious diversity and tolerance in post-revolutionary Tunisia, with a particular focus on the experiences of Jewish and Protestant Christian minorities. Despite Tunisia's reputation for relative religious freedom, highlighted by the awarding of the Nobel Peace Prize in 2015, challenges persist. Through combining religious freedom categories with ten anonymized interviews conducted in the Spring of 2023, the article aims to understand the current perceptions of tolerance and freedom of belief among these groups, shedding light on the broader implications for religious coexistence in Tunisia amidst its shifting political and social landscape. The research question we seek to answer is "How do members of selected religious minority groups experience tolerance for freedom of religion and beliefs in Tunisia at present, and how do these experiences reflect the broader social and political dynamics of post-revolutionary Tunisia?"

Keywords: Tunisia, religious minorities, coexistence, tolerance, Christians, Jews, Muslims.

1 Introduction

Many Tunisians would proudly argue that Tunisia is a land of peaceful reform. The "Jasmin Revolution" of January 2011 fitted perfectly with such a national imagination, where the long-term political oppressor, Zine El Abidine Ben Ali, was ousted without bloodshed, and the demonstrators' demands for political freedom prevailed. The picture, however, is somewhat more complicated. Tunisia has been a country of relative religious homogeneity, with the Maliki interpretation of Sunni Islam representing

1 Frank-Ole Thoresen is Associate Professor at Fjellhaug International University College, fthoresen@fjellhaug.no, ORCID iD: 0009-0006-8962-710X.

the majority and being the religion privileged by the state.[2] From independence in 1957, the first president, Habib Bourguiba, worked to establish a Tunisian national identity where a modern, indigenous, and tolerant interpretation of Maliki Islam played a key role. The American scholar Elisabeth Young labels this national myth an essential part of *Tunisianité*, namely what constitutes the national identity of modern Tunisia (Young, 2018, p. 37.49).

Jinan Limam, an expert in constitutional law and President of The Association for the Defence of Individual Freedoms, has argued that freedom of religion is fundamental to peaceful co-existence in any society (Limam, 2017, p. 77). In modern times, Tunisia has been characterized by relative religious freedom and peaceful coexistence. The Norwegian Nobel Committee even awarded four Tunisian organizations the Peace Prize in 2015. It stated that they had been instrumental to "establish a constitutional system of government guaranteeing fundamental rights for the entire population, irrespective of gender, political conviction or religious belief."[3]

The situation in Tunisia has nonetheless been more ambiguous. For instance, in 2002, the famous El Ghriba synagogue on the southern island of Djerba was hit by a terrorist attack, killing 21 people. During the 2012-2013 interval, probably more than 40 Sufi shrines and tombs were attacked, burned, and desecrated. Hence, although religion played a limited role during the revolutionary events, it soon became highly contested in the public discourse in the aftermath (Young, 2018, p. 16).

Recently, the government has taken some measures, acknowledging that freedom of religion and beliefs could be under pressure in Tunisia. For instance, in 2019, the Ministry of Religious Affairs established an Office for Religious Minorities to safeguard the security of religious minorities and their leaders. Further, in November 2020, the Ministry launched a new hotline to report on offensive behaviour against leaders of the three monotheistic religions in Tunisia: Muslims, Christians, and Jews.

This article examines religious diversity in post-revolutionary Tunisia, drawing on the experiences of informants representing two minority religions. Members of the Jewish population and the unregistered Protestant Christian community represent the minority groups in this study. The material comprises 10 interviews with individuals representing these two minority

---

2 There are four major schools of Islamic jurisprudence in Sunni Islam. Malikism is one of these schools, and it has a particularly strong following in North Africa.

3 Press release. NobelPrize.org. Nobel Prize Outreach 2025. Thu. 20 Mar 2025. https://www.nobelprize.org/prizes/peace/2015/press-release/

religious groups.[4] The article is further grounded in a hermeneutical approach, which involves negotiating interview data, text analysis, and theory.

Both Jews and Christians have experienced some degree of animosity during the past ten years. Accordingly, we ask: How do members of selected religious minority groups experience tolerance for freedom of religion and beliefs in Tunisia at present, and how do these experiences reflect the broader social and political dynamics of post-revolutionary Tunisia?

2 Previous research

Several reports on religious freedom in Tunisia have been published during the last five years.[5] The United States Department of State annually issues a report on international religious freedom, covering every recognized country in the world (US – Tunisia). This report gives an overview of various incidents experienced by individuals in the previous year.[6]

The most comprehensive report regarding the situation of Christians in Tunisia is an annual report by Open Doors, an NGO that covers the situation of Christians worldwide (WWR, 2023). This report gives a critical overview and an analysis of the situation for Christians in Tunisia. However, it does not focus on the situation of other religious minorities.

Further, the Religious Freedom Committee of the Tunisian Attalaki Association published a "Religious Freedom Report, Tunisia 2020". The report was published with the support of Minority Rights Group Europe and the Norwegian Agency for Development Cooperation (Attalaki 2020).

These reports are relevant and helpful to this research and will be consulted throughout the article. Although such reports focus on various incidents of infringement on religious freedom, none of them give an in-depth presentation of how individuals from minority groups experience the situation. This will be the focus of the research at hand.

The article will consult and discuss a range of other materials, including information on the political situation, judicial developments, and insights from religious studies. Anne Wolf *Political Islam in Tunisia: The History of Ennahda* (Wolf, 2017) and Elisabeth L. Young *Guardians of Religion: Islam, Nation, and Democratization in Post-Revolution Tunisia* (Young, 2018) have provided interesting perspectives.

---

4 The interviews were carried out during the Spring of 2023. All informants are anonymized and given fictitious names in the following.

5 For an overview, see for instance WWR, 2023, p.8.

6 United States Department of State, Bureau of Democracy, Human Rights, and Labor (2023). *Tunisia 2023 International Religious Freedom Report.*

3 Theoretical perspectives

In a 2019 report produced by the Danish Institute for Human Rights, authors Marie Juul Petersen and Katherine Marshall created a typology of the pervasiveness of violations of freedom of religion and belief (FORB) (Petersen and Marshall, 2019). The typology encompasses both state and non-state actors, examining how these actors shape the space for freedom of religion and the individual's beliefs. Petersen and Marshall identify four categories of violations: *Intolerance and exclusion*, *Discrimination*, *Severe violations* (persecution), and *Genocide.*[7]

According to the authors, the first category, intolerance, and exclusion, occurs in various ways in most societies and may or may not imply formal violations of FoRB. In this category, individuals may not face legal restrictions; however, followers of certain religions or beliefs may feel unwelcome or stigmatized, and the subjects may encounter various forms of societal pressure and challenges. The concept of *Tunisianité* may be particularly relevant in this regard within the Tunisian context.

In the second category, we find more systematic discrimination and violations of FoRB. There may be occasional violence incited by both state and non-state actors, or a situation where states refrain from interfering and protecting minorities. "The hallmark of 'discrimination' is a law – or established practice – which entrenches a treatment of, or a distinction against, a person based on the particular religious or belief community to which that person belongs" (Petersen and Marshall, 2019, p. 30).

The third category depicts a situation where discrimination develops into *severe violations*, and the intent is to subjugate certain religions or the religious beliefs of individuals. In this category, the state both supports and fails to prevent acts of violence. Furthermore, the state sanctions opposition against a preferred religion and systematically restricts the freedom to manifest or practice some or all other religions. At the same time, non-state actors systematically attack religious minorities, discriminate against them, and systematically interfere with individuals' or groups' freedom to practice their religion or belief.

---

7 Petersen and Marshall limit the term "persecution" to contexts of severe violations of FoRB, and state that "This denotes a situation in which there is systematic, organized violence, with the intent to drive away or subjugate particular religious or belief communities and individuals" p.31. There is no universally accepted definition of persecution. We notice, however, that this definition is narrow, excluding, for instance, all discrimination and violence against religious minorities that is not systematic and enforced with a particular intention. For a different perspective, see Tieszen (2010, p. 168).

The fourth and final category is genocide. "This is when the state commits, sponsors, or tolerates acts with intent to destroy a group, in whole or in part, or when non-state actors commit acts with the intent to destroy a group, in whole or in part" (Petersen and Marshall, 2019, p.32).

This research will use this typology to understand how religious diversity is negotiated in present-day Tunisia.

The World Watch List (WWL) is a report compiled by World Watch Research (WWR), the research department of Open Doors International. Considerable effort has been invested in developing a comprehensive methodology for this work, which benefits this article in several ways.

The WWL identifies five overall "blocks" for exploring the situation of minorities under pressure. These blocks are important spheres of life that are potentially influenced by the lack of freedom of religion. They are private life, family life, community life, national life, and church life. In addition, a sixth block, labeled violence, is introduced and cuts through the other five blocks. Violence is defined as "the deprivation of physical freedom or as serious bodily or mental harm to Christians or serious damage to their property" (WWL, 2022, p. 28). Further, WWR has developed 84 questions within these six blocks. In this research, we have consulted the most relevant questions for our in-depth interviews and adjusted them to suit the Tunisian context, taking into account more than one religious minority.

4 The political role of religion in recent history

In 1956, Tunisia was declared an independent state following more than seventy years of French colonial rule. Habib Bourguiba became the republic's first president, holding on to power for some thirty years until his Prime Minister, Zine El Abidine Ben Ali, took control through a bloodless "palace coup" in 1987. For the next twenty-plus years, Ben Ali's regime retained tight control of the country.

While most former colonized countries with a Muslim majority population chose to establish some sort of Muslim law following their independence, Tunisia became one of the few Muslim-majority countries with a mainly secular constitution. Freedom of religion was thus protected in Article 5 of the June 1st, 1959 Constitution (Limam, 2017, p. 77-78). In everyday life, however, the unwritten rules and regulations that dominate the private sphere and local government practices may be at least as important for an individual's freedom (Limam, 2017, p. 82).

During Ben Ali's rule, religious groups were often viewed as either a political threat or a potential political asset. Jewish and Christian groups neither represented much political potential nor posed a threat. If anything, they may have represented a risk for criticism and negative sanctions from various Muslim groups toward the government merely for being allowed to exist in the country. As such, they carry a degree of symbolic potential as dissenters in a majority Muslim context and, therefore, may be considered destabilizing elements. But, since they remained few and far between, such symbolic representation remained negligible. Thus, so long as they kept a low public profile, they were most often ignored and, to some extent, tolerated.

From the turn of the millennium onwards, Tunisia experienced a change toward a religious resurgence, and the importance of religious elements and symbols became increasingly visible to the public.[8] The British scholar Anne Wolf considers this a reaction against a general development in the Tunisian society of increased secularization, corruption, and materialism (Wolf, 2017, p. 107-111).

This development had at least two significant consequences. On the one hand, Ben Ali sought to strengthen the religious legitimacy of his regime, and support for the traditional Sufi orders became politically attractive. They did not have political ambitions, were not considered a political threat, and could potentially counter the growth of more radical Islamist impulses (Wolf, 2017, p. 107-112). Hence, although the Sufi groups neither supported nor opposed the regime in Tunisia, they could be seen as providing it with a certain religious legitimacy.

On the other hand, Islamist and Salafi-inspired groups were considered particularly threatening to the regime, as they carried both religious and political ambitions. The Ben Ali government, accordingly, sought to control and suppress such groups with any means available, and, for instance, the terrorist attack on the synagogue in Djerba in 2002 provided the government with increased legitimacy in this battle (Wolf, 2017, p. 112-125). There is, however, no doubt that discontent with political leadership, which suppressed all religious and political opposition and, at the same time, failed to deliver on financial expectations, became a factor in recruitment to the opposing groups with an Islamist inclination.

Despite such developments leading up to the revolution, religious groups played a minimal role during the protests and downfall of the government. It was after the regime had been toppled from power that a political power vacuum came into existence, and various groups with Islamist and Salafi inclinations gained a stronger foothold (Linan, 2017, p. 77-88). The fact that these groups had been politically suppressed by an

8 For instance, the number of students of Islamic studies at Zaytouna University grew steadily, and wearing the hijab in public became more widespread.

unpopular regime presumably added to their legitimacy among the population. The, at the time, Islamist Ennahda party managed to establish organizational structures within a matter of weeks, and also groups inspired by Salafism, such as Ansar al-Sharia and, later, Hizb al-Tahrir, suddenly had the opportunity to gain societal and political influence. Religious attire and symbols, such as the niqab and Sunna-style beard, soon became more common elements in public. Later, tensions regarding Salafi influences became prevalent within the Ennahda, and the movement developed more moderately and democratically (Wolf, 2017, p. 140-157).

This political and religious development has been significant for the situation of the religious minorities being studied.

5 Freedom of religion in the Constitution

From the middle of the 19th century onwards, Tunisia has had a Constitution safeguarding freedom of religion and beliefs. The Constitution has further stated that religion should not be utilized in a manner that furthers separation and discrimination. Considering the upheaval of Tunisian society following the revolution and the continuing renegotiation of Islamist and Salafi influences, establishing a new Constitution was met with considerable concern (Wolf, 2017, p. 141).[9] Nonetheless, in 2014, the outcome was a mainly secular Constitution, protecting the freedom to choose one's religious beliefs and exercise such beliefs through worship and observance (Limam, 2017, p. 77-78).

The Constitution still comprised a considerable ambivalence between the guarantee of freedom of religion, on the one hand, and the protection of Islam as the official state religion and Muslim national identity, on the other. This tension remained unresolved, and the interpretation of the Constitution in this matter was, in practice, often left to local governments and judiciaries.

In 2022, the newly elected Tunisian president issued a decree to change the Constitution. The wording regarding the religious foundation of Tunisia was altered once more. Islam is not identified as the official state religion in the new Constitution. Still, it states, "Tunisia is part of the Islamic Umma, and it is incumbent on the state alone to work to achieve the purposes of Islam in preserving the soul, honor, property, religion, and freedom" (Hafnaoui, 2022, p. 4). These are the objectives of the Sharia.

In one regard, the new Constitution can be considered a continuation of the legacy from the time of Bourguiba onwards. The wording closely

9 Controversies regarding women's rights were, likewise, an area of great concern.

follows that of earlier constitutions, with only minor alterations. However, earlier regimes have abstained from referencing Sharia as a basis for the Constitution in Article 1. Even the Islamist Ennahda-led government agreed not to include this in the 2014 Constitution (Young, 2018, 55-56). The 2022 revision appears to go as far as possible without introducing the term "Sharia." This may somewhat mirror the governmental challenge of balancing Tunisia between groups embracing liberal democracy and actors more inspired by Islamism.

According to more than 30 Tunisian NGOs and civil society associations, the new Constitution "undermines the notion of citizenship that unites Tunisians without discrimination based on faith, color, and gender, maintaining the requirement that the head of state be male and Muslim" (Hafnaoui, 2022, p. 4-5).

6 The religious legacy

The historical legacies of religious communities in Tunisia chosen for examination differ significantly. Representatives of both religious groups have been integral to the Tunisian social fabric for many centuries. However, neither indigenous Christianity nor Judaism has been a significant factor of religious influence in Tunisia since the pre-Islamic period.

6.1 Christianity in Tunisia

Christianity found a solid foothold in the North African region during the early years of Church history. Carthage, situated on the outskirts of Tunis, emerged as a significant theological centre for early Christianity. Influential Christian thinkers such as Augustin, Tertullian, and Cyprian were all based in the city at various times.

In the Roman period, the majority Roman Church enjoyed the most substantial support among the Romanized citizens of the urban population. The local Berber population often chose an alternative, minority interpretation of Christianity, as many became part of the Donatist movement. The Donatists were a separatist Christian movement representing an opposing theology, particularly regarding the question of restoration to the Church after giving in to persecution.

From the Arab expansion during the 8th Century onwards, the influence of the Church diminished throughout North Africa. An indigenous Christian presence survived in Tunisia, however, despite the growth of Islam, until at least the 15th Century (Talbi, 1990, p. 344-345). During the 19th Century, European migrants reintroduced Christianity to the country. According to statistics, there are presently between 20,000 and 30,000 Roman Catholic Christians and possibly between 2,000 and 3,000 Protestant Christians in Tunisia.[10]

6.2 Judaism in Tunisia[11]

The history of Judaism in Tunisia dates back at least to the 2nd Century AD, presumably extending further. Central to this history is the El Ghriba synagogue on the island of Djerba, which may have been one of the first synagogues to be raised outside the Holy Land. The synagogue is believed by some to date back as far as the 6th Century BCE (Hirschberg, 1974, Vol. I, p. 23). During times of Roman rule, the Jewish population in North Africa developed and flourished, with many Jews holding influential positions. Furthermore, during the Renaissance, many individuals fled persecution in Italy and Spain, finding refuge on the shores of North Africa. At other times, however, the conditions for the Jewish citizens were more challenging. Throughout history, various forms of discrimination have been imposed on the Jewish population during periods of both Christian and Muslim rule. At intervals, such discriminatory measures were harsh, while at others, they were more lenient.

The Jewish population in Tunisia has been sizeable throughout many centuries. By the turn of the 20th Century, the number of Jews residing in Tunisia is estimated to have been approximately eighty thousand. In the mid-20th century, the number had grown to approximately a hundred thousand people (Hirschberg, 1974, Vol. I, p. 134).[12] However, following the establishment of the state of Israel in 1948, the broader region of North Africa witnessed a persistent exodus of its Jewish population. The reasons for this development were twofold. On the one hand, many Jews embraced the opportunity to settle in a majority Jewish state and left to follow such an ambition. On the other hand, a wave of "Arabian nationalism" became widespread throughout North Africa, and sentiments of experienced animosity among the Jewish population grew. Although the new independent Tunisian government during the latter half of the 20th Century was not hostile

---

10 World Christian Database | Brill.
The numbers, however, are uncertain. The International Religious Freedom Report estimates that approximately 30,000 Christians reside in Tunisia. About 5,000 are Tunisian citizens, while the rest are foreigners. The majority of the Christians who are citizens are presumably Anglican or evangelicals (US-Tunisia 2023) p. 3.

11 For a comprehensive presentation of the history of the Jews in North Africa, see: Hirschberg, 1974, vol I and II.

12 See also Jews of Tunisia (https://www.jewishvirtuallibrary.org/jews-of-tunisia).

towards Jews, the growth of Muslim extremism combined with general negative sentiments pressured many to leave (Gilbert, 2010, p. 280).

The most well-known incidents in modern times are connected to the El Ghriba synagogue, which witnessed terrorist attacks in 1985, 2002, and 2023. The attacks resulted in more than twenty casualties and many more wounded. By the turn of the 21st Century, the number of Jews residing in Tunisia had dwindled to less than two thousand individuals. From that time onwards, the Jewish population in Tunisia remained at the same low level.[13] Most of the Jewish population in Tunisia resides on the island of Djerba and its surroundings.

The pattern of a group under pressure reappears when considering the situation of Tunisia's Jewish congregations. Wikipedia lists 223 different Jewish synagogues in Tunisia. Only twenty-eight of these are presently listed as active, while the rest are labeled as "destroyed," "disused," "in ruins," or "converted into buildings of other functions."[14] In January 2018, individuals attempted to set the school of the Jewish community in Djerba on fire, and some people encouraged acts of violence toward the Jewish population through social media. Following an explosion at Al Ahli Arab Hospital in Gaza in 2023, rioters attacked and set fire to a disused synagogue and shrine in Tunis (US – Tunisia, 2023, p. 11). The International Religious Freedom Report also refers to claims of anti-Semitism in prisons and judicial systems (US – Tunisia, 2019, p. 6-7).

However, the central government in Tunisia has promised to safeguard its Jewish population against anti-Semitism, and police guards are now present at many Jewish institutions. The government has also partially subsidized the maintenance of some synagogues in Tunis (US – Tunisia 2019, p. 9).

7 Informant experiences

7.1 Lack of tolerance for diversity

All my informants agree that some religions are considered "unwanted" by the general public in Tunisia. Followers of religious communities identified in this group are Jews, Christians, Shia Muslims, and the Bahai community. However, Salafi Muslims or other Muslim groups who are considered more inclined toward the use of violence are similarly not wanted as

---

13 Members of the Jewish community estimate the number to be approximately 1500.

14 List of synagogues in Tunisia (https://en.wikipedia.org/wiki/List_of_synagogues_in_Tunisia). See also Jarrassé, 2010.

part of Tunisian society. One of my Jewish informants states that many Jews are considering leaving Tunisia at present. Even though most Jews can make good money in Tunisia, they are treated as second-class citizens. The security situation for Jews has also been deteriorating over time.[15]

Muhammed, who is a Christian, explains the lack of tolerance for diversity by stating that Tunisians are like a tribe, with their own culture and rules that emphasize homogeneity and unity. "Difference is unwanted in Tunisia. Difference is unwanted in any way",[16] and "all religions that are not Sunni Islam are unwanted."[17] This often leads to experiences of societal alienation and a sense of not belonging for those who do not conform to the religious norm.

Change or mobility in both social status and religious identification tends to be taken as a dismissal of one's cultural inheritance. As such, it may be considered a form of contempt toward both family and cultural heritage. Religious change is particularly sensitive in this regard.

According to *Amira*, "If I want to insult you, I say, 'You are a Jew'. Christians are fine until they find out that you are a convert. That's when things go wrong." She continues to explain that being a Tunisian Christian doesn't make sense to most Tunisians and that the very fact that there are Tunisian Christians is a shock to many. The general understanding is that Christianity should not be part of the Tunisian social fabric. "There is no such thing as a Tunisian Tunisian (i.e. Arab) who is a Christian."[18]

Since its independence, Tunisia has been one of the few Muslim-majority countries with a secular Constitution. For decades, it has been considered one of the most Western-oriented countries in the region, if not the most. For obvious reasons, Tunisia has had particularly close ties to France, and one would expect that this history of Western orientation and exchange would facilitate diversity rather than homogeneity.

Muhammed, however, explains that a different kind of homogeneity, with its own dynamic, has been fostered. "You should be Muslim, but not too Muslim. You need to be culturally Muslim. But if you become too Muslim, then you belong to the terrorists or jihadists." As such, an ideal of "soft religion" has been fostered during the pre-revolution era. During the social and political upheavals of the revolution, this ideal was challenged by a powerful movement of Islamists and Salafis. On several occasions, acts of violence and vandalism were also instigated. Later, however, the development backfired,

---

15 In conversation with Samuel.
16 In conversation with Amira.
17 In conversation with Ahmed.
18 In conversation with Amira.

and the Tunisian ideal of soft religion reemerged, demonstrating its cultural robustness. Both the Islamist and Salafi movements lost popular support, but according to informants, even the more Salafi-oriented Muslims are considered preferable to both Jews and Christians.

7.2 Community and national life – central and local authorities

The secular history of Tunisia has implied constitutional rights for minorities that are not awarded in many other Muslim societies. Religious minorities have the right to commune for worship in buildings designated for that purpose. There is no legal prevention of proselytism, and conversion, even from Islam, is considered a constitutional right. Congregants do not have to register to participate in a congregation, and although the police are stationed at sites of worship, the general sentiment among Christian informants is that the police are there for protection rather than surveillance and that they most often demonstrate respect. Further, schoolchildren do not need to take part in Muslim religious education in the public school system if their parents are non-Muslims,[19] and religious minorities may also establish private schools.

Most of my informants generally trust the judicial system. Nonetheless, government practices may still be a challenge to religious minorities. The International Religious Freedom Reports for Tunisia depict that religious minority groups regularly complain that their rights are not protected. This may, for instance, mean that formal applications are stalled or that local authorities may not comply with the letter of the law. My informants from both groups do not expect that local authorities will always protect them if others violate their rights, since they belong to a religious minority.

The relationship with the government and the police is experienced as particularly ambivalent by my Jewish informants. Since the Jewish minority has been under pressure for decades, the Tunisian central government has been committed to giving necessary protection. Accordingly, there are police stationed at a few places like the El Ghriba Synagogue, the main synagogue in Tunis, and the Jewish neighbourhood in

19 If, however, the parents keep a low profile or remain "secret Christians," Islamic education will be compulsory for the children. Many are also reluctant to pull their children out of classes for fear of making their kids stand out as different and risk being bullied by peers or teachers. Ahmed claims that it is very risky to withdraw children from Islamic teaching in public schools because teachers may punish them by giving them poor grades or other problems.

Houmt Souk on the island of Djerba, where the majority of the Jewish population in Tunisia resides.

Jewish informants emphasize that they have legal protection like any other group. However, they also depict a situation in which police officers often treat them in a demeaning and condescending manner. Informants state that it would have been better without police protection. Samuel, for instance, states, "They are of no benefit to us." He further claims that before the revolution, the police were there to protect them, but this changed in later years. "Now they are just keeping a record of what we do to use it against us."

Similarly, there are security checkpoints throughout the country on the main roads, and according to my informants, Jews are regularly harassed and humiliated at such checkpoints. Also, if there are disagreements between members of the Jewish population and Arabs, there is no help in going to the police since they expect that "the police will turn against them, and they will not help."[20]

7.3 The judicial system – uncertainty and misconceptions

Most informants clearly state that Tunisia is a country where the law applies to everyone, and as such, minority groups are subject to legal protection. For instance, Asma, who is a Christian, claims that she will have full rights to inherit from her parents under the law.

It is worth noting, however, that my informants are often uncertain or confused about the jurisdiction for religious minority practices in Tunisia. In many cases, they hold contradictory convictions or are uncertain about what the law states.

For instance, some of my informants state that any form of evangelism or attempt to share one's faith with others is illegal and that they can only share their religious beliefs if others first ask them. Other informants claim that it is only unlawful to evangelize minors. Furthermore, some state that religious congregations are only open to those who already identify with said religion and that it, therefore, is not legal, for instance, to invite a Muslim to participate in a Christian worship service. According to the US Department of State, in the Religious Freedom Report for Tunisia 2023, "There is no legal prohibition of proselytism, but the law criminalizes forced conversions" (US – Tunisia, 2023, p. 4).

Another example of uncertainty is connected to regulations regarding locations for religious worship. Some informants claim that if religious

20 In conversation with Samuel.

worship takes place in someone's home, everyone present must identify as Christian. Ahmed further emphasized that it is not legal to have more than eight to ten people in such meetings and that there must not be more than ten Bibles present. Most informants told me that gathering for worship in house churches was not a problem. There had been some instances where the police interfered and stopped worship services in private homes, but that was before the revolution. Ahmed specifically stated that he does not believe that could happen today.

According to the Religious Freedom Report for Tunisia for 2021, "The law requires that all religious services be celebrated within houses of worship or other nonpublic settings. These restrictions extend to public advertisement of religious services." According to an agreement signed with the Roman Catholic Church in 1964, the Catholic Church is recognized and permitted to function in Tunisia. However, it is not legal to construct new churches.

Jewish informants also claim that they experience what they label "judicial discrimination." By this term, they describe a situation where they believe laws are designed to target them as a group. The most prominent example is the legal regulation of goldsmithing, a trade many Jewish families have been involved in for centuries. My informants describe a situation where the laws and regulations of trading with gold and jewellery are unclear and complicated to follow. A particular license from the government is also required, and such a license is very difficult to obtain. Thus, according to my informants, jewellers and goldsmiths break the law all the time, and this makes many Jews vulnerable. The local police can always decide to take action against them, and in case of conflicts, particularly with someone from the Arab population, the understanding is that the police will not support a Jew and that they can always find a reason to make life difficult for them.[21]

Informants seem to agree that the local police have become very powerful and can do what they want. A similar claim is also made by members of the majority Muslim population in conversation with the author. My Jewish informants nevertheless give voice to the experience that they are treated worse than others simply because of their ethnic origin.

One of my informants also states that it is not legal for police officers to become Christians. If a police officer converted to Christianity, that person would have to leave the police force.[22]

Several informants state that most Christians abstain from talking about their religious identity in the workplace and generally keep a "low profile" regarding religion. It is difficult to know whether this results from

---

21 In conversation with David and Samuel.

22 In conversation with Ahmed. I have not found any confirmation of such a claim.

misconceptions regarding the law or simply from fear and societal pressure. It is at least likely that it may be a combination.

7.4 Societal pressure

In most respects, Tunisia represents a traditional community-oriented society where the paramount value is vested in the corporate rather than the individual. The French anthropologist Louis Dumont characterizes such societies using the term "holism," in contrast to "individualism" (Dumont 1986, p. 25). In Dumont's understanding, holism is sociocentric, and the complex web of relations is considered a central value. In such societies, families will often be considered a sphere with its own rules and values, and accordingly, beyond the government's responsibility in most respects. My informants confirm such an understanding.

According to Muhammed, although the police generally do not interfere with religious matters, there are exceptions. The family and relatives of converts from Islam to Christianity will often threaten the convert by involving the police. "If the mother or the parents call the police, it is very, very crucial because the police always trust the parents. And if the child is not doing well with his parents, that is very bad, because in Islam, you can only go to heaven if your mother is satisfied with you and all that, so the role of the mother and the parents is very, very important, and they are believed by the police. So, if your family acts on it, even if there is nothing illegal about it, the cops can do other things to frame you. And that happens in Tunisia."

False accusations may, for instance, be that someone is accused of being involved with terrorist groups, proselytizing Muslims, or that they are using drugs or other issues that may cause trouble. According to Muhammed, in such cases, a person may be jailed for some days or a few weeks before they are most often let off.

My Christian informants unilaterally claim that the real problems for converts from Islam most often come from their families and relatives. Not only may they be subject to threats and false accusations, but it is also common that converts may experience various forms of exclusion from their families. This may include loss of inheritance, participation in family matters, and physical harm in some cases. The informant, Ahmed, tells of a girl who has just been told to leave her home because she became a Christian, while Amira reveals that she was beaten by her mother on a few occasions, but that "there have been no real problems with my family." In other words, such measures are expected and, to some extent, tolerated by Christians. Ali explained that several of his closest family members would not speak to him at all.

The backdrop is often that parents are under considerable pressure from the extended family. They are accused of bringing shame to their relatives when their offspring turn away from Islam. Parents will, therefore, use "every means available"[23] to bring their children back to the majority faith. Muhammed emphasizes, however, that the situation for converts is often particularly difficult during the first few years following conversion. He later experienced repeated "family discussions" over religion, which somehow brought him closer to his family. As time passed and he held onto his new-found faith, his parents gradually came to respect his religious convictions.

My Christian informants have different experiences with what may happen if, for instance, a wife becomes a Christian while her husband remains Muslim. In some cases, the husband may accept this, whereas in other cases, the wife will be beaten and threatened to make her return to Islam. No one will question the husband's right to beat his wife. Yet again, others will divorce a wife who becomes a Christian.

Asma explains, for instance, that she had to enter into an oral agreement with her husband that she should live as a hidden believer. In particular, the husband's family should not know that she was a Christian. She felt that she had no choice, as she had to respect her husband for as long as he was alive. After her husband died, everything changed. She became part of the local Christian community and established a Christian family with her children.

Ahmed has also experienced that converts from Islam, for instance, may face difficulties with their employer. There have been cases where the convert has been harassed and pressured to leave or told that all opportunities for future promotion or a higher salary are lost until they return to Islam.

Ali explains that he has become almost like an outcast in local society since he became a Christian more than 10 years ago. He and his family are most often not invited to take part in celebrations or local festivities, people do not often converse with him in public, and because they are Christian, most other children are not friends with his children.

Similarly, Jewish informants fear false accusations stemming from a combination of racist attitudes and jealousy. "If I were poor, nobody would care,"[24] but because many from the Jewish population do well financially, jealousy among individuals from the majority population may be spurred. A general sense of insecurity among the Jewish population also has the effect that they stay away from areas where there is no established Jewish population. There is protection in the community, and

23 In conversation with Muhammed.
24 In conversation with David.

although most people are considered to be kind and tolerant, there is a fear regarding how individuals and groups from the Muslim majority may treat them should they stay in areas without a historical Jewish presence.

Most informants state that Jews are often treated as second-class citizens. Some described experiences of violence and lack of protection from teachers in the public schools when they were children, and some of my informants have therefore decided that their children shall only attend the Hebrew school in the synagogue.

7.5 Muslim leaders

In many Muslim-majority areas globally, imams and other religious leaders are sometimes known to cause problems for religious minorities. The Open Doors country dossier for Tunisia states that religious leaders are a strong driver of Islamic oppression (WWR, 2023, p. 24). My informants do not identify this as an open problem. Ali states that there have been cases where imams have preached during Friday prayers and warned against associating with Christian converts from Islam, identifying that such people are living in the local community and that they should be shunned. My informants have, however, not experienced cases where imams, for instance, openly incite to violence. According to Ahmed, incitement to violence would be illegal, and if it should happen, the police would probably not accept it and act against the agitator.

7.6 Geographical variations

The situation for minorities in Tunisia may vary considerably depending on geographical location. Members of religious minorities residing in larger cities, particularly in Tunis, tend to experience a higher degree of acceptance and tolerance compared to many rural areas. The coastline is also considered more open to new impulses than the hinterland. Most of my informants live in bigger cities.

The southern part of the country, which is more rural, is considered far more religiously conservative, and as such, religious minorities may face more challenges in such areas.[25] According to Ahmed, "In the South, people may even kill you. They are very religious in the South".[26]

---

25 The southern island of Djerba, however, is historically a place of religious plurality and is presumably an exception in this regard.

26 This is probably based on presumption, rather than experience. I have not come across any stories of people in Tunisia who have been killed for their faith.

Ali has also experienced that a Christian brother in a suburban area in the South was attacked and beaten by a local mob for being Christian.[27]

Likewise, members of the Jewish population will avoid many areas in the rural hinterland. During the years following the revolution, several Jewish synagogues and graveyards, for instance, were attacked and demolished in such areas. A similar incident occurred in October 2023. In the wake of the terrorist attack by Hamas on Israel and the following war in Gaza, a pro-Palestinian mob attacked and set fire to a closed synagogue in central Tunisia (US – Tunisia, 2023, p. 1). Hence, even though my informants and probably most members of the Christian or Jewish communities do not experience much violence, it is likely that incidents regularly occur (WWR, 2023, p. 31-33).

7.7 Individual variations

The situation for religious minorities in Tunisia not only varies according to geographical location, but it also varies considerably depending on individual status.

Ali emphasizes that factors such as age, position, and personal networks can influence the level of hardships a person faces. Older people have a certain status in society, and those with networks that extend to the government or armed forces may have a degree of protection that more vulnerable individuals may not have. This is particularly the case when it comes to the risk of facing physical abuse.

It is also likely that women are more vulnerable than men in general, and this is also indicated in my material. Tunisian society may appear modern on the surface, but traditional values still prevail in many aspects of society. Women often depend on male relatives in various ways, and acceptance of individual choices is more limited.

How someone makes their religious faith known may also be of importance. Those who keep a low profile and rarely share their religious conviction with others are likelier to be left alone than those who, for instance, use religious symbols or witness more boldly. An example of how this may influence minorities is the testimony of Asma. She is a Christian convert from Islam, and she explains that her son wants to carry a piece of jewellery shaped like a silver cross around his neck. She is trying to convince him not to wear the piece of jewellery since she knows that such a

[27] He emphasizes, however, that this happened during the period after the revolution when the Islamist movement was on the rise. He describes this as a challenging time with much fear for the local Christians.

display of religious deviation will make the other children harass and bully him. There is little acceptance in society for such religious deviancy.

As stated by the journalist Priscilla Hwang, "Meanwhile a new and growing Tunisian Christian community is forced in to a difficult choice: remain hidden and be ignored, or be visible and become the target of hostility" (Hwang, 2016).

8 Prospects for religious minorities in Tunisia

Expectations and anticipations for the years to come are voiced distinctly differently among my informants. Those representing the Jewish community are far more restrained and concerned about the prospect of future developments than are my Christian informants.[28] Samuel, who is Jewish, explains that he wants to stay in Tunisia. This is his land, and he hopes the situation will improve for the Jewish population. Still, he states that everything was much better during the era of Ben Ali and that many younger Jews left the country in later years. The reason for this exodus is a combination of a lack of opportunities, difficulties connected to the jewellery trade, and negative sentiments toward Jews in the majority population. Opportunities seem much better abroad, and as most Jews have dual citizenship, they are free to leave.

David shares a similar perspective. He states that the security situation for Jews has become much more fragile after the revolution. However, he believes much will remain the same even if a new Constitution is in place. There will still be freedom of religion in general, even though a Jew can never become president. He is concerned about the extended power given to the president, but it is too early to say how things will develop. Although most people generally are kind and peaceful, he is not optimistic about the prospects for Jews in Tunisia.

My Christian informants are generally much more optimistic concerning the future of the Christian minority in Tunisia. Muhammed states that:

> "We have a good educational system in Tunisia. We have a lot of smart people, people who are educated and all that. So, people are aware. Everyone has screens, everyone has phones, so I think that helped a lot in enlarging the identity and acknowledging that in Tunisia, we are very different and diverse. We have a lot of languages; we have a lot of people from different countries. Even our history is very rich. I think people are beginning to open

---

28 The interviews were conducted before the war in Gaza began in October 2023. Pro-Palestinian support in connection with the war has, therefore, not influenced the responses of my informants.

> their eyes ... In ten years, I think Christians will not be a hundred percent accepted because it needs more time, but I think it will be acknowledged that, yes, we have Tunisian Christians. We may even have our own churches and all that."

Ahmed similarly emphasizes the importance of internet access. He claims that the situation changed after the Covid pandemic. During the period of social isolation, many people were forced to stay in their homes, and many spent a lot of time "online," where they were positively exposed to Christianity. Many also watched a lot of satellite TV, where they, for instance, were exposed to programs from the Christian satellite broadcasting SAT-7. Ahmed claims that such experiences have broadened the minds of many people. "Since Covid, everything has become more open." Furthermore, Tunisia's more challenging financial situation is straining the population, and many are migrating as a result. Thus, he believes that the combination of migration, widespread access to smartphones, higher proficiency in English, and increased cultural exposure will continue to lead to a more open society and greater acceptance for Tunisian Christians.

However, most of my informants are concerned about the new Constitution. Even though the general public becomes more open, a Constitution that may further restrict the space for religious freedom and human rights is feared to hinder positive developments.

Comparing the situations of the two groups, it is difficult to avoid the psychological aspect associated with change in later years. The Jewish community has been dwindling for many decades, and those left are a tiny remnant under considerable pressure. The group of Christians is in a different situation. Their numbers have grown, and most Tunisian Christians have converted within the last decade. Many Christian immigrants from sub-Saharan countries further increase their numbers. Hence, although both groups face challenges and, in many ways, share a common fate as second-rate citizens, their sentiments on the situation may still differ. Marginalization and harassment may be more difficult to tackle when there is a sense that your community is continuously shrinking.

9 Jewish and Christian minorities – differences and similarities

In our material, we may distinguish three main actors that cause infringements on the freedom of the two groups of religious minorities. These are 1) representatives of central and local authorities, 2) family and relatives, and 3) the local community.

First and foremost, my Christian informants fear reactions from family and relatives. Most often, they do not express a strong fear of negative actions by government representatives, but they expect that government representatives will not provide them with the necessary protection when facing discrimination. They also fear that the local police may cooperate with their relatives to scare them with the intention of turning them back to the majority faith. In other words, government officials most often play a secondary role.

My Jewish informants, on the other hand, do not face difficulties from family and relatives. Interreligious marriages between Jews and Muslims are not common, and most Jews live in majority Jewish contexts where they practice their faith together. The Jewish informants, however, generally lack trust in government representatives and experience systematic discrimination from police and other government officials who ideally should offer them protection. They also express a lack of confidence in the judicial system, and although the law applies to all, they fear that laws may be passed to target them as a group. Jewish informants would, therefore, consider government officials the main cause of their difficulties.

Both groups express more ambivalent feelings toward the local community. For many Christians, the local community, such as neighbours, friends, or schoolteachers, may not cause them any harm as long as their relatives support them. This is particularly true in larger cities, such as Tunis. Others experience exclusion and marginalization. Jewish informants describe the situation between the Jewish minority and the local communities as most often amicable, particularly in areas with a more significant historical Jewish presence. Yet, they also describe that jealousy and racist attitudes toward Jews are widespread, emphasizing the need for group protection. Thus, many areas in Tunisia are considered off-limits for Jews.

The situation for these two minority groups is, therefore, similar and different. The Christian minority, first and foremost, fears reactions from family and relatives, while the Jewish minority fears responses from government officials, particularly the police. Local communities may target both groups, but this is largely a geographically conditioned phenomenon. In big cities like Tunis, the population is more exposed to ethnic, cultural, and religious plurality, and they are generally more tolerant of diversity than is the case in the rural hinterland. In these areas, cultural homogeneity remains the norm.

10 Categorizing religious freedom violations in Tunisia

The testimonies of my informants demonstrate that religious minorities in Tunisia may experience infringements on their religious freedom in various ways. Informants have identified a general lack of tolerance for diversity in the Tunisian culture. This promotes a sense of alienation for those who do not concur or fit into the model of the majority interpretations. The expected model has historically been expressed through the concept of *Tunisianité*. As explained earlier, the concept was developed during the rule of the first independent president, Habib Bourguiba, and was fostered over the following decades, creating an image of national identity and contributing to the growth of Tunisian nationalism. *Tunisianité* may be defined by the combination of various symbolic elements constituting a preferred image of a Tunisian national "soul" or identity. Central to this image is Tunisia as a modern, progressive, and tolerant Muslim nation. Important aspects that form this concept include, for instance, the centrality of the Maliki school of Islam, women's rights, the ban on veiling, and the state being the guardian of religion.

Tunisianité has had the effect of constituting an image of a unified and homogenous society. All Tunisians should ideally be moderate and progressive Sunni Muslims, and Tunisian society should be characterized by inclusivity and tolerance. However, such tolerance has limits. Various religious minority groups have inherently represented "otherness" and a degree of exclusion from this national myth. Those who belong to religious minorities may therefore experience being treated as second-class citizens.

Negative reactions may include facing harassment by local authorities, fear and insecurity regarding their constitutional rights, and considerable societal pressure from their family and the wider community. In some instances, societal pressure may include occurrences of violence or isolation. Returning to the Petersen and Marshall model, we find informant experiences within all the three first categories.

Informants from both Jewish and Christian backgrounds face various acts of *intolerance and exclusion*. For Christian converts from Islam, experiences of intolerance and exclusion, particularly from the family, are common, while members belonging to the Jewish minority, in general, have such experiences with the police and government. Although experiences are depicted as common, it is presumably individuals who discriminate against them. As such, the discriminatory experiences represent more of an expression of general negative attitudes toward the Jewish population than a desired and systemic violation by the government.

We have also seen more *systematic discrimination* where, for instance, acts of violence occur, although not very often. If this happens within the family, the government is presumed not to protect the victim. In some areas, particularly in the southern hinterland, harsher forms of violence are expected to take place. Still, religious diversity is rare in such areas, and, e.g., converts from Islam will most often keep a lower profile. Members of the Jewish minority will most often stay away from such areas. The Jewish population remains vulnerable and fears that they will systematically be treated as less than equal to the majority population when conflicts arise.

The judicial system in Tunisia also privileges Islam in various ways, and the recently adopted Constitution expresses that the Tunisian state shall work towards "achieving the purposes of Islam." Different laws regulate the rights of religious minorities, and some of these may be considered discriminatory. Examples of such are laws preventing Christians from constructing new church buildings, while the same does not apply to the construction of new mosques, or that the president of Tunisia must be Muslim. My informants have also expressed a sense of uncertainty regarding how the law protects minority rights, which may pose a considerable challenge. Informants are often unaware of what the laws state. Hence, such uncertainty may contribute to causing fear and anxiety among religious minorities. Lack of confidence and uncertainty may also lead to members of minority groups withdrawing from exercising their legal rights out of fear of challenging the law. As such, judicial uncertainty hinders the empowerment of minorities.

Furthermore, they fear that local authorities may cause them problems, regardless of the law. Consequently, they fear that what is regarded as custom in many cases may take priority over the law. Members of the Jewish minority, in addition, suspect that laws may be discriminatory in the manner that they have been adopted to target them as a group in particular.

Although we may find infringements on freedom of religion and beliefs within all the first three categories in this typology, it should also be emphasized that, for instance, the use of violence and *severe violations* is not common in Tunisia and that religious minority groups have a level of legal protection that is rare in states with a Muslim-majority. It is, for instance, not illegal to proselytize for other religious convictions than Islam or to convert to different religions. The state presumably does not actively support acts of violence, and we do not find systematic attacks on religious minorities, even though such attacks may occur.

Thus, while infringements on the religious freedom of these two minority groups are common within categories one and two, defined as *intolerance/exclusion* and *discrimination*, *severe violations* are rare, and the fourth category in the Petersen and Marshall model, *genocide*, is not considered relevant to Tunisia.

11 References

American-Israeli Cooperative Enterprise (n.d.). Jews in Islamic countries: Tunisia. Jewish Virtual Library. Retrieved March 20, 2025, from https://www.jewishvirtuallibrary.org/tunisia

Attalaki (2020). *Religious Freedom Report Tunisia 2020.* Committee for Freedom and Equality.

Bismuth-Jarrassé, C., & Jarrassé, D. (2010). *Synagogues de Tunisie: Monuments d'une histoire et d'une identité.* Esthétiques du divers.

Dumont, L. (1986). *Essays on individualism: Modern ideology in anthropological perspective.* University of Chicago Press.

Gilbert, M. (2010). *In Ishmael's house: A history of Jews in Muslim lands.* Yale Univ. Press.

Hafnaoui, R. M. (2022). *Implications of the role of religion in Tunisia's new Constitution for non-Muslims. Cornerstone Forum*, (No. 323), Religious Freedom Institute. https://religiousfreedominstitute.org/wp-content/uploads/2022/09/Cornerstone-Forum-No.-323-Hafnaoui.pdf

Hirschberg, H. Z. (J. W.) (1974). *A history of the Jews in North Africa* (Vol. I, 2nd revised ed.). E. J. Brill.

Hirschberg, H. Z. (J. W.) (1981). *A history of the Jews in North Africa* (Vol. II, 2nd revised ed.). E. J. Brill.

Hwang, P. (2016, April). Underground: The plight of a religious minority living in a Muslim society. Divergent. Retrieved March 20, 2025, from https://www.divergent.com/underground-religious-minority-tunisia

Limam, J. (2017). Religious freedom in Tunisia: The scope of ambivalence. In A. Ferrari & J. Toronto (Eds.), *Religions and constitutional transitions in the Muslim Mediterranean: The pluralistic moment* (pp. 77-88). Routledge.

Norwegian Nobel Committee (2015, October 10). Press release: Nobel Peace Prize 2015 awarded to the Tunisian National Dialogue Quartet. NobelPrize.org. https://www.nobelprize.org/prizes/peace/2015/press-release/

Open Doors International / World Watch Research (2022). Complete World Watch List methodology. Open Doors International. https://opendoorsanalytical.org/wp-content/uploads/2022/10/Complete-WWL-Methodology-updated-October-2022.pdf

Open Doors International / World Watch Research (2023). Tunisia: Full country dossier. Open Doors International. https://www.opendoors.de/sites/default/files/country_dossier/tunisia_wwl_2023_country_dossier.pdf

Orthodox England (n.d.). The last Christians of North-West Africa: Some lessons for Orthodox today. Retrieved March 20, 2025, from http://www.orthodoxengland.org.uk/maghreb.htm

Petersen, M. J., & Marshall, K. (2019). *The international promotion of freedom of religion or belief: Sketching the contours of a common framework.* Danish Institute of Human Rights. Retrieved from https://www.humanrights.dk/sites/humanrights.dk/files/media/dokumenter/udgivelser/research/accessibility_checked_2020/rapport_internationalpromotion_updated.pdf

Talbi, M. (1990). Le Christianisme maghrébin. In M. Gervers & R. Bikhazi (Eds.), *Indigenous Christian communities in Islamic lands* (pp. 313-351). Pontifical Institute of Mediaeval Studies.

Tieszen, C. L. (2015). Towards Redefining Persecution. In C. Sauer and R. Howell (Eds.) *Suffering, Persecution and Martyrdom. Theological Reflections.* VKW.

United States Department of State, Bureau of Democracy, Human Rights, and Labor (2019). *Tunisia 2019 International Religious Freedom Report.* https://www.state.gov/wp-content/uploads/2020/05/TUNISIA-2019-INTERNATIONAL-RELIGIOUS-FREEDOM-REPORT.pdf

United States Department of State, Bureau of Democracy, Human Rights, and Labor (2021). *Tunisia 2021 International Religious Freedom Report.* Retrieved from https://www.state.gov/reports/2021-report-on-international-religious-freedom/tunisia/

United States Department of State, Bureau of Democracy, Human Rights, and Labor (2023). *Tunisia 2023 International Religious Freedom Report.* https://2021-2025.state.gov/wp-content/uploads/2024/04/547499-TUNISIA-2023-INTERNATIONAL-RELIGIOUS-FREEDOM-REPORT.pdf

Wikipedia (2025, February 17). List of synagogues in Tunisia. Retrieved March 20, 2025, from https://en.wikipedia.org/wiki/List_of_synagogues_in_Tunisia

Wolf, A. (2017). *Political Islam in Tunisia: The history of Ennahda*. Hurst.

Young, E. L. (2018). *Guardians of religion: Islam, nation, and democratization in post-revolution Tunisia* [Doctoral dissertation]. University of Michigan.

Zurlo, G. A., & Johnson, T. M (2025). *World Christian Database.* Brill. Retrieved March 20, 2025, from https://www.worldchristiandatabase.org

19 Wild wisdom for misconstrued mission

Protestantism and its persecution in Turkey, 1961-2025

James Bultema[1]

Abstract

In this essay, I argue that the Turkish Protestant movement, which has been emerging since 1961, has been variously misconstrued, manifested by polarized perspectives upon it and upon the persecution of it. On the one hand, the missionaries associated with the movement view themselves as virtuous and well-intentioned messengers of God, vulnerable to and oftentimes victims of governmental and societal persecution. On the other hand, both nominal and devout Muslim citizens of Turkey largely view the missionaries as threatening encroachers, themselves and their compatriots as the vulnerable ones, and the missionaries' converts as the casualties. These clashing perspectives underscore the complex interplay of such evangelistic mission and the related persecution, which cannot be adequately defined and described unilaterally. After synthesis and academic discussion, I also suggest what I refer to as "wild wisdom," which, when implemented in such situations and contexts, could result in less premature missionary attrition, increased missionary fruitfulness, and a more congenial cultural depiction of national Christians.

Keywords: Turkish Christians, Protestantism, persecution, securitisation, wisdom.

---

1 James Bultema (1962) is an independent researcher, residing in the Netherlands. His chief interest is the intersection of religious freedom and Christian mission in Islamic contexts. His PhD dissertation, "Free Enough to Grow: The Turkish Protestant Movement, 1961-2016" (2024), has informed this chapter. The dissertation is being published by Springer Nature, and a pre-publication copy is available upon request: jamesbultema@spccturkey.com, ORCID iD: 0009-0000-0505-4604.

1 Introduction

In 1990, just weeks prior to my wife's and my departure for long-term mission work in Turkey, the eminent British pastor and theologian John Stott preached at our home church in Santa Barbara, California. I had devoured many of his books, and so I was glad for an opportunity after that worship service to ask him a vital question. After informing him of our imminent departure for Turkey, I asked, "What words of wisdom would you be inclined to give us before we go?" He had a coffee cup in his hand, which he set down on a table as he seemed to think about his response. Then he said, "You're going out like sheep among wolves. Therefore, be as shrewd as snakes and as innocent as doves." In response, I remember thinking to myself, "*Is that all?* Is that all the advice that the chief architect of the Lausanne Covenant and the author of *Christian Mission in the Modern World* could share with me – just a single verse from the Bible?"

Although the following statement could by no means be proven, many, if not most, of the thousands of Protestant missionaries who have served the Lord in Turkey have been likened to living and working as essentially "sheep among wolves." Among them for the past 34 years, my wife and I have had this metaphor used with regard to us time and again. With biblical origin (Matthew 10:16), from Jesus himself, it is a fitting metaphor to include in a commissioning service for missionaries who are bound for Turkey, with its seemingly impenetrable and intimidating Islamic context, or in a prayer for those already serving there. Each time the metaphor is employed anew, it invariably evokes fresh belief and fervent concern, so much so that listening family members and close friends of the missionaries may have to reach for tissues or handkerchiefs as they tear up at the implied potential fate of their beloved sheep.

However, what eludes the reflections of virtually everyone in such situations is that, in Turkey, family members and friends of loved ones who have fallen prey to the enticement of foreign missionaries are often simultaneously hoping and praying that they will somehow be saved from those wolflike missionaries and that no other loved ones or any Muslims would suffer the same shameful apostatic fate. These converts tend to be viewed by fellow Turks as not victors in Christ, but rather victims of Christians – even traitors of the Muslim religion and the Turkish nation. As imprisoned missionary Andrew Brunson wrote after his release, "The Turkish media ... used me to paint a public image of Christians as traitors, terrorists, and enemies of Turkey" (Brunson with Borlase,

2019, p. 243). Furthering the mutual metaphor, Brunson added, "I am glad to have escaped the valley of the wolves" (p. 245).[2]

Since the movement's inception in 1961, when Turkey adopted a human-rights-based national constitution, the Turkish Protestant Church has grown to about 12,000 members from Muslim backgrounds, gathering in roughly 200 Turkish-speaking churches in cities around the country (Bultema, 2024). In this essay, I argue that the Turkish Protestant movement has been misconstrued in multiple ways, manifested by bipolar perspectives upon it and upon the persecution of it. Moreover, I suggest that a greater grasp and use of what I refer to as "wild wisdom" could result in less ill-timed missionary attrition, increased missionary fruitfulness, and a more agreeable depiction of Turkish Christians.

2 Protestantism in Turkey

A largely emic analysis of narrative, historical, and secondary data suggests that there are at least six types of contributing factors to these largely bipolar perspectives of missionaries and converts, on the one hand, and Kemalist and Erdoğanist Turkish citizens on the other (Yilmaz, 2021).[3] First, *historical factors* have contributed to their creation. Benny Morris and Dror Ze'evi elucidate the perceived Christian-missionary blame that fueled the Turkish-Armenian conflict of the late 19th and early 20th centuries (Morris and Ze'evi, 2023). They write, "In particular, the Ottomans were upset at American missionaries, of whom there were 176 in 1895, working with locals to run 125 churches and 423 schools with more than 20,000 pupils" (p. 44). Morris and Ze'evi go on to disclose how during the subsequent decade – and especially as a result of WWI – Turkish animosity toward the missionaries "only increased" (p. 411; see also p. 115). Remnants of this century-old upset and animosity toward missionaries endure to this day, and Turkish converts to Protestant Christianity are characterised as betrayers of true Turkishness, whether it be primarily secularist or Islamist.

While Turkish converts grasp, to varying extents, the grave implications of their conversion to Christianity, the post-1961 Protestant mission-

2 The metaphor is established earlier in the book, with Brunson recounting, "The wolf had caught me" (87).

3 The Kemalist and Erdoğanist citizen typologies are the two dominant ones discussed at length by Yilmaz (2021, pp. 27-32). The first is secularist, though nominally Muslim, while the second is staunchly Islamist (and, I should add, predates, in a more incipient form, the 22-year rule of President Erdoğan). In my dissertation, I define and describe these groups in terms of syntheses: the Turkish-secular, Turkish-Islamic, and the tiny Turkish-Protestant syntheses.

ary force has been mostly oblivious to their predecessors' attributed role in what most critical historians unhesitatingly label genocide. From the 67 in-depth interviews that I conducted with various missionaries as part of my research, only a few of them alluded in any way to the previous era of Protestant mission existence and endeavours in Turkey. One narrator who did allude to it opined that modern-era missionaries have "no idea what has gone on before, and they have never even heard of the American Board or the ancient churches."[4] Thus, the simmering national memory of missionary stigma continues to sway public opinion in Turkey, while most modern missionaries wonder why they are so suspiciously received.

Second, *cultural factors* have also contributed to the divergent missionary and Muslim-civilian perspectives. Let us consider their respective education on the topic. According to Ziya Meral, compulsory religious textbooks in Turkey include unfavourable descriptions of Christians and their beliefs and potentially incendiary warnings of missionary activities (Meral, 2015). However, if missionaries have any specific preparatory education for their service in Turkey, they study topics such as mission theory, World Christianity, cross-cultural understanding and communication, mission strategy, and basic Islam. My wife and I had an array of courses along these lines, but virtually nothing on Turkish culture. In my personal reading about Turkish culture back in 1990, I read about only admirable, agreeable aspects of it. All this to say that fundamental educational topics of Turkish citizens and of immigrating missionaries are poles apart, and the topics set up the two groups for bilateral misunderstandings and mistrust.

Turkish converts often find themselves uneasily in between these bipolar educational perspectives. One interviewee converted to Christianity as a minor, not long after his aunt and parents converted. He narrated that in his required religion classes, he had to memorize, in Arabic, Qur'anic verses and study Islamic ethics. Regarding Christianity, he was taught that its holy books had been corrupted. "When [the teachers] talked about Christianity, [they focused on] the Crusades ... [not on] Jesus' teachings. ... I was the only Christian at school; it wasn't safe for me to reveal that I was Christian."[5] Thus, cultural factors arising from education contribute to misunderstandings of Protestantism.

Third, *methodological factors* also contribute to the bipolar perspectives of Turkish society at large and missionaries on contemporary Protestant mission in Turkey. If I may appeal to my experience, time and again and in

---

4 KM and SM, personal communication, Nov. 9, 2007. My interviewees are anonymised to protect their identities.

5 ÇE, personal communication, Oct. 30, 2008. See fn. 4.

an array of situations, I have been proselytised by devout Muslim friends and acquaintances in the course of religiously oriented conversation. Despite the many variables, all the situations have had in common face-to-face interaction, replete with eye contact, gestures, and usually also physical touch. This method of persuasion reflects Turkish civility at its best.

Compare this approach with the most widely used method of the Protestant missionaries, dating back to 1962: mass mailings and (later) advertising of a Bible correspondence course (BCC). The first invitation letter, intending to prompt interest and provide the means of registration, solicited recipients to "read the greatest book in history," blatantly subordinating the Qur'an to the referent, which was the New Testament, or parts of it. Although contemporary missionaries have since employed a host of other missional methods, many of which are far more personal, this method remains in heavy use throughout Turkey. It must be added that the BCC has been notably fruitful over the years, enabling countless Muslims to secretly respond and register for Bible courses, with the eventual option of a personal visit. Perhaps resultantly, arsonists attacked the ministry in 2014, causing the burning of thousands of Bibles and other Christian books.[6] Reportedly, the attack itself was never seriously investigated; however, I would suggest that the attack stemmed from and stood for the vast methodological difference between Turkish- and American-styled proselytism, contributing to the bipolar perspectives on Protestantism and particularly its mission in Turkey.

Again, Turkish converts often find themselves caught in the crosshairs of compatriots' reprisals. The same news article tells also of such a situation that occurred years earlier in the same building.

> "Kadikoy International Church has been the site of other incidents of harassment or persecution, including an incident in August 2009 when a Turkish nationalist abducted a Turkish convert to Christianity at knifepoint. The attacker held a Turkish flag over İsmail Aydın's head, accused him of being a 'missionary dog' and threatened to slit his throat. After intervention by police, who told Aydın's attacker that killing him would damage Turkey's reputation, he released Aydın."[7]

Methodological factors by no means explain fully the clashing perspectives on Protestantism and its missional activities in Turkey, but they surely contribute to the formulation of a helpful explanation.

---

6 For an account of the arson attack, see https://morningstarnews.org/2014/12/suspected-arsonist-sought-in-fire-at-bible-distribution-center-in-istanbul-turkey/.

7 Ibid.

Fourth, *institutional factors* also add to the polarized perspectives of Christian missionaries and typical Turkish citizens. A commonality is that Turkish citizens and Protestant missionaries both have massive religious institutions or organisations operating on their behalf: the citizens have their Ministry of Religious Affairs[8] and the missionaries have their supporting (often mega) churches, agencies, networks, training programs, and so forth. The major difference, however, is that while the Ministry of Religious Affairs aims to sustain and strengthen Islamic orthopraxy among Turks domestically and abroad, the Christian missional institutions aim to religiously convert Muslims to Protestantism. This fact exacerbates the underlying reality of Turkish distrust of missionaries, and it helps to explain why numerous missionaries have been deported and disallowed back into Turkey. Moreover, Turkish converts are all too often attached to and even infected with reliance on a steady flow of funds from foreign Christian institutions, creating copious ethical quandaries for them. Thus, institutional factors also contribute to misconstruals of the Turkish Protestant movement – not only by Turkish citizens, but also by Christians who may unwittingly provide it with excessive support.

Fifth, *situational factors* contribute as well to the disparate perspectives of the Protestants and Turkish citizens. If Ottoman-era missionaries were faulted for empowering the Armenians and impelling a seditious mindset among them, then modern-day missionaries have been accused of empowering or even fostering secessionism among the Kurds. In 2008, eight years before his arrest and two-year imprisonment, I interviewed Andrew Brunson. One question I asked him pertained to the ethnic makeup of the Turkish-speaking church that he himself was leading. Brunson's answer was succinct: "We're full of Kurds."[9] If that was the case, then one must wonder whether this may have been an underlying contributive factor of his persecutive ordeal. I say this not to oversimplify or pretend to grasp the intricacies of Brunson's incarceration and eventual deportation, but rather to highlight the hyper-sensitivity of the Turkish government toward particularly Christian-foreign involvement with and assistance to Kurds, whom they typically view with intense suspicion. It must be added that many Kurdish converts are members, in some cases pastors, of Turkish

8 The Ministry of Religious Affairs, or *Diyanet*, is so well-funded and powerful that Yilmaz uses it for a third typology: "the liminal citizenship category of the two [other] antagonistic ideologies and regimes" (Yilmaz, 29-32). In other words, the *Diyanet* helps to bridge Turkey's secularists and Islamists.

9 Andrew Brunson, personal communication, Mar. 4, 2008. In this case, I chose to reveal Brunson's identity with respect to our personal communication, since his identity vis-à-vis the statement is crucial to the argument.

churches, and that other minorities in the country – most notably Alevis – populate Protestant churches.[10] My point here is that complex situational factors contribute variously to misconstruals of Protestantism. Ethnic distinctions among converts in local churches that may be worrisome to the local authorities may be winsome to missionaries and church leaders who value multiculturalism in local churches.

Sixth and finally, *functional factors* relating to religious freedom also contribute to the antithetical perspectives. By and large, Protestant missionaries in Turkey and converts who follow their lead focus on and tend to develop their functioning upon the explicit constitutional declaration of religious freedom, including the individual and communal rights of committing to and practicing a particular religion or belief, propagating that religion or belief, and converting from or to a religion or belief. Most Turks, however, give greater attention and importance to constitutional and legal restrictions that have been placed upon the expression of religious freedom in the country. Many of these restrictions are more implicit than explicit, based upon various Islam-favoring interpretations.

A conversation an early missionary named RM had with a Turkish detective illustrates the point very well, and it could apply to more conservative areas and cities of Turkey even today: "You can't do [Christian propaganda]," the detective said to RM. "This is Turkey."[11]

RM responded to the detective, "*Bey Efendi* (Sir), look,[12] your constitution says that there is total freedom of religion and you can share your faith ... in any way you want."

The detective simply responded to him: "This is Turkey. You don't understand."

While there are certainly misunderstandings that Turkish secularists, Erdoğanists, and variations of the two groups have regarding Protestant missionaries and Turkish Christians, there is also much about the Turkish Protestant movement, including its context and converts, that we foreign missionaries do not understand. Perhaps it is our tendency to think that we understand more than we actually do about historical, cultural, methodological, institutional, situational, and functional factors related to the Turkish Protestant movement that gets us

---

10 For a detailing of the non-Muslim and other minorities in Turkey, see Oran (2021, pp. 25-77).

11 RM, personal communication, April 17-18, 2007. This encounter took place in the early 1960s. See fn. 4.

12 At this point in the conversation, RM reportedly extended to the detective a pocket-sized copy of the new constitution. Pocket-sized copies of the current 1982 Turkish constitution can still be found for purchase.

into relational trouble with various Turkish citizens. The above findings suggest this to be the case, and they invite humble reflection.

3 Persecution in Turkey

Adding one more clause to the first introductory quote of Brunson, we have this: "The Turkish media ... used me to paint a public image of Christians as traitors, terrorists, and enemies of Turkey *when nothing could be further from the truth*" (Brunson with Borlase, 2019, p. 243).[13] To the extent that Brunson accurately described the intent of the media, I would be inclined to agree with him; I have met thousands of Christians living in Turkey, and none of them came across to me as a traitor, terrorist, or enemy of Turkey. However, I am also inclined to ponder the differing perspectives on persecution of Christians in the country. Is it possible that not only Protestant Christianity, but also persecution of Christians has been mutually misconstrued? Could what Christians view as pointless persecution be viewed by certain government officials and Turkish citizens as, for instance, crucial securitization? Herein, I present five selected episodes of persecution,[14] from different decades of the movement, all of which appear to have been construed contrarily from a Turkish perspective.

First, the reason RM found himself face-to-face with a Turkish detective, in the situation above, was that he had masterminded a mass-mailing campaign advertising free Bible Correspondence Courses to over 10,000 Turkish citizens in Istanbul. The fallout from that evangelizing effort led to his eventual blacklisting and banishment from Turkey – an act defined by Christians as persecution.[15] However, consider this mass-mailing campaign from the Turkish perspective. The mailing went out camouflaged by countless Turkish greeting cards, just prior to one of the two major Islamic holidays. I have to imagine for a moment my conservative Christian parents, in the US in the early 1960s, receiving in the mail a Qur'anic Correspondence Course advertisement on the verge of Christmas or Easter Sunday. I am certain that they, and thousands like them, would have been alarmed at such an occurrence, and, even in America, protective measures

13 The italics are mine.

14 At the outset of this section, I wish to emphasise that this episodic list is selective, for the sake of the argument, and does not represent the variations, afflictions, and repercussions of persecution of Christians in Turkey throughout the decades of the movement. Persecution has indeed scarred (and may have also strengthened) its members.

15 In addition to my personal communication with RM, this story is also recorded in Malstead (2020, pp. 25-7).

may have subsequently gone into effect. Thus, it is understandable that such an out-of-the-blue mass-mailing Christian campaign in the monopolistic Islamic city of Istanbul was viewed by recipients as essentially an attack on Islam.

Second, the first martyr of the Turkish Protestant movement is said to have been David Goodman, who, on an early June morning in 1979, was fatally shot at the entrance of his apartment in Adana. His story is narrated affectively, and also inspiringly, under the title "Sacred Surrender," in a volume by The Voice of the Martyrs (Drake & The Voice of the Martyrs, 2005, pp. 78-86). It must be added that neither the identity of the killer nor his motive for killing ever became known.[16] According to journalist Marvine Howe of the *New York Times*, the circumstances of David's murder were unclear, and thus he was considered to have been one of numerous victims of ambiguous violence between right and left political factions at that time (Howe, Dec. 26). During a period of just eight months that year, six other Americans were also killed due to political violence, and during 1978-1979 more than 2,400 Turkish citizens were also killed (Howe, Dec. 15). Thus, what Christians described as a sacred surrender to a religiously motivated persecutor, Turks, along with Howe, tentatively defined as a senseless slaughter by a politically motivated provocateur.

Third, Ataköy International Church, founded by foreign Protestant missionaries in 1987, was the first Republican-era church started openly in modern Turkey.[17] Beforehand, missionaries and at least one convert had started churches in diplomatic facilities, extant church buildings, or homes. The Ataköy Church, comprised of missionaries and converts and conducted bilingually, congregated in a meeting room of a two-star hotel. The foreign leaders had informed the Istanbul governorship of their meetings, and they had been officially registered. For two years the arrangement worked well, but then the official attitudes changed, and on the church's second anniversary, eleven armed police officers burst into the worship service and shut it down. Attendees' identification data were collected, the church leaders were questioned, and the meetings were thenceforth forbidden.[18]

The lead missionary in the church-planting venture, a lawyer from the UK, went to a law professor, the Evangelical Alliance, and a UK diplomat for assistance in dealing with the injustice the church had suffered. The

16 JP, personal communication, Oct. 2, 2007. See fn. 4.

17 BT, personal communication, Mar. 24, 2007. See fn. 4.

18 GB, personal communication, Mar. 5, 2008; and NP, personal communication, Jan. 10, 2009. See fn. 4.

law professor produced a legal abstract explaining that the church had complete freedom to assemble. However, in the final paragraph he wrote, 'You will have to prove this in a struggle with the authorities and you may encounter difficulties,'" which the lead missionary interpreted by recounting to me, "Put your head above the ramparts, and you might get shot" (GB, 2008).[19] The high-level diplomat, acting on the behest of the Evangelical Alliance, obtained from Turkish officials verbal permission for the church group to reorganize and restart regular meetings – but only on their owned or rented premises. The church's reinvented name was Güngören Church.

This is enough of the story to disclose starkly different perspectives upon it. Keeping in mind the various historical, cultural, methodological, institutional, situational, and functional factors that contribute to contrasting emic and etic interpretations of the Turkish Protestant movement, this episode of church closure was likewise antithetically interpreted. While the lead missionary felt as though he was "putting his head above the ramparts and getting shot at," the Turkish authorities believed that they were dealing with a threatening Western-Christian-Turkish-convert situation, indicated by not two or three, but eleven armed police officers bursting into the meeting room. We Christians may surmise that such a show of force to be terribly excessive, but research indicates that barely 6% of Turks have positive views of Christians, and the five most common traits that Muslims in general associate with Christians are selfishness, violence, greed, immorality, and arrogance (Pew Research Center, July 21, 2011).[20] The tragic probability is that those police were expecting to find inside of that room a corresponding scenario to those unconscionable traits.

Fourth, in October 2006, Turkish police arrested two Turkish Christians on "charges that they had insulted the Turkish state ... and its people ... by spreading Christianity" (Kremida, 2010).[21] Their arrests came after they had spent two-and-a-half years passing out Bibles and Christian literature in the Marmara region of Turkey, during which 35-40 Muslims had become Christians, 20-25 of them had been baptized, and three house churches had been

---

[19] Çetin Özek, untitled legal abstract addressed to "Messianic Believers" (Dec. 23, 1986), 25. Back then, adherents of the movement were called "Messianic Believers," rather than as Christians or Protestants.

[20] https://www.pewresearch.org/global/2011/07/21/chapter-2-how-muslims-and-westerners-view-each-other/.

[21] The first charge is against Article 301 and the second is against Article 216 of the Turkish penal code.

established.[22] They were finally arrested when an anonymous person made a telephone call to local authorities, reporting their activities. One can imagine the upset among the authorities that such a call caused. The two Christians were eventually acquitted of the charges; however, "they were found guilty of collecting information on citizens without permission" (Kremida, 2010), and they were sentenced accordingly.[23] In a separate case, they were charged with illegally collecting funds from church offerings (Kremida, 2010).[24] The two Christians had been doing these activities without having any kind of legal structure,[25] and thus it could be suggested that they were tempting trouble. On the one hand, then, Turkish authorities viewed these local procedures and legal proceedings as logical, based on their social means of reporting a complaint and codified penalties for wrongdoing. On the other hand, many or most Christians aware of the situation readily accused the Turkish authorities of persecution of Christians.

Finally, after President Trump compelled President Erdoğan to release Brunson from prison in 2018 (Brunson with Borlase, 2019), the Erdoğan Administration developed an action plan to undermine the ever-expanding work of Christians in Turkey, and the plan was sent to the government for execution (Bozkurt, 2024). Accordingly, a growing number of Protestant missionaries have been secretly coded as threats to public safety (N-82) or to national security (G-87), resulting in their deportation and debarment from reentry.[26] Unlike the legal cases of the two Turkish Christians (above), the assigning of these codes[27] has no basis in the Turkish legal system: the missional activities of those coded have not been criminal (ADF International, 2024). For these and related reasons, this extralegal assigning of codes reflects a grievous undermining of the rule of law. Particularly, Turkish citizens with foreign Christian spouses who have been coded face the agonizing reality of having to leave behind not just churches, ministries,

[22] Taştan, personal communication, Aug. 12, 2009. Taştan stated they were charged with Christian missionizing.

[23] This charge was against Article 135 of the penal code.

[24] See also https://www.persecution.org/2007/08/05/fears-of-new-turkish-persecution-update-on-hakan-and-turan/. Note the emphasis on defining this, as well as the other charges, as religious persecution. In a contemporaneous news article (alluded to in the linked one), it is likewise referred to as "Official Harassment."

[25] They have since gained legal status in Turkey as the Association for Propagating Knowledge of the Bible.

[26] Other codes have also been applied to Christian workers, but, in each case, with essentially the same result.

[27] The total number of these incidents of coding is close to 200, but those affected, severely or otherwise, reaches into the thousands: spouses, children, friends, coworkers, business partners, employees, church members, etc.

coworkers, and friends, but also their families of origin, relatives, and home cities and country (Bishai, 2024).

Taken as a whole, in this matter of coding Christian workers, Turkey seems to be reacting out of revenge, alarm, and arbitrary use of power. In its 2024 decision on a class-action case involving nine plaintiffs, Turkey's Constitutional Court was divided for the first time regarding an N-82 coding; the panel of judges was torn, 6 to 7 (ADF International, 2024). With the slightest majority possible, the deportations of the Erdoğan Administration were upheld. In this forlorn episode, then, religious persecution is palpable to Christians, discrimination is unmistakable, while Turkey maintains that it is simply exercising its national sovereignty and securitising its missionary-imperiled society.

In this section, I have posed five of myriad episodes of purported persecution of Christians in Turkey and have shown, to the best of my ability, the typical Turkish perspectives upon them. In doing so, I have sought to disclose the disparate nature of Protestant Christian and secularist-Islamist-Turkish viewpoints upon such episodes. Does this disparity matter? I suggest that it does. The disparity behooves us to be as precise as possible in our usage of the term persecution – avoiding overuse, underuse, or misuse of it – and to contextualise our usages in amenable awareness of contrasting interpretations of the situations and of the possibility of our own misinterpretations of them.

4 Synthesis and discussion

The Turkish Protestant movement along with its adherents' claims of persecution from official and societal sources compose a manifold reality, and most enlightened are those who circle the exhibit, so to speak, and study its many facets. Moreover, critical interaction with other observers of the exhibit deepens such enlightenment, as does engagement with researchers of similar movements and assertions of persecution. Therefore, herein, I will engage with a selection of related literature.

In *Protestant Missionaries to the Middle East: Ambassadors of Christ or Culture*, Peter Pikkert poses a false dilemma that runs throughout the work (Pikkert, 2008). The ambassadorial aspect of the missionaries' presence and labors in a country cannot be relegated to an either-or assessment. A critical analysis must take into account more than Christ-or-culture representation, which, to his credit, Pikkert's analysis does do, despite his title. However, with regard to the persecution of Christians, he writes, "Turkey's treatment of both Christian converts and Christian missionaries remains pathetic" (p. 162). Then he gives a lengthy, one-sided litany of persecutions to prove his point. However, in doing so, he commits a fallacy of overextrapolation that misleads readers from facts, for the Turkish government has made advances in the manifestation of religious freedoms – or else his longer litany of "Positive Responses in Turkey" could not have transpired. Moreover, segments of society across Turkey have largely come to accept Turkish Protestant churches existing and evangelizing within them (pp. 182-3). Thus, his claim of pathetic treatment must be qualified.

In "Christians in Turkey: Native Foreigners," Hratch Tchilingirian does not use the term persecution when discussing the Protestant community (Tchilingirian, 2021). After introducing the general topic with the phrase, "Even as some restrictions on religious minorities have been eased," Tchilingirian lists restrictions and legal problems that continue to bedevil the Protestants (pp. 546-7). Given the brevity of his essay, he does not delve deeper into the topic, but opting for specific terms, rather than resorting to the inflammatory, catch-all term persecution, may be a wiser approach in discussing such problematic situations, especially in religiously neutral academic settings.

To illustrate the point just made, Oran distils the thrust of his work with this sentence regarding minorities in Turkey and their difficulties: "Turkey has failed to respect and protect their rights, and minority citizens cannot feel secure" (Oran, 2021, p. 241). He then goes on to describe, in well-thought-out detail, the "knot of contradictions" that have countered and complicated "Turkey's transition from a national security state to a human rights state" (p. 249). The solution, Oran suggests, is the determined advance of democratisation and human rights. Notably, this solution would relieve the difficulties of not just Turkish Protestants, but also of other countercultural expressions of religion and belief that are represented in Turkey.

Christian Troll and Thomas Schirrmacher, wrestling with the extent to which "the human right of religious freedom ... may and must be limited by other human rights," take the topic further (Troll & Schirrmacher, 2015, p. 149). They argue for the adoption of nine ethical restraints on Christian mission, essentially, love, gentleness, noncoercion, peace, freedom, anti-fundamentalism, non-judgmentalism, impartiality, and honesty. If these restraints or a similar code of missional ethics[28] were to become publicised and practised values of Protestant missionaries and Turkish converts, one wonders how, over time, official and societal views of them would change.

---

28 See, e.g., *Christian Witness in a Multi-Religious World: Recommendations for Conduct* (World Council of Churches et al., 2017). This cogent, concise document could be adopted or adapted by the Turkish Protestant movement, as well as by other such movements.

In an effort to dispel a falsehood, Wolfgang Häde asks whether Christians in Turkey are part of a Western conspiracy (Häde, 2015). He presents a well-argued essay, suggesting that Christians contemplate the conspiratorial arguments and work to resolve mutual misunderstandings. Finally, he recommends accepting that such accusations are expressions of Christ's prophesied persecution. I would suggest that one recommendation is lacking, especially in an anthology on religious freedom and Christian mission: impartial advocacy for constitutionally-rooted human rights, particularly that of religious freedom. Those under the spell of social customs can at times be at odds with their national constitutions. To help Turkish people better integrate their customs and canon in this regard, the "human rights state" (Oran, 2021, p. 249) must be the concretizing vision.

Lastly, I am impelled to include *The Myth of Persecution: How the Early Christians Invented a Story of Martyrdom* (Moss, 2013). While it seems clear that Moss overstates her case for the sake of effect – even the title itself is obviously overstated – she makes some salient points. Too often assertions of persecution, sincere though they be, become instruments of polarisation, deepening the chasm between groups. Brunson's book is an example. Without passing any judgment on its basic content, its liberal use of the term persecution, as well as a host of other inflammatory terms, has the effect of vilifying Turkey and vindicating himself. In episodes of persecution, good judgment and moderation of rhetoric are prudent. Moss acknowledges rampant persecution of Christians in the world. "Many Christians live in situations that are oppressive and in which they are persecuted ... These flagrant human rights violations and their experiences demand our attention and action" (pp. 257-8). Yet, how we verbally address these situations can help or hinder progress from enmity to amity. Replacing the wedge of persecution with the warmth of participation, and the cuts of contention with the cure of common ground – these should be among the foremost goals in resolving persecution.

5 Wild wisdom

That memorable day, back in 1990, when the Rev. Dr. John Stott quoted to me Matthew 10:16 as his advice to my wife and me upon our soon departure for Turkey left me anticipating persecution – and this not from primarily Turkish sources, but from the devil himself (Stott, 1990).[29] Nevertheless, those words of Christ, via Stott, to "be as shrewd as snakes and as

[29] In this book, published that same year, Stott claimed that Satan is the ultimate source of persecution of Christians.

harmless as doves," for we are "like sheep among wolves," focuses attention on the animal kingdom, where "pursue-cution" is the way of life. Thus, I thought of Agur, to whom I had been introduced during the previous year,[30] and who introduces his listeners and learners to four small creatures that are "extremely wise."

This brief passage, Proverbs 30:24-28,[31] yields gems of wisdom that can enlighten and assist those who encounter various types of religious persecution. In essence, one can learn the wisdom of preparation from *ants*, for there are numerous ways that a person can prepare for persecution. Exploring historical, cultural, methodological, institutional, situational, and functional factors that interplay in one's life situation and its context, strengthening one's religious conviction vis-à-vis persecution, foreseeing constructive ways to respond to persecution, and building resilience – these are examples of practical ways that a religious worker can prepare for the possibility of persecution.

Hyraxes[32] can teach one the wisdom of protection; one is foolish to behave carelessly when one has "little strength" in threatening situations. One is wise to be mindful, tactful, and careful. Perhaps even RM – today in his mid-80s, but back then in his early 20s – would agree that his initial mass-mailing campaign in Istanbul, on the verge of an Islamic holiday, was ill-timed, if not ill-conceived. Indeed, throwing protection to the wind can readily translate into a very brief missionary career.

Locusts can teach one the wisdom – and the potential productivity – of unity. From my observations over the years, I have learned that many missionaries tend to be mavericks, unwittingly making themselves more, rather than less, susceptible to persecution. Christof Sauer espouses the wisdom of unity in "Christian Solidarity in the Face of Discrimination and Persecution" (Sauer, 2015). A unified, ethical response to episodes of persecution strengthens Christian witness and mission.

Finally, "*lizards* can be caught with the hand, yet they are found in kings' palaces." What veiled wisdom is here? If ants model preparation, hyraxes

---

30 Haddon Robinson, my homiletics professor in seminary, preached a sermon that year titled, "Lessons from Agur." Here is a more recent version of the sermon: https://www.youtube.com/watch?app=desktop&v=K0U2iBoMIfc.

31 Here is the text: "Four things on earth are small, yet they are extremely wise: ants are creatures of little strength, yet they store up their food in the summer; hyraxes are creatures of little power, yet they make their home in the crags; locusts have no king, yet they advance together in ranks; a lizard can be caught with the hand, yet it is found in kings' palaces" (New International Version; copied from https://www.biblegateway.com).

32 Robinson referred to these creatures as coneys, essentially a synonymous name.

model protection, and locusts model unity, then let lizards model comity, or "a state or atmosphere of harmony or mutual civility and respect."[33] In the verse, the comity is between the animal and hominal kingdoms, depicted by the lizard and king. Similarly, a missionary can exercise such comity by visiting key persons in an adopted society, such as the chief of police, the mayor, or the governor. Accordingly, throughout my 34 years in Turkey, I have visited countless leaders in our local societies, often with gifts to bestow in hand. I even traveled to the US with the mayor of the most populous municipality of Antalya in order to establish a sister-city relationship with my home city. I have considered such comity to be prudent.

However, there was one providential opportunity in which I failed to do this. In 1994, I became the interim (and then associate) pastor of the Union Church of Istanbul, and I considered myself to be "too busy" for such local visits, even with leading citizens. A new mayor had just been installed that same year in central Istanbul, and his office was very near to my own office. The inspired idea to arrange a visit with him had crossed my mind, as I recall, but it apparently did not rank high enough on my list of things to do. This is tragic, for the mayor's name was Recep Tayyip Erdoğan. To have established comity with him – perhaps even a lifelong friendship – to have been a "lizard on his palace wall" would have been a windfall of wisdom. But, alas, I was too busy with pastoral ministry.

On March 14, 2025, I discovered that both my wife and I were, just three days earlier, assigned N-82 deportation codes from the Turkish government. In the midst of our agonising uprooting, I wrote to President Erdoğan, essentially requesting the erasure of our codes, and blessing him, his family, and his country and people as sincerely and lavishly as I could, in obedience to Romans 12:14. But if he ever read my letter, I can imagine him thinking in response, "Who is this? Nobody whom I know."

6 Conclusion

An interplay of historical, cultural, methodological, institutional, situational, and functional factors contributes to Turkish and missionary misinterpretations of the Turkish Protestant movement and the persecution that its advocates and adherents have suffered. The diverse misinterpretations clash. In terms of the introductory metaphor, missionaries tend to think of themselves as essentially sheeplike ambassadors for Christ, "dwelling in the valley of the wolves," while savvy Turkish citizens contemplate forebodingly the well-financed missionary organisations and

33 See https://www.thefreedictionary.com/comity.

mega-churches, the slyly designed missionary communication and administration networks, the effective training programs, the clandestine collaboration with Kurds and refugees, and the demands of unrestricted religious freedom, and they construe these to be the canine claws and teeth of the missionaries themselves.

Regarding episodes of persecution that members of the movement have endured, these too have frequently been mutually misconstrued. This essay echoes the call for responsible rhetoric when recounting and discussing instances of persecution, prudently employing ethical self-restraints. It also calls for a pro-human-rights stance, including the more specific pro-religious-freedom stance. Moreover, the essay implicitly suggests refraining from a selfish focus upon one's own rights, with a blind eye toward the rights and interests of others, and forswearing allegations and actions that lead to polarization rather than to participation, and to contention rather than to common ground.

Finally, I propose that wisdom from the wild – ants, hyraxes, locusts, and lizards, not to mention other creatures who are "pursue-cuted" day by day – could conceivably assist missionaries and members of Turkish Protestant churches, which are planted and spreading throughout the country. The echo of Stott's advice, too, should be mentally entrenched, for snakes have an uncanny ability to evade traps and other threats, and – who fears a dove? Such "wild wisdom" can honey the presence and projects of missionaries and converts, even as they faithfully lift up the Son of Man, as Moses lifted up the snake, so that everyone who believes in the Son may have eternal life.[34]

7 References

ADF International (2024). Türkiye's Highest Court Rules in Support of Government's Expulsion of Nine Foreign Christians for Alleged 'Missionary Activities.' https://adfinternational.org/news/turkiye-christian-expulsion.

Bishai, Susan (July 2024). Religious Freedom Conditions in Turkey. In: *Country Update: Turkey*. United States Commission on International Religious Freedom. https://www.uscirf.gov/sites/default/files/2024-07/2024%20Turkey%20Country%20Update_0.pdf.

Bozkurt, Abdullah (June 13, 2024). Western Protestants in Turkey Labeled Threats to the Turkish State. In: *Middle East Forum*. https://www.meforum.org/western-protestants-in-turkey-labeled-threats-to.

Brunson, A, with Borlase, C. (2019). *God's Hostage: A True Story of Persecution, Imprisonment, and Perseverance*. Baker.

[34] John 3:14-15.

Bultema, James. (2024). *Free Enough to Grow: The Turkish Protestant Movement, 1961-2016.* [PhD diss.]. ETF Leuven.

Drake, B., & The Voice of the Martyrs (2005). Sacred Surrender. In: *Wear the Crown: Inspiring Stories and Photos of Modern-day Martyrs.* Genesis, 2005.

Häde, W. (2015). Christians in Turkey as Part of a Western Conspiracy? In: H. A. Gravaas et al. (eds). *Freedom of Belief and Christian Mission.* Regnum.

Howe, Marvine (Dec. 15, 1979). Four Americans Killed in Istanbul Ambush: Military Man and Three Civilians Shot Going Home from Allied Base. *New York Times* archives.

Howe, Marvine (Dec. 26, 1979). Turkish City Center of Terrorist Action: In Adana, Right-Left Forces Seem Evenly Matched, and Violence Is 'Almost a Way of Life.' *New York Times* archives.

Kremida, Damaris (Oct. 19, 2010). After Long Legal Battle, Christian Men Found Not Guilty of 'Insulting Turkishness.' In: *Baptist Press.* https://www.baptistpress.com/resource-library/news/after-long-legal-battle-christian-men-found-not-guilty-of-insulting-turkishness/.

Malstead, Y. (2020). *Istanbul, Here We Come.* YRM Publishing.

Meral, Z. (2015). *Compulsory Religious Education in Turkey: A Survey and Assessment of Textbooks.* Washington DC: United States Commission on International Religious Freedom. https://www.uscirf.gov/reports-briefs/spotlight/compulsory-religious-education-in-turkey-survey-and-assessment-textbooks.

Morris, B., & Ze'evi, D. (2023). *The Thirty-Year Genocide: Turkey's Destruction of Its Christian Minorities (1894-1924).* Harvard University Press.

Moss, Candida R. (2013). *The Myth of Persecution: How the Early Christians Invented a Story of Martyrdom.* HarperCollins.

Oran, B. (2021). *Minorities and Minority Rights in Turkey: From the Ottoman Empire to the Present State.* Lynne Rienner.

Pew Research Center (2011). How Muslims and Christians View Each Other. In: *Muslim-Western Tensions Persist.* https://www.pewresearch.org/global/2011/07/21/chapter-2-how-muslims-and-westerners-view-each-other/.

Pikkert, P. (2008). *Protestant Missionaries to the Middle East: Ambassadors of Christ or Culture.* WEC.

Sauer, C. (2015). Christian Solidarity in the Face of Discrimination and Persecution. In: H. A. Gravaas et al. (eds). *Freedom of Belief and Christian Mission.* Regnum.

Tchilingirian, H. (2021). Christians in Turkey: Native Foreigners. In: M. Raheb & M. A. Lamport (eds). *The Rowman and Littlefield Handbook of Christianity in the Middle East.* Rowman & Littlefield.

Troll, C., & Schirrmacher, T. (2015). Mission and Ethics of Mission 2014. In: H. A. Gravaas et al. (eds). *Freedom of Belief and Christian Mission.* Regnum.

World Council of Churches, Pontifical Council for Interreligious Dialogue, and World Evangelical Alliance (2011). *Christian Witness in a Multi-Religious World: Recommendations for Conduct.* https://www.worldevangelicals.org/pdf/1106Christian_Witness_in_a_Multi-Religious_World.pdf.

Yilmaz, I. (2021). *Creating the Desired Citizen: Ideology, State, and Islam in Turkey.* Cambridge University Press.

F. Applied Theology

20 Persecution as sacred and communal

A critical reflection on the fourth Lausanne Congress

Sara Afshari[1]

Abstract

In this short article, I reflect on my experience at the recent Lausanne Congress 4 in South Korea, focusing on how the Congress approached the issue of persecution of Christian. As someone who has personally faced persecution as a convert from a Muslim-majority country, I found that the Congress often reduced persecution to emotional appeals for evangelism or support. This approach, I argue, risks turning the suffering of Christians into a tool for marketing and evangelism rather than recognizing it as a sacred and shared experience within the Church. My short article calls for a shift in how we think about and respond to persecution. Instead of viewing it as just a problem to solve or a story to tell, we should see it as a sacred witness, a powerful way the Church bears the cross together. In short, we need a more thoughtful and holistic approach that honors the sacred, communal dimensions of suffering.

Keywords: Persecution, theology, community, commercialization, Lausanne Movement.

1 Introduction

The recent Lausanne Congress 4 in Incheon, South Korea, provided a significant platform to address contemporary challenges to Christian mis-

---

1 Dr. Sara Afshari is originally from Iran. She is a Research Tutor at Oxford Centre for Mission Studies and the current Admissions Tutor. She received her PhD from Edinburgh University in Media Religion and Culture. She is co-founder and former Executive Director of SAT-7 PARS, a Christian television channel in Farsi/Persian language. She has MTh in World Christianity from Edinburgh University and an MA in Media Communication from Wales University. Her recent book is titled: Religion, media and conversion in Iran: Mediated Christianity in an Islamic context. This article was originally published on 17 October 2024 on LinkedIn. Republished with permission. Email: safshari@ocms.ac.uk, ORCID iD: 0000-0003-4850-0306.

sion, including the pressing issue of persecution. However, as a convert from a Muslim-majority country where persecution is a lived reality, my participation in the Congress revealed the theological and missiological limitations in how the Lausanne movement, and much of the evangelical world, understands and engages with persecution. This reflection critiques the Congress's approach to persecution and offers an alternative theological vision that emphasizes the sacred andcommunal dimensions of suffering within the Church.

2 Lausanne and persecution: A narrow focus

One of the more concerning aspects of Lausanne 4 was its reduction of persecution to an emotional appeal, primarily linked to evangelism and/or the victimization of Christians. While the Congress certainly aimed to address persecution, the discussions often fell into a familiar framework – portraying persecuted Christians as either victims or tools for evangelism and church growth. This framing not only risks commodifying persecution but also neglects the sacred, communal nature of suffering in Christian theology.

Having lived through persecution myself, I have observed a disturbing tendency to commercialize the suffering of Christians, particularly converts, by turning their experiences into narratives designed to garner support, promoting church growth or demonize Muslim majority countries. This was evident in some of the stories shared at Lausanne, where persecution became a platform for boosting evangelism or church growth, mobilizing sympathy through evangelistic narratives that portrayed the enemy as being "defeated" by making them "one of us." The problem with this approach is that it reduces persecution to an evangelistic marketing tool, encouraging converts or persecuted individuals to frame their stories in such terms, rather than recognizing it as a sacred participation in the suffering of Christ.

Persecution, in its essence, is sacred because it links directly to Christ's own suffering on the Cross. It is through the Cross that Christians are called to bear witness to the world. As St. Gregory the Great highlighted, martyrdom is not simply about individual suffering but a communal act of witness involving the entire body of believers. The sacredness of persecution is also rooted in its connection to the Eucharist – the body and blood of Christ – where the suffering of the faithful is united with the suffering of Christ for the redemption of the world.

3 The Church as the heart of persecution

One of the key theological insights that was overlooked at Lausanne 4 is that persecution is not an individual experience, even though it may be experienced individually. When I reflect on my own story of persecution, I cannot see it as "my" story. I see it as the story of the Church. It was the Church, not just I, who suffered. When I was imprisoned and mistreated, it was the Church that sustained me and paid the ultimate price. Many of her members were arrested, and eventually, the church was shut down, losing many of its members to migration or to the world. Therefore, the pain of the Church was much greater than my own. This communal dimension, which also involves the Holy Spirit, is central to understanding the true nature of persecution.

Whenever people asked me to share my story, they wanted to hear about my individual experience, as though persecution were an isolated event in my life. Now, I live a fairly comfortable life in the West, yet my church is still struggling. Persecution is a communal experience, and any theological reflection on the subject must acknowledge this. The Church, like Christ, bears the Cross together. It is in this solidarity that the Holy Spirit moves, binding the persecuted and the community in a sacred unity that empowers the Church to give birth to new lights that shine with the resurrected Christ.

4 The missiological crisis: From witness to commodity

Another theological concern with Lausanne's (evangelical church) approach to persecution was its failure to engage with the broader missiological implications of suffering. The Congress largely viewed persecution through the lens of evangelism, treating it as a means to an end – the conversion of "the other". This misses the sacred nature of persecution as a witness to the faith and to the call of "let there be light", not just an opportunity for evangelism. A great example of such witness is the Coptic Church in Egypt.

In regions like Iran, where Christianity is growing, often in response to political disillusionment, the Church faces complex challenges. How will the Church sustain and support these converts once their faith is no longer defined by opposition to a hostile regime, but by the need for community-building and theological formation? Lausanne missed the opportunity to address such critical missiological questions, focusing instead on persecution as a story to be told, rather than a reality to be lived and responded to holistically.

Persecution must be understood as a sacred witness, not merely a tool for evangelism or a narrative for raising support. The Church's response to persecution should not be driven by emotional appeals or abstract theological concepts, but by a deep, incarnational solidarity with those who suffer. This solidarity is not just with individuals but with the Church – the body of Christ – that endures persecution as a collective witness to the world.

5 Theological failure and the need for a holistic response

Lausanne's failure to engage with the deeper theological dimensions of persecution reflects a broader crisis in evangelical theology, which often prioritizes evangelism over deeper theological reflection. This was evident in the organizational and theological tensions that surfaced during the Congress, including the apology issued after Ruth Padilla's talk. The Lausanne movement, once a platform for theological engagement and evangelical unity, seems to have shifted toward becoming an organization with its own preferred theology, one that struggles to engage meaningfully with the lived realities of persecuted Christians in non- Western contexts.

The Congress also revealed a troubling Western-centric bias in its approach to persecution. The experiences of persecuted Christians in the global South were often simplified, reduced to binary dynamics of "persecuted" versus "persecutor." This narrow focus overlooks the broader, systemic factors that shape the experiences of marginalized Christians and the Church in these regions. It reduces persecution to an emotional appeal rather than a call to a transformative, missional response that integrates the lived realities of those facing persecution daily and the future of the Church.

6 A call for a sacred, communal vision of persecution

To move beyond this theological and missiological impasse, the Church must begin to see persecution not just as a problem to be solved or a story to be told, but as a sacred witness – a participation in the suffering of Christ that unites the Church across time and space, calling for a deeper response within the context. The Holy Spirit stands with the persecuted, not just as a Comforter, but as the one who empowers the Church to bear witness to the truth of the Gospel in the face of systemic oppression and violence, and to find solutions to ease the pain within the context.

As mentioned earlier, persecution is not an individual experience. It is a communal reality that binds the Church together, just as the Trinity unites Father, Son, and Holy Spirit in perfect communion. In this sense, the persecuted are not isolated individuals but active agents in the Church's mission, bearing witness to the saving power of Christ through their suffering – "let there be light" (Genesis 1:3).

The Church's response to persecution must be rooted in this sacred, communal vision. It must move beyond emotional appeals and the commodification of suffering toward a holistic, missional approach that recognizes the profound spiritual transformation persecution can bring. Only then will the Church be equipped to support and sustain persecuted Christians in regions like Iran and beyond, offering not just sympathy, but a deep theological engagement with the realities of suffering, resilience, and hope.

In conclusion, persecution is sacred because it is a participation in the suffering of Christ. It is communal because it is the Church, not individuals, who bear this cross together. As the Church faces the challenges of persecution in the modern world, it must reclaim this sacred, communal vision, standing in solidarity with the persecuted and bearing witness to the hope of the Gospel.

21 "He would crush me with a storm"

Suffering in Job and observations in biblical theology

Duane Alexander Miller[1]

Abstract

In this essay, I explore the theme of unmerited suffering through a theological and pastoral reading of the book of Job, connecting it to the lived reality of persecuted Christians today. I begin with a biblical-theological reflection on Job, focusing on the heavenly court, the figure of the satan, and Job's anguished protest against divine silence and apparent injustice. I reflect on the difference between law and wisdom, the challenge of redemptive suffering, and Job's unwavering integrity. Drawing on my pastoral experience with persecuted Christians – particularly in Islamic contexts – I argue that Scripture-centered theology can offer true comfort and strength, far more than abstract academic analysis. I then explore how Job's insights resonate with the challenges these believers face today. I conclude by affirming that their suffering is seen, remembered, and honoured by God. Job's yearning for a redeemer ultimately finds fulfilment in Christ, and his story offers a pattern of faithful endurance and hope.

Keywords: Job, suffering, persecution, homily.

> "Even if I summoned him and he responded, I do not believe he would give me a hearing. He would crush me with a storm and multiply my wounds for no reason. He would not let me catch my breath but would overwhelm me with misery." – Job 9:16-18

---

1 Duane A. Miller is professor at the Protestant Faculty of Theology at Madrid (UEBE) and carries out doctoral supervision for the Oxford Centre for Mission Studies. He lives in Madrid with his wife and children. Email: drdamiller1232@gmail.com, ORCID iD: 0009-0002-2766-2955 – [Editorial note: As this contribution has the character of a homily, in order not to disturb the flow of reading, a different referencing system is used than for the rest of the volume.]

1 Introduction

The purpose of this chapter is to explore the nature of unmerited suffering in Job, and then to explore how we can connect that to contemporary instances of persecution – a type of unmerited suffering – in the world today. This approach is interdisciplinary, and readers who do not believe that biblical theology (the Job section) can inform an applied, pastoral theology (the persecution section) will not like it. The tone is more homiletic than academic, and that is intentional: as an Anglican priest I have known and worked with many persecuted Christians through the years, and I have yet to meet one that has benefited from a purely academic analysis of her situation. On the other hand, a personal and homiletical word, connecting their suffering with the world of the Bible – that has proved to be fruitful again and again.

2 Chapter outline

In Part 1 of this chapter I want to visit the topic of suffering (and persecution in particular) from the point of view of the Hebrew Bible, with a focus on the book of Job. We'll look at the heavenly court and the material realm and the difference between wisdom and law. We'll interrogate the errors of Job's colleagues and the strong denunciations that Job makes against God. We'll consider the reality that Job, in the end, does not in fact receive an answer from God, and what that says about suffering in the world today and the ethics of God.

In Part 2 we'll focus on the topic of persecution and ask what we can learn about the topic from Job. What are some applications that might be proposed from our biblical theology in relation to persecution?

Part 1

3 The heavenly court

We begin with a scene of the heavenly court – a place we know well from other passages of Scripture like Isaiah 6 and Psalm 82. While YHWH is the only deity there, he is accompanied by a plethora of celestial beings – the sons of God, angles, archangels, seraphim and cherubim, the 24 elders, four living creatures, etc. In Job we have the Sons of God reporting to YHWH, and among them we meet the satan. The reader is left with the possibility that the satan (a title, not a proper name) is one of those Sons of God.

We know the Sons of God from other passages of Scripture, as in Job 38:7 when we learn that these Sons of God predate the creation of humanity. In Psalm 29:1 the psalmist calls on the *bene elim* (Sons of the Mighty One, which is to say Sons of God) to join him in praise.

But we know that not all is well with the Sons of God. In Psalm 82 we read that Elohim (God) stands in the divine council – the heavenly court of which we are speaking – and rebukes certain of the *elohim*, referring to divine beings, but not rival gods. The context is God denouncing their unethical governance of portions of the earth which they had been assigned. Similarly, in Job 4:18 we find the statement that, "If God places no trust in his servants, if he charges his angels [*malakaw*] with error ...". We also know that some of the Sons of God are not obedient (Genesis 6:1-4). In this fragment we learn the certain of the Sons of God married and procreated with human women.

The psalmist reflects, "Who is man that you are mindful of him? You have made a little lower than the *elohim*" (8:4). Finally, there are also (at least) two passages[2] that allude to a rebellion in the celestial court or the mountain of God, but those go beyond the scope of this work.

With all of the preface we have the opening context – though much more could be said – for the initial conversation between YHWH and the satan.

4 The satan

The satan is also an officer of the heavenly court – at least in Job. We find the same word in only three other books of the Hebrew Bible. In Numbers 22 the celestial figure blocking (opposing) Balaam's donkey is the satan. With the development of the concept we find in a later writing (Zechariah 3) the satan is fulfilling the same role as in Job: accusing the righteous. Only in the late writing of 1 Chronicles 21:1 do we find the word *Satan* as a name rather than as title, and only here do we find this creature acting apart from the heavenly court. (It is worth noting that this passage is a retelling of 2 Samuel 24 where the same event is attributed to the wrath of God directed towards David. Clearly the Hebrews' theology of this figure is evolving over the centuries.)

But our interest is Job. The satan is a member of the heavenly court. YHWH is not displeased or surprised to see him, but asks for his report, as he has presumably done with the (other?) Sons of God.[3]

---

2 Ezekiel 28:11-19, Isaiah 14:12-15.

3 Some might ask, aren't these angels? I don't want to delve into the topic, but I do want to differentiate the *sons of God* from the *angels* in this article. There is a

4.1 The problem of good

The conversation between YHWH and the satan is straight forward. God boasts about the goodness of Job and the satan counters that it's easy to be righteous when you have everything you could desire. This is an ethical wager and is a serious claim on the level of moral theology and philosophy. Are people good only because they are rewarded for it? The question has gravity and is worthy of our (and YHWH's) attention, and "YHWH said to the satan, 'Very well, then, everything he has is in your power, but on the man himself do not lay a finger.' Then the satan went out from the presence of YHWH."[4]

When we hear of the suffering of the guilty we are neither surprised nor, for the most part, troubled. But this book of Job is asking the fundamental question about the suffering of the innocent. Furthermore, while we have the inside information about what is happening in the celestial court, Job certainly does not.

The satan goes about destroying all of Job's goods and family – excepting his wife, – and we read that Job handles this all stoically:

> "At this, Job got up and tore his robe and shaved his head. Then he fell to the ground in worship and said:
> "Naked I came from my mother's womb,
> and naked I will depart.
> YHWH gave and YHWH has taken away;
> may the name of YHWH be blessed."
> In all this, Job did not sin by charging Elohim with wrongdoing."[5]

I like how the narrator (clearly not Job) tells us that up until this point Job hasn't done anything wrong. That will change.

Fast forward: we have another day when the Sons of God are coming to give their reports at the celestial court and among them is the satan. The satan gives his report and does not even mention Job. But YHWH does, and the satan says, "A man will give all he has for his own life. But now stretch out your hand and strike his flesh and bones, and he will surely curse you to your face" (2:4, 5).

Hebrew word for angel (*malak*), but its role is not clear. It may be a type of celestial being inferior to the *elohim*; possibly it doesn't refer to a type of being at all, but to any celestial being who has been given a role (perhaps temporary) of relaying a message. But this distinction is incidental to our overall argument. The book to read on the topic of Heiser's *Unseen Realm* (details in bibliography).

4 Job 1:12.

5 Job 1:20-22.

Note that it is indeed YHWH who has the power to strike down Job, and the satan is only his agent – as we would expect of a royal courtier. He does his work, and Job's wife tells him to curse Elohim and die. (The Hebrew is "bless Elohim and die" as the pious scribes were not willing to actual write the words "curse God", but it was a euphemism like "ladies of the night.")

And our narrator concludes with a much more ambiguous verdict: "He replied, 'You are talking like a foolish woman. Shall we accept good from Elohim, and not trouble?' In all this, Job did not sin in what he said" (2:10). He did not sin *in what he said*, which leaves the reader with the possibility that he sinned in his mind or his heart.

4.2 Job and his companions make speeches to one another

Here we enter the main literary body of the work. All of a sudden, the name YHWH becomes rare and we often revert to the very ancient divine title *Shaddai*. The other common appellation for God is *El*, wither a generic name for a deity, or in the Canaanite pantheon the patron god of family patriarchs and the father of Baal and Asherah – his sister/wife. Of course, the generic deity title is also used often for the God of Israel.

These two divine titles are not unique to Israel, and Job is not an Israelite – indeed the setting is prior to the existence of people named Israel. This is significant because the final edition of the book as we have it claims to have a universal scope. And that is important because our concern is suffering. This book is intentionally *not* framed by Israel for Israel.

Job's companions start well, mourning with him in silence. But then we get these speeches wherein they try to explain that somehow Job has sinned, and that this is why all this suffering has befallen him. This is the easy case of merited suffering – not the suffering of the innocent. The tone of the speeches grows more vehement as they continue. "The lengthy speeches of Job's friends further remind us how debilitating and shameful a simple application of the sin-equals-suffering connection can be."[6]

Eliphaz insists that no innocent person has ever perished, and that evil only comes upon those who have done evil (4:7, 8). Perhaps Job has not sinned bodily, but with his words (15:4-6). He accuses Job of bitterness and prideful anger (5:2, 15:12-13). He will end with accusations of oppression and greed (22:5-9).

Bildad is a legalist *par excellence*. He points to the loss of Job's children as clear evidence of divine punishment (8:20, 21). He judges Job's claims of

6 Bartholomew, Ch. 8.

righteousness as blasphemous and ridiculous and thus meriting punishment, by implication (25:4-6).

Zophar is the most antagonistic of the correspondents, and Job refutes him forcefully. Like the others he knows that suffering must be merited – the suffering of the just is incompatible with the fact of God. Job must have hidden sins, Job is arrogant, Job must repent.

Is this verbal abuse persecution? "[P]ersecution need not always be violent; acts of silencing, shaming, or pressuring to dilute one's convictions are also persecution."[7] If this is correct then we can classify this as persecution. On the other hand, there are more cautious voices:

> "When disagreement is viewed as persecution, then these innocent sufferers must fight – rhetorically and literally – to defend themselves. In this polarized view of the world, disagreement and conflict – even entirely nonviolent conflict – is not just a difference of opinion; it is religious persecution."[8]

But we need not decide on this point right now.

These men understand one thing clearly: there is a law of the universe and God is forced to abide by it: the just will not suffer. They have misunderstood at least two things about suffering – at least from the story we've read so far – the wisdom tradition we find often enunciated in Proverbs is not law. There is indeed moral law. We don't want to at this point associate it with Torah since the story intentionally takes place before the revelation of Torah and in a land far from the holy mountain and among peoples who are not of the Covenant. But there is what would much later be called the Natural Law, proposing that the basic contours of morality are grafted into nature by its maker (Romans 2:14, 15). The wisdom tradition converses with legal tradition, but they are not the same thing.

There is also the issue of redemption. The first major story we find in the Bible about redemption is the well-composed and tightly narrated Joseph novella we find at the end of Genesis. The concept of redemptive suffering is proposed: what you meant for evil God has used for good, as Joseph says to his brother.[9] Redemption does not erase the pain of suffering or that fact the suffering of the innocent is very truly evil and confounding. But it does advance the idea that God can draw from detritus of genuine evil and craft from that wreckage something beneficial to the created order.

Meanwhile, Job has some very serious charges to make against God.

---

7 Theocharous, 195-196.

8 Moss, 9.

9 Genesis 50:20.

Job curses the day he was born – an affront to the entire material order and God's desire for its creatures to "be fruitful and multiply" and extend his reign beyond Eden, the sacred orchard he had planted for himself, to the ends of the earth.

In no particular order let's look at Job's denunciations of God. First, Job accuses God of being amoral – not immoral – meaning that he simply doesn't care about good and evil or the administration of this material realm. Consider 9:22-24: "It is all the same; that is why I say, 'He destroys both the blameless and the wicked.' When a scourge brings sudden death, he mocks the despair of the innocent. When a land falls into the hands of the wicked, he blindfolds its judges. If it is not he, then who is it?"

Later he will complain that not only is he being unjustly oppressed, but that sometimes the wicked actually flourish: "Why do the wicked live on, growing old and increasing in power? They see their children established around them, their offspring before their eyes. Their homes are safe and free from fear ... How often is the lamp of the wicked snuffed out? How often does calamity come upon them?" (21:7-9, 17). We can find similar statements in Ecclesiastes.

Not only is God amoral, but he is also cruel and vindictive: "He assails me and tears me in his anger and gnashes his teeth at me; my opponent fastens on me his piercing eyes ... All was well with me, but he shattered me; he seized me by the neck and crushed me. He has made me his target; his archers surround me. Without pity, he pierces my kidneys and spills my gall on the ground" (16:9, 12-14). While the Noachide Covenant has God pointing his divine armament (his bow) away from the earth in a gesture of peace, Job states that he is if the target of the divine arsenal.

El Shaddai is amoral, vindictive, and, to add insult to injury, unresponsive. The other ancient deities had holy mountains or sacred orchards where they could be approached, but El Shaddai does not: "If only I knew where to find him; if only I could go to his dwelling! I would state my case before him and fill my mouth with arguments. I would find out what he would answer me, and consider what he would say to me" (23:3-5).

Job doesn't even know what he has been charged with (10:2, 3), like Josef K in Kafka's *The Trial* (original title *Der Prozess*). "As persecution, assaults, and violence become personal experience, the individual's fear turns into hatred for the enemy and all the members of his or her group."[10] Job's wife is the only person who has been faithful to him so far.

What is remarkable about Job – and what makes him the hero of this story – is that despite all of this he maintains his integrity: "As surely as *El*

---

10 Hinton, 212.

lives, who has denied me justice, *Shaddai*, who has made my life bitter, as long as I have life within me ... I will not deny my integrity. I will maintain my innocence and never let go of it; my conscience will not reproach me as long as I live" (27:2-6).

That persecuted Job is the hero of the story recalls something that Tolstoy wrote much later: "Progress towards the welfare of mankind is made not by the persecutors but by the persecuted ... Only goodness, meeting evil and not being infected by it, conquers evil."[11]

There is a final ironic element that Job expresses his desire that a record be kept of his unmerited suffering as a testament against Shaddai (31:35-37), and we find ourselves reading that very testimony, even though Job will recant everything he has said after his theophany. Shaddai has indeed honoured this request, despite everything.

This says something to us about unmerited suffering. God does not shrink away from it nor is it a topic he is afraid of, nor does he regard it as unimportant, nor does he desire for it be ignored or forgotten. There is value in remembering suffering. There is value in grieving suffering. We ourselves can learn and benefit from the unmerited suffering of those who came before us – it is hard not to see in this dynamic a foreshadowing of the passion of the Christ.

Even prior to this we can imagine the people of Judah living in exile, identifying with Job, lamenting their disgrace and protesting, "we had not forgotten you; we have not been false to your covenant."[12] Nonetheless they will stay faithful to Torah.

4.3 His redeemer lives

There is a striking statement made by Job about his redeemer or *go'el*. We also meet a *go'el* in Ruth, where Boaz becomes the "kinsman redeemer" for the imperilled woman. More from the *Jewish Encyclopedia*:

> "Next of kin, and, hence, redeemer. Owing to the solidarity of the family and the clan in ancient Israel, any duty which a man could not perform by himself had to be taken up by his next of kin. Any rights possessed by a man

---

11 Tolstoy, *What I Believe*, quoted in Parrinder, 175.

12 Psalm 44:17. There are many proposed answers to the central question of the Hebrew Bible – *why the exile?* The most popular one is that of the Deuteronomist: idolatry. But there are plenty of other proposals, including this one: that the enormity of the punishment is incongruent with the faithfulness of the People of God. Habakkuk makes a similar point: "Why are you silent while the wicked swallow up those more righteous than themselves?" (1:13).

which lapsed through his inability to perform the duties attached to such rights, could be and should be resumed by the next of kin. This applied especially to parcels of land which any Israelite found it necessary to sell. This his go'el, or kinsman, had to redeem". (Lev. xxv. 25)

And:

"However, the chief of the go'el's duties toward his kinsman was that of avenging him if he should happen to be slain by some one outside the clan or tribe. This custom is found in all early or primitive civilizations ... Indeed, it is the only expedient by which any check could be put upon the tendency to do injury to strangers. Here again the principle of solidarity was applied to the family of the murderer, and the death of one member of a family would generally result in a vendetta."[13]

I don't want to read too much into which type of *go'el* Job was speaking of when he says:

"For I know that my *go'el* lives,
and that in the end he will stand on the earth.
And after my skin has been destroyed,
yet in my flesh I will see *Eloah*;
I myself will see him
with my own eyes – I, and not another.
How my heart yearns within me!" (Job 19:25-27)

Shaddai is obviously not Job's redeemer/vindicator, for he is amoral and distant and inaccessible and has made of Job an enemy. Rather, when we properly understand the context of the celestial court outlined earlier, the meaning becomes clear: Job is hoping that among the residents of the celestial court someone would take up his case and vindicate him – and perhaps all others who suffer innocently? Eloah will be made manifest, and Job's vindicator will defend him. The deity who is far off and inaccessible will be made to appear by Job's vindicator. He, in turn, will descend from the distant celestial court to "stand on the earth."

There is a lot to say here theologically about incarnation and soteriology. Job's conviction certainly came true but in a much more powerful way than he could have envisioned. And this tells us something again about the seriousness of suffering before *Eloah*. Not only did one of the many Sons of God come to advocate for him, but the eternal and unbegotten Son, second

13 "Go'el" in *Jewish Encyclopedia*. https://jewishencyclopedia.com/articles/6734-go-el. Accessed 13 March 2025.

person of the Trinity, was made flesh, having a divine nature received from the Father who is the fountainhead of all divinity, and a human nature received from his mother, a young Jewish maiden.

"For us for our salvation he suffered under Pontius Pilate, was crucified, buried and dead." What they meant for evil God has used for good. What was meant to be a curse becomes a conduit of life and salvation. The public humiliation of the vindicator is a prelude to his own vindication, exaltation and enthronement.

Yet the question is not answered: why is God taking so long to bring to completion his project of *apokatastasis panton* or "the restoration of all things" (Acts 3:21)? We remain with these questions: "Why have you forgotten me? Why must I go about mourning, oppressed by the enemy?" (Psalm 42:9) And, "O God, why have you rejected us forever?" (Psalm 74:1)

Job received no answer. Or perhaps we should say he received a response but no answer. He was given the opportunity to present his legal complaint against God, but relented. The best we can do is recognize that God is working on it. In some ineffable way which God does not explain the suffering of the Church appears to be a participation and fulfilment of the suffering of Christ (2 Corinthians 1:5, Colossians 1:24). What we do learn from our early section of Job is important here: we're in a war and we are one front of the war. We're not even the original front, which was in the celestial court when some creature rebelled against God.[14] The material realm was the opening of a second front in this cosmic war – at least as far as we know.

Job's hope that a go'el will arise for him and plead his case and his insistence on maintaining his rectitude and integrity, even in the midst of unjust suffering and despite all of his denunciations of God, lead to his vindication.

4.4 The Theophany

It is hard to know what to do with the theophany in chapters 38 through 41. Job is confronted with the complexity of nature. The modern reader has a difficulty: today we can answer many of these questions about zoology and meteorology and astronomy. The commentary for these chapters in the *Biblia de Jerusalén*[15] notes that these creatures are not domesticated or tamed – their life and energy lie beyond the purview of human

14 Cf. Isaiah 14 and Ezekiel 28, especially. The belief that there had been a rebellion in the divine court was common among the pantheons of the Near East.

15 Details in bibliography.

knowledge or authority. One ultimate question is this: can we, as creatures of this earthly realm, behold with wonder the ordered and beautiful world with which we have been entrusted?

Addressing Job's suffering, YHWH (yes, we find this name again but in the mouth of our narrator) not only magnifies the complexity of the created material order, but also alludes to the Sons of God, as if the beauty and intricacy of the material order was somehow part of a much larger story of which we humans know very little. Job confesses that he is vile, abandoning his lawsuit: "Job's final word to God is in beautiful contrast with much of his former unmeasured utterances."[16]

Nonetheless, YHWH continues with a further discourse: "Would you discredit my justice? Would you condemn me to justify yourself?" (40:8). God has already made his point, and Job has accepted it. But YHWH shifts into a discourse focused on the beasts of chaos – a remarkable rhetorical decision.

One tradition is to see this as God continuing to berate Job for his audacity in questioning God. But there is a better option for us: that God is here shifting to a more instructive tone, leaving Job not only with humiliation but also with material for reflection and meditation.[17]

But before the beasts of chaos, in 40:11 ff we hear an exhortation to Job:

"Unleash the fury of your wrath,
  look at all who are proud and bring them low,
look at all who are proud and humble them,
  crush the wicked where they stand.
Bury them all in the dust together;
  shroud their faces in the grave.
Then I myself will admit to you
  that your own right hand can save you."

Yes, Job: *You* execute justice. What would the world look like if all possibility of suffering were eliminated? It would entail by necessity the destruction of all humanity. All humans have at some time caused others to suffer. Which is to say, the possibility of suffering and the reality of free will are inseparable.

Who are the beasts of chaos? The masculine land beast is behemoth, and the feminine water beast is leviathan. Whether or not these chaos beasts have any relation to existing natural creatures that were then

16 MacLaren, 64.

17 This is following the insight in John Walton's fine lectures on Job (2017) which are noted in the bibliography.

mythologized is of no interest to us.[18] The chaos beasts are not members of the celestial realm, but of the material world. They are not really on anyone's side: in representing chaos they are dangerous to humans, who rely on stability and order to survive. In this chapter we learn that they are under the dominion of God. We will meet them later in the Bible when they will array themselves against the plans of God: the beast that arises from the sea, representing the gentile powers of Empire, and the beast emerging from the land representing the Temple.[19]

But in our text God takes pride in them. It appears he holds them to be exemplary for Job. As if to say, "Job, look at these powerful and resilient creatures. I take pride in them. Emulate their vitality and perdurance." Here is something to learn about suffering: be constant, be patient, be tenacious.

"God expects Job to realize, and Job is not slow at grasping the point, that the natural order – the principles on which the world was created – are analogous to the moral order – the principles according to which it is governed."[20] God is addressing evil and the suffering of the innocent: we are called to resilience and the emulation of these great powerful beasts.

4.5 The happy ending?

God reprimands the companions of Job saying: "I am angry with you and your two friends, because you have not spoken the truth about me, as my servant Job has." He tells them to make a sacrifice, and they do, and Job intercedes for them. There is something to learn about suffering here: a communal aspect – how both comfort and pain overflow into the people around us. These men have also learned something for they too have heard from Shaddai and (we hope) been transformed by the experience. They have learned to listen to the voice of the persecuted. They could, I believe, confess these words with a much later generation: "We are convinced that the people who are the victims of religious persecution and discrimination are the best sources of information and advice."[21]

---

18 For additional information on these creatures see "Leviathan and Behemoth" in *Jewish Encyclopedia.*

19 Revelation 13:1. "The land" is in Greek *gēs,* which would bring to mind the Hebrew *ha aretz*, which for Jewish Christians would not have simply meant "earth" or "the earth" but "the [Holy] Land," hence Jerusalem.

20 Clines, xlvi.

21 Committee on International Relations, 3.

Job intercedes for them. After being treated poorly in his time of unmerited suffering he has a humility that has been honed and attuned. They did evil unto him; Shaddai has used it for good. The good is not in having an answer or an explanation. The good is in knowing about God at a deeper and more painful level. No one in this book really gets to know God better, but they do learn something valuable: how to *interact* with God in a responsible and prudent manner.[22]

He never met his go'el, but he did see Shaddai in his own flesh. (We will learn later in the Bible that Job's go'el [and ours] was in fact perfected by his own suffering [Hebrews 2:10]).

Job's fortunes are restored, it seems. Perhaps the main reason I dislike how Christians tend to read Job is that they assume that this is a happy ending. That is not the lesson. His sons and daughters and his servants whom he loved are all dead. Is there restoration from unjust suffering? Yes. But the dynamic of redemption does not nullify or erase the gravity of real evil. Job would never be the same because suffering changes people. In the case of Job, it changed him for better, but the text implies that there is a choice to make here. I think we all know from our own lives that sometimes people suffer and they become bitter and angry.

Job got what he wanted: a chance to present his case before God. When given the opportunity he made his choice – and he could have chosen otherwise – to remain silent in that presence.

This chapter is not a commentary on Job, nor would I ever want to write a commentary on the book. There are many salient features – the narrator's panegyric to wisdom, the interventions of Ehud – which I have not even mentioned.

Regarding God's speeches, "On the surface they fail to address the issue of the suffering righteous, and they skirt Job's complaint that God fails to keep times of judgment [...]. Amazingly, they seem to ignore Job's avowal of innocence, for Yahweh neither condemns Job nor acquits him."[23]

But yes, in the end there is no answer. Or God will not give one. Maybe we don't need one. Maybe we would not understand it. Maybe an answer would nullify our path of faith. God is taking his time in the restoration of all things, but if we doubt how seriously he takes suffering we need only look to the Cross where the Word made Flesh suffered "for us and for our salvation." The texture of redemption and the journey back to paradise and the union of the worlds visible and invisible are impossible without, we are told, the suffering of the innocent.

---

22 I am indebted to Christine Hayes for this insight – see bibliography for details.

23 Hartley, 30.

Part 2

5 Suffering and persecution

So far I have presented a biblical theology vision of suffering based (primarily) on the book of Job. By biblical theology I mean that the text has spoken to us and we have taken our categories and concerns from the text itself. We have not started with a pre-existing vision of suffering derived from philosophy or ethics and then visited Job to mine the text for favourable evidence or to iron out apparent disagreements.

In this concluding section I want to observe the intersections of our study in Job and the reality of the persecution of Christians with an emphasis on Islamic contexts.[24] Why Islamic contexts? It is the type of persecution I have studied the most,[25] is one answer. But also, the people of Israel in exile were in lands that are today Islamic nations with small Christian minorities – which is to say there is a geographical continuity here as well.

I also note a sense of commonality between Job and Christians in Iraq (and other countries in the area), where converting to Islam would be much easier than being persecuted. But the Christians there, like Job, refuse to denounce their sense of vocation and ethics in the face of what honestly looks like an amoral God.

And to where shall they go? The dwindling Christian populations of Palestine and Iraq and Egypt: to where shall they go? How shall they submit their complaints to God? They do it in prayer, having (maybe) learned in some form from Job and others like him. But the physical places like the embassies of the West and the headquarters of the UN or the EU – the places are distant and show little interest in the well-being of these Christians.

Job could have run away from Shaddai. In his ancient setting you could leave one land for another and so move from the jurisdiction of one deity to another. (It appears this is what Jonah was trying to do.) The West sometimes tries to "help" these Christians by helping them leave their ancestral lands. Maybe the intention is good, but the result is the dissolution of ancient Christian communities *en toto*. Job stayed in his land, and a thoughtful, prudent response to persecution should first all ask how to help people do the same. In some cases there may be no other option, but that option

24 For a good summary of the lives on non-Muslims under Islamic rule see Andrew Bostom, *The Legacy of Jihad*, and Bat Ye'or, *The Decline of Eastern Christianity.* Full details are in the bibliography.

25 See Miller 2016.

should always be at the end of the list for governments, charities and especially churches.

In the face of persecution they are living out these words:

> "We are not to bend or yield before evil, nor to act like cowards or impotent weaklings: we are to overcome, to *surmount* evil, to go beyond it, to stand on a terrain that evil cannot reach, use weapons that evil cannot turn back on us, seek a victory that evil can never attain!"[26]

Some years ago I was visiting an ancient monastery in central Asia Minor.[27] Centuries ago, this place had thrived with scores of monks and a lively liturgical life. When I visited there were a handful of elderly monks, and I had the privilege to speak with one of them. I asked him for his favourite verse from the Bible, and he said, "I have not left you as orphans."[28] In this statement I see the faith of Job living on, though the monk knew much more about his redeemer than did Job. What can be done to provide spiritual companionship to Christians undergoing persecution at the hands of Muslims? It is another way of asking, how can emulate the example of Job's friends at first, before they – it appears – became complicit in his persecution.

We can also learn from the (negative example) of Job's friends once they abandoned a sorrowful and thoughtful companionship. As Saul is an example of how not to rule, they became an example of how *not* to respond to the persecution of Christians. Do we try to find fault? Do we ignore the source of persecution because it might make our own lives in Europe less comfortable? Are we too quick to say it is not "really" persecution because it's "really about natural resources" or "tribal grudges" because we don't want to anger local Muslims?

We also have the question of Satan – and now we can call a specific creature by one of its many names. While it is God that permits the persecution, it is Satan who executes it. Do we in the West take seriously the role of demonic powers in the persecution of Christians – especially in Islamic contexts? Or are we so devoted to interreligious dialogue and religious tolerance – are these bearing any fruit in rapidly Islamizing Europe? – that we refuse to identify the very real role of Satan in some of the dynamics of the Muslim world? Job's friends refused to acknowledge the truth – it was too painful and inconvenient for them.

---

26 Jacques Ellul, 173.

27 The results of that field work were published in the chapter "Word Games in Asia Minor" in *Muslim Conversions to Christ*. Details in bibliography.

28 John 14:18.

The so-called 'happy ending' – so often misunderstood in the West – tells us something too. Good times go and bad times come, but then good times can come again. There is a time for embracing, and a time to refrain from embracing. There is a time for peace and a time for war. The many Christian converts from Islam I've known over the years do not find actual physical persecution to be the hardest thing in their religious journey, over the long term. Those times come and they are very hard, but then they go. The hardest thing is the formation of a Christian identity – stable and firm.

One of the most common accusations levied against these Christians is that they have left their people and nation. It is an unfair accusation and almost never accurate. This is an example of "vilifying the target group for alleged crimes or misconducts," and, consequently, "marginalizing the targeted group's role in society."[29]

We must also note the faithfulness of his wife, for we read of more children and nowhere in the book is there talk of remarriage or concubines. She was, in a way, incidental to the main story. Had Job died she could have returned to her paternal home. But she lived in a poverty and took care of a diseased and angry man. She rarely receives the respects she deserves. Her faithfulness over the long term atones for her bad advice at first: her trajectory is a foil for the increasingly bellicose locutions of Job's friends.

When the persecuted Christians can say to Shaddai: I did my best, I was like behemoth and leviathan, I maintained my integrity – this can become a steppingstone towards a mature character a firm identity in his/her Redeemer who lives. And then, having passed through this persecution and suffering, the servant is able to fulfil his intercessional role for those who do not know the profundity of the darkness of God which he has experienced. He, like Job, can offer sacrifices of praise and thanksgiving and lamentation on their behalf, and they will be accepted by the deity of the mountain heights.

6 Conclusion

In this chapter we learned many things about and from the book of Job: the audience is universal; silence and companionship are appropriate responses; there is an invisible world whose events we know little (or nothing) about; God takes suffering seriously; our timing is not his; God allows the righteous to suffer; restoration is not erasure; we have a vindicator in the celestial court; our suffering will not be forgotten and God does not

29 Tony Beard, 64 and 68.

will that it should be; God is gracious when it comes to our accusations against him when we are suffering unjustly; the elimination of the possibility of evil requires the elimination of humanity; in suffering we are called to resilience and endurance and patience; those outside of the Covenant People do encounter God in unmerited suffering.

We learned about unmerited suffering in the book of Job. We learned about how humans react to it – whether they are suffering under it or observing it. We learned that God is governing realms and kingdoms of which we know little or nothing at all, but that they do overlap and influence each other at times. We learned about the importance of healthy companionship for those passing through suffering and persecution. These insights connect to the lives of today's martyrs and confessors, who suffer because of their refusal to renounce their own integrity in the face of God who appears to ignore them. These insights from an ancient text set in the Bronze Age still speak to us today.

7 References

Bartholomew, C. G. (2016). *When You Want to Yell at God: The Book of Job*. Transformative Word Series. Lexham Press.

Bat Ye'or. (1996). *The Decline of Eastern Christianity Under Islam: From Jihad to Dhimmitude: Seventh-Twentieth Century*. Farleigh Dickinson University.

Beard, T. (2020). *Let No One Despise You: Emerging Christians in a Post-Christian Society*. Wipf & Stock.

Biblia de Jerusalén. (2010). Desclée de Brouwer.

Bostom, A. G. (2005). *The Legacy of Jihad: Islamic Holy War and the Fate of Non-Muslims*. Prometheus Books.

Brueggemann, W. (2012). *Theology of the Old Testament: Testimony, Dispute, Advocacy*. Fortress.

Childs, B. S. (2011). *Biblical Theology of the Old and New Testaments: Theological Reflection on the Christian Bible*. Fortress.

Childs, B. S. (2019). *Old Testament Theology in a Canonical Context*. Fortress.

Clines, D. J. A. (1989). *Job 1-20*. Word Biblical Commentary, volume 17. Zondervan.

Committee on International Relations. (1998). *Freedom from Religious Persecution Act of 1997, Part II – Private Witness*. Washington DC: US Government Printing Office.

Ellul, J. (1969). *Violence: Reflections from a Christian Perspective*. Seabury Press.

Hartley, J. E. (1988). *The Book of Job*. New International Commentary on the Old Testament. Eerdmans.

Hayes, C. (2013). *Introduction to the Hebrew Bible*. Lecture Series. Available at youtube.com/playlist?list=PLh9mgdi4rNeyuvTEbD-Ei0JdMUujXfyWi&si=hEtzc6-B79xrO4aL.

Heiser, M. S. (2019). *The Unseen Realm: Recovering the Supernatural Worldview of the Bible*. Lexham.

Ibrahim, A. S., & Greenham A. (Eds.) (2018). *Muslim Conversions to Christ: A Critique of Insider Movements in Islamic Contexts*. Peter Lang.

Jewish Encyclopedia. (1901-1906). 12 vols. Funk & Wagnalls.
Kafka, F. (1925). *Der Prozess.* Verlag Die Schmiede.
MacLaren, A. (1932). *Expositions of Holy Scripture.* Vol. 3. Eerdmans.
Miller, D. A. (2016). *Living among the Breakage: Contextual Theology-making and ex-Muslim Christians.* Pickwick.
Moss, C. (2013). *The Myth of Persecution.* Harper One.
New Oxford Annotated Bible with Apocrypha: New Revised Standard Version. (2018). Oxford University Press.
Orthodox Study Bible. (2008). Thomas Nelson.
Parrinder, G. (Ed.) (2000). *The Routledge Dictionary of Religious & Spiritual Quotations.* Routledge.
Rodd, C. S. (1990). *The Book of Job.* Epworth Commentaries. Epworth Press.
Sagrada Biblia: Universidad de Navarra. (2016). University of Navarra.
Theocharous, M. (Ed.) (2024). *Suffering and Persecution: Rethinking Church in the 21st Century.* Langham.
Walton, J. (2017). *Theology of the Book of Job.* Lecture Series. Available at www.youtube.com/@tedhildebrandt_BeL

www.ingramcontent.com/pod-product-compliance
Lightning Source LLC
LaVergne TN
LVHW010528100826
845148LV00001B/124